Porsche 924 Owners Workshop Manual

Charles Lipton
and John H Haynes Member of the Guild of Motoring Writers

Models covered

All Porsche 924 models; Standard, Lux, Turbo, Carrera GT, and limited/ special edition versions; 1984 cc

Does not cover 2.5 litre 924 S introduced September 1985

ISBN **978 0 85733 964 5**

J H Haynes & Co. Ltd.
Haynes North America, Inc

www.haynes.com

British Library Cataloguing in Publication Data
Lipton, Charles Porsche 924 owners workshop manual. 1   Cars. Maintenance & repair – Amateurs' manuals I. Title 629.28'722 ISBN 1-85010-438-7

Acknowledgements

Special thanks are due to Volkswagen of America and its many kind and patient staff who helped us over many hurdles we would not have been able cross on our own. Mr Rudi Spielberger and his staff of service training instructors provided a great deal of insight into the brand-new Turbo models and also various tips and hints on making difficult tasks more understandable to the home mechanic. Their time is appreciated.

Ogner Porsche-Audi of Woodland Hills, California provided not only parts, but the time of their service people. We were able to pick up some simple shortcuts in the performing of basic tasks.

Dean Banks of Beck-Arnley Corporation provided us with his Porsche 924 and patiently endured our tampering with his car.

Several other people contributed much time and research in helping us get the most complete information available for this project. Even though we do not have the space to thank each one personally they know who they are.

Every care has been taken to provide the most complete and up-to-date information available on the repair and care of the Porsche 924. Although much time has been spent ensuring the correctness of the information in this manual, it must be understood that Porsche, as a manufacturer, is continually making minor improvements and detail changes to its production vehicles. These cannot be detailed exactly or completely.

We are proud of the thoroughness of the work that has gone into this manual, and of the excellent work carried out by our mechanics, Henry 'Spook' Caspers and Tom Schauwecker. Our thanks must also go to all those people at Sparkford, England who assisted in the production of this manual. However, no liability can be accepted by the authors or the publishers for loss, damage, or injury caused by errors in, or omissions from, the information contained in this manual.

About this manual

Its aim

The aim of this book is to help you get the best value from your car. It can do so in two ways. First it can help you decide what work must be done, even should you choose to get it done by a service station. It will also enable you to carry out routine maintenance tasks, and the diagnosis and course of action when random faults occur. However it is hoped that you will also use the second and fuller purpose by tackling the work yourself. This is not only satisfying, but on the simpler jobs it may even be quicker than booking the car into a service station and going there twice, to leave and collect it. Perhaps most important, much money can be saved by avoiding the costs a service station must charge to cover labour and overheads. To avoid labour costs a service station will often give a cheaper repair by fitting a reconditioned assembly. The home mechanic can be helped by this book to diagnose the fault and make a repair using only a minor spare part.

The book has drawings and descriptions to show the function of the various components so that their layout can be understood. Then the tasks are described and photographed in a step-by-step sequence so that even a novice can cope with complicated work.

The jobs are described assuming only normal tools are available, and not special tools unless absolutely necessary. However a reasonable outfit of tools will be a worthwhile investment. Many special workshop tools produced by the makers merely speed the work, and in these cases guidance is given as to how to do the job without them. On a very few occasions a special tool is essential to prevent damage to components; then its use is described. Though it might be possible to borrow the tool, such work may have to be entrusted to the official agent.

Using the manual

The manual is divided into thirteen Chapters. Each Chapter is divided into numbered Sections which are headed in bold type between horizontal lines. Each Section consists of serially numbered paragraphs.

There are two types of illustrations: (1) Figures which are numbered according to the Chapter and sequence of occurrence in that Chapter. (2) Photographs which have a reference number in their caption. All photographs apply to the Chapter in which they occur so that the reference figure pinpoints the pertinent Section and paragraph number.

Procedures, once described in text, are not normally repeated. If it is necessary to refer to another Chapter the reference will be given. Cross-references given without use of the word 'Chapter' apply to Sections and/or paragraphs in the same Chapter, eg, 'see Section 8' means also 'in this Chapter'.

When the left or right side of the car is mentioned it is as if one is seated in the driver's seat looking forward.

Contents

Introduction to the Porsche 924

The Porsche 924 began life as a concept vehicle. The Volkswagen Company had contracted the Porsche concern to produce a sports car with which VW-Audi might enter the field of mid-range priced sports cars. When VW ultimately decided against the manufacture of this design, Porsche acquired the rights of manufacture and the 924 was born.

The 924 differs from earlier Porsche designs in several significant ways. First, and the most obvious change, is the use of a water-cooled engine mounted at the front of the vehicle. The engine is not bolted directly to the transmission, that unit being found at the rear of the vehicle as a transaxle. This design feature gives the 924 a nearly perfect weight distribution and enhances the handling capabilities of the car.

Other features of the vehicle are unitized construction, fully-independent suspension, and redesigned seating. Some of the features are not new to Porsche, but an extension of previous styling practices.

The North American market versions of the 924 have the most variations. There are very few options available on these models. Options are generally limited to wheels, tires, air conditioning, and suspension options. The main difference between years and markets is in the engine.

From 1976 through 1977½ model years, North American versions of the 924 had engines of 95 hp. This was a result of fitting low compression pistons and the addition of emission control systems. The emission controls which were used vary according to the sales market. They are described in greater detail elsewhere in this manual.

Early North American models were fitted with a 4-speed gearbox, but an automatic transmission became an option in 1977.

A redesign of the emission controls and the higher-compression pistons brought the engine output to 110 hp in the 1977½ through 1979 models. Emission controls continued to vary according to the sales market.

The 4-speed gearbox was retained until the introduction of the 1979 models, when it was replaced with a 5-speed unit. The automatic transmission remained an option for all years.

The present engine configuration began with the 1980 models. Changing the emission control system to the oxygen sensor system and an additional raise in the compression ratio has lifted engine performance into the 120 hp range. Removal of pumps, valves and other emission control components has had the additional result of improved gas mileage figures.

A new 5-speed transmission accompanies the changes above and the automatic transmission remains an option.

Another addition for the 1980 model year was the Turbo model. Using an exhaust-driven turbocharger, the Turbo's engine produces 150 hp.

Specifications for the European version of the 924 have remained nearly unchanged for the entire run of production. The engine produces 125 hp and is connected to a 4-speed, 5-speed, or optional automatic gearbox.

In 1985 the versions of the 924 covered in this manual were discontinued, being superseded by the 924 S.

Porsche 924

Porsche 924 Turbo

Buying spare parts

Spare parts are available from a number of sources, for example: Porsche dealers, auto parts stores, and accessory shops. Our advice regarding spare parts sources is as follows:

Authorized Porsche dealers. This is the best and most completely stocked source of parts. Certain parts are unique to the 924 and can only be purchased through authorized dealerships. It is also the only parts source you should use while your car is under warranty. We did discover that there are a certain number of components which are available as VW, Audi, or Porsche parts, with prices reflecting the ranking of brand among the three. Although it is becoming the exception rather than the rule, a multi-make dealership with a knowledgable parts man can still save you money by selling you a VW part at a VW price, which just happens to be the same part for your Porsche. The above makes have begun to standardize their parts and prices so this may not be an advantage much longer. A knowledge of interchangeable parts, though, may save you a bit of hunting for a part you urgently need. Cultivate a good relationship with a knowledgable parts man.

Auto parts stores. These shops sell a combination of factory-supplier brand parts and parts manufactured by after-market constructors. Their speciality is in the supplying of the more commonly replaceable parts, such as clutch discs, brake pads, antifreeze, and oils. Auto parts stores also have certain remanufactured parts available on an exchange basis. This can save you a bit of money when working on your own car.

Accessory shops. These shops usually deal with the more decorative parts and accessories as well as gasket sets, spark plug wires and other general maintenance items.

Vehicle identification numbers

It is essential that you properly identify your vehicle when purchasing spare parts so that you get the right parts for the job you intend doing. Thus far there have been five different engines, four different transmissions, and two different rear suspension designs for the 924 in the US market alone and those do not include any of the many detail modifications.

The Vehicle Identification plate is located on the left hand windshield pillar and can be read from the outside of the car, through the windshield. The Vehicle Identification Number can also be found on a plate inside the engine compartment, adjacent to the battery.

The Chassis Number is stamped on the upper right hand MacPherson strut housing.

The Engine Identification Number is stamped into the engine, just to the left of the crankcase. It is adjacent to the clutch housing.

To find out the color and type of paint used on the vehicle, the *Paint Number* appears inside the engine compartment for 1979 and 1980 models. For models through 1978, the paint plaque can be found on the doorpost.

A Safety Compliance sticker is required for all vehicles sold in the USA. It is located on the rear door jam of the driver's door. It contains the manufacturing date (month and year), Gross Vehicle Weight Rating (GVWR) and Gross Axle Weight Rating (GAWR).

The Vehicle Identification Plate is located on the windshield pillar and can be read through the windshield

Adjacent to the battery is the Identification plate which also contains the Vehicle Identification Number

The chassis number is stamped on the upper right MacPherson strut mount inside the engine compartment

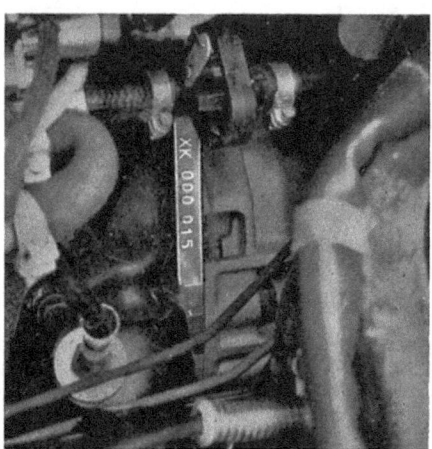

The engine number is stamped to the left of the crankcase, near the clutch housing

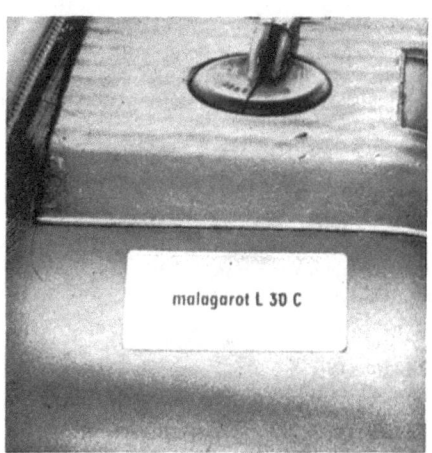

The paint number as it appears inside the engine compartment for 1979 and 1980 models. The paint number plate can be found on the doorpost for models through 1978

MANUFACTURED BY Dr. Ing. h.c. F. PORSCHE AG WEST GERMANY
DATE
GVWR ☐ GAWR front ☐ rear ☐
THIS VEHICLE CONFORMS TO ALL APPLICABLE FEDERAL MOTOR VEHICLE SAFETY AND BUMPER STANDARDS IN EFFECT ON THE DATE OF MANUFACTURE SHOWN ABOVE
VIN ☐
PASSENGER CAR

The safety compliance sticker contains valuable manufacturing data and can be found on the rear door jam

Tools and working facilities

Introduction

A selection of good tools is a fundamental requirement for anyone contemplating the maintenance and repair of a motor vehicle. For the owner who does not possess any, their purchase will prove a considerable expense, offsetting some of the savings made by doing-it-yourself. However, provided that the tools purchased meet the relevant national safety standards and are of good quality, they will last for many years and prove an extremely worthwhile investment.

To help the average owner to decide which tools are needed to carry out the various tasks detailed in this manual, we have compiled three lists of tools under the following headings: *Maintenance and minor repair*, *Repair and overhaul* and *Special*. The newcomer to practical mechanics may wish to start off with the *Maintenance and minor repair* tool kit and confine himself to the simpler jobs around the vehicle. As his confidence and experience grow, he can undertake more difficult tasks, buying extra tools as, and when, they are needed. In this way, a *Maintenance and minor repair* tool kit can be built-up into a *Repair and overhaul* tool kit over a considerable period of time without many major cash outlays. The experienced do-it-yourselfer will probably have a tool kit good enough for most repairs and overhaul procedures and will add tools from the *Special* category when he feels the expense is justified.

Maintenance and minor repair tool kit

The tools given in this list should be considered as a minimum requirement if routine maintenance, servicing and minor repair operations are to be undertaken. We recommend the purchase of combination wrenches (boxed one end, open-ended the other); although more expensive than open-ended ones, they do give the advantages of both types of wrench.

Combination wrenches - 5 through 24 mm
Adjustable wrench - 9 inch
Gearbox/rear axle drain plug key
Spark plug wrench (with rubber insert)
Spark plug gap adjustment tool
Set of feeler gauges
Screwdriver - 4 in long x 1/4 in dia (flat blade)
Screwdriver - 4 in long x 1/4 in dia (Phillips head)
Combination pliers - 6 inch
Hacksaw
Tire pump
Tire pressure gauge
Oil can
Fine emery cloth (1 sheet)
Wire brush (small)
Funnel (medium size)

Repair and overhaul tool kit

These tools are virtually essential for anyone undertaking any major repairs to a motor vehicle, and are additional to those given in the *Maintenance and minor repair* list. Included in this list is a comprehensive set of sockets. Although these are expensive they will be found invaluable as they are so versatile – particularly if various drives are included in the set. We recommend the ⅜ in square-drive type, as this can be used with most proprietary torque wrenches with an appropriate adapter. If you cannot afford a socket set, then inexpensive tubular box wrenches are a useful alternative.

The tools in this list will occasionally need to be supplemented by tools from the *Special* list.

Sockets to cover range in previous list
Reversible ratchet drive (for use with sockets)
Extension piece, 10 inch (for use with sockets)

Universal joint (for use with sockets)
Torque wrench (for use with sockets)
Vice grips – 8 inch
Ball pein hammer
Soft-faced hammer, plastic or rubber
Screwdriver - 6 in long x 5/16 in dia (flat blade)
Screwdriver - 2 in long x 5/16 in dia (flat blade)
Screwdriver - 1½ in long x 1/4 in dia (cross blade)
Screwdriver - 3 in long x 1/8 in dia (electricians)
Pliers - electricians side cutters
Pliers - needle nosed
Pliers - circlip (internal and external)
Cold chisel - 1/2 inch
Scriber (this can be made by grinding the end of a broken hacksaw blade)
Scraper (this can be made by flattening and sharpening one end of a piece of copper pipe)
Center punch
Pin punch
Brake drum nut wrench
Brake drum puller
Valve grinding tool
Steel rule/straightedge
Allen keys
Multi-spline keys
Selection of files
Wire brush (large)
Jack stands
Floor jack (hydraulic type on wheels)

Special tools

The tools in this list are those which are not used regularly, are expensive to buy, or which need to be used in accordance with their manufacturers' instructions. Unless relatively difficult mechanical jobs are undertaken frequently, it will not be economic to buy many of these tools. Where this is the case, you could consider clubbing together with friends (or a motorists club) to make a joint purchase, or borrowing the tools against a deposit from a local garage or tool hire specialist.

The following list contains only those tools and instruments freely available to the public, and not those special tools produced by the vehicle manufacturer specifically for its dealer network. You will find occasional references to these manufacturer's special tools in the text of this manual. Generally, an alternative method of doing the job without the vehicle manufacturer's special tool is given. However, sometimes, there is no alternative to using them. Where this is the case and the relevant tool cannot be bought or borrowed you will have to entrust the work to a franchised garage or the ordering ability of a friendly parts man.

Valve spring compressor (modified for 924 use)
Piston ring compressor
Balljoint separator
Universal hub/bearing puller
Impact screwdriver
Inclinometer
Emission control tester
Micrometer and/or vernier gauge
Dial indicator
Stroboscopic timing light
Tach/Dwell angle meter
Electrical multi-meter
Cylinder compression gauge
Lifting tackle
Light with extension lead

Last, but not least, always keep a supply of old newspapers and clean, lint-free rags available, and try to keep any working area as clean as possible.

Buying tools

For practically all tools, a tool factor is the best source since he will have a very comprehensive range compared with the average garage or accessory shop. Having said that, accessory shops often offer excellent quality tools at discount prices, so it pays to shop around.

There are plenty of good tools around at reasonable prices, but always aim to purchase items which meet the relevant national safety standards. If in doubt, ask the proprietor or manager of the shop for advice before making a purchase.

Care and maintenance of tools

Having purchased a reasonable tool kit, it is necessary to keep the tools in a clean and serviceable condition. After use, always wipe off any dirt, grease and metal particles using a clean, dry cloth, before putting the tools away. Never leave them lying around after they have been used. A simple tool rack on the garage or workshop wall, for items such as screwdrivers and pliers, is a good idea. Store all normal wrenches and sockets in a metal box. Any measuring instruments, gauges, meters, etc, must be carefully stored where they cannot be damaged or become rusty.

Take a little care when the tools are used. Hammer heads inevitably become marked and screwdrivers lose the sharp edge on their blades from time-to-time. A little timely attention with emery cloth, a file, or a sharpening stone will soon restore items like this to a good serviceable finish.

Working facilities

Not to be forgotten when discussing tools, is the workshop itself. If anything more than routine maintenance is to be carried out, some form of suitable working area becomes essential.

It is appreciated that many an owner mechanic is forced by circumstance to remove an engine or similar item, without the benefit of a garage or workshop. Having done this, any repairs should always be done in an enclosed garage.

Any dismantling should be done on a clean flat workbench or table at a suitable working height.

Any workbench needs a vice: one with a jaw opening of 4 in (100 mm) is suitable for most jobs. As mentioned previously, some clean dry storage space is also required for tools, as well as the lubricants, cleaning fluids, touch-up paints and so on which soon become necessary.

Another item which may be required, and which has a much more general usage, is an electric drill with a chuck capacity of at least 3/8 in. This, together with a good range of twist drills, is virtually essential for fitting accessories.

Wrench jaw gap comparison table

Jaw gap (in)	Wrench size
0.250	¼ in AF
0.276	7 mm
0.313	5⁄16 in AF
0.315	8 mm
0.344	11⁄32 in AF
0.354	9 mm
0.375	3⁄8 in AF
0.394	10 mm
0.433	11 mm
0.438	7⁄16 in AF
0.472	12 mm
0.500	½ in AF
0.512	13 mm
0.551	14 mm
0.563	9⁄16 in AF
0.591	15 mm
0.625	5⁄8 in AF
0.630	16 mm
0.669	17 mm
0.686	11⁄16 in AF
0.709	18 mm
0.748	19 mm
0.750	¾ in AF
0.813	13⁄16 in AF
0.866	22 mm
0.875	7⁄8 in AF
0.938	15⁄16 in AF
0.945	24 mm
1.000	1 in AF
1.024	26 mm
1.063	1 1⁄16 in AF; 27 mm
1.125	1 1⁄8 in AF
1.181	30 mm
1.250	1 ¼ in AF
1.260	32 mm
1.313	1 5⁄16 in AF
1.417	36 mm
1.438	1 7⁄16 in AF
1.500	1 ½ in AF
1.575	40 mm
1.614	41 mm
1.625	1 5⁄8 in AF
1.688	1 11⁄16 in AF
1.811	46 mm
1.813	1 13⁄16 in AF
1.875	1 7⁄8 in AF
1.969	50 mm
2.000	2 in AF
2.165	55 mm
2.362	60 mm

Jacking and towing

Jacking - floor jack

The spare tire and the jack are located in the luggage compartment beneath the floor mat.

Wedge-shaped indentations are stamped into the left and right sills beneath the doors. These mark the support points for the jack.

On the 924 Turbo models, the jack support points are wedge-shaped, as above, but they are partially hidden by a cover strip.

Jacking - jack stand and vehicle lift points

When raising a Porsche 924 for installing jack stands, or whenever placing a 924 on a service lift, the four support points are different from the jacking points above.

Front: The jack stands or lift pads must be placed on the longitudinal side member behind and inboard of the wheel.

Rear: Place the jack stands or lift pads on the U-shaped reinforcement brackets just ahead of the rear suspension.

Towing

There are towing eyes installed at the front and rear of the 924's body. Hook or tie tow lines to these points only, as they are reinforced and able to take the strain of towing. If you attempt to tow the car with a rope attached to the front axle, you stand the chance of pulling the steering gear out of the vehicle as well as severely bending the front air dam.

Proper position for the forward arm of a typical service lift

When using the scissor jack supplied with the car, position it at the stamped indentation as shown

Proper position for the rear arm of a typical service lift

A hydraulic floor jack raises the vehicle from the same point as the scissor jack above

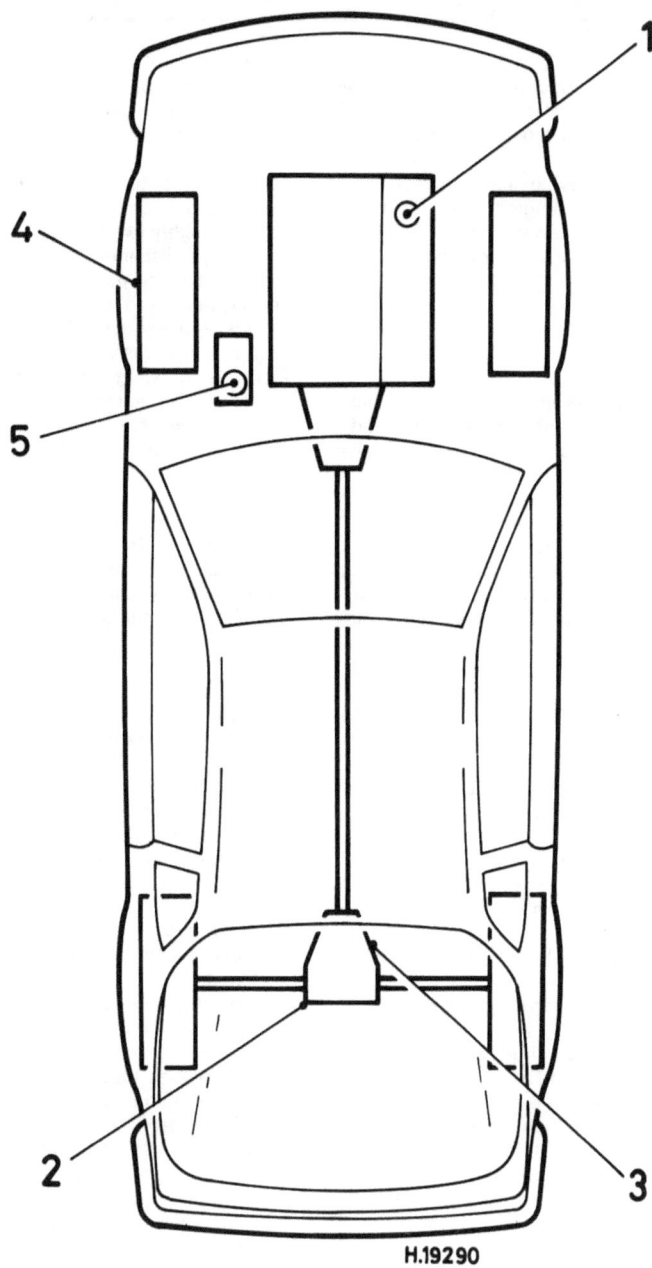

H.19290

Recommended lubricants and fluids

1 Engine	Multigrade engine oil, viscosity range SAE 10W-40, 10W-50, 15W-40 or 15W-50, to API SE or better
2 Transmission	
Manual	Hypoid gear oil SAE 80, API Spec. GL4 or MIL-L2105
Automatic	ATF 'Dexron'
3 Differential	
(Automatic transmissions only)	Hypoid gear oil SAE 90, API Spec. GL5 or MIL-L2105 B
4 Wheel bearings	Lithium-based multipurpose grease
5 Brake fluid	DOT 3 or 4

Safety first!

Professional motor mechanics are trained in safe working procedures. However enthusiastic you may be about getting on with the job in hand, do take the time to ensure that your safety is not put at risk. A moment's lack of attention can result in an accident, as can failure to observe certain elementary precautions.

There will always be new ways of having accidents, and the following points do not pretend to be a comprehensive list of all dangers; they are intended rather to make you aware of the risks and to encourage a safety-conscious approach to all work you carry out on your vehicle.

Essential DOs and DON'Ts

DON'T rely on a single jack when working underneath the vehicle. Always use reliable additional means of support, such as axle stands, securely placed under a part of the vehicle that you know will not give way.

DON'T attempt to loosen or tighten high-torque nuts (e.g. wheel hub nuts) while the vehicle is on a jack; it may be pulled off.

DON'T start the engine without first ascertaining that the transmission is in neutral (or 'Park' where applicable) and the parking brake applied.

DON'T suddenly remove the filler cap from a hot cooling system – cover it with a cloth and release the pressure gradually first, or you may get scalded by escaping coolant.

DON'T attempt to drain oil until you are sure it has cooled sufficiently to avoid scalding you.

DON'T grasp any part of the engine, exhaust or catalytic converter without first ascertaining that it is sufficiently cool to avoid burning you.

DON'T allow brake fluid or antifreeze to contact vehicle paintwork.

DON'T syphon toxic liquids such as fuel, brake fluid or antifreeze by mouth, or allow them to remain on your skin.

DON'T inhale dust – it may be injurious to health (see *Asbestos* below).

DON'T allow any spilt oil or grease to remain on the floor – wipe it up straight away, before someone slips on it.

DON'T use ill-fitting spanners or other tools which may slip and cause injury.

DON'T attempt to lift a heavy component which may be beyond your capability – get assistance.

DON'T rush to finish a job, or take unverified short cuts.

DON'T allow children or animals in or around an unattended vehicle.

DO wear eye protection when using power tools such as drill, sander, bench grinder etc, and when working under the vehicle.

DO use a barrier cream on your hands prior to undertaking dirty jobs – it will protect your skin from infection as well as making the dirt easier to remove afterwards; but make sure your hands aren't left slippery. Note that long-term contact with used engine oil can be a health hazard.

DO keep loose clothing (cuffs, tie etc) and long hair well out of the way of moving mechanical parts.

DO remove rings, wristwatch etc, before working on the vehicle – especially the electrical system.

DO ensure that any lifting tackle used has a safe working load rating adequate for the job.

DO keep your work area tidy – it is only too easy to fall over articles left lying around.

DO get someone to check periodically that all is well, when working alone on the vehicle.

DO carry out work in a logical sequence and check that everything is correctly assembled and tightened afterwards.

DO remember that your vehicle's safety affects that of yourself and others. If in doubt on any point, get specialist advice.

IF, in spite of following these precautions, you are unfortunate enough to injure yourself, seek medical attention as soon as possible.

Asbestos

Certain friction, insulating, sealing, and other products – such as brake linings, brake bands, clutch linings, torque converters, gaskets, etc – contain asbestos. *Extreme care must be taken to avoid inhalation of dust from such products since it is hazardous to health.* If in doubt, assume that they *do* contain asbestos.

Fire

Remember at all times that petrol (gasoline) is highly flammable. Never smoke, or have any kind of naked flame around, when working on the vehicle. But the risk does not end there – a spark caused by an electrical short-circuit, by two metal surfaces contacting each other, by careless use of tools, or even by static electricity built up in your body under certain conditions, can ignite petrol vapour, which in a confined space is highly explosive.

Always disconnect the battery earth (ground) terminal before working on any part of the fuel or electrical system, and never risk spilling fuel on to a hot engine or exhaust.

It is recommended that a fire extinguisher of a type suitable for fuel and electrical fires is kept handy in the garage or workplace at all times. Never try to extinguish a fuel or electrical fire with water.

Note: *Any reference to a 'torch' appearing in this manual should always be taken to mean a hand-held battery-operated electric lamp or flashlight. It does NOT mean a welding/gas torch or blowlamp.*

Fumes

Certain fumes are highly toxic and can quickly cause unconsciousness and even death if inhaled to any extent. Petrol (gasoline) vapour comes into this category, as do the vapours from certain solvents such as trichloroethylene. Any draining or pouring of such volatile fluids should be done in a well ventilated area.

When using cleaning fluids and solvents, read the instructions carefully. Never use materials from unmarked containers – they may give off poisonous vapours.

Never run the engine of a motor vehicle in an enclosed space such as a garage. Exhaust fumes contain carbon monoxide which is extremely poisonous; if you need to run the engine, always do so in the open air or at least have the rear of the vehicle outside the workplace.

If you are fortunate enough to have the use of an inspection pit, never drain or pour petrol, and never run the engine, while the vehicle is standing over it; the fumes, being heavier than air, will concentrate in the pit with possibly lethal results.

The battery

Never cause a spark, or allow a naked light, near the vehicle's battery. It will normally be giving off a certain amount of hydrogen gas, which is highly explosive.

Always disconnect the battery earth (ground) terminal before working on the fuel or electrical systems.

If possible, loosen the filler plugs or cover when charging the battery from an external source. Do not charge at an excessive rate or the battery may burst.

Take care when topping up and when carrying the battery. The acid electrolyte, even when diluted, is very corrosive and should not be allowed to contact the eyes or skin.

If you ever need to prepare electrolyte yourself, always add the acid slowly to the water, and never the other way round. Protect against splashes by wearing rubber gloves and goggles.

When jump starting a car using a booster battery, for negative earth (ground) vehicles, connect the jump leads in the following sequence: First connect one jump lead between the positive (+) terminals of the two batteries. Then connect the other jump lead first to the negative (–) terminal of the booster battery, and then to a good earthing (ground) point on the vehicle to be started, at least 18 in (45 cm) from the battery if possible. Ensure that hands and jump leads are clear of any moving parts, and that the two vehicles do not touch. Disconnect the leads in the reverse order.

Mains electricity and electrical equipment

When using an electric power tool, inspection light etc, always ensure that the appliance is correctly connected to its plug and that, where necessary, it is properly earthed (grounded). Do not use such appliances in damp conditions and, again, beware of creating a spark or applying excessive heat in the vicinity of fuel or fuel vapour. Also ensure that the appliances meet the relevant national safety standards.

Ignition HT voltage

A severe electric shock can result from touching certain parts of the ignition system, such as the HT leads, when the engine is running or being cranked, particularly if components are damp or the insulation is defective. Where an electronic ignition system is fitted, the HT voltage is much higher and could prove fatal.

Routine maintenance

For modifications, and information applicable to later models, see Supplement at end of manual

The following pages detail the maintenance procedures which will help you keep your Porsche 924 in proper working order. There are a number of common sense tasks which should be performed on a regular basis. These are detailed immediately below. Perform these tasks as noted but do not avoid doing them at the required interval checks. The interval maintenance will give you a clear picture of your vehicle's overall condition and the tasks which must be performed to bring it back to peak operating condition.

Weekly and/or whenever you refuel

1   Check the tire pressure. Do this when the tires are cold as heat is generated by running the vehicle and false pressure readings are given.
2   Check the engine oil level. The vehicle must be parked on level ground and must be turned off for at least five minutes before checking. If the oil level is below the 'min' mark on the dipstick (after removing the dipstick, wiping it off, reinserting it all the way into the hole and removing it for a reading) a quart of oil must be added immediately. See the proper oil specification listed under Recommended lubricants and fluids.
3   Check the engine coolant level. The coolant must be within the 'max' and 'min' lines on the translucent expansion tank. If the level is below the 'min' mark, fill the coolant system with a mixture of ethylene glycol-based antifreeze and water, mixed to the proportions proper for your climate. See Chapter 2 for all mixing and filling instructions as well as warnings on the safety of the coolant system under pressure. Do not remove the pressure cap on the expansion tank until you have read all mixing and warning instructions.
4   Check the tension of all engine drive belts. See the appropriate chapters for further information.
5   Check the hydraulic fluid levels in the brake fluid reservoir (all 924's) and the hydraulic clutch reservoir (Turbo). Fill with the proper fluid as required (Chapters 6 and 9).
6   Check the electrolyte level in the battery.
7   Check the fluid level in the windshield washer reservoir.

Maintenance intervals for engine systems, 1976 through 1979

Required after the first 1000 miles (1500 km)

1   Change the engine oil (Chapter 1).
2   Replace the engine oil filter (Chapter 1).
3   Check and adjust the valve clearances and replace the valve cover gasket (Chapter 1).
4   Check the cylinder head bolts for proper torque (Chapter 1).
5   Inspect the coolant system. Check coolant level and coolant hoses for tightness and condition (Chapter 2).
6   Check all V-belts for condition and adjust them as necessary.
7   Make a visual check of the fuel tank, fuel lines, connections, and components of the EEC system (Chapter 3).
8   Make a visual check of the exhaust system for signs of damage.
9   Check and adjust the engine idle and the CO level in the exhaust gases (Chapter 3).

Required every 7500 miles (12,000 km)

1   Change the engine oil (Chapter 1).

Required every 15,000 miles (24,000 km)

1   Change the engine oil (Chapter 1).
2   Replace the engine oil filter (Chapter 1).
3   Check and adjust valve clearances and replace the valve cover gasket (Chapter 1).
4   Inspect the coolant system. Check coolant level and coolant hoses for tightness and condition (Chapter 2).
5   Check all V-belts for condition and adjust them as necessary.
6   Replace the spark plugs (Chapter 5).
7   Check the timing of the ignition and adjust the timing with the proper electronic equipment (Chapter 5).
8   Make a visual inspection of the ignition wires, the distributor cap, and the ignition rotor and replace components as necessary (Chapter 5).
9   Replace the fuel filter (Chapter 3).
10 Make a visual check of the fuel tank, fuel lines, connections, and components of the EEC system (Chapter 3).
11 Make a visual inspection of the exhaust system for signs of damage and rusting (Chapter 3).
12 Check and adjust the engine idle and the CO level in the exhaust gases (Chapter 3).
13 Replace the air cleaner filter element (replace every two years if you drive less than 15,000 miles (24,000 km) every two years).

Required every 30,000 miles (48,000 km). Perform all 15,000 miles (24,000 km) tasks along with the tasks below

1   Check the tightness of the cylinder head bolts (Chapter 1).
2   Make a visual inspection of the crankcase ventilation hoses (Chapter 1).
3   Visually inspect and perform the required checks on the air pump, control valves, air hoses, and manifolds on models with this equipment (Chapter 3).
4   Replace the filter element for the air pump (Chapter 3).

Maintenance intervals for lubrication and general maintenance, 1976 through 1979

Required after the first 1000 miles (1500 km)

1   Manual transmission: Check the oil level in the transmission and top up as necessary (Chapter 7).
2   Automatic transmission: Check the levels of oil in the differential and ATF in the transmission body and top up as necessary (Chapter 7).
3   Check the play of the bearings in the front wheels and adjust as necessary (Chapter 9).
4   Adjust the free play of the clutch and brake pedals.
5   Check the operation of the lights, horn, windshield wipers and the windshield washer.
6   Check the adjustment of your headlights (Chapter 11).
7   Check and correct the pressure in your tires.

Required maintenance every 15,000 miles (24,000 km)

1   Lubricate the accelerator linkage at the pivot pins.
2   Make a visual inspection of the weatherstripping around the

doors, the rear hatch, and the sunroof (where installed). Remove all rubber residue from contact surfaces and lightly coat the seal surfaces with talcum power or a rubber lubricant. Replace any weatherstripping which is cracked or torn (Chapter 12).

3   Manual transmission: Check the oil level in the transmission and top up as necessary (Chapter 7).

4   Automatic transmission: Check the oil level in the differential and the ATF level in the transmission body and top up as necessary (Chapter 7).

5   Check the operation of the windshield washer. Flush out the reservoir and fill with fresh washer fluid.

6   Inspect the front suspension and steering gear for tightness, leaks in the hydraulic suspension units, crack and tears in the rubber boots, and tightness of the tie-rod connections. Make adjustments and tighten bolts as necessary. Replace the rubber boots as necessary (Chapters 8 and 9).

7   Adjust the clutch and brake pedal free play.

8   Make a visual inspection of the braking system, including the brake pads for wear the brake lines and hoses for leaks, and all connections for tightness. Correct problems as necessary (Chapter 9).

9   Check the operation of the lights, horn, windshield wipers, and the windshield washers.

10 Check the adjustment of your headlights (Chapter 11).

11 Check the steering lock and buzzer alarm for proper operation and make adjustments as necessary (Chapter 11).

12 Check the operation of the safety belt warning light and alarm buzzer. Make adjustments as necessary (Chapter 11).

13 Check the electrolyte level in the battery and top up as necessary.

14 Check the air pressure in the tires and inspect them for unusual or uneven wear patterns.

15 Perform a road test of your vehicle and check operation of the braking, clutch, steering, heating, and ventilation systems. Refer to the appropriate chapter to make any necessary corrections.

16 Check the operation of all instruments, control and warning lights as you drive. Make adjustments and corrections according to the information found in the appropriate chapters.

Required every 30,000 miles (48,000 km)

1   Manual transmission: Drain the transmission oil and fill with fresh oil (Chapter 7).

2   Automatic transmission: Change the oil in the differential and drain and refill the transmission body ATF (Chapters 7 and 13).

Maintenance intervals for engine systems, 1980-on (Oxygen sensor system)

Required after the first 1000 miles (1500 km)

1   Change the engine oil (Chapter 1).

2   Replace the engine oil filter (Chapter 1).

3   Check and adjust valve clearances and replace the valve cover gasket (Chapter 1).

4   Check and adjust the engine idle speed and the CO level in the exhaust gases (Chapter 5).

Required every 7500 miles (12,000 km)

1   Change the engine oil (Chapter 1).

Required every 15,000 miles (24,000 km)

1   Change the engine oil (Chapter 1).

2   Replace the engine oil filter (Chapter 1).

3   Check and adjust valve clearances and replace the valve cover gasket (Chapter 1).

Required every 30,000 miles (48,000 km)

1   Change the engine oil (Chapter 1).

2   Replace the engine oil filter (Chapter 1).

3   Check and adjust valve clearances and replace the valve cover gasket (Chapter 1).

4   Check the V-belts and the timing belt. Replace belts as necessary and adjust the others as required. New belts must be readjusted after the first 1000 miles (1500 km) of use.

5   Replace the spark plugs. If you drive less than 30,000 miles (48,000 km) in two years, replace spark plugs at two year intervals, as a minimum replacement figure (Chapter 5).

6   Replace the air cleaner filter element (Chapter 1).

7   Reset the oxygen sensor mileage counter and replace the oxygen sensor unit (Chapter 3).

Maintenance intervals for lubrication and general maintenance, 1980 – on (all models including Turbo)

Required after the first 1000 miles (1500 km)

1   Check the coolant level and inspect the hoses for tightness and condition (Chapter 2).

2   Manual transmission: Check the oil level in the transmission and top up as necessary (Chapter 7).

3   Automatic transmission: Check the oil level in the differential and the ATF level in the transmission body. Top up as necessary (Chapter 7).

4   Check the play in the front wheel bearings and adjust as necessary (Chapter 9).

5   Adjust the free play in the clutch and brake pedals.

6   Check the operation of the lights, horn, windshield wipers, and windshield washers.

7   Check the adjustment of the headlights and correct as necessary (Chapter 12).

8   Check the air pressure in the tires.

9   Make a road test check of the clutch, brakes, steering, heating, and ventilation systems. Correct problems as necessary.

10 Check the performance of all instruments, control, and warning lights during your driving check.

Required every 15,000 miles (24,000 km)

1   Check the coolant level and inspect all hoses and hose clamps for condition and tightness (Chapter 2).

2   Lubricate the pivot points of the accelerator linkage.

3   Inspect the weatherstripping around the doors, rear hatch, and sunroof (where installed). Remove all rubber residue from the contact surfaces and lightly coat the weatherstrip with talcum powder or rubber lubricant. Replace any weatherstripping which is cracked or torn (Chapter 12).

4   Manual transmission: Check the oil level and top up as necessary (Chapter 7).

5   Automatic transmission: Check the levels of oil in the differential and ATF in the transmission body and top up as necessary (Chapter 7):

6   Check the operation of the windshield wipers and windshield washer. Adjust the wipers as necessary. Flush the windshield washer reservoir and fill it with fresh fluid.

7   Check the front axle steering gear, tie-rod connections, the rubber boots, and other essential front axle components for tightness, condition and adjustment. Make adjustments and replace as necessary (Chapters 8 and 10).

8   Adjust the free play in the brake and clutch pedals.

9   Visually inspect the condition of all braking system components. Check for leaks, pinched hoses, loose connections and any signs of corrosion or other damage to the lines. Make adjustments and corrections as necessary (Chapter 9).

10 Check the operation of the lights and horn.

11 Check the adjustment of the headlights and correct as necessary (Chapter 11).

12 Check the operation of the steering lock and buzzer.

13 Check the operation of the seat belt warning light and warning buzzer.
14 Check the electrolyte level in the battery and top up as necessary.
15 Check the air pressure in the tires and inspect the tread for signs of unusual and improper wear.
16 Make a driving check for the operation of the clutch, brakes, steering, heating, and ventilation systems.
17 Check for correct operation of all instruments, controls and warning lights.

Required every 30,000 miles (48,000 km)

1 Manual transmission: Change the transmission oil (Chapter 13).
2 Automatic transmission: Change the oil in the differential and ATF in the transmission body (Chapters 7 and 13).

Troubleshooting

This section provides an easy reference guide to the more common faults which may occur in the operation of your Porsche 924. These faults and their most probable causes are grouped according to their respective systems, and are further cross referenced to the Chapter which deals with the problems.

Troubleshooting is a practice which requires only a little bit of logic and a basic understanding of what you are dealing with. A systematic approach to the problem at hand will save many hours of random searching and, possibly, a costly visit to a mechanic who is only going to employ the methods above and charge you well for the service.

Logic is a bit more than checking a system part by part. Begin any engine problem by thinking about what has happened since the car last ran well. Have you used a different brand of gasoline? Have you filled the gas tank recently? Could you have left the lights on overnight? Start with the most simple explanation, a change in normal practices or an error, and work toward the most difficult mechanical possibility.

Finally, take the time to find out why something has gone wrong. The solution to an empty fuel tank is different from a blown fuse, but each has a reason for happening. By understanding the cause of the problem, you can take steps to prevent the same problem from happening again. In the case of a blown fuse, for example, failing to find the cause of the fuses' blowing could result in the replacement of a several-hundred dollar electrical component instead of a twenty-five cent fuse the next time around.

Engine

1 Engine will not turn over or turns slowly

1 Turn the ignition switch to the "ON" position and switch on some of the electrical components such as lights, windshield wipers, and the radio. If these fail to function, the most probable cause is a defective or discharged battery. Check the condition of the battery and make sure the terminals are in contact and are clean.
2 If the headlights work normally, turn the ignition key to the "START" position with the headlights switched on. If the lights and the instrument panel lights dim, this indicates that the battery is in a discharged state or that the connections are poor.
3 If the headlights stay bright and the instrument panel lights don't dim when the ignition key is turned, this suggests a fault in the wiring between the ignition switch and the starter motor. Check the ignition wiring diagram which is appropriate to your model in Chapter 5. You may test the ignition switch by running a short wire between the power in and power out terminals of the switch. If this causes the engine to start, the ignition switch is faulty.
4 If the ignition switch is not at fault, check the starter solenoid and the starter motor (Chapter 5). If your vehicle has an automatic transmission, lift up the plate which surrounds the selector lever and make sure that the contact points on the switch contact are properly aligned and do not have dirt or other obstructions in the way.

2 Engine turns over but will not start

1 Once you have eliminated lack of fuel and crossed wires as a possible cause, perform the troubleshooting drill which follows Chapter 5. This will eliminate the ignition as the problem if all the tests are carried out and the engine still fails to start.
2 Perform a check of the injectors. This will eliminate the fuel pump and injectors as a source of the problem (Chapter 3).
3 Review Chapter 3 and test each of the components of the fuel starting system. Begin with the first component in the flow chart description and work through the components one at a time from the intake through ignition. Be logical and systematic.

3 Engine difficult to start when cold (outside temperature)

1 Check the output of the injectors (Chapter 3). If you can hear the pump operating but do not get good flow, the possible faults are dependent upon outside temperatures. If it is below freezing, the most common fault is ice in the fuel lines. Move the car to a garage and warm the car above freezing and attempt to start it again after an hour or so. Use a fuel system antifreeze additive to prevent further icing.
2 If the outside temperature is above freezing and the engine is difficult to start, see the steps below.

4 Engine difficult to start - cold engine

1 Once you have eliminated lack of fuel and lack of spark as problems, check the operation of the thermo time switch (Chapter 3).
2 If the thermo time switch checks out, check the output of the cold start valve (Chapter 3).
3 If the cold start valve checks out, examine the auxiliary air regulator's performance (Chapter 3).
4 Check your ignition timing (Chapter 5).

5 Engine difficult to start - hot engine

1 One you have eliminated lack of fuel and lack of spark as the cause of the problem, follow the elimination steps in the above cold start problem-solving to determine whether these components are working when they shouldn't be.
2 Check the output of the injectors (Chapter 3).
3 If your vehicle is a 1979 model, check the operation of the hot start solenoid (Chapter 3).
4 Check the idle adjustment and make any necessary adjustments (Chapter 3).
5 Check your ignition timing (Chapter 5).
6 Check engine compression (Chapter 1).

6   Poor performance during warm-up

1   Carefully check every join in the components of the fuel system for air leaks.
2   Check the performance of the cold start system components to ensure that they shut off or close at the proper time.
3   Check the continuity of ignition wires and components when cold and again at engine operating temperatures (Chapter 5).
4   Check the output of the injectors (Chapter 3).

7   Engine idles erratically and stalls

1   Check all components of the fuel system for air leaks (Chapter 3).
2   Check the output of the injectors (Chapter 3).
3   Check for water in the fuel. Drain about one quart of gasoline into a clear glass jar from the fuel line between the fuel tank and damper. Water will appear as a clear layer beneath the gasoline in the jar. If water is found, drain the fuel tank and fill it with fresh fuel from a reputable dealer.
4   Examine the wires of the ignition system for tight connection and the spark plugs for cleanliness and proper gap (Chapter 5).
5   Check the operation of the EGR valve (Chapter 3).
6   If none of the above steps solves the problem, perform a compression check on the engine (Chapter 1).

8   Lack of power, poor acceleration

1   Check the air cleaner filter to see if it is plugged or in need of replacement.
2   Check the condition of the spark plugs and check also the injectors. Be especially watchful for injector spray patterns and smooth operation of the sensor plate and operating lever (Chapter 3).
4   Examine the positive crankcase ventilation system and the evaporative emission control components for blockages, cuts or crushing of the hoses, and proper operation of the various components.
5   If your vehicle is equipped with an air pump, check the operation of the entire air injection system and the operation of the EGR valve (Chapter 3).
6   On cars with manual transmissions, check for clutch slip. Start the engine and select the highest forward gear. Engage the clutch while firmly holding down on the brake pedal at the same time. If the engine continues to run without stalling, the clutch is slipping.
7   On cars which have automatic transmissions, make a check of performance using the troubleshooting chart for automatic transmissions found in Chapter 7.
8   Check the ignition timing (Chapter 5).
9   Check the compression of the engine (Chapter 1).

9   Erratic performance during cruising

1   Check the operation of the fuel pump and the injectors. Use the tests in Chapter 3 to determine whether the fuel pump, accumulator, fuel filter, fuel distributor, or injectors may be at fault.
2   Remove the spark plugs and check their condition and gap. The color chart in Chapter 5 will help you to 'read' the type of charge being burned in the cylinders.
3   Check the cold starting system, particularly the cold start valve to see that it is shutting completely off and not operating at all under normal running conditions.
4   Check the vacuum line to the distributor for tight fit and lack of pinching or cuts in the tubing. Perform a test on a distributor test bench (Chapter 5) to determine whether the distributor is advancing properly. Check the operation of the vacuum amplifier.
5   Make sure that the air cleaner element is operating properly, is free of plugging, and is properly installed.

10   Car surges while decelerating

1   In cars which have manual transmissions and emission controls installed, check the operation of the decel valve.
2   Check the operation of the EGR valve.
3   On vehicles with automatic transmissions, check the throttle control cable on the transmission.

11   Poor engine braking

1   Check the throttle housing and its components for proper operation.
2   Check the operation of the decel valve, if your car has a manual transmission and emission controls installed (Chapter 3).

Coolant system

12   Overheating

1   Check the coolant level in the expansion tank. If the level is not between the upper and lower lines cast into the sides of the translucent tank, prepare a mixture of antifreeze according to the mixing directions in Chapter 2. Do no remove the coolant system pressure cap from the top of the expansion tank until you have reviewed the instructions and warnings in Chapter 2.
2   If the system is losing coolant on a regular basis, carefully inspect all hoses and connections for hose condition and loose or overtightened hoses. See Chapter 2 for the proper check procedures.
3   Check the operation of the electric fan and the thermo switch (Chapter 2).
4   If the engine overheats rapidly, but the lower section of the radiator remains cool, remove and perform the appropriate tests on the thermostats (Chapter 2).
5   Check the spark plugs for evidence of a very lean air/fuel mixture.
6   Check the ignition timing (Chapter 5).
7   If the engine continues to run hot after all of the above tests and checks, drain the coolant system and flush it with a proprietary cleaner. Make sure that the cleaner is suitable for use in alloy engines before using. If calcium deposits or rust and scale are a problem, use distilled water in place of tap water.

13   Coolant too cool

1   Perform an operational check of the thermostat (Chapter 2).

Electrical

14   Battery discharges rapidly

1   Check the alternator drive belt for proper adjustment and condition. Adjust or replace as necessary (Chapter 5).
2   Check the electrolyte level in the battery and top up with distilled water if necessary.
3   Check the lighting circuits for shorting or grounding out (Chapter 11).
4   Check the output of the voltage regulator (Chapter 5).
5   Have a competent service center check the alternator output.

15   Wiper motor fails to work

1   Check the operation of the proper fuse and relay and replace as necessary (Chapter 11).
2   Check all connections for tight fit and evidence of any frayed or broken wires.
3   Have a competent service center check the operation of the motor and replace if necessary.

16   Wiper motor works very slowly and draws excess current

1   Check the motor for dirt and grit around the shaft and clean it as necessary (Chapter 11).

2 Check the drive linkage for binding, bent parts, or lack of proper lubrication at the pivot points.
3 Examine the motor for binding, worn bearings, or other signs of abuse or wear. Have a competent service center check the motor and replace as necessary.

17 Wiper motor works slowly but draws little current

1 Have the motor checked out by a competent service center.

18 Wiper motor works but blades remain static

1 Check the linkage and replace if faulty or damaged (Chapter 11).
2 Check the wiper arm holding nuts for tightness and the splined drive pivots for damage or stripping out.

19 Headlights do not come on

1 Check the headlight sealed beam units for burning or broken filaments.
2 Check the headlight relay (Chapter 11).
3 Check the operation of the headlight switch.
4 Check the wiring for breaks and bad connections.

20 Headlights come on but fade (engine stopped)

1 Recharge the battery and perform checks on the battery charge if the problem persists (Section 14).

21 Headlights give poor illumination

1 Make sure the lenses are clean.
2 Examine the reflectors for dirt and corrosion, replacing any units which show those signs.
3 Check the adjustment of the headlights and make any necessary corrections (Chapter 11).
4 If the headlight lens is old and the unit has discolored, replace the unit (Chapter 11).
5 Check all electrical connectors for clean, tight fitting.

22 Lights flash on and off, especially over bumps

1 Examine all wiring and connectors for loose connections or breaks. Make sure that the system grounds are properly installed (Chapter 11).

23 Headlights do not raise when they are turned on

1 Check the linkage for binding and lack of lubrication (Chapter 12).
2 Check the operation of the motor.
3 Check the operation of the fuse and relay for the motor.

24 Horn does not work

1 Check the fuse and horn relay (Chapter 11).
2 Remove the pad in the center of the steering wheel and examine the horn switch for tight connections and good contact between the two plates of the horn button (Chapter 11).
3 Have the horn tested and adjusted by a competent service center.

25 Horn does not shut off

1 Remove the pad on the steering wheel and separate the two leads from the horn button (Chapter 11).
2 Check the horn relay for condition and operation.

26 Poor tone in the horn

1 Check all horn wiring for loose connections (Chapter 11).
2 Disconnect each horn in turn to determine which horn is bad. Replace that horn.

27 Fuel level gauge reads 'maximum' continuously

1 Remove the fuel tank sending unit and test (Chapter 3).
2 Remove the gauge and test.
3 Check all wiring for defects.

28 Fuel level gauge gives no reading

1 Check all wiring in this system for proper connectors and proper grounding (Chapter 11).

29 No reading on tachometer

1 Have the tachometer and transistorized ignition control unit tested by a qualified mechanic.

30 Tachometer reading inaccurate or wildly fluctuating

1 Have the tachometer and transistorized ignition control unit tested by a qualified mechanic.

Clutch

31 Clutch judders when engaged

1 Check the condition of the bonded mounts for the engine, drive-line tube, and the transmission (Chapters 1 and 7). Tighten or replace mounts as necessary. On 1978 and later models, check the condition of the engine shock absorber beneath the engine.
2 Examine the clutch lining for thickness. If there is useable lining material shown, remove the clutch disc and pressure plate and inspect these components according to the instructions in Chapter 6. Correct any oil leaks which might be causing problems and replace clutch components as necessary.
3 With the clutch disc and pressure plate removed, check the condition of the pilot bearing in the center of the flywheel and correct any problem as necessary.
4 Inspect the drive shaft and drive shaft dampers for proper installation and condition.

32 Clutch drags or does not allow gears to engage

1 Check the adjustment of the clutch cable (standard models) and make any necessary corrections (Chapter 6).
2 If the car has sat idle for some time, the clutch friction plate may be seized on the splined shaft. This is the result of a small amount of rust or corrosion holding the plate on the shaft. It is not a major problem and will go away with increased use of the car. To free the clutch disc from the shaft, engage the transmission in top gear, engage the parking brake and depress the clutch pedal. Engage the starter and allow the engine to turn over. If the clutch disc is badly seized, the engine will not turn. This solution is a temporary measure and the clutch disc and pressure plate should be removed and inspected (Chapter 6), as well as inspecting the splined shaft and cleaning the splines with a wire brush.

3 If the above solution does not free the clutch disc, it will be necessary to remove the clutch disc and pressure plate. Inspect all parts carefully and replace parts as necessary.

33 Clutch slips

1 Check the adjustment of the clutch operating cable and make any corrective adjustments required (Chapter 6).
2 Inspect the clutch disc friction lining thickness (Chapter 6).
3 Remove the clutch disc and pressure plate and look for signs of oil leaks, hard spots, and other evidence of abuse or wear (Chapter 6).

Manual transmission

34 Transmission balks on downshifts, gear shifts slow

1 Synchromesh bodies are worn or do not have proper clearances after reassembly. The transmission will have to be stripped down and repaired (Chapter 7).

35 Gears jump out of mesh

1 The shift forks are worn or out of adjustment; the grooves in the selector rod are worn; or there is excessive end float at the end of the gear shafts. In any case, the transmission must be stripped down and inspected for the appropriate repairs to be made (Chapter 7).

36 Excessive transmission noise

1 Check the oil level and top up as required.
2 If the noise persists, the cause is most likely worn parts in the transmission. Strip the transmission and inspect all parts for the appropriate repairs to be made (Chapter 7).

37 Difficulty in engaging gears

1 Check the adjustment of the clutch (Chapter 6).
2 Check the adjustment of the shift linkage. Inspect all pivoting and rubbing components for binding and bending.
3 If the above adjustments do not solve the problem, the correction to this matter lies in the condition of internal transmission parts. Strip the transmission and inspect all parts for the appropriate repairs to be made (Chapter 7).

Automatic transmission

38 No drive

1 In all gears: ATF level too low (Chapter 7).

39 Erratic drive performance

1 In all forward gears: ATF level too low (Chapter 7).

40 Erratic shifts when engaging D or R from N

1 Idle speed set too high (Chapter 3).
2 ATF level too low (Chapter 7).

41 Upshift too long from 1 to 2

1 ATF level too low (Chapter 7).

42 Upshift too long from 2 to 3

1 ATF level too low (Chapter 7).

43 Kickdown malfunctions

1 Control pressure cable out of adjustment (Chapter 7).

44 Poor acceleration

1 Ignition, fuel supply, or compression problems (Chapters 1, 3, 5).
2 Throttle cable out of adjustment (Chapter 3).
3 Control pressure cable out of adjustment (Chapter 7).

45 Top speed cannot be reached

1 Ignition, fuel supply, or compression problems (Chapters 1, 3, 5).
2 Throttle cable out of adjustment (Chapter 3).
3 Control pressure out of adjustment (Chapter 7.)

Final drive components (except transmission)

46 Excessive vibration

1 Check all of the mounts of the engine, drive shaft housing, and transmission for tightness. Make any necessary corrections (Chapters 1 and 7).
2 Remove the drive shaft and have it checked for balance and distortion (Chapter 7). This requires a dynamic balance test.
3 Examine the rear wheel bearings and the axle shafts for tightness and alignment (Chapter 10).

47 Knock or 'clunk' when taking up drive or changing gear

1 Check the mounts of the engine, drive shaft housing, and transmission for tightness (Chapters 1 and 7). Make any necessary corrections.
2 Check the tightness of the gears in the planetary gear set in the final drive (Chapter 7).
3 Twist the axle shafts back and forth to check for wear in the axle shaft splines.

48 Rear axle noisy on turns

1 Check the planetary gearbox for wear (Chapter 7).

49 Rear axle noisy under all conditions

1 Check the ring and pinion gears for proper adjustment and the planetary gear set in the differential for wear. This will require removing and stripping the transmission (Chapter 7).

Brakes

50 Brake pedal travels almost to the floor before the brakes operate

1 Check the fluid level in the master cylinder reservoir and top up as required (Chapter 9).
2 Check the brake pads (front) and the brake linings (rear) for wear and replace if necessary (Chapter 9).
3 Make a visual inspection of the brake linings and hoses for fractures or leaks. Tighten connections to proper torque specifications or replace damaged parts as required.

4   Check the operation of the master cylinder and the brake booster and replace or rebuild parts as required (Chapter 9).

51   Brake pedal feels springy

1   New brake pads not yet bedded in.
2   Scored or unevenly worn brake drums and discs may also be a cause. Inspect the drums and discs according to the instructions in Chapter 9 and have the drums and discs skimmed or replaced according to the results of the inspection.
3   Examine the mounting of the master cylinder for looseness and tighten the nuts as required (Chapter 9).
4   Check the clearance on the booster rod to master cylinder piston rod connection. Adjust as necessary (Chapter 9). Make sure that the brake booster and master cylinder are manufactured by the same company, or they will not be compatible.

52   Brake pedal feels spongy and soggy

1   Bleed the system to remove any possible air in the hydraulic lines. If the brake fluid is over two years old, drain the entire braking system and fill it with new hydraulic fluid from a previously-unopened can (Chapter 9).
2   Examine the calipers, fittings, lines and hoses of the braking system for leakage, loose connections, broken or punctured hoses, or worn seals. Replace parts and rebuild calipers as necessary. Remember to rebuild front brake calipers and/or wheel cylinders as a set on an axle (all front or rear at once) (Chapter 9).
3   Check for leaks in the master cylinder by looking for air bubbles in the brake fluid reservoir. Rebuild the master cylinder as necessary (Chapter 9).

53   Excessive brake pedal pressure is required to slow car

1   Check the brake pads and brake shoe linings for glazing. This problem is usually caused by improper breaking-in or repeated hard stops. The glaze can usually be broken by sanding the surface slightly with fine sandpaper. Do not breathe the dust from this procedure.
2   Check the brake booster unit, including the vacuum lines and the check valve for proper operation (Chapter 9).
3   If neither of these checks provides a solution, the problem may be one of the material on new brake pads being of a harder material than the old ones; contamination of the friction surfaces by grease, oil or brake fluid; or pads in need of replacement.

54   Brakes pulling to one side

1   This is an unusual problem with the 924, as the negative scrub radius characteristics of the suspension and the diagonal braking circuits should prevent such an occurrence. The first check, therefore, is to make sure that the brake lines and hoses are not broken, plugged, or leaking.
2   If the problem persists, have the alignment of the car checked by a competent service facility.

55   Brakes bind, drag, or lock

1   Check the adjustment of the rear brake shoes and slacken the adjusting nuts if necessary (Chapter 9).
2   Check the adjustment of the handbrake (Chapter 9).
3   Examine the master cylinder and brake booster for incorrect operation. Make sure that the check valve in the brake booster vacuum line is installed in the proper direction (Chapter 9).

Steering and suspension

56   Steering vague, car wanders and 'floats' at speed

1   Check tire pressures.
2   Check the operation of the shock absorbers (Chapter 10).
3   Check the play in the ball joints (Chapter 10).
4   Have the suspension geometry checked and aligned if necessary.
5   Make sure that the tires on your car are not mixed between radial and crossply construction. All tires must be of the same construction and of equal rolling radius.

57   Steering heavy and stiff

1   Check tire pressures.
2   Check the adjustment of the steering gear tension adjusting bolt on the pinion cover plate. Adjust as required (Chapter 8).
3   Have the toe-in of the front suspension checked and adjusted by a competent service facility.

58   Wheel wobble and vibration

1   Check the wheels for bent rims, and the tires to make sure they have no bulges or other obvious out-of-round conditions.
2   Check that the wheel nuts are correctly tightened in a cross pattern and torqued to the proper setting (Specifications, Chapter 9).
3   Check the balance of the wheels. This can be done quickly by a tire store or similar shop.
4   Check the free play in the ball joints (Chapter 10).
5   Check the front wheel bearing's adjustment (Chapter 10).

59   General suspension and steering rattle

1   Check all steering gear mounting bolts for tightness (Chapter 8).
2   Check all bushings in the front suspension for wear and separation of the metal pieces from the rubber bushes (Chapter 10).
3   Check the adjustment of the steering gear tension adjusting bolt on the pinion cover plate. Adjust as required (Chapter 8).
4   Check that the two steering column bearings are not worn out, by grasping the center of the steering column beneath the dashboard and trying to shake the steering column up and down.
5   Examine all suspension mounts for wear in the bushings or loose fittings (Chapter 10).

Chapter 1 Engine

For modifications, and information applicable to later models, see Supplement at end of manual

Contents

Specifications

Specifications common to all models (Standard)

Engine

Type	Water-cooled, overhead camshaft, 4 cylinder, 4 stroke, internal combustion engine (Otto cycle), with the cylinders arranged in-line
Bore mm (in)	86.5 (3.41)
Stroke mm (in)	84.4 (3.32)
Displacement cc (cu in)	1984 (121.06)
Firing order	1, 3, 4, 2
Crankcase...................................	Cast iron crankcase (engine block) with aluminum alloy oil pan.
Crankshaft..................................	Forged steel
Crankshaft bearings	Plain bearings (measurements and clearances available in text)
Engine weight (bare)	142 kg (313 lb)
Piston-pin bush..............................	Press fit, bronze
Pistons	Cast light alloy (measurements and clearances available in text)
Piston pins	Floating pins, steel; with circlips
Piston rings	2 compression and 1 oil scraper ring
Cylinder head	Light alloy
Valve seat inserts...........................	Shrink fit into cylinder head casting
Insert material, intake.......................	Gray cast iron
Insert material, exhaust	Cast steel
Valve guides................................	Press fit into cylinder head, bronze special alloy
Valve arrangement	1 intake, 1 exhaust, overhead location
Exhaust valve...............................	Reinforced seat
Valve springs...............................	2 coil springs (inner/outer arrangement)
Valve operation.............................	By overhead camshaft and bucket-type cam followers
Camshaft...................................	Billet case-hardened steel
Camshaft bearings...........................	Machined into cylinder head, no shells
Camshaft drive	Fiberglass-reinforced, toothed belt driven by a corresponding pulley on the oil pump (crankshaft end)
Drive belt dimensions	9.5 x 888 mm

Engine cooling ....

Pressurized cooling system, water/ethylene glycol coolant, electric fan with thermo switch (Chapter 2).

Engine lubrication

Lubrication	Pressure type lubricating system with a rotary (sickle-type) pump
Oil filter	Full flow
System oil pressure (at 5000 rpm).............	4 bar (58 psi) minimum at 80° to 100°C (176° to 212°F)
Oil pressure monitor.........................	Indicator lamp and pressure switch
Maximum oil temperature	150°C (302°F)
Oil consumption	1.5 liters/1000 km (1.5 US qts/600 miles)

Specification differences for Turbo models

Engine
Type .... Engine is turbocharged via an exhaust-driven turbocharger (Chapter 4)
Piston rings .... 2 compression rings, no oil scraper ring
Oil pressure (at 5000 rpm)................................. 4 bar (58 psi) minimum at 80° to 100°C (176° to 212°F)
Drive belt dimensions...................................... 9.5 x 1050 mm
Engine weight (bare) .... 165 kg (364 lb)

Specifications according to market

1976-1977½, US market:
Engine
Compression ratio 8.0:1
Horsepower at rpm .... 95.4 at 5500
Kilowatts power at rpm .... 71 at 5500
Torque in ft-lb at rpm .... 109.2 at 3000
Torque in m-kg at rpm .... 15.1 at 3000
Maximum engine speed...................................... 6500 prm

Valve clearances
Warm engine (engine oil at about 80°C or 176°F)
    Intake .... 0.20 mm (0.008 in)
    Exhaust .... 0.45 mm (0.018 in)
Engine cold
    Intake .... 0.10 mm (0.004 in)
    Exhaust .... 0.40 mm (0.016 in)

Timing with 1 mm (0.04 in) valve clearance
Intake opens .... 5° BTDC
Intake closes .... 37° ABDC
Exhaust opens... 43° BBDC
Exhaust closes .... 7° ATDC

1977½-1979 US market:
Engine
Compression ratio 8.5:1
Horsepower at rpm .... 110 at 5750
Kilowatts power at rpm .... 82 at 5750
Torque in ft-lb at rpm .... 111.3 at 3500
Torque in m-kg at rpm .... 15.8 at 3500
Maximum engine speed...................................... 6500 rpm

Valve clearances
Warm engine (engine oil at about 80°C or 176°F)
    Intake .... 0.20 mm (0.008 in)
    Exhaust .... 0.45 mm (0.018 in)
Engine cold
    Intake .... 0.10 mm (0.004 in)
    Exhaust .... 0.40 mm (0.016 in)

Timing with 1 mm (0.04 in) valve clearance
Intake opens .... 6° BTDC
Intake closes .... 42° ABDC
Exhaust opens... 47° BBDC
Exhaust closes .... 2° ATDC

1980-on, US market:
Engine
Compression ratio 9.0:1
Horsepower at rpm .... 115 at 5750
Kilowatts power at rpm .... 85 at 5750
Torque in ft-lb at rpm .... 111.3 at 3500
Torque in m-kg at rpm .... 15.9 at 3500
Maximum engine speed...................................... 6500 rpm

Valve clearances
Warm engine (engine oil at about 80°C or 176°F)
    Intake .... 0.20 mm (0.008 in)
    Exhaust .... 0.45 mm (0.018 in)
Engine cold
    Intake .... 0.10 mm (0.004 in)
    Exhaust .... 0.40 mm (0.016 in)

Timing with 1 mm (0.04 in) valve clearance
Intake opens .... 6° BTDC
Intake closes .... 42° ABDC
Exhaust opens.. 47° BBDC
Exhaust closes .... 2° ATDC

1976-on, European market:
Engine
Compression ratio 9.3:1
Horsepower at rpm .... 125 at 5800
Kilowatts power at rpm .... 92 at 5800
Torque in ft-lb at rpm .... 121.7 at 3500
Torque in m-kg at rpm .... 16.8 at 3500
Maximum engine speed... 6500 rpm

Valve clearances
Warm engine (engine oil at about 80°C or 176°F)
    Intake .... 0.20 + 0.5 mm (0.008 + 0.002 in)
    Exhaust .... 0.45 + 0.5 mm (0.018 + 0.002 in)
Engine cold
    Intake .... 0.10 + 0.5 mm (0.004 + 0.002 in)
    Exhaust .... 0.40 + 0.5 mm (0.016 + 0.002 in)

Timing with 1 mm (0.04 in) valve clearance
Intake opens .... 6° BTDC
Intake closes .... 42° ABDC
Exhaust opens.. 47° BBDC
Exhaust closes .... 2° ATDC

Turbo, US market:
Engine
Compression ratio 7.5:1
Horsepower at rpm .... 150 at 5500
Kilowatts power at rpm .... 110 at 5500
Torque in ft-lb at rpm .... 147 at 3500
Torque in m-kg at rpm .... 21 at 3500
Maximum engine speed... 6500 rpm

Valve clearances
Warm engine (engine oil at about 80°C or 176°F)
    Intake .... 0.20 mm (0.008 in)
    Exhaust .... 0.45 mm (0.018 in)
Engine cold
    Intake .... 0.10 mm (0.004 in)
    Exhaust .... 0.40 mm (0.016 in)

Timing with 1 mm (0.04 in) valve clearance
Intake opens .... 6° BTDC
Intake closes .... 42° ABDC
Exhaust opens.. 47° BBDC
Exhaust closes .... 2° ATDC

Turbo, European market:
Engine
Compression ratio 7.5:1
Horsepower at rpm .... 170 at 5500
Kilowatts power at rpm .... 125 at 5500
Torque in ft-lb at rpm .... 180 at 3500
Torque in m-kg at rpm .... 25.5 at 3500
Maximum engine speed... 6500 rpm

Valve clearances
Warm engine (engine oil at about 80°C or 176°F)
    Intake .... 0.20 mm (0.008 in)
    Exhaust .... 0.45 mm (0.018 in)
Engine cold
    Intake .... 0.10 mm (0.004 in)
    Exhaust .... 0.40 mm (0.016 in)

Engine identification codes

1976-1977½, 95 Hp engines
49 States and Canada .... 924 XH
California .... 924 XF
1977½-1979, 110 Hp Engines
49 States and Canada .... 924 XG
California... 924 XE

1980-on, 115 Hp engines
US, Canada, Japan .... 924 VC
1976-on, 125 Hp engines
Europe... 924 XK
Great Britain, Australia .... 924 XJ
Turbo, US and Europe.. M 31/02

Tolerances and torque specifications

Tolerances and wear limits

	new	wear limit
Engine, pistons, cylinder		
Cylinder-to-piston clearance, mm	0.03	0.08
in	0.0011	0.0031
Weight difference of pistons	not greater than 14 gm	
Piston ring side clearance, mm	0.04 to 0.07	0.10
in	0.0016 to 0.0028	0.004
Piston ring end gap, mm	0.3 to 0.5	1.0
in	0.012 to 0.020	0.04
Connecting rod weight	815 to 927 gm	
Maximum permissible weight difference	not greater than 8 gm	
Connecting rod bushing diameter, mm	24.012 to 24.018	
in	0.9454 to 0.9456	
Piston pin diameter, mm......................................	23.996 to 24.000	
in	0.9447 to 0.9449	
Connecting rod bushing-to-piston pin radial play, mm..........	0.01 to 0.02	
in............	0.0004 to 0.0008	
Crankshaft runout, mm	max. 0.06	
in	max. 0.0024	
Connecting rod bearing journal diameter, new, mm	47.95 to 47.97	
in	1.888 to 1.889	
Connecting rod bearing-to-crankshaft radial play, mm	0.02 to 0.07	0.1
in	0.0008 to 0.0028	0.004
Connecting rod bearing-to-crankshaft end play, mm	0.05 to 0.08	0.4
in	0.0020 to 0.0012	0.016
Crankshaft bearing journal diameter, mm......................	63.95 to 63.97	
in	2.518 to 2.519	
Crankshaft bearing-to-crankshaft radial play, mm...............	0.02 to 0.08	0.16
in	0.0008 to 0.0031	0.006
Crankshaft bearing-to-crankshaft end play, mm.................	0.1 to 0.19	0.25
in	0.004 to 0.007	0.010
Cylinder bore, maximum permissible out-of-round, mm	0.04	
in	0.0016	
Cylinder head		
Cylinder head, maximum permissible distortion, mm............	0.1	
in	0.004	
Intake valve, seat width, mm	2.2 to 3.0	
in	0.087 to 0.118	
Intake valve, seat angle	45°	
Exhaust valve, seat width, mm	2.2 to 3.0	
in................................	0.087 to 0.118	
Exhaust valve, seat angle	45°	
Valve stem diameter		
Intake, mm	8.97	
in..	0.353	
Exhaust, mm	8.95	
in	0.352	
Valve rock in guide (see Section 20)		
Intake, mm	0.4	0.8
in..	0.0157	0.0315
Exhaust, mm	0.5	1.0
in	0.020	0.040
Engine compression		
Bar..	8 to 11	6
Psi	114 to 156	85
Maximum allowable pressure difference between individual cylinders		
Bar..	3	
Psi	43	

Torque specifications – general

	ft-lb	m-kg
Camshaft cover nuts......................................	5.8	0.8
Camshaft bearing cap bolts	7.0	1.0
Camshaft bearing cap nuts	11.6 to 15.2	1.6 to 2.1
Cylinder head bolts, warm	86	12
cold	72	10
Oil pressure sensor......................................	11	1.5

Timing belt pulley-to-camshaft	58	8
Timing belt tension pulley bolt	29	4
Rear coolant system flange	7	1
Upper thermostat housing	7	1
Thermostat housing-to-cylinder head	14	2
Water pump pulley bolts	14	2
Spark plugs	21	3
Distributor clamping nut	14 to 16	2.0 to 2.2
Temperature sensor	6	0.8
Intake manifold and lifting bracket-to-cylinder head	17	2.4
Exhaust manifold-to-cylinder head	18	2.5
Exhaust manifold guard	14	2
Timing belt guard bolts	7	1
Throttle housing-to-intake manifold	16	2.2
Water pump, small diameter bolts	7	0.9
Water pump, large diameter bolts	16	2.2
Oil drain plug	29	4
Oil pan, small diameter bolts	6	0.8
Oil pan, large diameter bolts	11	1.5
Flywheel-to-crankshaft	65	9
Timing pulley-to-crankshaft	180	25
V-belt pulley-to-lower timing belt gear	14	2
Oil pump bolts	7	1
Oil pickup mounting bolts	7	1
Oil pickup strut	7	1
Oil filter mounting boss-to-crankcase	14	2
Oil filter	Hand-tight	Hand-tight
Bearing cap bolts	58	8
No. 5 bearing cap, socket head bolts	47	6.5
Connecting rod cap nut	43	6.0
Engine support-to-engine block	30	4.2
Engine mount to engine support	44	6.1
Engine mount-to-body	30	4.2
Clutch bellhousing, small bolts	33	4.5
Clutch bellhousing, large bolts	54	7.5
Catalytic converter-to-exhaust pipe	14	2
Catalytic converter heat shield	7	1
EGR Filter support bolts	14	2
EGR filter bolt	14	2
Air pump bracket bolt	33	4.5

Torque specifications – variations for Turbo and oxygen sensor (1980) models

Flywheel-to-crankshaft	72	10
Adapter-to-oil pan	72	10
Oil return line, turbocharger-to-oil pan	61	8.5
Oil return line, turbocharger-to-mount	61	8.5
Oil filter adapter-to-filter mount	14	2
Oil filter mount-to-engine block	43	6
Oil line banjo bolts-to-filter mount	41	5.5
Oil feed line-to-oil filter mount	61	8.5
Oil line-to-turbocharger mount	29	4
Adapter-to-turbocharger mount	29 to 33	4.0 to 4.5
*Cylinder head bolts, in steps	29, 58, 80	4, 8, 11
*Camshaft bearing cap nuts	11 to 14	1.6 to 2.0
Fuel injector adapter-to-cylinder head	16 to 18	2.2 to 2.5
Fuel injector-to-adapter	4 to 5	0.6 to 0.7
*Fuel line banjo bolt-to-mixture control unit	14	2
*Injector line banjo bolts-to-injectors	7	1
*Injector line banjo bolts-to-mixture control unit	6.5	0.9
*Fuel line banjo bolt-to-mixture control unit and control pressure regulator	6.5	0.9
*Fuel line banjo bolt-to-control pressure regulator	10	1.4
*Fuel line banjo bolts-to-cold start valve and mixture control unit	6.5	0.9
*Frequency valve fuel line-to-mixture control unit	6.5	0.9
*Fuel line-to-frequency valve	8.5	1.3
*Oxygen sensor-to-front exhaust pipe	36 to 43	5 to 6
Control line banjo bolt-to-waste gate	14	2
Plug-to-oil filter mount	87	12
*Oil filter	Hand-tight	Hand-tight
Turbocharger-to-turbine housing	3.5	0.5
Turbocharger compressor housing	5	0.7
Exhaust manifold flange-to-turbocharger	25	3.5

*Applies to Turbo and oxygen sensor models. All others apply to Turbo only.

1 Engine – general description

1 As stated in the Introduction to this book, the engine of the Porsche 924 is a radical departure from those found in earlier examples of the Porsche marque. Not only is the engine mounted at the front in the 924, it is water-cooled.

2 The engine unit is easily lifted from the engine compartment via the lifting loops provided. The loops will be found between the cylinder head and the intake manifold and are held in place by the nuts holding these two units to one another.

3 There are several different versions of the engine produced for the US market and a single type which has been available in the European market. The basic descriptions of these engines will be found in the Specifications Section.

4 There are also two different versions of the Turbo model, one for the US and one for Europe. These differences will not affect the tasks which can be performed.

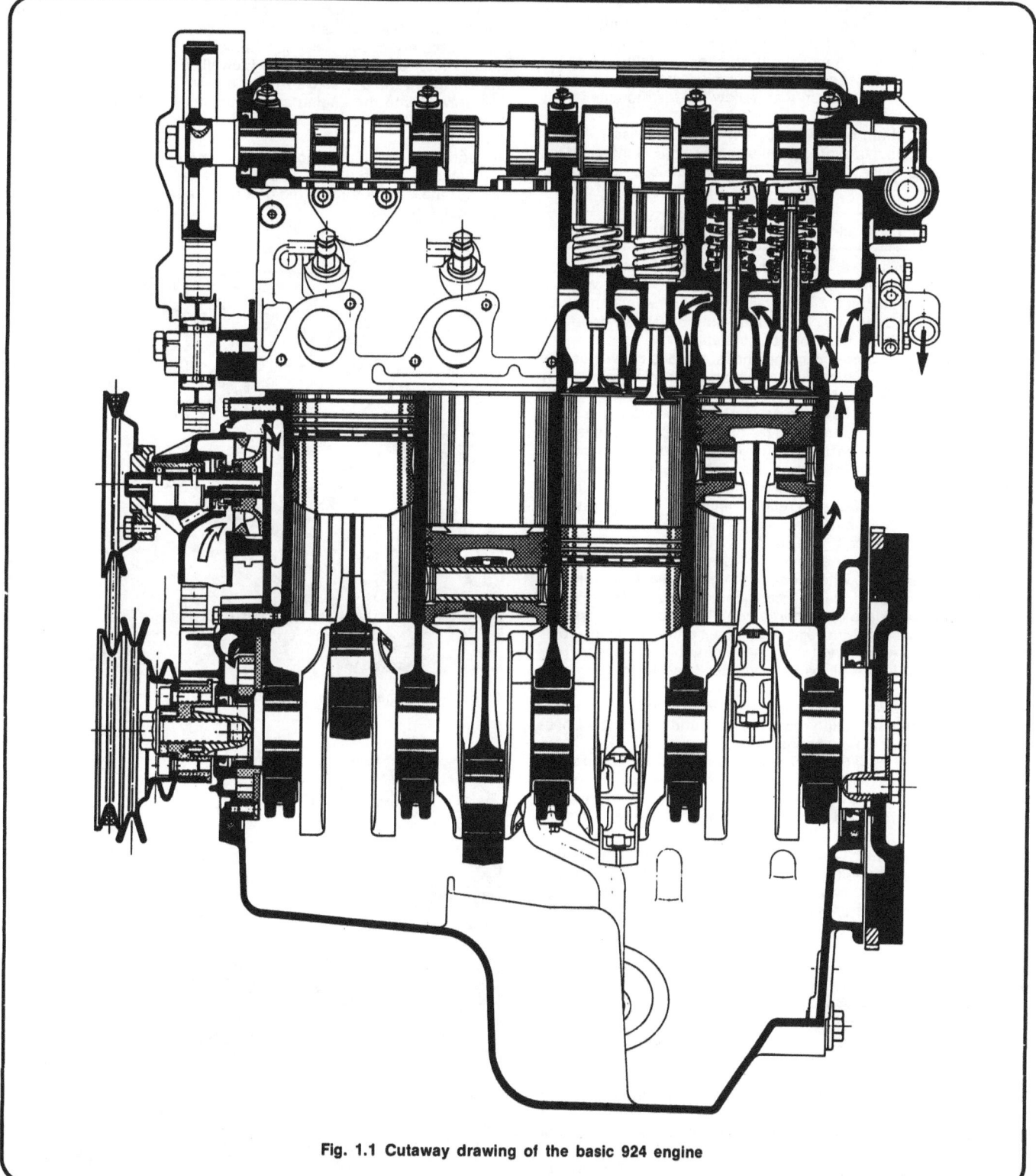

Fig. 1.1 Cutaway drawing of the basic 924 engine

2 Work which may be performed with the engine installed

1 All work to be performed upon ancillary equipment may be carried out with the engine installed. To locate removal instructions, check the Table of Contents or the Index of this book.

2 Many basic engine work tasks can easily be performed with the engine installed. The rule of thumb to be used here is: if the tasks to be performed do not involve removal of the oil pan or any item within the engine block itself, you do not need to remove the engine to perform those tasks.

3 This chapter is organized to give a series of instructions in a constant flow, in the order the tasks would be performed in an engine-removal situation. If the task you wish to carry out is not dependent upon engine removal, but is engine related, clear the surrounding area of those parts which block access to the component you will have to work on, then follow the instructions in this chapter.

4 Remember to drain the oil or coolant where necessary. If your car is air conditioned, take precautions concerning discharge of the system. Refer to these cautions in Chapter 2 before continuing.

3 Engine repairs and alternatives – special note

1 This chapter will cover the removal, stripdown, assembly, and installation of the Porsche motor. There are alternative ways to ending up with a complete, rebuilt engine which we will mention. After assessing your abilities, tools, and alternatives, we hope you will make the decision best for your situation.

Machine shops: Some machine shops and dealers will accept the engine from your vehicle for service work. In this way you will save the mechanic's fees for engine removal and stripdown of the ancillaries. You will still have the costs of machine work and parts, as well as the cost of the mechanic's time, but they will be somewhat reduced from the cost of bringing the whole car to the shop.

Exchange/purchase of a 'long block': Auto parts stores make available rebuilt engines in several configurations. The 'long block' is the most complete, offering a rebuilt engine (crankshaft, pistons, and connecting rods), plus a rebuilt cylinder head (valves, valve guides, springs, camshaft, etc), and may be thought of as being completely rebuilt from the camshaft cover to the oil pan. These units are expensive but, when compared against machine work and the cost of 'down time', can be considered quite reasonable.

Exchange/purchase of a 'short block': The short block consists of a rebuilt crankshaft with replaced pistons and connecting rods. They are complete from the top of the engine block to the oil pan, but do not include the oil pan or cylinder head in the purchase price.

Purchase of a 'master kit': The master kit consists of proper sized pistons and connecting rods on a reground crankshaft. These are usually sold on an exchange basis..

Purchase of a 'bare block': The bare block is not a built-up unit, but an engine block which has been bored for new cylinders and has the crankshaft bearing surfaces sized and cut as necessary. These are usually required in the replacement of cracked, or broken or overbored engine blocks.

2 If you choose any of the exhange/purchase options listed above, remember that your engine number is part of your vehicle's registration. If you change your engine block, make sure to change those details on your registration. Failure to do so could prove most embarassing some time when you least expect it.

4 Engine – removal

1 Disconnect both leads from the battery.

2 Raise the vehicle and place it on jack stands.

3 Remove the front wheels (Chapter 9).

4 Place work covers on the fenders to prevent damage.

5 Remove the bolts from the lower engine guard and remove the guard.

6 Drain the engine coolant (Chapter 2) and engine oil (Section 12).

7 Loosen the clamps on the various coolant system hoses and remove them (Chapter 2).

8 Pull the windshield washer hose from the T-fitting on the hood.

9 Unplug the engine compartment lamp, if installed.

10 Mark the hood location on its mounting brackets.

11 Remove the hood. This will take two people. Have an assistant hold the hood in place while you remove the bolts.

12 Remove the hoses connected to the coolant expansion tank at the ends opposite the expansion tank. Remove the nut from the mounting strap and lift out the overflow tank and the mounting strap, after it has been unhinged from the mounting plate.

13 Slide the windshield washer tank from its mount and place it ahead of the right front wheel well (photo 5.11 Chapter 2).

14 Using a pair of pliers or a special grooved pliers, loosen the clamps from the alternator cooling hose and remove it.

15 The battery positive lead is connected to the starter motor via a cable which passes through the firewall. The cable is removed by punching out the protective rubber grommet from the back side of the firewall into the engine compartment. Pull the cable through, bend open the wire clip securing it to the firewall and unclip it (photo).

16 Unplug the multiple lead plug at the engine wiring harness. This is located next to the ignition coil. Disconnect the wire from terminal 1 of the distributor and the ground wire from the ignition coil at terminal 1 (photo).

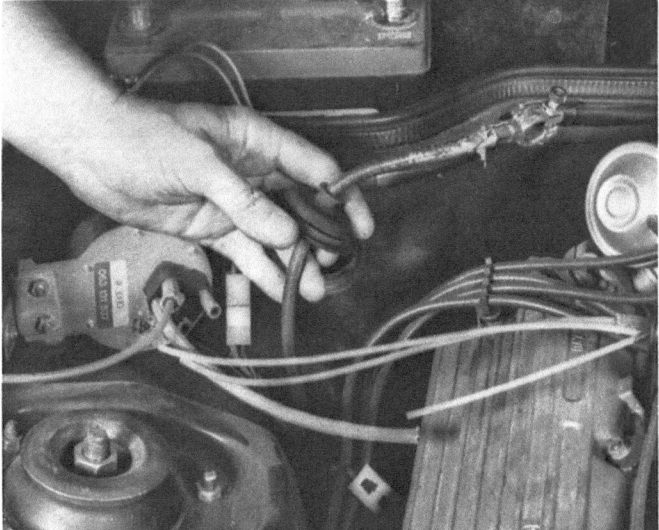

4.15 Pressing the positive lead grommet into the engine compartment

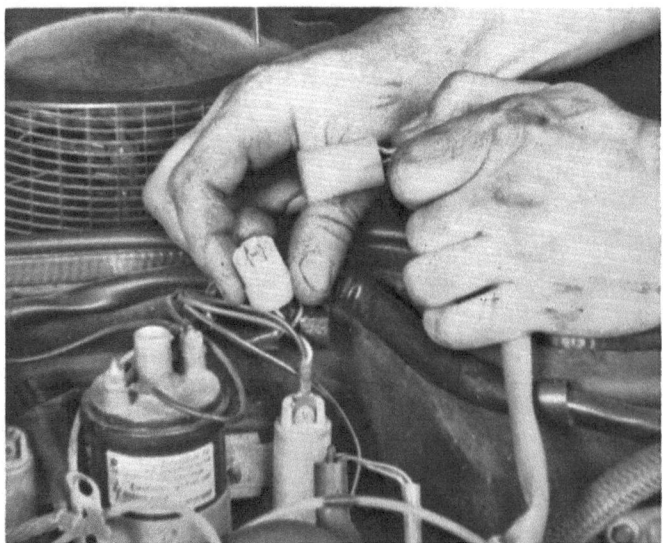

4.16 Disconnecting the multiple lead plug

17 Remove the hose from the brake booster unit to the intake manifold. Make sure that the clamps are suitably loosened before pulling the hose loose (Chapter 9).

18 Loosen the clamp on the engine side of the heater regulating valve and separate the hose and valve. The regulating valve and heater hoses will remain in the vehicle when the engine is removed. Loosen the clamp on the engine side of the heating system intake hose and pull it loose (Chapter 2).

19 Loosen the nuts on the throttle cable support and unscrew the throttle cable. Unhook the end of the cable from the operating lever of the throttle housing (Chapter 3).

20 Pull the oil dipstick out and wipe it off before setting it aside.

21 Loosen the clamp on the crankcase vent hose at the intake manifold end and pull the hose loose.

22 Disconnect the electrical plug from the mixture control unit. This is installed only on 1978 and earlier models (photo).

23 Remove the molded rubber duct between the mixture control unit and the throttle housing (Chapter 3).

24 Loosen the lock nuts on the clutch adjuster and remove the cable from the adjuster plate (Chapter 6).

25 Clamp the fuel return line at the fuel tank with a standard squeeze clamp (Chapter 3).

26 Using tape and an indelible ink pen mark all of the fuel lines at the mixture control unit and at the injectors. Label all of the plastic hoses for the vacuum systems and the electrical plug connectors on the engine and its ancillary parts.

27 Detach the fuel feed line from the fuel filter and plug the end of the filter to prevent dirt from entering the fuel system. Remove the fuel feed line from the mixture control unit (Chapter 3).

28 Remove the fuel lines from the fuel distributor and set the lines aside. Place the banjo bolts in an out-of-the-way spot and dispose of the metal seals. These must be replaced when the lines are connected (Chapter 3).

29 Remove the electrical connector from the fan and pull the clip from the fan shroud (Chapter 2).

30 Remove the cooling fan motor and shroud (Chapter 2).

31 Remove the air filter housing and mixture control unit (Chapter 2).

32 If your vehicle is air conditioned, it is not necessary to discharge the system if the unit is of the factory type (Chapter 2). If your air conditioning system is of the aftermarket-supplier type and manufacture, check with that company or its representatives to see if the system must be discharged. Note, nevertheless, that discharge of the air conditioning system should only be done by a qualified air conditioning technician with the proper tools and equipment.

For air conditioned vehicles with factory-type systems, perform the following tasks. If your model is not in this group, move to paragraph number 36.

33 Loosen the V-belt on the compressor and remove it (Chapter 2).

34 Remove the compressor from its bracket and carefully lay it aside. Do not attempt to disconnect the compressor hoses. The contents of the hoses are under pressure and could cause injury. If the hoses are loosened, the system must be evacuated and recharged by an air conditioning specialist.

35 Remove the nut which holds the refrigerant hose bracket to the engine mount.

36 Install a homemade wooden support block at the front tunnel reinforcing brace so that it supports the central tube (Chapter 6).

37 Remove the exhaust gas recirculation line from the exhaust pipe and the EGR filter (Chapter 3).

38 Remove the 'Thermag' nuts which hold the exhaust pipe to the exhaust manifold (Chapter 3).

39 Remove the nuts and bolts from the front exhaust pipe to primary muffler/catalytic converter flange and remove the forward exhaust pipe (Chapter 3).

40 Remove the sheet metal guard installed above the front pipe (Chapter 3).

41 Remove the clamping bolt from the universal joint at the bottom end of the steering column and pull the clamp away from the serrated end of the steering pinion (Chapter 8).

42 Remove the bolts from the front crossmember and also remove the bolts from the steering stabilizer mounts on the frame. Carefully lower the crossmember and allow it to rest on the compression of the MacPherson struts of the front suspension (Chapter 10).

43 Roll your engine lift into place. Attach a lifting chain to the front and rear lift straps on the engine and raise the engine lift to put tension on the chain (photo).

44 Make a survey of the entire engine compartment. Mark, then disconnect, any electrical connectors, hoses, or other connections you may have missed before. Do not unbolt the engine mounts.

45 When you are sure that all connections except the engine mounts have been disconnected, place several blocks of wood between the crossmember and the engine. This will enable the oil pan to clear the crossmember during engine removal. About 3 to 3½ inches of wood blocks should be sufficient, but too many blocks of wood will bend suspension pieces. Do not force wood blocks into place, or try to get the crossmember to lower any more than it will under gentle pressure.

46 Remove the entire left-hand engine mount, first from the body and then from the engine. Remember, the left-hand mount is the mount on the driver's left (photo).

47 Remove the bolts from the engine bellhousing (Chapter 6).

48 Remove the bolts from the body end of the right-hand mount.

49 On vehicles with automatic transmission, it is necessary to remove the inspection cover from the bellhousing and remove the bolts which hold the rubber/metal damper to the flywheel. Turn the engine with a socket applied to the bolt on the center of the oil

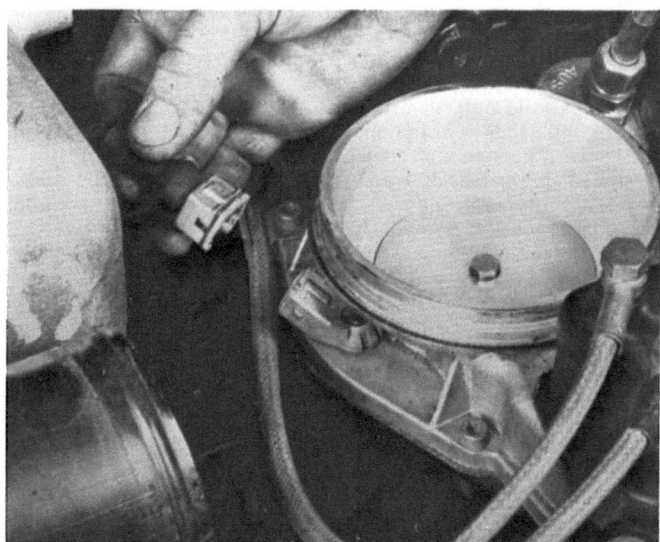

4.22 Disconnecting the electrical plug from the mixture control unit

4.43 The engine lift and chains installed on the engine

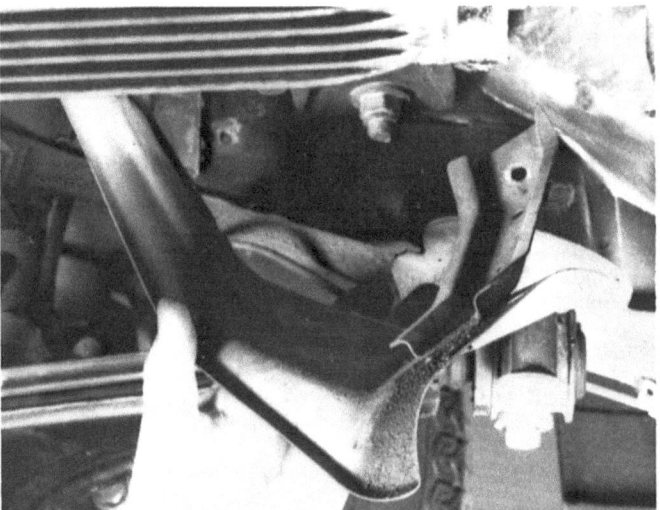

4.46 Removing the left hand engine mount

4.52 Lifting the engine

pump pulley. Loosen the bolts two turns each in a cross pattern.
50 Vehicles with manual transmission have the driveshaft connected to the clutch disc via a splined coupling. When removing the engine, the clutch disc will be slid from the splined end of the driveshaft and the clutch disc and pressure plate will be removed with the engine.
51 Removing the engine can be done by one person, but the help of another will make the removal process safer and reduce the chances of propeller shaft, clutch, body, or windshield damage.
52 Slowly raise the engine, sliding it forward to disengage the splines from the clutch center. Pay careful attention to the clearances between the oil pan and crossmember. As you raise the engine, and once you are sure that the engine is held in place only by the lifting chains, turn the engine to the driver's right to clear all other blocks and raise it clear of the body (photo).
53 When the engine is clear of the body, pull the engine lift away from the vehicle and lower the engine to about waist height.
54 Remove the pressure plate and clutch disc. Loosen the bolts in a cross pattern and about two turns each in order (Chapter 6).
55 Remove the starter (Chapter 5).
56 Remove the alternator (Chapter 5).
57 Loosen the flywheel bolts in a cross pattern, two turns each in order. Remove the bolts and the flywheel (Section 8).
58 The engine is now ready for stripping, and should be placed on a firm workbench or mounted on an engine stand.

5 Engine ancillaries - removal

1 Before beginning the engine stripdown, clean your work area and make sure that you will have adequate and clean storage space.
2 Make a walk-around inspection of the engine. Check that all hoses, lines, and electrical connections are marked for easy installation.
3 Remove the alternator V-belt and the alternator (Chapter 11).
4 Remove the spark plug wires and the spark plugs (Chapter 5).
5 Remove the air pump (Chapter 3).
6 Remove the bolts from the right-hand motor mount and remove the mount.
7 Remove the exhaust manifold and its heat shield.
8 Remove the two bolts from the timing belt cover and remove the cover. Remove the tensioning pulley and the timing belt.
9 Remove the water pump pulley (Chapter 2).
10 Remove the thermostat housing (Chapter 2).
11 Remove the water pump (Chapter 2).
12 Remove the rear coolant flange from the cylinder head (Chapter 2).
13 Remove the transverse tube hoses and then remove the transverse tube (Chapter 2).
14 Remove all EGR and vacuum hoses (Chapter 3).
15 Remove the following:

The engine wiring loom.
The EGR filter and its mounting bracket (Chapter 3).
The crankcase vent tubes.
The throttle control housing (Chapter 3).
The control pressure regulator (Chapter 3).
The cold start valve (Chapter 3).
The auxilliary air regulator (Chapter 3).
The intake manifold (Chapter 3).
The ignition distributor (Chapter 5).
The distributor drive housing (Chapter 5).
16 The engine is now ready for engine work.

6 Engine - removal (Turbo)

1 Disconnect both leads from the battery.
2 Raise the vehicle and place it on jack stands.
3 Place fender covers on the fenders to prevent damage.
4 Remove the front wheels (Chapter 9).
5 Push the positive cable of the battery into the engine compartment (Section 4.15).
6 Disconnect the wiring harness plugs at the firewall. Disconnect the wires from terminals 1 and 4 of the ignition coil. Loosen the clamp holding the ignition coil to its mounting bracket, remove the coil and set it in the tray formed by the firewall and dashboard bulkhead.
7 Pull off the windshield washer hose at the T-fitting on the hood.
8 Unplug the engine compartment light.
9 Remove the hood (Section 4.10 and 4.11).
10 Loosen the clamps and remove the molded rubber boot from the pressure ducting and the mixture control unit (Chapter 3).
11 Remove the bolt on bracket for the throttle cable adjuster, unhook the cable from the operating lever of the throttle housing and move the cable and adjusting bracket aside (Chapter 3).
12 Loosen the clamps and remove the vacuum hose from the intake manifold to the brake booster. Remove the entire hose along with all parts connected between the two ends (Chapter 9).
13 Pull the rubber hold down straps off the air cleaner housing and remove the upper housing and the air cleaner element. Dispose of the element and replace it with a new one when you reassemble the engine.
14 Remove the molded rubber boot from the mixture control unit and the air filter housing (Chapter 3).
15 Remove the bolts from the lower air cleaner housing and remove the housing from its bracket.
16 Clamp the fuel return line shut with a clamp at the fuel tank (Chapter 3).
17 Remove the fuel lines from the fuel distributor (Section 4.28).
18 Remove the three nuts from the lower bracket of the mixture control unit. Loosen the clamp at the top of the rubber bellows to keep dirt and grit out of the turbocharger (Chapter 3).

19 Set the mixture control unit aside. Do not disconnect the fuel lines.

20 Remove the mixture control unit mounting bracket.

21 Remove the plate which holds the hydraulic line for the clutch to its mounting bracket (Chapter 6).

22 Remove the bolts which hold the lower engine protection guard in place and remove the guard.

23 Drain the engine coolant (Chapter 2) and engine oil (Section 12).

24 Remove the four bolts from the connecting flange between the catalytic converter and the final muffler (Chapter 3).

25 Unhook the muffler suspension from its rubber mount, remove the clamp on the final muffler along with the suspension bracket at the end of the transmission and remove the final muffler (Chapter 3).

26 Remove the waste gate pipe between the exhaust manifold and the waste gate by removing the holding nuts and pulling the pipe free. Scrape away left-over gasket material and sealants with a putty knife or gasket scraper. Do no use a razor blade (Chapter 4).

27 Remove the two mounting bolts for the waste gate.

28 Remove the banjo bolt for the control line. Early production models of the Turbo also have a vent line installed, which should be removed at this time.

29 Remove the mounting nuts between the turbine housing and the exhaust pipe.

30 Remove the catalytic converter. This involves removing the four mounting nuts at the exhaust pipe and loosening the bracket (Chapter 3).

31 Remove the four mounting nuts from the oil cooler mount and pull the oil cooler free of the mounts. Do not detach the hoses from the cooler.

32 If your vehicle has headlight washers, remove the pump from its mount and suspend it in an out-of-the-way location with a loop of string or wire.

33 Remove the clamping bolt from the universal joint at the lower end of the steering column. Pull the clamp free of the serrated end of the steering pinion (Chapter 8).

34 Remove the steering stabilizer mounts from the frame. Set the bolts, strap and nylon bush aside. Leave the rubber bush in place on the stabilizer (Chapter 10).

35 Remove the nuts from the control links on the stabilizer ends (Chapter 10).

36 Remove the nuts from the pivot bolts on the control arms and press out the pivot bolts. Slide the threaded ends of the control links from the control arms (Chapter 10).

37 Remove the bolts which hold the front axle crossmember to the body and allow the entire front suspension to rest its weight on the tie rods. Do not place any additional weight on the tie rods or front axle (Chapters 8 and 10).

38 Remove the starter motor (Chapter 5).

39 Remove the waste gate mounting bracket on the central tube.

40 Unbolt the clutch slave cylinder from its mount and free it from the mounts without disconnecting the hydraulic lines.

41 Disconnect the coolant hoses from the radiator and then from the flanges at the other end of each hose (Chapter 2).

42 Remove the coolant hoses from the thermostat housing.

43 Detach the coolant hose between the overflow tank and the vent line. Slide the overflow tank from its mount and set it aside.

44 Disconnect the electric plugs and remove the coolant system fan and shroud. If your vehicle is air conditioned, remove the cooling fan for the condenser as well.

45 If your vehicle is air conditioned, refer to Section 4, paras. 32 thru 35.

46 Roll your engine lift into place and install the lifting chain. Raise the lift until the weight of the engine rests on the lift chain. Do not extend the engine mounts or raise the front of the car, as the car could fall on you when the motor mounts are removed (photo 4.43).

47 Remove the shift lever boot and the shift lever cover. The boot is a snap fit into the console and the shift lever cover can easily be pulled from its shaft by wiggling it back and forth several times while pulling upward (Chapter 7).

48 Remove the two guide bolts which are immediately ahead of hole for the shift lever in the console.

49 Remove the spring clips which hold the shift lever shaft locating pins in place. Separate the plates on the shifter and remove the shift lever shaft.

50 Remove the axle shafts from the transmission and suspend them in a horizontal position to prevent bearing damage (Chapter 6).

51 Remove the self-locking nuts on the bonded metal/rubber mounts of the transmission. Dispose of the self locking nuts and install new nuts on the assembly.

52 Run a universal transmission jack or an hydraulic floor jack with a secure piece of wood on the lifting face beneath the transmission. Raise the transmission slightly to take the weight of the transmission off its mounts.

53 Remove the transmission mounting bolts and remove the mounts.

54 Remove the four bolts holding the central tube of the clutch bellhousing.

55 Slide the entire transmission and central tube assembly to the rear. Be very careful not to crush the brake line of the left rear wheel, which will be hit if the transmission is raised too high.

56 Block the wheels of your floor jack to prevent its rolling and secure the transmission to the trunk floor with a chain to prevent its falling.

57 Loosen the clamp on the engine side of the heater control valve and pull the hose from the valve (Chapter 3).

58 Loosen the hose clamp on the heater intake hose at the rear coolant system flange and pull the hose free (Chapter 3).

59 Remove the bolt from the lower end of each engine mount.

60 Lower the engine to disengage the mounts from their mounting points.

61 Turn the engine slightly so that the engine may be raised.

62 Raising the engine and removing it from the engine compartment is a task which may be performed by one person if necessary; however an assistant will greatly reduce the possibility of damage to the body, engine compartment components, or the windshield.

63 Check that all connections between the engine and the car have been disconnected. When you are sure that this is the case, raise the engine slowly while your assistant turns the engine so that the engine mounts clear their mounting spots and pulls the engine slightly forward so that the clutch bellhousing does not damage the components left on the firewall.

64 Raise the engine above the forward section of the body and roll the engine stand clear of the vehicle.

65 Lower the engine to about waist height for further work.

66 Disconnect the wiring harness at the clutch bellhousing.

67 Remove the lock nut and clamping bolt from the release lever shaft (Chapter 6).

68 Screw in a bolt of 8 mm diameter and the proper thread pitch into the end of the release lever shaft and pull the shaft out of the bellhousing with the bolt.

69 Remove the clutch bellhousing bolts. Note that the bolts are of differing lengths and of two different diameters. Make a note as to the location of each bolt when removing them.

70 Remove the clutch bellhousing and release shaft (Chapter 6).

71 Remove the pressure plate and clutch disc from the flywheel. Loosen the bolts in a cross pattern about two turns each in order until the bolts can be removed. Do not drop the pressure plate or clutch disc when you remove them.

72 Loosen the flywheel holding bolts in a cross pattern, about two turns each time until they can be removed.

73 Remove the flywheel.

74 It is now possible to strip the engine, once it has been placed on a firm work bench or mounted on an engine stand.

7 Engine ancillaries – removal (Turbo)

1 Follow the procedures laid out in Section 5, paras. 1 thru 4.

2 Remove the fuel lines from the mixture control unit and remove the control unit. Screw the banjo bolts into the fuel distributor to prevent dirt from entering. Dispose of the seals and replace them with new ones when reassembling the engine for installation (Chapter 3).

3 Loosen the two clamps which hold the upper pressure duct's rubber adapter to the throttle housing. Remove the entire turbo-charger assembly from the engine (Chapter 4).

4 Unbolt the fuel line looms and remove the fuel lines from the injectors. Screw the banjo bolts back into the tops of the injectors to prevent dirt from entering them. Dispose of the seals and replace

them with new ones when reassembling the engine for installation (Chapter 3).

5   Mark all of the connections of the engine wiring loom, unplug all the connections and remove the loom.

6   Remove the two banjo bolts from the timing belt cover and remove the cover. Using a socket and wrench of the proper size, turn the bolt on the water pump pulley until the number 1 cylinder comes up on top dead center. This is further indicated when the dot on the upper timing belt pulley aligns with the pointer cast into the camshaft cover.

7   Remove the bolt from the timing belt tensioning pulley and remove the pulley. Remove the timing belt.

8   Remove the three bolts from the water pump pulley and remove the pulley (Chapter 3).

9   Remove the following:

The water pump (Chapter 2).

The thermostat housing halves and the thermostat (Chapter 2).

The right-side engine mount.

The exhaust manifold (Chapter 3).

The throttle housing from the intake manifold (Chapter 3).

The intake manifold (Chapter 3).

The hoses from the transverse tube and then remove the tube (Chapter 2).

The left-side engine mount.

The rear coolant flange from the cylinder head with the switches still in place (Chapter 2).

The ignition distributor (Chapter 5).

The distributor drive housing (Chapter 5).

10 The engine is now ready for engine work.

8   Engine flywheel – removing, installing, and component replacement

1   The flywheel may be removed with the engine installed in the vehicle by removing the clutch bellhousing and sliding the transmission to the rear (Chapter 6).

2   The flywheel is held to the rear of the crankshaft by six bolts. These should be loosened about three turns each in turn, using a cross pattern (photo). When all of the bolts are completely unthreaded, remove the bolts and six-holed washer.

3   Remove the flywheel by grasping it firmly with both hands and pulling it off the crankshaft (photo). Do not drop the flywheel.

4   There are two versions of the center needle bearing which Porsche calls Version I and Version II (Fig. 1.2). The Version I bearing may be replaced by a Version II bearing.

5   The bearing should be checked for grooving, tightness of the needles, and the general condition of the bearing surfaces. If the bearing needs replacement, it may be pulled from the flywheel with an appropriate puller. This procedure can be performed with the flywheel in the vehicle by removing the clutch disc and pressure plate.

6   Installation of the new needle bearing may be done with a socket and mallet. Drive the bearing into its sleeve.

7   If the bearing sleeve is found to need replacement when the bearing is removed, it may be pulled out with an appropriate puller, and its replacement driven in with a socket and mallet. If a Version II sleeve is used, install the new seal after the needle bearing is driven into the bearing sleeve.

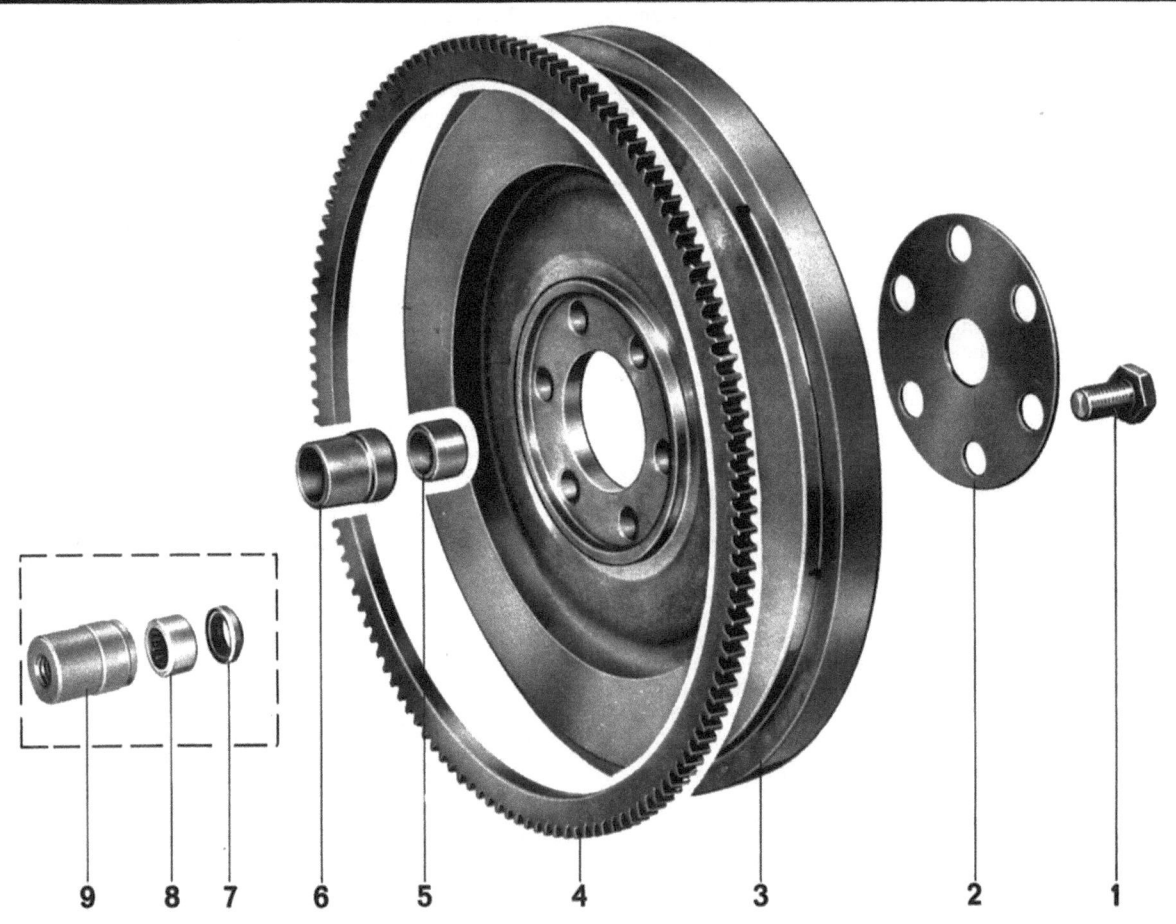

Fig. 1.2 Components of the flywheel, standard models. Turbo models will not have toothed starter ring

1 Bolt	4 Starter gear ring (standard	6 Bearing sleeve (version I)	8 Needle bearing (version II)
2 Washer	engine)	7 Seal (version II)	9 Bearing sleeve (version II)
3 Flywheel	5 Needle bearing (version I)		

8.2 Removing the flywheel bolts

8.3 Removing the flywheel

8.12 Aligning the mounting marks on the flywheel and crankshaft end

8.13 The proper order for torqueing of the flywheel bolts

8 If the splines of the starter ring gear are badly worn or chipped, the ring gear may be replaced. Drill a hole into the ring gear with a large drill bit, but only far enough for the tip of the bit to nearly contact the flywheel surface. Do not drill through the ring gear into the flywheel.

9 Use a mallet and cold chisel to break the ring by cutting between the splines and into the drilled hole. This will break the ring and allow it to be lifted off.

10 To install the new ring gear, heat it to 230°C (450°F) and install it squarely on the flywheel. Use a flat faced punch and mallet to drive the ring gear up to the stop on the flywheel. Drive it on squarely; do not allow it to twist or cock to one side.

11 Installation of the flywheel is the reverse of the removal procedure.

12 Place the flywheel on the crankshaft so that the marks on the flywheel and the crankshaft end align (photo). Some of the six holed washers installed on early models had slots which also had to be placed over the two marks, so that the alignment could be checked without removing the washer. If the washer you have has these slots, make sure that they are located so that they show the lines.

13 Install the six bolts and tighten them in a cross pattern until snug. Torque the bolts in a cross pattern to 65 ft-lb (9 m-kg) (photo).

14 Mark the bolt heads and washer with white paint lines. This will enable you to quickly check whether or not the bolts have turned in the flywheel (photo).

9 Timing belt – removal and installation

1 The timing belt may be removed and installed while the engine is in the vehicle by removing the alternator V-belt and the timing belt cover. The remaining procedures are for both installed and removed engines.

2 Turn the large bolt in the center of the oil pump so that the stamped dot on the upper timing belt pulley aligns with the pointer on the camshaft cover.

3 Loosen the nut on the timing belt tensioning pulley and remove the bolt and the pulley. Remove the timing belt.

4 Installation is the reverse of the removal procedure, if the engine has not been rebuilt or turned over while the belt was removed.

5 If you have just rebuilt the engine, turn the engine via the center bolt of the oil pump so that the notch on the V-belt pulley aligns with the pointer on the oil pump.

6 Align the pointer on the camshaft cover with the dot on the timing belt pulley.

7 Install the timing belt. Install the timing belt tensioning pulley

8.14 Marking the bolt heads as a guard against loosening

9.2 Proper alignment of the pointer and dot

9.7 Testing the timing belt for proper tension

and bolt. Turn the tensioning pulley in the direction of the engine rotation (counterclockwise) until the belt can just barely be turned 90 degrees with your fingers on the 'long' side of the belt. Torque the tensioning pulley bolt to 29 ft-lb (4 m-kg) (photo).

10 Engine lubrication – general description

1   The operating parts of your Porsche's engine are lubricated with oil. The types of oil required and the weight of the oils are listed in the Recommended Lubricants section at the front of this book.
2   Your engine relies on its oil passages and other equipment being kept clean. The oil filter keeps contaminants, small metal chips, and dirt out of the oil. It must be replaced at the specified intervals to maintain peak efficiency.
3   Oil is drawn out of the oil pan through a pickup which is deep within the sump of the engine. From here, oil flows to the sickle-type oil pump and on through the engine.

11 Engine oil – checking oil level

1   The engine must be stopped and the car must be parked on level ground in order to perform this check. Allow the car to sit for at least five minutes after stopping the engine for the most accurate readings.
2   Raise the hood of the car.
3   Locate the dipstick on the left side of the engine and pull it out of its tube.
4   Wipe the oil from the dipstick and insert it back in the tube.
5   Remove the dipstick once again and look at the level of oil on the dipstick end. If the oil is between the 'max' and 'min' lines, there is sufficient oil for safe operation of your engine. If the level is below the 'min' line or if there is no oil on the dipstick, add enough oil to bring the oil level within the two lines.
6   Look at the oil which is on the dipstick. If it seem gritty or extremely black, you may be due for an oil and filter change. Check your maintenance log.
7   Oil is introduced into the engine through the cap on the camshaft cover marked 'Oel'. Remove the cap (it is a twist-on type) and pour oil into this hole.

12 Engine oil – changing the oil and oil filter

1   Engine oil is best drained immediately after a run, when contaminants will still be in suspension. Take care to avoid scalding yourself with the hot oil, however.
2   Raise the hood of the car and remove the cap on the camshaft cover (twist-on type).
3   Place a drip pan beneath the oil pan of the car to catch the oil you will remove. Center the pan beneath the oil drain plug which is at the rear of the oil pan.
4   Remove the oil drain plug and allow the oil to flow into the drain pan.
5   If you are changing the oil filter as well, unscrew the filter with a strap wrench and drop it into the oil pan. The filter is full of oil, so watch for dripping. Clean up any oil spills.
6   Install a new seal on the drain plug. Before installing the drain plug in the oil pan, clean the drain plug hole with a clean, lint-free cloth to absorb any extra oil in the threads of the drain hole. Install the drain plug and torque it to 29 ft-lb (4 m-kg).
7   Before installing the oil filter, pour about one pint of new oil into the threaded portion of the filter. Allow the filter to sit upright for a few minutes so that the oil may be absorbed by the filter material. This will eliminate the possibility of the engine running without oil for up to 45 seconds, which is the possible result when an oil filter is installed dry.
8   Hold the filter upright with the threaded end facing up and lightly coat the rubber ring of the filter with fresh oil. This will enable the rubber ring to form a better seal on the oil filter boss. Hold the oil filter next to the filter boss and invert it over the threaded boss. Quickly screw the filter into place to prevent any of the oil in the filter from leaking out. Tighten the filter as much as you can by hand. Do not force the filter beyond this tightness, as there is a good chance of breaking the filter or deforming the sealing surface.

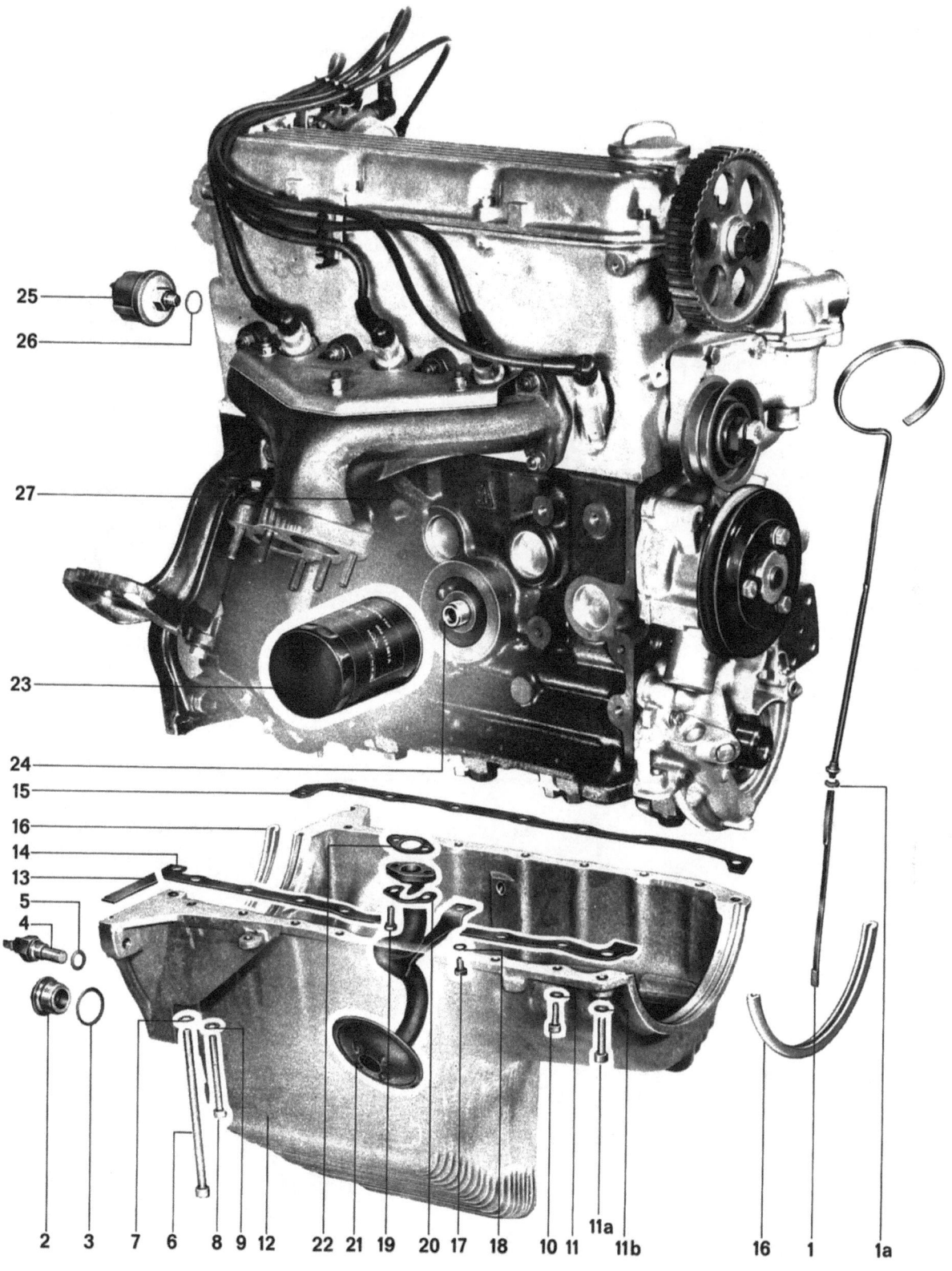

Fig. 1.3 Components of the engine lubrication system

1 Oil dipstick	6 Socket head bolt	11a Socket head bolt	16 Gasket, oil pan	22 Gasket
1a Seal	7 Flat washer	11b Flat washer	17 Socket head bolt	23 Oil filter
2 Plug	8 Socket head bolt	12 Oil pan	18 Flat washer	24 Oil filter location
3 Seal	9 Flat washer	13 Gasket, end piece	19 Socket head bolt	25 Oil pressure switch
4 Temperature sensor	10 Socket head bolt	14 Gasket, oil pan	20 Lock plate	26 Seal
5 Seal	11 Flat washer	15 Gasket, oil pan	21 Oil intake pipe	27 Cylinder block

9 Fill the lubrication system with the proper amount of the recommended oil. Oil is poured into the engine through the filler hole on the camshaft cover (photo).
10 Replace the cap on the camshaft cover.

---

13 Oil pump – removal and installation

1 Although these steps appear in the engine stripdown sequence, they may be done while the engine is installed in the vehicle.
2 Remove the six socket head bolts which hold the V-belt pulley to the timing belt pulley on the front of the oil pump.
3 Remove the timing belt pulley by removing the bolt from the end of the crankshaft which holds it in place along with the washer. Pull the pulley off of the crankshaft (photo).
4 Remove the six bolts which hold the oil pump to the engine and pull the pump straight out of the engine. Do not attempt to rock the

oil pump and use no sharp objects to break the seal of any gasket sealer. The pump may be levered with a flat blade screwdriver in the notch provided in the casting (photo).
5 Scrape the remains of the old gasket from the engine block and the back of the oil pump with a putty knife or a gasket scraper. Never use a razor blade as it is made of a harder metal and can damage the sealing surface.
6 Using Special Tool 10-221 or a flat blade screwdriver, remove the oil seal from the crankshaft boss in the oil pump. The crankshaft oil seal must be replaced every time the oil pump is removed, as well as any time it begins to leak.
7 The oil pump is not a rebuildable component for the home mechanic. If your oil pump is in need of replacement, exchange it for a factory-rebuild unit or purchase a new one.
8 Installation is the reverse of the removal procedure.
9 Coat the new oil pump gasket with gasket sealer and mount it on the rear of the oil pump. Place the oil pump on the engine block such that the bolt holes are aligned and the pump drive ring engages the drive tabs on the crankshaft.

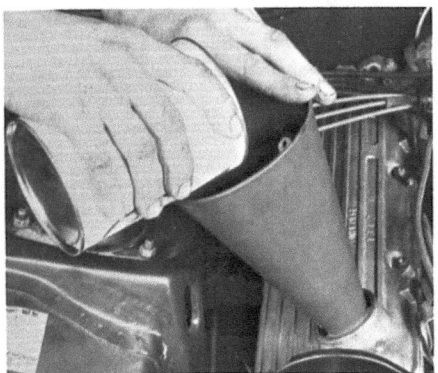
12.9 Filling the lubrication system

13.3 Removing the timing belt pulley center bolt

13.4 Using a screwdriver to lever the oil pump from the engine

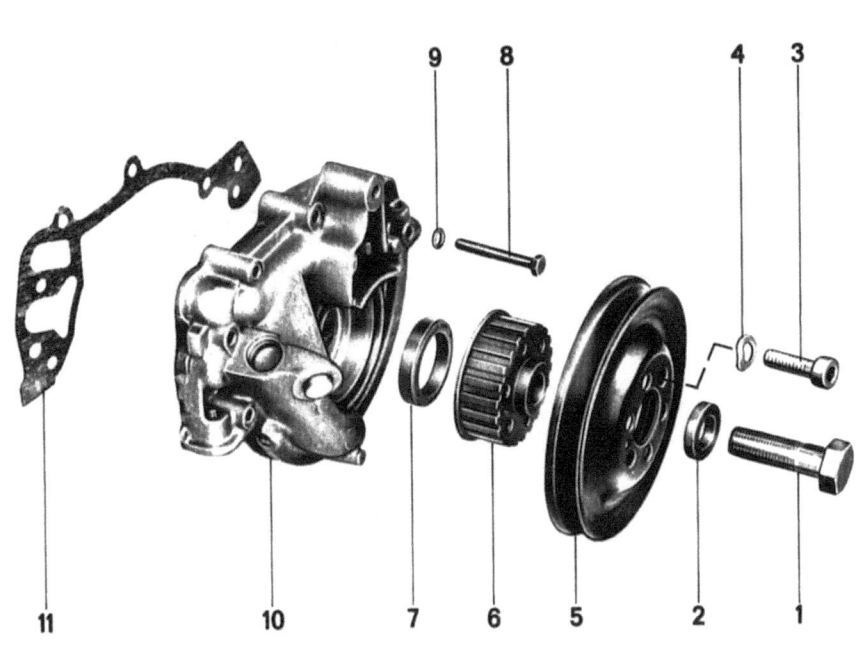

Fig. 1.4 Oil pump and components

1 Bolt	5 V-belt pulley	9 Flat washer
2 Washer	6 Timing belt pulley	10 Oil pump
3 Socket head bolt	7 Oil seal	11 Gasket
4 Washer	8 Bolt	

10 Install the bolts in their proper holes (remember that the bolts are of different lengths) and torque them in a cross pattern to 7 ft-lb (1 m-kg) (photo).

11 Intall the crankshaft oil seal and drive it into place with Special Tool 2033 or a socket of the proper size. Press the seal in until it fully contacts the stop in the pump body.

14 Crankshaft front oil seal - removal and installation

1 The crankshaft front oil seal is located in the front of the oil pump and may be removed and installed without removing the oil pump or the engine.

2 Lever the old seal from the end of the crankshaft with Special Tool 10-221 or a flat blade screwdriver.

3 Installation of the seal may be done with Special Tool 2033 or a socket of the proper size. Press the oil seal into the oil pump until it seats squarely against the stop (photo).

15 Oil pan and oil pickup - removal and installation

1 Although the following steps were written to be part of the engine removal and stripdown sequence, these parts may be removed from the engine while it is installed in the vehicle. To gain sufficient clearance, remove the bolt holding the steering gear-to-steering column clamp and disconnect the steering column. Remove the tie rod ends of the steering knuckles and the bolts which hold the front crossmember to the body and remove the crossmember. Loosen the left-side engine mount, but do not remove it.

2 The oil pan should be removed every 100 000 miles (160 000 km), to clean any sludge and other accumulations from the sump of the engine.

3 If the engine is in an engine stand, turn the engine over so that the oil pan faces up.

4 Remove the socket-head bolts which hold the oil pan to the engine block. Note that the bolts are of two different lengths and two different diameters. Make notes on the location of each of the bolts for ease in reassembly.

5 Remove the bolts which hold the oil pan to the clutch bellhousing (manual transmission) or the damper bellhousing (automatic transmission).

6 Remove the oil pan from the engine (photo). If the removal proves difficult because of gasket sealer or an old gasket, pull on the oil pan at the two cast-in strengthening webs which are just ahead of the bellhousing mounting locations. If this does not loosen the oil pan, rap the web area with a soft-faced mallet on each side. Break the seal from the rear of the engine forward. Do not insert any screwdrivers, chisels, knives, or any other sharp object into the join between the oil pan and the engine block. All of the above named objects are manufactured of metals which are harder than the aluminum alloy of the oil pan and you will ruin the sealing surfaces of the oil pan and engine block.

7 Scrape old gasket material from the engine block and oil pan with a putty knife or a gasket scraper. As mentioned above, any other scraper will most probably ruin the sealing surfaces of the oil pan and engine block.

8 Clean the inside of the oil pan thoroughly with cleaning solvent and allow it to dry completely before installing and filling with oil. If the solvent has not evaporated entirely, the residue will cause some of the oil in the oil pan to break down and limit the protective qualities of your engine oil.

9 The oil pickup is held in place by two bolts at the pipe flange of the pickup and by a single bolt which holds a steadying arm to the underside of the engine block.

10 Remove the bolt from the steadying arm.

11 Bend back the ears of the locking plate with a flat blade screwdriver and remove the two bolts. Dispose of the locking plate and replace it with a new one when installing the pickup.

12 Scrape the remains of the gasket from the engine block and the flange of the oil pickup with a gasket scraper or putty knife.

13 Installation is the reverse of the removal procedure.

14 Coat the oil pickup seal with gasket sealer and place it on the flange of the oil pickup. Install the oil pickup in its proper location and locate the new locking plate on the flange. Thread the bolts into place just enough to hold the oil pickup in the block.

15 Install the bolt on the steadying arm.

16 Tighten the bolts a couple of turns each so that the gasket sealer is compressed and the pickup seats squarely on its mounting boss. Make sure that you have not put too much gasket sealer on the gasket. If more than a trace oozes out of the join between the oil pickup flange and its mounting boss, remove the oil pickup and scrape off excess gasket sealer from the gasket and the bore of the oil pickup.

17 Torque all three mounting bolts to 7 ft-lb (1 m-kg). Bend the locking ears of the locking plate tightly against the flats of the bolt head. Place the end of a flat blade screwdriver against the lower section of the locking tab and strike the end of the screwdriver several times with a mallet to push the lower portion of the locking head against the bolt (photo).

18 Lightly coat the flat gaskets for the oil pan with gasket sealer and set the gaskets into place on the oil pan's sealing surfaces. Make sure that the short gasket end pieces at the rear of the oil pan are perpendicular to the long gasket pieces on the sides and that the join between the pieces is tight with no gap, if possible (photos).

19 Install the round rubber gaskets at each end of the oil pan. Press them into place at the center and work out toward the ends. If the gasket sticks out above the seal surface at the ends, remove it and install it again in the same fashion until it is securely installed and the ends are flush with the upper sealing surface. Put a small dab of gasket sealer on each of the ends to help sealing (photo).

20 Place the oil pan in its proper location on the engine and thread in the four bolts in the corners of the pan enough to hold it in place.

21 The longest and larger diameter bolts are installed in the rearmost mounting holes of the oil pan. The longest of the smaller diameter bolts are installed in the next bolt hole forward on each side. The two bolts which are longest of the ones that are left are installed in the forward corners of the oil pan and the remaining 13 bolts and washers are installed in the middle holes.

22 Beginning in the middle and working outward toward both ends of the oil pan in a cross pattern, torque each of the socket head

13.10 Torqueing the oil pump mounting bolts

14.3 Installation of the front oil seal

15.6 Removing the oil pan

15.17 Bending the ears of the locking plate to secure mounting bolt

15.18a Installing the oil pan gasket

15.18b Check the gasket end pieces for tight fitting

15.19 Installing the round rubber gaskets

mounting bolts to 5 ft-lb (0.8 m-kg). Once this has been done for all of the smaller diameter bolts, loosen them all about one-half turn and re-torque them in the same pattern. This will allow the gasket sealer to be compressed and ensure proper torque values. Torque the larger socket head bolts to 11 ft-lb (1.5 m-kg).

16 Oil pressure sensor – removal and installation

1   Although part of the lubrication system, the oil pressure sensor is found at the rear of the cylinder head, below the distributor drive housing.

2   Disconnect the two screw connectors from the electrical wires on the top of the pressure sensor. Mark the wires for proper installation.

3   Insert a wrench of the proper size between the sensor body and the cylinder head and engage the flats of the hex fitting. Unscrew the sensor and remove it.

4   Installation is the reverse of the removal procedure.

5   Install a new seal on the threaded end of the pressure sensor and coat the threads with a heat proof sealer and thread the sensor into place (photo).

6   Torque the sensor to 11 ft-lb (1.4 m-kg). Be careful not to break the sensor body from the threaded portion.

7   Connect the wires to the sensor body.

16.5 Threading in the oil pressure sensor

17 Oil pressure sensor – testing

1 Testing of the oil pressure sensor requires a special shop tool which is unique to the Porsche line. If you suspect your sensor to be defective, have it checked by a Porsche garage.

18 Cylinder head repairs and alternatives – special note

1 Although we will cover the rebuilding of the cylinder head in the pages which follow, there are alternatives which may give economic and/or time advantages over performing the work yourself.

Machine shop: By following the inspection procedures in the test, you can purchase those new parts you know you will need and take the cylinder head and parts to a machine shop and have them perform the cutting, replacement, and cleaning of the head. You will save the costs involved with the machine shop personnel making all of the measurements, as well as the cost of the additional time they would spend picking up the parts. However, there are certain steps which even a medium-sized machine shop cannot do. The best example of this is installing new valve guides in the aluminum head. This task requires special equipment which larger machine shops (and your Porsche dealer) will have access to but is not found in many of the smaller shops, except for those which specialize only in this type of work.

Exhange/purchase of rebuilt parts: Many auto parts stores offer rebuilt cylinder heads which have been completely remanufactured by a large machine facility. The cost of these heads, against the exchange of your worn head, is usually quite a bit less than having a machine shop perform the work, cutting and cleaning and having you perform the reassembly of the cylinder head components. The other advantage is the reduction in the time your car is 'down for parts'. Some people do not like to trade parts and prefer to keep their engines as a 'set'. The decision will have to be yours.

19 Cylinder head – removal and stripdown

1 Remove the timing belt (Section 9) and the distributor (Chapter 5). If the engine is still in the vehicle, drain the cooling system (Chapter 2).
2 Remove the nuts holding the camshaft cover in place and lift the camshaft cover from the cylinder head (photo).
3 Remove the timing pulley bolt and its washer from the timing pulley and draw the pulley off the end of the camshaft. Remove the Woodruff key which locates the pulley on the camshaft. If the Woodruff key is bent, nicked, or otherwise damaged, replace it with a new one when reassembling.
4. Remove the two bolts from the rear of the number 5 bearing cap (photo).
5 Remove the two nuts which hold the camshaft oil tube on the bearing caps, lift the oil tube from the mounting studs and lift the oil feed end from the number 1 bearing cap. The oil feed end is a press fit, held firmly in place by an O-ring. A gentle tug may be necessary to remove it. Replace the two nuts on their studs and tighten them (photo).
6 Beginning with the two nuts on the number 3 bearing cap, loosen the nuts two turns at a time in a crosspattern which works outward. All nuts should then be loosened at the same time. This will allow the valve spring tension on the camshaft to be released evenly and prevent bending of the camshaft or breakage of the bearing caps.
7 Remove the bearing caps in numerical order and place them on a sheet of clean newspaper. The bearing caps are numbered with a stamp (photo). Note also that the bearing surfaces are located at an offset in the cap and may be reinstalled only one way. If the caps cannot be lifted out, strike the sides gently with a soft-faced mallet to loosen them.
8 Remove the rubber gasket strip from the number 1 and 5 bearing caps (photo).
9 Lift the camshaft from the cylinder head carefully. Do not allow the bearing surfaces on the camshaft to come in contact with the

19.2 Removing the camshaft cover

19.4 Removing the bolts from the number 5 bearing cap

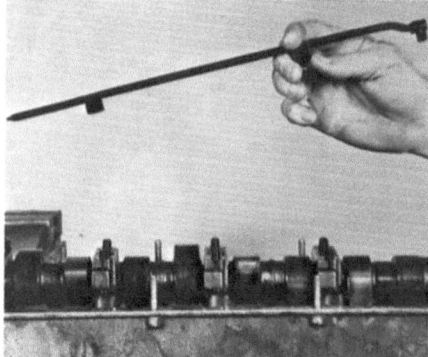
19.5 Removing the oil feed tube

19.7 Removing the camshaft bearing caps

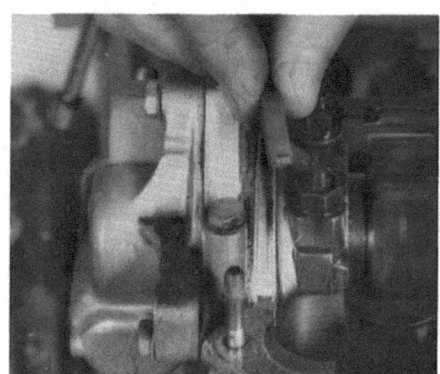
19.8 Removing the rubber gasket strips from the end bearing caps

19.9 Lifting out the camshaft. Leaving the timing belt pulley in place will cause problems in later steps

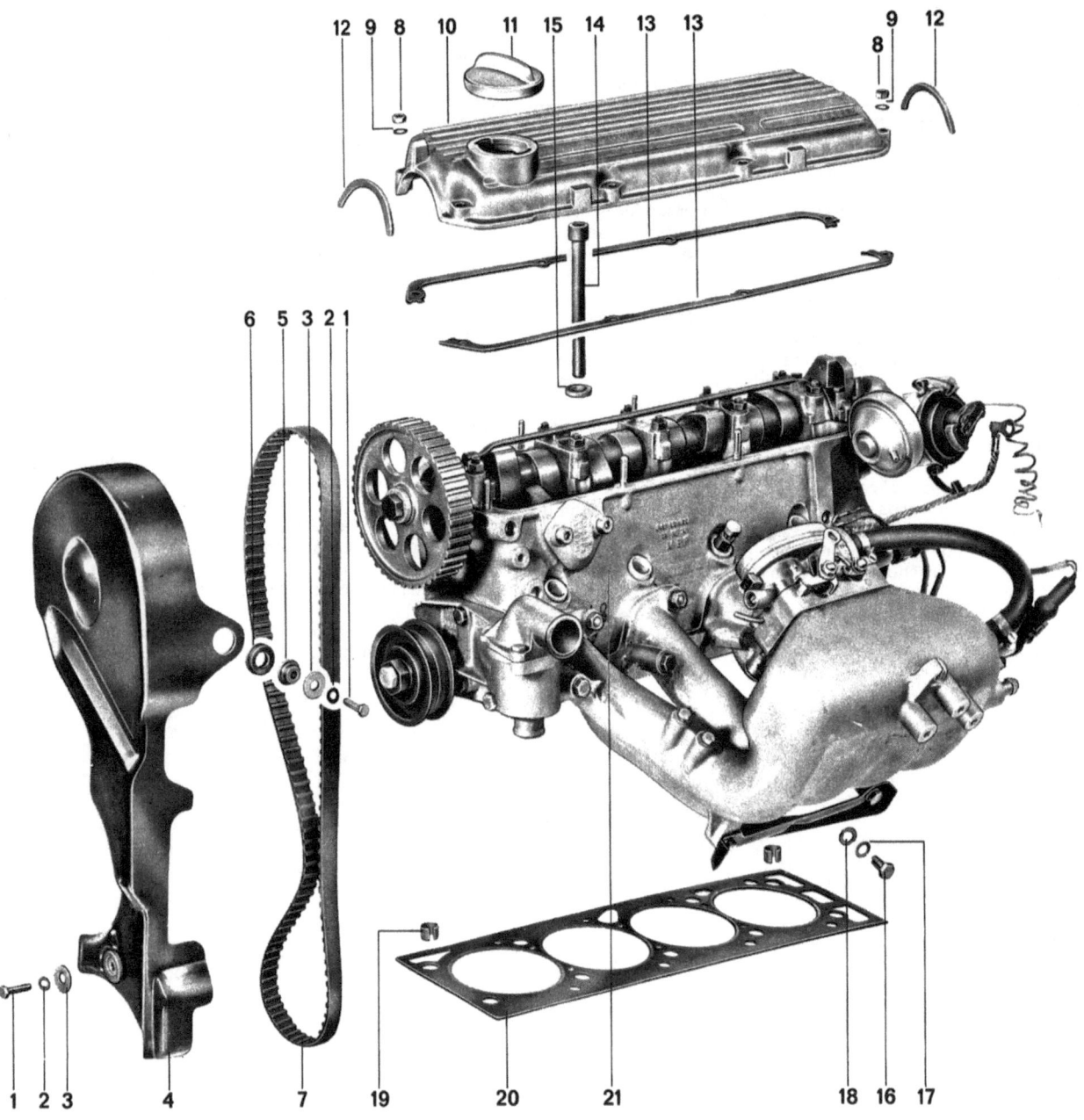

Fig. 1.5 Cylinder head: major external components

1	Bolt	7	Timing belt	12	Gasket	17	Lock washer
2	Wave washer	8	Nut, camshaft cover	13	Gasket	18	Flat washer
3	Flat washer	9	Flat washer	14	Head bolt	19	Head locating dowel
4	Timing belt guard	10	Camshaft cover	15	Flat washer	20	Cylinder head gasket
5	Bearing bushing	11	Oil filler cap	16	Bolt	21	Cylinder head
6	Rubber bearing						

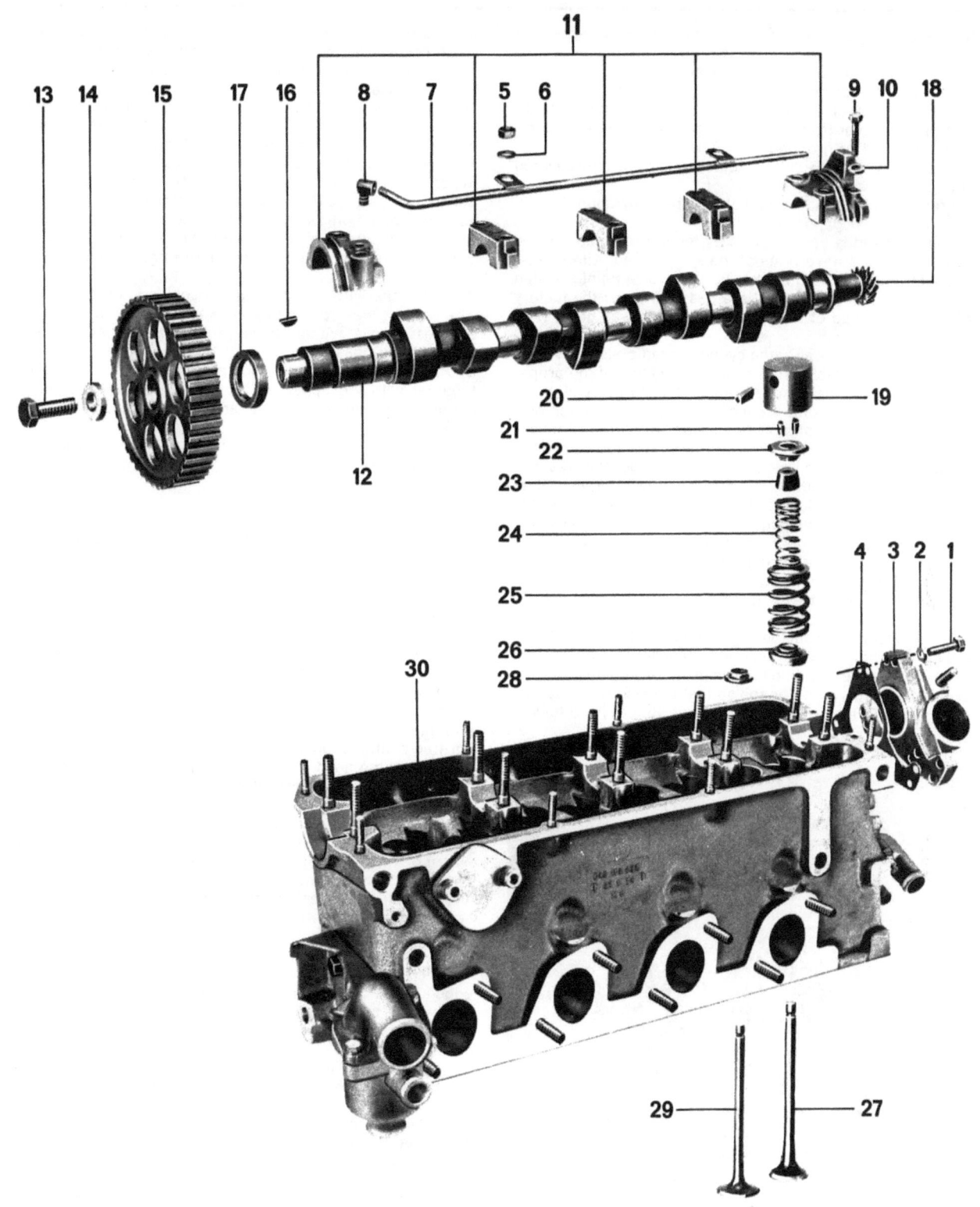

Fig. 1.6 Cylinder head: major internal components

1	Bolt	7	Oil feed tube	14	Flat washer	19	Tappet	25	Valve spring (outer)
2	Flat washer	8	Connector	15	Upper timing	20	Adjusting screw	26	Rotocap (exhaust valves)
3	Distributor	9	Bolt		belt pulley	21	Collet (keeper)	27	Exhaust valve
	drive housing	10	Flat washer	16	Woodruff key	22	Valve spring collar	28	Spring seat (inlet valves)
4	Gasket	11	Bearing cap	17	Oil seal	23	Valve stem oil seal	29	Inlet valve
5	Nut	12	Camshaft	18	Distributor	24	Valve spring (inner)	30	Cylinder head
6	Washer	13	Bolt		drive gear				

studs for the bearing cap, or damage to the bearing surfaces may result (photo).

10 Slide the oil seal from the front end of the camshaft. This should be a slip fit onto the camshaft end.

11 Place the camshaft on a clean piece of newspaper or a cloth. Do not allow the drive gear from the distributor drive end of the camshaft to be knocked or dropped.

12 The tappets, complete with their adjusting screws, may be lifted out of the cylinder head.

13 When removing the tappets, do not mix them. Arrange them in order on a clean newspaper or cloth.

14 The cylinder head is held in place by ten socket-head screws. Models through 1979 have bolts of the six-pointed 'Allen' type. These were replaced in 1980 models by the twelve-point serrated socket type. Not all 1980 models have this change as the factory installed the earlier type of bolt until their supply was gone, then switched to the later bolt.

15 The best tool for removal of the cylinder head bolts is an Allen key bit for use with a ratchet; however an Allen key of the proper size may be used in a pinch and levered on the short side of the 'L' shaped end with a closed-end wrench slipped over the end to provide a long enough lever (photo). The proper wrench for the serrated head sockets may be obtained through most tool suppliers. Although the 'Allen' key and wrench method of removal works, it is necessary to obtain the proper bit for a rachet/torque wrench when installing the head. If you do not obtain the proper tool, your only alternative must be taking the engine block and head to a mechanic to be properly torqued. Failure to do so will lead to head warpage immediately upon rebuild and running in.

16 Loosen the bolts according to the directions in Fig. 1.7. Turn each bolt two turns and move on. Continue this until all of the bolts can be removed.

17 Lift the cylinder head from the engine block with two hands. To break the hold of the gasket sealer, grasp the front and rear ends of the cylinder head while standing at the side of the engine. Rock the cylinder head toward you at the top so that the side opposite you breaks free first. Having an assistant rap the cylinder head toward

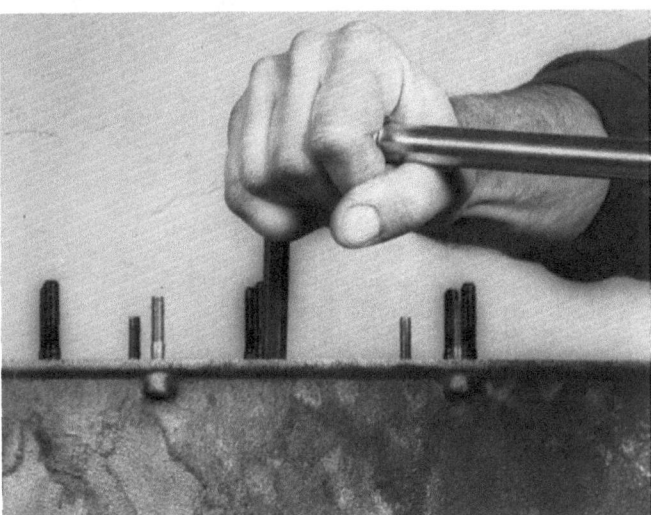

19.15 Using an Allen-type wrench and bar to remove the cylinder head bolts

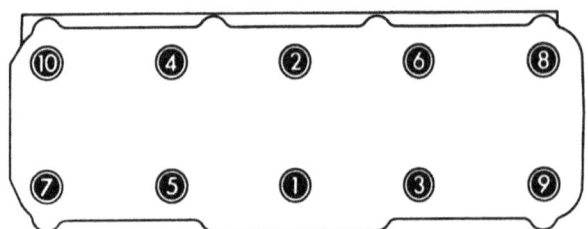

Fig. 1.7 Cylinder head bolt loosening and tightening sequence
LOOSEN in order from highest to lowest numbered bolt. TIGHTEN in order from lowest to highest numbered bolt

the top of the side opposite you may help break the seal if simple pulling does not provide the desired result. Do not attempt to strike the side of the cylinder head, as it cannot be dislodged sideways due to the locating dowels.

18 Do not set the cylinder head on a dirty surface. Dirt and grit can harm the sealing surface. Set the head on clean newspaper or cloth in an area free of sharp tools, other parts, and dirt.

19 The valves of the 924 models are deeply set into the cylinder head. When seen from the top, the valve stem, with its springs and collars, is down inside a tube. Conventional valve spring compressor tools will not allow the springs to be compressed sufficiently so that the keepers can be removed. Most larger auto parts stores carry the proper compressor or the proper adapter for your compressor.

20 Install the valve spring compressor and compress the spring. The easiest way to remove the keepers is with a magnet. This ensures removal without having to turn the cylinder head over to knock them loose.

21 Remove the valve spring compressor. Remove the valve springs, together with the upper spring retainer, the valve stem seal, the springs, the lower spring retainer, and the rotocap, if the valve is an exhaust valve.

22 Remove the valves and lay them out in the order they were installed in the cylinder head.

20 Cylinder head – measurements, checks, and overhaul

1 Once the cylinder head has been removed and stripped, it should be chemically cleaned or 'boiled out'. As this process is normally employed for iron-alloy engine parts, you must be sure that the chemical cleanser used is for aluminum-alloy parts; the former type of cleaner solvent will embrittle the cylinder head.

2 When the cylinder head cleaning is complete and the head has been thoroughly dried with compressed air (DO NOT use any cloths or rags for this as you will fill water and oil passageways with lint), place the head on a workbench, upon a layer of newspaper or lint-free cloths (shop cloths, etc) to prevent damage to the mating surfaces of the head. Begin your inspection and measurements on the combustion chamber side of the head.

Cylinder head distortion

3 First, the cylinder head must be checked for distortion and the extent of any distortion found must be known, for, if the distortion is beyond acceptable limits, the head will have to be replaced. Using a straight edge and feeler gauge, the test is as follows: Place the straight edge on the cylinder head so that it passes through the diameter of each combustion chamber circle on the head. Do not press down on the straight edge. Sight across the flat surface of the cylinder head and check for light appearing between the straight edge and the cylinder head in the area between the cylinder circles. This is the area of greatest stress on the cylinder head gasket because of the engine compression and the close proximity of the cylinders.

4 If you see no light at these points, check for light appearing in the areas from the edge of each of the outside cylinder circles to the outboard edges of the cylinder head. If light is seen at any of these points, measure the extent of the distortion by inserting the leaves of the feeler gauge into the space. If the thickness of the leaves which may be inserted into the space total more than 0.1 mm (0.04 in) the head must be machined.

5 Take the cylinder to your Porsche dealer or a competent repair shop. The sealing surface of the head must be machined smooth and flat. Your machinist will have to know where you found the distortions, what the distortion measurement was, the wear limit for the sealing surface, and the maximum allowable roughness and waviness permissible in completing this work. The first two figures will come from your notes, but the second two will always be:

    Wear limit A = 139.55 mm (5.494 in)
    Max. allowable surface roughness + waviness = 0.015 mm (0.0006 in)

6 If the cylinder head cannot be machined properly within the wear limit given above, the head must be replaced. Your machinist should be able to tell you whether or not this is possible before he begins work. Complete all measurements before having the head

machined, but if in any doubt, contact your machinist before continuing.

7 When the flatness of the sealing surface has been established, go on to the next tests.

Valves and valve seats

8 Clean each of the valves with chemical cleaner or a very fine wire brush. Do not mix up the valves as it will be important to know which cylinder they were mounted in for later testing.

9 Measure each of the valves to make sure they each comply with the measurements shown in Fig. 1.8. Check each of the valve stems for bending and make sure each of the valve heads is perpendicular to the valve stem.

10 Carefully examine the heads of the valves for pitting and burning, especially the heads of the exhaust valves. The valve seats should be examined at the same time. If the pitting on the valve and seat sealing surface is very slight, the marks can be removed by lapping the valves and seats together with coarse and then fine lapping compound.

11 Lapping the valves is carried out as follows: Make sure that each of the sealing surfaces on the valve is not cupped, but is straight. If the sealing surface is cupped inward, replace the valves with new ones and use these for lapping in. Smear a small amount of coarse lapping compound on the sealing surface of the valve seat and insert the valve into its guide. Press the suction end of a hand lapping tool on the face of the valve. Twist the lapping tool back and forth by rolling the dowel of the tool between the palms of your hands. Raise the tool and valve every few minutes and turn it about one half turn and begin twisting the tool once again. When an even matt color is distributed over the sealing surface of both the valve and valve seat, wipe the residue of the coarse paste from both surfaces and perform the same procedure with fine lapping compound. When a dull, light gray matt coating is evenly distributed on the sealing surfaces of the valve seat and the valve, the lapping operation for that valve is complete.

12 Where the valves or seat show bad pitting, the valve seats and the intake valves may be machined. Fig. 1.9 shows the necessary machining details. If you have the proper equipment for this task, the above information should be all you need for a proper job. If you do not have proper equipment, employ the services of a competent machine shop.

13 Carefully clean away every trace of lapping compound, taking great care to leave none in the ports or the valve guides. Clean the valves and valve seats with a rag tip dipped in kerosene (or gasoline); then apply a clean, lint-free cloth, and finally, carefully blow-dry the area with an air hose.

Valve guides

14 The wear of the valve guides must be checked with new valves. If possible, obtain one new intake and exhaust valve on loan.

15 Clean the inner surfaces of the guide with a broach (a small-diameter brush which resembles a bottle brush).

16 Install a dial indicator in the cylinder head so that the plunger of the indicator is in line with an imaginary line running through the diameter of the valve to be checked (photo).

17 Push the valve stem to open the valve. The end of the valve stem must be flush with the upper edge of the guide. Rock the valve back and forth along the imaginary diameter line which aligns with the plunger on the dial indicator. If the amount of rock exceeds the values below, the valve guide must be replaced, subject to the condition which follows:

Amount of permissible rock in the valve guides:
Intake valves = 0.8 mm (0.0315 in) maximum
Exhaust valves = 1.0 mm (0.0394 in) maximum

18 To see whether or not the valve guide may be replaced, place the cylinder head upright on the workbench with the combustion chambers facing down. Make sure that the sealing surfaces are protected by setting the cylinder head on several sheets of news-

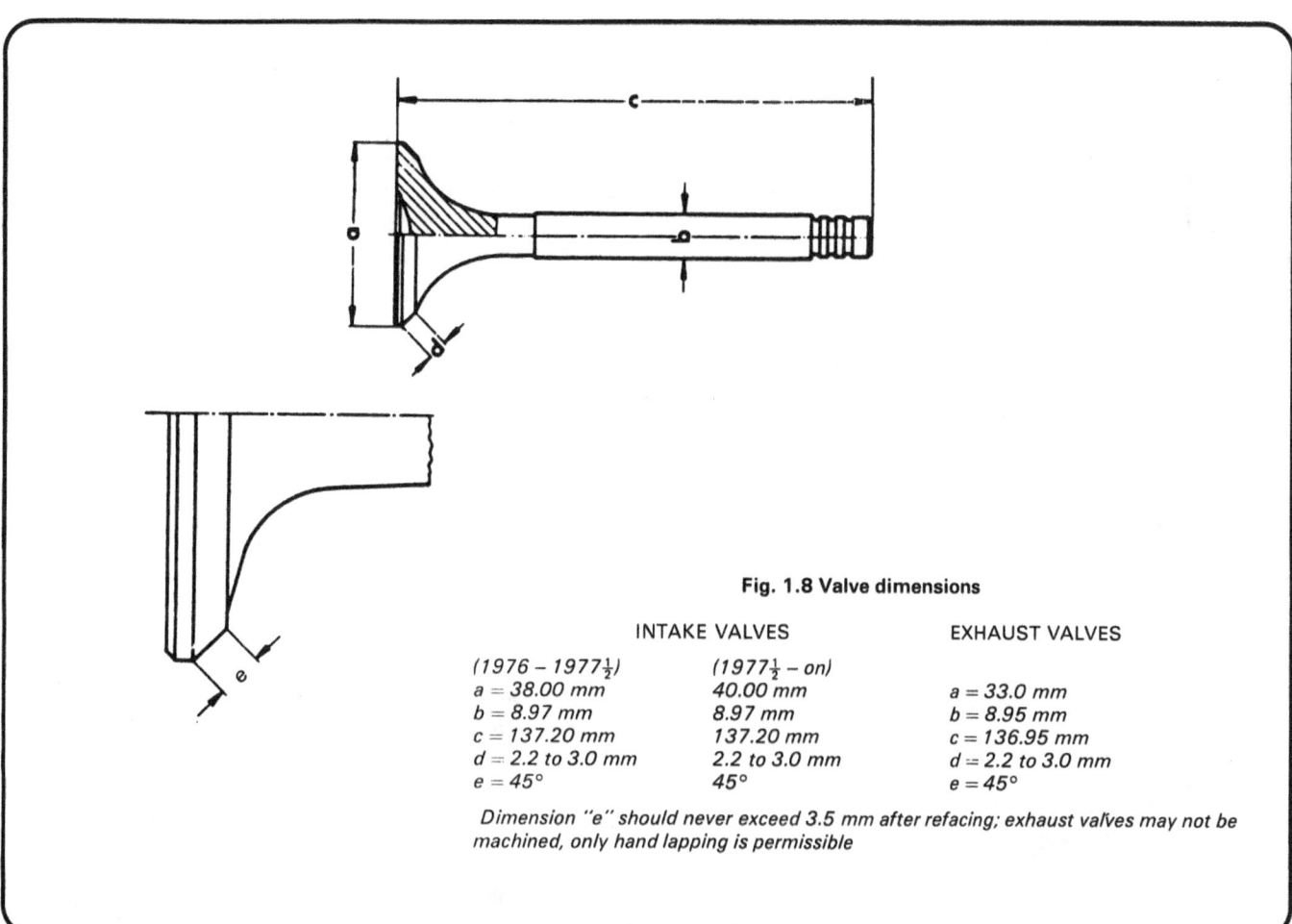

Fig. 1.8 Valve dimensions

	INTAKE VALVES		EXHAUST VALVES
	(1976 – 1977½)	*(1977½ – on)*	
	$a = 38.00$ mm	40.00 mm	$a = 33.0$ mm
	$b = 8.97$ mm	8.97 mm	$b = 8.95$ mm
	$c = 137.20$ mm	137.20 mm	$c = 136.95$ mm
	$d = 2.2$ to 3.0 mm	2.2 to 3.0 mm	$d = 2.2$ to 3.0 mm
	$e = 45°$	45°	$e = 45°$

Dimension "e" should never exceed 3.5 mm after refacing; exhaust valves may not be machined, only hand lapping is permissible

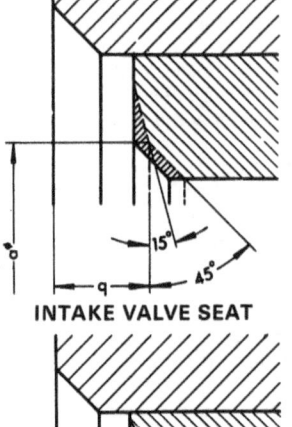

INTAKE VALVE SEAT

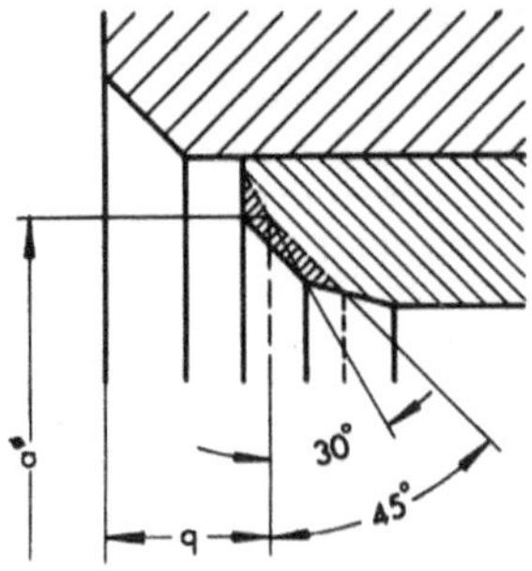

EXHAUST VALVE SEAT

Fig. 1.9 Machining dimensions for valve seats

	INTAKE VALVE SEAT		EXHAUST VALVE SEAT
	(1976 – 1977½)	(1977½ – on)	
	a = 36.5 mm	38.5 mm	a = 31.5 mm
	b = 3.5 mm	3.3 mm	b = 3.9 mm

Worn or burned valve seats may be machined until reaching the maximum depth limit (b). If depth "b" is exceeded, the head must be replaced. If you machine the valve seats, the valve adjusting screw must be replaced with screw 046 109 453 C (Fig. 1.11)

Removed Production Guide	Identification Production Guide	Outside Diameter (mm)	Replacement Guide with Circlip	Identification Replacement Guide	Outside Diameter (mm)
Int. 048 103 415 Exh. 046 103 415	no groove no groove	14.048 - 14.059	048 103 419 A 046 103 419 A	one groove one groove	14.248 - 14.259
Int. 048 103 419 Exh. 046 103 419	one groove one groove	14.248 - 14.259	048 103 423 A 046 103 423 A	two grooves two grooves	14.448 - 14.459

Fig. 1.10 Standard and replacement valve guides

New adjusting screw	Identification	Old adjusting screw	Identification
Part No.		Part No.	
046.109.453 D	1 notch	046.109.453 B	blue
046.109.453 E	2 notches	046.109.453 A	red
046.109.453 F	3 notches		
046.109.453 G	4 notches	046.109.453	yellow
046.109.453 C	no notches	046.109.453 C	white

The number of notches indicates thickness of valve adjusting screws.
High notch number = thick adjusting screw.

Note

If cylinder head has been repaired, i.e. valves replaced and ground or camshaft replaced, valve clearance must be checked and adjusted on warm engine after about 1,000 miles/1600 km. After repairs on cylinder head valve clearance can also be adjusted on cold engine. Final check must be on a warm engine.

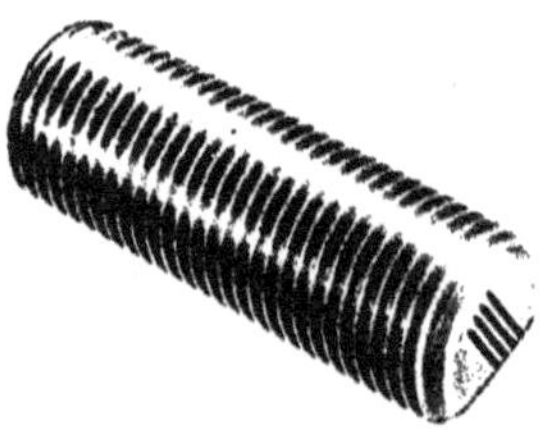

Fig. 1.11 Standard and replacement valve adjuster screws

20.16 Checking valve rock to determine valve guide wear

paper or rags. Inspect the ends of the valve guides and count the number of grooves cut into the guide above (but not including) the valve guide circlip (if installed). Check this information with the chart in Fig. 1.10. If any of the valve guides in need of replacement has two grooves the cylinder head must be replaced.

19 Have a Porsche dealer or competent mechanic perform the installation of new guides. The guides are of a material harder than the aluminum alloy of the cylinder head. If the guides are not inserted straight into the head, the valve guide hole will be elongated and the installation faulty.

20 Have the same people who install the guides ream the bores of the guides. Instruct them to clean the reamer often, and specifically not use any type of oil for this operation.

21 If you replace standard valve guides, which have no circlip, with valve guides which have a circlip, you must also replace the lower valve spring retainer with one which has a groove cut in it to clear the circlip (Porsche part number 046 109 629).

Valve adjusting screw

22 If the measurements and tests above indicate the need for recut valve seats the valve adjusting screw must be replaced.

23 There are two types of identification system which have been used by Porsche for this part. The earlier versions of the 924 used a color coding system which had three types of adjusters which could be installed and a fourth for use in reworking situations. The factory-installed adjusting screws are identified with dots of blue, red, or yellow paint and each color corresponds to a Porsche part number (Fig. 1.11). The rework adjuster screw is identified by a white paint dot.

24 Later production models use adjuster screws with a different identification system. The factory-installed adjusters number four, and are identified by one to four notches cut into the end of the screw. The rework adjuster is identified by no notching at the end. As can be seen by Fig. 1.11, the two systems identify the same parts, but the identification type has been changed. Some Porsche dealers may still have earlier adjusters in stock and the chart is included for interchangeability information.

Tappets

25 Without mixing up the order of the tappets, inspect each one for excessive wear and scoring along the sides of the cylinders. Inspect the tappet bores in the head for roundness and to ensure that their bore size is within specification. If the tappet bore exceeds the larger figure shown, or if the bores are badly elongated, the cylinder head must be replaced.

26 If you are in doubt as to the condition of any of your tappets, consult your local Porsche dealer. There are a variety of problems and your dealer is best qualified to handle your specific situation.

Camshaft

27 Inspect the lobes of the camshaft and the bearing surfaces for grooves, scoring and other wear.

28 The camshaft must also be checked for radial runout. Mount the camshaft in the centers of a lathe (if available) and set up the dial indicator with the plunger directly on the center bearing. Slowly turn the camshaft on its centers. The total permissible radial runout is 0.02 mm (0.0008 in). If your measurment exceeds this figure, replace the camshaft. Make sure that you give full identification of your vehicle to your parts source. There have been four different engines in four different states of tune (US market) and it is essential that you properly identify your engine to obtain the correct camshaft.

29 Once you have completed the information you need for machine work and/or the purchase of replacement parts, you will be able to reassemble the cylinder head.

21 Cylinder head – assembly and installation

1 When all machine work has been completed and the cylinder head has been thoroughly cleaned, it is time to begin reassembly of the cylinder head.

2 If you are reusing your valves and tappets, set them out alongside the cylinder head in their respective cylinder locations.

3 Begin at the front and work toward the rear of the cylinder head when re-installing valves and their components.

4 Fit the valve into the head so that the head of the valve rests squarely against the valve seat. Install the lower spring seat.

5 When all valves have been installed in the cylinder head in this fashion, make sure that the cylinder head is lying on a flat, level, protected surface and that the sealing face of the cylinder head is on the flat surface with the installed valve's stems facing up. Using an appropriate installation tool (Porsche Special Tools 10-204 and US 1918 or their equivalent), install the valve stem seals on the valve stems.

6 Because the top of the valve stem is grooved, the valve stem seal can easily be damaged when it is pushed into position. To prevent this damage, valve seal packages have a plastic sleeve as part of the kit, which is placed over the top of the valve stem. To install each valve seal, place the plastic sleeve over the end of the valve stem and lubricate the seal with oil. Slip the seal over the plastic sleeve and press it into place with the pushing tool, which is a tube of a slightly larger diameter than the seal with a pad on top to help place the pressure. Carefully push the seal on to the valve stem.

7 Install the inner and outer valve springs and the upper spring retainer on each valve. The tight coils of the inner spring should face the cylinder head.

8 Install the spring compressor and compress the valves until the upper two-thirds of the collet groove in the valve show above the upper spring cap. The easiest way to install the collets (keepers) is with a small screwdriver. Place a small blob of grease on the flat of the screwdriver and place the collet half on the grease with the outer diameter of the collet facing the blade and the thick section of the wedge facing toward the handle. Insert the collet into the space left by the cap and place the upper edge of the collet under the edge of the collet groove in the valve. Install the other half of the collet in the same manner and see that the gaps between the two collet halves are equal on both sides. Place a shop rag over the collets and the top of the valve stem and loosen the spring compressor. If your installation has been successful, the collets will be locked in place, and if not, the collet halves will be in the rag. It is very important that you cover the collets with a rag when loosening the spring compressor as flying collets can be destructive as well as difficult to find.

9 When all of the valves have been installed, lubricate the tops of each valve stem with white general purpose grease (photo). Lubricate the sides and top of the tappets with the same grease and install each of the tappets in the same hole from which it was removed. The adjuster screw hole, which has the hex head drive hole, must face the left or the low side of the tappet hole (photo). Since the valves must be reset, back the adjusting screws fully out until they are just threaded in the tappet.

10 Install the oil pressure sensor according to the instructions in Section 16. Torque the sensor to 11 ft-lb (1.5 m-kg).

11 Lightly lubricate the tops of the tappets with white general pur-

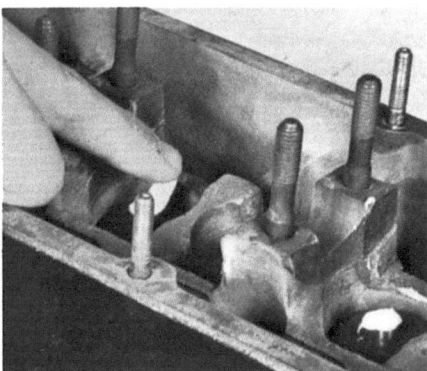
21.9a Lubricating the tops of the valves

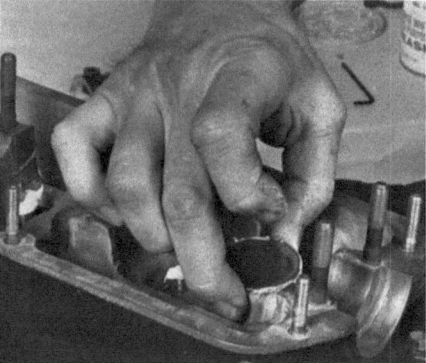
21.9b Inserting the tappets

21.11 Setting the camshaft into place

21.13 Installation of the oil feed tube

21.16 Positioning the dial indicator to check camshaft end play

21.17 Installing the camshaft front oil seal

pose grease. Lubricate the camshaft lobes and the bearing surfaces of the camshaft with assembly lubricant and set the camshaft into the bearings on the cylinder head. The distributor drive gear (or the end of the camshaft without a Woodruff key slot) is installed at the rear of the cylinder head (photo).

12 Lubricate the bearing surface of the bearing caps. Install the number 2 and 4 bearing caps in place. The bearing surface bores are offset in the bearing caps and when the bearing caps are properly installed their stamped number, which indicates the order in which they are found installed in the cylinder head, may be read in an upright position from the rear of the cylinder head. Install one flat washer and nut on each of the studs of these two bearing caps and tighten them down in a cross pattern.

13 Install the number 1, 3, and 5 bearing caps and tighten them down in the same manner as outlined above. When all of the nuts have been tightened snug, remove the nuts on the left side studs on both the number 2 and 4 bearing caps and install the upper camshaft lubrication tube. The tube has an O-ring which seals the connector in the fitting on the number 1 bearing cap. Make sure that the O-ring is not cut or damaged during installation of the tube. Make sure that the oil tube's feed end is a snug fit in the hole (photo).

14 Install the nuts back on the number 2 and 4 bearing caps and tighten them snug. Torque the nuts to 11.6 to 15.2 ft-lb (1.6 to 2.1 m-kg). Torque the nuts in a crossing pattern, beginning with the number 3 bearing cap and working out.

15 Install the two bolts at the rear of the number 5 bearing cap and torque them to 7 ft-lb (1 m-kg).

16 Set up a dial indicator in the manner shown in the accompanying photo and measure the camshaft end float (photo). End float is determined by pressing the camshaft all the way to the front of the cylinder head, setting the dial indicator to zero, and pressing the camshaft to the rear with your thumbs on the lobes of the camshaft. The indicated figure on the dial is the end float and must not exceed 0.2 mm (0.00787 in).

17 Using Special Tool 10-203, or another appropriate seal installation tool, install the oil seal at the front of the camshaft. Lubricate the lips of the seal before installing (photo).

18 Install the Woodruff key in the slot provided at the front end of the camshaft. Align the slot in the timing belt sprocket with the Woodruff key and press the sprocket into place. Install the plain washer and bolt at the end of the camshaft and tighten the timing belt sprocket bolt to 58 ft-lb (8 m-kg) (photo).

19 Before installing the cylinder head on the engine block, make sure that the two centering bushings on the engine block are in place (photo). If they are not, set each one in the bushing mounting hole and lightly tap it into place with a soft-face mallet.

20 Coat the engine head gasket with a light coating of gasket sealer. Do not leave sealer on any of the metal reinforcing rings which are around many of the holes on the gasket material. Place the head gasket on the engine block and press it into place over the two centering bushings and press the coated sections of the gasket against the engine to promote good adhesion of the gasket.

21 It is much easier for two people to set the cylinder head in place. Although the weight of the casting makes one-man installation possible, with two people setting the cylinder head into place, much more time and control is available to get the head properly centered over the locating bushings before setting it down (photo).

22 Install the cylinder head bolts and screw them in finger tight. Following the sequence in Fig. 1.7, tighten each of the bolts two turns each until they are tight. Using a torque wrench, tighten the bolts in the same sequence, to the torque given in the Specifications. Regular Allen bolts will have to be retightened after 1000 miles – see Section 29. For 12-point serrated socket bolts, see Chapter 13.

23 If the installation of the cylinder head is being done as part of an engine rebuild all the work on the block (Section 23 thru 28) should be done first. To install the head, fit the camshaft cover and tighten the nuts on the camshaft cover snug (photos). This will keep the valve train clean while you install the various components to the front of the engine prior to timing belt installation.

24 Install the thermostat housing (Chapter 2).

25 Install the timing belt (Section 9).

26 Adjust the valve clearances (Section 22).

27 Check the ignition timing and idle adjustment to take account of the new efficiency of your engine (Chapters 2 and 5).

21.18 Torqueing the upper timing belt pulley, using a flat blade screwdriver to counterhold

21.19 Positioning the cylinder head centering bushings

21.21 Setting the cylinder head on the engine block

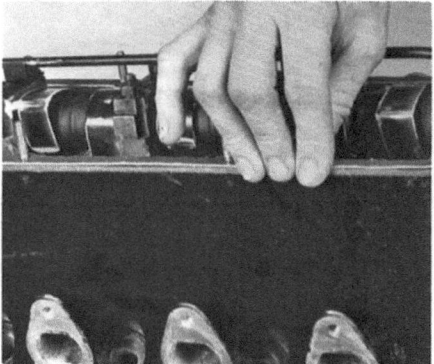
21.23a Installing the camshaft cover gaskets

21.23b Installing the camshaft cover gasket end pieces

21.23c Installing the camshaft cover

22 Cylinder head – adjusting valve clearances

1 When the engine is completely rebuilt and the timing belt installed, the clearance of the valves and tappets may be adjusted.
2 Remove the camshaft cover nuts and the camshaft cover.
3 Turn the engine via the bolt head of the oil pump to bring the first cylinder to top dead center. The valves are arranged with the number 1 cylinder intake valve at the front of the engine, followed by the number 1 cylinder exhaust valve, and the valves are so ordered in the same manner, intake ahead of exhaust.
4 Using one of the valve adjusting tools shown in Fig. 1.12, or an Allen key (see Chapter 13), adjust the valve clearances to the values given in the Specifications. Proceed as follows.
5 With the piston at top dead center (both valves closed) insert the leaves of the feeler gauge into the space between the top of the tappet and the camshaft lobe. The feeler gauge must be set for the desired clearance. Insert the adjusting tool into the hole in the tappet and engage the screw. Turning the tappet adjusting screw one turn will add or subtract 0.05 mm (0.002 in) of clearance. Clearance has been properly adjusted when the leaves of the feeler gauge may be pushed and pulled through the space. Perform this adjusting task for each cylinder from front to back in the engine.

23 Engine block – piston, connecting rod, and crankshaft removal

1 Before removing the pistons from the engine block, use a ridge reaming tool to remove the excess build up of carbon from the cylinders (photo).
2 Use a prick punch to number the connecting rods by punching the correct number of dots (1 through 4) on both the connecting rod and caps on the side opposite the stamped part numbers on the lower end of the connecting rod (photo). Remember that the number 1 piston and cylinder are at the front.
3 Turn the engine so that the cylinders face downward and the

exposed crankshaft faces up. Turn the crankshaft so that the number 1 and 4 pistons are at bottom dead center.
4 Remove the nuts from the bearing caps and remove the caps from the number 1 and 4 connecting rods. Do not mix the bearing caps.
5 Making sure that the connecting rods of the number 1 and 4 cylinder stay hard against the throws of the crankshaft, turn the crankshaft, bringing the number 1 and 4 cylinders to top dead center and the number 2 and 3 cylinders to bottom dead center.
6 Remove the nuts from the bearing caps and remove the caps from the number 2 and 3 connecting rods. Do not mix the bearing caps.
7 Turn the crankshaft through another half turn, removing the bearing caps of the throws from the number 1 and 4 connecting rods and pressing the number 2 and 3 connection rods to top dead center.
8 Beginning at the front of the engine, remove the pistons and connecting rods in numerical order. Press out each piston and connecting rod with the engine block turned upside down and using only the pressure of your hands. Make sure that the pistons do not turn to the side in their bores and score or chatter on the walls. Use a prick punch and hammer to label each connecting rod and its bearing cap. Punch the appropriate number of dots on the unmarked flats on the connecting rod and bearing cap which abut each other when the bearing cap is installed. (There is a cast-in raised piece on the connecting rod and the bearing cap which must be facing the same side.)
9 The forward cylinder is the number 1 cylinder and the rearmost one is the number 4 cylinder.
10 Set the pistons, together with their numbered connecting rods and caps, on a clean sheet of newspaper in numerical order. Unless later measurement and testing proves otherwise, these pistons may be reused, as long as they are reinstalled in the same cylinders in the engine block.
11 Before moving on to the crankshaft removal, make sure that the engine is turned completely over and the crankshaft is facing up.
12 Using Special Tool 10-221 or a flat blade screwdriver, remove the

23.1 Removing carbon build-up with a ridge reamer

23.2 Connecting rod identification numbers

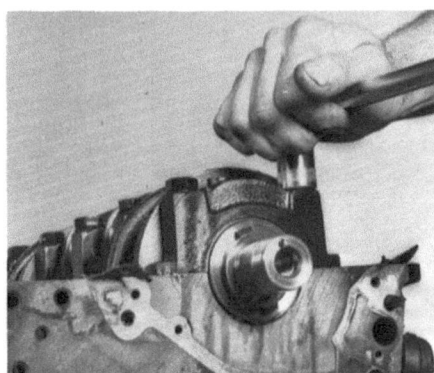

23.14 Removing the bearing cap bolts

23.15 Removing the crankshaft bearing caps

23.16 Lifting the crankshaft from the engine block

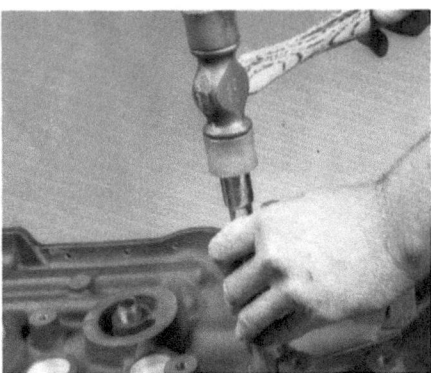

24.5 Installing new freeze plugs after engine cleaning

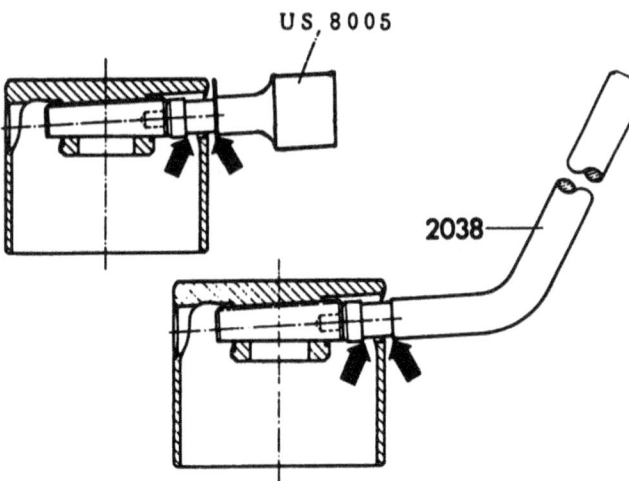

Fig. 1.12 The two variations of valve adjusting tools

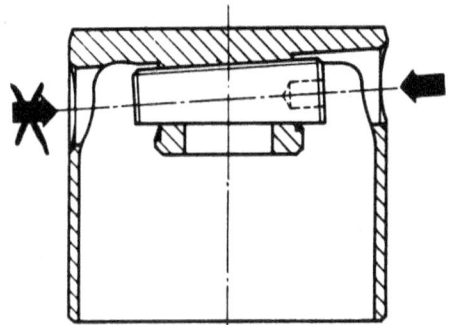

Fig. 1.13 Insert the valve adjusting tool and tighten only one way

oil seal from the flywheel end of the crankshaft.

13 Remove the socket head screws from the number 5 bearing cap.

14 Beginning with the number 3 bearing cap, loosen the bolts on the bearing caps in a cross pattern, two turns each in order until the bolts may be lifted off (photo).

15 Remove the bearing caps in numerical order from front to back. If the bearing caps do not lift off their locating pegs, rap the sides of the caps with a soft faced mallet to free them (photo).

16 Lift the crankshaft out of the engine block and set it on a clean sheet of newspaper (photo).

17 Remove the bearing shells from the engine block and place them with their corresponding bearing cap. Do not mix them up.

24 Engine component cleaning and inspecting

1   Before taking measurements, checking clearances, and making decisions on machine work, give all of your engine parts a thorough cleaning.

2   Remove carbon deposits from piston tops and the cylinder head with a fine wire brush.

3   Remove oil and sludge buildup with standard engine cleaning solvent.

4   If you find that there are large deposits of rust and calcium scale in the water jacket of the engine block and cylinder head, have them 'boiled out' by an engine cleaning service. In this process the engine block and cylinder head are lowered into an acidic bath which removes all internal deposits from the castings. See Section 20.1. Remember to remove the freeze plugs from the engine block before having such work done. The freeze plugs are removed by punching through the middle of the plug with a flat blade screwdriver and levering the plug out of its spot in the engine casting.

5   When the engine block is returned from the cleaning service, place it back on the engine stand, install new freeze plugs (photo), mask off all mating surfaces and openings in the casting, and paint the engine block with a reliable brand of engine paint. Your 924 engine block is made of iron and will look better and be easier to clean if it is painted.

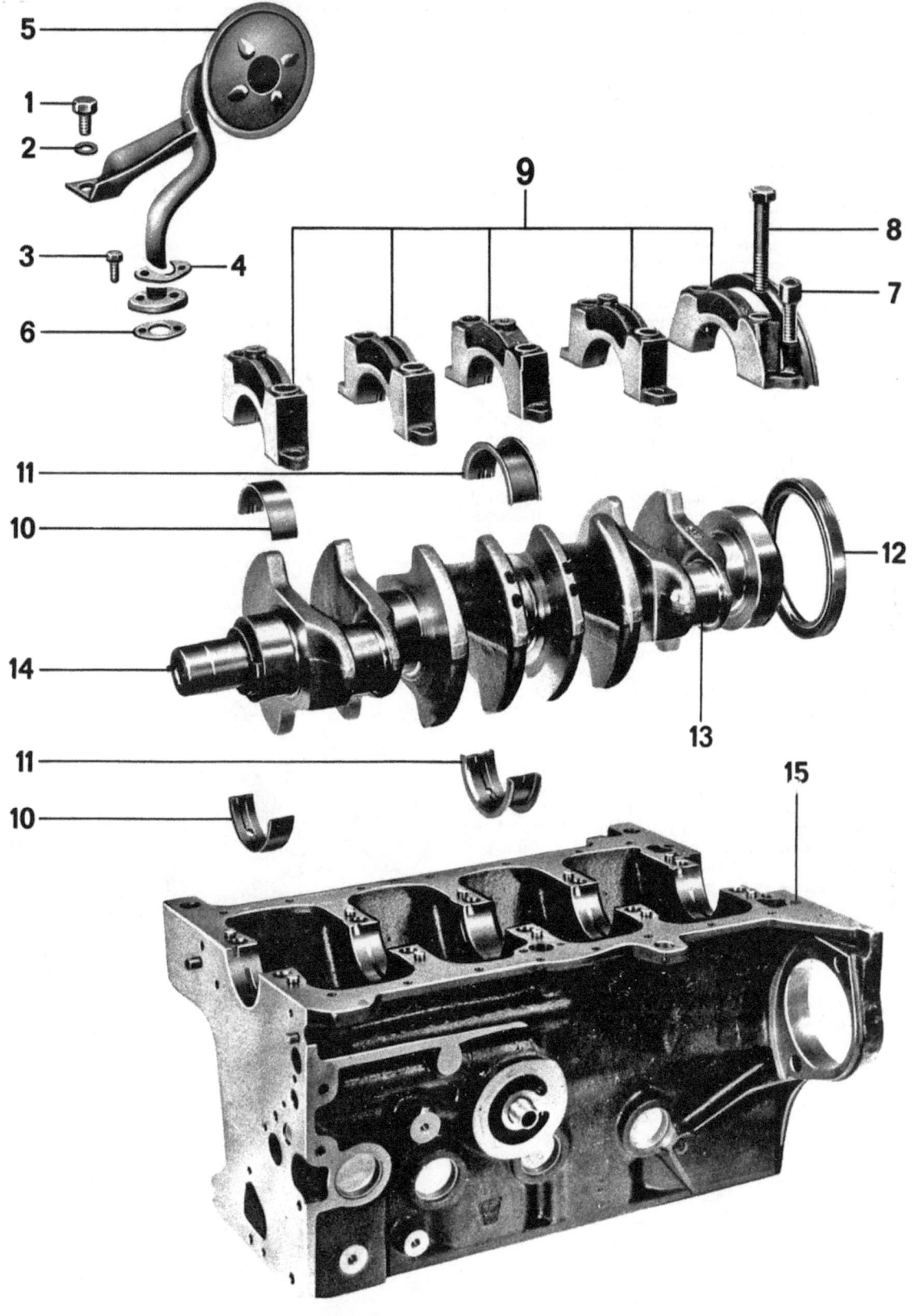

Fig. 1.14 The crankshaft and its mounting components

1	Bolt	6	Gasket	10	Bearing shell 1, 2, 4 and 5	12 Oil seal
2	Flat washer	7	Socket head bolt			13 Crankshaft
3	Bolt	8	Bolt	11	Bearing shell 3, thrust bearing	14 Driving dog
4	Lockplate	9	Bearing cap			15 Locating bushing
5	Oil pickup					

25 Engine block - measurements and checks

1   When the engine block has been stripped and cleaned, place it back on your engine stand with the cylinders facing up.

2   Assemble your tapered bore gauge and insert it in the cylinder bore of the number 1 cylinder (photo).

3   Measure the diameter along the front to the rear and side to side axes of the cylinder bore. As shown in Fig. 1.15, these measurements must be done at a distance of 10 mm (approx. 3/8 in) from the top of the cylinder, at the center of the cylinder bore, and at a point about 10 mm (approx 3/8 in) from the bottom of the bore.

4   Divide a sheet of notebook paper into a grid four spaces down by seven across and record the piston/cylinder numbers (1 through 4) down the left-hand side of the grid. In the first three spaces, record the three measurements (in millimeters) for each of the bores.

5   On the right side of the engine block, just above the place where the alternator is located, you will find a three digit number stamped into the front right side of the engine block. Record this number in the fourth space (honing group). Using this number for each of the bores, refer to the chart in Fig. 1.16 or 1.17 to determine the bore of the cylinders when the engine was assembled at the factory. Write this diameter (in millimeters) in each of the fifth spaces.

6   When this has been done for all four cylinders, compare each of the three measurements you made on each cylinder to the measurement made at the factory (space 5) and record the largest difference between your measurements and the original bore in the sixth space.

7   If the largest deviation (difference) in diameter is less then 0.08 mm (0.003 in), the cylinders do not need to be honed or rebored.

8   If the largest difference in diameter is greater than 0.08 mm (0.003 in), the cylinder will need to be bored.

9   The boring of the cylinder is dependent upon the size of piston available from your Porsche dealer. Move to the size number immediately below the group your cylinder was previously bored to and note the three sizes of piston available. An example of this: your cylinder was previously bored to a size within the 'Standard' group, but is now in need of a rebore. Move one size group down the chart to the '1' group. The most desirable piston size in this group is the smallest, therefore you would seek that size from your Porsche dealer. If, however, your dealer can fill your order with one of the other sized pistons from the same group, you will still realize maximum economy from your engine. It is, of course, possible to replace a 'Standard' group piston with a '3' group piston, but you will forfeit much of the life of your engine. If, for example, a rebored engine lasts 80,000 miles, you would give up the potential of 160,000 additional miles of use from your engine by overboring to a much larger size.

10 Once you have purchased new pistons, take the engine block to a reliable machine shop to be bored to the appropriate size. Instruct your machine shop to bore the cylinders to the diameter which corresponds to the piston diameter of your new pistons in Fig. 1.16 or 1.17.

11 Other checks which should be performed on the engine block are general checks for cracks and breaks in the engine block metal, nicks and deep scratches in the gasket surfaces of the various parts attached to the engine block, and make sure that the cylinder head to engine block surface is level and flat. A good machine shop may be able to grind smooth any surfaces in need of truing.

26 Pistons and connecting rods - disassembly, inspection, assembly

1   Lay out the pistons, connecting rods, and their bearing caps on a cleared area of your workbench. Do not mix up the piston order if there is a chance you will be reusing the same pistons and/or connecting rods. If you must bore the cylinders, set the pistons aside, after you have used them to perform the various tests on the connecting rods.

2   Lever the circlips from the number 1 piston. Perform all tests on this unit and then each of the others in numerical order (photo).

3   The piston pin is a tight fit in the connecting rod bush, but it may be easily removed by inserting a screwdriver—whose handle diameter is larger than the center hole of the pin—into the center

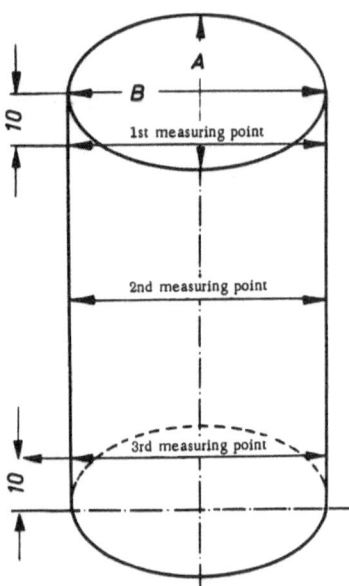

Fig. 1.15 Cylinder bore measuring points

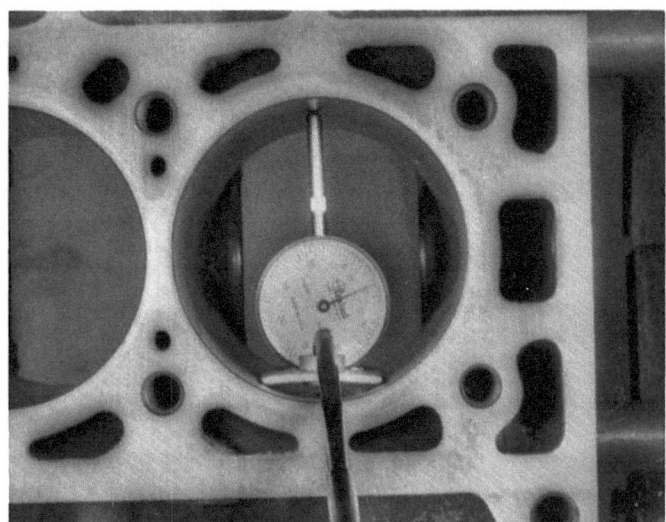

25.2 Installing the tapered bore gauge

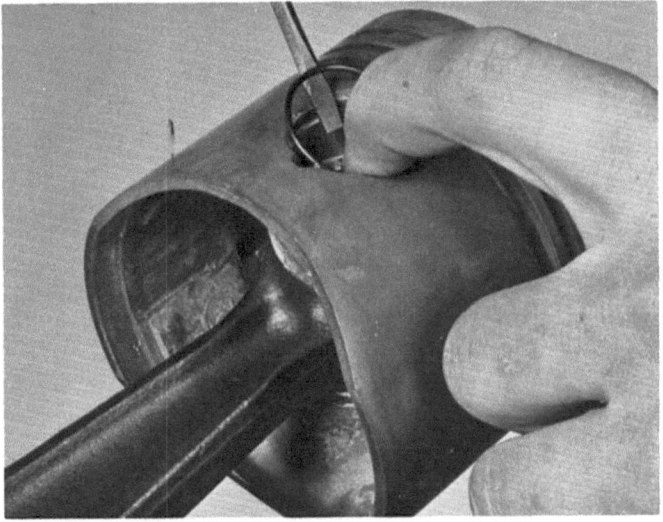

26.2 Removing the piston pin circlip

Size	Piston Dia. (mm)	Cylinder Bore (mm)	Honing Group Number
Standard	86.48	86.51	601
	86.49	86.52	602
	86.50	86.53	603
1st Oversize	86.73	86.76	626
	86.74	86.77	627
	86.75	86.78	628
2nd Oversize	86.98	87.01	651
	86.99	87.02	652
	87.00	87.03	653
3rd Oversize	87.48	87.51	701
	87.49	87.52	702
	87.50	87.53	703

Fig. 1.16 Piston size tolerance chart (standard models)

Size	Tolerance Group		Piston Diameter (mm) Mahle	Cylinder Bore Diameter (mm)	Honing Group Code
Standard	86.5	I	86.45	86.51	601
		II	86.46	86.52	602
		III	86.47	86.53	603
1st Oversize	86.75	I	86.70	86.76	626
		II	86.71	86.77	627
		III	86.72	86.78	628
2nd Oversize	87.0	I	86.95	87.01	651
		II	86.96	87.02	652
		III	86.97	87.03	653
3rd Oversize	87.5	I	86.45	87.51	701
		II	86.46	87.52	702
		III	87.47	87.53	703

Fig. 1.17 Piston size tolerance chart (Turbo models)

hole of the piston pin. Pull the blade of the screwdriver to draw the piston pin out of the piston and connecting rod.

4   Press the piston pin into the connecting rod upper bush without the piston and center it in the bush. Using a feeler gauge, measure the amount of play between the connecting rod bush and the piston pin. The play must be between 0.01 and 0.02 mm (0.0004 and 0.0008 in). If the play you find is greater than these figures, measure the outer diameter of the piston pin and the inner diameter of the connecting rod bush.

5   The outer diameter of the piston pin must be between 23.996 and 24.000 mm (0.9447 and 0.9449 in) and the inner diameter of the connecting rod must be between 24.012 and 24.018 mm (0.9454 and 0.9456 in). If the piston pin diameter is less and/or the connecting rod diameter is more than the figures above, check with your local Porsche dealer on the availability of these individual parts.

6   The radial play between the connecting rod and the crankshaft, as well as the side clearance check, are covered in Section 27.

7   If you intend to reuse the pistons, the following measurements must be made.

8   Measure about 16 mm (5/8 in) from the bottom edge and at a right angle to the centerline of the piston pin (photo). Record this measurement for all four pistons and check the chart in Fig. 1.16 or 1.17. Based upon your engine's bore group number the piston diameter is critical. None of the pistons may vary in diameter from the piston diameter shown by more than 0.04 mm (0.0016 in), or all must be replaced.

9   If you use the same pistons, remove the piston rings from the pistons and check each one in the cylinder bore, about 16 mm (5/8 in) from the bottom of the cylinder wall. The piston ring gap, when checked with a feeler gauge must be between 0.3 and 0.5 mm (0.012 and 0.020 in), with a wear limit of 1.0 mm (0.039 in) (photo).

10 If you use new pistons or piston rings, the same piston ring gap test will have to be performed. A piston ring gap which is too small can be corrected by careful filing of the ring gap surfaces.

11 Assembly of the pistons and connecting rods is an easy task which requires a little care and alignment to do properly.

12 The connecting rod nuts and bolts must be replaced with new ones. To remove the old connecting rod bolts, place a deep well socket, whose inside diameter is slightly greater than the outside diameter of the bolt head, in the protected jaws of a vice. Insert the bolt head into the socket and hold the connecting rod with one hand so that the bolt will travel straight into the socket. Using a hard faced hammer, drive the bolt out of the connecting rod. When both connecting rod bolts have been removed, install new bolts by driving the new bolts into the connecting rod with a hammer and punch. Make sure the splines of the bolts are driven completely into the connecting rod (photos).

13 Note that there are cast-in pins on the connecting rod and its cap. The machined edges on this side also have a number stamped into them (photo). The pips must face forward when the connecting rod is installed in the engine. There is also a directional arrow on the piston crown which points to the front of the engine (photo). The arrow and the pips must both point in the same direction when the piston is installed on the connecting rod. The cast in pip on the bearing cap must also face the same direction when it is installed.

14 Install the piston on the connecting rod and align the hole in the piston and connecting rod. The piston pin may be installed with thumb pressure while holding the piston in your hands.

15 Install the new circlips with needle nose pliers. The circlip gap should face into the slot (photo).

16 Clean the piston ring grooves with a groove cleaning tool. A piece of broken piston ring will do the job just as well, but protect your fingers – it may be sharp. This is essential when reusing pistons, but should also be done to new pistons to remove any debris from the machining process (photo).

17 Install the piston rings. This must be done with an installation tool (photo), or as described in Chapter 13.

18 Check the piston ring side clearance with a feeler gauge. Insert the edge of the feeler gauge leaves between the upper edge of the piston lands and the piston ring (photo). If the piston and rings are new, the gap must be between 0.04 and 0.07 mm (0.0016 and 0.0028 in). The maximum wear limit for all instances and combinations of new and used pistons and rings is 0.1 mm (0.004 in). If the gap exceeds this measurement consult your Porsche dealer. It is most likely that this situation will occur when the piston is reused, but, as circumstances vary, your Porsche dealer will have the best solution.

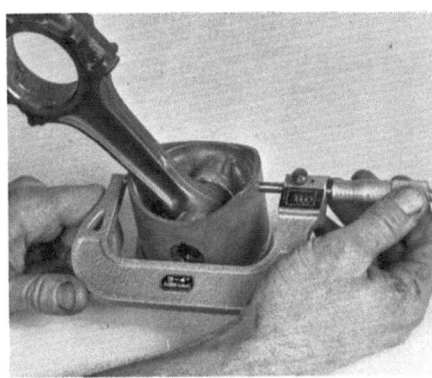

26.8 Proper method of piston measurement

26.9 Proper method of checking ring gap

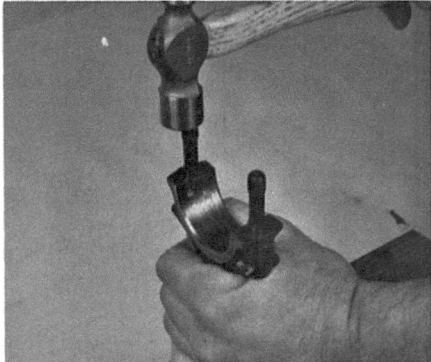

26.12a Removing the old connecting rod bolts

26.12b Installing new connecting rod bolts

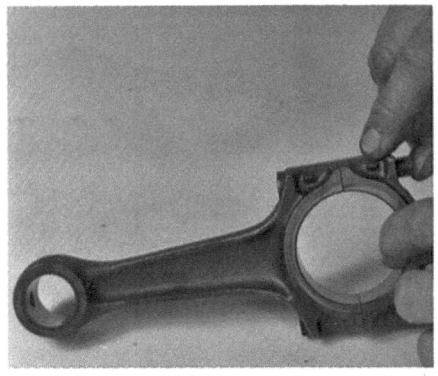

26.13a Location of the connecting rod's directional pips

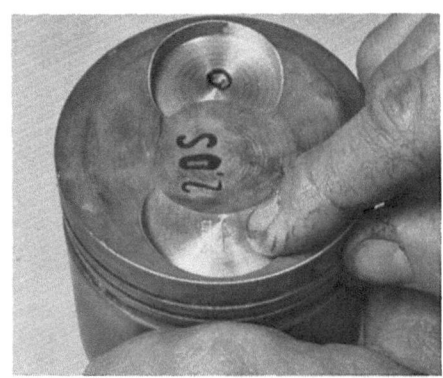

26.13b Location of the piston's directional arrow

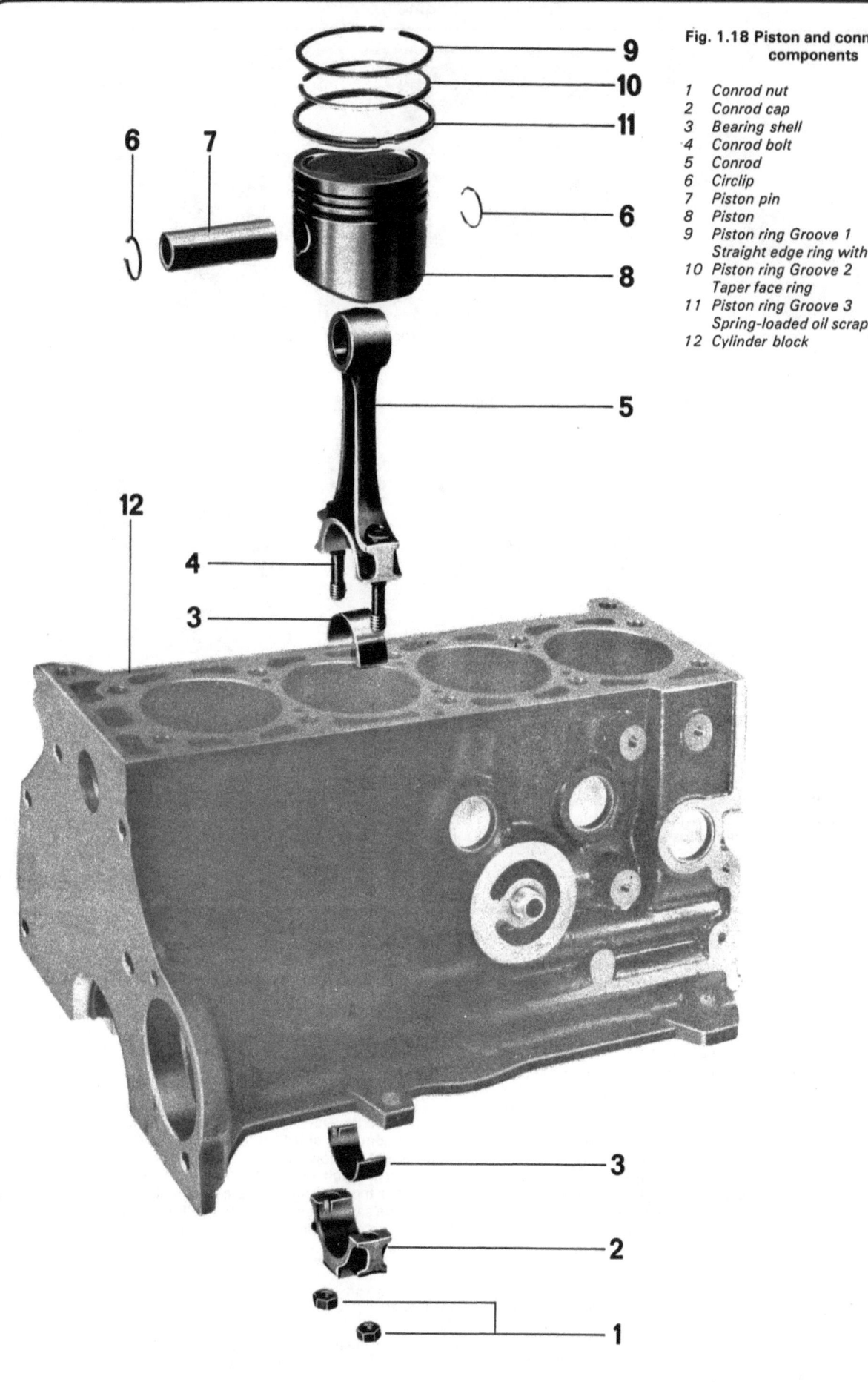

Fig. 1.18 Piston and connecting rod components

1 Conrod nut
2 Conrod cap
3 Bearing shell
4 Conrod bolt
5 Conrod
6 Circlip
7 Piston pin
8 Piston
9 Piston ring Groove 1
  Straight edge ring with inside chamfer
10 Piston ring Groove 2
  Taper face ring
11 Piston ring Groove 3
  Spring-loaded oil scraper ring
12 Cylinder block

26.15 Installing new piston pin circlips. Hand location prevents circlips from flying out

26.16 Cleaning the piston ring grooves with a groove cleaning tool

26.17 Installing piston rings with a ring expander tool

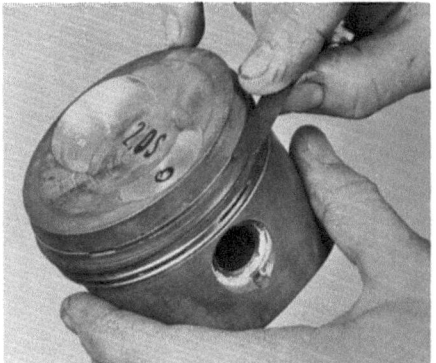

26.18 Measuring piston ring side clearance

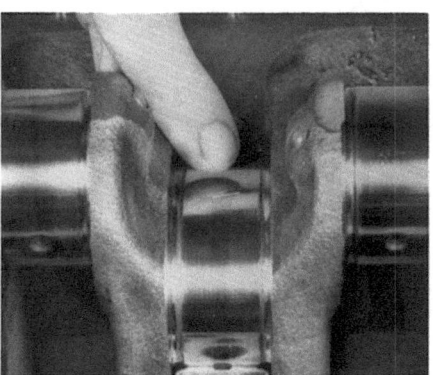

27.3 The flattened piece of Plastigage ready for measuring

27.7a Measuring the crankshaft journals

19 Once all of the connecting rods have been installed in the pistons and the rings are installed and the gaps correct, adjust the rings so that the ring gaps are spaced 120° apart, that is, the three ring gaps should divide the circle of the piston into thirds. Do this for all pistons and set them aside for installation in the engine.

27 Measuring the crankshaft and connecting rods

1 The first step in the measurement process is to clean and dry the crankshaft, connecting rods, and their bearings. When all parts are free of dirt and other material which can cause inaccurate measurement, turn the engine so that the crankshaft bearing bosses face up.
2 The easiest way to measure radial clearances in the main bearings is with a 'Plastigage' strip. This is obtainable in three sizes, but, for the purposes of these tests, the PG1 size (green packet, 0.0025 to 0.0075 in) is the only one which will be needed.
3 Place the clean bearing shells in their proper bosses and set the crankshaft into place. Lay a strip of 'Plastigage' strip onto the first bearing journal so that the strip is in line with the longitudinal axis of the journal. Set the bearing cap and its bearing shell in place and tighten the bearing cap bolts. Torque the bolts to 58 ft-lb (8 m-kg). Remove the bolts and the bearing cap. Take the 'Plastigage' sleeve and measure the width of the flattened strip at the ends and middle of the strip. The width of the strip corresponds to the thickness as shown in the key on the 'Plastigage' sleeve (photo).
4 Scrape off the 'Plastigage' with a thumbnail and continue these tests for all main bearing journals.
5 If the measured thicknesses exceeds the figures below, either the crankshaft or the bearings are worn. Your Porsche dealer will be the best source for deciding the proper replacement bearings or the proper regrind for the crankshaft.

6 The two other items which must be checked are the roundness of the crankshaft main and connecting rod bearings and the radial play in the connecting rod lower end bearings.
7 Checking for roundness of the journals may be done with simple shop micrometers and by referring to the 'Tolerances and wear limits' section of this Chapter; however, we recommend that you leave this job to a trained professional. The tolerances of the Porsche engine are essential to good high performance and long life. An experienced mechanic knows all of the little tips and warning signs your crankshaft can tell him. This book cannot detail his years of experience (photos).
8 One check which can be performed before taking the crankshaft to be checked for roundness is the radial play of the connecting rod lower ends.
9 Install the crankshaft in the engine block and install all of the bearing caps. Torque the bearing caps in a cross pattern to 58 ft-lb (8 m-kg). Turn the engine block so that the cylinders face up. Lubricate the cylinder walls heavily with new oil and install the pistons and connecting rods (Section 28).
10 Install all of the bearing caps on the connecting rods and tighten the nuts until they are snug. Turn the crankshaft over in the stand to bring the number 1 and 4 cylinders to the BDC position. The pistons should be at the lowest end of their stroke and the throws of the crankshaft as high out of the inverted block as possible.
11 Remove the bearing cap from the number 1 connecting rod and perform the same procedure with the 'Plastigage' as you did in your check on the crankshaft main bearing journals. The allowable radial play figures are as follows:

Connecting rod bearing-to-crankshaft:	new	wear limit
Maximum clearance, mm ..0.02 to 0.07		0.1
in ....0.0008 to 0.0028		0.004

12 Torque the connecting rod bearing cap nuts to 43 ft-lb (6 m-kg).

Main bearing:	new	wear limit
Maximum clearance, mm ...0.02 to 0.08		0.16
in .....0.0008 to 0.0031		0.006

27.7b Measuring the connecting rod journals

27.15 Measuring crankshaft end-play

28.1a Honing the cylinder bores

28.1b A proper cross-hatch pattern

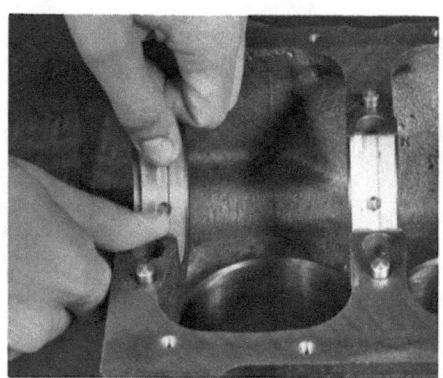

28.3 Installing new crankshaft bearing shells

28.4 Setting the crankshaft into the engine block

13 When you have completed the check for the number 1 connecting rod, perform the same tests on the number 4, 2, and 3 connecting rods, in that order.

14 Check the connecting rod side clearance by pushing each connecting rod bearing cap toward the rear of the engine and measuring the space between the crankshaft throw and the connecting rod with a feeler gauge. The side clearance must be as follows:

Connecting rod-to-crankshaft	new	wear limit
Maximum clearance, mm ...0.03 to 0.05		0.4
in .....0.001 to 0.002		0.016

15 When all of the crankshaft-to-connecting rod clearances have been checked, and before disassembling the engine block for machining, press the front end of the installed crankshaft toward the rear as much as possible. Check the gap between the number 3 bearing cap and the number 3 crankshaft throw with a feeler gauge (photo). The end play must be as follows:

Crankshaft end play	new	wear limit
End play, mm ....0.10 to 0.19		0.25
in ....0.004 to 0.0075		0.0098

16 If your measurements exceed the wear limit, discuss this with your Porsche dealer as well. The proper solution to your crankshaft fit will require these measurements.

28 Engine block – rebuilding

1 Before assembly is begun, the engine block must be honed with a three-stone hone and drill. A proper cross hatch pattern on the cylinder walls helps retain oil lubrication (photos). If you are unsure about performing this task yourself, have a qualified mechanic perform the honing for you.

Crankshaft
2 Turn the engine in the engine stand so that the crankshaft bearing surfaces face up.

3 Install the bearing shells in the machined bearing surfaces of the engine block and the bearing caps. The bearing shell and the caps and engine bosses are notched. Make sure that the oil holes of the bearing shells and their mounting surfaces align (photo).

4 Set the crankshaft in the bearing bosses of the engine block. The long 'nose' of the crankshaft faces the front of the engine (photo).

5 Set the crankshaft bearing caps in place and install the bolts. Tighten the bolts in a cross pattern and then torque them to 58 ft-lb (8 m-kg), also in a cross pattern. Install the two socket head bolts in the number 5 cap and torque to 47 ft-lb (6.5 m-kg) (photo).

Pistons and connecting rods
6 Oil all cylinder walls with engine oil. Install the clean bearing shells to their locations in the connecting rods and caps. Oil the shells.

7 Beginning with the number 1 piston and connecting rod install the pistons. Assuming that the pistons have been installed on the connecting rods according to the directions in Section 26, proper installation continues as follows:

8 Install a ring compressor on the rings of the piston. Tighten the compressor and insert the piston in the cylinder so that the cast-in directional pip faces the front of the engine, as does the arrow on the piston.

9 Set the compressor into the cylinder slightly. Rap on the top of the piston with the wooden handle of a mallet or hammer to drive it into the cylinder (photo).

10 Make sure that the connecting rod bolts do not contact the sides of the cylinder or the machined surface of the crankshaft. Guide the connecting rod so that it seats squarely on the crankshaft throw. If the crankshaft throw is not at BDC, turn the crankshaft until the crankshaft throw and the connecting rod protrude the farthest they can from the bottom of the engine block.

11 Turn the engine over, so that the crankshaft throw and connecting rod face up.

12 Install the bearing cap and bearing cap nuts. Torque the nuts to

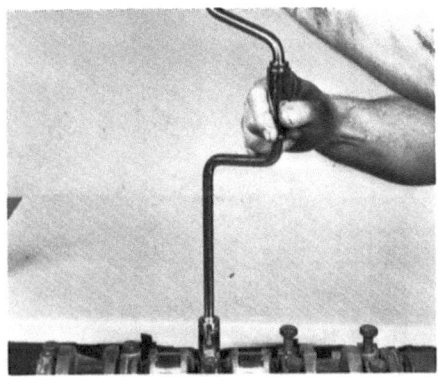

28.5 Evenly tightening the bearing cap bolts. The use of a speed wrench helps avoid over-tightening

28.9 Installing the pistons in the cylinder

28.12 Tightening the connecting rod nuts

43 ft-lb (6.0 m-kg) (photo).
13 Perform the same steps for numbers 4, 2, and 3 pistons, in that order.

Oil seal
14 Install the rear crankshaft oil seal. Set the seal in place and drive it squarely into the engine block until the seal has firmly contacted the shoulder of the seal holder.

Other components
15 Install the oil filter, oil pickup, and oil pan (Sections 12 and 15).
16 Install the cylinder head (Section 21).
17 Install the ancillary parts (Sections 5 or 7).
18 Installation of the engine in the vehicle is the reverse of the operation described in Sections 4 and 6. The nut and bolt torque specifications will be found at the front of this chapter. The only thing which must be added is a suggestion to use fender pads when installing the engine, to prevent scratching and denting of the bodywork.

---

29 Break-in and maintenance of a rebuilt engine

1 When your engine is rebuilt and installed in your vehicle, it will need the same gentle break-in and care as an engine in a new car. Avoid hard acceleration and do not run the engine over 3500 rpm until the tasks below have been completed at 1000 miles (1500 km).

If you use your vehicle for many long highway trips, do not remain at the same speed constantly. Run at 55 mph for fifteen minutes or so, then 50 mph for a similar period of time then, perhaps, 60 mph. In this way the engine parts will mate to one another at all speeds and excess heat will not be built up.
2 After the first 1000 miles (1500 km) have elapsed, perform the following tasks:
3 Change the oil and the oil filter (Section 12). Take the drain pan aside and examine your engine oil for metal fragments and other warning signs that something may not have been assembled properly. A certain amount of small metal fragments in the oil is normal, but larger chunks and many chips are not.
4 Check all coolant hoses and their clamps for tightness and condition.
5 Check all mounting bolts for proper torque.
6 Run the engine until normal operating temperature is reached. If regular Allen bolts are securing the cylinder head, tighten them as follows. Following the sequence in Fig. 1.7, slacken the first bolt about 30°, then retighten it to the specified final torque. Repeat on each bolt in turn. (There is no need to retighten the 12-point serrated socket bolts if these have been angle-tightened as described in Chapter 13.)
7 Adjust the valves (Section 22).
8 Make a general inspection of the engine and its ancillary parts to make sure everything has bedded in well. Look for signs of air leakage, oil leakage, and coolant leakage.
9 When the engine is deemed to be tight and running well revert to the maintenance schedule of the 'Routine maintenance' section found in the front of this book.

Chapter 2 Cooling, interior heating and air conditioning

Contents

Specifications

Radiator .... Alloy construction with crossflow, header tank centrally mounted. Turbo model has header tank mounted to the left of the radiator.

Cooling fan .... Electrically operated fan controlled by a thermo switch in the upper tank of the radiator. Switch is on at 92° C (198° F) and off at 87° C (189° F)

Thermostat .... Bellows operated
    warm water test .... Opening begins at 82° ± 2°C (180° ± 3.5°F) opening ends at 93°C (200° F)
    installed performance .... Opening begins at 87° ± 2°C (189° ± 3.5°F)
    opening stroke .... 8 mm (0.31 in.) minimum

Pump .... Mounted to the front of the engine block and driven by V-belt which also drives the alternator.

System pressure .... Pump tester must hold 1 bar (14 psi) on dial indicator when the engine is at operating temperature, but not running.

System cap pressure .... Pump tester must indicate 0.9 to 1.15 bar (12.8 to 16.4 psi) on dial when high pressure valve opens.

Cooling system capacity .... 7.0 litres (12.3 Imp pints) approx

Cooling system antifreeze mixing chart

Temp. to	% antifreeze/% water
–13°F (–25°C)	40/60
–23°F (–30°C)	44/56
–31°F (–35°C)	50/50

Torque specifications

	ft–lb	m–kg
Thermostat upper housing to lower housing, bolt	7	1.0
Thermostat housing to engine	14	2.0
Water pump to engine:		
smaller diameter, shorter	6	0.9
larger diameter, longer	16	2.2
Timing belt adjustment pulley, bolt	29	4.0

	ft-lb	m-kg
V-belt pulley, water pump	14	2.0
Timing belt guard, bolts	7	1.0
Transfer tube mounting bolts	14	2.0
EGR filter mounting bolts	14	2.0
EGR filter support bracket, bolts	14	2.0
Coolant temperature sensor to rear coolant flange	6	0.9
Thermo time switch to rear coolant flange..................	20	2.8
Rear coolant flange to engine	7	1.0

1 Coolant system - general description

1 The purpose of the Porsche 924 cooling system is to carry away heat created by the combustion process and transfer the heat into air. With engine location, this is one of the two major items which distinguish the 924 model line from all earlier Porsche designs.
2 The coolant system consists of a water pump; which circulates coolant (water and non-phosphate ethylene glycol) throughout the system under a small pressure; a radiator to remove the heat from the coolant by drawing air over the tubes and fins; a fan to move the air over the radiator when forward motion of the vehicle is not sufficient to carry away the heat; a thermostat to raise the system pressure and the boiling point of the coolant; and various other sensors described in greater detail throughout this Chapter.
3 The coolant system is dependent on the hoses and other parts being in proper repair and the system is filled with water of low mineral content to prevent calcium deposits from forming in the system. If you live in a climate warmer than those shown in the mixing chart, mix antifreeze and coolant in the minimal amounts shown. Antifreeze contains rust and deposit inhibitors essential to the free running of coolant through the system and increases the ability of the water to gain and retain heat, then lose it in the radiator.
4 Never work on any part of the cooling system unless the engine has cooled down. There is a real danger of burns caused by retained heat or scalding by escaping steam if this precaution is not observed.

2 Coolant - draining, mixing, filling

1 Do not drain coolant from the system unless the engine is cold.
2 Disconnect the negative lead from the battery.
3 Place a container of at least 8 liters (2½ gallons) capacity beneath the left side edge of the radiator.
4 Set the heater controls on their warmest setting.
5 Remove the pressure cap on the coolant tank (photo).
6 Loosen the drain plug located on the lower left side of the radiator, and allow coolant to drain.
7 Mix water and ethylene glycol-base antifreeze in the proportion necessary to prevent freezing at the lowest average temperature seen in your vehicle's area of operation (see Specifications for mixing chart).
8 Reinstall the drain plug on the radiator.
9 Remove the plastic bleeder plug from the upper hose by loosening the clamp and pulling out the plug.
10 Add the coolant mixture by pouring it through the filler hole in the expansion tank.
11 Start the engine and allow it to run at a fast idle speed for about one minute. When the coolant at the bleeder plug no longer bubbles, replace the plug and tighten the clamp.
12 Allow the engine to run until normal operating temperature is reached. When the needle on the temperature gauge on the dashboard reads normal operating temperature, this is proof enough. Fill the cooling system with as much of the remaining coolant mixture necessary to fill the system to the line on the expansion tank.

3 Coolant - draining, mixing and filling (Turbo)

1 Drain coolant from cold engines only.
2 Disconnect the negative lead from the battery.
3 Move the heater controls to the hottest position.
4 Place a container of at least 8 liters (2½ U.S. gallons) capacity beneath the drain screw on the left side of the radiator.
5 Remove the drain screw and allow the coolant to drain.

6 Replace the drain screw, complete with a new seal, and torque the screw to 11 ft-lb (1.5 m-kg).
7 Leave the heater controls set on their hottest setting and loosen the bleeder screw about one turn. The bleeder screw is located inside the turn of the fuel lines and is immediately to the left of the timing belt guard, in the casting.
8 Fill the engine at the overflow tank with coolant mixed according to the mixing chart (Specifications Section).
9 Reconnect the battery and start the engine. Allow it to run at a fast idle for about one minute.
10 Tighten the bleeder screw when air bubbles no longer emerge from the bleeder screw opening.
11 Run the engine until it reaches operating temperature.
12 Check the bleeder screw and drain screw for leakage.
13 Turn the engine off and fill the coolant tank to the "Maximum" mark.
14 When checking the coolant level, it should be between the "Minimum" and "Maximum" lines. Always check coolant level when the engine is cold.

4 Coolant hoses - removal, inspection, installation

1 Every one of the coolant system hoses is held in place by worm-drive hose clamps. Loosening the clamp and pulling the hose from the flange to which it is mounted in the standard method of removing the hoses (photo).
2 If the hoses seem to be sealed on due to heat, age, or inside deposits, gently twist the hoses from side to side carefully. Some hose flanges, particularly those on the radiator, are aluminum and will deform and/or crack easily around the base. Use great care and judicious use of force when working these hoses loose. Pushing a thin screwdriver between the hose and the pipe stub, and working it around full circle, will usually release the hose.
3 If the above methods do not work, carefully cut the hose from the flange end about 1 in. (about 26 mm) into the hose, separate the pieces at the slit and carefully peel the hose from the flange. Remember that a steel razor blade (which is the best cutting tool for this job) will score most of the metal flanges as they are made of softer metal. If you do score the flange, the score may be the site of a fatigue crack later in the life of the engine. Consider replacement of the damaged part; better yet, take a little time and care so that the flange will not be scored.
4 Any hose which does not pull straight off its mounting flange should be considered a likely candidate for replacement.
5 Check every hose for flexibility. If the hose shows several large or many small cracks when squeezed, replace the hose. Check also to see if the hose springs back into shape, or slowly reforms itself. Replace the hose if it has lost its flexibility. Finally, check the inside of the hoses for rust and calcium deposits. These choke the flow of coolant and could eventually lead to overheating problems. If the water in your area is considered quite "hard", you can increase the life of your cooling system by substituting distilled water for tap water.
6 Installation of the hoses is the reverse of the removal procedure.
7 Remember that worm-drive hose clamps strip out very easily when overtightened. An overtightened hose clamp may also deform the flange it is holding the hose to and cause leakage problems. Use new hose clamps and tighten them only until the hose cannot be removed from the flange by gentle tugging.

5 Radiator - removal and installation

1 Disconnect the negative lead from the battery.

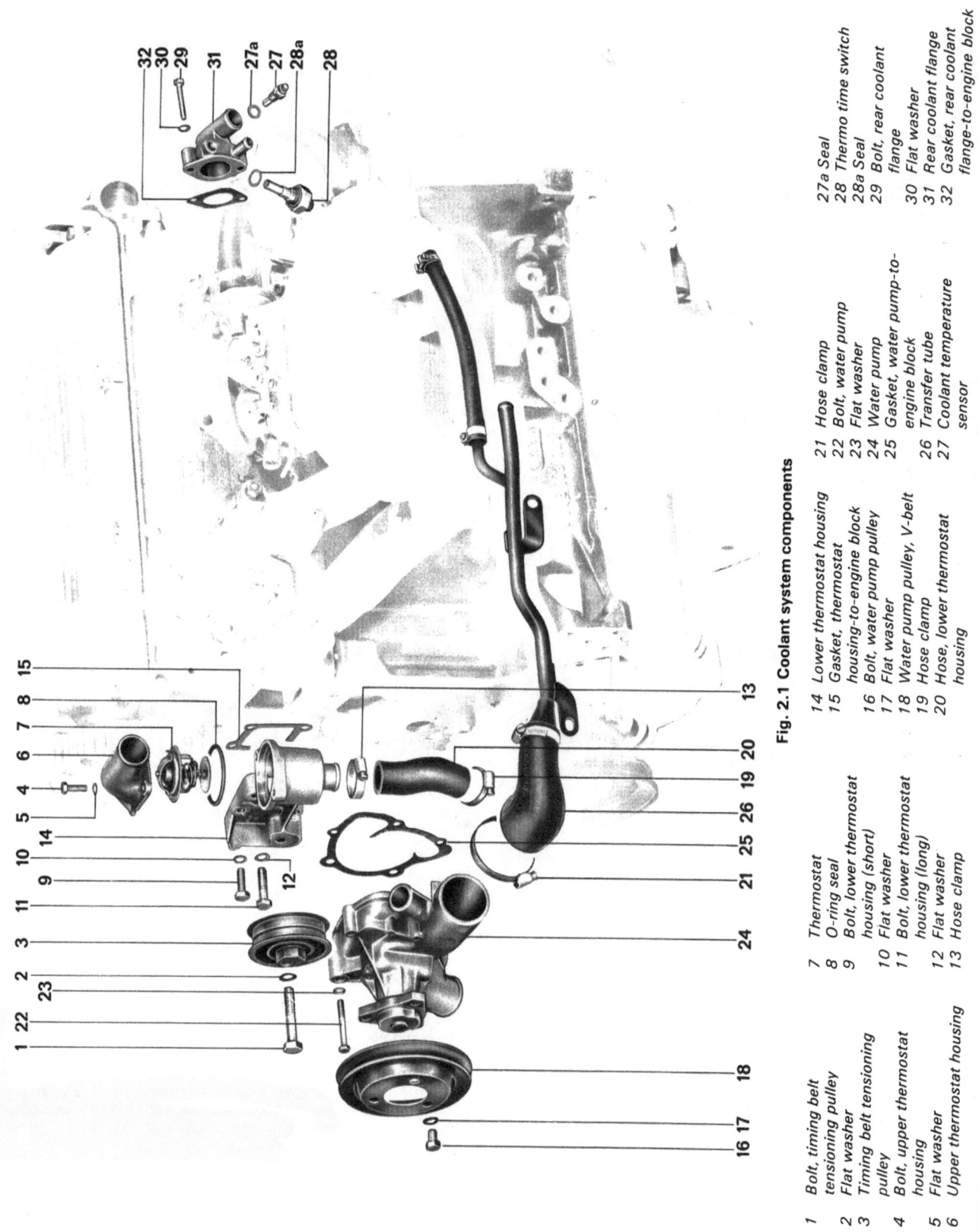

Fig. 2.1 Coolant system components

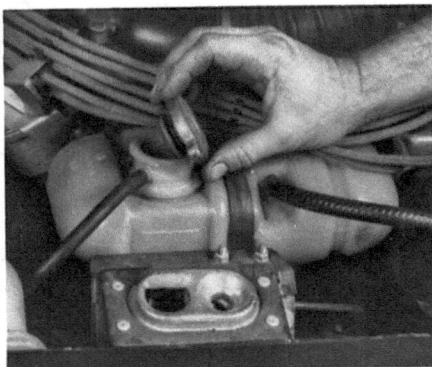

2.5 Removing the pressure cap from the coolant tank

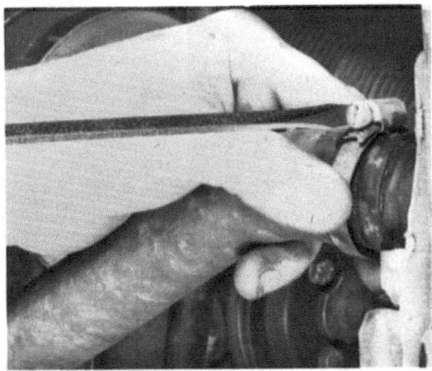

4.1 The recommended way to remove coolant system hoses and their clamps

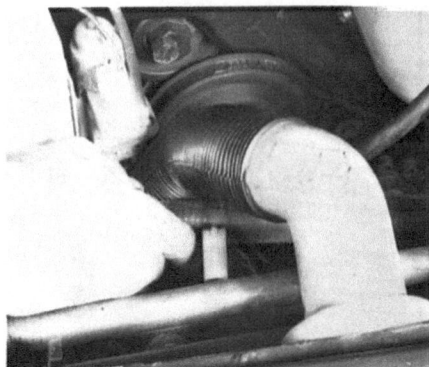

5.6 Removing the hoses for the expansion tank

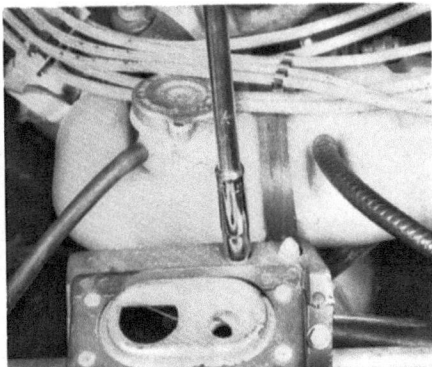

5.7a Removing the expansion tank hold down strap

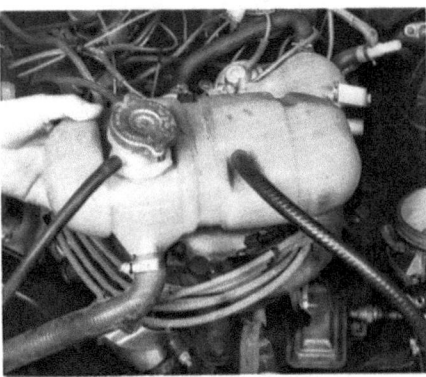

5.7b Removing the expansion tank

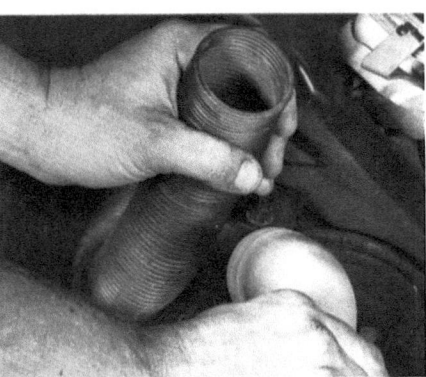

5.10 Disconnecting the alternator cooling air hose

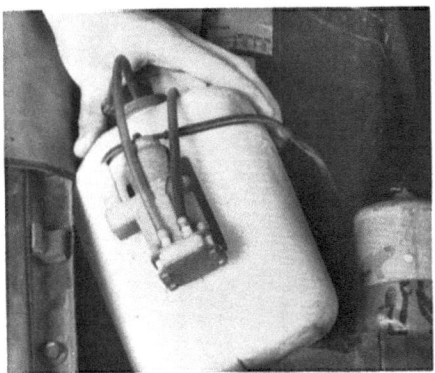

5.11 Relocating the windshield washer tank

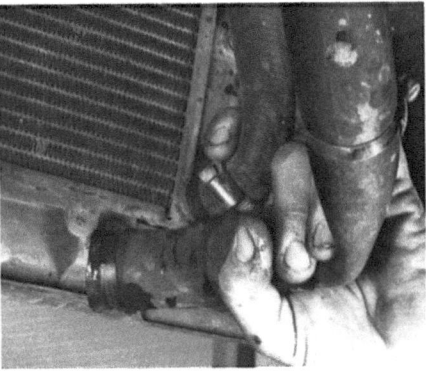

5.13 Separating the coolant hoses from the radiator

5.15 Unbolting the radiator

2   Remove the pressure cap on the expansion tank. If the vehicle is warm from operation of the engine, turn the cap to the first notch and let excessive pressure escape. It is best to turn the cap while holding it with a rag or cloth which covers the cap. Hot steam will burn skin as it escapes. Once pressure has been relieved, remove the cap (photo 2.5).

3   Raise the vehicle and place it on jack stands.

4   Drain the coolant system (see Section 2 or 3).

5   Remove the four bolts from the engine guard and remove the lower guard.

6   Follow all of the hoses leading from the expansion tank and remove each hose at the end opposite the expansion tank (photo).

7   Remove the expansion tank hold down strap and pull out the expansion tank and all attached hoses together (photos).

8   If your model has air injection (check Chapter 3) remove the air cleaner housing with its holder.

9   Leave the molded rubber boot in place on the mixture control unit, but remove the socket head screws which attach it to the air box and place it to one side.

10 Remove the alternator cooling air hose from the intake manifold (molded plastic) over the radiator and the end of the metal shroud on the alternator. If the proper type of pliers are not available, a standard set of slip-joint pliers should be used to squeeze the clamps holding the hose in place so that it may be removed (photo).

11 Slide the windshield washer tank out of its holder and set it in the open space ahead of the wheel well (photo).

12 Remove the thermo switch (see Section 8).

13 Remove the hoses which service the radiator at the radiator end and allow them to hang free (photo).

14 Disconnect the fan plug wires. Remove the bolts which hold the fan shroud to the radiator and disconnect the fan wiring harness clips before sliding the shroud toward the engine for clearance (see Section 10).

15 Remove the four radiator mounting bolts and lift the radiator out of the engine compartment (photo).

16 Installation is the reverse of the removal procedure.

17 Always install a new seal at the thermo switch connection.
18 Check the radiator hoses and their connections for any signs of leaks. Replace any cracked, brittle, or swollen hoses with new ones before installing the radiator.

2 Pump up the tester until the high pressure valve in the cap opens. The valve should open at a value of between 0.9 and 1.15 bar (12.8 – 16.4 psi) indicated on the dial of the pressure gauge (Fig. 2.3).

6 Radiator pressure cap – checking

1 Mount the radiator pressure cap on the tester (see Section 7 for a description of the proper tool).

7 Coolant system – pressure test

NOTE: This test will require a special pressure testing tool. The tool (illustrated in Fig. 2.4) is an air pump mounted in combination

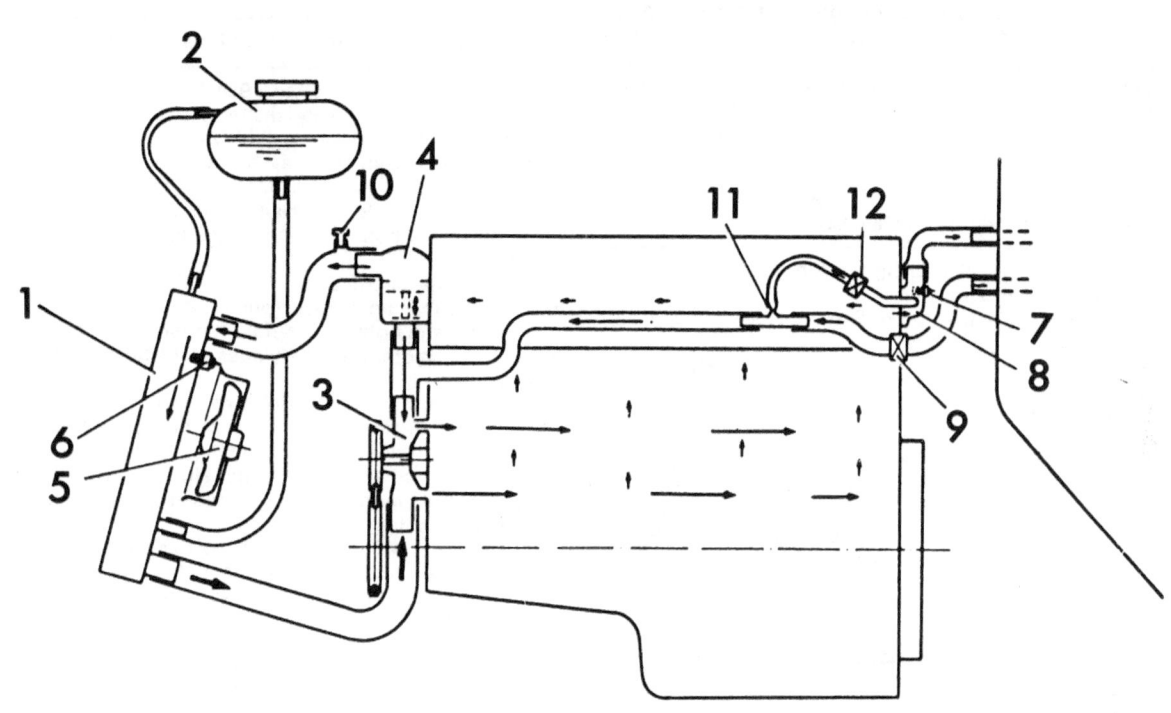

Fig. 2.2 Coolant flow

1 Radiator	5 Electric fan	8 Heater connection (inlet)	11 Operational vent
2 Expansion (overflow) tank	6 Thermo switch	9 Heater control valve	12 Temperature switch (EGR
3 Water pump	7 Temperature sensor	10 Vent	system)
4 Thermostat			

Fig. 2.3 Porsche tool VW 1274 set up for testing the radiator pressure cap

Fig. 2.4 Porsche tool VW 1274 set up for testing coolant system pressure

with a pressure gauge. It carries number VW 1274 in the Porsche tool list, but a similar tool is made by any number of manufacturers and sold through auto parts stores.

1   Remove the pressure cap from the coolant expansion tank and start the engine. Allow the engine to reach operating temperature (as indicated by the temperature gauge in the instrument cluster on the dashboard), then shut the engine off.

2   Install the pressure tester on the coolant expansion tank in place of the pressure cap. Pump up the pressure in the system with the air pump until a reading of 1 bar (14 psi) is indicated on the dial of the gauge.

3   If the pressure remains steady and does not drop for a period of fifteen minutes, the system is pressure tight. If a pressure drop occurs, make a systematic check of all components of the coolant system (including the radiator) for evidence of leaks. Replace any defective components you find. The Contents Section of this chapter will direct you to removal and installation instructions for all components. If an external leak cannot be found, suspect an internal cylinder head gasket leak.

8   Thermo switch - removal and installation

1   The thermo switch is located along the top rear section of the radiator and is on the left side.

2   Place a pan under the vehicle, just beneath the thermo switch, to catch any fluid.

3   Slide the rubber cap from the switch and disconnect the two leads (photos).

4   Remove the thermo switch with a proper size wrench.

5   Installation is the reverse of the removal procedure.

6   Although there is a specified torque for the thermo switch, we could discover no way to use a torque wrench due to tight clearances. We recommend that you tighten the thermo switch snugly, but do not place any force on the wrench. The boss which holds the switch is of alloy and will deform quite easily.

7   To check that you have installed the wires on the proper posts, bridge the two connectors with a screwdriver. The cooling fan blades must turn in a clockwise direction when viewed from the front of the vehicle. If this does not happen, reverse the leads and perform the test again.

9   Thermo switch - testing

1   Remove the thermo switch from the radiator (Section 8).

2   Fill a saucepan with water and heat the water to about 92° +2°C (197° + 3.5°F). Use a standard kitchen thermometer to keep track of the water temperature. Stir the water with the thermometer but do not allow the bulb to rest on the bottom of the pan.

3   While the water is heating, connect the two leads of an ohmeter to the flat plugs of the thermo switch. The reading should be ∞ ohms.

4   When the water has reached the proper temperature, remove the pan from the heat source and submerge the bulb end of the thermo switch in the water. The reading on the ohmeter should be 0 ohms. Do not submerge the entire thermo switch, especially the plug end of the switch.

5   Leave the bulb of the thermo switch immersed and monitor the drop in water temperature with the thermometer. At 87° ± 2°C (189° ± 3.5°F) the ohmeter reading should return to ∞ ohms.

10   Cooling fan(s) - removal and installation

NOTE: Early versions of the 924 have a single fan and motor mounted in a shroud behind the radiator. Later models will have two fans and motors and the shroud will be split between the two fan circles so that each fan may be removed separately.

1   Disconnect the negative lead from the battery.

2   Raise the vehicle and place it on jack stands.

3   Remove the bolts which hold the lower engine guard in place and remove it.

4   Unplug the electrical connector at the fan motor and disconnect the clip on the fan shroud (photo).

5   Remove the bolts which hold the fan motor to the shroud and push the fan motor until the blades of the fan are about 3/4 in. from the radiator.

6   Loosen the attaching bolts of the fan shroud and carefully remove the fan, motor, and shroud by lifting out through the bottom of the vehicle. Make sure not to hit the radiator at the front, nor to hit the sway bar at the rear of this slot through which you must maneuver the fan, motor and shroud. Take great care not to drop the motor (photos).

7   Installation is the reverse of the removal procedure.

8   Install the fan motor with the water drain hole facing down. Make sure that the wiring harness is properly located and in no danger of being crushed or cut by any part in the vicinity.

9   Check the fan's direction of rotation. Remove the rubber cap from the thermo switch and bridge the two connectors of the switch. The fan must rotate in a clockwise direction when seen from the front.

11   Thermostat - removal and installation

1   Disconnect the negative lead from the battery.

2   Place blocks at the wheels to prevent rolling. Drain at least 2 liters (1.8 U.S. quarts) from the cooling system (see Section 2).

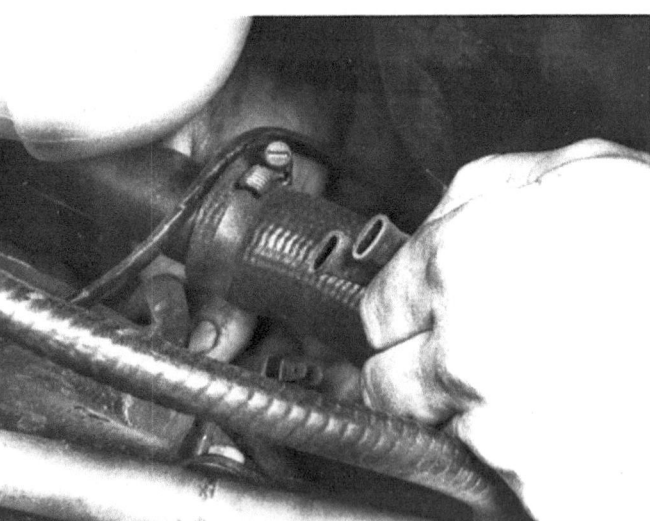

8.3a Removing the rubber cap from the thermo switch   8.3b Unplugging the thermo switch leads

3 Gently remove all fuel hoses from the loom at the front of the camshaft cover.

4 Remove the bolt from the thermostat housing which holds the fuel hose loom ahead of the loom mentioned above and place all of the hoses behind the bleed plug for the cooling system where they will be out of the way.

5 Remove the second bolt from the thermostat housing and lift the upper housing away (photo).

6 The thermostat may be removed at this point without removing any other parts. If you wish to have a less restricted view of the thermostat and lower housing, remove the upper housing from its hose by loosening the clamp and pulling the upper housing free (photo).

7 Remove the O-ring from the groove in the lower thermostat housing and discard it. Always replace the O-ring with a new one whenever the seal between the upper and lower thermostat housings is broken.

8 Inspect the thermostat and replace it as necessary (see Section 13).

9 Installation is the reverse of the removal procedure (photo).

10 Torque the two bolts on the thermostat housing to 7 ft-lb (1 m-kg) (photo).

10.4 Unplugging the cooling fan connector

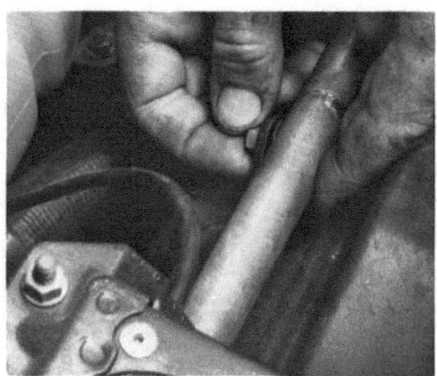
10.6a Removing the fan shroud mounting bolts

10.6b Removing the fan, motor, and shroud as a unit

10.6c Removing the cooling fan from the shroud

11.5 Removing the upper thermostat housing

11.6 Removing the thermostat

11.9 Installation of a new thermostat

11.10 Applying the appropriate torque to the thermostat housing bolts

12 Thermostat – removal and installation (Turbo)

1   The thermostat housing is located at the left, forward corner of the engine, alongside the timing belt guard. The bleed screw is located at the top of the upper thermostat housing.
2   Disconnect the negative lead from the battery.
3   Block the wheels of the vehicle if it is not on a lift, and then drain about 2 liters (1.8 U.S. quarts) of coolant from the system before removing the thermostat (see Section 3).
4   Loosen the clamp on the upper hose and pull it free.
5   Remove the two bolts and remove the upper thermostat housing (photo 11.5).
6   Remove the thermostat (photo 11.6).
7   Remove the O-ring from the groove on the lower thermostat housing. Replace the O-ring every time the seal between the upper and lower thermostat housings is broken.
8   Check the thermostat according to the instructions in Section 13.
9   Installation is the reverse of the removal procedure.
10 Torque the bolts on the thermostat housing to 7 ft-lb (1 m-kg) (photo 11.10).

13 Thermostat – checking

1. Remove the thermostat according to the directions in Section 11 or 12. If the thermostat is open, it is defective and must be replaced. Make sure you have a working thermostat before you begin this test, to save time.
2   The tools required for this task are a saucepan and a thermometer.
3   Fill the saucepan with enough water to allow the thermostat to float in an upright position without touching the bottom of the pan.
4   Place the pan on a stove burner and heat the water slowly. Stir the water occasionally with the thermometer. Do not allow the thermometer to rest on the bottom of the pan.
5   When the water temperature reaches approximately 82° ± 2°C (180° ± 3.5°F), the thermostat should begin to open. When the thermostat opens, the flat plate below the spring moves outward.
6   When the water temperature reaches about 93°C (200°F) the opening stroke of the thermostat should be completed.
7   If a second saucepan is available, fill it with cool tap water, otherwise dump out the hot water in the saucepan you have and fill it quickly with cool water. If you have the second saucepan, place the thermostat in the cool water.
8   The thermostat should now begin to close. Watch to be sure that the thermostat closes with the relief valve moving at least an 8 mm (0.31 in.) stroke. If closing is not complete or if the stroke is not over the minimum required, the thermostat must be replaced (Fig. 2.5).

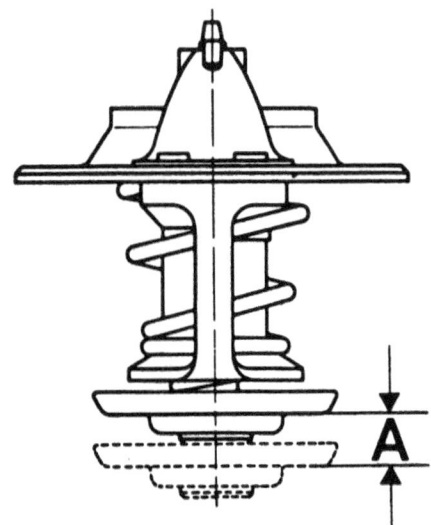

Fig. 2.5 Thermostat opening stroke
Distance "A" must be equal or better than 8 mm (0.31 in)

14 Thermostat housing – removal and installation

1   The thermostat housing need only be removed when it is damaged, for cleaning out, or when the engine block is being stripped down for reworking. Perform all of the tasks in Section 16 down to paragraph 13. This will clear the front end of the engine block to give access to the thermostat housing.
2   Loosen the clamp holding the upper coolant hose to the upper thermostat housing and remove the hose.
3   Gently disengage the fuel hoses from the forward loom on the camshaft cover.
4   Remove the bolt on the upper thermostat housing which holds the fuel hose loom ahead of the one mentioned above.
5   Place the fuel lines behind the bleed plug (photo).
6   Remove the other bolt from the upper thermostat housing and remove the upper housing (photo 11.5).
7   Remove the thermostat.
8   Remove the O-ring from the lower thermostat housing and throw it away. Replace the O-ring any time the seal between the upper and lower thermostat housings is broken.
9   Loosen the clamp on the short hose on the lower thermostat housing, but do not try to remove it as yet (photo 14.5).
10 Remove the four bolts which hold the thermostat housing to the engine block. Note that the bolts are of two different lengths and must be placed in the same holes when installing the thermostat housing (photo).
11 Pull the lower thermostat housing away from the engine block. Lift the housing straight up to slide it from the short hose (photo).
12 Scrape the gasket from the back of the thermostat housing and its mating surface on the engine block. Use a metal spatula or putty knife for this task. Razor blades, chisels, and the like are made of harder metals than your engine block and may cause chips and gouges which will prevent proper sealing of the surfaces.
13 Installation is the reverse of the removal procedure.
14 Coat the new gasket with sealer and install it on the back of the thermostat housing.
15 Torque the four bolts holding the thermostat housing to the engine block to 14 ft-lb (2 m-kg). Make sure that the proper length bolts are in their proper holes (photo).
16 Make sure that the short hose is squarely fitted to the lower thermostat housing, then tighten the clamp.
17 Make sure that the thermostat has passed the checks outlined in Section 13 before reinstalling the old one.
18 Torque the two bolts holding the upper and lower housings to 7 ft-lb (1 m-kg).
19 Continue assembly of the various engine pieces as outlined in Section 16.
20 Fill and bleed the cooling system.

15 Thermostat housing – removal and installation (Turbo)

1   The thermostat housing does not have to be removed, except in instances where the housing needs to be replaced or in the process of stripping down the engine block for rework.
2   Perform all of the tasks in Section 17 through paragraph 15.
3   Loosen the clamp on the upper hose and pull it free.
4   Remove the two bolts from the thermostat housing and lift off the upper housing (photo 11.5).
5   Remove the thermostat (photo 11.6).
6   Remove the O-ring from the groove in the lower housing and throw it away. Replace the O-ring with a new one any time the seal between the upper and lower thermostat housings is broken.
7   Remove the four bolts holding the lower thermostat housing to the cylinder block. The bolts are of two different lengths, so take note of which length bolts are installed in which holes for ease in reassembly (photo 14.10).
8   Pull the thermostat housing away from the engine block (photo 14.11).
9   Scrape the old gasket off with a gasket scraper or putty knife. Razor blades are made of a harder metal and will damage the mating surfaces on the block and the thermostat housing.
10 Installation is the reverse of the removal process.
11 Coat the new gasket with gasket sealer and install it on the back of the thermostat housing.

14.5 Pulling back the fuel lines and loosening the hose clamp on the lower thermostat housing

14.10 Removing the thermostat housing mounting bolts

14.11 Pulling the thermostat housing from the engine block

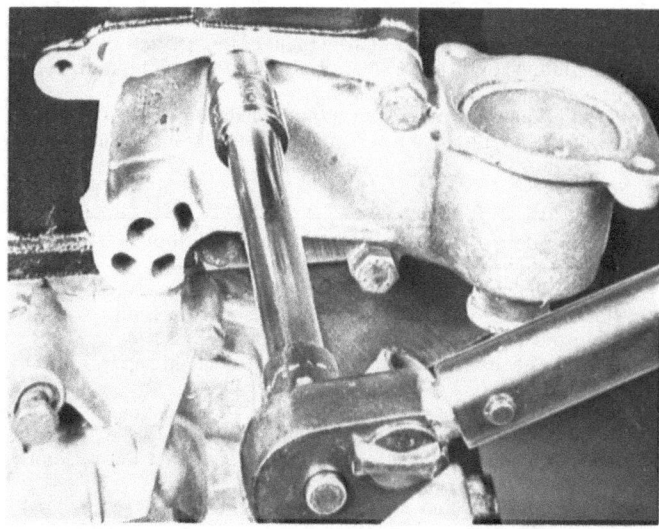

14.15 Applying the appropriate torque to the thermostat housing mounting bolts

12 Install the four bolts in their proper locations and tighten them finger tight. Torque the four bolts in a cross pattern to 14 ft-lb (2 m-kg) (photo 14.15).

13 Follow the installation instructions in Section 17 for the remaining special instructions in reassembly.

16 Water pump – removal and installation

1 Disconnect the negative lead from the battery.

2 Block the wheels of the vehicle if it is not on a lift.

3 Place a socket on the nut of the oil pump pulley and turn the engine until cylinder 1 is at top dead center. This may be double-checked by seeing that the mark on the camshaft timing belt pulley aligns with the pointer on top of the camshaft cover (Chapter 1).

4 Drain the coolant system (see Section 2).

5 Follow each of the hoses from the overflow tank and disconnect them at the end opposite the tank (photo 5.6).

6 Remove the holding strap and the overflow tank. The strap is held in place by a single nut and stud (photo 5.7a).

7 Slide the windshield washer reservoir from its bracket and place it ahead of the right front wheel well (photo 5.11).

8 Remove the alternator cooling hose from the molded plastic intake manifold by squeezing the clamp with pliers and pulling the

hose free. If a little more working room is desired, remove the other end of the hose from the sheet metal shroud on the alternator (photo 5.10).

9 Remove the two bolts which hold the timing belt guard to the engine and remove the guard.

10 Loosen the adjusting nut and bolt on the air pump (on cars so equipped). Tilt the air pump so that the tension is removed from the drive V-belt and remove the belt.

11 Loosen the adjusting nut and bolt on the alternator and slacken the V-belt tension. Remove the V-belt.

12 Loosen the bolt on the timing belt tension pulley and allow the timing belt to go slack. Remove the bolt and tensioning pulley.

13 Remove the loosened timing belt by sliding the belt first from the camshaft drive pulley and then removing it from the lower toothed pulley.

14 Remove the three bolts from the V-belt pulley on the water pump at the water pump end. It is not necessary to pull them loose at this time; they may be left in place until the water pump is unbolted from the block.

16 The water pump is held to the engine block by 5 bolts, which differ in length and diameter. Note the location of each bolt as you remove it for ease in reassembly.

17 Pull the water pump free of the engine block and disconnect the hoses at this time.

18 Inspect the hoses (see Section 4).

19 Installation is the reverse of the removal process.

20 Coat the surface of the new water pump gasket with gasket sealing compound and install the gasket on the back of the water pump. Make sure that the mating surfaces have been thoroughly cleaned and that all traces of the old gasket have been removed.

21 Install the hoses on their appropriate flanges and press the water pump against the engine block to seat the gasket in its proper location.

22 Install the bolts in their proper holes and tighten finger tight.

23 Torque the three shortest (and smaller diameter)bolts 6 ft-lb (0.9 m-kg).

24 Torque the two long bolts (with larger diameters) to 16 ft-lb (2.2 m-kg).

25 Install the timing belt and tensioning pulley. Make sure that the mark on the camshaft pulley is aligned with the pointer on the camshaft cover and that the number 1 cylinder is at top dead center.

26 Adjust tension on the timing belt by turning the tensioning pulley in the direction of belt travel until the 'long' side of the belt can just be turned 90°, showing the teeth of the belt forward. Torque the bolt on the pulley to 29 ft-lb (4 m-kg).

27 When installing the V-belt pulley on the water pump torque the three bolts to 14 ft-lb (2 m-kg).

28 Install the timing belt guard and torque the bolts to 7 ft-lb (1 m-kg).

29 Adjust the V-belts on the alternator and air pump as follows: 0.20 to 0.39 in (5 to 10 mm) deflection for the V-belt on the alternator and 0.20 to 0.32 in (5 to 8 mm) for the air pump's V-belt deflection. Neither of these units has a specified torque for the adjusting bolts. Tighten until firm.

30 Fill the cooling system with a fresh mixture of water and antifreeze and bleed the system according to the instructions in Section 2.

17 Water pump – removal and installation (Turbo)

1 Disconnect the negative lead from the battery.

2 Block the wheels of the vehicle if it is not on a lift.

3 Drain the coolant system (see Section 3).

4 Replace the drain screw with a new seal installed and torque it to 11 ft-lb (1.5 m-kg).

5 Loosen the clamps on the air cleaner housing hoses.

6 Disconnect the rubber hold-down straps on the air cleaner housing and remove the upper section. Disconnect the hoses by gently pulling them free.

7 Remove the air filter element. If the element is dirty from use, replace it with a fresh element, even if its mileage interval has not passed.

8 Remove the four bolts from the lower filter housing section and remove the section.

9 Remove the three nuts from the mixture control unit at the join with the air box beneath it. Do not move the mixture control unit at this stage.

10 Remove the bolt which holds the fuel line loom in place ahead of the engine and gently lift the mixture control unit upward and turn the mixture control unit and the strap holding the loom about 180° and set the mixture control unit just behind the alternator. Be careful not to bend or crimp the metal fuel lines and do not allow the flexible sections of the fuel lines to close off completely.

11 Remove the coolant line mounting nut. Loosen the hose clamps and remove the coolant hose. Check the hose as outlined in Section 4 and replace as necessary.

12 Loosen the adjusting bolt on the alternator, slacken the tension on the V-belt and remove the belt.

13 Remove the bolts holding the timing belt guard to the engine block and remove the guard. If your model has air conditioning installed, it will be necessary to remove the V-belt for the compressor. It is removed in the same manner as the alternator V-belt, outlined above.

14 If the number 1 cylinder is not at top dead center, place a socket on the center bolt on the oil pump pulley and turn the engine until it comes up on top dead center. This can be double checked by making sure the mark on the camshaft pulley is aligned with the pointer cast into the camshaft cover.

15 Remove the timing belt by loosening the bolt holding the tensioning pulley in place, turning the pulley to release the belt tension, then removing the bolt and tensioning pulley. It should now be possible to slide the timing belt from the camshaft pulley and then from the lower pulley.

16 Remove the three bolts which hold the water pump pulley to the three pointed bracket. Remove the water pump pulley.

17 Loosen all clamps for the hoses at the water pump.

18 Pull as many of them from the flanges as possible.

19 The water pump is held in place by five bolts which are of differing length and diameter. Note the location of each bolt as you remove them for ease in reassembly.

20 Pull the water pump free of the engine block and disconnect the rest of the hoses.

21 Scrape the old gasket from the engine block and the back of the water pump with a gasket scraper or putty knife. Razor blades are made of a harder metal than the engine and water pump castings and may cause grooves or gouges to the mating surfaces, so they must not be used.

22 Inspect the hoses as outlined in Section 4 and replace them as necessary.

23 Installation is the reverse of the removal procedure.

24 Coat the new gasket with gasket sealer and place it on the back of the water pump. Before pressing the water pump into place, slip on those hoses which, because of clearance problems will be difficult to install later.

25 Locate the water pump and press it into place to set the gasket sealer. Install the five bolts in their proper locations and tighten them finger tight.

26 Torque the three shorter (and smaller diameter) bolts to 6 ft-lb (0.9 m-kg) and the longer (and larger diameter) bolts to 16 ft-lb (2.2 m-kg).

27 Install the timing belt and tensioning pulley. Make certain that the mark on the camshaft pulley is still aligned with the pointer on the camshaft cover. Remember also that the number 1 cylinder must be at top dead center.

28 Adjust tension on the timing belt by turning the tensioning pulley in the direction of the belt travel until the 'long' side of the belt can just be turned 90°, showing the teeth of the belt forward. Torque the bolt on the pulley to 29 ft-lb (4 m-kg).

29 When installing the water pump pulley on the three pointed bracket, torque the three bolts to 14 ft-lb (2 m-kg).

30 Install the timing belt guard and torque the bolts to 7 ft-lb (1 m-kg).

31 Adjust the V-belts for the alternator to the following deflections along the 'long' side of the belt: 0.39 in (10 mm) when measured between the pulleys and with the thumb pressure on the belt for the alternator, and 0.20 in (5 mm) when measured between the V-belt pulley on the oil pump and the drive pulley on the compressor for the compressor.

32 Tighten evenly the nuts on the mixture control unit.

33 Install the four bolts in the lower air filter housing and tighten them evenly.

34 Fill the cooling system and bleed it according to the instructions in Section 3.

18 Water pump – inspection

1 The water pump of the 924 series is not considered to be a rebuildable item at the home mechanic or dealer level of service. The following checks will tell you whether or not your vehicle's water pump should be replaced with a new or rebuilt unit.

2 Turn the shaft by grasping the three pointed pulley mount and turning back and forth. After doing this several times, turn the mount clockwise several times. If the pulley mount fails to turn smoothly under light pressure and/or if you feel a 'gritty' or 'notchy' motion, replace the water pump.

3 Grasp the three pointed mount once again and attempt to wiggle the shaft back and forth. If the bearing surfaces of the shaft are worn, a definite 'klunk' will be felt. Replace the water pump if this is felt at all.

4 Inspect the join between the water pump body and the shaft. If any leaks are found, replace the water pump. In some water pumps very small droplets of water may be forced out between the pump

body and shaft by pressing the shaft very hard against the pump body. Disregard any small (barely visible) droplets of water, but larger amounts of water are signs of upcoming pump replacement.

19 Transfer tube – removal and installation

1 The transfer tube runs beneath the intake manifold and is accessible only from the bottom of the vehicle.
2 Disconnect the negative lead from the battery.
3 Raise the vehicle and place it on jack stands.
4 Drain the coolant system (Section 2 or 3).
5 Remove the four bolts which hold the lower guard of the engine in place and remove the guard.
6 Disconnect the metal hoses from the EGR filter. See Chapter 3 for further information on this piece. It is located beneath the intake manifold on the left side of the engine.
7 If the EGR filter hoses are to be disconnected for a number of days either remove the hoses from the vehicle or tie the disconnected ends with string so they do not hang loose and stand the possibility of cracking.
8 Remove the three bolts from the EGR filter mounts and remove the EGR filter.
9 Remove the intake manifold lower support bracket after removing the center bolt. This is the bolt left in place after the EGR filter has been removed.
10 Loosen the clamps on the hoses at the rear of the transfer tube and pull them loose at the transfer tube flanges.
11 Loosen the clamp on the conical hose at the front of the transfer tube at the flange on the water pump. Do not remove the hose at this stage.
12 Remove the two mounting bolts on the flat mounting brackets.
13 Remove the transfer tube by pulling it free at the rear and then disconnecting the front hose from the water pump flange. Guide the transfer tube out through the underside of the vehicle (photos).
14 Inspect the tube for crimping, dents or cracks. Any crimps serious enough to restrict coolant flow are grounds for replacement of the transfer tube. Cracks are also cause for immediate replacement. Do not forget to check the flat mounts for cracking around the bolt holes and at the point where they join the tube.
15 Sight through the tube, checking for deposits which can restrict coolant flow. If the inner surface appears very rough and scaly, replace the transfer tube.
16 Check all of the hoses as described in Section 4.
17 Installation is the reverse of the removal procedure (photo).
18 Torque the two transfer tube mounting bolts to 14 ft-lb (2 m-kg).
19 Torque the intake manifold support bracket bolt to 14 ft-lb (2 m-kg).
20 Torque the EGR filter mounting bolts to 14 ft-lb (2 m-kg).
21 Carefully tighten the flange nuts on the metal lines to the EGR filter.

20 Rear coolant flange – removal, stripdown, rebuild, installation

1 The rear coolant flange is located just beneath the distributor. It houses the coolant temperature sensor as well as the thermo time switch for the cold starting system. Access may be gained through the space between the engine and the firewall. If proper care is taken with tools, there is no need to remove the distributor and distributor drive housing.
2 Disconnect the negative lead from the battery.
3 Block the wheels of the vehicle if it is not on a lift.
4 Drain the coolant system (See Section 2 or 3).
5 Although the coolant temperature sensor and the thermo time switch may be removed separately, they may be left installed in the rear coolant flange to ease disassembly. Remove the two bolts holding the rear coolant flange to the engine block.
6 Loosen the clamp on the hose and pull the hose free.
7 Unplug the wires from the coolant temperature sensor and the thermo time switch.
8 Remove the rear coolant flange from the engine block (photo).
9 Scrape the gasket and sealer from the engine block and the rear coolant flange with a metal spatula or scraper. A razor blade should not be used as it is of a harder metal and can easily scratch the mating surfaces.

19.13a Pulling the forward transfer hose from the water pump

19.13b Removing the transfer tube

19.17 A properly installed transfer tube shown on a bare engine

10 Remove the coolant temperature sensor and the thermo time switch.
11 Installation is the reverse of the removal procedure.
12 Torque the coolant temperature sensor to 6 ft-lb (0.9 m-kg) (photo 21.9).
13 Torque the thermo time switch to 20 ft-lb (2.8 m-kg) (photo 22.8).
14 Coat the new gasket with a light coating of gasket sealer and place it on the rear coolant flange.
15 Install the rear coolant flange and bolts (photo).
16 Torque the bolts on the rear coolant flange to 7 ft-lb (1 m-kg).
17 Do not forget to connect the plugs for the coolant temperature sensor and the thermo time switch.
18 Fill and bleed the cooling system (Section 2 or 3).

---

21 Coolant temperature sensor – removal and installation

1 As stated in Section 20 the coolant temperature sensor may be most easily removed as a unit with the rear coolant flange. It may be removed separately as follows:
2 Disconnect the negative lead from the battery.
3 Place blocks beneath the wheels if the vehicle is not on a lift.
4 Disconnect the plug from the coolant temperature sensor.

5 Drain about 2 liters (1.8 U.S. quarts) from the cooling system in order to remove the coolant temperature sensor (Section 2 or 3).
6 Remove the coolant temperature sensor with an appropriate size wrench.
7 Installation is the reverse of the removal process.
8 As the only types of testing carry serious danger of burns or scalding, it is recommended that the coolant temperature sensor be tested by replacement with a new unit.
9 Install the coolant temperature sensor and torque to 6 ft-lb (0.8 m-kg) (photo).
10 Fill the cooling system and bleed it before running the engine (Section 2 or 3).

---

22 Thermo time switch – removal and installation

1 As stated in Section 20 the thermo time switch may be most easily removed as a unit with the rear coolant flange. The thermo time switch is part of the fuel control system and any tests and inspections are covered in Chapter 3.
2 Disconnect the negative lead from the battery.
3 Place blocks beneath the wheels if the vehicle is not on a lift.
4 Disconnect the plug from the thermo time switch. It is easily identified as the larger of the two fittings.

20.8 Removing the rear coolant flange

20.15 Installation of the rear coolant flange

21.9 Applying the appropriate torque to the coolant temperature sensor

22.8 Applying the appropriate torque to the thermo time switch

5 It is necessary to drain about 2 liters (1.8 U.S. quarts) from the cooling system to remove the thermo time switch.
6 Remove the thermo time switch with an appropriate size wrench.
7 Installation is the reverse of the removal procedure.
8 Torque the thermo time switch to 20 ft-lb (2.8 m-kg) (photo).
9 Fill and bleed the cooling system (Section 2 or 3).

23 Heater - general description

1 The heater in the passenger compartment makes use of the heated coolant in the cooling system to provide warming for the interior air.
2 Coolant is drawn from the cooling system and passes through a heat exchanger in the passenger compartment beneath the dashboard. An electrically-powered fan passes interior air mixed with an amount of fresh outside air over the heat exchanger and ducts it into the passenger compartment.
3 This Section is concerned only with the coolant circulation aspects of the heater. The electrical motor is covered in Chapter 11.

24 Heater hoses - checking

1 The hoses of the heating system are manufactured of the same materials as the cooling system hoses. See Section 4 for further information.

25 Heater control valve - removal and installation

1 The heater control valve is located beneath the ignition coil and just ahead of the firewall in the engine compartment. It is on the outflow side of the heater and may be found by following the larger (and lower) tube at the rear of the transfer tube (Section 19).
2 Disconnect the negative lead from the battery.
3 Block the wheels of the vehicle if it is not on a lift.
4 Place a container of at least 8 liters (2½ U.S. gallons) capacity beneath the drain screw located on the left side of the radiator.
5 Move the heater controls to their hottest position.
6 Loosen the drain screw and drain the radiator and heater.
7 Disconnect the control valve operating cable.

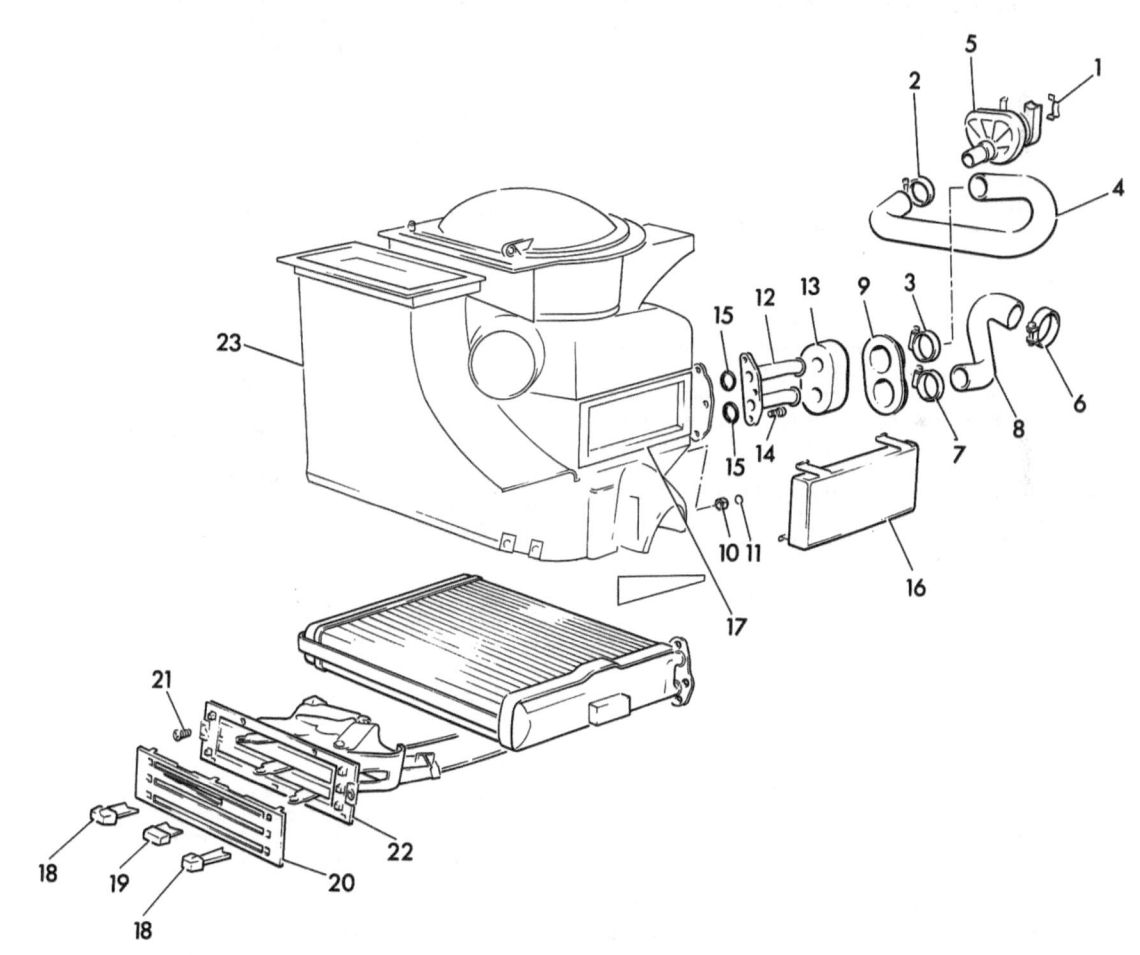

Fig. 2.6 Heater components

1	Spring clip	7	Hose clamp	13	Damping block	19	Button, center

1   Spring clip
2   Hose clamp
3   Hose clamp
4   Heater hose, outflow
5   Heater valve
6   Hose clamp
7   Hose clamp
8   Heater hose, intake
9   Double grommet
10 Nut, heater flange
11 Flat washer
12 Heater flange
13 Damping block
14 Bolt, heater flange
15 Seals
16 Heat exchanger cover
17 Heat exchanger
18 Button, upper and lower
19 Button, center
20 Fascia plate
21 Sheet metal screw
22 Fresh air and heater
       control panel
23 Heater fan housing

8 Loosen the hose clamp on the hose entering the rear of the valve and pull the hose loose.
9 Remove the control valve by prying the clip at the front of the valve loose and removing it, then pulling on the valve to free it from the forward hose.
10 Installation is the reverse of the removal procedure.

26 Heater control valve and operating cable - checking

1 The heater control valve and/or its operating cable must be replaced any time their operation is not smooth and easy.
2 Remove the control cable from the control valve and operate the control lever in the passenger compartment to determine whether or not the cable has become kinked, rusted, or seized in its housing. If the cable is difficult to operate, and lubrication does not change this condition significantly, replace the cable.
3 Replacement of the cable must be done by removing the three heater control knobs, removing the facia plate (which is held by plastic clips), and then removing the screws which hold the controls in place and pulling them slightly forward.
4 Slip out the old operating cable. Install the new cable, first threading it through the firewall and then hooking up the end to the control lever. Reinstall the controls, facia plate and knobs.
5 If installation of a new operating cable proves not to be the solution to rough or sticky operation, the control valve must be replaced (Section 25).

27 Heat exchanger - removal and installation

1 Disconnect the negative lead from the battery.
2 Drain the coolant system (Section 2 or 3).
3 Remove the heater control valve (Section 25).
4 Loosen the clamps of the heater hoses and remove them.
5 Remove the center console in the passenger compartment (See Chapter 12).
6 Remove the cover from the right side of the heater housing. The cover is held in place by spring clips which must be disengaged with the flat blade of a screwdriver to prevent breakage.
7 Remove the screws, nuts, and seals which hold the flange which passes through the firewall to the heat exchanger. Dispose of the seals and replace them with new seals when installing the heat exchanger.
8 Remove the heat exchanger from the right side of the heater housing, sliding it out along its installation rails.
9 Installation is the reverse of the removal procedure.
10 Fill the coolant system according to the directions in Section 2 or 3.

28 Heat exchanger - inspection

1 The heat exchanger must be checked carefully for signs of leaks. These are most easily identified by discolorations and whitish deposits left by evaporating coolant.
2 Look through the inlet and outlet tubes for signs of rust or calcified deposit buildup. If the inner surface of the tubes is heavily scaled, replace the heat exchanger.
3 Further scale buildup can be prevented by avoiding the use of 'hard' or high mineral content water and mixing in proper amounts of antifreeze into the coolant. Antifreeze contains inhibitors to prevent rust and scale. Distilled water is a good choice instead of tap water but its cost, and the variations in mineral content of water throughout the world, will make its use a personal decision by the owner of the vehicle.

29 Air conditioning system - general description

1 The air conditioning systems used by Porsche for their 924 model lines are of the modular type and constructed in such a way that they may be installed by a dealer or at the factory and also removed completely without affecting the operation of any other system in the vehicle. Do not mistake a factory-type of air conditioning system for an aftermarket system. Many of the latter were installed by individual dealers on an 'as ordered' basis. If you are in doubt as to whether or not your vehicle's air conditioning system is of the factory or aftermarket type, check with a dealer in auto air conditioning or your local Porsche garage.
2 This manual discusses only the two types of factory air conditioning installed in 924 models. If your vehicle's air conditioner is from an aftermarket supplier, seek the help and advice of an automotive electrical or air conditioning repair shop.
3 The earlier air conditioner was installed in 924 models through the 1978 production year. A description of the various parts, their removal and installation is discussed first in this Chapter. In 1979, Porsche switched to an air conditioning unit manufactured by the Nippondenso company. This will be discussed only in terms of its differences from the earlier system.

30 Refrigerant warning

1 Your Porsche's air conditioner uses Freon R 12-type refrigerant. This substance is non-toxic in its natural state, but improper use of equipment and tools and use of the wrong tools can create conditions which are quite dangerous.
2 Freon R 12 is heavier than air and will collect in the low spots of your garage floor. If you should work in one of these low spots within an hour or two of filling or draining your air conditioning system, there is a distinct possibility of inhaling large amounts of Freon gas, which will result in suffocation.
3 Always keep your work area well ventilated so that any Freon gas leakage will be dispersed and will not gather.
4 Never work on a vehicle with air conditioning in an area with a naked flame of any type close by. Smoking materials, gas-operated appliances and naked flame methods of leak location will burn the Freon R 12 refrigerant, discharging a poisonous gas. Never smoke around a recently discharged air conditioner.
5 Finally, Freon R 12 was selected for use in your vehicle's air conditioner because of its unique ability to absorb and lose great amounts of heat quickly. The major by-product of this process is the production of high pressure and high heat areas in the system.
6 Take great care when performing any task on an air conditioned vehicle. A sudden release of pressure in an area as small as the engine compartment of your car will produce serious results.
7 Since the draining and filling of the air conditioning system requires many specialized tools, and because this must be the first step in any other work performed on the air conditioner, we strongly recommend that you seek the services of a qualified Porsche garage or air conditioning repair shop.
8 For your convenience and information, the remainder of this chapter will identify the components of the air conditioning system and the adjustments which can be made without the depressurization of the system.

31 Air conditioner - components

Compressor

1 Driven by a V-belt from the engine through an electro-magnetic clutch, the compressor draws refrigerant from the evaporator and compresses it. This raises the temperature and forces the compressed charge into the condenser.
2 The compressor is located on the lower left side of the engine and the V-belt is driven from a pulley mounted ahead of the oil pump accessory drive pulley. Tension is placed on the belt by a screw type tensioner and held constant by a locknut on the tensioner.

Condenser

3 Mounted ahead of the coolant system radiator, the condenser receives the high pressure, high temperature vapor from the compressor. As the refrigerant loses heat, the resulting liquid is kept at high pressure and passes into the receiver-drier.
4 Factory-type condensers have a two-part fan shroud and two cooling fans. The right side fan is used for passing cooling air over the condenser. It is removed and installed the same as the radiator cooling fan (Section 5).

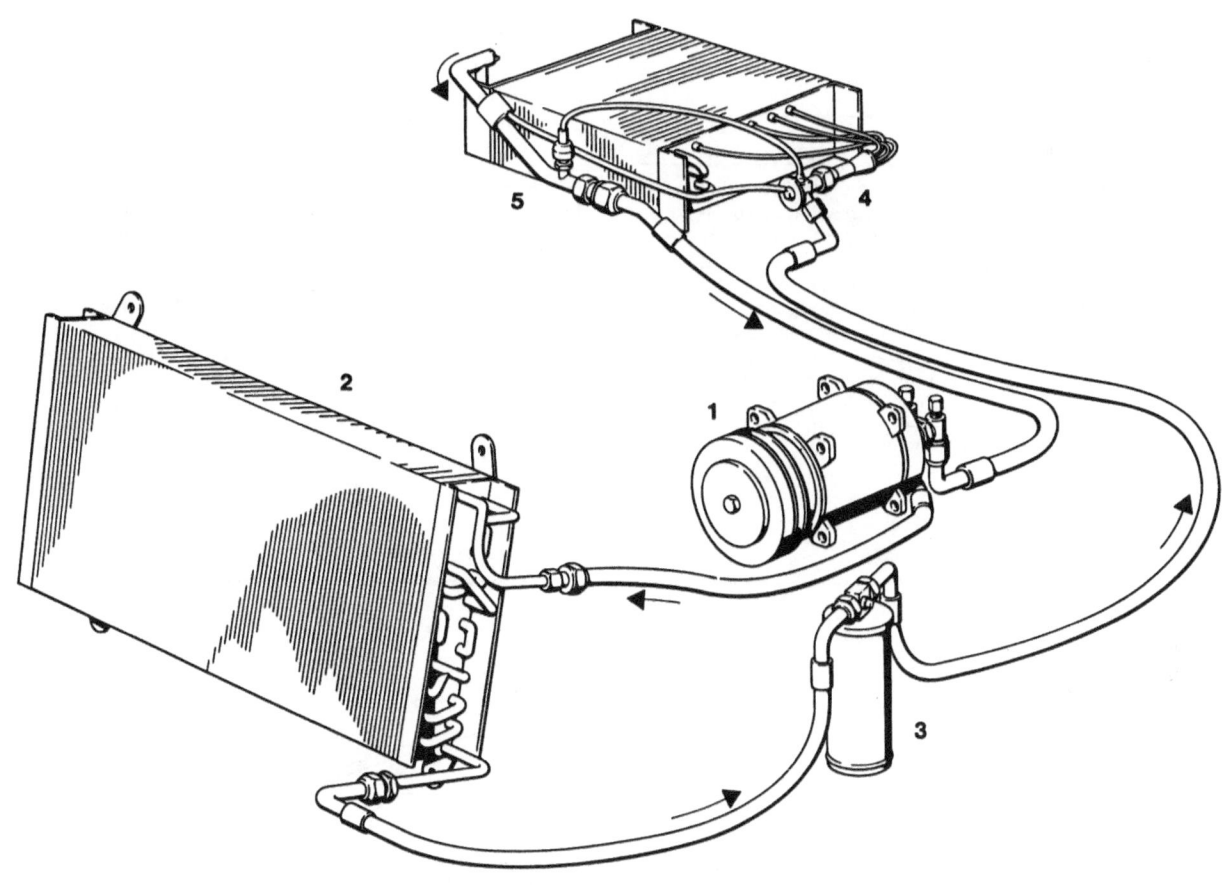

Fig. 2.7 Air conditioning system components

1	Compressor	3	Receiver-drier
2	Condenser	4	Expansion valve
		5	Evaporator

Receiver-drier

5   The receiver-drier acts as a reservoir for the high pressure refrigerant liquid and removes water vapor from the refrigerant before it is delivered to the expansion valve. It is located ahead of the left front wheel well.

6   A sight glass is installed to monitor the refrigerant charge and a safety seal is mounted atop the container. The seal is designed to rupture in the event of high temperatures being created by the pressurized liquid.

Expansion valve

7   Found on top of the receiver-drier, the expansion valve allows a metered amount of refrigerant into the refrigerant lines. Working with the temperature sensor coil mounted on the outlet side of the evaporator, the valve assures constant metering in a continuous flow.

8   The refrigerant passing through the expansion valve loses heat and pressure as it continues to the evaporator.

Evaporator

9   Located beneath the glove box in the dashboard, the evaporator acts as a heat exchanger, cooling fan-blown air and absorbing the heat of the passenger compartment air as the blower fan draws the air over it.

10 As the evaporator absorbs heat the refrigerant is changed from a cool liquid to a cold vapor. From the evaporator, the refrigerant is drawn back into the compressor and the cycle begins again.

32 Air conditioner – general operating note

1   The air conditioner in your 924 must be operated for at least 5 minutes every month, regardless of the outside weather. Failure to run the system will lead to the shaft seal on the compressor drying out. In most instances, the seal will have to be replaced at the cost of removing and stripping down the compressor.

33 Compressor V-belt – adjustment and replacement

1   The compressor's V-belt adapter is a banjo type of adjuster, whose threaded end points toward the thermostat housing.
2   Loosen the bolt at the center of the banjo section of the adjuster.
3   Loosen the nut until the V-belt can be removed.
4   If the V-belt needs replacement, loosen the nut until the adapter is at its full minimum position (nut screwed down toward the compressor as far as it will go), remove the old belt from the two pulleys

and slip a new V-belt into place on the pulleys.
5   Adjust the V-belt by tightening the nut and checking belt tension with your thumb between the two pulleys. When the V-belt deflection under light pressure is 0.25 in (5 mm) between the pulleys, tighten the lower belt.

34   Condenser cleaning

1   When dirt and other road debris collects on the condenser, the effectiveness of the cooling process is seriously impaired. Because the condenser is located just inside the air duct beneath the front bumper, it collects road debris much more easily than a radiator.
2   Most loose dirt and other accumulation may be removed by blowing compressed air over the fins of the condenser. This will remove most of the accumulations of sand, leaves, and other debris.
3   If great amounts of sand and dirt are left in the fins, or if some of the fins are bent, they may be straightened and the additional deposits removed by combing the fins with a fin comb. This tool is available at most auto parts stores and will aid the effectiveness of your condenser.

35   Air conditioning system – Nippondenso model, 1979–on

1   The chief difference in the Nippondenso system, and its most noticeable feature, is the inclusion of a separate fan and blower ducting beneath the glovebox.
2   The only other major change has been in the compressor where the number of compressing cylinders has changed from five to six.

36   Air conditioning vacuum system – general notes

1   The air conditioning system is paired to a vacuum system, the components of which operate the varous flaps and gates in the air conditioning system when it is operating. Figure 2.8 shows the various components.
2   This system is a part of the air conditioning system and thus should also be left to an air conditioning specialist.
3   If one of the connections is accidently pulled loose during any other work on your 924, simply press the hose back into its connector. The vacuum system is self-regenerating.

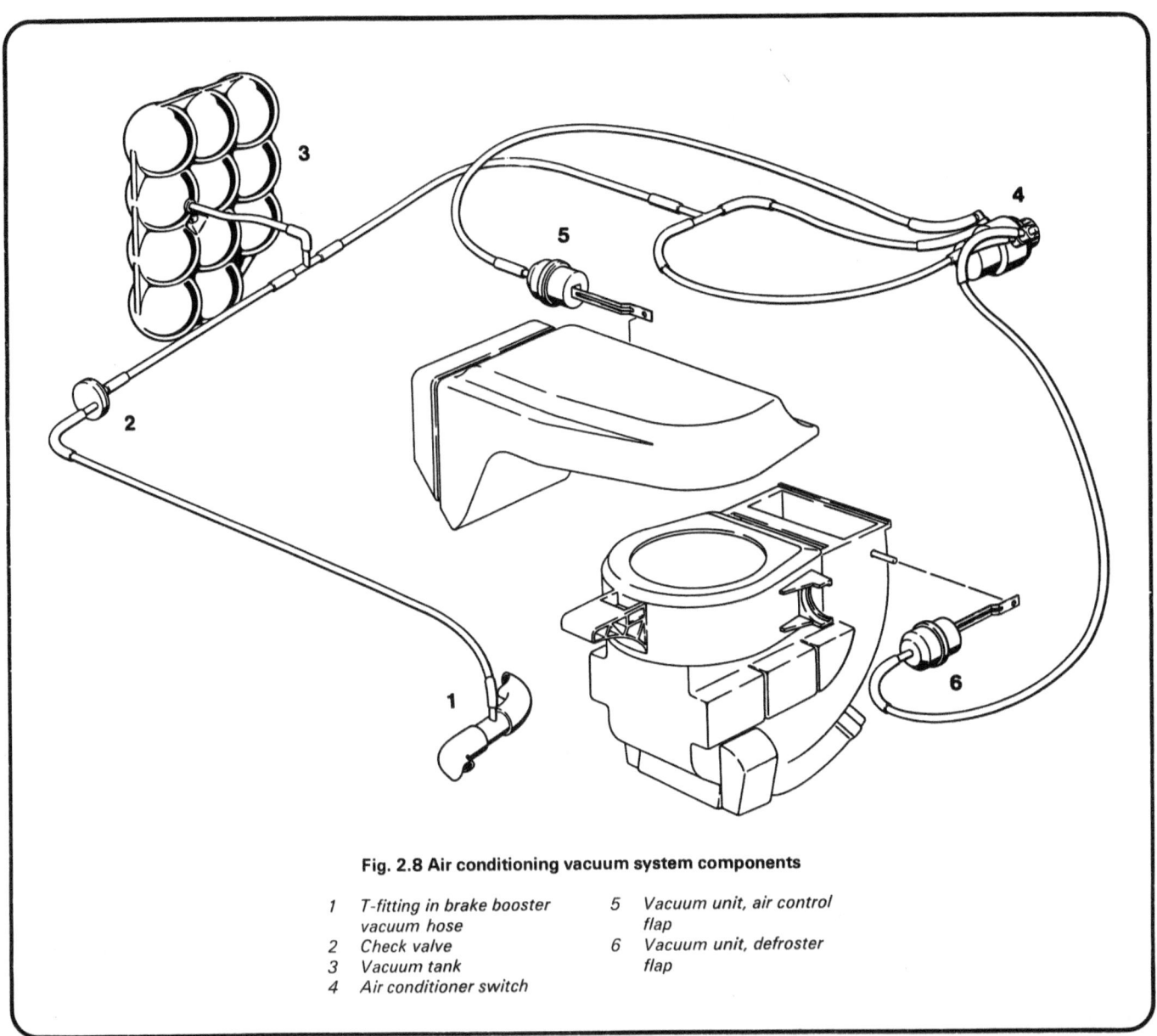

Fig. 2.8 Air conditioning vacuum system components

1	T-fitting in brake booster vacuum hose	5	Vacuum unit, air control flap
2	Check valve	6	Vacuum unit, defroster flap
3	Vacuum tank		
4	Air conditioner switch		

Chapter 3
Fuel, emission control and exhaust systems

For modifications, and information applicable to later models, see Supplement at end of manual

Contents

Specifications

General
Fuel tank capacity
924.. 62.0 litres (13.6 Imp gallons)
924 Turbo and Carrera GT .... 84.0 litres (18.5 Imp gallons) – includes 7.0 litres (1.5 Imp gallons) reserve

Fuel grade .... 98 RON

All models with CIS (K-Jetronic) Injection (1976–79)

System pressure
Test value... 4.5 to 5.2 bars
Adjusting value.. 4.7 to 4.9 bars

CO setting
1976–78, except California, but including all UK models .... 1.5 ± 0.5%
1976–78, California only .... maximum 0.7% measured ahead of the catalytic converter
1979, except California .... 0.5 to 1.0%
1979, California only .... 0.8 to 1.2% measured before catalytic converter with air pump and/or carbon canister disconnected and hoses plugged

'Warm' control pressure .... 3.6 ± 0.2 bars (control pressure regulator fully actuated)

'Cold' control pressure .... 1.5 ± 0.2 bars at room temperature of 20°C (68°F)

Injection valve opening pressure .... 2.5 to 3.6 bars

Idling speed
1976–77 .... 925 ± 75 rpm
1978-80 .... 950 ± 50 rpm

Thermo switch (cold start valve) .... 35 ± 5°C

Leak test
Minimum pressure after 10 min .... 1.7 bar
Minimum pressure after 20 min .... 1.5 bar
Fuel pump delivery rate.................................. 750 cc per 30 sec.

All models with Lambda injection (1980) and Turbo

System pressure (test value) .... 5.4 to 6.0 bar

CO setting (at idle) .... 0.5 to 1% by volume

'Warm' control pressure .... 3.65 ± 0.20 bars with engine stopped (no vacuum)

'Cold' control pressure .... 2.2 ± 0.20 bars at room temperature of 20°C (68°F)

Injection valve opening pressure .... 2.7 to 3.8 bars

Idling speed .... 900 ± 50 rpm

Charge pressure controlled (full throttle enrichment) 2.9 ± 0.20 bars

Leak test
Minimum pressure after 60 min .... 1.0 bar

NOTE: The Lambda system of fuel injection is basically similar to the K-Jetronic system on earlier models. The Lambda equipped vehicles have no EGR equipment, but rely on an oxygen sensor to help regulate emissions. Test procedures are the same as those for the CIS vehicles, but the above values must be used rather than those found throughout the text.

Torque specifications

	ft–lb	m–kg
Fuel pump, banjo fittings	14	2
Mixture control unit, air flow sensor housing-to-air box (socket head screw)	7	1
Fuel feed line, banjo bolt	7	1
Fuel return line, banjo bolt	7	1
Adapter, control pressure line............................	11	1.5
Fuel distributor injector lines...........................	7	1
Fuel distributor-to-air flow sensor housing	3	0.35
Air flow sensor plate-to-operating lever	4	0.55
Stop bracket-to-air flow sensor housing	3.5	0.50
Operating lever counterweight-to-operating lever	4	0.55
Fuel distributor plug	9 to 11	1.3 to 1.5
Oxygen sensor	35 to 45	5.0 to 6.0
Throttle housing-to-inlet manifold, warm-up regulator, lower hollow bolt	7	1
Warm-up regulator, upper hollow bolt......................	11	1.5
Cold start valve...	6	0.8
Auxiliary air regulator..................................	6	0.8
Deceleration valve nuts	7	1
Air pump-to-engine block	33	4.5
Vacuum tank-to-bracket...................................	7	1
Vacuum amplifier mounting bolts	7	1
Diverter valve, socket head screws	6	0.8
EGR valve mounting bolts	7	1
EGR filter mounting bolts.................................	14	2
Catalytic converter, flange mounting bolts................	14	2
Catalytic converter, guard plate.........................	7	1
Steel bracket, exhaust hanger............................	7	1
Lord mounts, nut	7	1
Muffler clamp, final muffler	14	2
Clamp, slip fitting	14	2
Flange nuts, primary muffler	14	2
Flange nuts, front exhaust pipe-to-exhaust manifold	14	2

To simplify referral to the contents of this Chapter it has been broken down into three distinct divisions. *Division A* covers fuel systems using the CIS (K-Jetronic) injection system; *Division B* covers fuel systems using the Lambda injection system; *Division C* covers the emissions control and exhaust systems applicable to all injected models.

Information on the turbocharger system used in the Porsche 924 Turbo can be found in Chapter 4.

A: Fuel system – Continuous Injection System (CIS)

1 General description

1   The system is fitted to all 924 models through 1979. All 1980 and Turbo models use the Lambda system which is essentially the same. Refer to the notes following the Specification Section, and Section 34 for further details.

2   Although it is sometimes known as the K-Jetronic system it does not depend upon electronics, but on the passage of air through a cone and the position of a sensor plate in that air stream. The only electrical components are bi-metallic heaters and solenoids. The fuel pump is also driven by an electric motor but there are no mini-computers or other electronic devices as in the previous Bosch systems fitted to Porsche vehicles.

3   Refer to Fig. 3.1 which shows a diagrammatic layout of the system. Air passes through the air cleaner into the airflow meter and from there via two throttle butterfly valves into the inlet manifold. The idea of two butterfly valves is not a two stage idea but to divide the airflow. The valves move simultaneously and at equal angles.

4   The engine inlet and exhaust valve arrangements are identical with a carburettor engine.

5   As the air passes through the airflow meter, the sensor plate is lifted from the rest position. The angle at which it becomes stable depends upon the speed of the airflow, which is of course governed by the engine speed. There is a law of hydraulics and pneumatics which states that a body free to move in a vertical conical air passage will move according to a straight line graph assuming a stable position governed by the airflow volume. This simple law shows that the up-and-down movement of the sensor plate may be used to measure the correct volume of fuel required by the engine.

6   The sensor plate is mounted on a lever, hinged at the end. In the center of this lever a rod, bearing on the lever, operates in the fuel metering unit. This plunger has grooves machined in it which open and close ports in the wall of the plunger bore of the metering unit. These ports connect the input side of the metering unit which receives fuel from the tank via the pump, accumulator and filter, to the output side of the metering unit which has the four injector lines connected to it. As the sensor plate fits in the inlet air stream, the plunger lifts and fuel is supplied to the injectors in a volume directly proportional to the airflow, which in theory gives perfect combustion. Unfortunately, the engine requires a different air/fuel ratio for differing conditions, and the required ratio is not a straight line graph. The actual requirement is a wave form centering on a straight line. A slightly rich mixture at idle, a lean mixture at cruising speed and a rich mixture for acceleration and full load. This is obtained by altering the shape of the cone bore slightly so that it

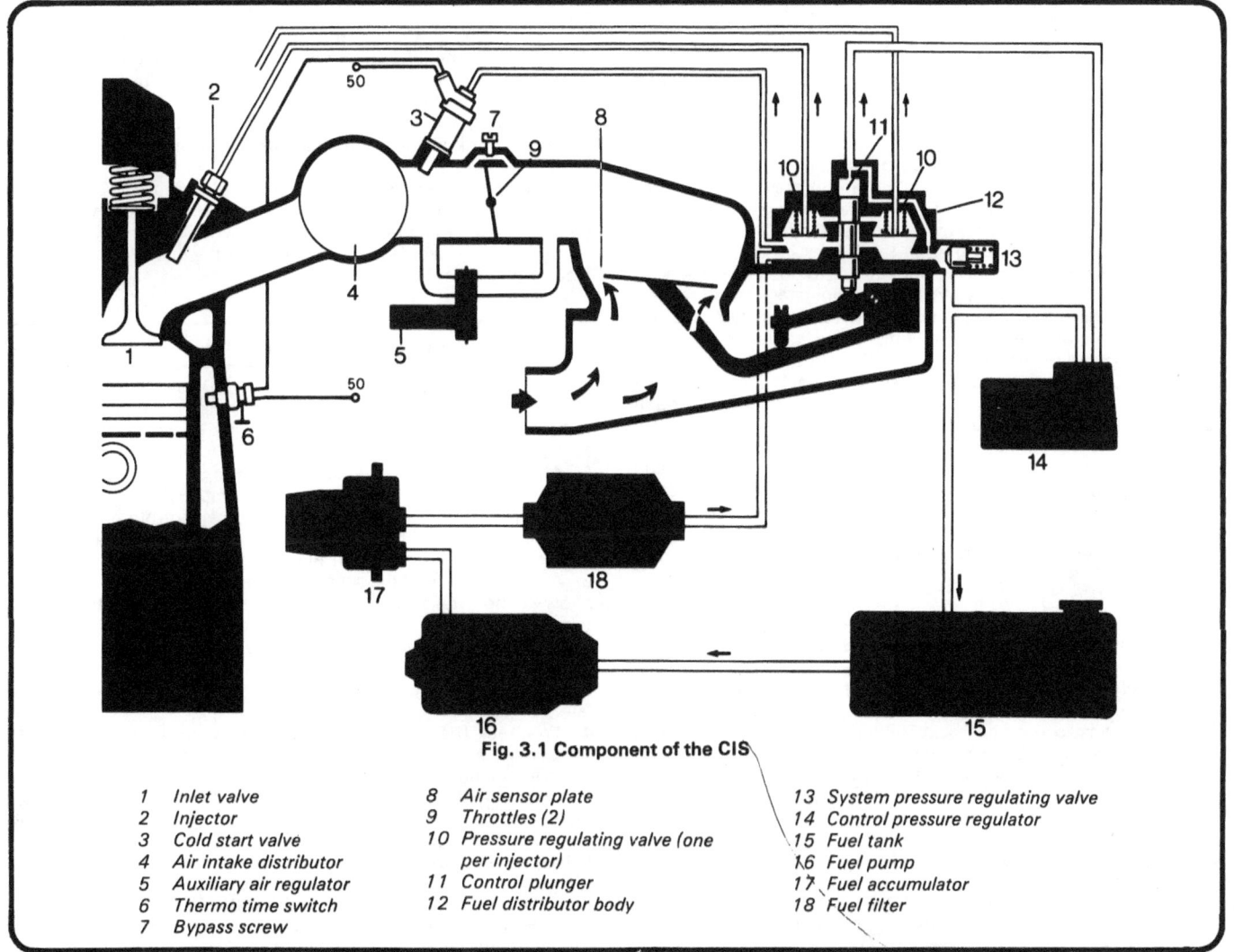

Fig. 3.1 Component of the CIS

1	Inlet valve	8	Air sensor plate	13 System pressure regulating valve
2	Injector	9	Throttles (2)	14 Control pressure regulator
3	Cold start valve	10	Pressure regulating valve (one	15 Fuel tank
4	Air intake distributor		per injector)	16 Fuel pump
5	Auxiliary air regulator	11	Control plunger	17 Fuel accumulator
6	Thermo time switch	12	Fuel distributor body	18 Fuel filter
7	Bypass screw			

has a slight wine glass shape. The irregularities in the bore are not defects but the results of very careful calculation and patient experiment.

7　When the ignition is switched on the pump operates and quickly raises the system pressure to approximately 3.5 kgf/cm^2 (50 lbf/in^2). The pump runs at an almost constant velocity supplying 1.5 litres/minute (2.6 Imp quarts/minute). The amount of fuel required is dependent on the opening of the meter valve, so provision is made at the side of the metering unit, for a spring loaded valve which opens at approximately 4.9 kgf/cm^2 (70 lbf/in^2) allowing the fuel to return to the tank via a return pipe.

8　As the engine is turned by the starter the airflow lifts the sensor arm, opens the fuel ports to the injector lines, and fuel pressure builds up in the injector lines. The injectors are spring loaded and open between 2.4 and 3.5 kgf/cm^2 (35 and 50 lbf/in^2). Once open they stay open, squirting fuel into the inlet manifold continuously in the vicinity of the inlet valve ports. The volume of fuel supplied per second is governed by the volume of airflow at that time so the combustion is nearly complete if the system is tuned correctly.

9　Obviously there are starting problems for an engine tuned to run efficiently at a high temperature. There are various minor problems too, which are dealt with in the text.

10　There must be some way of keeping the fuel meter in contact with the sensor arm. This is done by introducing hydraulic pressure to the top of the plunger from the control pressure valve, or warm-up valve as it is sometimes known.

11　Surges and pressure variations are dealt with by an accumulator in the pipe line between the pump and the fuel meter unit. This device also maintains residual pressure in the system for a short time to assist hot starting. Under each of the injector outlets from the fuel meter is a small pressure regulating valve to keep the pressure difference on both sides of the port constant and maintain a smooth continuous supply of fuel to the injectors.

12　The supply of additional air to the inlet manifold when the engine is cold at idle speeds, when the throttles are closed, is insufficient. This is overcome by a simple gate valve connected between the air cleaner and the manifold. The gate is closed by a bi-metallic strip heater as the engine warms up. The operation of this valve and its testing are described in the text.

13　A very rich mixture for starting from cold is supplied by a fifth injector in the inlet manifold operating at full pressure for a very short period, varying from 3 to 10 seconds according to the temperature of the coolant. This period is regulated by a thermo-switch. The operation is described later in the text.

14　The tests and adjustments require the use of meters, measuring glasses, a thermometer, a voltmeter or ohmmeter, a tachometer, pressure gauge with adaptors and an exhaust gas analyzer. Given the correct meters the tests are simple and adjustments easily within the grasp of the owner/driver. Without the gauges the job cannot be done, so how much you can do yourself depends on the availability of proper equipment. We have described the method of testing the components under the component headings. Slow running and CO adjustments are dealt with under running adjustments. There are a few hints on the maintenance of plastic pipes and a test routine for electric circuits.

15　Fig. 3.1 gives an exploded view. The latter is somewhat diagrammatic but it shows what is connected to which, and will assist those who have an unconnected hose and no idea where to make the connection.

2　Components and hoses - removal and installation

1　The details for the removal and installation of each unit is given under the unit heading but there are a few general rules to observe if the engine is to run successfully after overhaul.

2　If the engine is to be dismantled, or removed from the chassis, then obviously the fuel system must be dismantled. It is easy to pull off leads and hoses but quite another thing to put them all back, so, before starting, get a notebook and pencil, plus some labels and tape. Using your own code, label each wire or pipe as it is taken off. Remember that not only has the CIS to go back correctly but the ignition, cooling system, indicator lights, starter and alternator leads, radiator fan and thermal switch and possibly the headlamp leads have to also. So, label everything for ease of reassembly. If you do not you will find a surprising number of ways of making

connections incorrectly, some of them possibly expensive.

3　The first lead to disconnect, and the last one to reconnect, is the battery ground strap.

4　Porsche has a very firm ruling about plastic hoses. If they are removed from the connectors then new ones must be fitted. The old ones must NOT be used. It will probably be necessary to heat the plastic hose over the connector in order to pull it off. Do NOT cut it off or you may damage the metal connector and a new hose will leak. Heat the plastic with a hair drier on its hottest setting or a soldering iron, not a naked flame, until it is sufficiently soft to manipulate and then pull the hose away.

5　It is now necessary to fit a new hose. This must be done without warming the hose. The hose should be gripped in a suitable circular clamp with the amount of hose required to cover the metal of the joint protruding. Push the hose on cold and then remove the clamp and leave the joint alone. Porsche has a special clamp tool VW P-385 if you have access to one. If you do not and cannot make up a tool yourself, we suggest you take the old hose complete with connectors to your dealer and ask for a new hose to be fitted to the old connections.

6　It is necessary to fit new washers and gaskets when rebuilding joints, and to torque connections correctly where a limit is given. Gaskets and joint washers can be damaged by overtightening and leak just as those not tightened enough.

7　Always replace frayed or worn electric wiring. Do NOT use insulation tape except as an emergency repair, and always fit the correct terminal tags. If you do not have the tools or ability to do this then go to someone who has and get the job done properly.

Air cleaner - removal, servicing and refitment

8　The air cleaner consists of right and left body halves and an air cleaner element. The body is held to the frame by bolts and rubber bushings. The right is held to the left by four clips. The airflow meter is bolted to the top part of the air cleaner housing.

9　To remove the filter cartridge undo the clips holding the right to the left half and lift the left half away from the right half. Remove the filter element and take it away from the vehicle. Wipe the inside of the casing with a clean rag slightly moistened with oil (photo).

10　Replace the air filter element with a new one of the same type (photo).

11　Servicing should be carried out at 15 000 mile (24 000 km) intervals under normal operating conditions, but under dusty operating conditions we would recommend a weekly look at the element until the amount of dust entering is determined. After that a sensible interval may be worked out.

3　Air sensor unit - tests and adjustments

1　This unit is known also as the Air Flow Meter. This is a strictly incorrect definition as it does not measure the quantity of air in units but responds to the rate of air flow and passes on the information to the fuel metering unit.

2　An aluminum casting is bolted to the top of the air cleaner casing and connected by means of a hose clamp to the black plastic air conducting casing at the top. The mixture control unit or, as the later models have it, fuel metering valve, is bolted to the top of the Air Sensor Unit as shown in Fig. 3.2.

3　A cross-section of the sensor unit and the fuel distributor is also shown. The intake air lifts the sensor plate, moving the sensor beam, which then moves the smaller lever which is pivoted to the sensor beam and this in turn lifts the control plunger. It will be seen that a screw adjustment controls the angle between the lever and the beam. This is the adjustment for CO content, about which more later.

4　To check the position of the sensor plate it is necessary to remove the air intake casing, but before doing this run the engine for a few minutes to build up residual pressure in the fuel lines.

5　Undo the clamp and take off the air intake casing. The sensor plate may now be seen. Check the position of the plate relative to the bore. There must be a gap of 0.10 mm (0.004 in) all around, between it and the bore. The plate surface must also be even with the bottom of the air cone when the residual pressure is removed.

6　If the level is not correct then the plate should be lifted using a magnet or with the fingers, but be careful not to scratch the bore. The clip underneath must be bent to adjust the level, using small

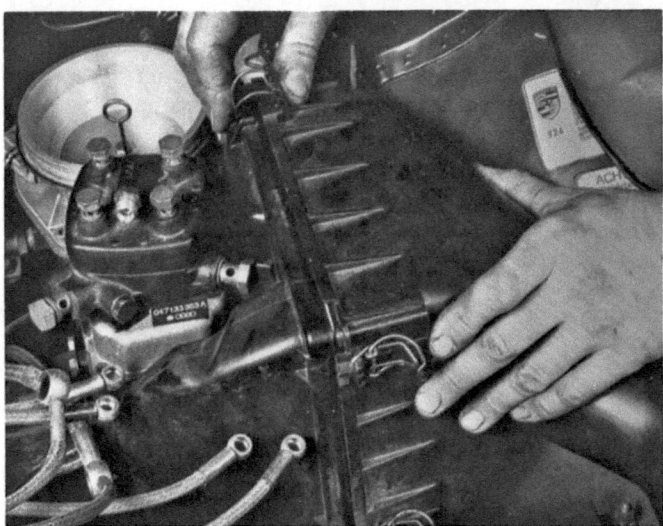

2.9 Unhooking the airbox clips

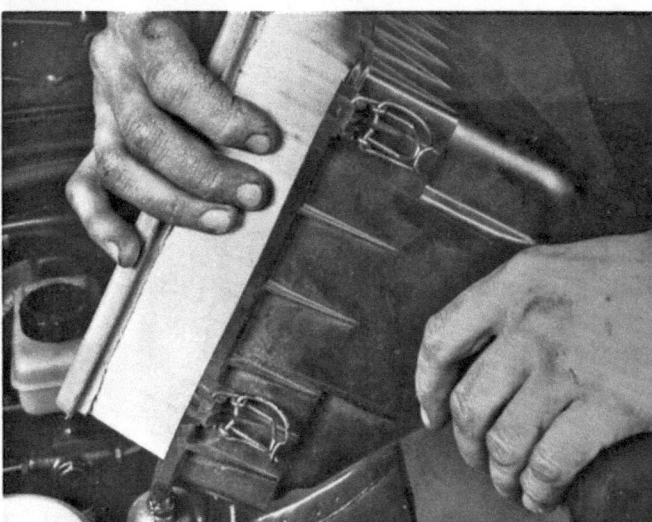

2.10 Installing a new aircleaner element

pliers. Pull the plate up as far as it will come and the job can be done without dismantling anything else. The tolerance is 0.5 mm (0.019 in.) but it isn't possible to measure it accurately, so judge the level as best you can by eye.

7   Centering the plate can be easy or difficult. Try the easy way first. Undo the center bolt; it is fairly stiff as it is held by Loctite. Take the bolt out and clean the threads. Now try to center the plate with the bolt loosely in position. If this can be done then remove the bolt, put a drop of Loctite on the threads and refit it holding the plate central. Torque the bolt to 4 lb-ft (0.5 m-kg) (Fig 3.3).

8   If the plate will not center then the sensor unit must be removed from the vehicle. It is probably easier to remove the mixture control unit from the sensor unit than to undo all the pipes, but if you do, be careful that the plunger does not drop out when you separate the units. Disconnect the sensor unit from the top of the air cleaner. Take the sensor unit out and turn it upside down. Now check that the sensor beam is central in its bearings. If it is not, loosen the clamp bolt on the counterweight and it may be possible to center the beam in its bearings and at the same time the sensor plate in the cone. If this is possible, remove the bolt, clean the threads, put a drop of Loctite on them and install the bolt with the beam and plate in the correct positions. Failing this a new sensor unit must be purchased, for if the plate is not central you will not be able to properly adjust the air flow.

9   Once the plate is central and level, the unit reassembled, the mixture control unit refitted, and the system recharged with residual pressure by turning the ignition on for a few seconds, it is possible to check the action of the air sensor unit. Turn the ignition off again and, using a small magnet, lift the plate to the top of its movement. There must be a slight, but even, resistance, but no hard spots. Now depress the plate quickly. This time there should be no resistance to movement.

10 If there is resistance to movement, or hard spots in both directions then probably the plate is not correctly central, so check again. If the resistance or hard spot happens only when lifting the plate then the problem is with the plunger of the fuel mixture unit. Remove the mixture unit from the sensor casing and carefully remove the plunger. Wash it well in clean fuel to remove any residue, refit it and try again. If this does not cure the problem then it is probable that a new mixture control unit is needed. *DO NOT* try to remove the hard spot with abrasives; this will only make matters worse. A visit to your Porsche dealer is indicated. He may be able to cure the problem but be prepared to purchase a new mixture control unit.

4   Mixture control unit – operation and testing

NOTE: Before replacing the mixture control unit, refer to Section 31 for additional information.

1   This unit is also called the Fuel Metering Valve. That is what it does. As the sensor beam moves up and down the control plunger opens and closes the ports and regulates the flow of fuel to the injectors. However, there is much more to it than that. Refer to Fig. 3.4. This shows a cross-section of the unit in diagrammatic form. Fuel is supplied from the pump to the lower half of the unit. From there it goes to the plunger bore and then back to the top half of the unit. There are four pipes to the injectors, each with its own small pressure control valve. Fuel in excess of the requirements goes back to the tank via the pressure regulating valve and the return pipe.

2   It will be seen that a pipe goes from the top of the plunger bore to the control pressure regulator (this is also called the warm-up valve). When the engine is cold the pressure regulator is open allowing fuel from the top of the plunger to return to the tank. This reduces the pressure on the top of the plunger to a little below the system pressure, allowing the plunger to rise slightly and open the ports made for the same movement of air through the sensor. Thus, when the engine is cold the mixture is enriched a little in this way. As the engine warms up the control pressure regulator valve closes and the pressure on the top of the plunger becomes system pressure, moving the plunger down a little and returning the mixture to normal.

3   The metering ports can control the supply of fuel to the injectors accurately only if the pressure dfference on either side of the port is kept constant. If the pressure varies the amount of fuel flowing through the same area of port will vary. For this reason a simple valve is arranged under each injector outlet pipe. Refer to Fig. 3.4. This shows in diagrammatic form the flow of the fuel through the mixture control unit. The hexagonal chamber is divided into top and bottom halves by a thin metal diaphragm. Fuel flows in via the plunger valve and goes to both sides of the diaphragm. From the lower half it flows via the pressure regulating valve back to the tank so that the pressure in the lower half is always system pressure. The diaphragm prevents a small valve on the bottom of the outlet pipe from the top half from opening, until pressure has built up enough to press the diaphragm down and allow for the spring to open the valve. About 0.1 kgf/cm^2 (1.5 lbf/in^2) is used up deflecting the diaphragm, so in this way the pressure in the upper half is always 0.1 kgf/cm^2 (1.5 lbf/in^2) below that in the lower half, even if the system pressure alters, and so the pressure diference remains constant and the port opening controls the flow accordingly.

4   The pressure regulating valve for the system pressure is included in the mixture control unit. Refer to Fig. 3.5. A hexagonal plug on the corner of the fuel distributor casing may be screwed out and inside will be found a copper ring, shims for adjusting the pressure on the spring, the spring, a piston and a rubber ring. Be careful not to scratch the bore or the piston since these are mated on assembly and a new piston means a new distributor body. If the piston is stuck, either blow it out with compressed air or work it out

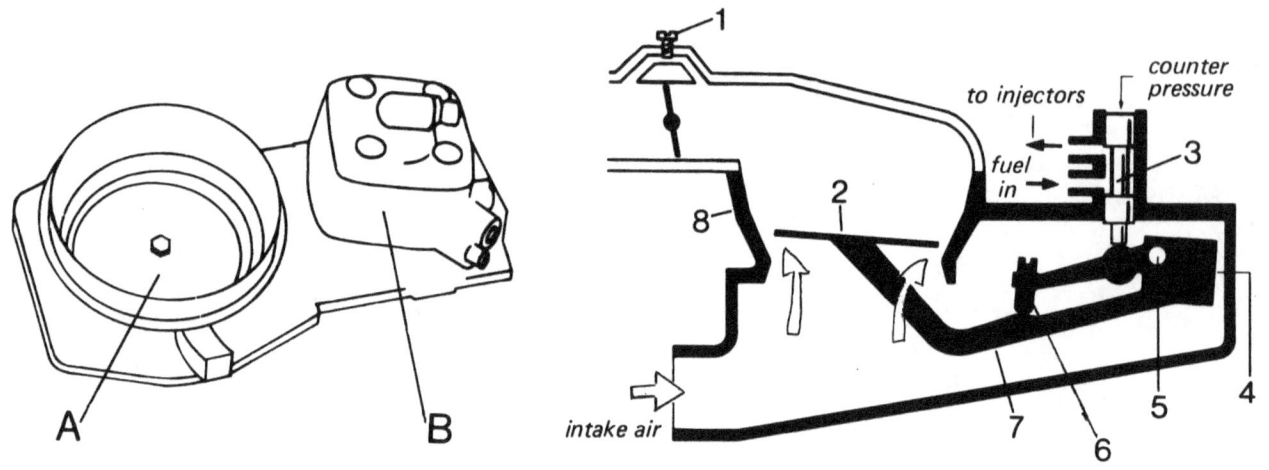

Fig. 3.2 Two views of the air sensor unit

A Sensor plate	2 Sensor plate	5 Pivot	7 Sensor beam
B Fuel distributor	3 Control plunger	6 CO adjusting screw	8 Air cone
1 Bypass screw	4 Balance weight		

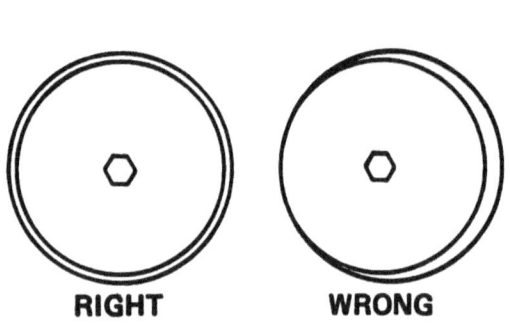

Fig. 3.3 Centering of the air sensor plate

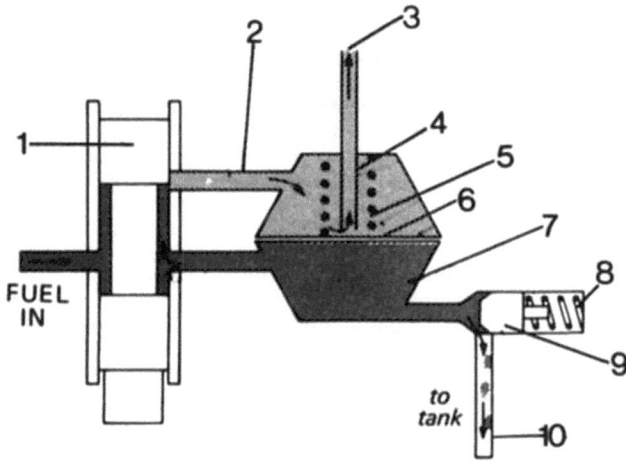

Fig. 3.4 Cross section view of the control pressure valves in the fuel distributor

1 Metering valve
2 Inlet to upper part of valve and injector line
3 Pipe to injector
4 Valve spring
5 Location of valve (not shown) which regulates injector pressure
6 Diaphragm
7 System pressure chamber
8 System pressure regulating valve spring
9 System pressure regulating valve piston
10 Return fuel line to fuel tank

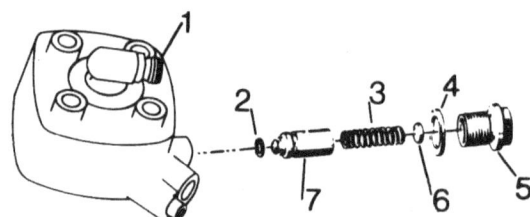

Fig. 3.5 Exploded view of the pressure regulating valve

1 Fuel distributor body	5 Plug
2 Rubber ring	6 Shims for pressure
3 Spring	adjustment
4 Copper ring	7 Valve piston

using a piece of soft wood. The pressure may be adjusted by altering the thickness of the shims. Add or subtract a 0.1 mm (0.004 in) shim to change the pressure 0.06 kgf/cm^2 (0.9 lbf/in^2); add to increase, subtract to decrease. A 0.5 mm (0.019 in) shim changes the pressure 0.3 kgf/cm^2 (4.4 lbf/in^2). When refitting always use a new copper ring and a new rubber ring.

5   From the tests on the air sensor plate movement the operation of the plunger will have been checked. If it is suspect then, as stated in paragraph 4, the fuel distributor body must be disconnected from the air sensor unit plate and lifted clear. Be careful that the plunger does not fall out, and get damaged. Carefully extract the plunger and wash it in clean fuel. When refitting it the small shoulder goes in first. Do not attempt to cure any hard spots by rubbing with abrasive. If washing in clean fuel does not cure the problem then a new assembly is required.

6   There are three pressure tests and one quantitive test in order to check the operation of the fuel distributor. For these a special pressure gauge is required and a batch of four 100 cc (2.8 Imp oz) measuring glasses. Before these tests are carried out the pump delivery must be checked and the filter examined.

7   The pressure gauge should be capable of reading pressures from 0 to 7 kgf/cm^2 (0 to 100 lbf/in^2). It must be fitted between the fuel distributor body and the control pressure regulator. Take the pipe off the control pressure regulator and connect it to the input side of the gauge. A further pipe is required to connect the gauge to the control pressure regulator and there must be a tap on the regulator side of the gauge. In effect the original line is connected to one side of a T-piece with the tape and extension pipe on the other side and the gauge on the stem of the T-piece. The official Porsche tool number is 1318 (Fig. 3.6).

8   To check the system pressure close the tap by the gauge, run the engine at idle speed and read the gauge. If the pressure is not between 4.5 to 5.2 kgf/cm^2 (65 to 75 lbf/in^2) then it must be adjusted. Porsche states that the fuel distributor body should be changed, but before that we suggest you try to adjust the pressure relief valve as described in paragraph 4. The problem will be getting the correct shims.

9   The control pressure may be checked 'hot' or 'cold'. To check it cold means the engine should not have been run for several hours.

10 For a cold check connect the gauge as in paragraph 7 but open the tap. Remove the electric leads from the control pressure regulator. Check the air temperature around the engine. Now start the engine, run it at idling speed for a few moments and check the pressure. Fig. 3.7 gives a graph within which the pressure should lie according to the air temperature. If the pressure is outside these limits Porsche recommends that the control pressure indicator be replaced, but we recommend that you check the system pressure and the fuel return line for blockage if the 'cold' regulator pressure is high before doing anything drastic. If the pressure cannot be cured this way then a new control pressure regulator is necessary as it cannot be repaired, because too high a control pressure at cold start will prevent the plunger moving up to give that extra rich mixture. Conversely, too low a pressure will give too rich a mixture.

11 The 'hot' check means that the engine oil is between 50 and 70°C (122 and 158°F). The gauge connections are as for the 'cold' check but this time leave the electric wires on the control pressure regulator. Start the engine and run at idling speed for a few minutes. The control pressure should build up to 3.4 to 3.8 kgf/cm^2 (49 to 57 lbf/in^2). If the pressure is outside this limit then the control pressure regulator must be replaced.

12 If all is well on the two previous tests, check the whole system for pressure leaks. With the gauge as for the 'hot' control pressure regulator test run the engine until the gauge reads between 3.4 and 3.8 kgf/cm^2 (49 to 57 lbf/in^2). Switch off the engine and leave the gauge connected for ten minutes. It should now read not less than 1.8 kgf/cm^2 (27 lbf/in^2). If the pressure is between 1.8 and 2.0

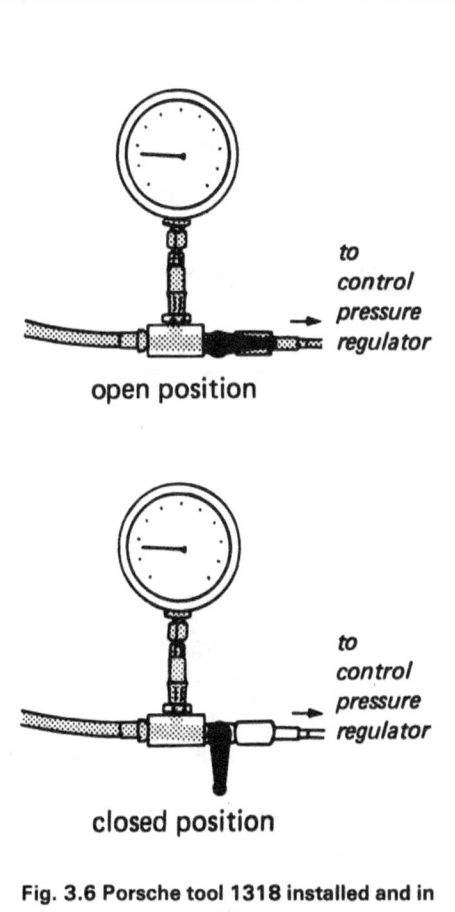

Fig. 3.6 Porsche tool 1318 installed and in use

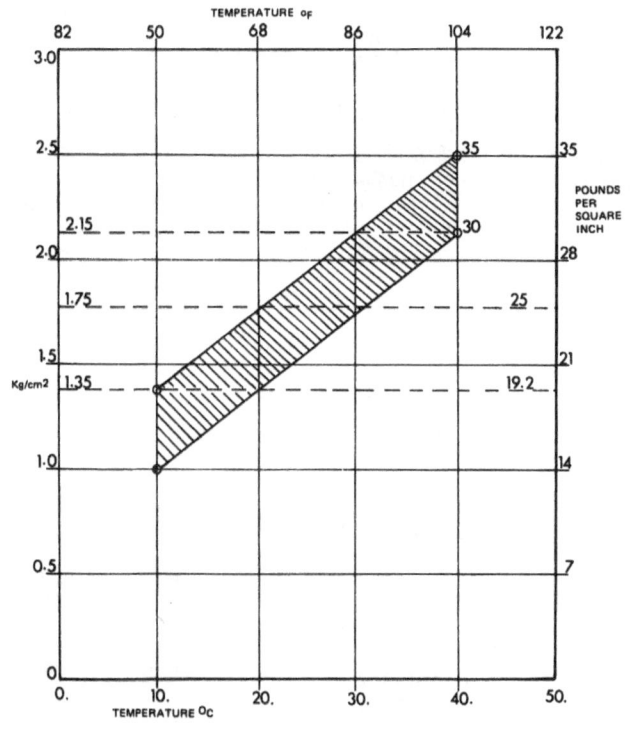

Fig. 3.7 Acceptable control pressures at different outside temperatures

EXAMPLE: at 20°C (68°F), pressure must be 1.35 to 1.75 kg-cm^2 (20 to 25 psi)

kgf/cm² (27 and 29 lbf/in²), wait a further ten minutes. It should not have fallen below 1.6 kgf/cm² (23 lbf/in²). If the system fails these tests then there is a leak somewhere and trouble with starting will be experienced when the engine is warm as the residual pressure will be lost and the system may even vapor lock. The obvious action is to check all the hoses and joints first. Then check the pump to see that the check valve is working correctly (Section 8) and the accumulator (Section 9). There is one other unit that is suspect. If the pressure drops with the tap in the gauge line open, but does not drop if you close the tap after running the gauge up to between 3.4 and 3.8 kgf/cm² (49 and 57 lbf/in²) and then waiting ten minutes, the control pressure valve is at fault and must be replaced.

13 The last test on the fuel distributor unit is a quantitive test which will also check the injectors (Section 11). Pull the injectors out of the inlet manifold and place each one in a 100 cc measuring glass (Fig. 3.8). On the relay/fuse board connect contacts 30 and 87 by means of a lead made up of 1.5 mm² wire (1979–on models only). Run the pump and lift the sensor plate slightly (you will have to remove the air duct from the top to do this) so that fuel begins to emerge from the injectors. Run the pump until one glass contains 100 cc and switch off. The other three glasses should have more than 85 cc in them. If one or more have less than this change the injector of the low one with the injector which gave 100 cc and repeat the test. If the same fuel line shows a low level again, then the fuel distributor is defective; if the same injector shows low again then the injector is at fault (Section 11). If the fuel distributor is at fault then probably one of the pressure control valves is not working properly. Clean the external parts of the system and take the defective fuel line off the distributor. There may be a fault in the line or the banjo joint, or dirt in the control valve pipe, but failing this a new assembly is required. Before buying one it would be worth having the system checked by an expert.

5 Control pressure regulator – operation

1 The function of this regulator, known also as the warm-up valve, is to control the pressure on the top of the control plunger. The functions and tests of the unit are described in Section 4 inclusive, in some detail. The following paragraphs describe its construction.
2 It is bolted to the rear of the intake housing. There are two pipes to it, one from the control pressure regulator and the second to the fuel return line.
3 Refer to Fig. 3.9. This is a diagrammatic section of the unit. Fig. A shows the regulator when the engine is cold. Fuel flows from the top of the control plunger in the fuel distributor into the control pressure regulator and out again to the return line to the tank. The valve is held open against the spring by an arm composed of a bi-metallic strip. When the engine is started current flows through

the heater element and the bi-metallic strip moves to the position shown in Fig. B. The spring now closes the valve and fuel no longer flows; the unit is now inactive (photo).
4 The control pressure regulator is not repairable and unlikely to become inoperative. If it does not seem to respond to the tests described in Section 4 check the value of the resistance by connecting an ohmmeter across the terminals. It should be 20 ohms. It will be zero or infinity if incorrect and you need a new unit.

6 Fuel supply units – location, removal and installation

1 The tank is situated at the rear of the vehicle. See Section 27 for removal procedures.
2 Situated under the vehicle just in front of the tank are the damper unit, pump and accumulator. One other unit completes the supply system; a full flow filter which is located in the engine compartment.
3 The fuel travels from the tank via a hose with two clips to a small drum-like unit. This is the silencer, or in American terms, the damper. It has a baffle inside and is a sealed unit. If the baffle comes loose or the casing is damaged and leaks fuel, it must be replaced. Its purpose is to even out surges in the fuel system and suppress noise. If it is left out of line the fuel supply can be heard very plainly in the car. From the other side of the silencer another hose connects the silencer to the pump. This is also held by two clips. The silencer is not bolted to the frame but supported by the hoses. The fuel leaves the pump via a check valve inside a banjo joint and travels to an accumulator. The pump is driven by an electric motor, the supply for which is plugged into the side of the pump.
4 Depending on the year of manufacture, there will be one of three fuel pump-accumulator configurations found in your vehicle.
5 The earliest Porsche 924 models had the fuel pump mounted to a vibration-damped plate alongside the fuel tank and connected by hose to two 20 cc accumulators. The accumulators were clamped to a plate which was held to the frame by the two bolts. Later 924's (circa 1978) had the pump and one 40 cc accumulator clamped to the plate which previously held the two smaller accumulators.
6 As of 1979, the fuel pump was once again mounted to the vibration-damped plate alongside the fuel tank and a single 40 cc accumulator was clamped to a modified mounting plate ahead of the fuel tank.
NOTE: Porsche 924's of 1976–78 manufacture have an early-style fuel distributor. This is not compatible with accumulators available as replacement parts.
      Bosch code 0438 100 039 (old number)
      Bosch code 0438 100 005 (new number)
Only the 005 fuel distributor is now available. Replacing the accumulator requires that the 039 distributor be replaced with the 005 unit

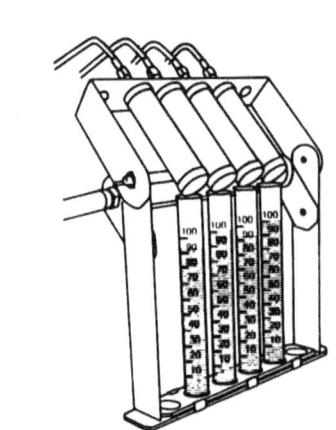

Fig. 3.8 The standard tool for testing injectors. A similar tool may be constructed for home use

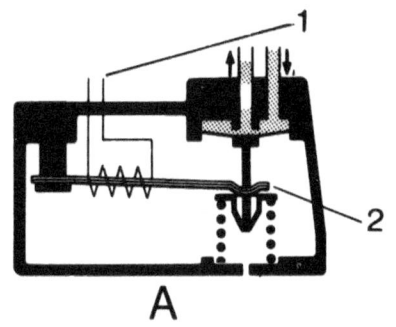
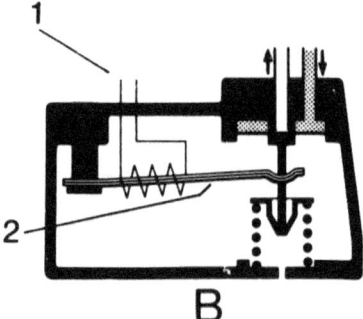

Fig. 3.9 Cross section view of the control pressure regulator

A   Warm-up position   1   Heater resistance
B   Normal running position   2   Bi-metallic strip

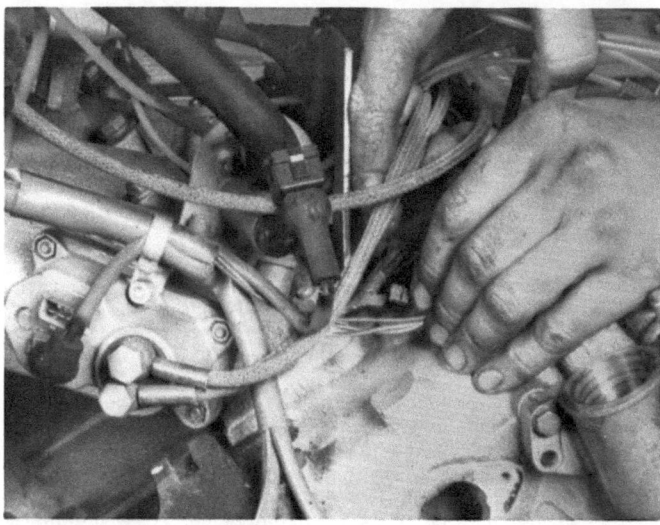

5.3 Location of the control pressure regulator

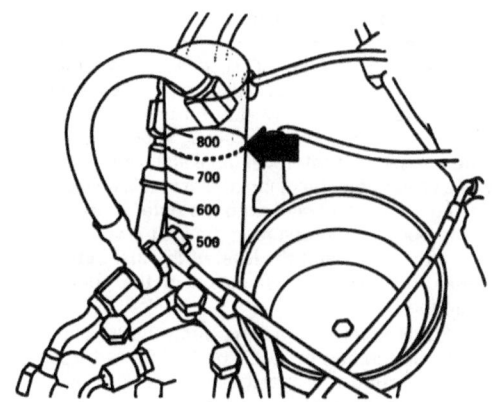

Fig. 3.10 Testing fuel pump output

as well as new lines. Conversely, replacing the fuel distributor necessitates the replacement of the accumulator in all pre-1979 models.

7   From the accumulator the fuel travels to the filter in the engine compartment. The accumulator has a double purpose: it irons out surges and also maintains a residual pressure in the system for a considerable time. This assists hot starting and also prevents vapor locks in the system as the power unit cools down when it has been switched off.

8   The filter is bolted to the side of the engine compartment alongside the left wheel well. Fuel enters at one end and leaves at the other. The body is held in a circular clip. There is an arrow on the body which must point in the direction of fuel flow when installing a new filter. This should be done every 24,000 km (15,000 miles).

9   There are two things of paramount importance when servicing the supply units. If the pump is to be removed, disconnect the battery ground lead before disconnecting the pump leads. Gasoline and sparks are not good companions. Clean the exterior of all units, pipes, connectors and hoses BEFORE starting work. This is tiresome, but not nearly so tiresome as cleaning out the system if grit gets into the pipes.

10 Once the system is clean, wash your hands and keep a clean rag handy. This has two functions, to wipe your hands and to catch fuel which spills.

11 When the pipes to the silencer, pump and accumulator are undone fuel will come out, so the pipes must be plugged. There is bound to be some spillage as you undo the unions so do not smoke or allow a flame or anything hot to come into contact with spilled fuel which could start a fire. Have the plugs ready and a container to catch fuel, for you will have to plug two pipes each time. Plug the tank side first. If you have everything ready very little fuel will be wasted. It is a good idea to have an assistant to bring whatever you have forgotten while you hold your finger over the end of the pipe, or to hold the fire extinguisher.

12 A word of warning about joints. Except for banjo joints the others have a hexagon on the pipe and on the unit; use a proper wrench on each one, not an adjustable wrench or a pair of pliers. Always fit new washers or gaskets. Banjo joints should be torqued to a maximum of 7 lb-ft (1 m-kg). Read also the notes on repairs to plastic hoses in Section 2, paras. 2 to 5.

7   Fuel supply - tests and fault finding

1   If the engine is not getting enough fuel, or none at all, then a logical routine should be followed. The tests described below are not exhaustive, but should help you to locate and cure the trouble.

2   Before we begin, a word of warning. Using the electrical system with the ignition switched on but the engine not running can lead to burning out of the alternator diodes. To avoid this possibility slip the plug out of the alternator (See Chapter 11).

3   Refer to Fig. 3.10. Undo the fuel return line from the fuel distributor and put it in a jug which will hold a quart, or, preferably, a 1000 cc measuring glass.

4   On pre-1979 models the fuel pump may be activated by lifting the sensor plate, but on 1979 and later vehicles you must locate the fuse relay box under the dash and find the fuel pump relay. It is second from the right and has a 16 amp fuse on top of it. Pull it out and locate terminals 30 and 87 on the board.

5   Make up a jumper lead of one piece of 1.5 mm² cross-section wire and an 8 amp bottle fuse. Get someone to hold the measuring glass and the return pipe. Switch on the ignition and using the jumper lead connect 30 and 87 for exactly 30 seconds. Disconnect and see how much fuel arrived in the measure. It must be at least 750 cc. If not then you have problems; either with the pump or a faulty filter/accumulator.

6   Reinstall the relay. Remove the HT lead from the coil and tie it safely out of the way. This time repeat the test operating the starter, with the ignition switched on. Check the amount delivered. It must be at least 750 cc. If you had this amount the first time but not the second then the relay on the fuse is at fault. If you did not obtain 750 cc either time, then the relay is probably all right but the fault is elsewhere.

7   The official way now is to start replacing things but a little thought may save a lot of expense. The standard fuse is 16 amps. The fuse in the jumper lead was 8 amps. The maximum correct requirement of the pump should be 8.5 amps, and normal consumption 6.5 amps. If the fuse has not blown then it may be that there is no voltage at all at the pump, or that there is an intermittent fault. If the 8 amp fuse has blown then the motor is working too hard or has an electrical fault.

8   It is best to have two people for the electrical tests. Remove the plug from the fuel pump and connect a voltmeter across the plug terminals. Switch the ignition on and read the voltmeter. There should be the full battery volts at these terminals. If the voltage is less, then the problem is in the switch or the wiring. However, it isn't as easy as that. Look at the correct current flow diagram, Chapter 11. See Chapter 5 which goes into detail on the supply to the pump. If the voltage supply is correct, then rig up jumper leads from the plug to the motor with an ammeter in one of them. Switch on and check the current consumption. A high consumption (6.5 amps plus) could mean a number of faults. Perform the following checks:

a) Switch off, undo the inlet hose to the fuel filter and hold it in a container. Switch on again and check the current. If fuel is flowing rapidly and the current consumption has dropped then examine your vehicle records. It is time the filter was replaced.

b) If test (a) gives no answers, this time repeat the test but disconnect the hose from the pump to the accumulator at the accumulator. If the fuel flows now with a reasonable current consumption then the accumulator is suspect.

c) If tests (a) and (b) give no cure, then either the pump or something between it and the tank is at fault. At this point remove the pump and the silencer. Fuel should flow easily through the silencer. This then leaves the pump to be tested. The tests for the individual items are described in Sections 9 thru 11. The pump is described in Section 8.

8 Electric fuel pump – construction

1   The pump is a roller cell type. This consists of a rotor in which there are five cut-outs, each of which holds a roller. The rotor is mounted on the armature shaft. The rotor is held in a pressure chamber (see Fig. 3.11), and as the motor spins, the rollers, which are a loose fit in the cut-outs, are pressed by centrifugal force against the pressure chamber walls. It will be seen from the diagram that fuel is collected by the roller between it and the wall, carried onto the outer space and then forced into the pump body. The pressure at the inlet is small, due only to the head between the pump and the level of the fuel in the tank. Refer to Fig. 3.12 which shows a cross-section of the pump and motor in diagrammatic form.

2   As stated, fuel is forced into the pump body. The armature and brush gear are immersed in fuel. The fuel flows through the motor body and out through the check valve. The purpose of this check valve is to stop fuel flowing back into the pump from the fuel system when the pump is turned off. The system pressure at that point is considerable and the valve holds to a pressure of approximately 2 kgf/cm² (29 lbf/in²). It is not a true one-way valve but serves only to maintain, in conjunction with the accumulator, a residual pressure in the system. It may be taken out and serviced if necessary.

3   Inside the pump between the pump body and the fuel inlet is a spring loaded relief valve. If excess pressure builds up in the pump body the fuel is pumped back into the supply port and enters the cycle again. This valve is built-in and cannot be serviced.

4   It may be thought that having the brush gear immersed in high octane fuel is dangerous, but since air is not present the liquid is not inflammable. The fuel cools and lubricates the pump and for this reason the pump should not be run unless it is full of fuel or it will seize up and overheat. It could then be very dangerous.

5   Apart from replacing the check valve, the pump may not be repaired; it must be replaced by a new one if faulty. The check valve may be removed for examination while the pump is in position in the vehicle.

6   Electric current is supplied to the armature only; the field is supplied by permanent magnets. The brush gear may not be serviced, nor may the commutator. If these are faulty, causing the pump to run erratically, then the pump must be replaced. The motor should be tested for open circuit or short circuit by using an ammeter on the terminals (Fig. 3.13).

9 Fuel accumulator – construction and testing

1   Removal and fitting are described in Section 6. Refer now to Fig. 3.14.

2   The accumulator has several roles. It damps down the fuel surge from the pump, cuts down pump resonance, help to maintain system pressure thereby avoiding vapor lock and assisting hot starting and eases back pressure on the pump when the engine stops.

3   The operation is simple. Refer to Fig. 3.14. The pump forces fuel into the accumulator body past the damper plate. The diaphragm is pushed inwards against the spring until it comes hard against the stop. At this point system pressure begins to build up to the operating valve. Without the accumulator in the circuit the pressure would build up in micro seconds but, with it in the circuit the build up is approximately 1 second long. When the pump is switched off the spring forces the diaphragm back slowly to the original position, pushing fuel through the small hole in the reed valve and maintaining pressure in the system for half an hour.

4   The only problems that can occur with it are leaks or a ruptured diaphragm for which there is no repair, only replacement of the unit.

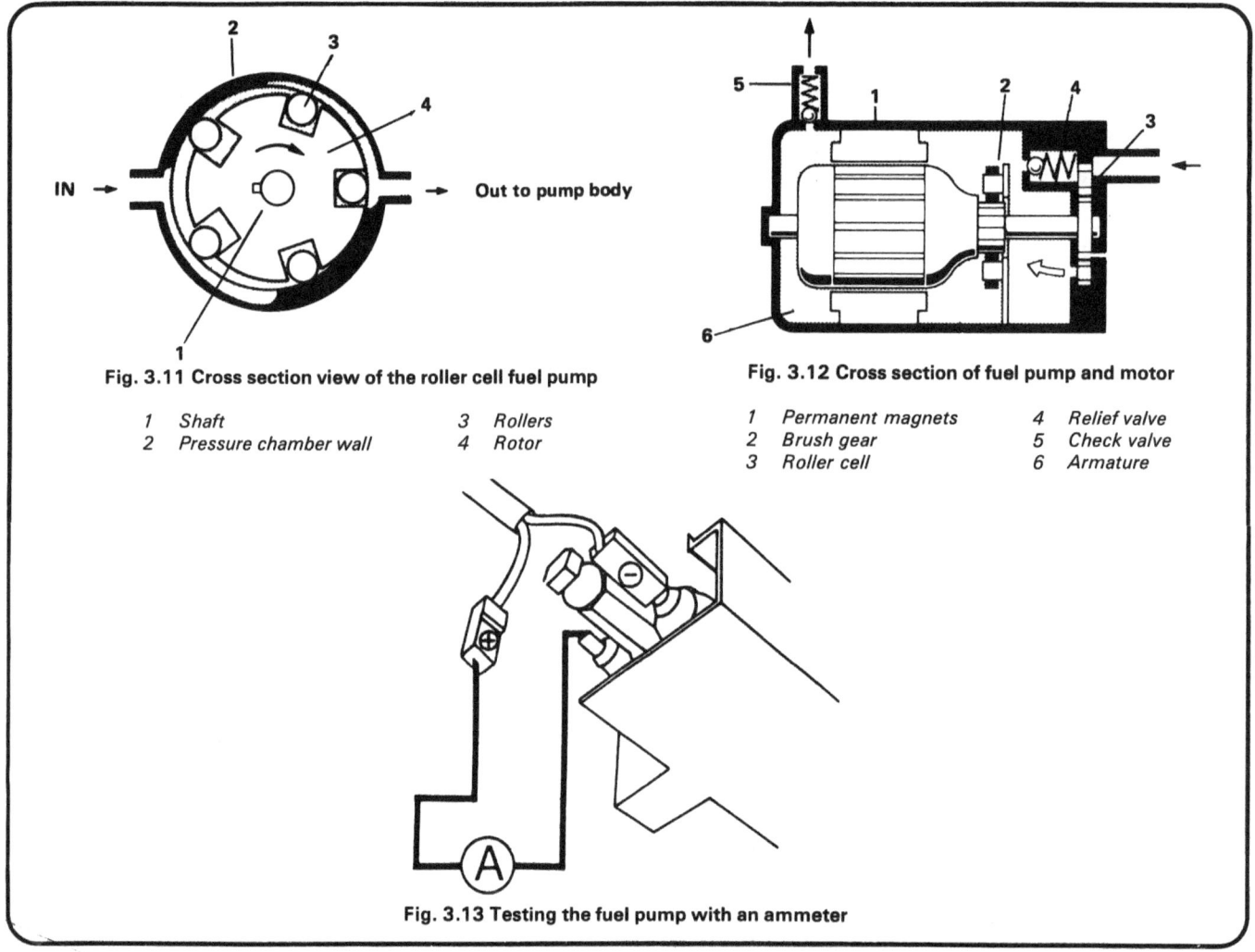

Fig. 3.11 Cross section view of the roller cell fuel pump

1	Shaft	3	Rollers
2	Pressure chamber wall	4	Rotor

Fig. 3.12 Cross section of fuel pump and motor

1	Permanent magnets	4	Relief valve
2	Brush gear	5	Check valve
3	Roller cell	6	Armature

Fig. 3.13 Testing the fuel pump with an ammeter

10 Fuel filter – construction and servicing

1   The fuel filter is attached to the side of the engine compartment by a clip. It will be seen that there is an arrow on the casing. This must always point in the direction of the fuel flow.

2   The filter should be replaced with an new one every 48,000 km (30,000 miles). No other servicing is necessary, or possible. Fit new washers on the joints when replacing the filter. Clean the exterior carefully before removing the pipes and use a proper fitting wrench, not an adjustable wrench, to turn the nuts.

3   Inside the tubular casing is a rolled nylon paper cartridge, so wound that flow is only maintained in the direction shown by the arrow. The filter is situated on the injection system side of the pump, not as you might imagine before the pump, as a clogged filter in that position could cause the pump to run dry with disastrous consequences (Fig. 3.15).

11 Fuel injectors – description and checking

1   There is one injector fitted per cylinder. These are pushed into bushes in the inlet manifold. These injectors spray onto the back of the inlet valve ports so they are working in a lower pressure than atmospheric pressure, thus the tendency is for them to be pulled in rather than blown out at high speeds. They are pulled out quite easily. Inspect the rubber seal in the intake manifold. If it is broken or cracked, remove it and fit a new one. Moisten the new seal with fuel before installing it and likewise moisten the injector before fitting it into the seal. Fig. 3.16 shows the push-in injector as well as the thread-in type for the Turbo.

2   The injector may give trouble for one of four reasons. The spray may be irregular in shape; the nozzle may not close when the engine is shut down, causing flooding when restarting; the nozzle filter may be choked giving less than the required ration of fuel; or

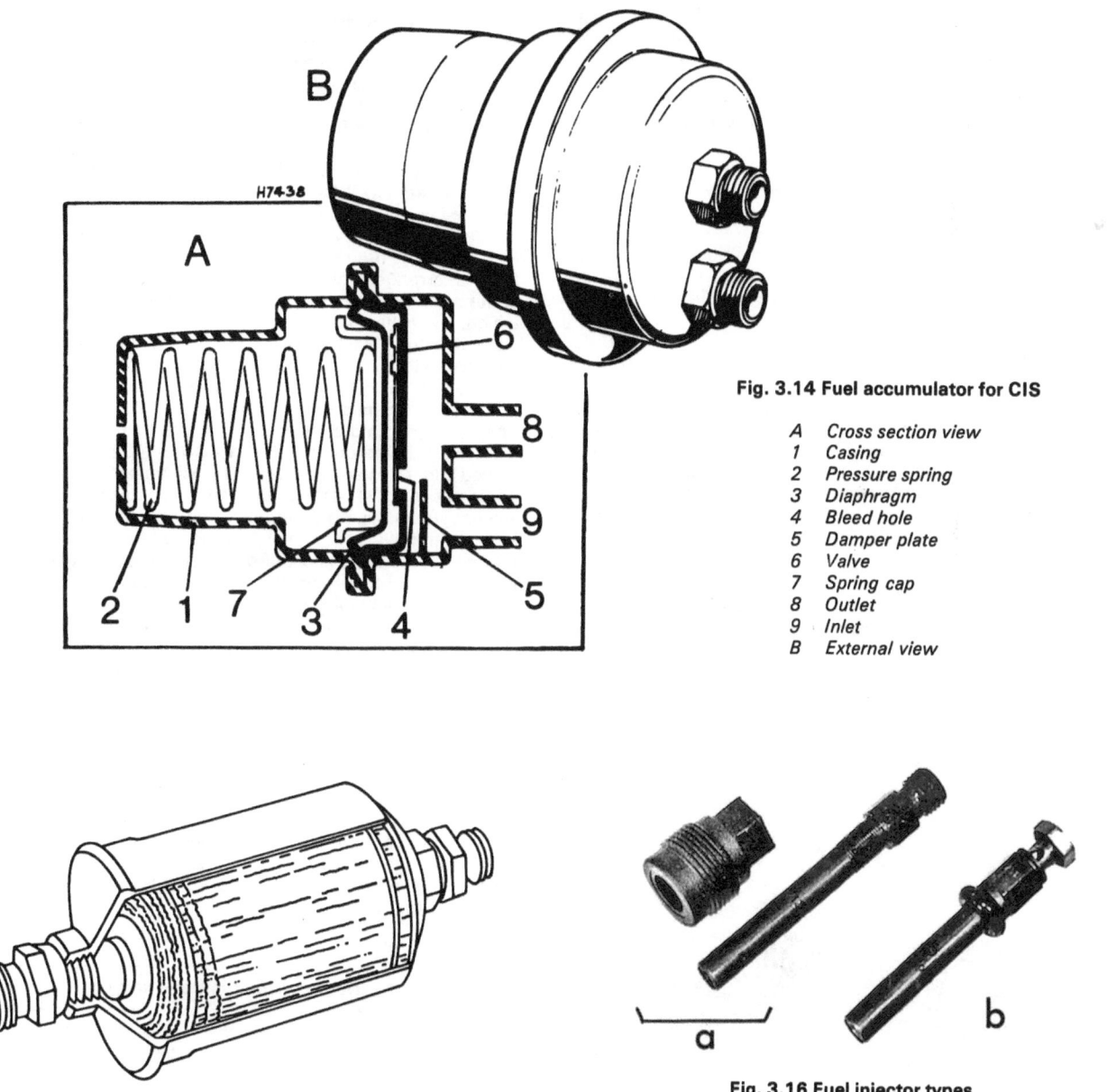

Fig. 3.14 Fuel accumulator for CIS

    A   *Cross section view*
    1   *Casing*
    2   *Pressure spring*
    3   *Diaphragm*
    4   *Bleed hole*
    5   *Damper plate*
    6   *Valve*
    7   *Spring cap*
    8   *Outlet*
    9   *Inlet*
    B   *External view*

Fig. 3.15 Cutaway drawing of the fuel filter

Fig. 3.16 Fuel injector types

    A   *Screw-in type for Turbo models*
    B   *Press-in type for standard models*

the seal may be damaged allowing an air leak.

3 If the engine is running roughly and missing on one cylinder, allow it to idle and pull each plug lead off and refit it. If that cylinder is working properly there will be an even more adverse effect on the idling speed when the lead is pulled off, which will promptly improve once the lead is refitted. If there is little difference when the lead is removed then that is the cylinder giving trouble. Stop the engine and check and service the spark plug. Now have a look at the injector. Pull it out of the seal and hold it in a 100 cc measuring glass. Plug up the injector hole and start the engine. Let it tick over on three cylinders and look at the shape of the spray. It should be of a symmetrical cone shape. If it is not the injector must be changed because the vibrator pin is damaged or the spring is broken. Shut off the engine and wait for 15 seconds. There must be no leak or dribble from the nozzle. If there is the injector must be replaced as dribble will cause flooding and difficult starting. If the spray is cone shaped and no dribble occurs then the output should be checked. Turn back to Section 4.13. This will tell you how to do a comparative test.

4 Fig. 3.17 shows a cross-section of the injector. It cannot be dismantled for cleaning. If an injector is removed from the line the new one should be installed and torque tightened to 18 lb-ft (2.5 m-kg). The operating pressure is between 2.1 and 3.1 kg/cm² (38 and 45 lb/in²). It is not possible to check this without special equipment. If this is available the opening pressure of the four injectors should not vary more than 0.6 kg/cm² (8.5 lb/in²).

12 Throttle valve housing - description, removal and installation

1 The housing is bolted to the air intake distributor (inlet manifold). The other end has a circular clip holding the air connector from the sensor unit. To remove it from the vehicle, unclip the air connector and ease it away. Remove the bolts holding the housing to the air intake distributor and ease the assemblies apart. If it is necessary to remove the unit from the car disconnect the accelerator cable from the operating arm (photos).

2 Refit in the reverse order except for the cable. When the accelerator pedal is right down, there should be a 1 mm (0.04 in) play at the operating lever, as the throttle valve may be strained (photo).

3 There is no adjustment between the twin throttle valves, and when the pedal is fully up the throttle flaps are shut.

4 Between the throttle spindles on the side of the casing is the idle adjustment screw. This is discussed in Section 14.6.

13 Air intake distributor - removal and installation

1 This casting conveys the mixture from the throttle housing to the inlet ports.

2 Before commencing work on its removal, take off the battery ground strap.

3 Consult Section 12 and remove the throttle valve housing. It is much easier to remove the air intake distributor if the throttle housing is taken off it.

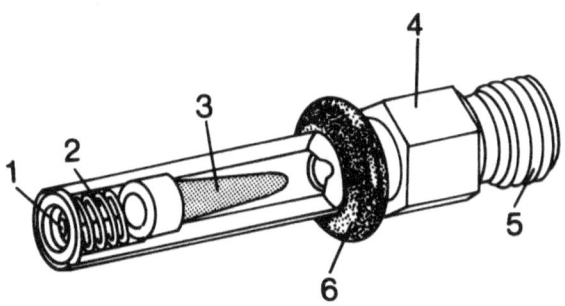

Fig. 3.17 Cross section view of a fuel injector

1	Pin	4	Injector body
2	Spring	5	Connection for hose
3	Filter	6	Seal

4 Depending upon the operating market there will be different hoses and leads so remove all electric leads and hoses, labelling them as you do.

5 For USA vehicles remove the EGR vacuum hose and pipe and then undo the holding bolts and remove the EGR valve.

6 Pull out the injectors and tie them out of the way. Label them 1 to 4. At the end of the casting is the cold start valve. This should have been disconnected but take it out and store it safely.

7 For USA vehicles remove the decel valve. (Section 61).

8 From above remove the two outer holding bolts. From under the vehicle remove the four lower bolts. A good socket wrench with a universal balljoint drive will help when removing and refitting. Always clean off all old gasket material and use new gaskets when refitting the casting to the cylinder block. Torque the bolts to 18 lb-ft (2.5 m-kg) (photos).

9 Reassembly is the reverse of removal. Reconnect the ground lead last.

14 Cold start equipment - general description

1 The system described so far is for normal operation with the engine warm. Starting from cold presents its own problems and to overcome these three extra items are provided.

2 To supply extra fuel a fifth injector, called the cold start valve, is screwed into the end of the air distributor. It is supplied with fuel from the fuel distributor. The valve is held shut by a spring during normal operation. When the ignition is turned on and the starter operated, a solenoid in the cold start valve opens the valve and fuel is injected into the air distributor when the engine is cold.

3 This fuel is not required for a hot start, nor for long from a cold start, so arrangements are made to limit the open time by means of a thermo time switch, the main portion of which is a bi-metallic strip which, when heated, opens a contact and cuts out the supply of current to the cold start valve. The solenoid ceases to operate and the valve closes.

4 The thermo time switch is screwed into the coolant system and if the coolant temperature is above 35°C (95°F) the contacts remain open and the cold start valve does not operate at all.

5 If the temperature is below 35°C (95°F) then the contacts are closed and the valve operates while the starter turns. However, if the engine does not start the system soon becomes flooded and then it will not start at all. To overcome this problem a heater resistance, in series with the starter supply, warms up the bi-metallic strip in the thermo time switch and the contacts are opened by this means. With a very cold engine the heater resistance has to do all the heating. This may take up to 10 seconds. If the coolant temperature is approaching 35°C (95°F) then the time period may be as little as three seconds. In this way the problem of flooding is resolved.

6 The normal operation slow running adjustment is by the opening and closing of a balance tube connecting the two sides of the throttle flaps in the throttle housing. The amount of air for slow idle with a warm engine is insufficient for a cold start, so an auxilary air valve is connected by hoses to the air intake by the air cleaner and the air distributor. This is a gate valve rotated by an electrically heated bi-metallic strip. It is fully open when the engine is cold and closes gradually during the first five minutes of operation.

7 The construction and tests for these units is given in Section 15.

8 The supply of electricity to the valves is discussed in Section 17 for the auxilary air valve and in Sections 15 and 16 for the cold start valve and thermo time switch.

15 Cold start valve - construction and testing

1 Fig 3.18 shows a cross-section of the cold start valve. There are several ways of testing it. The following seems the safest and most conclusive.

2 Remove the plug from the cold start valve and wrap it in insulation tape to prevent any sparks — there will be fuel vapour present. Take out the two screws holding the valve to the inlet air distributor, and take the valve out of the distributor casing. The valve must be left connected to the fuel supply. Wipe the nozzle of the valve. Pull the HT lead out of the center of the coil and tie it out of the way. Switch on the ignition and operate the fuel pump for one minute.

12.1a Unbolting the throttle valve housing

12.1b Removing the throttle valve housing

12.1c Disconnecting the throttle cable

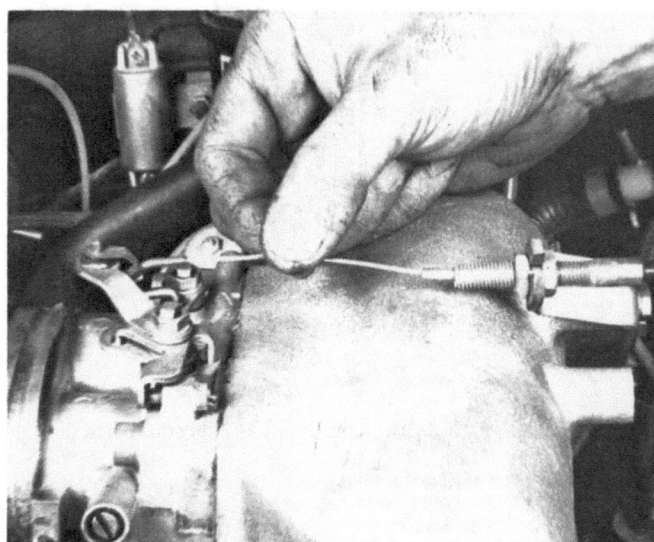

12.2 Adjusting the throttle cable free play

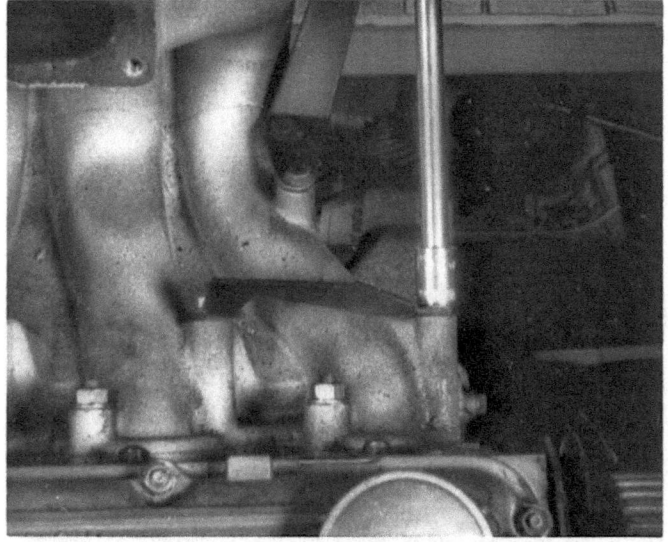

13.8a Remove the outside bolts of the air distributor first

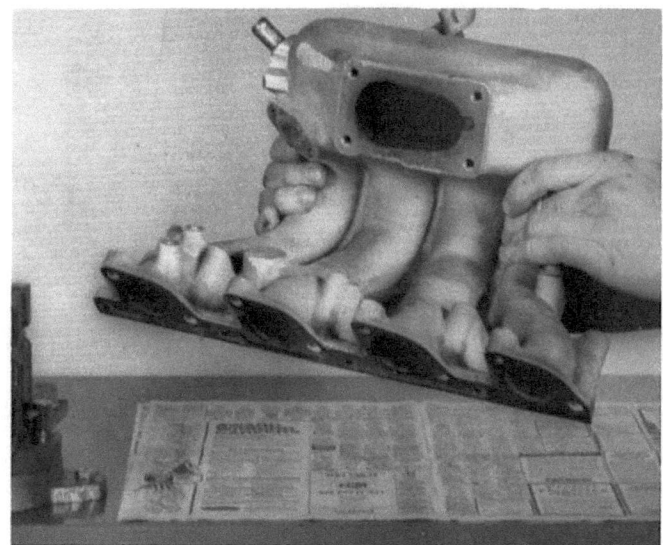

13.8b Removing the air intake distributor

There must be no fuel dripping from the nozzle. If there is, the valve is faulty and must be replaced. Switch off the ignition (photos).
3. Now put the stem of the valve in a glass jar. Reconnect the plug to the valve. Refer to Fig. 3.19. Take the plug off the thermo time switch and put a jump lead over the plug terminals. Switch on the ignition and have an assistant operate the starter. The valve should squirt a conical shaped spray into the jar. If the spray is correct the valve is working properly. If the spray pattern is irregular the valve is damaged and should be replaced. If the valve is working properly reinstall it in the intake distributor and proceed to test the thermo time switch.

16 Thermo time switch - construction and testing

1 Fig 3.20 shows a cross-section of the switch which is self-explanatory. It is not possible to repair the unit; if it is faulty it must be replaced.
2 To test the switch remove the plug from the cold start valve and bridge the contacts with a test lamp or a voltmeter. The test must be done with a cold (coolant below 35°C (95°F)) engine.
3 Remove the HT lead from the center of the coil and have an assistant operate the starter for ten seconds. Depending on the

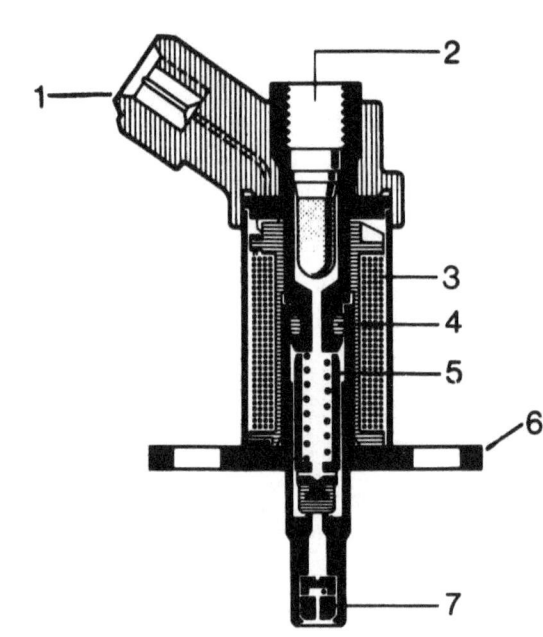

Fig. 3.18 Cross section view of cold start valve

1 Plug connections
2 Fuel inlet
3 Solenoid
4 Seal

5 Plunger
6 Flange
7 Nozzle

Fig. 3.19 Testing cold start valve output

15.2a Disconnecting the cold start valve electrical connection

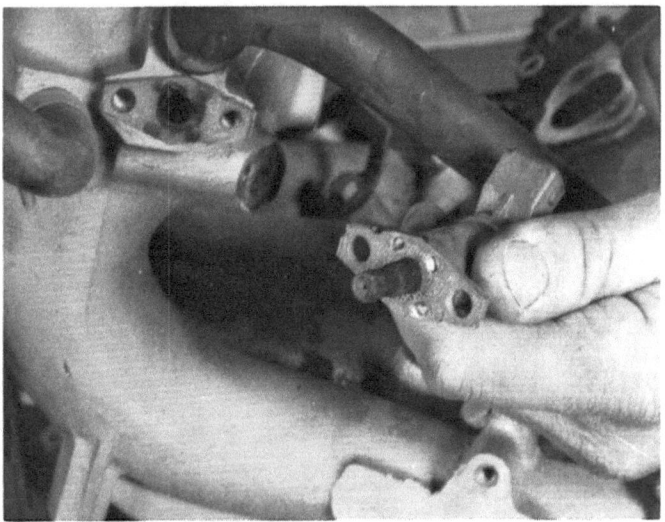

15.2b Removing the cold start valve

coolant temperature the bulb should light, or the voltmeter register, for a period of between 3 and 10 seconds, and then cease to register. If the circuit is not broken in ten seconds the switch must be replaced. If the bulb does not light at all, and you are sure the engine is cold, then check that there is voltage supplied to the switch. If there is no voltage then the fuel pump must be checked, as described in Section 18.

17 Auxiliary air regulator – construction and testing

1   Figs. 3.21A and 3.21B show a cross-section and profile of the auxiliary air regulator. The hole in the rotating valve allows air to pass while the engine is cold. When the ignition is switched on the heater resistance causes the bi-metallic strip to deform, turning the rotating valve until the air passage is closed. It remains in this position during normal operation.

2   To check the operation remove it from the engine, disconnect the hoses and look through the inlet pipe. If the unit is cold there must be a clear passage. Connect it to a 12V supply for five minutes and watch the operation through the inlet. At the end of the five minutes the valve should be closed. If it does not operate correctly check the resistance of the heater unit. This should be 30 ohms.

3   If the valve operates correctly but the system is still giving trouble check the supply voltage to it. This should be battery voltage. If this is not available then check the fuel pump relay as described in Section 18.

18 Fuel pump relay – location and testing

1   The fuel pump relay location is shown in Fig. 3.22. Fig. 3.24 is a simplified extract from the current flow diagram. It will be seen that the relay also supplies current to the control pressure regulator and the auxiliary air valve heater units. This explains why, although the

motor requires only 6.5 amps, a 16 amp fuse is fitted. Remove the plug of the air sensor before starting. If the pump motor has zero voltage when the ignition is switched on, then first locate the fuse on the top of the relay and check that it has not blown. If the fuse is in order remove the relay and with the ignition switches on test the voltage between terminals L13 and ground on the relay board. No voltage difference means no supply to the relay from the battery. Trace the circuit back with the help of the current track diagram.

2   If there is no voltage at L13 use the jumper described in Section 7.5 and see whether the pump works now. If it does, the fault is in the relay, or in the circuit which should operate it. Refer to Fig. 3.24 which shows the relay in more detail. Voltage at L13 with a fuse in good order but no voltage at terminal T in the engine compartment means that the relay has not closed. Remove the relay again, switch on and check the voltage between L16 and L15 and between L12 and terminal 15 and ground. There should be battery voltage between L16 and L15 but L15 should be grounded. Switch off and check the continuity between L12 and terminal 1 of the coil. If all these are in order then the relay is faulty and must be renewed.

3   If the fuse is blown do NOT fit a new fuse and try again. This time you may damage something badly. Locate the T-junction and disconnect the wire from the air auxiliary valve and the warm-up valve. Take the relay out of the board, and using your jumper lead, connect L13 to L14 (Fig. 3.25). Switch the ignition on and check whether the pump is running. If it is, remove the jumper lead and refit the relay with an 8 amp fuse in it. Switch it on again. If the pump runs then the relay is all right and the trouble is in the supply to the warm-up valve on the auxiliary air valve. If the 8 amp fuse in the jumper lead, or the relay blows, then the trouble is in the wiring between the relay board and the pump, or in the pump itself. Check the wiring insulation and test the pump (Section 8).

4   If the pump runs correctly with the relay installed, refit the 16 amp fuse to the relay. Isolate the auxiliary air valve and check the heater unit. Do the same for the control pressure valve. When you

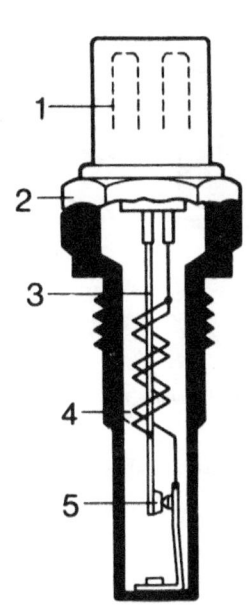

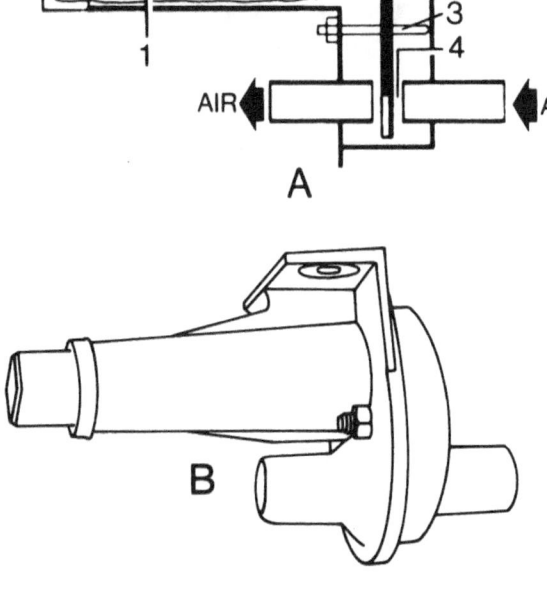

Fig. 3.20 Cross section view of thermo time switch

1	Electrical connections	4	Heater resistance
2	Switch body	5	Contacts
3	Bi-metallic strip		

Fig. 3.21 Auxiliary air regulator

A	Cutaway view	3	Pivot
1	Heater resistance	4	Rotating disc valve
2	Bi-metallic strip	B	Exterior profile

1. Fan relay
2. Fuel pump relay
3. Air conditioner relay
4. Headlight cleaner relay
5. Seat belt warning relay
6. Rear window defogger relay
7. Headlight flasher and dimmer combination relay
8. Extra high beam relay
9. Horn relay
10. Intermittent wiper action relay
11. Turn signal/emergency flasher relay

Fig. 3.22 The relay box, showing the position of the fuel pump relay (2)

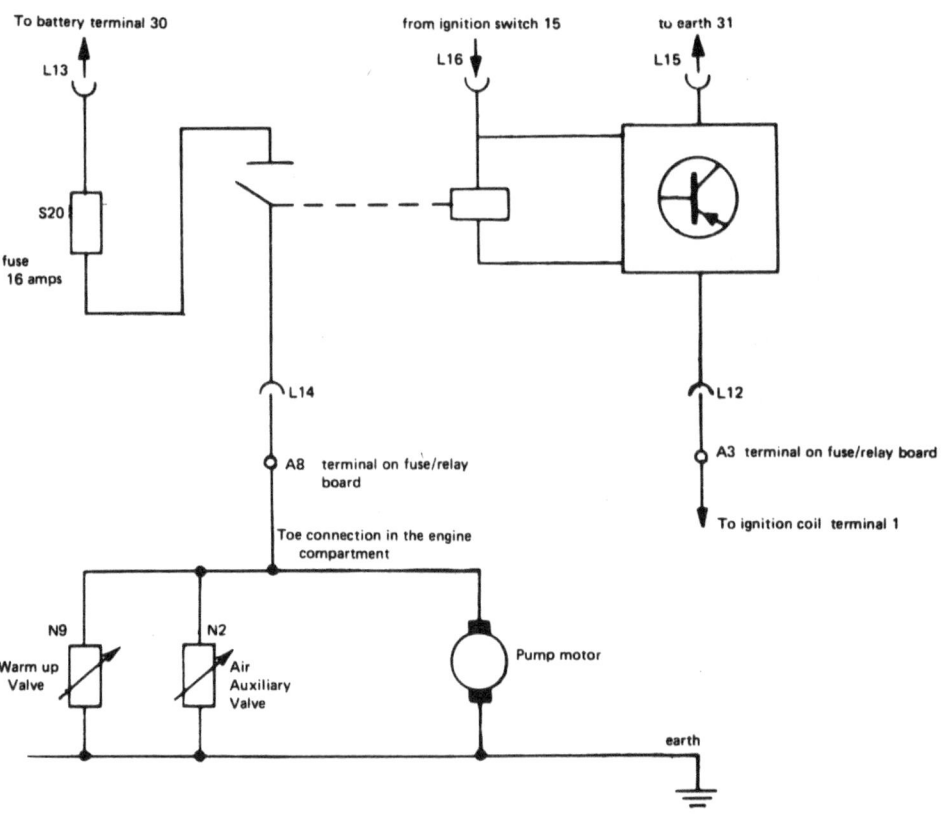

Fig. 3.23 Wiring diagram for fuel pump relay

are satisfied that they are working properly reconnect them to the T-junction. It may be that the 16 amp fuse just got tired and gave in, but refitting a fuse without finding out what caused it to blow is an expensive way of going about things.

19 Electrical connections – cold start valve and thermo time switch

1 Fig. 3.26 gives a simple diagram of the circuit for the cold start valve. Supply is from terminal 50 on the starter solenoid to the positive terminal of the thermo time switch and then to the solenoid of the cold start valve. As long as the electro thermal relay remains closed (F26) the solenoid is activated and the valve operates. When the points open the solenoid is cut out of the system and the valve shuts.

20 Electric solenoid (1979 models only)

1 To aid in the warm start behavior of the 924 with CIS injection, an electric solenoid valve has been installed in the system. It is triggered by a temperature switch in the coolant return line.
2 The solenoid is connected to the fuel return line and the control pressure line (Fig. 3.27). When the engine is started, current flows from the starter (terminal 50) to the cold start valve, and from there to the solenoid. When water temperature in the coolant return line

reaches 45°C (138°F) the temperature switch grounds the solenoid. The valve opens and fuel flows from the control pressure line into the fuel return line. In this way extra pressure is produced in the fuel lines and the fuel distributor when extra fuel is needed for starting and pressure is dropped to normal levels once the engine is running well. Testing of these parts is as follows:
3 Make sure the engine has not been run for several hours.
4 Unplug the electrical leads from the temperature switch and remove it from its hose. Connect an ohmmeter to the leads on the temperature switch and you should receive a reading of continuity. Heat a pan of water to a boil and place the temperature switch in the water. Resistance read on the ohmmeter should be zero.
5 Remove the solenoid from its housing and reconnect the wires of the temperature switch and have an assistant turn the ignition on. Do not activate the starter. The solenoid should immediately pop into the open position.
6 If this does not happen, the solenoid is defective and must be replaced. Double check to see that the temperature switch has not cooled below its opening point. If it has, heat the switch in hot water again and recheck the behavior of the solenoid.
7 If the switch proves to be defective, the solenoid cannot be checked until it has been replaced.

21 Running adjustments for the CIS

1 There are two simple adjustments; idle speed and CO content at idle speed.

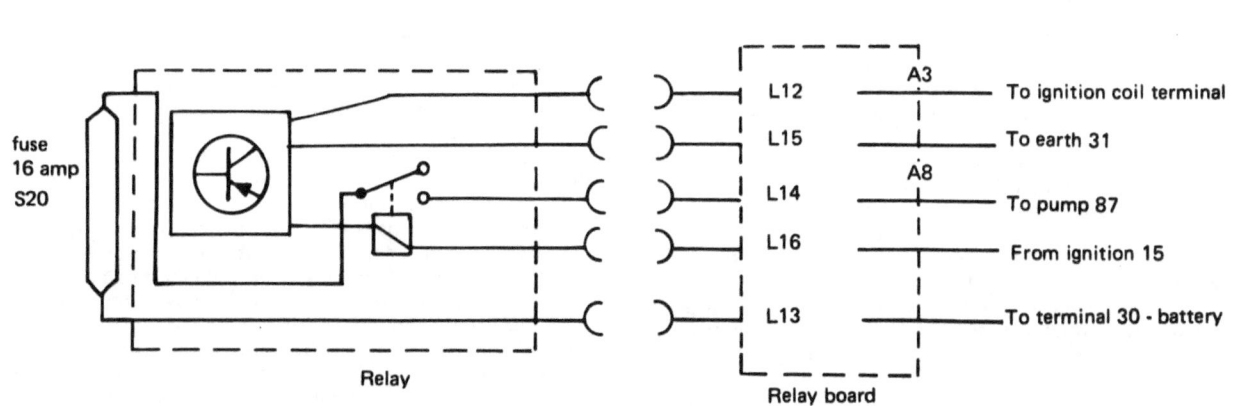

Fig. 3.24 Circuit connections for relay pins on fuel pump relay

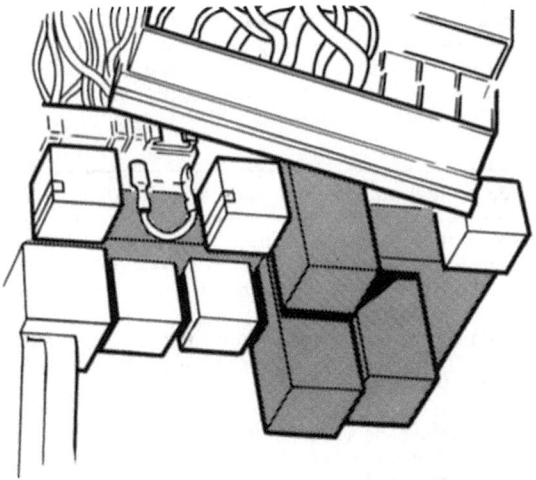

Fig. 3.25 Proper installation of the jumper wire

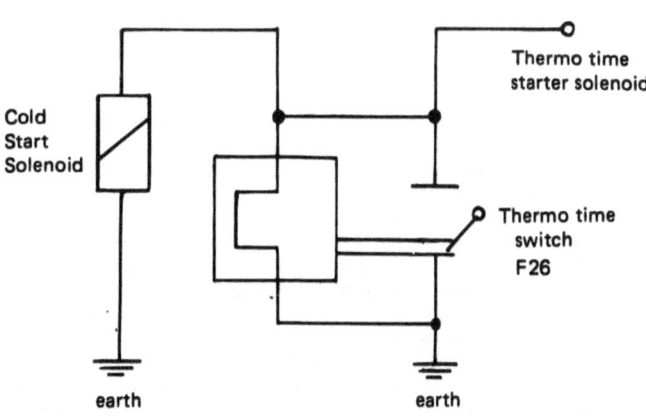

Fig. 3.26 Circuit diagram of cold start valve and thermo time switch

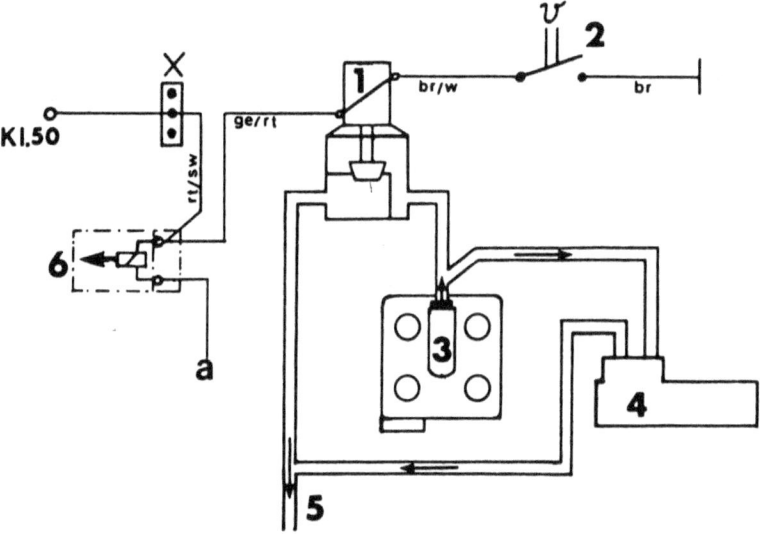

Fig. 3.27 Fuel system electrical connections (1979 – on)

1	*Solenoid*	4	*Control pressure*
2	*Temperature switch*		*regulator*
3	*Fuel distributor*	5	*Fuel return line*

6	*Cold start valve*
a	*Connection to thermo*
	time switch

2   Run the engine until the oil temperature is between 50 and 70°C (120 to 170°F). Connect a tachometer to the engine. Check that the auxiliary air valve is closed, pull the hose off and look through or probe it with a thin piece of wire. Turn the head lamps on to high beam to provide a small load, or switch on the air conditioner. Read the tachometer. It should be between 900 and 1000 rpm. If it is not, then turn the screw located on the top of the throttle housing between the throttle shafts to adjust the speed. Clockwise decreases speed, counter-clockwise increases speed.

3   The adjustment of the CO content is equally simple but you must have the correct equipment. The actual adjustment is done by altering the relationship of the sensor plate beam and the small lever attached to it which actuates the fuel distributor plunger. On top of the sensor plate housing, between the black plastic air duct and the fuel distributor body, is a small rubber plug. Remove this and the grub screw which does the adjustment can be seen. A special VW tool P377, is used to fit into the hexagon socket on the top of the screw but a long 3mm socket-head key will do the job. The plug has a small wire loop on it to make removal more easy.

4   If you have an American vehicle fitted with emission control then disconnect the purge hose between the air cleaner and the activated charcoal container at the air cleaner end. If there is a decal the permissible content will be shown on it.

5   This test must be done with a reputable gas analyzer. Porsche specifies an infra-red type, the SUN EPA 75 performance analyzer. Whichever one is used it has to measure accurately to 0.1%.

6   Run the engine up as for the idle speed adjustment and then, having connected up the analyzer, insert it into the tail pipe (this includes vehicles with catalytic converters) and read the meter. If the volume % is outside the limit remove the plug described in paragraph 3, fit the tool and turn the screw; clockwise for a richer mixture, anti-clockwise for a weaker mixture. Try not to push the sensor beam down when turning the screw. Remove the tool, replace the plug and accelerate the engine gently and read the analyzer again. Repeat until the reading is within the specified limits. Do NOT accelerate the engine while the tool is in position, you will damage the air sensor. Now recheck the idle speed, adjust if necessary and repeat the CO adjustment. Carry on until both are correct.

7   The question of CO percentage volume is a thorny one. Canada and USA except California are content with 1.5% for manual transmission and 1.0% for automatic gear boxes, but California demands 0.3% for both types. The rest of the world accepts 2% maximum. We recommend strongly that you consult your local dealer or the highway authority to check these figures. Sections 30 and Specifications have further details.

22   Fault finding on the CIS

1   Before you do anything to the CIS, check that the ignition system is functioning correctly and the valve tappet clearances are correct. Check the ignition timing and the dwell angle, ensure that the spark plugs are clean and correctly gapped, that the battery is fully charged, and that there is fuel in the tank.

2   Inspect all the hoses and electrical connections to the CIS system and clean any dirt or grease from the components of the CIS before you attempt to do anything to them. If you allow any dirt to get into the system the result could be very expensive.

3   A tachometer, voltmeter, ohmmeter and a pressure gauge, 0 to 7.03 kgf/cm² (0 to 100 lbf/in²) are required, plus the use of an exhaust gas analyzer if the system is to be checked completely. However, much can be done with just a test lamp and an ohmmeter.

4   Get a notebook and pencil and write down what you are going to do in the correct order, and what the result was. If in the end you have to go to your Porsche dealer for help he will then know what has been checked and may save valuable time.

5   Start with the electrical system. Is the pump working, are all the connections to the cold start valve, thermo time switch, control pressure regulator and so on supplied with the correct voltage? Check the various heater elements to see that the resistance is correct, or at least that they are working. For more information see also the Troubleshooting section in the introduction part of the manual.

23   Electric fuel pump - removal and installation

1   Remove the negative lead from the battery.

2   Raise the vehicle and place it on jack stands.

3   Clamp off the hose on the gas tank side of the pump with a standard hose clamp.

4   Loosen the hose clamps at either end of the pump.

5   Unplug the connector *or* unscrew the leads at the end of the pump (each Bosch pump has one type of power connection or the other) (photo).

6   If your vehicle has a fuel pump guard (installed in those models which have a fuel pump and a single 40 cc accumulator on the same bracket), loosen the two nuts which hold it in place and remove it.

7   Models with the fuel pump and accumulator on the same bracket will find the remainder of their instructions immediately below. If your car has the fuel pump mounted on a bracket along-side the fuel tank, skip to paragraph 13.

8 The bracket holding the fuel pump and accumulator together has two sub-assemblies; the bracket holding the pump and the accumulator and the bracket attaching it to the vehicle frame. The two are connected by lord mounts (rubber bushes with studs on each end).

9 Remove the nuts from the lower studs of the lord mounts and lift the holding bracket away.

10 Detach the fuel line between the pump and accumulator. Hold the banjo fitting with a wrench while removing the banjo bolt or the fittings may crack.

11 Loosen the holding strap on the fuel pump and remove it from the bracket.

12 Pull off the feed line from the gas tank. Catch any gasoline which spills and wipe up any drops of gasoline on the floor.

13 If your vehicle has the fuel pump mounted to a bracket alongside the fuel tank, the remaining steps follow.

14 Remove the banjo bolt from the end of the fuel pump. Hold the hex fitting on the fuel pump with another wrench to prevent cracking of the fitting (photo).

15 Loosen the clamp holding the pump to its bracket and remove the pump (photo).

16 Remove the hose on the feed side of the pump and clean any spilled gasoline (photo).

17 Installation is the reverse of the removal process.

18 The banjo bolts must be torqued to 14 ft-lb (2 m-kg) and new seals must be installed every time the banjo bolts are removed. Do not overtighten or the seals could be damaged and leakage will result.

24 Electric fuel pump – electrical testing

1 Disconnect the electrical connector at the air flow sensor. 1979 and later models do not have this connection.

2 Disconnect the electrical connectors at the fuel pump (as appropriate).

3 Switch on the ignition. Do not engage the starter motor.

4 Connect a voltmeter to the ends of the plug connector or the screw ends on the wires. A reading of not less than 11.5 volts should be seen.

5 Measure current consumption by connecting one lead on the fuel pump to one lead of the plug and placing a voltmeter in the circuit between the other two leads. A reading of not more than 8.5 amps should be seen.

6 If current consumed is greater than the above figure, replace the fuel pump.

7 Restore all connections to their proper locations after switching off the ignition.

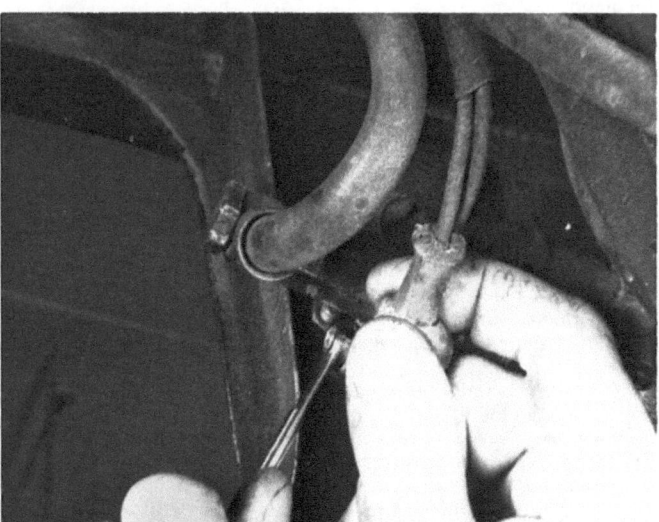
23.5 Unscrewing the fuel pump power leads

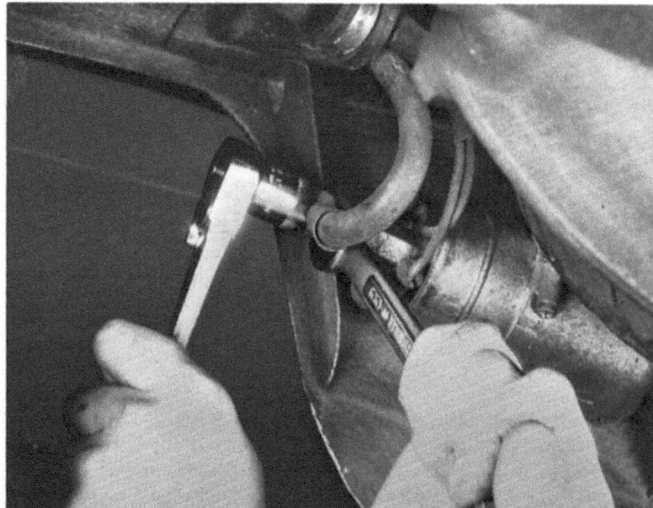
23.14 Unbolting the fuel pump banjo fittings

23.15 Removing the fuel pump mounting clamp

23.16 Removing the feed side connection of the fuel pump

25 Fuel tank sending unit - removal and installation

1 Disconnect the negative lead from the battery.
2 Remove the carpeting over the fuel tank.
3 Remove the sound deadening blanket and plywood cover over the gas tank.
4 Remove the plastic cover from the fuel tank sending unit. It is located on the left side of the fuel tank area. A flat-blade screwdriver may be used to gently pry on an edge, but be careful not to scratch the paint or deform the cover (photo).
5 Unplug the three wires from the spade connectors on top of the sending unit. Hook the wiring loom in an out of the way location.
6 A special wrench, part number 2012, may be used to unscrew the sending unit. If one of these is not readily available, use a large channel lock pliers or other such wrench whose jaws cross the diameter of the sending unit hole and engage the slots on each side (photo).
7 The sending unit is loosened by a quarter turn counter clockwise. Lift it out slowly, allowing the gasoline to drain out.
8 Installation is the reverse of removal. Make sure that the sending unit is completely engaged before connecting the wires. The loom is hooked up in the following order:
— (blank): brown
G: purple/black
W: yellow/black
The letters are stamped on the raised portion in the center of the sending unit top.

26 Fuel tank sending unit - testing

1 The fuel tank sending unit will have to be removed from the gas tank for this task. The only additional tool necessary is an ohmmeter.
2 Place the sending unit on your bench in an upright position (spade connectors at the top).
3 Check for continuity by placing one lead of the ohmmeter on the case and the other on the "W" spade. Continuity should be shown on the meter. This means the low level signal lamp in the systems monitoring nacelle on the dashboard is receiving its signal from the sending unit.
4 Keeping the two leads in the same locations as above, invert the fuel sending unit. The needle on the ohmmeter should drop to zero. This indicates that the signal lamp is receiving current only when the sending unit float is at a low level in the tank.
5 Testing for the low level reading on the gas gauge is accomplished by touching the ohmmeter leads to the "W" spade with one and the "G" spade with the other. A reading of approximately 85 ohms should be recorded.
6 With the two leads in the same position, invert the fuel sending unit. A reading of approximately 4.75 ohms should be recorded. This indicates that the "full" end of the gas gauge is being signalled by the unit.

27 Fuel tank - removal and replacement

1 Disconnect the negative lead of the battery.
2 Remove the final muffler (Section 66).
3 Remove the transmission (Chapter 7).
4 Drain the fuel from the tank. Clamp the hose leading to the fuel pump, disconnect it at the first clamp after the gas tank (not the suction hose nipple at the tank), and allow the gasoline to drain into an appropriate container which complies with national regulations.
5 Remove the carpeting, sound blanket, and plywood cover from the luggage compartment.
6 Remove the plastic cover from the sending unit and disconnect the three wires (photo 25.4).
7 Loosen the side trim (left side) and remove the filler pipe cover (photo).
8 Loosen the clamps on the vent hoses and pull the hoses off their mounting nipples (photo).
9 Loosen the clamps on the fuel supply hoses at the tank and pull them free.
10 Remove the nuts and washers from the tank holding strap,

remove the straps and lift out the gas tank.
11 Do not attempt to close leaks and hoses in the gas tank as the remaining gasoline vapor is highly explosive. There are several means of repairing gas tanks, some are better for specific locations than others. If in doubt as to the proper course of action, consult a local repair garage or your local Porsche dealer.
12 Before reinstalling the gas tank, purchase and replace the anti-chafe strip along the bulkhead forward of the tank, the four anti-chafe blocks on the corners of the tank and holding strap, and the rubber blocks which are found between the gas tank and underside of the luggage compartment. The nuts which anchor the holding strap are self-locking and must be replaced with new nuts every time they are removed.
13 Installation is the reverse of the removal procedure.

28 Fuel silencer unit - removal and replacement

1 The fuel silencer unit, known also as the damper, is the small drum-shaped object immediately after the first section of the gas tank suction hose and before the fuel pump. Its purpose is to silence the flow of fuel as it enters the pump and also provide a bit of pressure in the lines when the car is not running.
2 This sealed unit has one moving part—a baffle. If the unit ceases to function properly, leaks or is punctured, it will need to be replaced.
3 Clamp the suction hose from the gas tank.
4 Loosen the two clamps which hold the hoses to each end of the damper unit. Pull the hoses loose.
5 Remove the damper unit.
6 Installation of the damper unit is the reverse of the removal procedure. Be sure to clean up all gasoline spilled in this task.

29 Fuel filter - removal and installation

1 The fuel filter is located on the left side wheel well slightly behind the air flow sensor housing on normally aspirated models. Turbo models have their fuel filter located in the fresh air intake plenum. This is the area immediately behind the firewall and just ahead of the windshield wiper assemblies on the left side (photo).
2 Fuel filters should be replaced every 30,000 miles (48,000 km).
3 To remove the filter, first remove all dirt and grit from the filter connections. This will prevent the entry of foreign matter into the fuel hoses while they are disconnected.
4 If the fuel filter is held to its bracket by a plastic strap, cut the strap. Those filters held in place by metal clamping bands should have the band loosened.
5 Loosen the nut on each end of the fuel filter. Use a second wrench to hold the hex fitting on the filter body in place and to prevent cracking of the filter body (photo).
6 Remove the hoses and lift the fuel filter free of the vehicle. Clean up all spilled gasoline immediately.
7 The new filter is installed with the arrow stamped on the filter housing pointing in the direction of fuel flow. The fuel filter works as a one-way valve and incorrect installation will stop fuel flow.
8 When replacing the fuel line fittings, hold the hex fitting on the filter with a second wrench to prevent damage to the new filter (photo 29.5).
9 Replace the strap, if the old one was cut. Do not overtighten the metal clamps, as it is possible to crush the filter body.

30 Adjusting idle speed/CO - CIS systems

1 The engine must be in proper tune and the timing set before these adjustments can be carried out successfully.
2 Start the vehicle and run the engine until operating temperature is reached. Oil temperature should be 80 to 90°C (180 to 190°F).
3 Connect the exhaust gas test line to the tail pipe or muffler (US, Canada, Japan) or to the test connection just ahead of the catalytic converter (California and all other vehicles with a catalytic converter).
4 Connect the CO tester according to manufacturers instructions.
5 If your car has an air injection hose (Fig. 3.40) detach it and plug the end.

25.4 Levering the plastic cover from the fuel tank sending unit

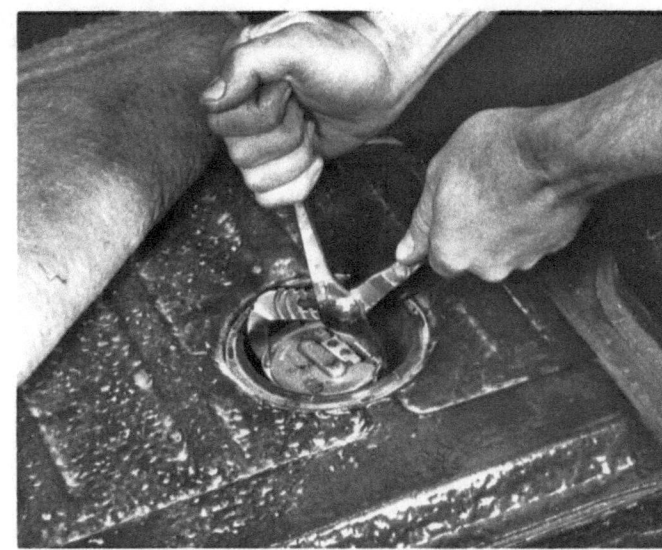

25.6 Using channel lock pliers to remove the fuel tank sending unit

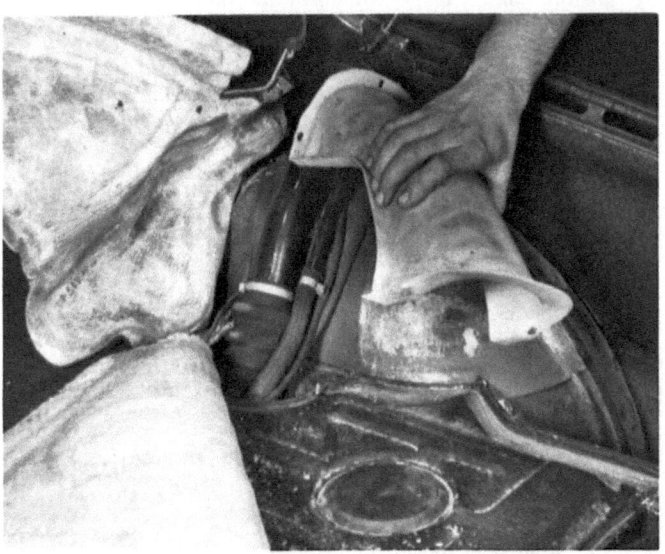

27.7 Removing the filler pipe cover

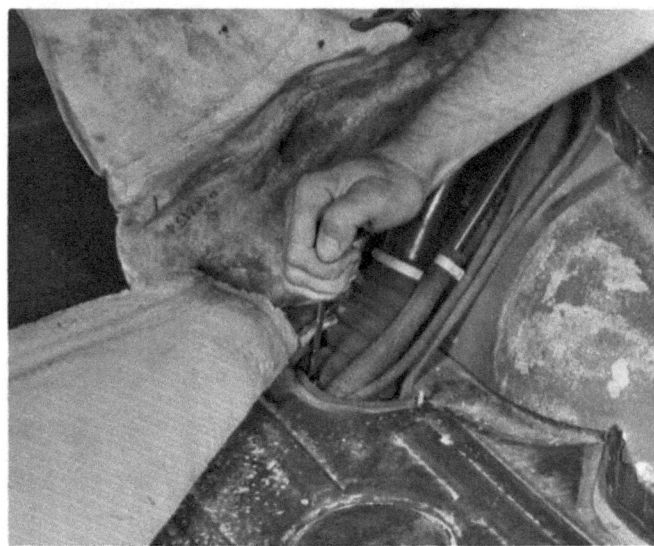

27.8 Loosening the vent hose clamps

29.1 Location of the fuel filter in standard models

29.5 The proper loosening and tightening technique for the fuel filter connections

6   Clamp the EEG lines to the air filter and charcoal canister.
7   If your car has a diverter valve detach the air hose at the diverter valve and plug the end.
8   Connect the tachometer according to the directions supplied with the unit.
9   Turn the bypass screw on the throttle housing until the specified rpm is reached. (Specifications)
10 Remove the plug in the mixture control unit between the fuel distributor and the air flow sensor venturi.
11 Insert adjusting wrench P 377 or an appropriately sized socket head screw key (photo).
12 Observe the following cautions:
   a) Make all CO adjustments from lean to rich. If the mixture is too rich, turn the adjusting screw counter-clockwise further than necessary, and then clockwise until the proper mixture is reached.
   b) Never press on the adjusting wrench when turning the adjusting screw. This will give incorrect readings on the test equipment or stall the engine.
   c) Turn the regulating screw in very small increments. A small turn on the idle regulating screw will change the CO readings significantly.
13 When the specified setting has been reached, remove the wrench and install the plug in the idle regulating screw adjustment hole. It is necessary to plug this hole to obtain proper results in the following steps.
14 Accelerate the engine briefly (approximately 3500 rpm for 15 to 20 seconds).
15 Wait until the CO tester reacts. The proper adjustment results are found in the Specifications section of this chapter.
16 Repeat the adjustment steps as necessary to reach the proper CO amounts.

31   Mixture control unit – removal and installation

1   Disconnect the negative lead from the battery.
2   Loosen the clamps on either end of the air hose which is directly above the air sensor unit venturi. Remove the air hose (photo).
3   Loosen and remove the banjo bolts on the fuel distributor and set them aside. Make careful notes on the location of each banjo fitting (photo).
4   Remove the control pressure line which enters at the center of the fuel distributor (photo).
5   Remove the fuel feed line and the fuel return line by loosening and removing the banjo bolts and banjo fittings on the sides of the fuel distributor (photo).
6   Catch the escaping fuel in a container and wipe up all spilled gasoline.
7   Detach the plug on the air flow sensor housing. Models from 1979 do not have this plug (photo).

8   Remove the six socket head screws and lift out the mixture control unit.
9   Installation is the reverse of the removal procedure with the following points which must be observed:
10 All banjo fittings must be rebuilt using new seals (soft metal washers).
11 The mating surface between the mixture control unit and the air flow sensor housing requires a new O-ring.
12 The joint between the air flow sensor housing and the air box requires a new gasket.
13 Torque the socket head screw to 7 ft-lb (1.0 m-kg).
14 Torque the banjo bolt on the fuel feed line to 7 ft-lb (1.0 m-kg).
15 Torque the banjo bolt on the fuel return line to 7 ft-lb (1.0 m-kg).
16 Torque the adapter for the control pressure line to 11 ft-lb (1.5 m-kg).
17 Torque the four banjo bolts on the fuel control to injector lines to 7 ft-lb (1.0 m-kg).
18 When replacing the air hose on top of the air sensor venturi, make sure the hose is firmly seated on the machined edge of the venturi all the way around. Air leaks will result in inaccurate readings at the sensor plate and an improper fuel mixture.

32   Mixture control unit – stripdown and rebuild

1   The mixture control unit consists of the fuel distributor and the air flow sensor unit.
2   Place the 'bend' of the operating lever in the protected jaws of a vise, with the venturi end of the air flow sensor housing at the top and facing you.
3   Remove the sensor plate and its mounting bolt (photos).
4   Open the jaws of the vise slightly and place the air flow sensor housing on top of the jaws with the operating lever hanging between the vise jaws.
5   Remove the three screws which hold the fuel distributor to the air flow sensor housing (photo).
6   Take the fuel distributor in your hand and invert the entire mixture control unit. Remove the fuel distributor by twisting gently to break the seal between it and the air flow sensor housing. These pieces must remain inverted until the two units are separated to prevent the control piston from falling out. If the control piston is dropped it must be replaced (photo).
7   Lift out the control piston and set aside.
8   Strip off the O-ring and dispose of it. It must be replaced with a new one (photo).
9   Remove the plug from the adjusting screw (idle screw) access hole in the air flow sensor housing.
10 With the air flow sensor housing placed on a bench, operating lever up and the venturi facing away from you, loosen the lock nut on the left-hand end of the stop bracket.

30.11 Installing the adjusting wrench in the air sensor unit   31.2 Removing the rubber air hoses from the mixture control unit

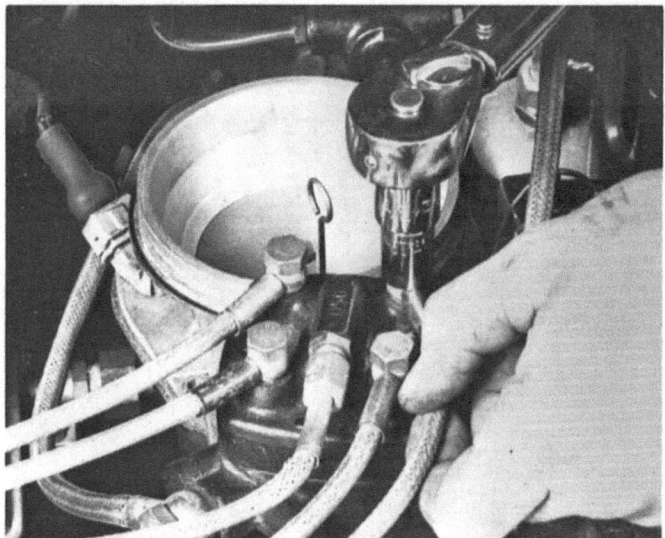

31.3 Removing the fuel injector banjo bolts

31.4 Removing the control pressure line

31.5 Removing the fuel feed and return lines

31.7 Unplugging the air flow sensor plug (1978 and earlier models)

32.3a Unbolting the sensor plate. Note the position of the air flow sensor housing in the vise

32.3b Removing the sensor plate

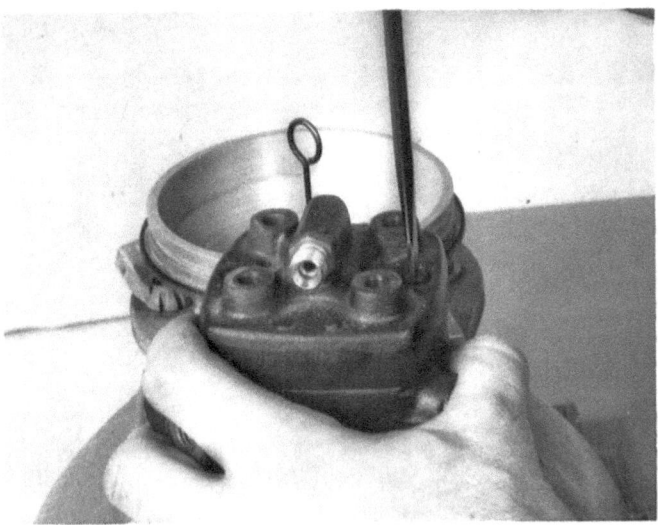

32.5 Unscrewing the fuel distributor bolts

32.6 Separating the fuel distributor and the air flow sensor unit

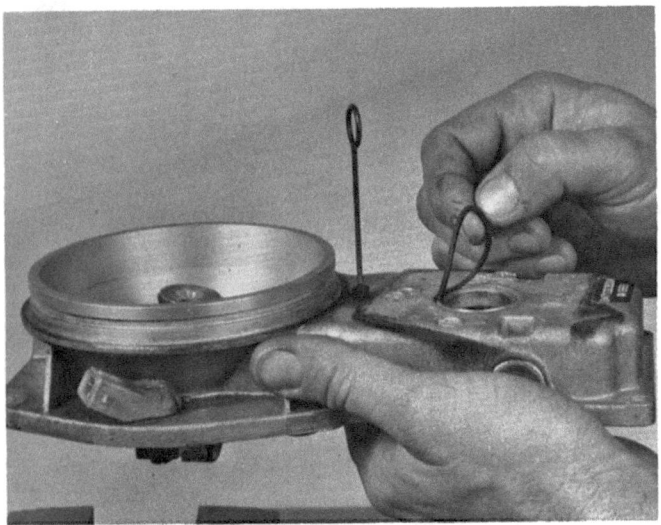

32.8 Removing the old O-ring from the air flow sensor unit

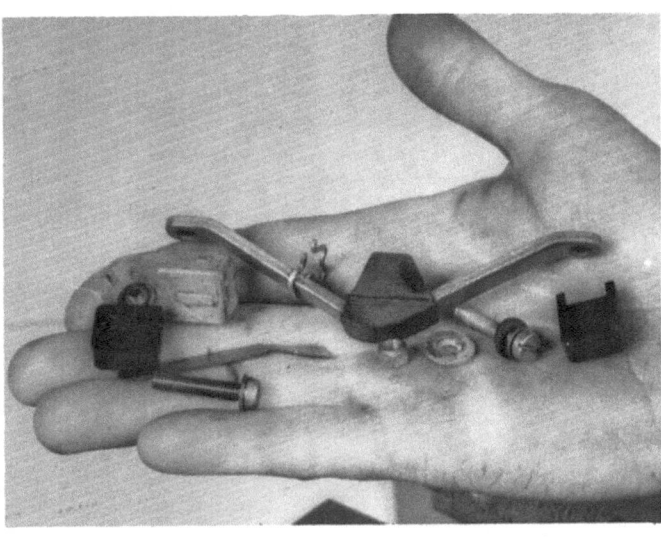

32.17 All parts of the stop bracket which must be removed

11 Remove the self-locking nut (replace this with a new self-locking nut when rebuilding) and plain washer.

12 From the bottom side of the air flow sensor housing (the side which is now facing you), remove the bolt, plain washer, insulator plate, and the insulator block. There is a protective sleeve which fits into the bore of the insulator block. This should be removed if it does not come out with either the insulator block or bolt.

13 Models prior to 1979 will have a plug connector on the right side bolt. Later models have simply a self-locking nut and plain washer.

14 If your air flow sensor housing has a plug connector, check to see whether the nut is separate or cast into the plug body.

15 Remove the nut and plain washer or nut and plain washer connector from the right-side bolt.

16 From the bottom, remove the bolt, plain washer, and sleeve.

17 Remove the stop bracket, leaf spring, and clip, then remove the insulator block (photo).

18 With the air flow sensor housing still laid on its top and the air flow sensor venturi faced away from you, remove the circlip from the round boss at the right side of the casting. Carefully extract the circlip as the plug it holds down is spring loaded (photo).

19 Remove the flat end plug, seal, and ball from the right side.

20 Remove the circlip from the left side boss and remove the flat end plug, seal, spring and ball.

21 Press the operating lever down at the venturi end to gain access to the screw on the end of the counterweight. Remove the screw

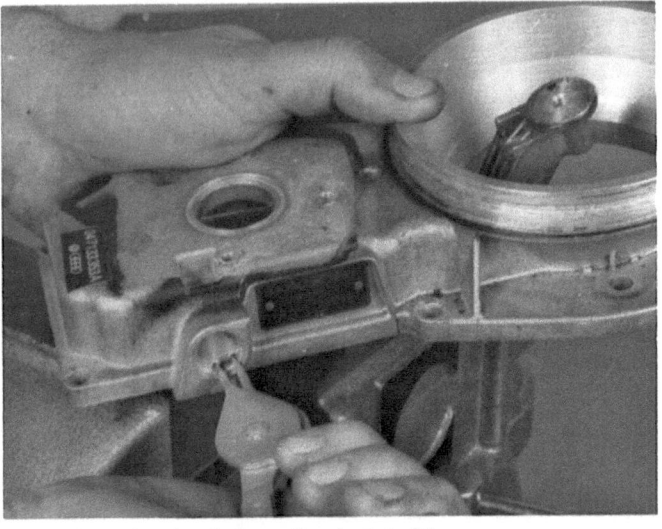

32.18 Removing the circlip on the pivot shaft boss

and counterweight, then gently press out the shaft which the operating lever rides on (photos).

22 If the operating lever pivot shaft cannot easily be pressed from the air flow sensor housing, turn the adjusting screw on the pivot lever two turns clockwise, then four turns counter-clockwise if the tension on the pivot is not eliminated by the latter action. Turning the pivot screw in this manner will determine which way relieves the tension on the pivot shaft.

23 Holding the operating lever with the threaded boss at the end away from you, turn the adjusting screw clockwise until the two levers can be separated (photos).

24 Inspect the pivot shaft for gouging and radial marking.

25 Inspect the air flow sensor housing venturi for roundness and make sure there are no nicks, gouges, or any other damage to the interior surface of the venturi.

26 Inspect the pivot arm for proper play in the needle bearing, the condition of the bearing needles, and the condition of the adjusting screws' socket and threads. Replace parts as necessary.

27 Inspect the air flow sensor plate for warpage and make sure that the central hole is round. Check carefully around the central bolt hole for evidence of overtightening (grooves around the central hole and 'wavy' appearance of the metal).

28 Assembly of the mixture control unit is the reverse of the strip-down with the following items to be observed:

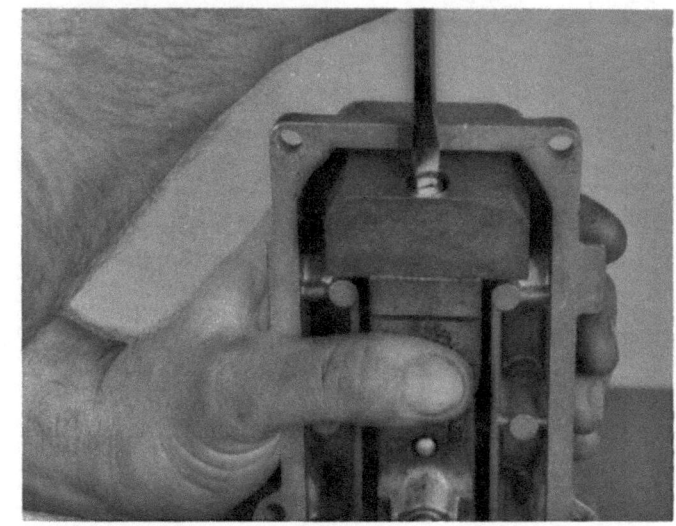

32.21a Removing the counterweight bolt from the operating lever

32.21b Removing the operating lever counterweight

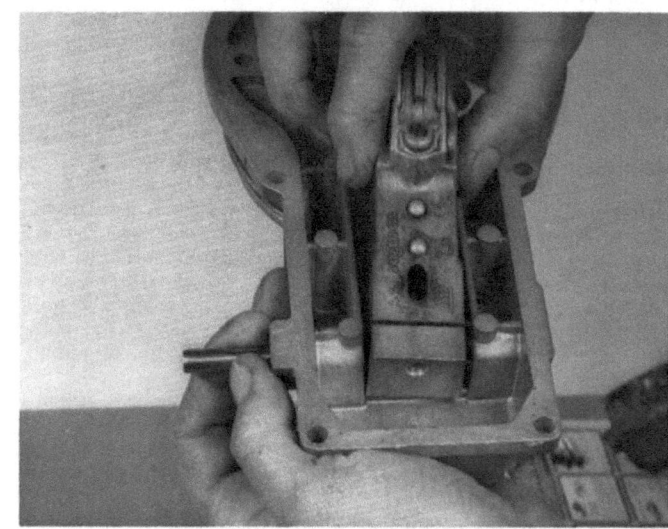

32.21c Removing the operating lever pivot shaft

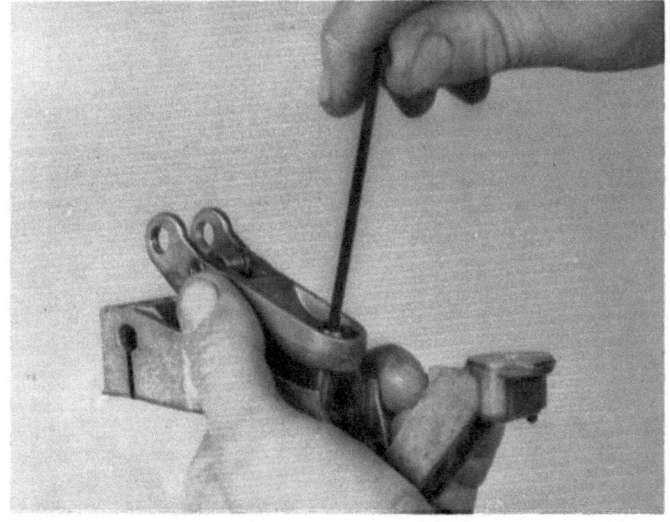

32.23a Loosening the adjusting screw

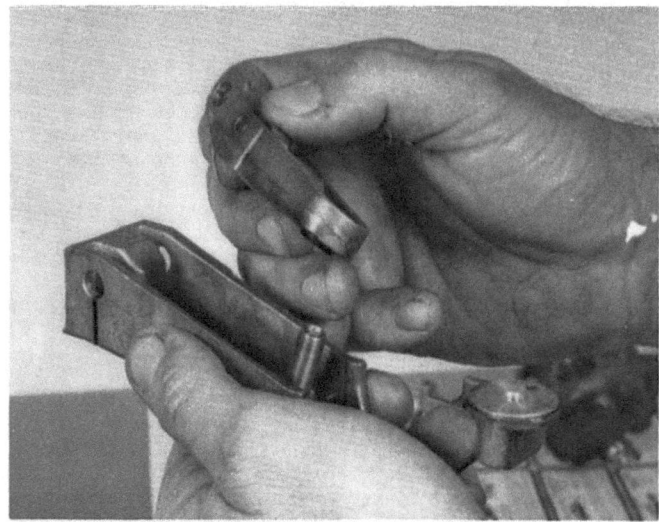

32.23b Separating the pivot lever from the operating lever

29 The circlips on the ends of the pivot arm must be installed with the sharp edged side facing outward. This is for both circlips, one on each side, ahead of the end plates (photo).

30 Torque the screw on the counterweight to 4 ft-lb (0.5 m-kg).

31 Torque the screws which hold the stop bracket to the air flow sensor housing to 4 ft-lb (0.5 m-kg).

32 When the air flow sensor plate is installed and located properly in the venturi of the air flow sensor housing, torque the center bolt to 4 ft-lb (0.5 m-kg) (photo).

33 The join between the fuel distributor and the air flow sensor housing requires a new O-ring seal. Do not reuse the old one.

34 The three screws holding the fuel distributor to the air flow sensor housing must be torqued to 3 ft-lb (0.35 m-kg).

35 Further reassembly instructions are found in the installation instructions of Section 31.

33 Fuel distributor - inspection and assembly

1 The following procedures can only be performed when the fuel distributor has been removed from the air flow sensor housing. Disconnecting all fuel lines and removing the fuel distributor from the vehicle is also necessary (Section 32).

2 Screw all banjo bolts into their proper holes and wipe down all surfaces of the fuel distributor. Make sure that the control piston has been removed and set aside. Do not drop the control piston; if it has been dropped, it must be replaced.

3 Remove all of the banjo bolts and clean them separately to further assure that no dirt enters the fuel distributor.

4 Remove the plug from the boss alongside the fuel return and remove the flat metal seal, two shims, and a spring.

5 Remove the control piston from this hole by tapping the open hole gently on the palm of your hand. If this fails to dislodge the piston, a tapered wooden dowel should be used to remove it. We found that a wooden chopstick from a Chinese restaurant worked quite well! The tapered dowel should be of a soft wood so it may be forced in for a snug fit without damaging the bore of the hole (photo).

6 Remove the O-ring from the end of the piston with a fingernail. Do not use any metal objects for this purpose.

7 Futher disassembly of the fuel distributor should not be attempted. Porsche dealers do not have any of the proper internal parts available to them, nor do they have the training or tools to assist you in work beyond this point. If, after disassembly, cleaning and testing, the fuel distributor is still found to be giving unacceptable performance, it must be replaced.

8 1976 to 1978 models of the 924 had fuel distributors of Bosch code number 0438 100 039. This has been superseded by Bosch code number 0438 100 005 as a replacement for the earlier model and is standard equipment on subsequent models. The later style fuel distributor is used in conjunction with the later style pressure accumulator. Updating the fuel distributor should be accompanied by an updating of the fuel pressure accumulator. Your spare parts outlets will be able to help you obtain the proper parts. Vehicles with Lambda systems do not have the above problem and all fuel system parts may be ordered from the 931-prefix parts book.

9 Inspect the bore of the fuel distributor which houses the pressure regulating piston for scoring and scratching.

10 Inspect the rubbing surfaces of the piston for signs of excessive wear, scratching, and scoring. Replace if necessary.

11 With fingernails only, install a new O-ring on the tapered part of the piston. Be careful not to damage the piston.

12 Install the spring on the piston, lubricate the O-ring with a light coating of gasoline and install the piston in the bore.

13 Place the two shims in the 'cup' of the plug. The order must be the thin (0.1 mm) shim first and the thick (0.5 mm) shim next. The thick shim must contact the spring.

14 Install a new metal seal on the plug. Do not reuse the old one.

15 Install the plug in the fuel distributor body and torque to 9 to 11 ft-lb (1.3 to 1.5 m-kg).

16 Check the pressure of the system when the fuel distributor is reinstalled. The pressure may be raised by adding shims behind the spring and thick shim.

32.29 Check the operating lever for centering in the air flow sensor unit

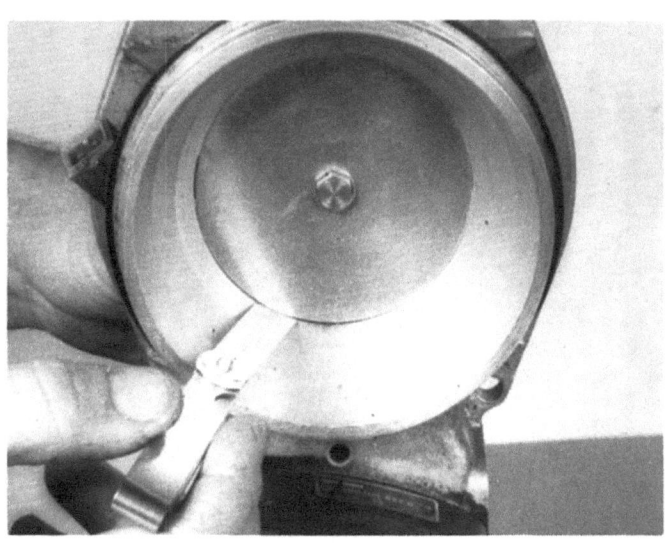

32.32 The proper method of checking the centering of the sensor plate

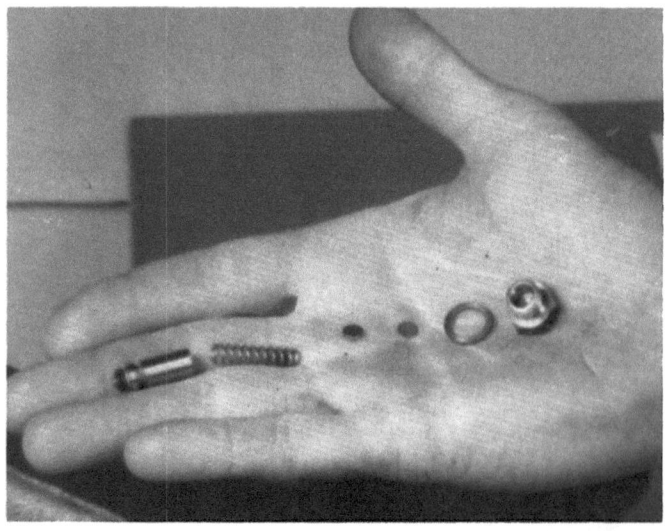

33.5 The parts which must be removed from the control piston hole

B: Fuel system – Lambda injection system

34 General description

1   As explained in the note attached to the Specifications Section, the Lambda injection system is basically the same as the K-Jetronic (CIS) system described above. The two are so alike that test procedures for the CIS units may be performed on the Lambda system, substituting the proper test values (photo).
2   While CIS injection relies on the EGR (exhaust gas recirculation) method of emission control, the Lambda system uses an oxygen sensor to regulate the amounts of fuel and air in the mixture entering the combustion chamber, giving cleaner burning and fewer unburned hydrocarbons.
3   The advantages of the oxygen sensor system are threefold:
   a) The EGR system lowers mileage figures and reduces the overall flexibility of the powerplant, the oxygen sensor system does not.
   b) The additional components required to make the EGR system operative add weight, additional production costs, and the probabilities of component failure.
   c)The air pump robs the vehicle of horsepower (because some power is diverted to driving the pump) and increases fuel consumption.
4   The oxygen sensor system consists of an oxygen sensor which measures the oxygen in the exhaust, an electronic control unit (located beneath the steering column), and a frequency valve which adjusts the air-to-fuel ratio. A pair of micro switches change the control unit signal at idle and provide full load enrichment at full throttle. A relay also provides full load enrichment whenever engine speeds exceeds 3500 ± 150 rpm (See Fig. 3.28).

35 Oxygen sensor – description, removal, installation

1   The oxygen sensor is attached to the exhaust pipe on a threaded flange extending out from the body of the pipe. It is covered by a rubber shield, and a wire projects through the top (photo).
2   The sensor body is made of a ceramic material (Zirconium dioxide) and the inner and outer surfaces are covered with a layer of platinum. The inner surface of this sealed tube (Fig. 3.29) is exposed to outside air, while the outer surface extends into the exhaust gases.

3   The difference in the oxygen amounts of the outside air and the oxygen content of the exhaust gases causes a small voltage signal to be produced. This signal is sent to the electronic control unit which regulates the amount of fuel supplied to the engine.
4   When the sensor detects a low amount of oxygen in the exhaust system a rich mixture is indicated and a high sensor voltage (about 900 mv) will be sent to the electronic control unit. The amount of fuel supplied to the engine will be reduced.
5   Fuel reductions go on until the amount of oxygen in the exhaust system rises, indicating a leaner mixture. The oxygen sensor will begin to send a low voltage signal (about 100 mv) to the electronic control box. The control box will increase the quantity of fuel until the sensor voltage increases and the cycle begins again.
6   An illustration of this continuous cycle appears in Fig. 3.31. This cycle of lean and rich fuel-to-air ratio goes on whenever the engine is running. Lean and rich must also be relative terms. The fluctuations which occur are too small to be noticed in any testing by the home mechanic.
7   To remove or install the oxygen sensor unit, do the following:
8   Raise the vehicle and place it on jack stands.
9   Remove the rubber cap on the plug terminal for the oxygen sensor and unplug.
10 Pull the metal safety shield from the sensor body.
11 Unscrew the oxygen sensor, taking extreme care not to damage the ceramic body.
12 Installation of the sensor is the reverse of removal. The threads of the sensor body should be coated with an anti-seize paste (be careful not to get any on any other place but the threads) and the unit must then be torqued to 35 to 45 ft-lb (5 to 6 m-kg).

36 Oxygen sensor mileage counter – resetting

1   The oxygen sensor must be replaced every 30,000 miles (48,000 km). To remind you of this, Porsche has installed a mileage counter on the left front wheel housing which will activate a light in the instrument cluster when this mileage has been reached. As soon as a new oxygen sensor is installed the special mileage counter may be reset.
2   To reset the counter, raise the vehicle and place it on jack stands.
3   Remove the engine guard.
4   Locate the mileage counter and press in the reset button with a screwdriver.
5   Switch on your ignition to make sure the red light has gone out.
6   Replace the engine guard.
7   Lower the car.

34.1 Note the similarities between the Lambda system components and the CIS components (Fig. 3.1). The chief distinguishing characteristic between the two systems is the bright metal color of the Lambda system's fuel distributor

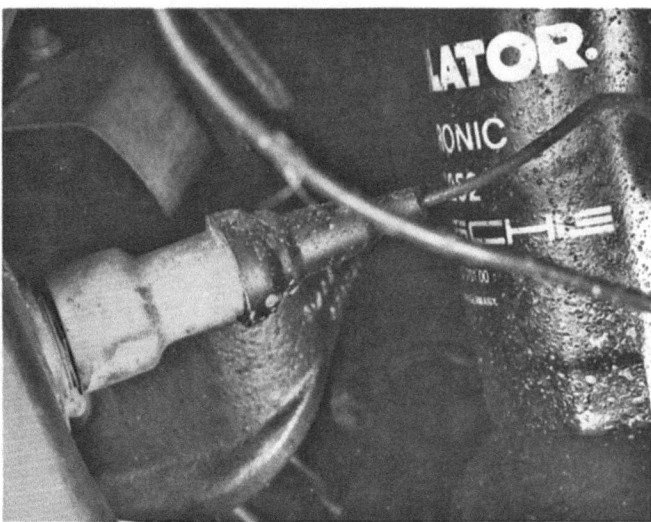

35.1 The oxygen sensor installed in the exhaust pipe of a Turbo model

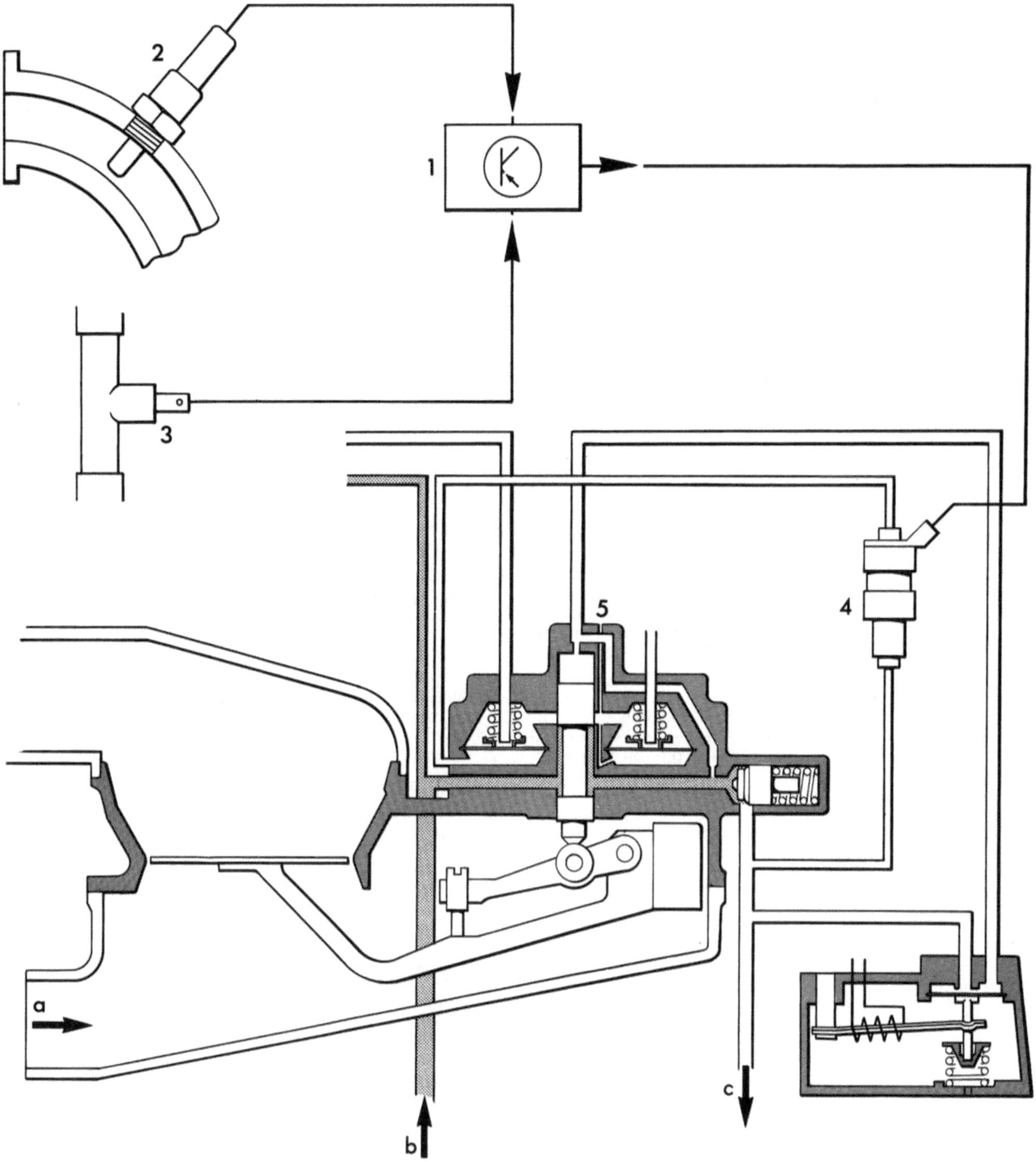

Fig. 3.28 Oxygen Sensor (OS) System

1	Electronic control unit	3	Thermoswitch	a	Route of intake air
2	Oxygen sensor (mounted in exhaust pipe)	4	Frequency valve	b	Fuel supply line
		5	Fuel distributor (lower chamber)	c	Fuel return line

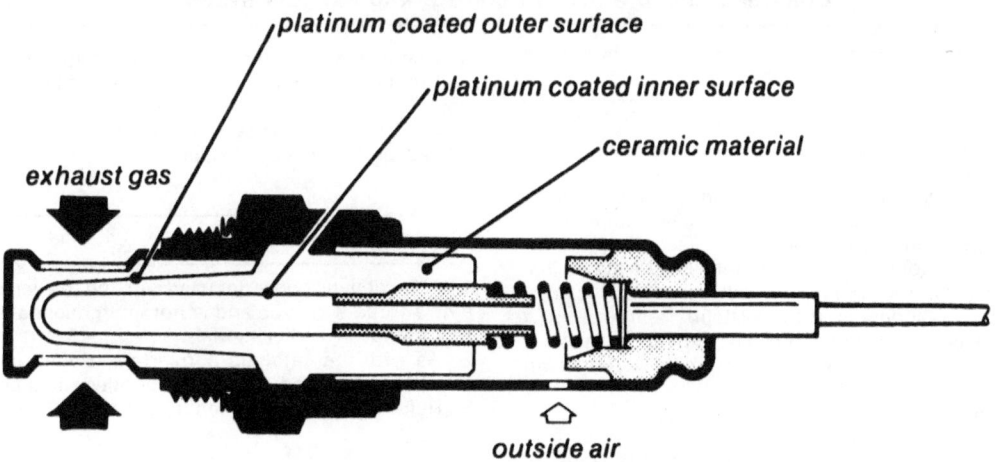

platinum coated outer surface

platinum coated inner surface

ceramic material

exhaust gas

outside air

Fig. 3.29 A cutaway view of the oxygen sensor

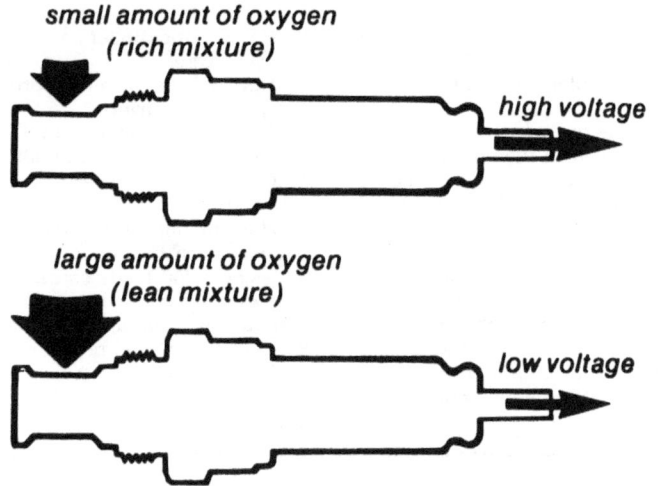

small amount of oxygen
(rich mixture)

high voltage

large amount of oxygen
(lean mixture)

low voltage

Fig. 3.30 An explanation of the oxygen sensor's workings

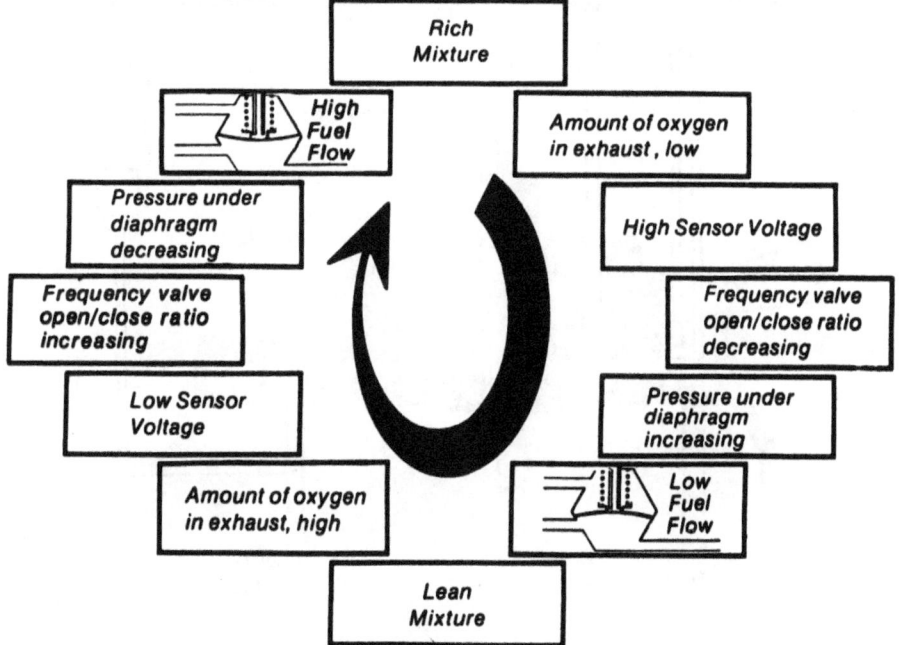

Rich Mixture

High Fuel Flow

Amount of oxygen in exhaust, low

Pressure under diaphragm decreasing

High Sensor Voltage

Frequency valve open/close ratio increasing

Frequency valve open/close ratio decreasing

Low Sensor Voltage

Pressure under diaphragm increasing

Amount of oxygen in exhaust, high

Low Fuel Flow

Lean Mixture

Fig. 3.31 The closed loop cycle controlled by the oxygen sensor and the computerized control unit

37 Oxygen sensor control unit – replacing

1   The oxygen sensor control unit is located beneath the steering column just behind the dashboard facia. Its functions have already been outlined in Section 35.
2   The procedures for testing of this unit may only be done with the specialized test computers found in Porsche-VW dealerships. Tests with the types of meters found in the home mechanic's shop may be used to eliminate other sources of failure, but Porsche states that inadvertant connection of the wrong leads will lead to serious damage to the electrical components in the system.
3   The control unit is not repairable, it may only be replaced.
4   To replace the control unit, loosen the three screws on the control unit.
5   Remove the plugs.
6   Remove the screws and the control unit.
7   Installation of the new unit is the reverse of the removal procedure.

38 Frequency valve – description

1   The frequency valve is located on an injection system branch line connecting the fuel return line to the inlet side of the fuel distributor unit. (See Fig. 3.32).
2   When a rich condition is sensed by the oxygen sensor, the control unit closes the frequency valve. This causes the pressure in the fuel distributor to increase in the lower chamber. The increased pressure forces the steel diaphragm upward, reducing the amount of fuel in the top chamber, reducing, in turn the amount of fuel being pumped to the injectors. (See Fig. 3.33).
3   A reading of lean by the oxygen sensor leads to opening of the frequency valve by the control unit. This allows fuel to be siphoned from the intake side of the lower fuel distributor chambers and dumped into the fuel return line. The resulting drop in pressure on the lower chamber causes the diaphragm to drop, increasing the amount of fuel in the upper chamber. Consequently, more fuel is pumped to the injectors. (See Fig. 3.34).

4   Removal and replacement of the frequency valve requires several special tools and special training available to the mechanics at your Porsche dealer. This is one job that, due to the highly specialized nature of the parts and tools, and the infrequency of failure, should be left to your dealer.

39 Catalytic converter

1   The catalytic converter used with the oxygen sensor system is of a new three-way type and is not interchangeable with the converters found on earlier models.
2   As with the catalytic converters of earlier systems, this unit should be replaced every 30,000 miles (48,000 km).
3   Removal and replacement directions will be found in Section 62.

40 Idle adjustment

1   Proper adjustment of this system requires that you have access to a CO tester and a separate tachometer.
2   Remove the rubber cap from the oxygen sensor and disconnect the plug wire.
3   Hook up the exhaust probe line at the test connection ahead of the catalytic converter.
4   Start the engine and run it up to operating temperature. The oil temperature should be about 80°C (176°F).
5   Connect the CO tester according to the instructions supplied with the unit.
6   Hook up the hand-held tachometer according to the instructions supplied with the unit.
7   Using a flat blade screwdriver, turn the control screw (bypass screw) on the throttle housing until the proper idle speed is reached. For this unit the speed is 900 ± 50 rpm.
8   Remove the plug between the fuel distributor and the air sensor venturi housing.
9   Install a Special Tool P 377 or the proper size socket head screw key (photo 30.11).

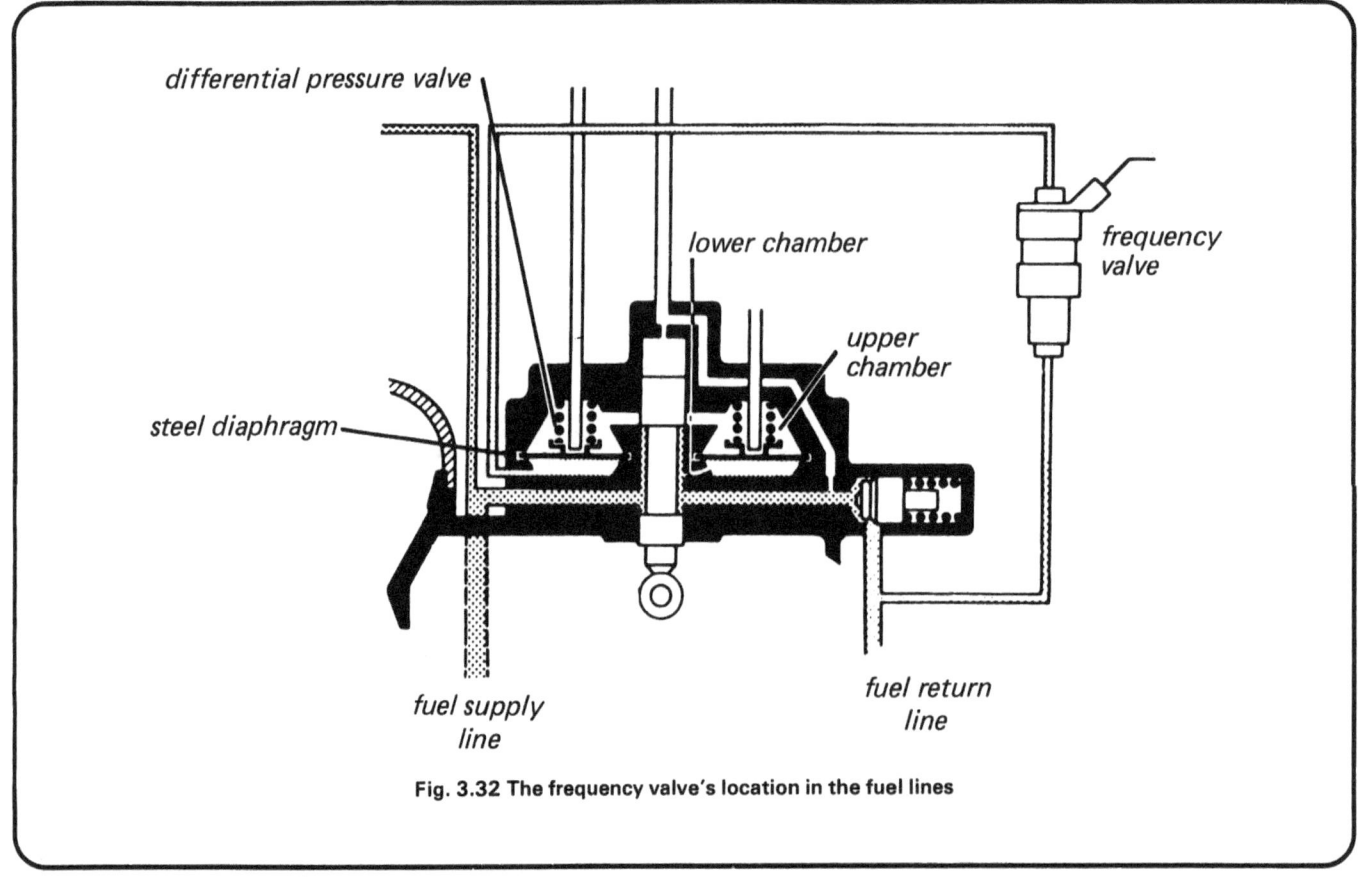

Fig. 3.32 The frequency valve's location in the fuel lines

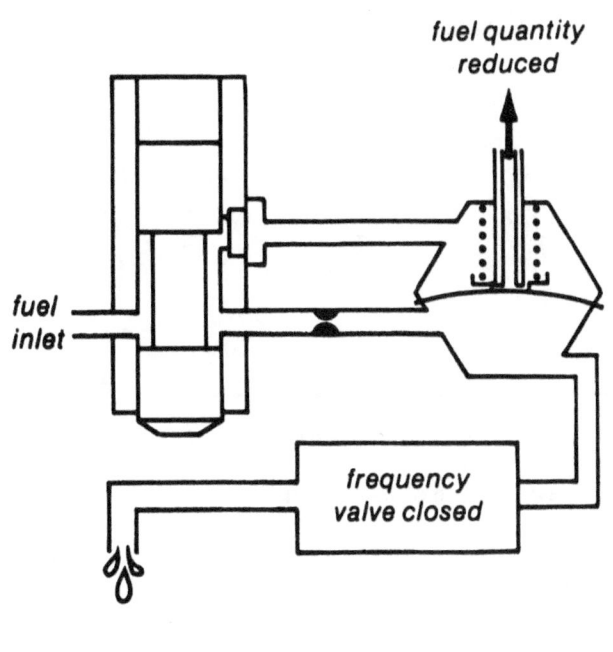

Fig. 3.33 Fuel control with the frequency valve closed (leaning the mixture)

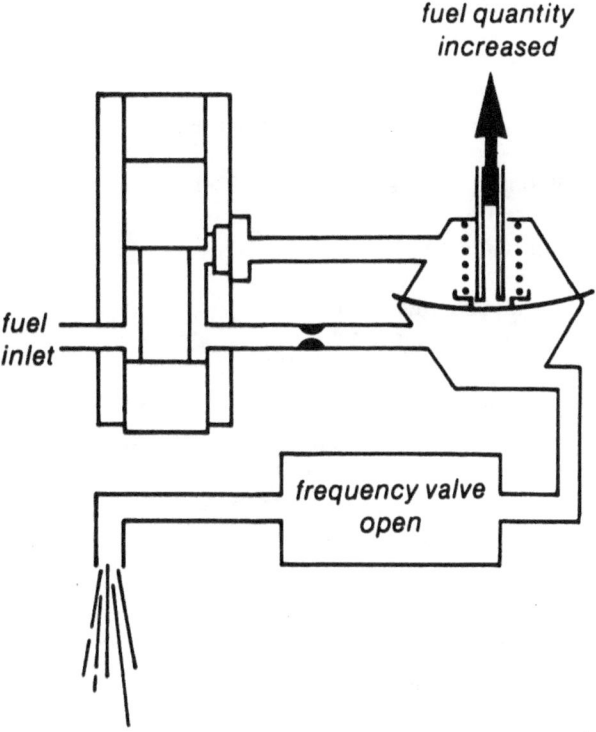

Fig. 3.34 Fuel control with the frequency valve open (richening the mixture)

10 Observe the following points when adjusting the system:

a) Adjust the CO level from lean to rich. If the level is too rich, turn the idle control screw counter-clockwise further than necessary to over-lean the mixture, then rotate the screw clockwise until the proper levels are reached.

b) Never press down on the adjusting wrench when making changes to the level of the idle screw. This will result in inaccurate readings and may stall the engine.

c) Turn the idle screw in small increments. Small changes in the idle screw height will make large changes in the CO readings.

d) Work as quickly and as accurately as possible. Slow work will allow the intake ports to heat excessively.

11 Turning the idle screw clockwise richens the mixture, counterclockwise provides a leaner mixture.

12 Remove the idle screw adjusting wrench.

13 Replace the plug over the idle screw. Failure to do this will give false CO level readings in the following steps.

14 Accelerate the engine for a brief period (about 3500 rpm for 15 to 20 seconds should be more than sufficient).

15 Wait until the CO tester shows the CO concentrations at idle speed (radiator fan should switch off). Check the CO levels (values given in Specifications) and repeat the adjusting procedures as necessary.

16 Connect the plug wire to the oxygen sensor and install the rubber cap.

17 Switch off the engine.

18 Disconnect the CO exhaust probe and reinstall the plug.

C: Emission controls and exhaust system

41 Emission controls and exhaust system - overview

1 Porsche 924 models constructed for the US, Californian, Canadian, and Japanese markets are different in several distinct ways from the models destined for the European markets. Federal and state mandates on pollution control have meant that the 924s destined for these markets must be specially equipped for cleaner burning engines and fewer exhaust emissions.

2 The emission control system can be divided into several distinct parts:

Evaporative Emission Control (EEC), which prevents evaporated fuel and fuel vapors from entering the atmosphere.

Exhaust Gas Recirculation (EGR), which limits the level of potentially hazardous pollutants exhausted into the atmosphere.

Air Injection (AI), which further reduces the amounts of unburned fuel in the exhaust gases.

Catalytic Converter (CAT), which helps to further reduce the amounts of pollutants exhausted into the atmosphere.

Oxygen Sensor System (OS), which was introduced in the Turbo and all 1980 models as a replacement to the EGR and AI systems above. This system has helped to increase gas mileage, reduce pollutants and reduced the number of moving parts which robbed the engines of horsepower and smooth running.

3 The three pollutants which must be controlled by law are CO (carbon monoxide), hydrocarbons, and nitrogen oxides (NOx). The various systems listed above have specific impacts on the elimination of specific pollutants. This can best be seen in the chart, Fig. 3.35.

4 To meet the emission levels set by separate state and federal agencies, several of the methods listed above must be used in different combinations to meet the standards of different segments of the markets. Fig. 3.36 lists the various markets in which emission controls were used and lists by year and area which devices were originally installed in vehicles for each market.

42 Evaporative Emission Control (EEC) - overview

1 The EEC system prevents the evaporated fumes from the fuel and crankcase from entering the atmosphere. Its function is to trap fuel vapors from the fuel system and the crankcase and return them to the induction system to be burned.

2 Evaporative emissions are high in unburned hydrocarbon content and a properly working EEC system prevents these.

3 The EEC system consists of a fuel tank shaped to allow fuel expansion without allowing fuel vapors to escape into the air; a charcoal canister to trap evaporated fuel from the engine and crankcase when the vehicle is at rest; and a control valve which

SYSTEM	POLLUTANT		
	Hydro-carbons	CO	NOx
Evaporative Emission Control (EEC)	X	—	—
Exhaust Gas Recirculation (EGR)	—	X	X
Air Injection (AI)	X	—	—
Catalytic converter (CAT)	—	X	X
Oxygen sensor system (OS)*	X	X	X

Although the OS system controls all pollutants, a catalytic converter is necessary to bring pollutant levels within the California regulations for emission control

Fig. 3.35 The various emission control systems and the pollutants they control

All 924 models 1976 – 1979 inclusive	49 US states	California
Exhaust gas recirculation	X	X
Catalytic converter	X	X
Air injection	—	X
Deceleration valve*	X	X

Manual transmission vehicles, only.
All models from 1980 – on use the Oxygen Sensor System on all models and for all markets where emission controls are necessary

Fig. 3.36 The emission control systems and the markets for which they are installed

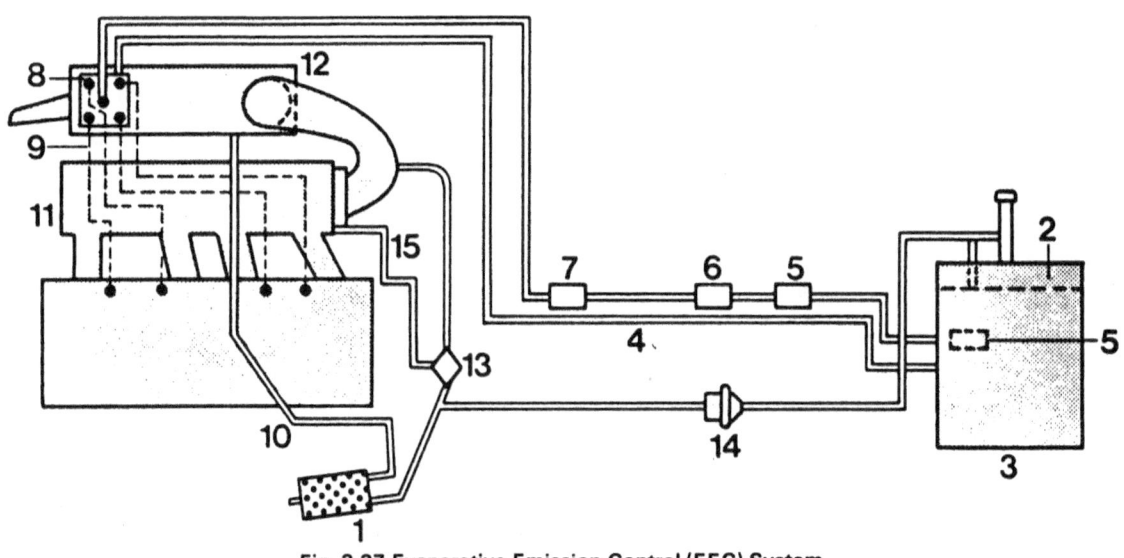

Fig. 3.37 Evaporative Emission Control (EEC) System

1	Charcoal canister	5	Fuel pump	11	Intake manifold
2	Expansion chamber		(two pumps on 1980 – on	12	Air cleaner
3	Fuel tank		models)	13	Control valve
4	Fuel return line	6	Accumulator	14	Safety valve
		7	Fuel filter	15	Vacuum control line
		8	Fuel distributor		
		9	Fuel injection lines		
		10	Vent line		

directs the flow of fumes.

4   As fumes are created by heat and evaporation they are ducted into the charcoal filter where they are trapped by the activated charcoal in the canister. When the vehicle is at rest, idle, or full throttle, the control valve directs the flow of fumes into the charcoal filter to be stored.

5   When the engine is at partial throttle, the control valve changes the flow of the fumes into the throttle housing so that the fumes may be burned. The opening of the control valve into this circuit causes fresh air to be drawn through the charcoal filter and mixed with the trapped fumes. In this way the proper air/fuel ratio is assured and the filter is a self-cleaning unit.

43   Charcoal canister – removal and installation

1   The charcoal canister is located inside the left front wheel well on most 924 models; however, some early California market versions have a smaller canister located in the 'tray' just behind the firewall and ahead of the windshield wiper motor on the left side of the vehicle. Check the wheel well location first.

2   Remove the two bolts holding the canister to its mounts and lift the canister outward.

3   Loosen the three clamps on the incoming hoses and remove them.

4   Installation is the reverse of the removal procedure.

5   See Fig. 3.38 for the order of installation of the three hoses. The numbered connections are hooked up as follows:

   Hose 1: (front connection) fresh air line
   Hose 2: (center connection) line from fuel tank
   Hose 3: (rear connection) to tee fitting on PCV/air cleaner line

44   Control valve – removal and installation

1   The control valve may not be installed on many early models. All 1980 and Turbo models definitely have these valves, but Porsche is unable to verify the earliest date of installation.

2   Loosen the three clamps which hold the hoses to the control valve. (See Fig. 3.39.)

3   Pull the hoses loose and remove the control valve.

4   Installation is the reverse of the removal procedure. Make sure the control valve is installed in the proper direction.

45   Air Injection – overview

1   The air injection (AI) system reduces the levels of unburned hydrocarbons and dilutes the exhaust gases, reducing the percentages of the other pollutants in the exhaust.

2   By injecting a flow of air into the exhaust gases leaving the exhaust ports, hot gases are reburned, using up the remainder of the unburned hydrocarbons in the exhaust gas mixture (Fig. 3.40).

3   The Porsche 924 air pump is bolted to an adjustable bracket mounted on the right front corner of the engine block. It is operated by a V-belt which is driven by a pulley on the oil pump. The V-belt is kept under proper tension by moving the air pump in its slotted mount.

46   Air pump – drive belt adjustment and replacement

1   The air pump is driven by a cord reinforced V-belt which drives off a pulley on the oil pump.

2   The V-belt should have a flex in the center of about 0.20 to 0.32 in. (5 to 8 mm) when pressed with the thumb. If the flex is more or less than the above figures, the V-belt must be adjusted.

3   Loosen the nut on the bolt holding the slotted side of the mounting bracket.

4   Loosen slightly the nut on the pivot side of the bracket and lever the air pump body carefully with a long screwdriver or tire iron.

5   Place tension on the belt until the proper flex is present when the V-belt is pressed with the thumb.

6   Tighten the pivot bolt and recheck the tension, then tighten the

Fig. 3.38 Location of the charcoal canister and its hoses

Fig. 3.39 The EEC control valve

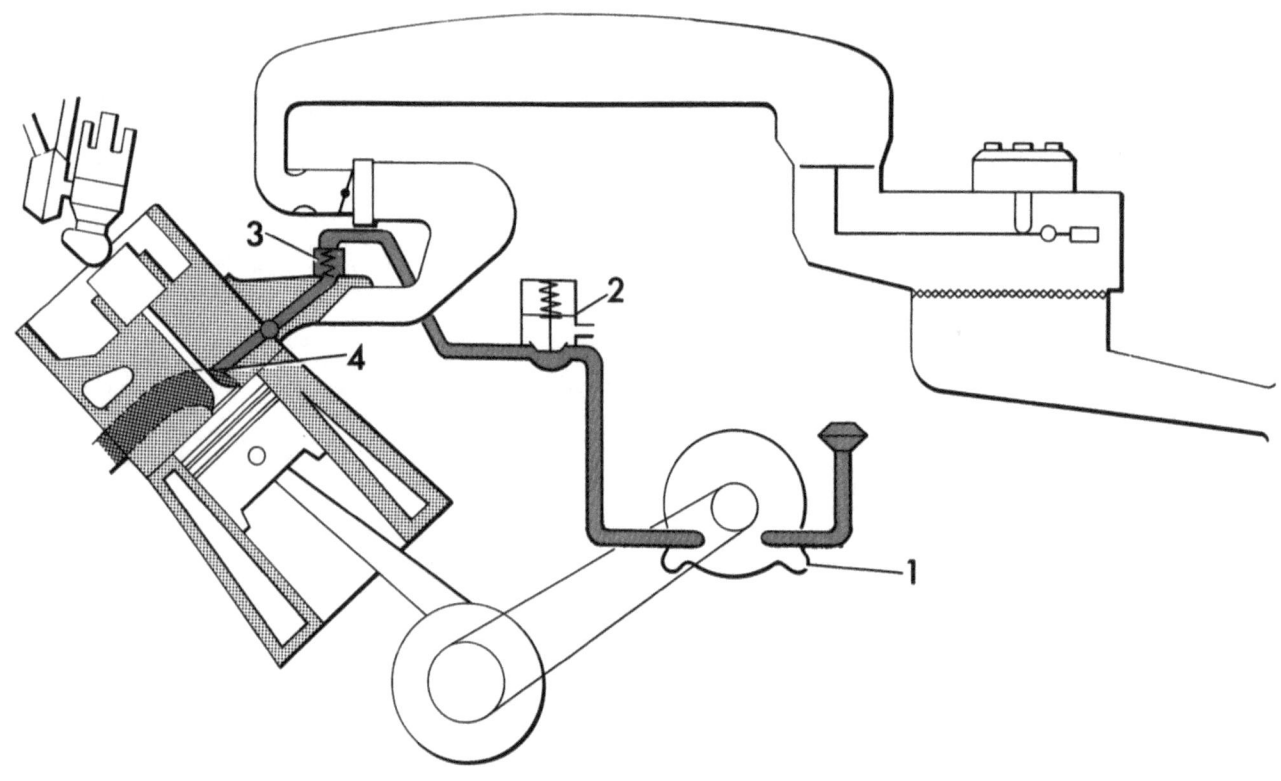

Fig. 3.40 Air injection (AI) System

1   *Air pump*   2   *Diverter valve*   3   *Check valve*   4   *Exhaust port*

bolt on the slotted side and check the belt tension once again.
7   The V-belt is replaced by sliding the slotted end of the bracket down to the right until all tension is relieved then removing the worn belt and slipping the new one on to the same two pulleys. Adjust the tension on the new belt as above.

47 Air pump – air filter removal and installation

1   The air pump filter does not have a disposable element. Whenever the filter requires replacement, the entire canister and filter must be replaced as a unit.
2   Loosen the clamp and pull the air filter canister from the hose.
3   Install the new air filter on the hose and tighten the clamp. Be careful when setting the new air filter into its proper location and make sure that it is not in contact with any of the surrounding parts. The air filter canister is constructed of steel and will wear away any of the things around it, which are made of softer materials.

48 Air pump – removal and installation

1   Loosen the clamps on the air pump ends of the pressure and suction hoses and pull the hoses free.
2   Loosen the air pump bracket mounting bolts and swing the air pump to the right, slackening the tension on the V-belt.
3   Remove the V-belt.
4   Remove the nuts from the two holding bolts and slip out the bolts.
5   Lift the air pump out of the engine compartment.
6   Installation is the reverse of the removal procedure.
7   The bolts which hold the air pump bracket to the engine block are torqued to 33 ft-lb (4.5 m-kg). All other bolts should be carefully tightened; no torque figures are given.

49 Check valve – removal and installation

1   Remove the molded rubber airflow housing from the throttle housing.
2   Loosen the clamp and pull off the hose.
3   Remove the check valve from the casting with an open end wrench of the proper size.
4   If the gasket between the check valve and casting does not pull out with the check valve, remove it. Dispose of this gasket and use a new one when installing the check valve.
5   Installation is the reverse of the removal procedure.
6   Make sure that a new gasket is used between the check valve and casting.
7   There is no torque setting for the check valve. Do not over-tighten, rather tighten it only until snug. Forcing the housing with 'muscle power' will cause a warpage along the seal surface and air leakage will result.

50 Exhaust Gas Recirculation (EGR) system – overview

1   The EGR system reduces the levels of NOx in the exhaust gases by injecting inert gas into the combustion chamber. The inert gas used is the already-burned gas taken from the exhaust side of the engine, which is injected in small amounts into the intake side, mixing it with the air/fuel mixture about to be burned.
2   NOx is produced by hot, rapid combustion. Addition of the inert exhaust gas slows the combustion process and allows a more complete burning of the air/fuel mixture.
3   Figs. 3.41 through 3.43 show the various configurations of the EGR systems used throughout Porsche 924 production and give the direction of flow in each of the systems. When troubleshooting the EGR system, check each part of the system in the order in which they appear on the appropriate chart. This will guarantee that each

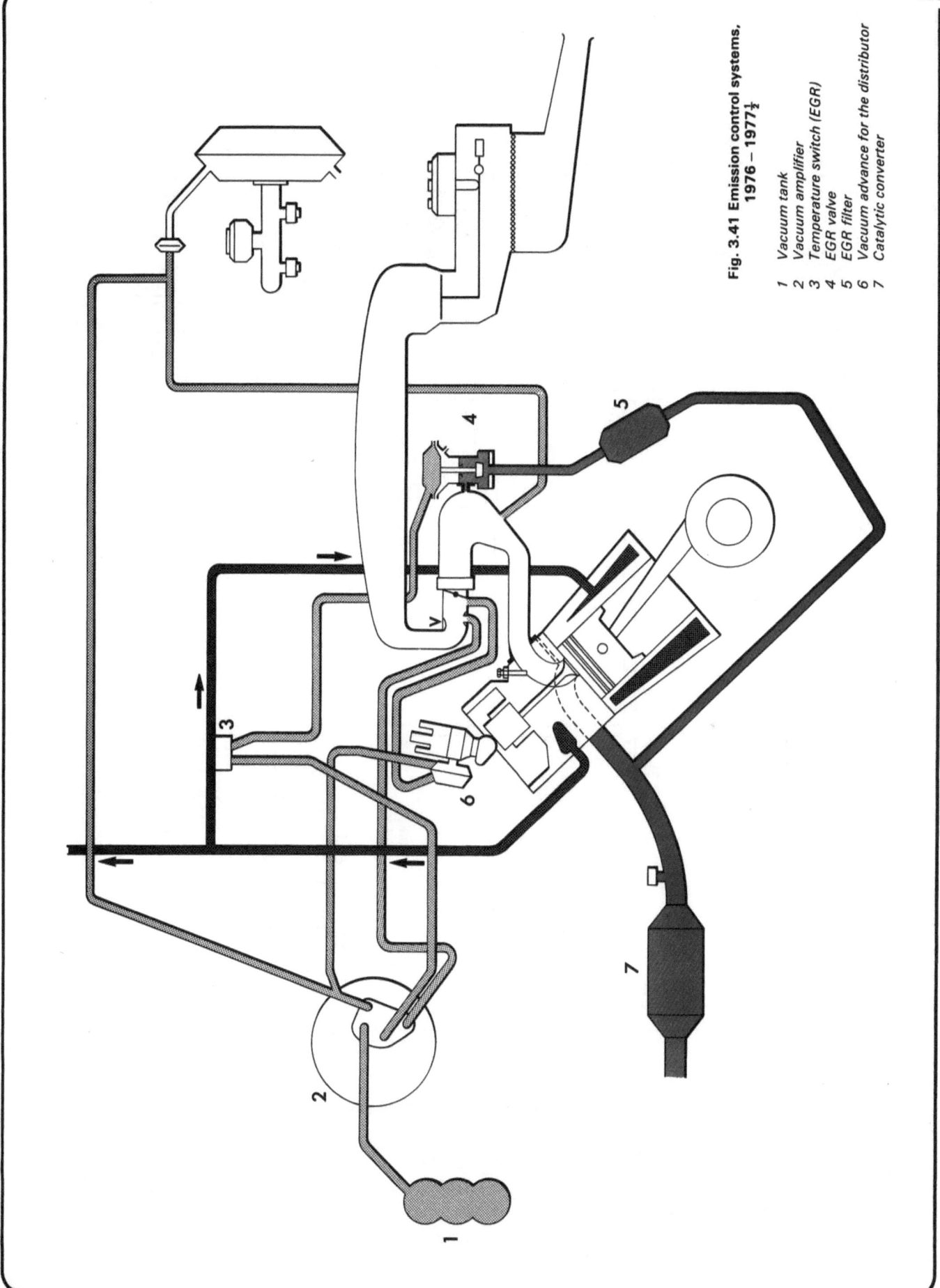

**Fig. 3.41 Emission control systems,
1976 – 1977½**

1 Vacuum tank
2 Vacuum amplifier
3 Temperature switch (EGR)
4 EGR valve
5 EGR filter
6 Vacuum advance for the distributor
7 Catalytic converter

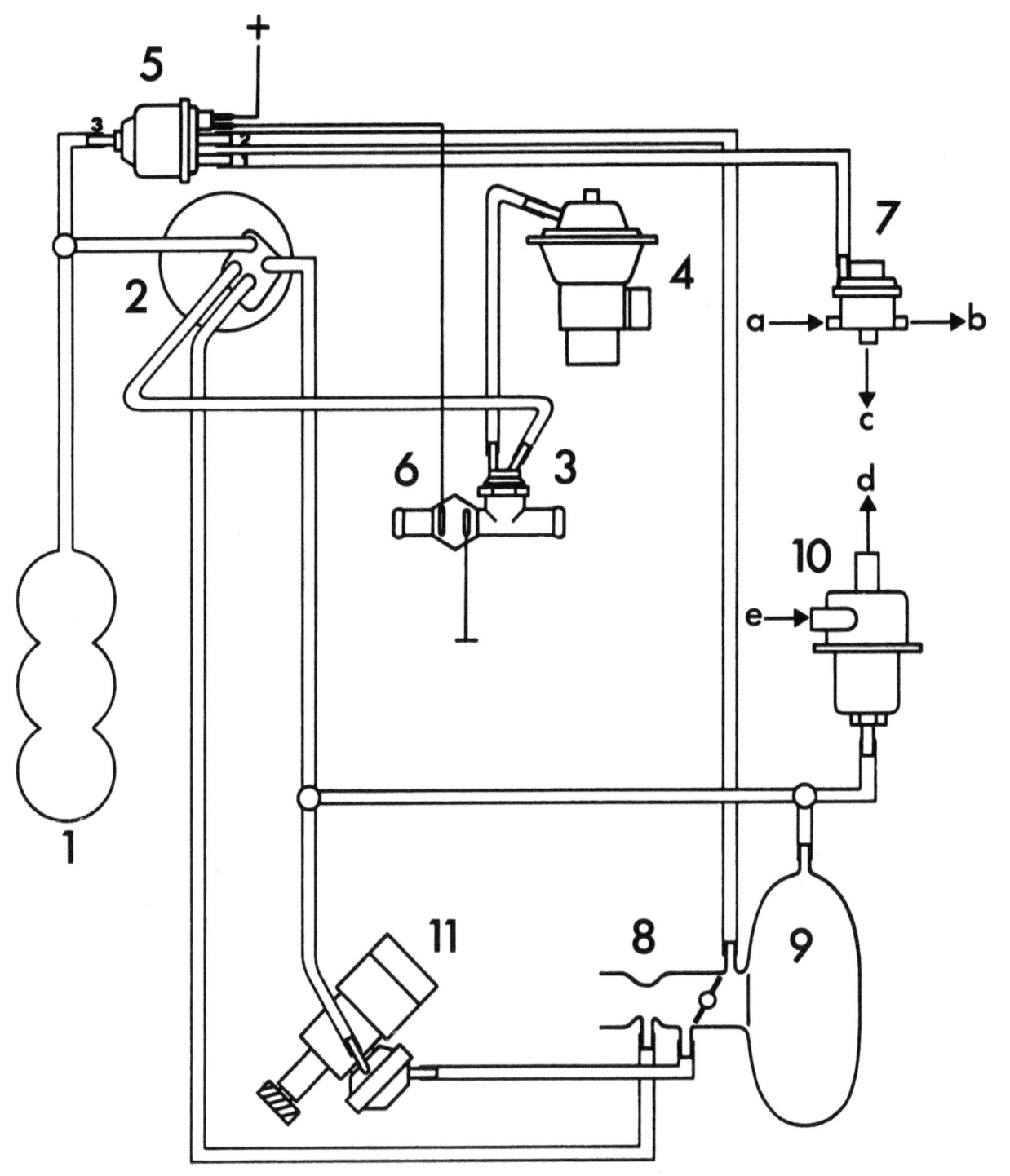

Fig. 3.42 Exhaust Gas Recirculation (EGR) System, 1977½

1	Vacuum tank	
2	Vacuum amplifier	
3	Temperature valve for EGR	
4	EGR valve	
5	Two-way valve for AI system (California only)	
6	Temperature switch	
7	Diverter valve (California only)	
8	Throttle valve housing	
9	Intake manifold	
10	Deceleration valve (all manual transmission models)	
11	Ignition distributor	

Connections

a	From the air pump
b	To the air cleaner housing
c	To the check valve
d	To the intake manifold
e	From the air intake duct

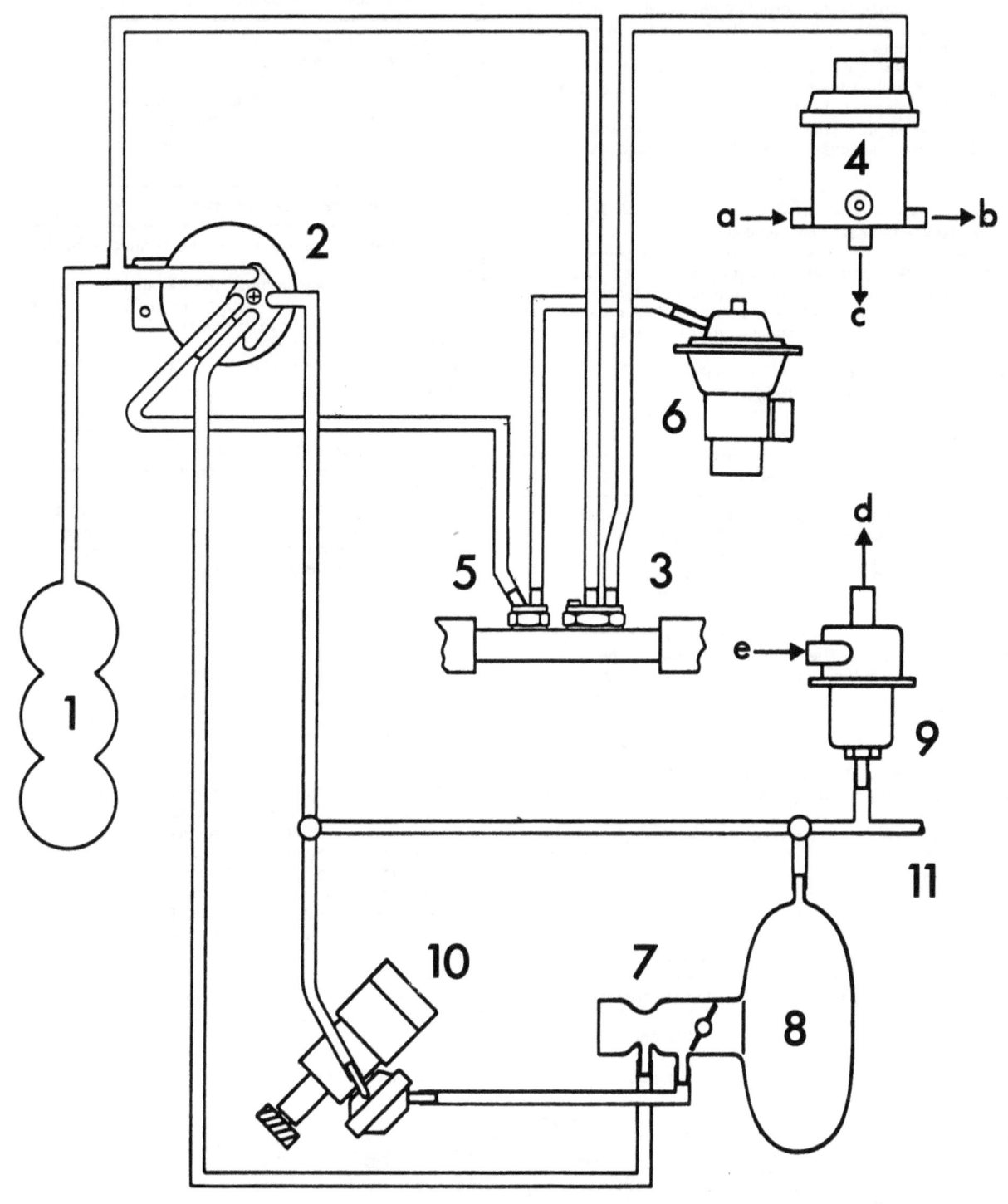

Fig. 3.43 Exhaust Gas Recirculation (EGR) System, 1978 – 1979

1	Vacuum tank	
2	Vacuum amplifier	
3	Temperature valve for AI system (California only)	
4	Diverter valve (California only)	
5	Temperature valve for EGR system	
6	EGR valve	
7	Throttle valve housing	
8	Intake manifold	
9	Deceleration valve (all manual transmission models)	
10	Ignition distributor	
11	Brake booster connection	

Connections

a   From the air pump
b   To the air cleaner housing
c   To the check valve
d   To the intake manifold
e   From the air intake duct

part of the system before the one you are checking is in working order and that the cause of your problem lies 'downstream' in the flow. This will also save time and money, as parts will not be replaced indiscriminately.
4   Instructions for the removal and installation of individual parts of the EGR system follow the flow charts and are arranged in the order in which they appear in the charts.
5   Always refer to the flow chart appropriate to the year of manufacture and the original market in which your vehicle was sold.

51   Vacuum tank – removal and installation

1   The vacuum tank is located in the right front wheel housing.
2   Pull the vacuum line from the top of the vacuum tank after you have carefully removed any dirt from the outside of the connection.
3   Remove the two nuts holding the vacuum tank to its mounting bracket and remove the tank.
4   Installation is the reverse of the removal process.
5   Torque the nuts to 7 ft-lb (1 m-kg).

52   Vacuum amplifier – removal and installation

1   Detach the four vacuum lines from the vacuum amplifier.
2   Loosen and remove the two bolts attaching the vacuum amplifier to its mounting bracket and remove it.
3   Installation is the reverse of the removal procedure.
4   Torque the two mounting bolts to 7 ft-lb (1 m-kg).
5   The proper installation of the vacuum hoses is as follows:
6   Think of the four connectors on the vacuum amplifier as positions on the face of a clock. The following locations will be given as you see them standing at the vacuum amplifier from the front of the vehicle and looking toward the rear of the car (photo).
7   Three o'clock position: vacuum supply (this hose runs to the connecting hose between the intake neck and the brake booster).
8   Six o'clock position: to the throttle housing (connect it to the left connection as seen when facing the rear of the car).
9   Nine o'clock position: connected to the EGR valve via the temperature valve.
10   Twelve o'clock position: to the vacuum tank (this is the vacuum line which emerges from the fender well alongside or slightly behind the vacuum amplifier).

53   Temperature valve – removal and installation

1   Loosen the hose clamps on either side of the temperature valve and remove the vacuum hoses (photo).
2   Pull off the hose from the vacuum amplifier and remove the temperature valve.
3   Installation is the reverse of the removal procedure.

54   Diverter valve – removal and installation (California only)

1   Loosen the three clamps which hold the hoses to the diverter valve. Pull the hoses off.
2   Remove the two socket head screws which hold the diverter valve to the throttle housing and remove the diverter valve.
3   Installation is the reverse of the removal procedure.
4   Torque the two socket head screws to 6 ft-lb (0.8 m-kg).

55   EGR valve – removal and installation

1   Detach the vacuum hose from the connector at the top of the EGR valve (photo).
2   Loosen the nut and remove the exhaust gas line.
3   Remove the bolts which attach the EGR valve to the throttle housing and remove the EGR valve.
4   Installation is the reverse of the removal procedure.
5   Torque the two bolts which attach the EGR valve to the throttle housing to 7 ft-lb (1 m-kg).

56   EGR valve – operational check

1   Remove the EGR valve (Section 55).
2   Apply a vacuum to the vacuum side of the valve and check that the ball of the valve lifts completely off of the seat.
3   Replace the valve if it does not perform in this manner. A properly operating valve is reuseable.

57   EGR filter – removal and installation

1   Remove the molded rubber airflow housing from the air flow sensor housing venturi to the throttle housing and set it aside.
2   Detach the exhaust gas recirculation line which runs from the EGR valve to the EGR filter. Be sure to hold the hex fitting on the filter to prevent breaking of the fitting or twisting of the metal hose (photo).
3   Detach, in the same manner as above, the metal line which runs from the EGR filter to the front exhaust pipe.
4   Remove the three bolts which secure the EGR filter to the engine block and remove the filter (photo).
5   Installation is the reverse of the removal procedure.
6   Torque the three mounting bolts to 14 ft-lb (2 m-kg).
7   Tighten the two fittings carefully. There is no torque listed for these flange nuts. They must be tightened 'snug', but remember that overtightening will distort the fittings and cause leakage.

58   Electric switch – removal and installation

1   The electric switched two-way valve is installed on all 1977½ to 1979 vehicles destined for the California market. It is mounted to

52.6 Correct installation of the hoses in the vacuum amplifier

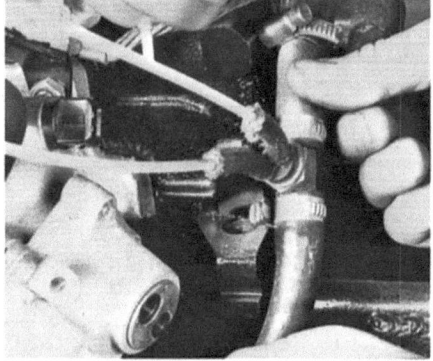

53.1 Location of the temperature valve and its mounting clamps

55.1 Location of the EGR valve

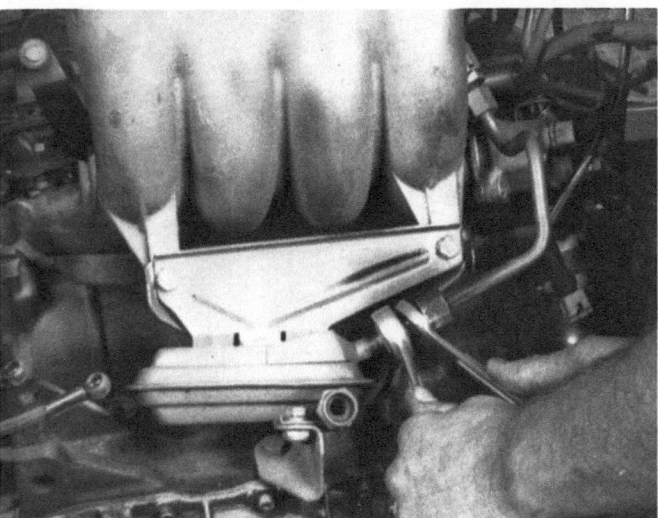

57.2 The proper technique for loosening the fittings on the EGR filter

57.4 Removing the EGR filter

the same bracket as the vacuum amplifier.
2   With tape and a pen label all of the vacuum connections and the electrical connector.
3   Remove the vacuum hoses.
4   Unplug the electrical connector.
5   Loosen the screw and remove the electric switch.
6   Installation of the electric switch is the reverse of the removal procedure.
7   The upper vacuum hose connection goes from the electric switch to the throttle housing. It is marked with a red ring on the valve.
8   The lower connection goes from the electric switch to the blow-off valve. This connection is marked with a blue ring on the valve.

59   Check valve - inspection

1   The check valve must open in the direction of injection flow into the exhaust manifold and must also close completely in the opposite direction.
2   Blow into the valve in the direction of air flow. The valve should open and allow air to pass through.
3   Blow into the other end of the valve. The valve should not allow any air to pass. If leakage is detected, replace the check valve.

60   EGR system - elapsed mileage switch

1   Since the EGR system consists of several parts which are subject to wear and, consequently, a change in performance, it is necessary to have the entire EGR system checked over by an authorized Porsche garage every 30,000 miles (48,000 km).
2   To inform you when a check is necessary, an elapsed mileage switch is installed behind the speedometer. This will illuminate the EGR light on your vehicle's dashboard when the proper mileage interval has elapsed.
3   The switch may be reset after a proper inspection of the EGR system by pressing the exposed pin on the housing fully down with a punch or small screwdriver. The EGR light should no longer light up when the ignition is turned on.

61   Deceleration valve - removal and installation

1   1977½ through 1979 models have a deceleration valve installed in vehicles with manual transmissions. Owners of automatic transmission models do not need to refer to this Section.
2   To remove the deceleration valve, loosen the two clamps which hold the hoses to the deceleration valve.
3   Remove the two nuts which attach the deceleration valve to the intake manifold and remove the valve.
4   Installation is the reverse of the removal procedure.

62   Deceleration valve - checking

1   Loosen the clamp and remove the hose which connects the intake manifold to the deceleration valve at the valve end.
2   Insert a plug in the end of the hose.
3   Have a second person start the engine and accelerate it briefly to 3500 rpm.
4   On a prearranged signal, have your assistant suddenly lift off the throttle so that there is a sharp drop from 3500 rpm to idle. Place a finger over the hose connection to see if suction can be felt.
5   If no suction is felt, repeat the steps once again. If the same results are found, replace the deceleration valve.

63   Catalytic converter (CAT) - overview

1   Although the various emission control devices work quite well in controlling pollutants, they are not effective in reducing them to certain levels prescribed in State or Federal statutes. The purpose of the catalytic converter (CAT) is to further reduce the emissions of NOx and CO from the exhaust gases.
2   The CAT system has no moving parts. The converter has a ceramic core cast in a waffle pattern and this is coated with platinum. These materials act as a catalyst in a reaction which reduces the amounts of pollutants and produces water vapor as a by-product.
3   The CAT system should be checked every time the car is tuned up. A life of 30,000 miles (48,000 km) is the normal service period of the converter unit, but it must be replaced before this interval should it fail the tests found below.

64   Catalytic converter - removal and replacement

1   The catalytic converter is mounted just behind the two-pipe front exhaust section and takes the place of the primary muffler. (Fig. 3.44).
2   Remove the bolts which attach the guard plate to the body and remove the guard plate.
3   Remove the six mounting bolts (three on each end) from the mounting flanges and remove the catalytic converter.
4   Scrape off all gaskets and sealing materials from the flanges.
5   Installation is the reverse of the removal procedure.
6   Always use new sealing gaskets.
7   Torque the six nuts on the flanges to 14 ft-lb (2 m-kg).
8   Torque the bolts on the guard plate to 7 ft-lb (1 m-kg).

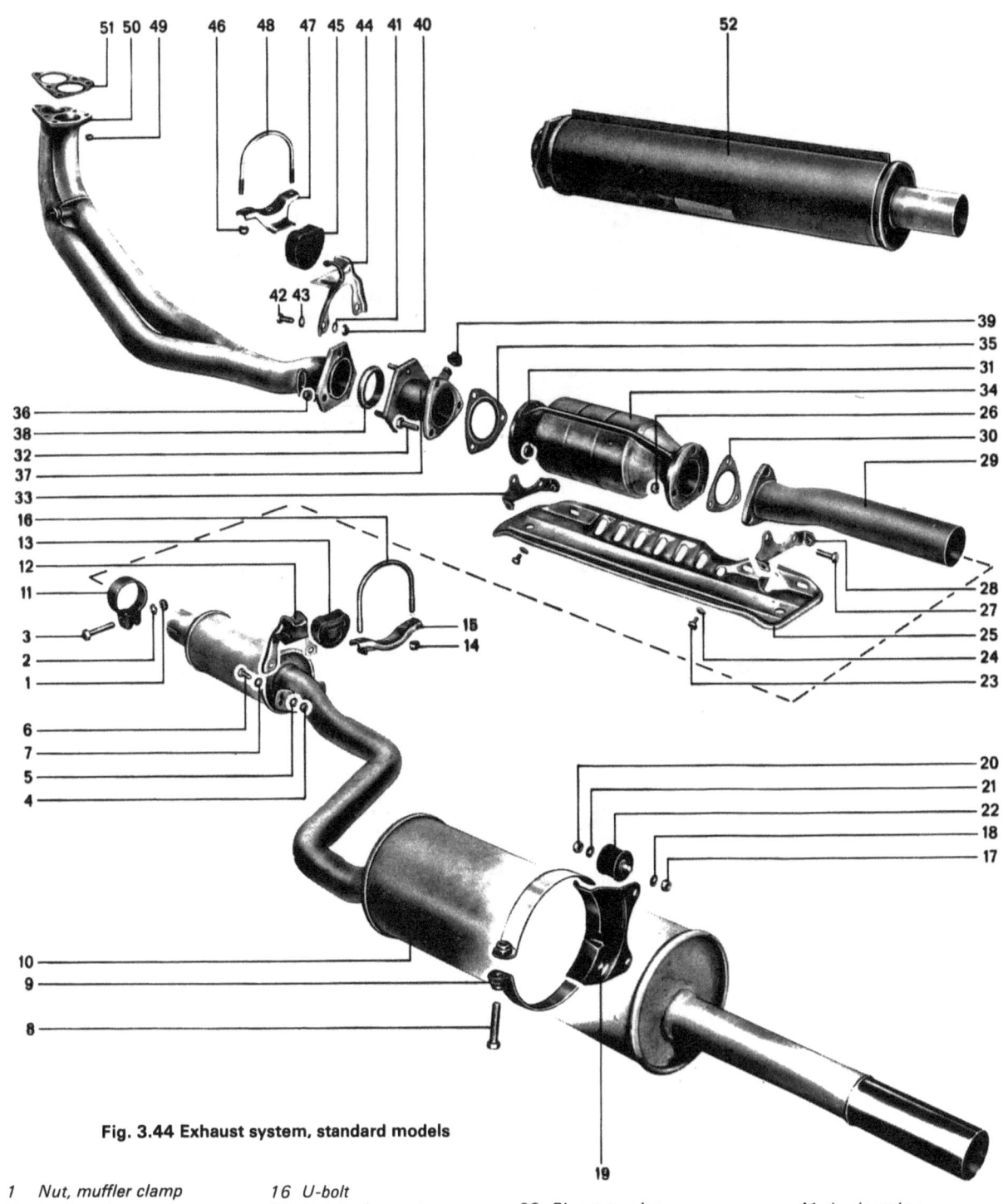

Fig. 3.44 Exhaust system, standard models

1	Nut, muffler clamp	16	U-bolt	29	Pipe extension	41	Lockwasher
2	Lockwasher	17	Nut, lord mount	30	Gasket, catalytic	42	Bolt, hanger bracket
3	Bolt, muffler clamp	18	Lockwasher		converter-to-pipe	43	Flat washer
4	Nut, hanger bracket	19	Final muffler hanger		extension	44	Hanger bracket
5	Lockwasher		bracket	31	Self-locking nut	45	Rubber bush, hanger
6	Bolt, hanger bracket	20	Nut, lord mount	32	Bolt, short pipe		bracket
7	Flat washer	21	Lockwasher	33	Holder, catalytic	46	Self-locking nut
8	Bolt, final muffler	22	Lord mount		converter guard	47	Lower bracket, U-bolt
	clamp	23	Bolt, catalytic	34	Catalytic converter	48	U-bolt
9	Final muffler clamp		converter guard	35	Gasket, catalytic	49	"Thermag" nuts, self-
10	Final muffler	24	Flat washer		converter-to-short pipe		locking
11	Muffler clamp	25	Catalytic converter	36	Self-locking nut	50	Front exhaust pipe
12	Hanger bracket		guard	37	Short pipe	51	Gasket, front exhaust
13	Rubber bush, hanger	26	Self-locking nut	38	Seal		pipe-to-exhaust manifold
	bracket	27	Bolt, pipe extension	39	Plug nut	52	Primary muffler (Europe
14	Self-locking nut	28	Holder, catalytic	40	Nut, hanger bracket		only)
15	Lower bracket, U-bolt		converter guard				

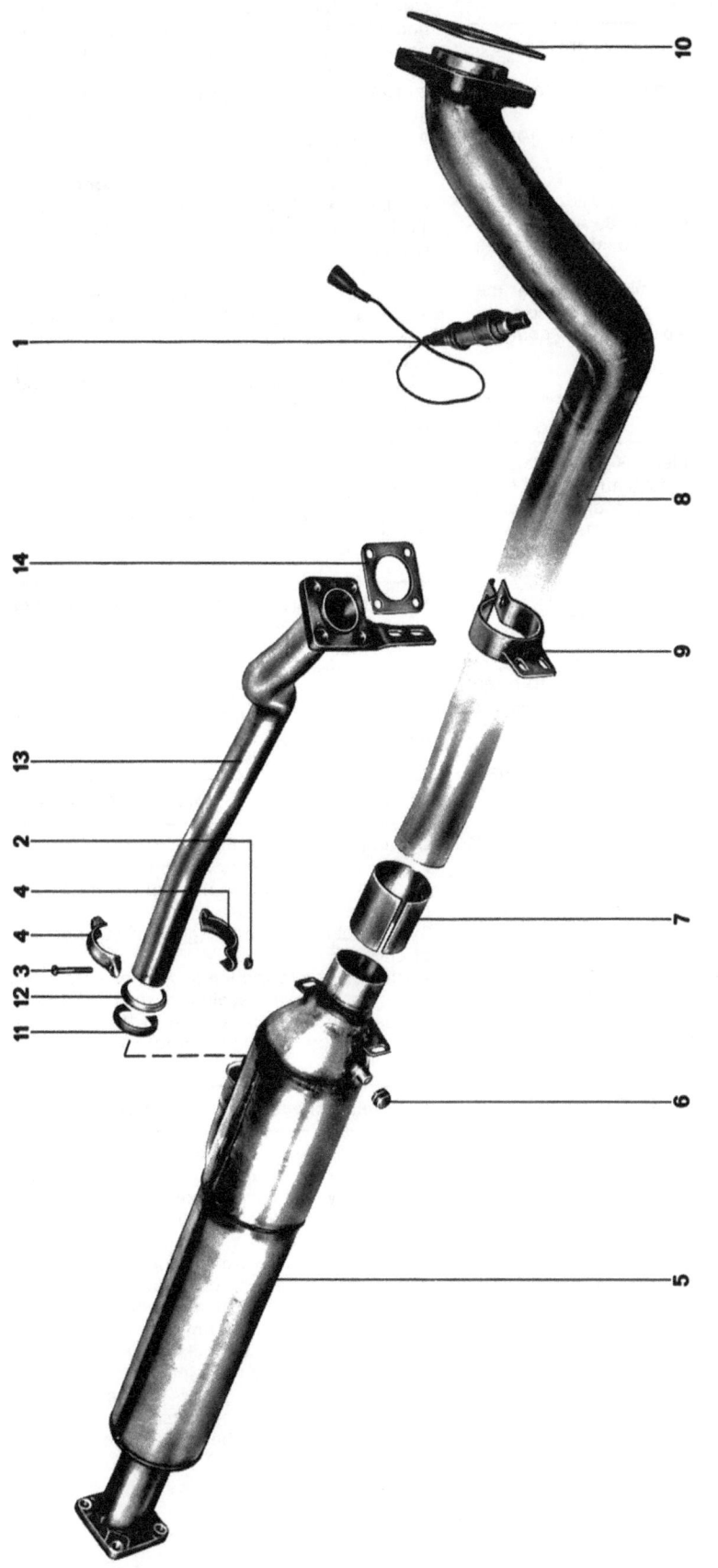

Fig. 3.45 Exhaust system, Turbo

1 Oxygen sensor with connector wire
2 Locknut, bypass line clamp
3 Bolt, bypass line clamp
4 Bypass line clamp
5 Catalytic converter
6 Capped nut

7 Sleeve
8 Front pipe
9 Hanger clamp
10 Gasket, front pipe-to-
   turbocharger

11 Sealing ring
12 Support
13 Bypass line
14 Gasket, bypass line-to-
   waste gate

65 Catalytic converter – operational check

1 Run the engine until normal working temperatures are reached. Oil temperature should be 80° to 90°C (180° to 190°F).
2 Hook up your exhaust gas analyzer according to the manufacturers' written instructions.
3 Connect the exhaust gas analyzer probe to the fitting in front of the catalytic converter.
4 Run engine at idle speed.
5 Read the CO% level on you analyzer. Adjust the CO% level referring to the Specifications pages and to Sections 30 and 40.
6 Connect the exhaust gas analyzer probe to the tail pipe on the final muffler and read again.
7 The value of CO% must be smaller at the tail pipe than at the connection ahead of the catalytic converter. If this is not the case, replace the catalytic converter. Reset the elapsed mileage counter.

66 Oxygen sensor system

1 The oxygen sensor system controls emissions by altering the air/fuel ratio. As the sensor in the exhaust directly affects fuel flow, the description and adjustment instructions have been included in the fuel supply sections at the beginning of this chapter. See Section 35.

67 Exhaust system

1 The exhaust system consists of all exhaust pipes, hanger brackets, and protective heat shields which begin with the sealing gasket between the exhaust manifold and two pipe exhaust line and ends at the tail pipe. The purpose of the system is to exhaust hot gases, which contain some substances potentially dangerous when they are inhaled, away from the passenger compartment and into the atmosphere. It is important that the exhaust system be kept in good working order and free from breaks, leaks, and rusting through.
2 The exhaust system for those markets where the installation of a catalytic converter is possible consists of several additional pieces not included in those intended for the European market. Fig. 3.44 gives good examples of both types.
3 Any work which is performed on the exhaust system should be done only after the vehicle has not been run for three or more hours. The various components in the system retain heat and may cause serious burns if not handled properly.

68 Final muffler – removal and installation

1 The final muffler consists of the entire portion of the exhaust system from the flanged pipe-to-secondary muffler slip fitting (on models with catalytic converters) or from the primary muffler-to-secondary muffler slip fitting (European-market vehicles) to the tip of the tail pipe.
2 Remove the two nuts and washers which hold the Lord mounts to the rear hanger bracket. It will be easier to remove the other nuts and bolts if you leave the threaded studs of the Lord mounts in the bracket.
3 Loosen the clamp at the forward end of the small secondary muffler.
4 Remove the two nuts and flat hanger strap from the U-bolt just behind the secondary muffler.
5 Unhook the steel bracket from the rubber mount at the rear of the secondary muffler.

6 Pull the entire final muffler assembly toward the rear of the vehicle. This should disengage the secondary muffler from the slip fitting. If the unit cannot be pulled free and appears to be rusted on, have an assistant rap along the front side of the secondary muffler while you pull from the rear.
7 Remove the steel bracket from the secondary muffler.
8 Remove the clamp from the final muffler.
9 Inspect the rubber hanger for dryness, loss of elasticity, and cracking. Replace if necessary.
10 Inspect the Lord mounts for bonding separations, dryness, cracking, and loss of elasticity. Replace if necessary.
11 The self-locking nuts which hold the flat hanger strap to the U-bolt must be replaced any time they are removed.
12 Installation is the reverse of the removal procedure.
13 Torque the nuts holding the steel bracket to the rear of the secondary muffler to 7 ft-lb (1 m-kg). On vehicles with standard transmissions, use the top set of holes, bottom for those with automatic transmissions.
14 Loosely install all other nuts and bolts and ensure that the final muffler is squarely placed before tightening all fasteners to their required torque settings.
15 Torque the self-locking nuts on the U-bolt to 14 ft-lb (2 m-kg).
16 Torque the nuts on the Lord mounts to 7 ft-lb (1 m-kg).
17 Torque the bolt on the final muffler clamp to 18 ft-lb (2.5 m-kg).
18 Torque the nut on the clamp at the slip fitting to 14 ft-lb (2 m-kg).

69 Exhaust system – catalytic converter removal and installation

1 Removal of the catalytic converter is covered in Section 64.
2 For information on the removal of the short flange pieces and connectors, see Section 70 on the removal of the primary muffler. The fittings of the remaining pieces are the same as this section of the system.

70 Primary muffler – removal and replacement

1 Remove the final muffler assembly (Section 68).
2 Remove the three bolts from the flange at the front of the primary muffler and remove the muffler, the forward steel bracket, and the metal seal.
3 Inspect the rubber hanger mount for dryness, cracking, and loss of elasticity.
4 Inspect the round metal seal for a tight fit, and for nicks, chips, and cuts along the sealing surfaces.
5 Installation is the reverse of the removal process.
6 Torque the bolts on the forward flange to 14 ft-lb (2 m-kg).

71 Front exhaust pipe – removal and installation

1 Remove the final exhaust pipe and muffler.
2 Remove the catalytic converter (when installed), Section 62, or the primary muffler (Section 70).
3 Remove the five nuts holding the front exhaust pipe to the exhaust manifold.
4 Lift out the forward exhaust pipe.
5 Scrape the heat-proof gasket from the front flange of the front exhaust pipe and the exhaust manifold.
6 The five nuts which hold the front exhaust pipe to the exhaust manifold are of the self-locking type and must be replaced with new nuts whenever they are removed.
7 Installation is the reverse of the removal procedure.
8 Use new self-locking nuts.
9 Use a new gasket between the exhaust manifold and the front exhaust pipe.
10 Torque the nuts on the front of the pipe to 14 ft-lb (2 m-kg).

Chapter 4 Turbocharger

For modifications, and information applicable to later models, see Supplement at end of manual

Contents

Specifications

Type	Exhaust gas driven turbocharger with waste gate and pop-off valves installed in the system to prevent overpressurization and lag in throttle response time.
Manufacturer	KKK, Type K 26-2664 G 4.10

Boost pressure

test	10 to 11 psi (0.70 to 0.80 bar)
control switch, testing values:	
minimum (value at which electrical current is flowing)	15.6 to 20 psi (1.1 to 1.4 bar)
maximum (value at which electrical current is stopped)	21 psi (1.5 bar)

System pressure	10 to 11 psi (0.70 to 0.80 bar)

Torque specifications

	ft–lb	m–kg
Exhaust manifold-to-cylinder head	18	2.5
Exhaust manifold/turbocharger bracket nuts	25	3.5
Turbocharger turbine housing, bolt	5	0.7
Turbocharger turbine housing, nut......................	3.5	0.5
Control line-to-waste gate	14	2.0
Oxygen sensor-to-front exhaust pipe.....................	36 to 43	5.0 to 6.0
Oil return line, turbocharger-to-oil pan	61	8.5
Oil return line, turbocharger-to-mount	61	8.5
Oil feed lines, turbocharger mount	40	2.9
Adapter, turbocharger mount	40 to 45	2.9 to 3.3

1 Turbocharger – general description

1 Many ways of producing a great deal of horsepower from the 924's engine are known. The problem with most of them is their adverse effect on gas mileage, pollutant emissions, or both. Turbocharging has been discovered to be one of the best ways to increase the horsepower output of the 924's engine without producing uncontrollable amounts of the regulated emissions and without an adverse effect on gas mileage.

2 Basically, the Porsche turbocharging system consists of two fans mounted on a common shaft. One fan is driven by the burned exhaust gases as they rush from the exhaust manifold and expand. The other fan pulls in fresh air and compresses it before it enters the intake manifold. By compressing the air/fuel mixture before it is again compressed by the rise of the piston, a larger charge of this mixture can be let into the cylinder and more power output achieved.

3 In practice the 924 Turbo (or 931 as it is known in Porsche production) works as follows:

4 Fresh air is drawn through the air filter at the front of the engine compartment and then passes through the air sensor unit of the Lambda injection system. This particular system is the same as the K-Jetronic system, both of which are described in Chapter 3. However, it differs slightly from the injection system found on the normally-aspirated engines. The Turbo's Lambda system features a

larger venturi in the air flow sensor housing and a slightly different configuration of the injectors are used. See Chapter 3 for an illustration of the two types of injectors.

5 After passing through the venturi of the air flow sensor housing, the fresh air charge is drawn into the KKK-manufactured turbocharger where it is compressed to a maximum of 10+ psi. The vanes of the turbocharging fan are driven by the exhaust gases passing over its counterpart which lies on the same shaft passing through a sealed wall and separating the induction and drive sections of the turbocharger.

6 Pressurized air is then ducted through the large cast alloy pipe to the induction manifold, where fuel is injected into the air charge and air/fuel mixture is ducted through the head (which has been redesigned for the Turbo models) and into the combustion chamber.

7 Dished pistons which give a compression ratio of 7.5 : 1 under normal aspiration are used for the Turbo. These give a rounded, slightly hemispherical shape to the combustion chamber and allow for more complete burning of the air/fuel charge.

8 Burned gases pass through the exhaust valve to the exhaust manifold where the oxygen sensor is located. This sensor adjusts the entering air/fuel charge based upon the oxygen content of the burned gases (see Chapter 3).

9 The hot exhaust gases, which are under pressure from the charge as it enters the combustion chamber, are further pressurized by the

heated gases attempting to expand. As the hot gases are forced from the exhaust manifold, they pass over the blades of the driving rotor (which, if you remember, is driving the intake side of the turbocharger) and are then ducted into the exhaust pipe, through a catalytic converter and out the tail pipe.

10 This is the basic cycle. There are several additions to the turbocharging system which aid in rapid throttle response and prevent over pressurization of the system.

11 To limit the pressure in the system, a waste gate is installed on the exhaust side of the turbocharger. This dumps additional exhaust gases directly into the catalytic converter whenever the pressure produced on the intake side exceeds the 10+ psi figure.

12 Whenever the throttle is lifted, as in slowing or preparing to stop, the decreased demand for boost air on the intake side causes a build-up of pressure which causes a drag on the turbine blades. This has been the cause of the time delay in acceleration normally associated with turbocharged engines.

13 To prevent the time delay and to maintain turbine speed, Porsche adds a pop-off valve between the intake and exhaust sides of the system downstream of the intake compression side of the turbocharger. Pressure build-up on the intake side is bled into the exhaust side of the system by the pop-off valve. This increases turbine speed and eliminates the loss of boost mentioned above.

14 If you choose to work on your turbocharging system, do so only after your vehicle has sat unused four to six hours. The turbocharger is driven by exhaust gases which are quite hot and the turbo housing, which is made of cast iron, absorbs and retains much of this heat.

15 Do not attempt disassembly of the turbocharger unit itself. This is not even a function which is performed at the dealership level of repair; your Porsche dealer is authorized only to replace a defective unit, not to rework any unit suspected of faulty performance.

2 Waste gate – removal and installation

1 Raise the vehicle and place it on jack stands.

2 Remove the lower engine guard.

3 Remove the rubber cap from the oxygen sensor and unplug the wire which leads into it.

4 Unbolt and remove the starter.

5 Detach and remove the bypass line which connects the waste gate and exhaust manifold (Fig. 4.4).

6 Remove the nuts holding the turbine housing to the exhaust pipe (Fig. 4.5).

7 Remove the bolts from the flange connecting the final exhaust system to the turbine housing (Fig. 4.6).

8 Remove the catalytic converter and final muffler assembly and set it aside.

9 Loosen the heat shields over the bypass line.

10 Loosen the bypass line mounting clamp.

11 Remove the bolts on the holder and control line at the waste gate and remove the exhaust pipe complete with the waste gate (Fig. 4.7). Some early production models have a 4 vent line which must be disconnected before removal can be accomplished (Fig. 4.8).

12 Installation is the reverse of the removal procedure.

13 Coat the threads of all bolts and studs with Bosch paste VS 140 16 ft or other suitable, heat resistant thread sealing compound.

14 Torque the nuts on the flange holding the exhaust pipe to the turbocharger housing to 25 ft-lb (2.5 m-kg).

15 Torque the hollow bolt (control line-to-waste gate) to 14 ft-lb (2 m-kg).

16 Tighten all other nuts and bolts until tight. Make sure that pressure is evenly applied (bolts on either end of clamps tightened evenly) and wipe away all excess thread sealant.

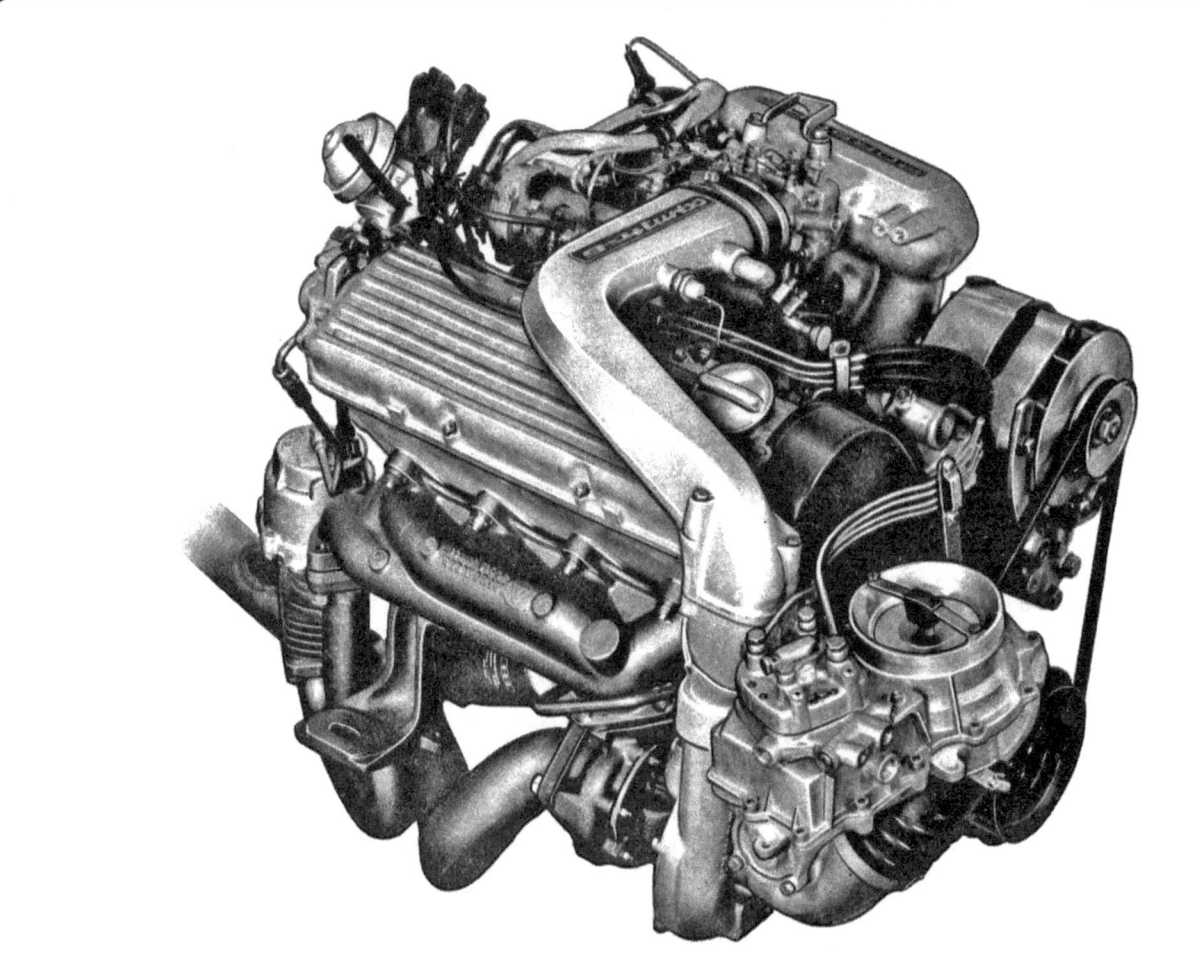

Fig. 4.1 The Porsche 924 Turbo engine with the turbocharger installed

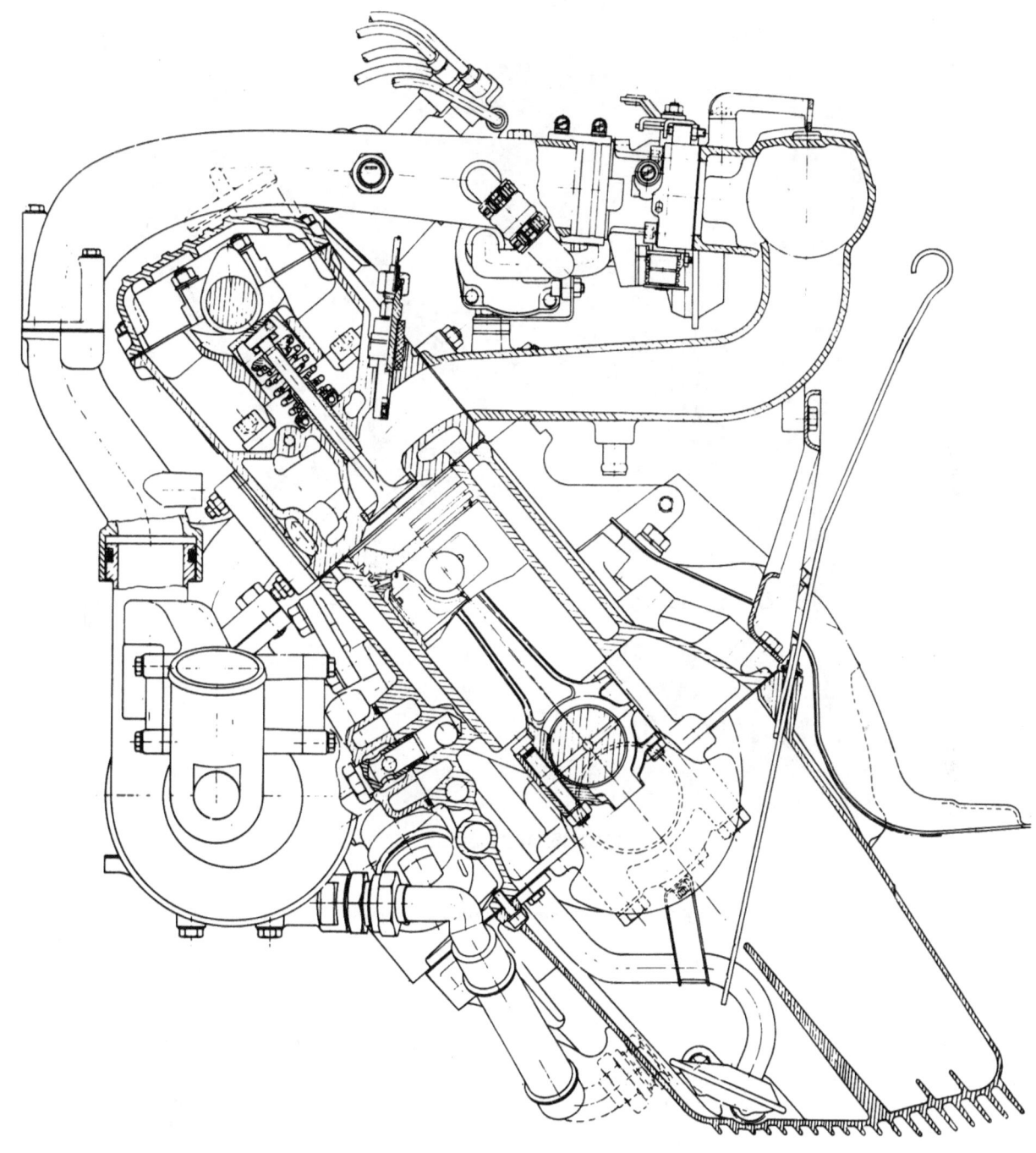

Fig. 4.2 A cutaway drawing of the engine and turbocharger system

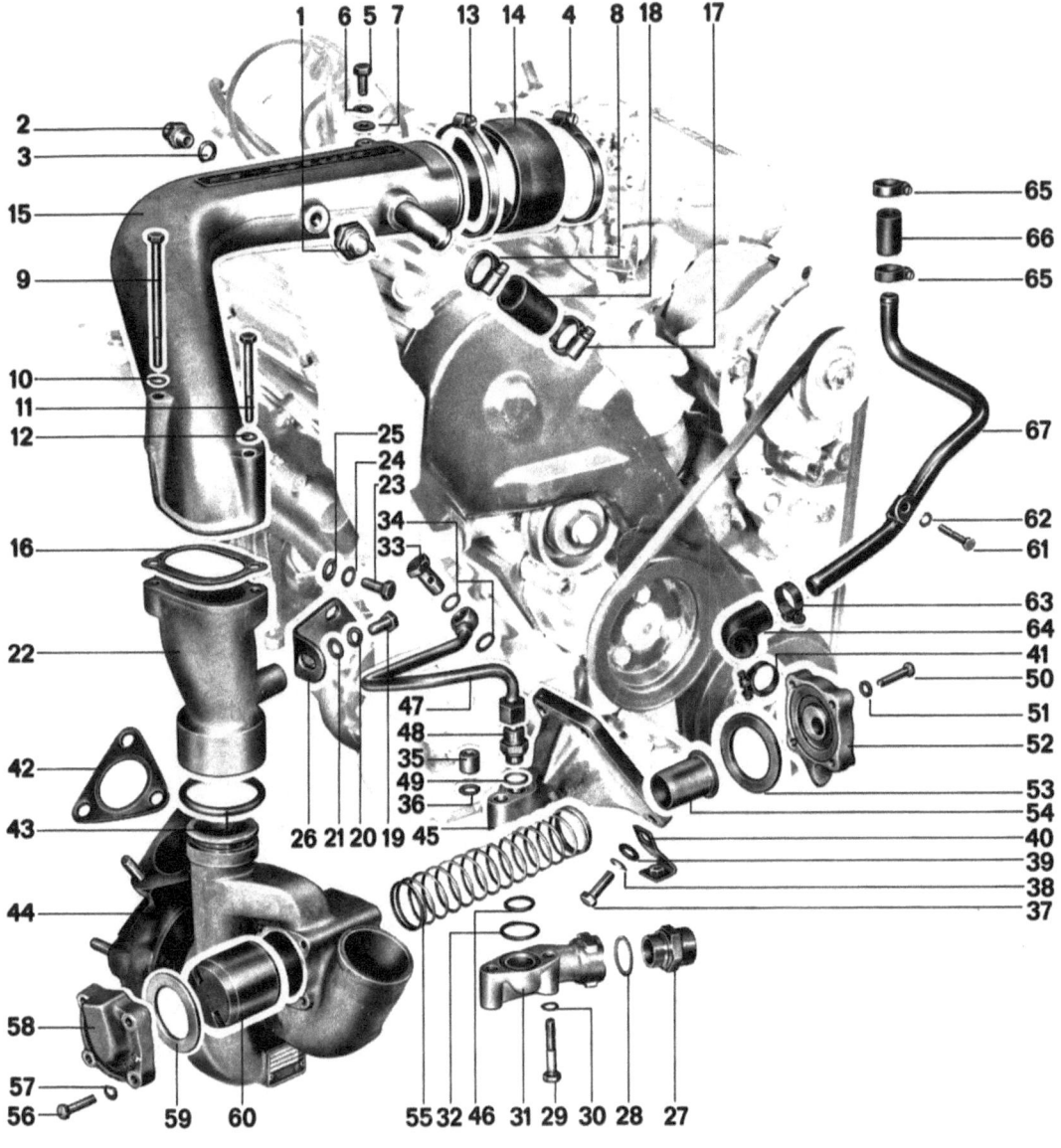

Fig. 4.3 Components of the turbocharger system

1	Boost pressure control switch with seal
2	Adapter, control line
3	Adapter seal
4	Hose clamp, upper pressure duct-to-throttle housing
5	Upper pressure duct bolt
6	Wave washer
7	Flat washer
8	Hose clamp
9	Bolt, upper-to-lower pressure duct
10	Flat washer
11	Bolt, upper-to-lower pressure duct
12	Flat washer
13	Hose clamp, upper pressure duct-to-throttle housing
14	Rubber sleeve
15	Upper pressure duct
16	Gasket
17	Hose clamp
18	Hose
19	Lower pressure duct bolt
20	Wave washer
21	Flat washer
22	Lower pressure duct
23	Bolt, lower pressure duct holding bracket
24	Wave washer
25	Flat washer
26	Lower pressure duct holding bracket
27	Oil line adapter
28	Adapter seal
29	Bolt, oil distributor block
30	Flat washer
31	Oil distributor block
32	Seal
33	Banjo bolt
34	Flat seals
35	Socket-head nut
36	Flat washer
37	Bolt, oil hose holder
38	Wave washer
39	Flat washer
40	Oil hose holder
41	Hose clamp
42	Gasket, turbocharger-to-exhaust pipe
43	O-ring seal
44	Turbocharger unit
45	Turbocharger mount
46	Seal
47	Oil feed line
48	Oil feed line adapter
49	Adapter seal
50	Bolt, pop-off valve cover
51	Lockwasher, spring type
52	Pop-off valve cover, with control line connection
53	Gasket, pop-off valve cover
54	Spring guide
55	Spring
56	Bolt, pop-off valve cover
57	Lockwasher, spring type
58	Pop-off valve cover
59	Gasket, pop-off valve cover
60	Piston, pop-off valve
61	Bolt, control line bracket
62	Lockwasher, spring type
63	Hose clamp
64	Hose
65	Hose clamp
66	Hose
67	Control line

Fig. 4.4 Location of bypass line nuts

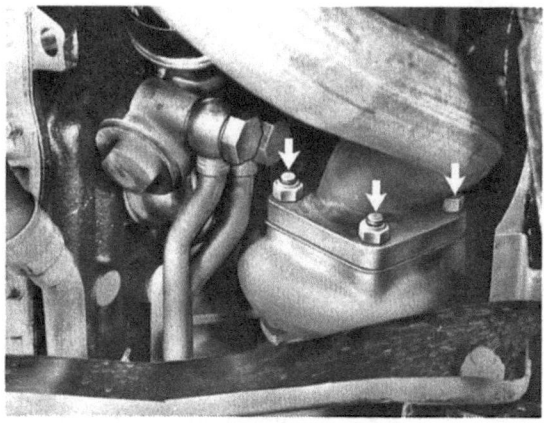

Fig. 4.5 Location of exhaust pipe nuts on the turbine housing

Fig. 4.6 Exhaust flange nuts

Fig. 4.7 Location of the holder for the exhaust pipe

Fig. 4.8 Vent line location. These were installed only on early Turbo production models

3 Turbocharger – removal and installation

1 Raise the vehicle and place it on jack stands.
2 Remove the engine guard.
3 Remove the rubber cover from the oxygen sensor unit and unplug the wire.
4 Remove the starter.
5 Disconnect and remove the bypass line between the exhaust manifold and the waste gate.
6 Remove the exhaust system and waste gate as described in Section 2.
7 Do not damage the oxygen sensor. It is very expensive to replace and is easily broken when struck.
8 Disconnect the oil lines leading to the engine oil cooler and the banjo bolt at the oil filter flange for the turbocharger's oil feed line. Plug all lines to prevent dirt from entering the engine oiling system (Fig. 4.9).

9 Place a pan beneath the oil filter flange to catch any escaping oil and then remove the oil filter flange.
10 Loosen the clamps on the oil lines which pass through the turbocharger area and pull forward all oil lines which interfere with the turbocharger's removal (Fig. 4.10).
11 Disconnect the turbocharger oil return line. It is necessary to hold the hex fitting closest to the turbocharger housing to prevent breakage or distortion of the oil return line (Fig. 4.11).
12 Loosen the clamps connecting the upper pressure duct to the intake manifold and also the clamp on the air hose fitting on the left forward edge of the upper pressure duct (Fig. 4.12).
13 With a piece of tape and an indelible pen, mark the electrical connection on the boost pressure control switch and unplug the wire (Fig. 4.12).
14 Remove the control line from its adapter. Hold the hex fitting on the adapter when loosening the hose to prevent twisting and possible breakage of the hose (Fig. 4.12).

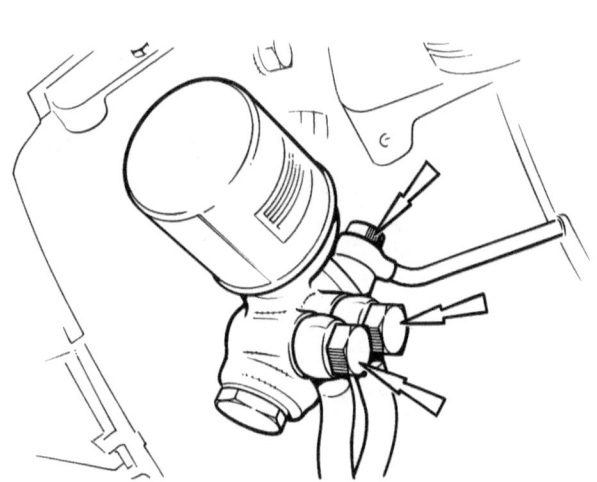

Fig. 4.9 Oil feed line connections

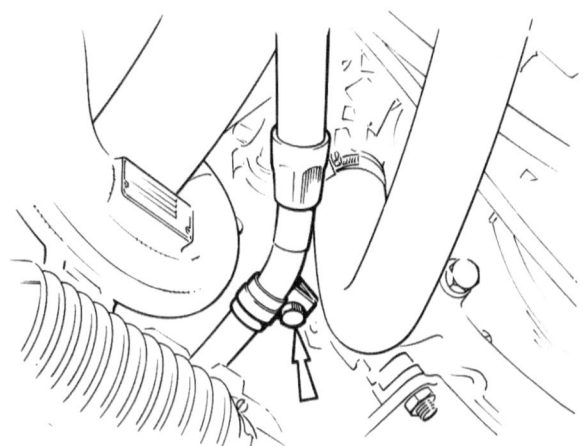

Fig. 4.10 Oil line holding clamps

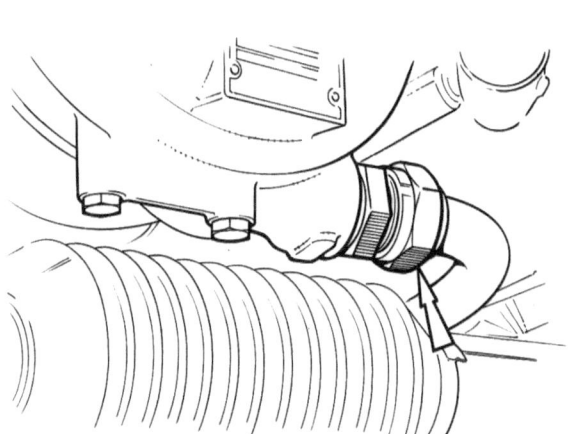

Fig. 4.11 Oil return line fitting

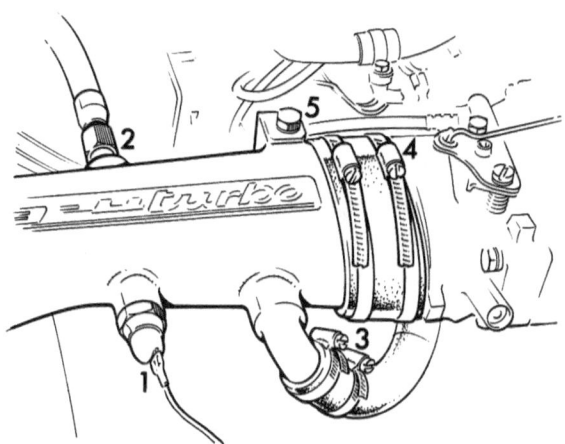

Fig. 4.12 Upper pressure duct

1	Boost pressure control switch	4	Hose clamps
2	Control line	5	Upper pressure duct mounting bolt
3	Air hose fitting		

15 Remove the single bolt on the mounting bracket at the top of the upper pressure duct (Fig. 4.12), then remove the two bolts which hold the upper and lower pressure ducts together. Lift out the upper pressure duct and set aside (Fig. 4.13).

16 Remove the mounting bolts from the air cleaner housing. Loosen the clamp holding it to the air flow sensor housing dust cover and remove the entire air cleaner housing as a single unit.

17 Remove the three mounting nuts from the bottom of the air flow sensor housing at the fuel distributor end of the casting (Fig. 4.14).

18 Loosen the clamps on the air flow sensor housing dust cover and move the air flow sensor housing to one side (Fig. 4.15).

19 Unscrew the mounting bolt from the lower pressure duct and remove the pressure duct and its sealing O-ring (Fig. 4.16).

20 Remove the two nuts from the exhaust manifold/turbocharger mount directly behind the flange for the lower pressure duct (Fig. 4.17), and loosen the two socket head nuts from the bolts on either side of the oil feed line located on the turbocharger mount. It may be

necessary to hold the bolt head with another wrench while loosening the socket head nuts (Fig. 4.18).

21 Loosen the clamp on the hose which is on the fitting to the front of the turbocharger unit. Do not remove the hose as yet; it must be disconnected as the turbocharger is lifted from the vehicle (Fig. 4.19).

22 Disconnect both ends of the right side stabilizer arm (Chapter 8).

23 Disconnect the steering gear from the control arm.

24 Disconnect the turbocharger at its base and turn the turbocharger unit so that the mounting flange faces front (Fig. 4.20).

25 Pull the hose from the waste gate connection.

26 Installation is the reverse of the removal procedure; however, it is very important that the following instructions be strictly adhered to and that only this order is followed:

27 Before installing the turbocharger, make sure that the socket head nuts are loose on the base.

28 Push on the lower hose while the turbocharger is being placed in position.

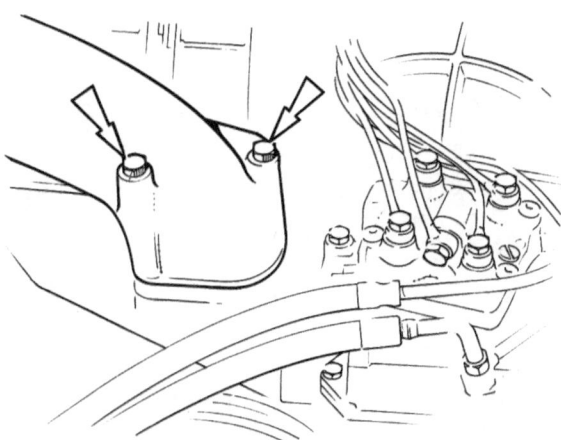

Fig. 4.13 Mounting bolts, upper-to-lower pressure ducts

Fig. 4.14 Air flow sensor mounting nuts

Fig. 4.15 Hose clamps, air flow sensor housing dust cover

Fig. 4.16 Lower pressure duct mounting bolt

29 Tighten the nuts on the exhaust manifold/turbocharger mount and then install and tighten the nuts on the base.
30 Torque the exhaust manifold/turbocharger nuts to 25 ft-lb (3.5 m-kg).
31 Tighten the socket head nuts evenly. Use the proper size hex key and be sure to hold the bolt head with a wrench to ensure proper tightening.
32 Use all new seals on the oil lines.
33 Torque all banjo bolts holding oil lines to the oil filter mounting block to 41 ft-lb (5.5 m-kg).
34 Torque the oil feed line to the oil filter block to 61 ft-lb (8.5 m-kg) if it was removed.
35 Torque the oil line to the turbocharger mounting bolts to 29 ft-lb (4 m-kg).
36 Use a new O-ring seal on the lower pressure duct to turbocharger join. It may be necessary to lightly lubricate the O-ring with a silicone rubber preservative and slide the lower pressure duct over the outlet of the turbocharger.
37 Install a new gasket in the join between the upper and lower pressure ducts. Loosely install all mounting bolts and hose clamps and make sure that the ducts are properly aligned before tightening everything down.
38 Tighten the bolts holding the upper and lower pressure ducts together evenly. Next, do the same for all other mounting bolts. Do not overtighten.
39 Torque the steering gear mounting bolts to 14 to 17 ft-lb (2.0 to 2.4 m-kg).
40 Before the vehicle can be run again, the turbocharger oiling system must be primed. This is done by removing the plugs from the manifold pressure limiting switch and the spark plugs from the engine, then running the engine on the starter motor only for 15 seconds.

Fig. 4.17 Exhaust manifold/turbocharger mounting nuts

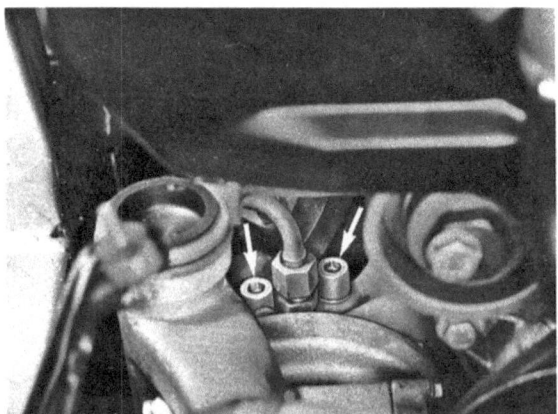

Fig. 4.18 Socket head nuts

Fig. 4.19 Turbocharger, location of the forward hose

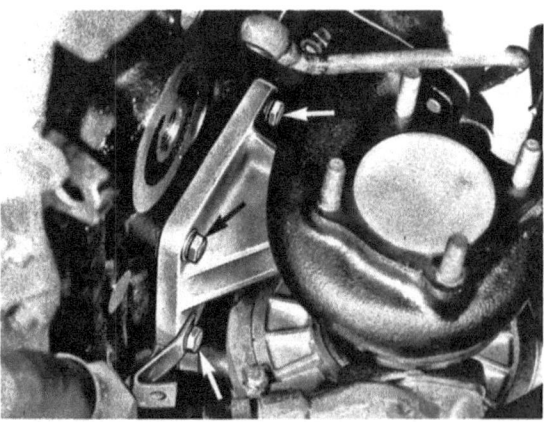

Fig. 4.20 Turbocharger base mounting bolts

4 Turbocharger - checking axial play

1 Install a dial indicator on the exhaust turbine housing so that the plunger end of the indicator is resting on the end of the turbine wheel shaft and is in line with the shaft direction (Fig. 4.21).
2 Set the indicator to zero.
3 Press the turbine wheel shaft toward the dial indicator and note the value.
4 Press the turbine wheel shaft away from the indicator and note this value.
5 The difference between the two readings is the value of the end play. The maximum end play which may be noted and still allow usage of the turbocharger is 0.006 in. (0.16 mm). If the end play value exceeds this figure, replace the unit.

5 Turbocharger - checking radial play

1 Install a dial indicator on the exhaust turbine side of the turbocharger housing so the end of the indicator rests against the hub. Set the indicator dial to zero (Fig. 4.22).
2 Press the hub toward the indicator and note the value.
3 Press the hub away from the indicator and note this value.
4 The difference between these two values is the radial play. Maximum radial play allowed is 0.017 in. (0.42 mm). If the radial play exceeds this figure, replace the turbocharger unit.

6 Turbocharger - boost test

1 Unplug the lead from the boost pressure control switch (Fig. 4.23).
2 Install the Porsche pressure gauge tester in the passenger compartment on the passenger's side and route the hose into the engine compartment.
NOTE: The pressure gauge tester referred to in this section is Porsche tool 9103. It is a special glycerine-filled unit which gives more accurate readings than the standard pressure gauges normally available. If you cannot gain access to this tool, we suggest that you seek the services of your local Porsche dealer as no alternative to this particular shop tool appears to be available.
3 Screw the boost pressure control switch into the adapter and tighten slightly. Be sure to hold the adapter with a wrench while tightening. Connect the electric plug.
4 Install the adapter seal into the control switch hole. Be sure to use a seal on the adapter before installation.
5 When installing the pressure gauge tester be sure not to clamp the hose or to pinch it in a closed door.
6 Connect the line adapter and test line making sure to hold the adapter with a wrench during the tightening (Fig. 4.24).
7 The actual boost pressure test must be carried out on the road or with the vehicle on a chassis dynamometer. The values to be met are 10 to 11 psi (0.70 to 0.80 bar).
8 Accelerate to within 500 rpm of red line in first and second gears while an assistant takes the boost pressure reading during acceleration from 4500 to 5500 rpm. The reading must be done while accelerating through these two rpm values only. Disregard any readings made during deceleration or obtained when accelerating cleanly outside these rpm limits.
9 If the boost pressure value exceeds the given limits, the waste gate must be replaced.

7 Boost pressure control switch - checking

1 Unplug the wire and remove the boost pressure control switch from the upper pressure duct.
2 Carefully clamp the boost pressure control switch in the jaws of a vise with jaw protectors installed.
3 Connect a 'buzz box' audible circuit tester, or a 12v bulb connected to two lengths of electrical cable (Fig. 4.25), between the switch housing and the connecting terminal. The buzzer should sound, or the light should come on.
4 Take a rubber valve stem (the type used for tubeless tires) and remove the valve core. Slide the rubber end over the threads of the switch.
5 Connect an air hose to the proper hole on the metal end of the

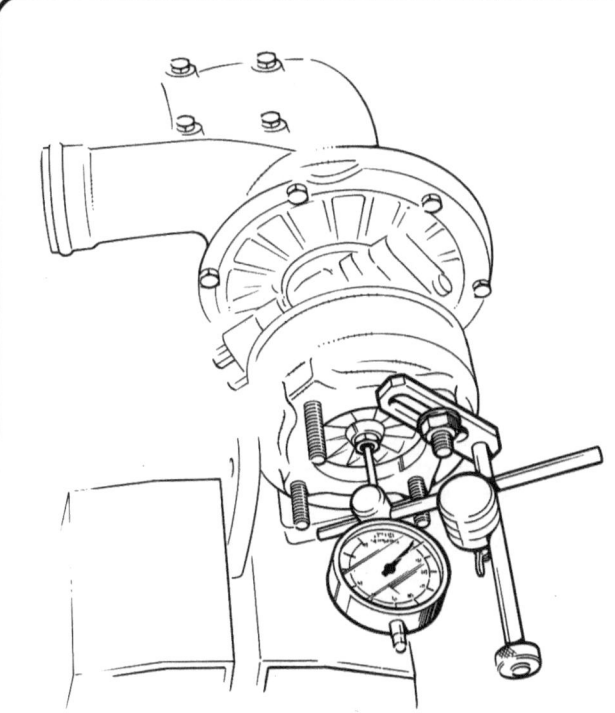

Fig. 4.21 Test equipment installed to test turbocharger axial play

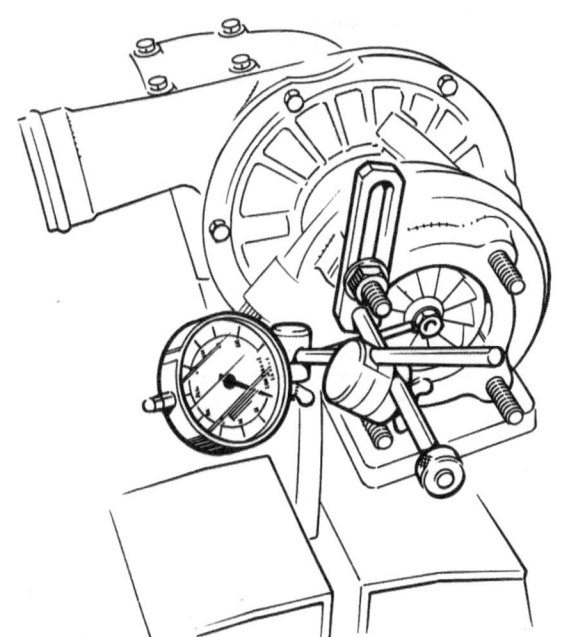

Fig. 4.22 Test equipment installed to test turbocharger radial play

Fig. 4.23 Boost pressure control switch

Fig. 4.24 Correct installation of the boost pressure test gauge
adapter

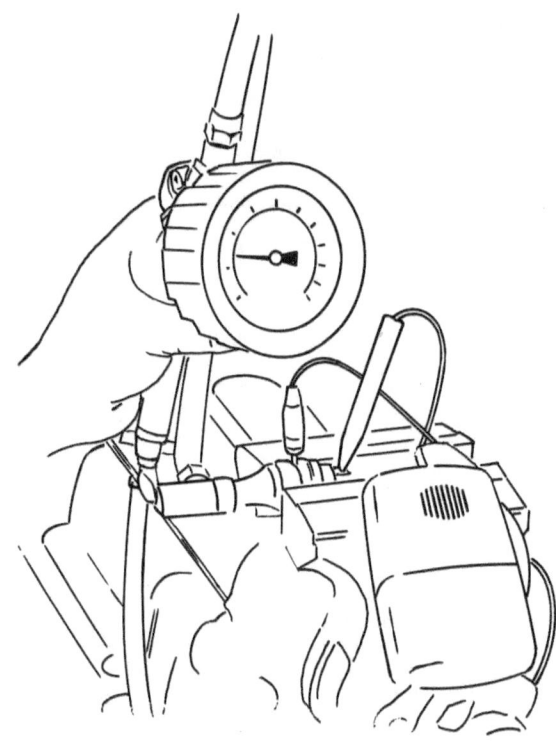

Fig. 4.25 Connection of 'buzz box' circuit tester and pressure
gauge for checking boost pressure control switch

pressure gauge and press it on to the threaded end of the valve stem.
6   Slowly build pressure up until the reading is approximately 21 psi
(1.5 bar). The buzzer should stop sounding, or the light should go off.
7   Allow the pressure to drop slowly until the buzzer begins to
sound, or the light comes on, again. The pressure should be 15.6 to
20 psi (1.1 to 1.4 bar).
8   If the boost pressure control switch fails either of these tests, it
must be replaced.

8   Pop-off valve – piston, spring, or guide sleeve removal and installation

1   Remove the turbocharger unit as explained in Section 3.
2   Set the turbocharger housing on a workbench and arrange it so

that the inlet duct of the intake fan is facing you.
3   Loosen the right-hand cover on the pop-off valve, but do not
remove the bolts and cover. The cover is spring loaded and may
cause serious injury if not properly removed.
4   Hold the cover in place with the pressure of one hand while
loosening the bolts equally around the corners of the cover. When
the last bolt is backed all the way out, remove all four bolts and set
aside. Carefully allow the spring to slowly extend itself and remove
the cover when there is no tension.
5   Remove the spring guide, spring and piston.
6   Inspect the spring guide and piston for nicks, gouges, and other
signs of excessive wear. Replace if excessive wear is apparent.
7   Installation is the reverse of the removal procedure.
8   Lubricate the pop-off piston with a thin coat of oil.
9   Tighten the four bolts on the pop-off valve cover in a cross pattern. Do not overtighten.

Chapter 5 Ignition and starting system

For modifications, and information applicable to later models, see Supplement at end of manual

Contents

Specifications

For details of early mechanical breaker type ignition, refer to Chapter 13

1976-1977½, U.S. models, 90 hp engine

Firing order... 1-3-4-2

Ignition timing .... 10° ATDC at 925 ± 75 rpm with vacuum hoses installed

Timing mark... ' – ' (+10 and –10 indicate degrees before and after proper timing mark)

Full advance, test.. 42° at 4500 rpm with vacuum hoses disconnected

Spark plug, type
    Bosch .... 200 T 30 (WR 6 D5)
    Beru .... 200/14/3 A (RS S7)

Spark plug, gap... 0.028 to 0.032 in (0.7 to 0.8 mm)

Distributor type .... Bosch 047 905 205, centrifugal and vacuum advance and retard control, no speed governor

Transistorized ignition control unit type .... Bosch 046905 351

Ignition coil type... Bosch 046 905 105, with two ballast resistors 0.4 and 0.6 ohms

1977½-1980, U.S. models, 110 hp engine
As above except for:

Ignition timing .... 3° ATDC at 950 ± 50 rpm with vacuum hoses installed

Timing mark... ' –3 '

Full advance, test.. 41° at 4500 rpm with vacuum hoses disconnected

Distributor type .... Bosch 047 905 205 C, centrifugal and vacuum advance and retard control, no speed governor

1976-1980, European models, 125 hp engine

Firing order... 1-3-4-2

Ignition timing .... 10° BTDC at 950 ± 50 rpm with vacuum hoses disconnected

Spark plug, type
    Bosch .... W 225 T 30 (W 5 D)
    Beru .... 225/14/3 A 1 (14 – 5 D)
    Champion N6YC

Spark plug, gap... 0.028 in (0.7 mm)

Turbo Models	All models except UK	UK models
Firing order	1 – 3 – 4 – 2	1 – 3 – 4 – 2
Ignition timing	20° BTDC at 2000 ± 50 rpm	9° BTDC at 900 rpm 25° BTDC at 2000 rpm
Timing mark	' – 20 '	On flywheel
Spark plug, type		
Bosch	WR 7 DS	W 3 DP
Champion	N 8 GY	N 2 G
Spark plug, gap		
Bosch	0.024 in (0.6 mm)	0.028 in (0.7 mm)
Champion	0.024 in (0.6 mm)	0.024 in (0.6 mm)

Torque specifications

	ft – lb	m – kg
Starter motor-to-engine	54	7.5
Ballast resistor clips, nut	6	0.8
Spark plugs	21	3
Distributor hold down plate, nut	14 to 16	2.0 to 2.2

---

1 Ignition/starting system – overview

1   The ignition/starting system is actually three separate systems which must work together in an integrated manner so that the engine runs smoothly. These three systems are:
   1) Starting system, which activates the starter motor.
   2) Ignition system, which provides the spark to the spark plugs.
   3) Fuel injection electrical system, which meters the amounts of fuel added to the air before combustion.
2   The fuel injection system is explained in Chapter 3 and the electrical circuitry for fuel injection is discussed in Chapter 11. It is included here only to show the inter-relationship of the three systems.
3   All three of these systems must be kept in top working order if each is to perform at its best level. What appears to be a lack of spark may actually be an improper fuel charge, for example. When troubleshooting ignition problems, keep this inter-relationship of systems in mind.
4   This chapter is divided into the ignition system and its components, followed by a description of the starting system and its components. It is necessary to follow a specific pattern of tests when troubleshooting these systems. The final part of this chapter, then, is a flow chart which outlines the testing procedures and their order.

---

2 Ignition starting system – current flow

1   When the ignition key is turned in the ignition lock to the 'start' position, the current flows simultaneously to the components of the three systems as follows:

Starting system
2   Power flows from the positive lead of the battery to the number 30 connector of the starter motor. At the same time, power flows from the ignition lock to the number 50 connector on the starter solenoid. This closes the two switches which allow current to flow to the starter motor and also to the ballast resistor (resistor wires in later models) and on to the ignition system.
3   When the solenoid closes the two switches in the motor, the drive pinion of the starter motor is electrically engaged in the teeth of the ring gear on the flywheel.
4   The engine is now being mechanically turned over.

Ignition system
5   Power first reaches the ignition through the connection running from the number 16 connector on the starter to the ballast resistor (resistor wires in later models) then on to the number 15 connector on the ignition coil.

6   Power is also directed to the number 15 connection of the transistorized ignition control unit and the number 15 connection of the ignition coil (via the ballast resistors or resistor wires) from the electrical connections in the ignition switch. Once the engine is running and the starter is disengaged, this circuit remains completed and the starter-to-ignition coil connection is broken.
7   From the transistorized ignition control unit, current travels through the ballast resistor (resistor wires) to the number 15 connector of the ignition coil. The lead from the number 6 terminal of the transistorized ignition control unit is connected to the number 1 terminal of the ignition coil. This connection activates the transistor circuit which sends the power impulses through the coil to the distributor. Section 8 contains a more precise explanation of the inner workings of the transistorized ignition control unit.
8   When the circuit is activated, high voltage electrical power then leaves the ignition coil through the high tension lead to the distributor. The distributor rotor then transfers this current through one of the spark plug high tension leads to the appropriate spark plug, which sparks and ignites the air/fuel mixture within the cylinder.

Fuel injection electrical system
9   When the engine begins turning with the ignition in the 'start' position, electrical pulses from the transistorized ignition control unit energize the fuel pump relay. The fuel pump relay energizes, in turn the fuel pump, control pressure regulator, and the auxiliary air regulator via relay terminals 30 and 87, through the number 2 fuse (16 amp) in the fuse box. Terminal 50 activates the cold start valve and warm start solenoid.
10 All of the above functions take place immediately and simultaneously when the ignition key is turned in the ignition lock. Each system, as you can now see, depends on the other two systems to be in proper working order if starting and running of the engine is to take place.

---

3 Starting system – general description

1   The starting system consists of the starter motor, the solenoid, and the voltage regulator.
2   The purpose of the voltage regulator in the starting system is to regulate alternator output according to electrical loads and the state of charge of the battery. Refer also to Chapter 11.
3   The starting system is very simple in operation and performs in the manner described in Section 2.

---

4 Voltage regulator – removal and installation

1   Remove the negative lead from the battery.
2   Disconnect the air hose on the alternator at the fitting on the alternator guard (photo).

3   Place a drip pan beneath the vehicle and drain the engine oil (Chapter 1).
4   Remove the oil filter and catch any oil which drips from the mounting boss.
5   Remove the three bolts which mount the guard to the rear of the alternator (Fig. 5.1).
6   Remove the guard.
7   Unscrew the voltage regulator and remove it (Fig. 5.2).
8   Installation is the reverse of the removal procedure.
9   Tighten all bolts evenly and snugly.
10 Fit a new oil filter, referring to Chapter 1 and taking care to prime the oil filter.

Note: while it is not essential to drain the engine oil in order to remove the oil filter, it would be wise to take the opportunity of carrying out an oil and filter change while involved in removing the voltage regulator.

---

5   Voltage regulator – measuring voltage output

1   Raise the hood and connect a voltmeter to the battery terminals.
2   Start the engine and hold the speed at 2000 rpm.
3   Turn on the headlights and the rear window defogger.
4   Read the voltage. The output should be between 13.5 and 14.5 volts. If the voltage is not within these limits, replace the voltage regulator and perform the tests again. If the readings still do not fall within the specification limits, remove the alternator and have its output checked by a reputable Porsche dealer.

6   Starter motor – removal and installation

1   Remove the negative lead from the battery.
2   Raise the vehicle and place it on jack stands.
3   Remove the bolts which attach the shroud to the body (photo).
4   Remove the two nuts which hold the starter motor to the engine. Press the bolts out toward the rear of the vehicle.
5   Pull the starter motor forward and then down (photo).
6   Remove the two wires from the starter motor and remove the motor from the vehicle (photo).
7   Installation is the reverse of the removal procedure.
8   Make sure that the solenoid is at the top of the motor when installing.
9   Do not overtighten the connectors when hooking in the two wires. Overtightening will cause twisting of the cable end and may lead to breakage of the fitting.
10 Place the starter motor in its place and press in the two bolts. The hex head bolt is installed in the upper hole and the 'T'-shaped bolt in the lower hole. Both are installed from the rear side of the bellhousing with the threaded ends facing forward.
11 Install the nuts on the bolts and torque the nuts to 54 ft-lb (7.5 m-kg) (photo).

7   Starter motor and solenoid – testing

1   There is no way that these two parts can be tested without expensive diagnostic equipment. Most auto parts stores and auto

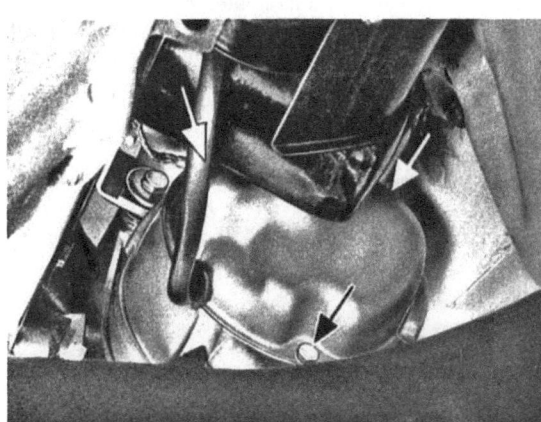

Fig. 5.1 Location of the three alternator shroud bolts

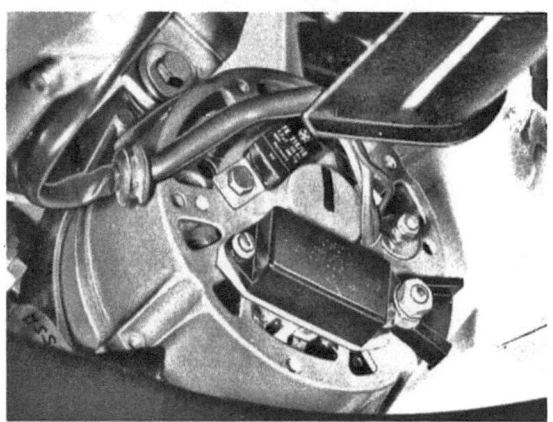

Fig. 5.2 Voltage regulator exposed and ready for removal

4.2 Removing the alternator air hose

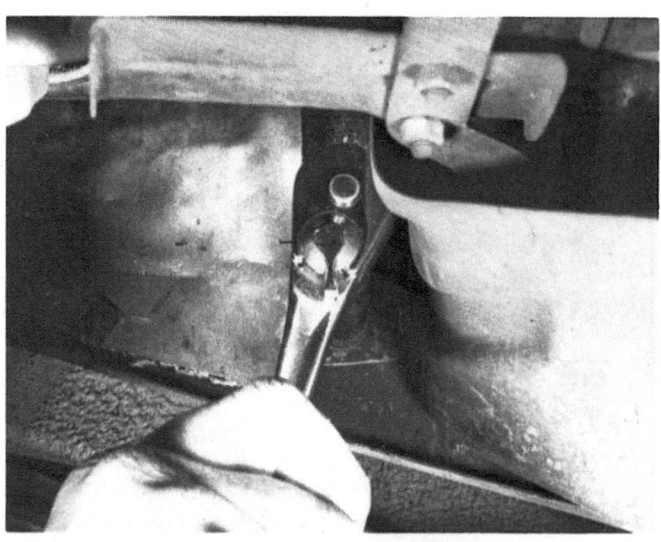

6.3 Removing the protective shroud from the starter

6.5 Removing the starter motor

6.6 Starter motor wires ready for removal

6.11 Applying the specified torque to the nuts on the starter motor holding bolts

service centers have the proper equipment on hand and can perform the necessary tests in a matter of minutes and at nominal cost. If the starter or solenoid have failed it is advised that they should be traded for an exchange rebuilt unit.

8 Ignition system – general description

1 The ignition system is of the transistorized type and consists of a transistorized ignition control unit, a single ignition coil, and a distributor. Figures 5.3 and 5.4 give an illustration of the various components and their relationships to one another.
2 The transistorized ignition control unit takes the place of the points in a conventional ignition system. The purpose of the transistor in the system is to act as a switch for the ignition current.
3 A transistor has the ability to control the flow of large amounts of electrical current by applying small amounts of current to a third circuit acting as a 'gate'. By turning current on and off at the gate,

impulses of current are directed through the wiring to the spark plug at high amp rates.
4 In the Porsche system, the power is directed as follows: (see Figure 5.3 for the number locations).
5 The transistor has three terminals: the emitter, which is connected to ground; the collector, which picks up a 12 volt charge via the coil primary lead; and the base, which turns the current on and off. The base terminal and its circuit function will be seen more clearly in the example.
6 The emitter terminal corresponds to terminal 5 on the ignition control unit in our example.
7 The collector terminal and its related circuitry is terminal 6 on the ignition control unit and the wiring which connects it to terminal 1 on the ignition coil. The collector terminal receives its 12 volt charge through this circuit.
8 The base terminal corresponds to either terminal 1 or 2 in our example. The other terminal would be the circuitry for the tachometer and is not included in this example.

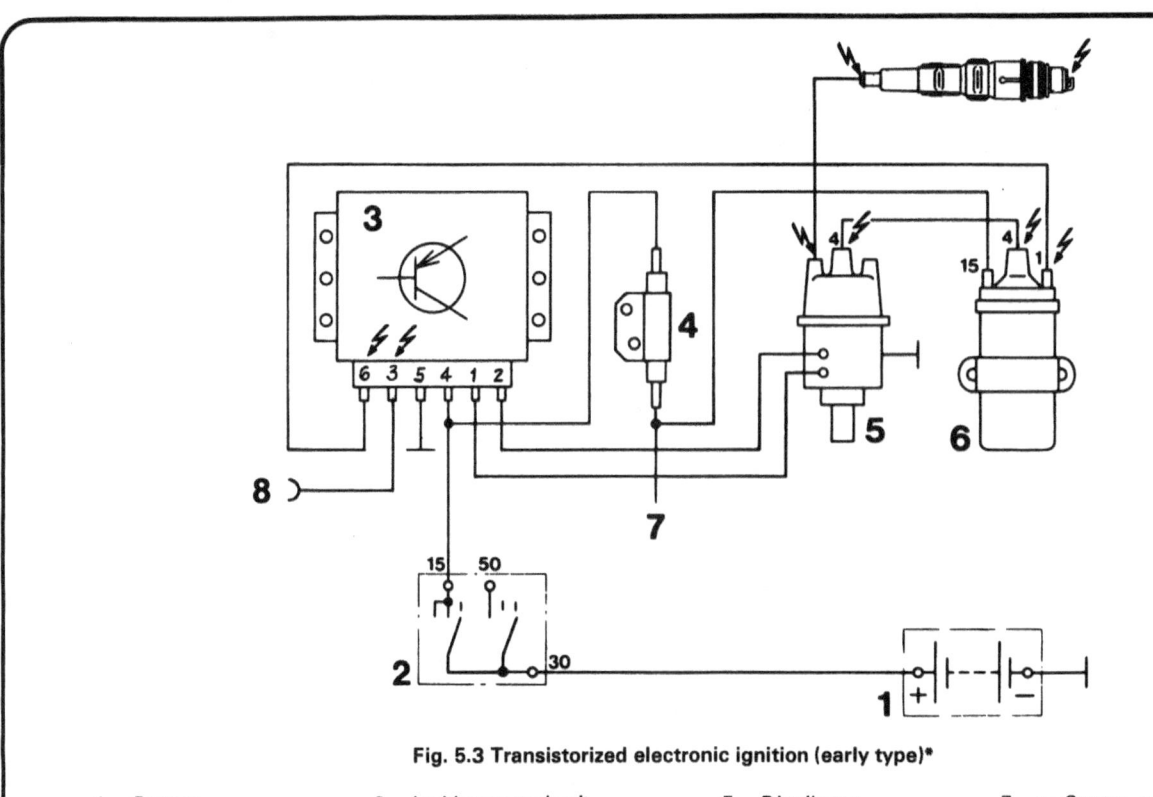

Fig. 5.3 Transistorized electronic ignition (early type)*

| 1 | Battery | 3 | Ignition control unit | 5 | Distributor | 7 | to Starter, terminal 16 |
| 2 | Ignition lock | 4 | Ballast resistor | 6 | Ignition coil | 8 | to Tachometer |

* 'Lightning bolt' symbols denote high voltage connections. Review Section 9 for further information

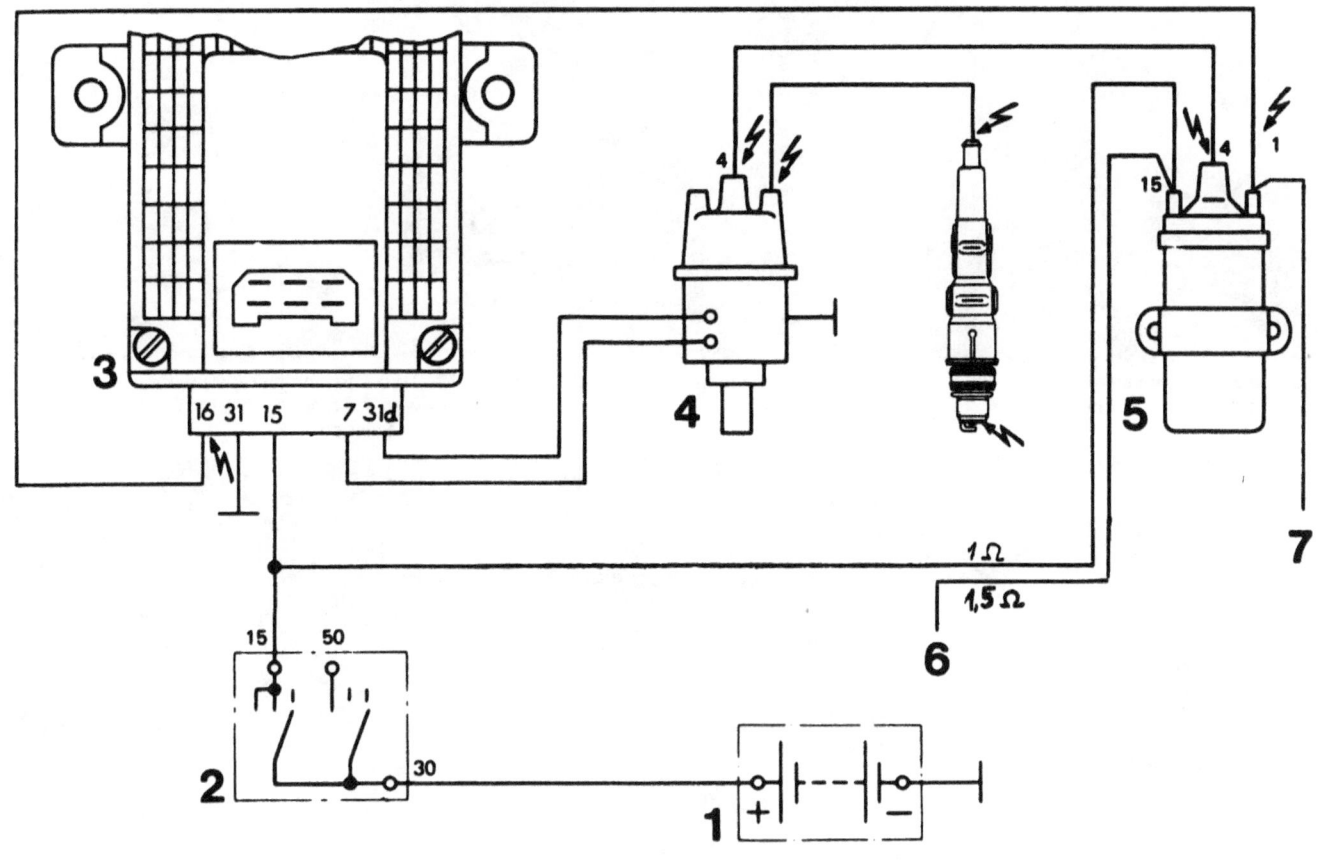

Fig. 5.4 Transistorized electronic ignition (late type)*

1	*Battery*	3	*Ignition control unit*
2	*Ignition lock*	4	*Distributor*

5	*Ignition coil*	7	*To tachometer*
6	*To starter, terminal 16*		

* *'Lightning bolt' symbols denote high voltage connections. Review Section 9 for further information*

9   In practice, the transistor passes a current to the coil via the ballast resistor (two resistor wires in later models). In general practice, the amount of current passing in most standard systems, regardless of make, is 4 amps. The flow is kept 'on' by the trigger circuit, which feeds 1/10 amp or less into the base terminal.

10 When the sensor rotor in the distributor is turned by the gear drive on the camshaft, one of the four points on the rotor will pass over the base terminal pickup inside the distributor, interrupting the power flow.

11 Disrupting the flow of current in the base terminal circuit causes a 'switch off' condition in the trigger circuit of the transistor. A surge of current then leaves the coil via the number 4 terminal on the coil, passes through the distributor/ignition rotor to the appropriate spark plug lead. This surge of current finally passes through the spark plug, jumping the gap at the terminal which is connected to ground.

12 This type of ignition circuitry is known as inductive discharge ignition. As the system requires no points which can arc, the 'switch off' condition happens very abruptly with no leakage of current. This means more power at the spark plug and a very rapid build up of high current even at very high engine revs. In theory, no engine which relies on rotating mass as the means of producing power can turn faster than the ignition system can produce spark. Ignition remains 'dead on' at all times and under all conditions once it is set up correctly.

9   Ignition system – cautionary note

1   The efficiency of the transistorized ignition system means that very high levels of voltage at high rates of amperage are being

produced. Great care is necessary when installing or removing components of the system even when the engine is switched off.

2   When performing running adjustments on the ignition there is an even greater danger of electrocution. The 'lightning bolt' symbols found in Figures 5.3 and 5.4 point out the 'hot' leads.

3   The electrical current produced by this system can be very dangerous if mis-handled. Treat the ignition system with a bit of respect and caution, and you should have no trouble in safely performing the tasks which follow.

10   Distributor – removal and installation

1   Disconnect the negative lead from the battery.

2   Remove the number 1 spark plug and set the piston at TDC.

3   Mark the ignition wires plugged into the distributor cap and remove them. Disconnect the electrical plug from the distributor body (photos).

4   Remove the nut on the distributor hold-down plate. Remove the hold-down plate.

5   Disconnect the vacuum hoses after marking them for proper location.

6   Remove the distributor by pulling it straight out of the distributor drive housing.

7   Installation is the reverse of the removal procedure.

8   Align the line on the rotor with the scribed mark on the distributor housing. You must remove the distributor cap for this part of the installation. Replace the cap when the distributor is in place to prevent dirt from entering the distributor (Section 11) (photo).

9   Make sure that cylinder 1 is in the TDC position (Chapter 1).

10 Install the distributor into the distributor drive housing. As the drive

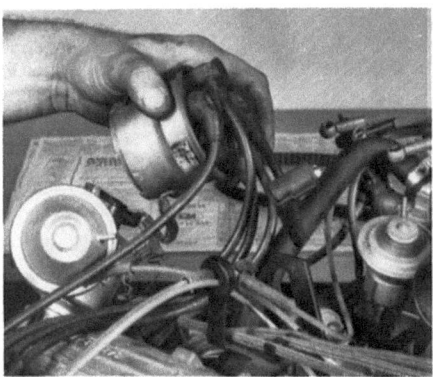
10.3a The distributor cap removed to show location of the ignition wires

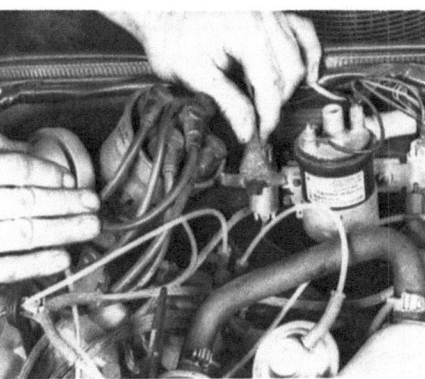
10.3b Disconnecting the electrical plug from the distributor

10.8 The ignition rotor in proper alignment with the mark on the distributor body for installation

10.10 Installing the distributor in the distributor drive housing

10.11a Installing the distributor hold-down plate and nut

10.11b A properly installed distributor

gears mesh, the rotor will turn out of alignment with the distributor housing mark. Anticipate this by moving the rotor a few degrees out of alignment before installing the distributor (photo).
11 Install the distributor hold-down plate and nut (photos).
12 After installation has been completed, adjust the timing of the ignition (Section 20).

11 Distributor cap – removal and installation

1 Remove the negative lead from the battery.
2 Mark the ignition wires according to their location on the cap and unplug them.
3 Pry the spring clips from either side of the cap. Finger pressure should be sufficient for this task. Use of a screwdriver or other similar tool may cause a breakage of the distributor cap (photo 10.3a).
4 Installation is the reverse of the removal procedure.

12 Ignition wires – removal and installation

1 Disconnect the negative lead of the battery.
2 If you intend to re-use the ignition wires, mark them according to the proper cylinders.
3 Unplug the wires from their rubber bases. Do not remove any wires by tugging above the caps. This will cause wire breakage and separations in the leads.
4 Remove the wires from the distributor cap first, then from the spark plugs.
5 When installing new ignition wires start with the shortest wire and move to the longest. If your engine has wiring looms installed, snap the wires into the looms after both ends of each wire have been connected.

13 Ignition rotor – removal and installation

1 Disconnect the negative lead from the battery.
2 Remove the distributor cap with the ignition wires in place (Section 11) (photo 10.3a).
3 Remove the ignition rotor by lifting it straight off its shaft.
4 Installation is the reverse of the removal procedure. The shaft is keyed for proper location of the rotor.

14 Ignition coil – removal and installation

1 Disconnect the negative lead from the battery.
2 Loosen the hold-down nuts and remove the leads from the number 1 and 15 terminals. Label the wires with tape and an indelible ink pen to prevent mixing up the wires on installation (photo).
3 Remove the heavy wire connecting the coil to the distributor by pulling close to the connector. Pull on the collar of the rubber cap to prevent wire breakage (photo).
4 Loosen, but do not remove the nuts holding the ballast resistor clips (photo).
5 Loosen the nut on the coil holding clamp and lift out the coil.
6 Installation is the reverse of the removal procedure.
7 Torque the nuts on the ballast resistor clips to 6 ft-lb (0.80 m-kg).

15 Ignition coil – checking

1 Check the battery terminals to ensure proper connection.
2 Make sure that the ignition is off.
3 Connect an ohmmeter between terminals 1 and 15. The value of this test is the primary resistance. The primary resistance value should be 1.0 to 1.3 ohms (0.95 to 1.4 on Turbo).
4 Connect the ohmmeter to the number 1 and 15 terminals of the coil. This will give the secondary resistance value. The value of secondary resistance should be 5.5 to 8.0 kilohms.

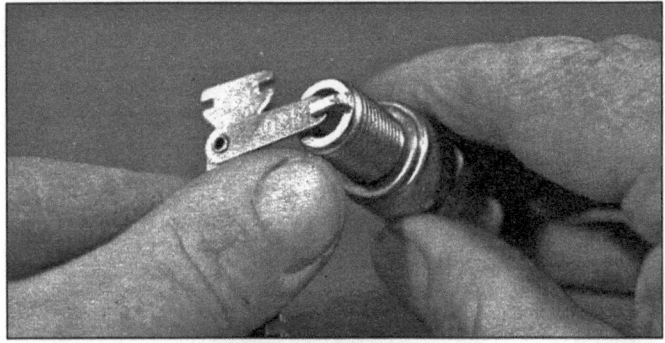

Measuring plug gap. A feeler gauge of the correct size (see ignition system specifications) should have a slight "drag" when slid between the electrodes. Adjust gap if necessary

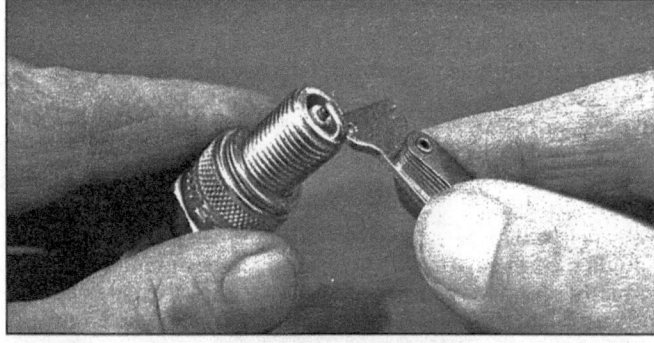

Adjusting plug gap. The plug gap is adjusted by bending the earth electrode inwards, or outwards, as necessary until the correct clearance is obtained. Note the use of the correct tool

Normal. Grey-brown deposits, lightly coated core nose. Gap increasing by around 0.001 in (0.025 mm) per 1000 miles (1600 km). Plugs ideally suited to engine, and engine in good condition

Carbon fouling. Dry, black, sooty deposits. Will cause weak spark and eventually misfire. Fault: over-rich fuel mixture. Check:carburettor mixture settings, float level and jet sizes; choke operation and cleanliness of air filter. Plugs can be re-used after cleaning

Oil fouling. Wet, oily deposits. Will cause weak spark and eventually misfire. Fault: worn bores/piston rings or valve guides; sometimes occurs (temporarily) during running-in period. Plugs can be re-used after thorough cleaning

Overheating. Electrodes have glazed appearance, core nose very white - few deposits. Fault: plug overheating. Check: plug value, ignition timing, fuel octane rating (too low) and fuel mixture (too weak). Discard plugs and cure fault immediately

Electrode damage. Electrodes burned away; core nose has burned, glazed appearance. Fault: pre-ignition. Check: as for "Overheating" but may be more severe. Discard plugs and remedy fault before piston or valve damage occurs

Split core nose (may appear initially as a crack). Damage is self-evident, but cracks will only show after cleaning. Fault: pre-ignition or wrong gap-setting technique. Check: ignition timing, cooling system, fuel octane rating (too low) and fuel mixture (too weak). Discard plugs, rectify fault immediately

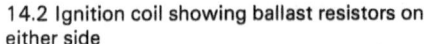

14.2 Ignition coil showing ballast resistors on either side

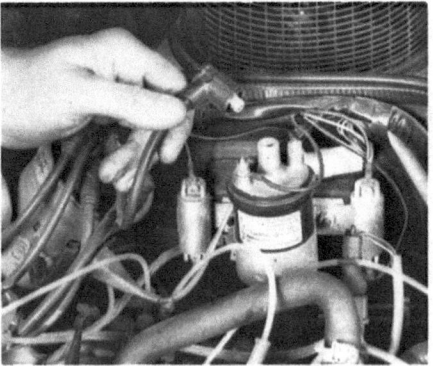

14.3 Removing the coil-to-distributor wire

14.4 Loosening the ballast resistor clips

5. If the primary and secondary values are not met, replace the ignition coil. It is necessary that both values be met to ensure proper ignition.

16 Transistorized ignition control unit - removal and installation

1 Disconnect the negative lead of the battery.
2 Remove the nuts holding the ignition control unit to the wheel well (photo).
3 Lift the ignition control unit and disconnect the plug connector.
4 Installation is the reverse of the removal procedure.

17 Spark plugs - removal and installation

1 Disconnect the negative lead from the battery.
2 Remove the spark plug leads by pulling up on the covers. Do not pull on the wires.
3 With a padded spark plug socket, unscrew the spark plugs and remove them.
4 Replace old spark plugs with new plugs of the proper type and which are correctly gapped. The Specifications Section lists the proper type of spark plug and gas specification for your model.
5 Installation is the reverse of the removal procedure.
6 Torque spark plugs to 21 ft-lb (3 m-kg).

18 Ballast resistors - removal and installation (1976-1977½)

1 Disconnect the negative lead from the battery.
2 Unscrew the connectors at either end of the ballast resistors and remove the leads. Mark the leads for proper installation.
3 Remove the nuts which hold the mounting clips in place and remove the ballast resistors. The resistance value of each resistor is stamped on the mounting clips. Note which resistor is being removed from each mounting stud (photo 14.2).
4 Installation is the reverse of the removal procedure.
5 Torque the hold down nuts to 6 ft-lb (0.80 m-kg).

19 Resistor wires - 1977½ on

1 1977½ and later versions of the 924 do not have ballast resistors ahead of the ignition coil in the electrical circuit. These have been replaced by two resistor wires of 1.0 and 1.5 ohms resistance (Fig. 5.4).
2 These are removed and installed simply by unscrewing their connector clips. Do not shorten these wires; replace them if they break.
3 If, at any time, these wires are removed in conjunction with other work, take time to label each wire and its proper location.

16.2 An early-type control unit, showing the two nuts which must be disconnected before removal

20 Adjusting ignition timing

1 Run the engine until normal operating temperatures are reached. Oil temperature should be 180 to 190°F (80 to 90°C).
2 Connect a hand held tachometer according to the manufacturer's instructions. The car's tachometer is run from the ignition control unit and may not give as exact a reading.
3 Leave the hoses connected to the vacuum advance unit on the distributor unless stated otherwise in the Specifications Section.
4 Make sure that the ignition is turned off, then install a timing light according to the manufacturer's instructions.
5 Start the engine and check the idle speed on the hand held tachometer. If the idle speed is not well within the idle speed specified for your model, refer to Chapter 3 for instructions in adjusting the idle speed.
6 Sight the beam of the timing light into the open slot of the bellhousing. The slot is located on the upper left side of the bellhousing.
7 The flywheel usually has three marks; the center mark of the three is the timing mark. See the Specifications Section to determine which timing mark is correct for your model. The timing mark should appear in the slot and align with the reference mark at the proper idle speed.
8 If the timing mark does not appear in the beam of the strobe light as a steady image, loosen the nut on the distributor hold down plate and turn the distributor back and forth until a steady image is seen. Tighten the nut and torque it to 14 to 16 ft-lb (2.0 to 2.2 m-kg). Recheck this torque once the engine has cooled.
9 Ignition timing should be checked for proper advance at an engine speed of 4500 rpm. This must be done on a distributor test machine when the vacuum hoses are disconnected. Check the specifications section for the amount of advance proper for your model (Fig. 5.5).

Centrifugal advance curve: 125 Hp, European models

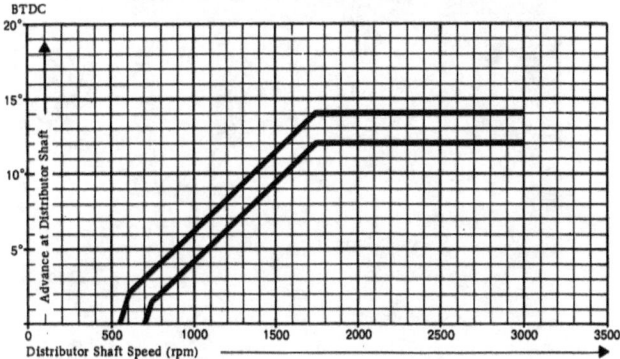

Vacuum advance curve: 125 Hp, European models

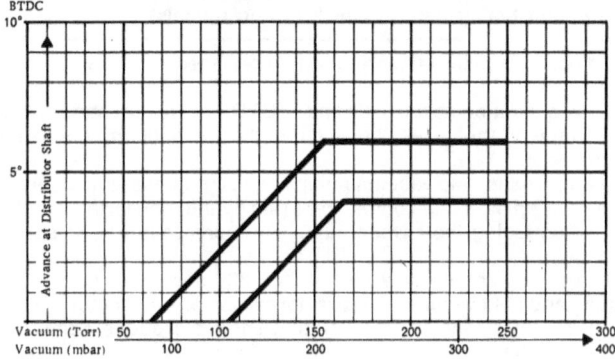

Centrifugal advance curve: 95 Hp, US models (1976 – 1977½)

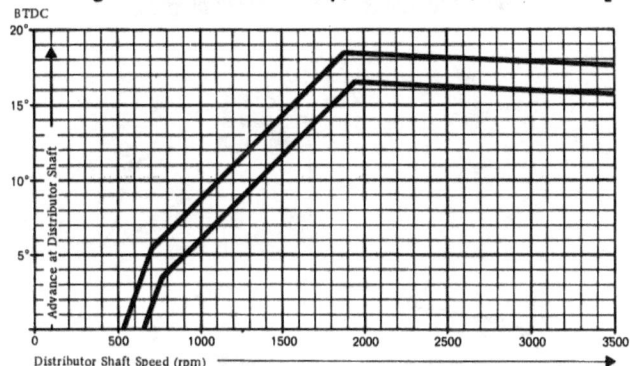

Vacuum advance curve: 95 Hp, US models (1976 – 1977½)

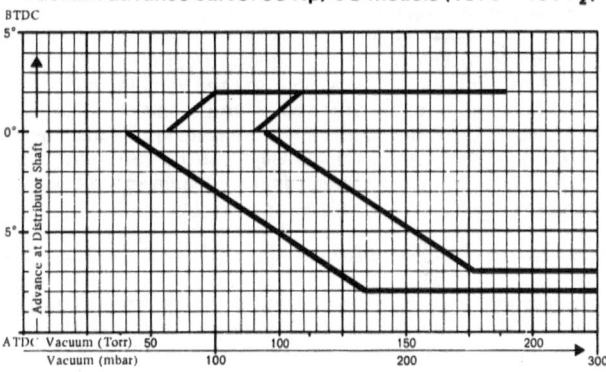

Centrifugal advance curve: 110 Hp, US models (1977 – 1979)

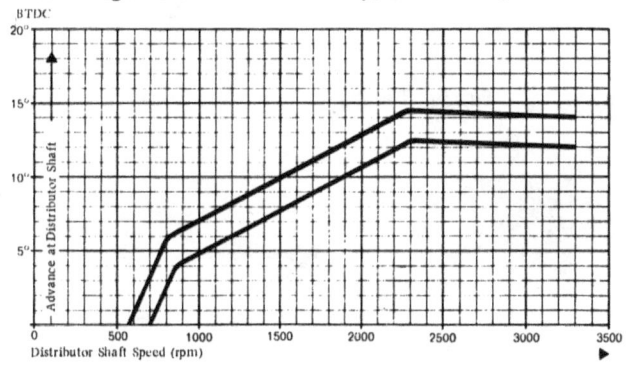

Vacuum advance curve: 110 Hp, US models (1977 – 1979)

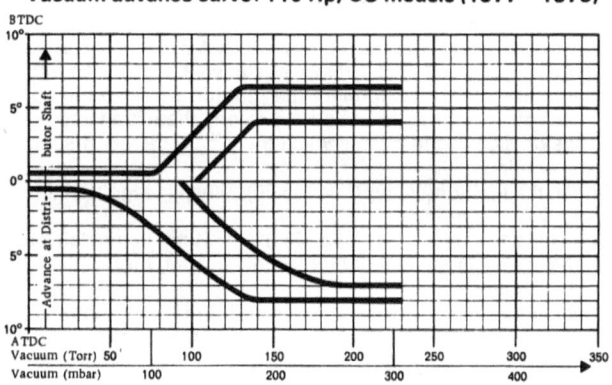

Centrifugal advance curve: Turbo, US models

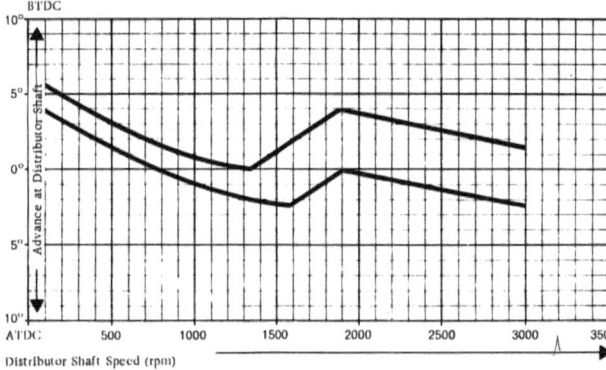

Vacuum advance curve: Turbo, US models

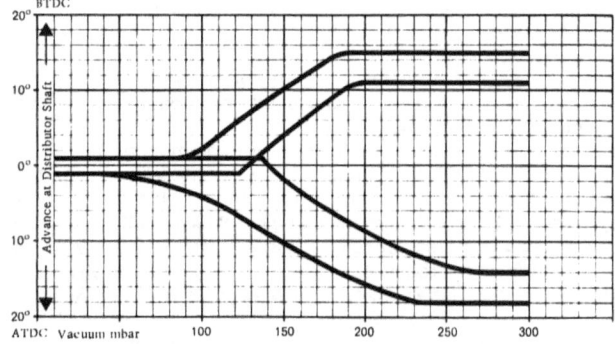

Fig. 5.5 Distributor test bench curves

Instructions: When operated on a test bench, the distributor of your vehicle must produce oscilloscope readings within the boundaries shown in the following charts. Make sure that you refer to the charts appropriate to your model

21 Ignition timing control check (Turbo models)

1   Adjust the ignition timing to the proper specifications (Section 20).
2   Timing must be between 3° and 9° BTDC at an idle speed of 900 ± 50 rpm with the hoses connected to the two vacuum fittings on the distributor.
3   Using a hand held vacuum pump and vacuum gauge, produce a vacuum of 250 m-bar at connection 1 (the connection farthest to the right when facing the advance unit). An increase in engine speed will result.
The timing should now be between 32° and 38° BTDC.
4   If a hand held vacuum pump is not available, connecting fittings 1 and 2 with a long piece of tubing should produce adequate vacuum in the system.

22 Transistorized ignition – troubleshooting

1   Performance of this procedure requires that the battery be fully charged, fuel is in the gas tank, and that the vehicle and the surrounding air is at a temperature between 0° and 40°C (32° and 104°F). Temperature will seriously affect the readings obtained in this test. Remember the warnings about high voltage (Section 9) and follow the tests in strict order. Jumping from component to component will not give a useable set of readings.

Starter turns, but the engine will not start or has poor output.

2   Connect a spark plug meter to ignition coil terminal 4 and set the gap to 12 mm (Fig. 5.6). Start the engine. If 12 mm of spark is not available, go to paragraph 11. If 12 mm of spark is available, continue.
3   With the ignition off, check the resistance of the distributor cap, distributor rotor, ignition wires, and spark plugs. Resistance of the ignition wires (including connectors) should be approximately 6 kOhms. Connect the tester as shown in Fig. 5.7. The resistance of the distributor rotor, when it is tested as shown in Fig. 5.8, should be approximately 5 kOhms. Connect the ignition wires to the spark plugs and test for spark. If no spark is present, there is a fault on the high tension side of the circuit which must be repaired. If spark is present, continue.
4   Check the ignition timing (Section 20). When the ignition timing is properly set, continue.
5   Check the fuel system (Chapter 3). If fuel is not being delivered, make the necessary corrections. When proper fuel delivery is assured, continue.
6   Check the resistors and the ignition coil with the ignition off and the resistors or resistor wires disconnected at both ends. The 0.4 Ohm resistor should give a reading of 0.35 to 0.45 Ohms and the 0.6 Ohm resistor should show 0.55 to 0.65 Ohms. Checking the ignition coil primary windings is done by hooking the leads to terminals 1 and 15 of the ignition coil. A reading of 1.0 to 1.35 Ohms (Turbo: 0.95 to 1.4 Ohms) should result. To test the ignition coil secondary windings, connect the tester to terminals 1 and 4. Readings of 5.5 to 8.0 kOhms should be found. See Fig. 5.9 for the location of the connection points. Replace any component whose resistance values are not within the values above. When all readings are within the given values, continue.
7   Check the battery voltage. Minimum voltage must be 11 volts or more. Charge or replace the battery as necessary. With the ignition switch on, check the voltage between terminal 15 of the ignition coil and ground (Fig. 5.10). Minimum voltage must be 5 volts or more. If a greater drop is noted, check all wires from the battery to the ignition switch, to the resistor, ignition coil, and the ignition control unit for the source of the voltage drop. Make repairs as necessary. If normal readings are found, continue.
8   Check the delivered voltage to the ignition control unit by connecting terminal 4 of the plug to ground through a volt meter (Fig. 5.11a). On Turbo models, connect terminals 15 and 31 of the plug through a volt meter (Fig. 5.11b). The voltage reading obtained in this test should equal the battery voltage reading. If the two readings are not the same, check the wiring from the ignition switch to the ignition control unit for voltage drop. If the values are equal, continue.

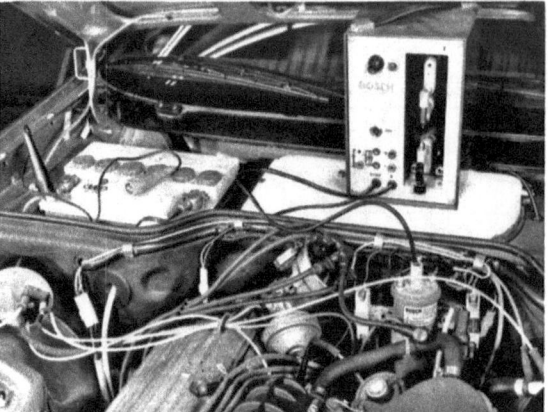

Fig. 5.6 Installation of the spark plug gap meter

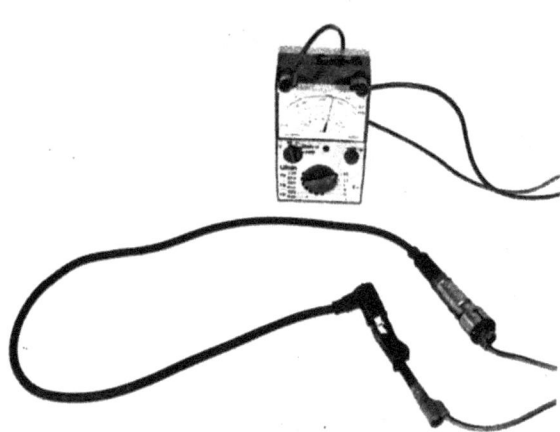

Fig. 5.7 Testing ignition wire resistance

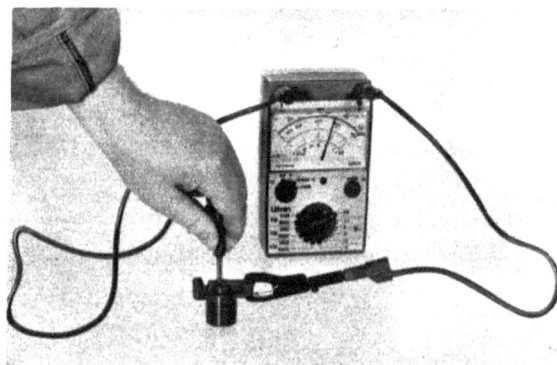

Fig. 5.8 Testing the resistance of the distributor rotor

9   With the ignition on, check the voltage between terminal 1 of the ignition coil and ground (Fig. 5.12). Maximum voltage should be 2.0 volts. If the voltage read is greater than this value, replace the ignition control unit. If the voltage value is good, continue.
10 Check the ignition dwell angles (Fig. 5.13). They are as follows:
Idle: 52° to 70° at 1500 ± 50 rpm (Turbo: 54° to 78° at 1500 ± 50 rpm)
Fast: 42° to 68° at 5000 ± 50 rpm (Turbo: 66° to 80° at 5000 ± 50 rpm) rpm)
If the dwell angle is not correct, go to paragraph 11. If the dwell angle is correct, continue. The engine must now start and/or the engine output must be good. If this is not true, there is a mechanical defect.

Fig. 5.9 Connection points for resistor and resistor wire tests

Fig. 5.11a The delivered voltage test (standard models)

Fig. 5.10 Volt meter connection points for testing battery voltage

Fig. 5.11b The delivered voltage test (Turbo)

Fig. 5.12 Testing coil voltage to ground

Fig. 5.13 Checking the ignition dwell angles

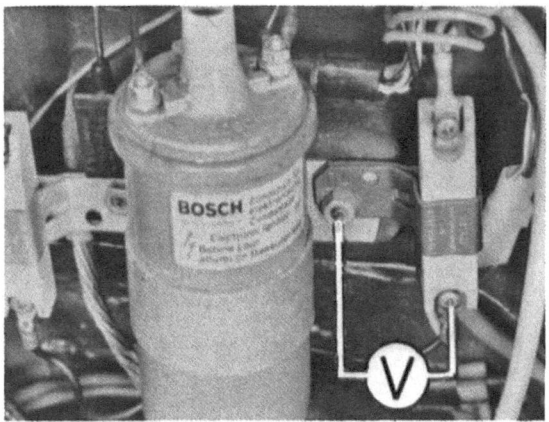

Fig. 5.14 Connections for the starting boost test

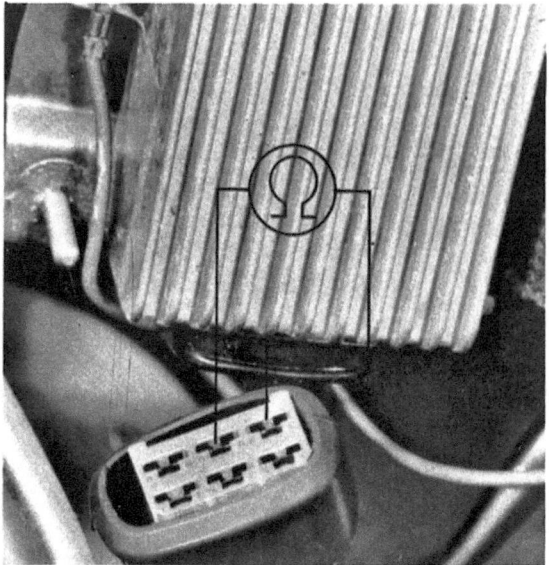

Fig. 5.15 Measuring the sensor resistance. The connections are the same for Turbo

Fig. 5.16 Checking resistance at the sensor coil

11 Check the starting boost by connecting a volt meter to the 0.4 Ohm resistor or resistor wire as shown in Fig. 5.14. Operate the starter. The meter must register battery voltage. If this does not happen, there is a break in the supply wiring or the relay solenoid which must be located and corrected. If the boost is good, continue.

12 Measure the sensor resistance including the wiring at the ignition control unit plug between terminals 1 and 2 (Turbo: terminals 7 and 31 d) (Fig. 5.15). The ignition must be turned off. Resistance should be between 890 and 1285 Ohms (Turbo: 485 and 700 Ohms). If these readings are not obtained, replace the distributor. If the resistance values are good, continue.

13 With the ignition off, check the sensor coil, including the sensor wire, for a ground short at the ignition control unit plug as follows (Fig. 5.16):
connect terminal 1 to ground (Turbo: terminal 7 to ground)
connect terminal 2 to ground (Turbo: terminal 31 d to ground)
If resistance does not equal ∞, replace the distributor. If resistance does equal ∞, continue.

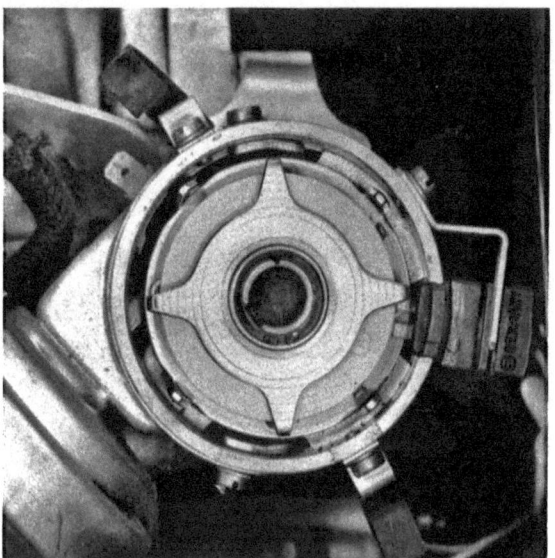

Fig. 5.17 Inspection of the sensor for proper gap between rotor and stator

14 Check the sensor system for mechanical damage. Check for a visible gap between the rotor and stator (Fig. 5.17). If the sensor system does not look like it is in proper working order, replace the distributor. If the sensor system appears to be in proper working order, return to paragraph 6 and test out through paragraph 10 once again.

Chapter 6 Clutch

Contents

Specifications

Mechanical clutch, all standard 924

Clutch type .... Single plate diaphragm clutch, dry-type, mounted at rear of engine. Operated via cable.

Pressure plate type...................................... MF 215 K

Clutch disc type .... 215 PSD

Contact pressure .... 490 to 560 m–kg

Clutch disc thickness
    new .... 10.1 to 10.5 mm
    wear limit... to 8.5 mm if wear is symmetrical

Adjustments
    clutch lever adjustment (outboard lever) .... 138 ± 2 mm
    pedal free play.. 20 to 25 mm

Hydraulic clutch, all Turbo

Clutch type .... Single plate diaphragm clutch, dry-type, mounted at rear of engine. Operated by hydraulic cylinder.

Pressure plate type...................................... MFZ 225

Clutch disc type .... 225 TD

Friction lining thickness
    new .... 8.1 ± 0.3 mm (0.319 ± 0.012 in.)
    wear limit... 6.3 mm (0.248 in.) if the wear pattern is symmetrical

Lateral runout
    maximum permissible .... 0.6 mm (0.024 in.)

Contact pressure .... 720 to 790 m–kg

Adjustments
    free play, push rod to master cylinder piston .... 0.5 mm
    free play, clutch pedal movement (as a way of determining the proper free play of above figure).......................... 3 mm
    outer edge of spring disk to knife edge bearing.............. 55 mm

Torque specifications

Mechanical clutch, all standard 924	ft–lb	m–kg
Pressure plate to flywheel	23	3.2
*Transmission mount to transmission	18	2.5
*Transmission mount to body	30	4.2
Rear wheel drive shafts to transmission drive flanges	30	4.2
Back up light switch	18 to 23	2.5 to 3.2

Bellhousing to engine:	ft-lb	m-kg
small	33	4.5
large	54	7.5
†Transmission bonded mount bolts	30	4.2
†Transmission bonded mount self-locking nuts (use new nuts)	30	4.2
†Guide bolts	6.5	0.9
Clutch bellhousing to central tube	30	4.2
Clutch lever clamp bolt	11	1.5

* (4-speed transmissions only)
† (5-speed transmissions only)

Hydraulic clutch, all Turbo

	ft-lb	m-kg
Guide sleeve to clutch bellhousing	9	1.2
Clutch and gear ring	16 to 18	2.2 to 2.5
Flywheel to crankshaft	65	9.0
Bellhousing to engine:		
small	33	4.5
large	54	7.5
Release lever shaft, bolt	7	1.0
Release lever shaft, nut	5.5	0.75
Hydraulic slave cylinder to bellhousing	14 to 17	1.9 to 2.3
Clutch bellhousing to central tube	30	4.2
Transmission mount to transmission	30	4.2
Transmission mount to rear axle cross tube	30	4.2
Drive shaft	30	4.2

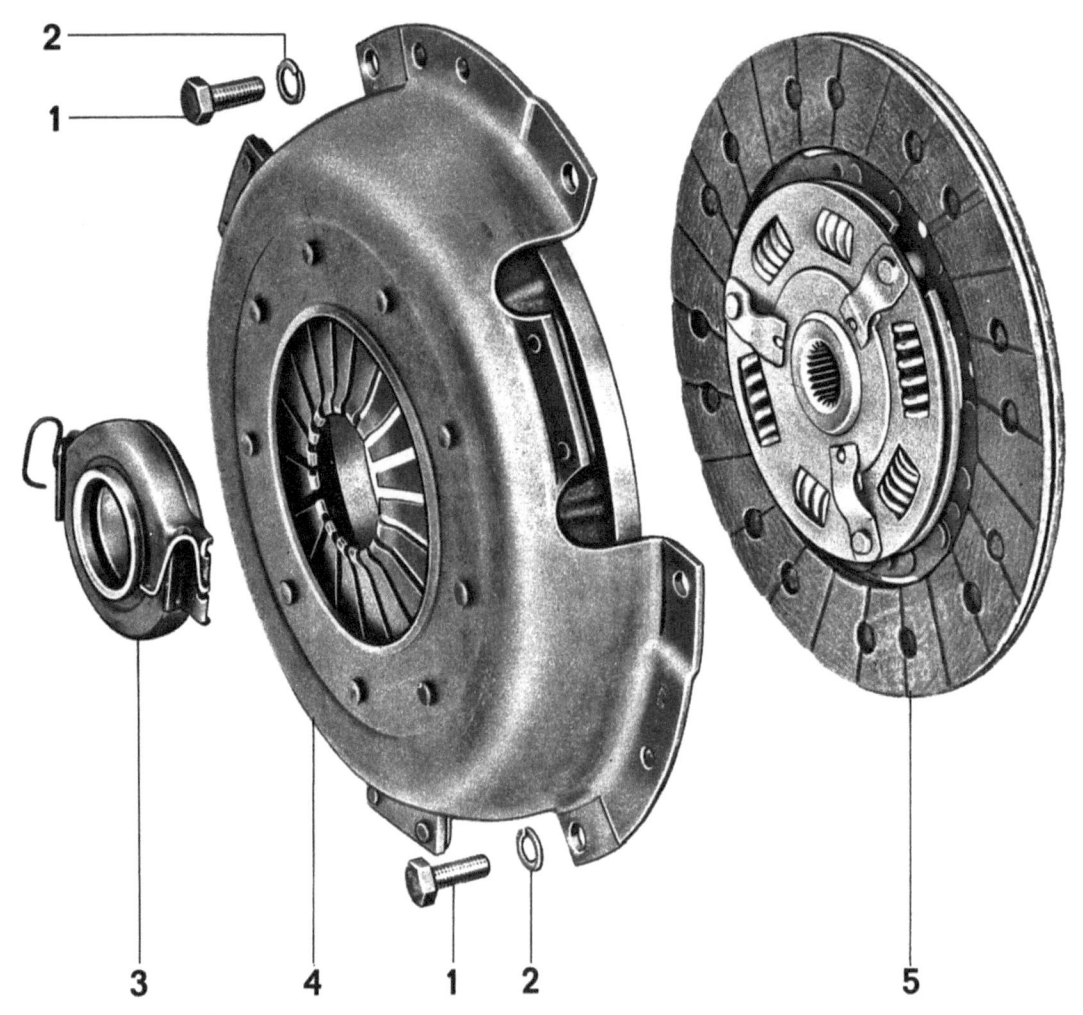

Fig. 6.1 Clutch disc and pressure plate, mechanical and hydraulic clutches

1	Pressure plate-to-flywheel bolts	2	Lock washer, spring type	4	Pressure plate
		3	Release bearing	5	Clutch disc

1 Mechanical clutch - general description

1   The clutch is of the single disc, diaphragm type. The clutch disc is run 'dry'.
2   Engagement and disengagement of the clutch is via a cable which operates a lever on the side of the clutch bellhousing. Depressing the clutch pedal disengages the clutch from the driving plate on the engine flywheel.

2 Clutch disc - inspection (while installed)

1   Disconnect the negative lead from the battery.
2   Raise the vehicle and place it on jack stands.
3   Remove the single bolt from the inspection cover and remove the cover by pulling down slightly and back to disengage the clips.
4   Check the clutch disc for even wear; that the friction material is within the wear limits established; for smooth operation of the clutch actuating mechanisms.
5   Turn the engine at the lower pulley and take thickness measurements at several points on the disc to ensure even wear.

3 Clutch disc - removal and installation (4-speed transmission)

1   Disconnect the negative lead from the battery.
2   Raise the vehicle and place it on jack stands.
3   Using Porsche tool VW 10-222 or an engine hoist, raise the engine by the front engine lifting loop so that the engine is supported by the hoist and not resting on the engine mounts.
4   Loosen the nut on the clutch cable adjuster and remove the clutch cable (photos).
5   Remove the lower engine guard by removing the four bolts.
6   Disconnect the wire at the engine temperature sensor.
7   Remove the clutch bellhousing inspection cover (Section 2) (photo).
8   Loosen the clutch pressure plate mounting bolts about two turns each. Loosen them in a crossing pattern, loosening the bolt immediately across from the previous bolt then moving to the bolt immediately to the left. The engine may be turned by turning the crankshaft pulley bolt. If engine turning is difficult, remove the spark plugs (photo).
9   Place a homemade wood block tool (Figure 6.2) between the driveshaft central tube and the front cross connection. This tool is necessary to the success of this task as it prevents the driveshaft and tube from falling against any parts and being damaged (photo).

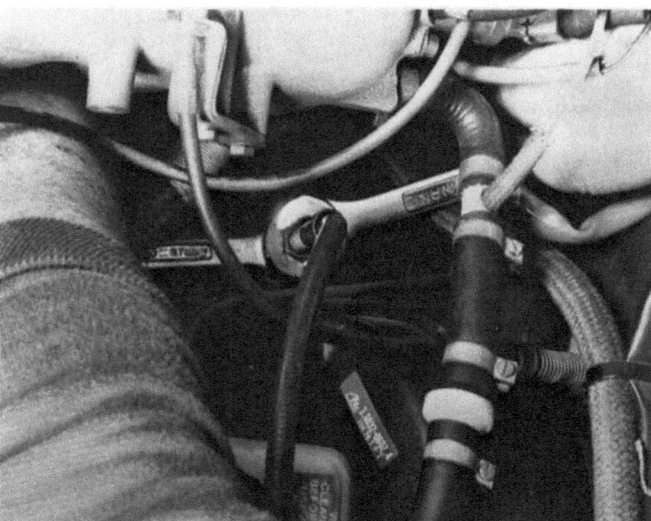

3.4a Loosening the adjusting nuts on the clutch adjuster bracket

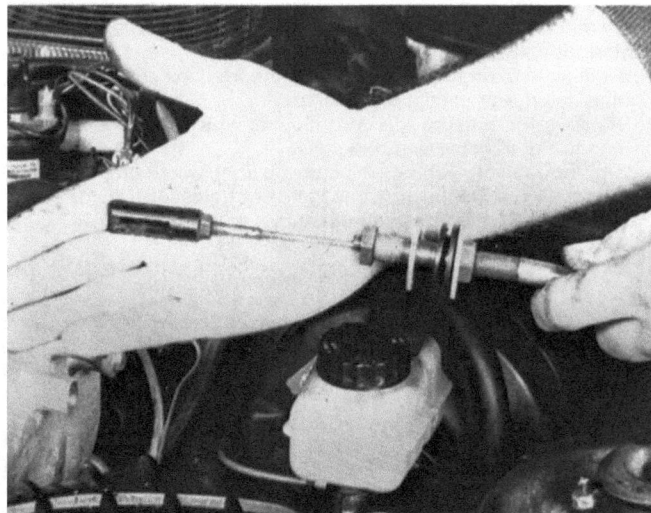

3.4b Removing the clutch cable

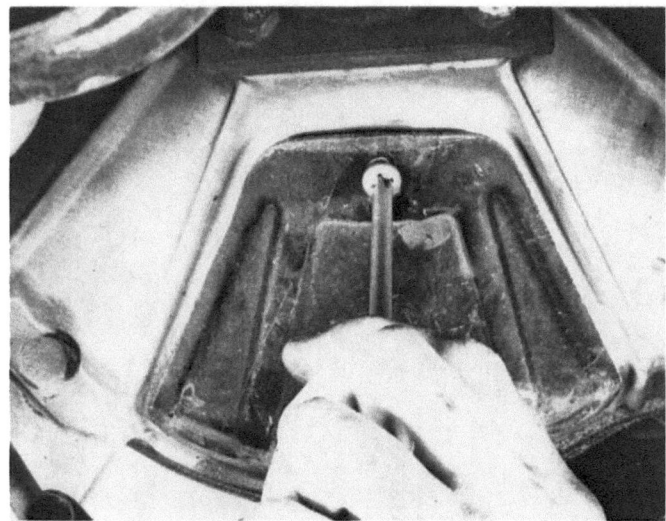

3.7 Removing the clutch inspection plate

3.8 Loosening the pressure plate bolts

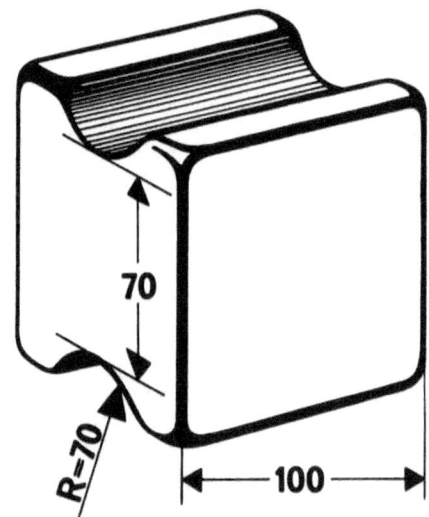

Fig. 6.2 Homemade wooden support block for clutch removal

10 Remove the clutch bellhousing-to-engine bolts from beneath the vehicle (photo).

11 Detach the front and rear exhaust pipe hanger brackets from the central tube. (See photos, Chapter 3).

12 Remove the three bolts which hold the front exhaust pipe to the primary muffler or catalytic converter.

13 Remove the nuts on the Lord mounts which hold the exhaust system to the transmission end plate.

14 Unplug the connector to the back up light switch on the rear of the transmission. Unclip the wires from their holder on the side of the transmission so that they are not damaged. (See Chapter 7).

15 Remove the back up light switch.

16 Unsnap the rubber sleeve and bellows for the shift lever from the console. Carefully rock the shift lever cover back and forth while pulling upward to remove the cover complete with bellows.

17 Remove the circlip from the shift shaft pivot located on the shift lever. Pull off the selector rod and the wave washer. Remove the two bolts holding the shift lever to the central tube (photos).

18 Using a twelve-point socket head wrench, detach the axle shafts at the transmission (Chapter 7). Use a loop of string or wire to hang the shafts in a horizontal position. This will prevent damage to the shafts or their bearings.

19 Support the transmission with a wheeled floor jack or several blocks of wood so that the weight of the transmission is taken off the mounts.

20 Remove the transmission mounts.

21 Slide the entire transmission, central tube and clutch bellhousing to the rear of the vehicle about 85 mm. The clutch disc, pressure plate, and clutch release bearing may be removed through the slot between the engine and bellhousing in the following way:

22 Remove the pressure plate bolts by loosening them about two turns each in a crossing pattern until all pressure is relieved and the bolts may be removed (photo 3.8).

23 Hold the clutch plate inside the pressure plate and lift down and away from the clutch bellhousing (photo).

24 Remove the release bearing by unsnapping the spring clips which hold it in place and lifting it out of the bellhousing.

25 Inspect the friction surface on the flywheel for wear. Clean the flywheel surfaces with acetone or naptha; do not use degreasers or any petroleum based cleaners. If the friction surface is excessively or unevenly worn, the flywheel must be replaced.

26 Installation is the reverse of the removal procedure.

27 Lubricate the needle bearing in the end of the crankshaft with approximately 3 grams (3 cc) of NGLI grade number 3 lithium grease. Do not substitute any other type of grease, as an unsuitable type will cause needle bearing damage.

28 The clutch disc must be installed with the stamped lettering "Schwungradseite" facing the flywheel (photo).

29 Center the clutch disc with a phenolic centering mandrel (available at most auto parts stores, purchase the same one as for any Volkswagen) or a mandrel made from a piece of Porsche driveshaft and install the pressure plate.

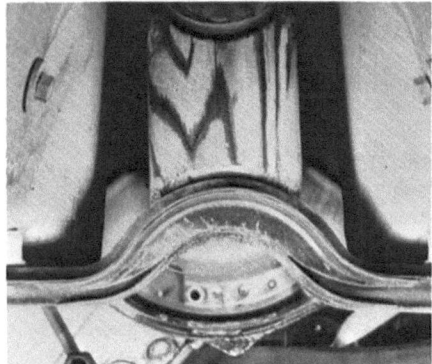

3.9 Installation of the homemade wooden block

3.10 Removing the clutch bellhousing bolts

3.17a Disconnecting the shifter rod from the shift lever

3.17b Removing the shift lever-to-central-tube mounting bolts

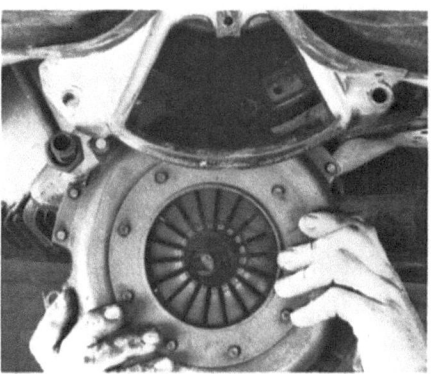

3.23 Removing the clutch disc and pressure plate

3.28 Installing the clutch disc

30 Tighten the bolts on the pressure plate in a cross pattern, two turns at a time until they are snug. Torque the bolts, again in a cross pattern, to 23 ft-lb (3.2 m-kg) (photos).
31 Torque the transmission mount to transmission bolts to 18 ft-lb (2.5 m-kg) and the transmission mount to body bolts to 30 ft-lb (4.2 m-kg). (See photos, Chapter 7).
32 Torque the socket head bolts on the rear wheel drive shafts to 30 ft-lb (4.2 m-kg).
33 Torque the back up light switch to 18 to 23 ft-lb (2.5 to 3.2 m-kg).
34 There are two different sizes of bolts which hold the bellhousing to the engine. The smaller bolts, which hold the bellhousing to the oil pan, which is of aluminum construction, are torqued to 33 ft-lb (4.5 m-kg). The larger bolts hold the bellhousing to the steel engine block and are torqued to 54 ft-lb (7.5 m-kg) (photos).
35 Do not remove the wood block tool until you have installed and torqued all bolts.
36 Referring to Section 9, check the clutch adjustment.

4 Clutch disc – removal and installation (5-speed transmission)

1 Disconnect the negative lead from the battery.
2 Raise the vehicle and place it on jack stands.
3 Remove the shift lever and its boot (photos 3.17a and 3.17b).

4 Unscrew the mounting bolts of the shift guide and remove them.
5 Detach the shift centering springs at the guide.
6 Loosen the adjusting nuts for the clutch cable and remove the cable from its adjusting bracket (photos 3.4a and 3.4b).
7 Using Special Tool VW 10-222 or an engine hoist, lift the engine by its lifting loops so that the weight of the engine rests on the hoist and not on the engine mounts.
8 Remove the lower engine guard by removing the four bolts.
9 Remove the entire exhaust assembly from the exhaust manifold-to-front exhaust pipe flange back. See Chapter 3. Make sure that the two exhaust hangers are unhooked from their rubber hanger bushings.
10 Using a twelve-point socket wrench, remove the axle shafts from the transmission (Chapter 7). Suspend the axle shafts in a horizontal position to prevent damage to the internal bearings.
11 Remove the self-locking nuts from the bonded transmission mounts.
12 Place a floor jack or several blocks of wood beneath the final drive section of the transmission and raise them so that the weight of the transmission rests on the wood blocks or jack and not on the transmission mounts. Do not raise the transmission too far or you may crush the brake line for the left rear wheel.
13 Remove the bolts from the bonded transmission mounts and make sure that the transmission unit is firmly held by the floor jack or wood blocks.

3.30a Applying the appropriate torque to the pressure plate bolts

3.30b A properly installed clutch disc and pressure plate

3.34a Applying the appropriate torque to the small-diameter bolts (alloy oil pan)

3.34b Applying the appropriate torque to the large-diameter bolts (iron engine block)

14 Remove the four bolts holding the central tube to the clutch bellhousing.

15 Slide the transmission and central tube assembly to the rear of the vehicle. About 85 to 100 mm is needed between the end of the central tube and the clutch bellhousing so that the next steps can be completed.

16 Remove the bolts from the clutch housing (photo 3.10).

17 Remove the clutch bellhousing.

18 Loosen the bolts on the pressure plate about two turns each in a cross pattern. Continue this process until all bolts are completely disengaged from the flywheel and remove the pressure plate and clutch disc together (photos 3.10 and 3.23).

19 Inspect the friction surface of the flywheel as well as the seal. Replace as necessary.

20 Clean all clutch parts with acetone or naptha. Do not use commercial degreasers or petroleum based cleaners.

21 Installation is the reverse of the removal procedure.

22 Lubricate the needle bearing in the end of the crankshaft with approximately 3 grams (3 cc) of NGLI grade number 3 lithium grease. Unsuitable grease will cause needle bearing damage.

23 Install the clutch disc with the word "Schwungradseite' which is stamped into the metal facing the flywheel (photo 3.28).

24 Install the pressure plate and center the clutch disc with a phenolic clutch centering tool (available at most auto parts stores, the one you'll need is the same as that for any Volkswagen) or a mandrel made from a piece of Porsche axle shaft.

25 Install the pressure plate to flywheel bolts and tighten them each in turn about two turns each in a cross pattern until they are snug. Torque them in a cross pattern to 23 ft-lb (3.2 m-kg).

26 Install the clutch bellhousing (photo). When you install the bolts for the bellhousing, note that they are of two sizes. The smaller bolts attach the bellhousing to the oil pan which is of soft aluminum. Torque these bolts to 33 ft-lb (4.5 m-kg). The larger bolts attach the bellhousing to the engine block which is of steel. Torque these bolts to 54 ft-lb (7.5 m-kg) (photos 3.30a and 3.30b).

27 Slide the transmission and central tube assembly forward and install the four bolts which hold the central tube to the clutch bellhousing. Torque the bolts to 30 ft-lb (4.2 m-kg).

28 Install the bolts which hold the transmission bonded mount to the transmission and torque them to 30 ft-lb (4.2 m-kg).

29 Install new locknuts on the lower studs on the bonded mounts and torque them to 30 ft-lb (4.2 m-kg).

30 Install the bolts on the guide of the shift lever and torque them to 6.5 ft-lb (0.9 m-kg).

31 When all bolts have been torqued, make a careful visual check to make sure you have not pinched any wires in the installation of the bellhousing and to ensure that the insulating blanket between the central tube and the floor of the passenger compartment remains 17¾ in. (450 mm) from the rear edge of the forward central tube flange.

32 Adjust the clutch play (Section 9).

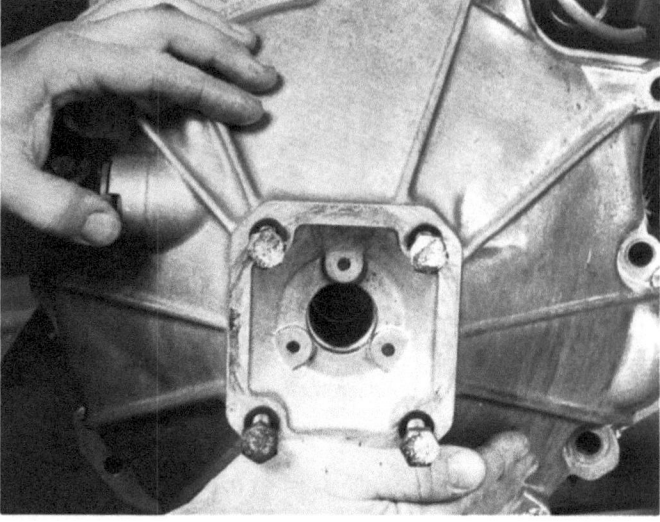

4.26 Installing the clutch bellhousing

Fig. 6.3 Measuring clutch plate lining thickness

5 Clutch disc – checking

1 This series of tests can only be performed on a clutch disc which has been removed from the vehicle. It is possible to check friction lining thickness and the condition of the rivets and lining without removing the disc. See also Section 2.

2 Clean the friction lining and all other surfaces with acetone or naptha only. Do not use any degreasers nor should any petroleum based cleaners be used.

3 Check the splined clutch center for broken teeth and other signs of wear.

4 Make sure that the clutch center turns against the springs when it is rotated (axial play) but does not exhibit any ability to be pushed from side to side on the round hole in which it rides (radial play).

5 Check all rivets for looseness. Look carefully for any signs of 'working', which occurs when two pieces are able to move against each other even though the rivet appears to be tight under normal inspection. Working rivets will be surrounded by a small ring composed of microscopic bits of friction material and metal. Treat working rivets as loose rivets. Since the friction material cannot be re-riveted or bonded, any loose or working rivets mean replacement of the clutch disc. If in doubt as to the condition of any rivet, replace the disc.

6 Carefully check the surfaces of the friction linings. Replace the clutch disc if you find evidence of oil spattering, cracking of the lining material, tears, or wearing of the surface in any noticeable amount.

7 Check the thickness of the clutch disc linings (Fig. 6.3). New values and wear limits are given in the Specifications. If the disc is to be re-used, wear must be even and symmetrical. Replace the disc if in doubt.

8 Place the disc on a spindle which will hold it firmly and squarely, then mount the spindle in a lathe or other device (such as vee blocks) so that the spindle may turn.

9 Place a dial indicator on the friction surface of the clutch disc at the 200mm diameter line and rotate the disc. A deviation of 0.6 mm (lateral runout) or more means that the disc must be replaced (Fig. 6.4).

6 Pressure plate – checking

1 Clean the pressure plate with acetone or naptha and blow dry with compressed air if available. Do not use any other commercial solvents or cleaners, especially those containing petroleum products.

2 Check the friction surfaces for burned spots and rub them out lightly with emery cloth. Blow out the assembly with compressed air again to remove all traces of loose friction material.

Fig. 6.4 Measuring lateral runout of the clutch disc

Fig. 6.5 Pressure plate. The diaphragm springs point inward

3 Check the ends of the diaphragm (center) springs for signs of wear. Traces of wear less than 0.0118 in. (0.3 mm) in depth are of no concern. Greater wear will necessitate replacement of the pressure plate (Fig. 6.5).

4. Place a steel straight edge across the diameter of the friction surface at three different points and check for flatness of the friction plate surface. A change in flatness (cupping or twisting) greater than 0.0118 in. (0.3 mm) will require replacement of the pressure plate (Fig. 6.6).

5 Check the friction surface for burns, cracks and wear of the material. These friction plates are not rebondable nor can a new friction surface be riveted on. If any of these conditions are present, the pressure plate must be replaced.

6 Check the spring connections for cracks. Any spring between the pressure plate and cover which shows signs of cracking will necessitate replacement of the pressure plate.

7 Finally, check the rivets for tightness. If any rivets are loose or damaged, replace the pressure plate. Check also for signs of 'working' around the rivet holes. A rivet which is loose enough to allow the two pieces of metal to move, but is not yet loose enough to be turned or twisted with your fingers, will leave a small rim composed of dark microscopic metal chips around the rivet hole. A 'working' rivet should be treated as a loose rivet.

Fig. 6.6 Checking the flatness of the pressure plate friction surface

---

7   Clutch bellhousing – stripdown and assembly

1 The following tasks may be performed while the clutch bellhousing is installed in the vehicle. The illustrations show all work being performed on a workbench for clarity.

2 Loosen the clutch lever clamping bolt on the bellhousing.

3 If work is being performed with the bellhousing in the vehicle, remove the release bearing. If you are removing the bellhousing from the vehicle, remove the release bearing after placing the bellhousing on a workbench (Section 8).

4 Unbolt the central tube from the clutch bellhousing.

5 Turn the bellhousing and remove the clutch lever and the grip ring.

6 Unhook the return spring with a screwdriver (photo).

7 Remove the clutch release lever bearing from the bellhousing by prying gently with a screwdriver.

8 Remove the clutch release lever from the inside.

9 The internal bushing is removed by inserting an extractor through the release bearing hole.

10 Inspect the release bearing guide tube for scratches, gouges, and other noticeable wear. If any of the above conditions exist, remove the guide tube. The mounting bolts may be reused as long as their lockwashers are also installed (photo).

11 Installation is the reverse of the removal procedure. Lubricate all rubbing surfaces with MoS$_2$-based grease as you progress.

12 Install the release bearing guide tube. Remember to install the lockwashers on the bolts.

13 Install the internal bushing with an appropriate installation tool and drive it into the bellhousing until it is flush with the surrounding metal.

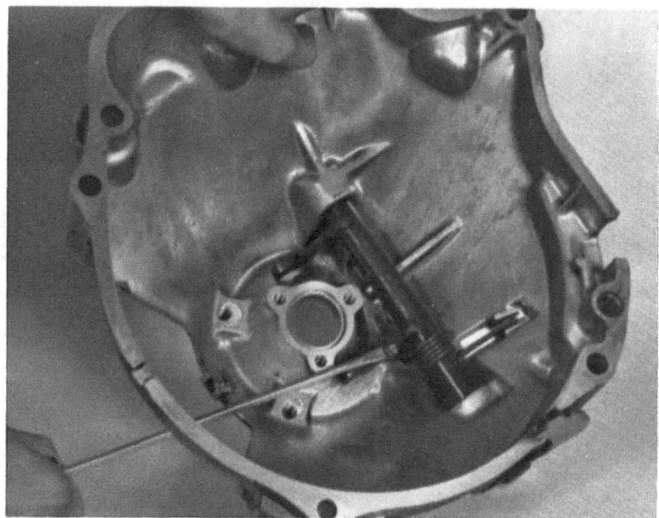

7.6 Removing the return spring

14 Install the clutch release lever from the inside. Be sure that the return spring is properly positioned on the shaft. Do not hook the spring over its mounting tab at this time.

15 Place the new clutch release lever bearing over the clutch release lever and drive it into the bellhousing until the other flange of the bearing is flush against the bellhousing.

16 Hook the ends of the return spring over the mounting tabs and make sure the connection is secure.

17 Torque the release bearing guide tube bolts to 7 ft-lb (1 m-kg).

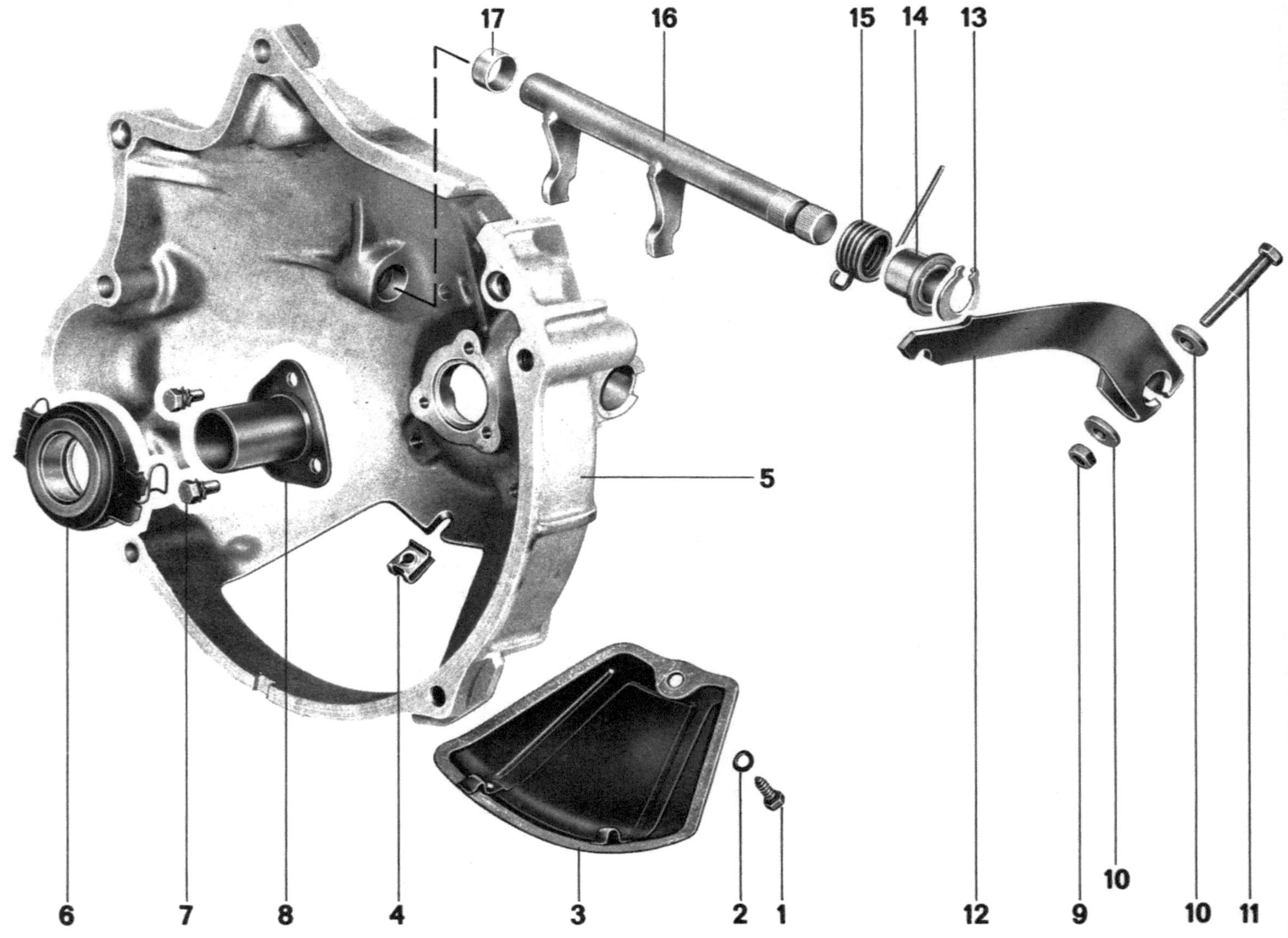

Fig. 6.7 Clutch bellhousing and components; mechanical clutch

1 Sheet metal screw
2 Wave washer
3 Inspection cover
4 Snap nut
5 Clutch bellhousing
6 Release bearing
7 Bolts with lockwashers
8 Release bearing guide tube
9 Clutch lever clamping nut
10 Flat washers
11 Clutch lever clamping bolt
12 Clutch lever
13 Grip ring
14 Clutch release lever bearing
15 Return spring
16 Clutch release lever
17 Inner bushing

7.10 Inspecting the release bearing guide tube for damage

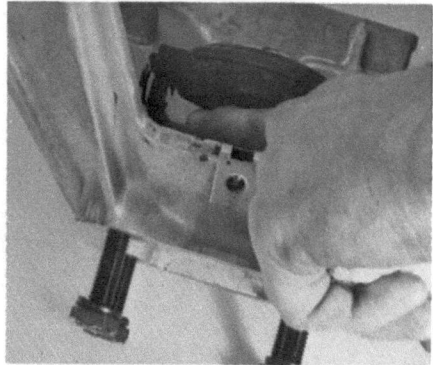

8.2 The release bearing as seen installed. The mechanic's finger points to the spring clip holding the release bearing in the clutch housing

8.4 Inspecting the release bearing

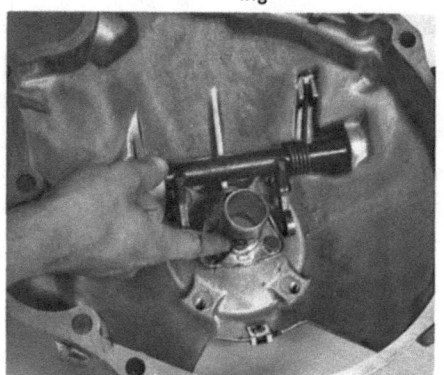

8.6 Lubricating the guide tube before installing the release bearing

8.7 A properly assembled bellhousing

18 Torque the bolts which attach the clutch bellhousing to the central tube to 30 ft-lb (4.2 m-kg).
19 Install the clutch lever and torque the clamping nut to 11 ft-lb (1.5 m-kg).
20 Lubricate the release bearing guide tube with MoS₂-base grease before installing the release bearing (Section 8).

8 Release bearing removal and installation

1 The clutch and pressure plate should already be removed (Sections 3 and 4).
2 Reach through the inspection hole and with a pair of needle-nose pliers or a screwdriver, carefully pry the spring clips on the release bearing from the tabs on the release lever. Operate the release lever back and forth as necessary to help the removal process. Do not nick or gouge any surface in this procedure (photo).
3 Pull the release bearing off its guide tube.
4 Inspect the sliding surface of the release bearing for gouges, nicks, and wear. If the surface shows signs of wear, replace the bearing. Whenever you replace the clutch disc and/or the pressure plate, it is a good routine practice to replace the release bearing as well, regardless of condition (photo).
5 Installation is the reverse of the removal procedure.
6 Coat the sliding surface of the bearing and the guide tube with MoS₂-base multipurpose grease before reassembly (photo).
7 Take care, once again, not to nick or gouge any surfaces inside the bellhousing when installing the bearing. Make certain that the spring clips are squarely seated (photo).

9 Adjusting the clutch

1 If the clutch has not been removed or inspected, the first three steps must be performed prior to the actual adjustment of the clutch.
2 Disconnect the negative lead from the battery.
3 Raise the vehicle and place it on jack stands.

4 Remove the inspection cover from the clutch bellhousing.
5 The adjustment of the operating lever on the clutch bellhousing must be carried out first if it has been disturbed.
6 Insert a large screwdriver through the inspection hole and position the release bearing on the diaphragm spring of the pressure plate.
7 Turn the outboard lever until the pointed end of the outboard lever is 138 ± 2 mm from the lower edge of the clutch cable adjuster bracket. See Figure 6.8 for an illustration. Remove the screwdriver.
8 It is now possible to adjust the clutch play.
9 Loosen the lock nuts at the clutch cable holder.
10 Screw the adjuster back and forward in its adjuster bracket until:
  a) the point of the outboard lever is 138 ± 2 mm from the lower edge of the cable adjuster bracket, and:
  b) the free play at the clutch pedal is 20 to 25 mm. Free play is the distance the pedal may be pushed before it begins to operate the clutch. See Figure 6.8 for an illustration of the proper free play distance.

10 Clutch cable – removal and installation

1 The clutch cable must be replaced any time its operation is impaired by crushing of the outer housing, rust or dirt in the inner housing, or if the inner cable ever stretches farther than adjustments can be made to compensate.
2 Raise the hood and disconnect the negative lead from the battery.
3 Loosen the two locknuts on the cable adjusting bracket and pull the cable out of the bracket.
4 Loosen the locknut on the threaded lower end of the cable (where it enters the pivot piece on the outboard lever) and unscrew the cable end from the pivot piece. The pivot piece may be unhooked from the outboard lever to make this task easier.
5 Remove the pivot piece from the clutch pedal lever, loosen the locknut and remove the threaded end of the clutch cable.
6 Remove the clutch cable from the passenger compartment by pulling it through the firewall into the engine compartment.

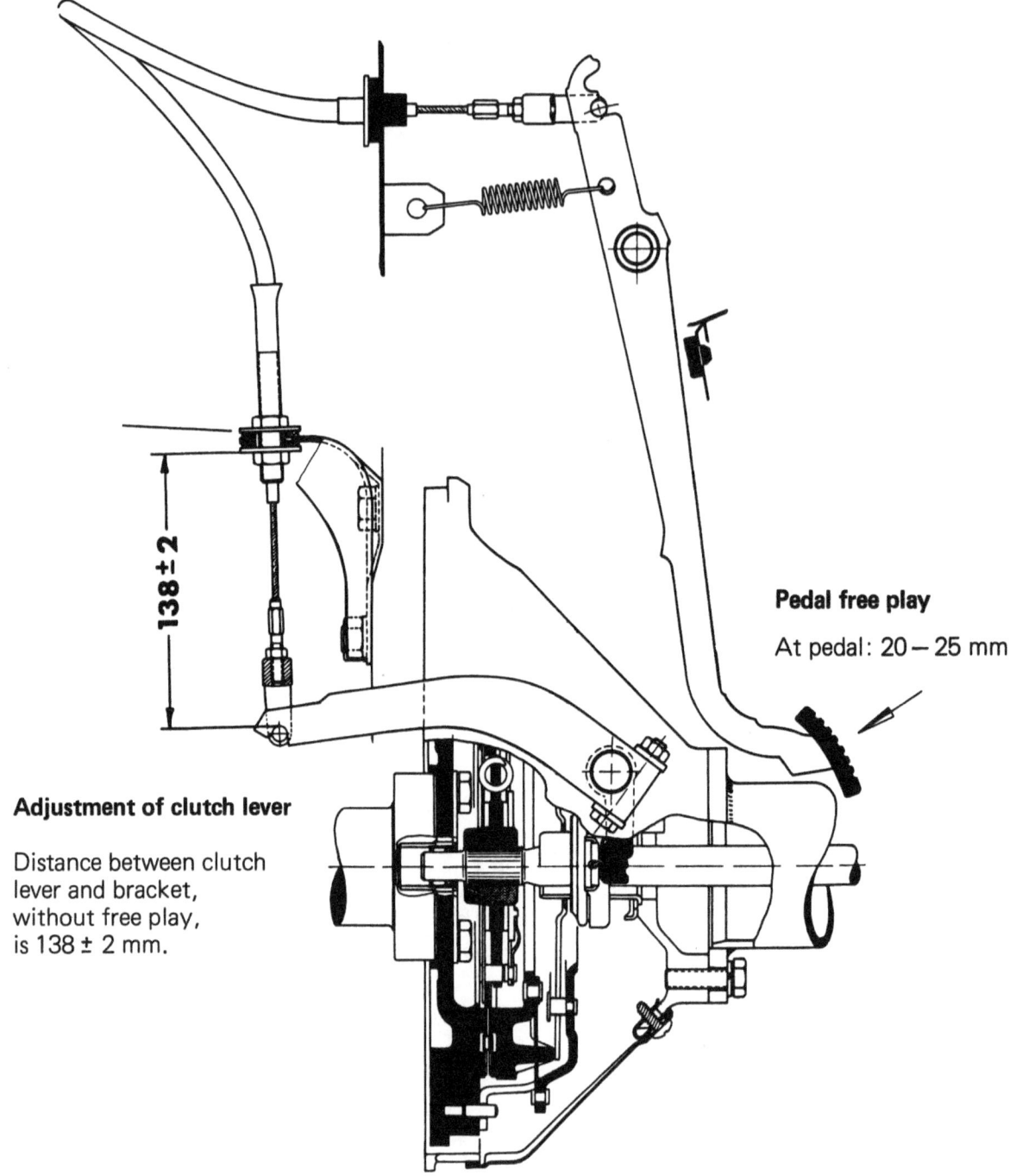

Adjustment of clutch lever

Distance between clutch
lever and bracket,
without free play,
is 138 ± 2 mm.

Pedal free play

At pedal: 20 – 25 mm

Fig. 6.8 Adjusting the mechanical clutch

7   Installation is the reverse of the removal procedure.
8   Tighten the locknuts on the pivot ends securely.
9   Adjust the cable according to the directions in Section 9.

11 Hydraulic clutch - general description (Turbo)

1   Like the mechanical clutch, the hydraulic clutch is of the single
disc, diaphragm type. It differs from the former in that the engagement and disengagement of the clutch disc is done by hydraulically-
operated pushrods acting on the clutch disc.

12 Clutch disc - inspection (Turbo)

1   Disconnect the negative lead from the battery.
2   Raise the vehicle and place it on jack stands.
3   Remove the inspection cap (Fig. 6.10).
4   Measure the distance between the front of the throw-out lever and
the edge of the inspection hole (Fig. 6.11). As the clutch disc wears,
this distance will increase. When the wear limit is reached, the clutch
disc must be replaced without delay.
5   Install the inspection cap, lower the vehicle and reconnect the
battery.

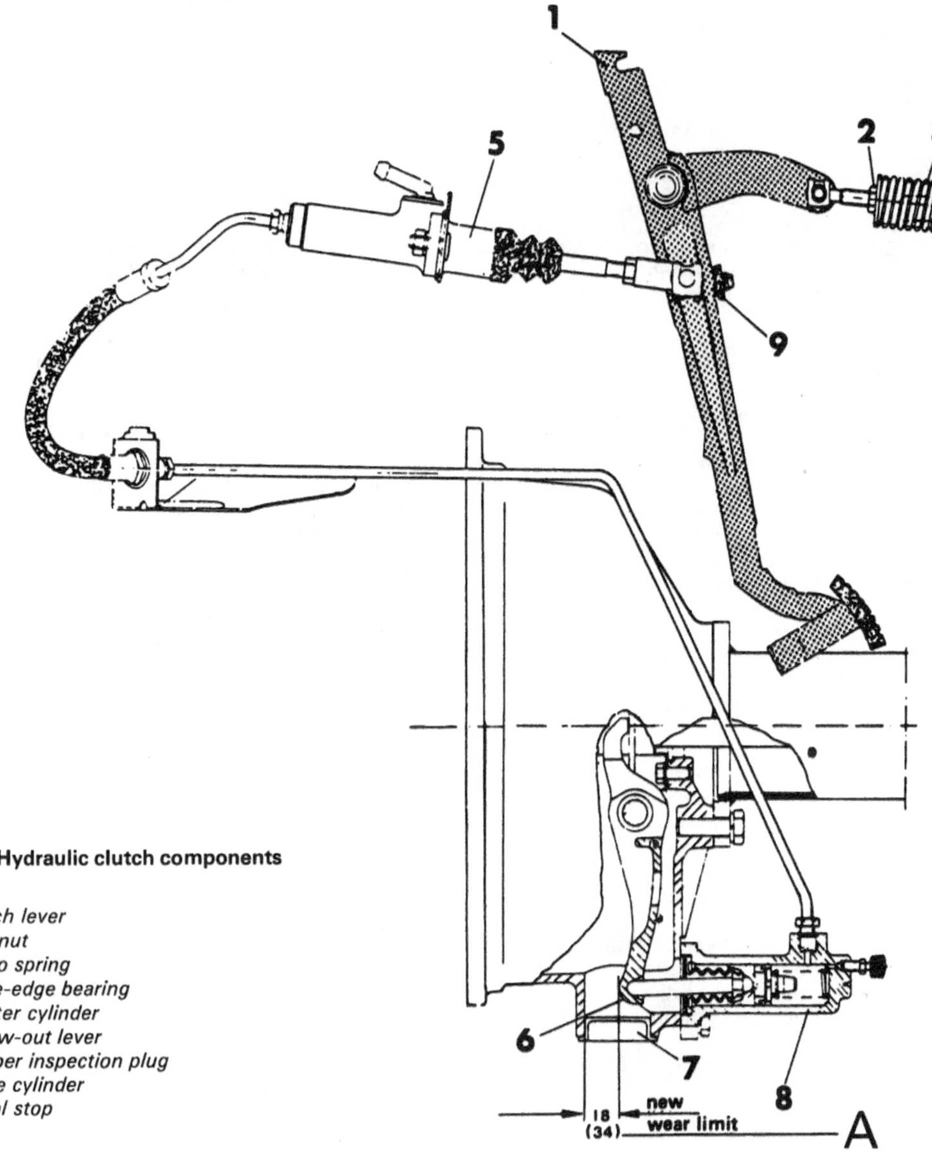

Fig. 6.9 Hydraulic clutch components

1   Clutch lever
2   Locknut
3   Servo spring
4   Knife-edge bearing
5   Master cylinder
6   Throw-out lever
7   Rubber inspection plug
8   Slave cylinder
9   Pedal stop

18
(34)

new
wear limit

A

Fig. 6.10 Location of the clutch disc inspection cap (Turbo)

Fig. 6.11 Measuring the clutch disc lining

Distance 'A' equals: New clutch disc – 18 mm   Wear limit – 34 mm

13 Clutch disc – removal and installation (Turbo)

1   Remove the molded cover and boot from the shift lever.
2   Remove the bolts from the guide.
3   Disconnect the spring from the base of the guide.
4   Disconnect the negative lead from the battery.
5   Remove the clutch hydraulic hose from its holder after removing the clip.
6   Raise the vehicle and place it on jack stands.
7   Using Special Tool VW 10-222 or an appropriate engine hoist, attach the engine at its fitting strap points and raise it slightly so that the weight of the engine is borne by the hoist rather than the engine mounts.
8   Remove the lower engine guard.
9   Loosen and remove the waste gate pipe between the exhaust manifold and the waste gate.
10 Remove the nuts which hold the turbine housing to the exhaust pipe.
11 Remove the exhaust system from the catalytic converter back. See Chapter 4.
12 Remove the waste gate. See Chapter 4. Some of the first Turbo models produced have a vent line at the waste gate which will be accessible only after the exhaust pipe has been lowered.
13 Unhook the rear exhaust pipe bracket from the rubber hanger which holds it.
14 Using a twelve point socket head wrench, remove the bolts which hold the axle shafts to the transmission. Suspend the axle shafts in a horizontal position to prevent damage to the bearings.
15 Remove the self-locking nuts from the bonded transmission mounts. Dispose of these nuts and replace them with new self-locking nuts every time they are removed.
16 Position a floor jack or several blocks of wood beneath the final drive section of the transmission and raise the transmission slightly so that the weight of the entire transmission rests on the floor jack.
17 Remove the transmission mount bolts and raise the transmission slightly again. Be careful not to crush the brake line for the left rear brake when raising the transmission. Do not raise the transmission far enough for contact to take place.
18 Remove the nuts from the starter holding bolts and pull the starter out of its mount. Disconnect the wiring from the starter.
19 Loosen the wiring harness on the clutch bellhousing.
20 Remove the release lever shaft after removing the lock nut on the clamping piece.
21 Remove the four bolts holding the central tube to the clutch bellhousing.
22 Loosen the two bolts holding the slave cylinder to the clutch bellhousing and carefully pull the slave cylinder out of its mounting boss. Do not disconnect or twist the hydraulic line running into the slave cylinder.
23 Slide the central tube and transmission toward the rear of the vehicle. Check occasionally to make sure that no brake lines are being crushed. The critical area is around the central tube forward flange.
24 Remove the release lever shaft by pulling it out with an 8 mm threaded shaft or stud.
25 Remove the bolts from the clutch bellhousing. Mark each bolt according to location, as each one is different and must be reinstalled in the proper location. Move the clutch bellhousing with the release lever rearward until it can be removed without hitting the clutch assembly.
26 Installation is the reverse of the removal procedure.
27 Using a MoS₂-base multipurpose grease, lubricate the guide sleeve, central shaft splines, grooved ball bearing in the flywheel, and clutch release bearing with a light, uniform coating of grease. Set these parts aside where they will not have dust and dirt blown on them before they are installed.
28 Install the clutch disc and pressure plate together. Center the clutch disc with a phenolic clutch centering tool (available at most auto parts stores, suitable for all VWs) or Special Tool 9102 to center the clutch disc. Tighten the bolts holding the pressure plate to the flywheel in a cross pattern, two turns each until they are snug. Torque the bolts to 16 to 18 ft-lb (2.2 to 2.5 m-kg).
29 Mount the clutch bellhousing and release lever together at the rear of the engine and install two mounting bolts finger tight.
30 The release bearing lever shaft must be aligned against its stop.

To achieve this, first align the needle bearing and bore in the clutch bellhousing, then gently move the release lever back and forth until it seats. The machined surface of the release bearing lever shaft must face the mounting bolt.
31 Install the mounting bolt after the release lever shaft has been aligned correctly and counterlock it with a nut. Torque the nut to 5.5 ft-lb (0.75 m-kg) and the bolt to 7 ft-lb (1 m-kg).
32 Install the rest of the clutch bellhousing mounting bolts in their correct order and tighten them finger tight.
33 Torque the bolts in a cross pattern. The bolts are of varying length, but of only two diameters. Torque the smaller diameter bolts to 33 ft-lb (4.5 m-kg) and the larger diameter bolts to 54 ft-lb (7.5 m-kg).
34 Make sure that the insulation sheet on the central tube is in its proper location when the central tube is slid forward. The forward edge of the insulation sheet must be 17¾ in. (450 mm) from the rearmost face of the forward flange when the central tube is placed in its proper location.
35 Slide the central tube and transmission forward and install the splines of the driveshaft in the clutch center. If the splines do not align, rotate the crankshaft slightly by turning the center bolt on the oil pump pulley with a socket and wrench.
36 Check the wiring on the backup light still fits properly.
37 Torque the slave cylinder mounting bolts to 14 to 17 ft-lb (1.9 to 2.3 m-kg).

14 Clutch bellhousing – stripdown and assembly (Turbo)

1   Remove the clutch bellhousing and continue these tasks at a workbench.
2   Check the condition of the guide sleeve for wear. If any scratches or worn spots are apparent, replace the guide tube, torquing the three mounting bolts to 9 ft-lb (1.2 m-kg).
3   Inspect the needle bearings for wear. Bearings which show signs of uneven or excessive wear should be replaced. Old bearings may be driven out of the release lever by placing the lever in the protected jaws of a vise and driving out the bearing and race. Install new bearings with a mandrel and drift them in flush with the edges of the release lever.
4   When you prepare the bellhousing for installation, lubricate the guide tube's outer surface with MoS₂-based multipurpose grease and the needle bearings with white lubricating paste.

15 Clutch disc – checking (Turbo)

1   See Section 5. Also check the condition of the rubber torsion damper (when fitted). Replace the disc if the damper is damaged (photo).

15.1 Clutch disc with rubber torsion damper, fitted to later Turbo models

16 Pressure plate – checking (Turbo)

1   See Section 6. Also inspect the starter ring gear round the edge of the plate. Replace the plate if the ring gear is damaged.

17 Hydraulic master cylinder – rebuilding (Turbo)

1   When performing this task, observe the following general points.
2   Remove the master cylinder and drain the hydraulic fluid into a sealable container. Hydraulic fluid is poisonous.
3   Place the master cylinder in the protected jaws of a vise with the operating pushrod facing upward.
4   Remove the protective rubber boot.
5   Remove the circlip from the end of the cylinder bore.
6   As you remove the various parts of the master cylinder from the bore, lay them out in the order removed and the direction in which they were installed on a piece of clean, dry paper.
7   Inspect the bore of the cylinder for chatter marks, nicks, and scoring. If any of these marks are evident, the master cylinder must be replaced.
8   Open the master cylinder rebuild kit and lay out the replacement parts in the same locations and directions as the parts you removed.
9   Using the directions packed with the rebuild kit, supplemented by the way in which you removed the parts, install the new parts of the kit.
10 Lubricate all rubbing surfaces with hydraulic fluid (DOT 3 brake fluid) or brake assembly lubricant. Make sure that all parts are clean and that they have not been cleaned with any petroleum based solvents.
11 When the master cylinder is reinstalled, the hydraulic system must be bled (Section 19).

18 Hydraulic slave cylinder – rebuilding (Turbo)

1   Raise and support the vehicle. Remove the two bolts which secure the slave cylinder to the clutch bellhousing.
2   Disconnect the hydraulic pressure line at the top of the slave cylinder by unscrewing the flange nut on top of the slave cylinder and withdrawing the flange and nut.
3   Place a plug in the end of the line to prevent dirt from entering the clutch hydraulic system.
4   Remove the rubber cap from the bleed screw and remove the bleed screw.
5   Drain the hydraulic fluid into a container. Like brake fluid, this is highly poisonous and should not be taken internally, nor should the vapor be inhaled for long periods of time. Hydraulic fluid also removes paint, so wipe up all spills immediately.
6   Remove the domed circlip.
7   Pull out the pushrod. The rubber cover and retaining ring will come out at the same time. Remove the retaining ring and separate the parts.
8   Remove the piston and seal. These are under spring pressure and should rise above the side of the cylinder so that they can be removed with the fingers, but if the piston appears to be seized in the bore, wedge a piece of soft wood or plastic into the center of the piston and pull it out.
9   Remove the rubber seal cup from the piston.
10 Remove the spring.
11 Inspect the bore of the cylinder for chattering, nicks, and scratches. If these are found the cylinder must be replaced.
the cylinder must be replaced.
12 Flush out the cylinder with new hydraulic fluid. Never use solvents or petroleum based cleaners.
13 The build up process is the reverse of the strip down procedure, with a change or two.

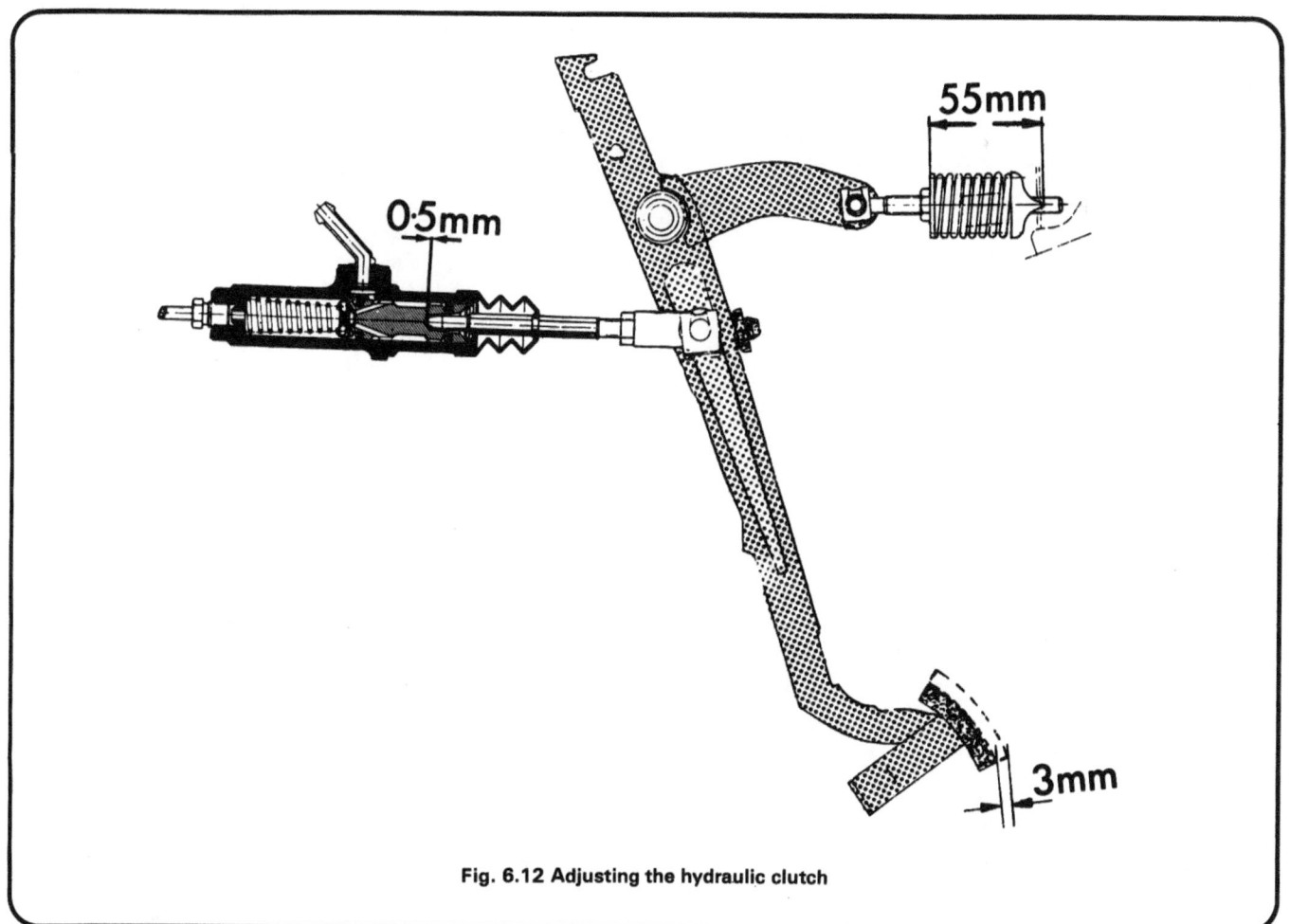

Fig. 6.12 Adjusting the hydraulic clutch

14 Install the bleed screw and rubber cap.
15 Lubricate the inner bore of the cylinder with hydraulic fluid (DOT 3 brake fluid) or brake assembly lube.
16 Place the slave cylinder body in the protected jaws of a vise with the open end facing up.
17 Open the cylinder rebuild kit and lay out the parts.
18 Install the spring with the wide end being placed in first.
19 Inspect the new piston. Note that there is a narrow, tapered end with a groove immediately behind it.
20 Lubricate the seal cup (new) with brake fluid or assembly lubricant and install the cup in the groove of the piston with the open side of the cup facing the tapered end.
21 Insert the tapered end of the piston into the narrow end of the spring and press the piston into the cylinder far enough to seat the lips of the seal cup in the bore of the cylinder.
22 Slide the new rubber cover over the notched end of the pushrod so that the narrow end of the cover sits squarely in the groove of the pushrod and the wide end is farther up the pushrod.
23 Install the new circlip.
24 Place the bellows end of the rubber cover into the piston and press the pushrod into the cylinder until the wide end of the cover sits squarely on the shouldered portion of the cylinder bore.
25 Install the domed circlip with the dome facing inward and press it squarely into place with your thumbs. Use a small screwdriver to gently press on the circlip and seat it more firmly in the bore of the cylinder.
26 Bleed the hydraulic system when you reinstall the slave cylinder.

19 Clutch hydraulic system – bleeding (Turbo)

1 Carefully clean the surfaces of the clutch master cylinder reservoir. This will prevent dirt from entering the hydraulic system.
2 Remove the rubber cap from the bleed screw on the hydraulic slave cylinder and clean the bleed nipple thoroughly.
3 Obtain a length of plastic tubing and a container. Place about ½ in. of hydraulic fluid (DOT 3 brake fluid) in the bottom of the container, slide one end of the plastic tubing over the bleed nipple and submerge the other end in the fluid.
4 Remove the cap from the clutch master cylinder reservoir and fill it to the 'maximum' line with hydraulic fluid. Replace the cap every time filling is required.
5 Have an assistant pump the clutch pedal. Instruct him to depress the pedal fully each time.
6 When the assistant has depressed the pedal three times, have him hold down on the pedal while you open the bleed screw.
7 Close the bleed screw and begin again.
8 When the hydraulic fluid coming from the hose is free of air bubbles, the system is bled.
9 Tighten the bleed screw and replace the cap.
10 Do not allow the amount of hydraulic fluid in the reservoir to fall below the 'minimum' mark at any time.
11 Fill the reservoir to the 'maximum' mark before replacing the cap at the completion of the bleeding process.

20 Clutch play – checking and adjusting (Turbo)

1 Clutch play cannot be checked at the pedal as with the standard 924's as the hydraulic system is self adjusting.
2 There are several checks which should be made, however, to ensure proper clutch operation.
3 The master cylinder pushrod should have 0.5 mm (0.020 in.) of play against the piston. This play is translated into 3 mm (0.125 in.) at the clutch pedal. This play can be adjusted at the pushrod locknut toward the top of the clutch pedal lever (Fig. 6.12).
4 There is a servo spring on a knife-edge bearing which reduces the amount of pedal effort required to operate the clutch. When the clutch is engaged and no pressure is placed on the pedal, the distance between the outer edge of the knife-edge bearing and the outer side of the disc on the other side of the spring should be 55 mm (2.165 in.). If this is not the case, the distance may be adjusted by loosening or tightening the nut at the disc.

Chapter 7 Transmission and transaxle

For modifications, and information applicable to later models, see Supplement at end of manual

Contents

Specifications

Transmission gear ratios
4-speed transmission, US and Europe:

Code letters
  Europe and US to 1977½ .....YR (088/6)
  US from 1977½ ....XT (088/A)

Gear	No. of teeth	Gear ratio	Overall ratio
1st gear	10:36	3.600:1	12.384:1
2nd gear	16:34	2.125:1	7.310:1
3rd gear	25:34	1.360:1	4.678:1
4th gear	30:29	0.966:1	3.324:1
Reverse	12:42	3.500:1	
Axle gear			
Europe and US to 1977½	9:31	3.444:1	
US from 1977½	9:35	3.889:1	

5-speed transmission, type 016 Z, US (1979). Europe (1978–79):
Code letters .... VB

Gear	No. of teeth	Gear ratio	Overall ratio
1st gear	14:39	2.785:1	13.925:1
2nd gear	19:32	1.684:1	8.420:1
3rd gear	27:30	1.111:1	5.555:1
4th gear	31:25	0.806:1	4.030:1
5th gear	35:21	0.600:1	3.000:1
Reverse	21:46 – 14:16	2.503 1	
Axle gear	7:35	5.000:1	

5-speed transmission, type 016 Z modified for use in Turbo
Code letters .... VB

Gear	No. of teeth	Gear ratio	Overall ratio
1st gear	12:38	3.167:1	14.929:1
2nd gear	18:32	1.778:1	8.381:1
3rd gear	23:28	1.217:1	5.737:1
4th gear	29:27	0.931:1	4.388:1
5th gear	35:21	0.600:1 (US) 0.706:1 (UK)	2.828:1
Reverse	22:48 – 12:16	2.909:1	2.828:1
Axle gear	7:33	4.714:1 (US) 4.125:1 (UK)	

5-speed transmission, type 016/9
Code letters .... VR

Gear	No. of teeth	Gear ratio	Overall ratio
1st gear	10:36	3.600:1	14.800:1
2nd gear	16:34	2.125:1	8.736:1
3rd gear	25:34	1.360:1	5.590:1
4th gear	30:29	0.966:1	3.971:1
5th gear	37:27	0.729:1	2.996:1
Reverse	12:24:42	3.500:1	
Axle ratio	9:37	4.111:1	

All manual transmissions

Clutch..	Single plate dry disc (Chapter 6)
Axle drive	Spiral bevel pinion and differential
Power transmission	Double constant velocity joints and drive shafts (Chapter 10)

Automatic transmission, US and Europe (1977–on)

Code letters .... RL (US), RK (Europe)

Gear	Gear ratio (US)	No. of teeth	Overall ratio	Gear ratio (Europe)
1st gear	2.552:1	—	—	2.714:1
2nd gear	1.448:1	—	—	1.500:1
3rd gear	1.000:1	—	—	1.000:1
Reverse	2.462:1	—	—	2.428:1
Axle ratio				
US	—	11:41	3.727:1	
Europe	—	11:38	3.455:1	

Clutch..	Hydrodynamic torque converter
Converter ratio..	2.44:1

Oil capacities

4-speed transmission:

Capacity, transmission and differential	2.6 liters (2.75 US qt.)
Type	Hypoid oil SAE 80 or 80 W 90 API Spec. GL 4 or MIL-L-2105

5-speed transmission (all types):

Capacity, transmission and differential	2.5 liters (2.64 US qt.)
Type, standard models.....................................	Hypoid oil SAE 80 or 80 W 90 API Spec. GL 4 or MIL-L-2105
Type, Turbo	Hypoid oil SAE 90 API Spec. GL 5 or MIL-L-2105 B

Automatic transmission:
Capacity, transmission and torque converter

Total	6 liters (1.59 US gal.)
Oil change	2.8 liters (2.96 US qt.)
Type	ATF Dexron only
Capacity, differential	1 liter (1.06 US qt.)
Type	Hypoid oil SAE 90 API Spec. GL 5 or MIL-L-2105 B

Torque specifications

	ft–lb	m–kg
4-speed transmission:		
Axle shaft flange center bolt	18	2.5
Transmission side plate	20	2.7
Selector shaft cover	6	0.8
End plate...	17	2.4
Differential drive shaft bolt..............................	17	2.4
Drive pinion bolt	17	2.4
Oil filter screw	18	2.5
Oil drain plug	18	2.5
Reverse shaft bolt	18	2.5
Reverse lever mounting bolt	25	3.5
Selector rod locking bolt	22	3.0
Threaded cap, reverse selector rod........................	22	3.0
Ring gear bolt	61 to 72	8.5 to 10
Drive shaft guide tube bolt	9	1.2
Axle shaft flange bolt	30	4.2
Selector rod bolt	15	2.1
Back-up light switch	22	3.0
Muffler holder-to-transmission	33	4.5
Exhaust pipe hanger-to-transaxle system	7	1.0
Central tube housing-to-transmission case, large bolts......	61	8.5
Central tube housing-to-transmission case, small bolts	30	4.2
Shift lever plate-to-central tube	15	2.1
Drive shaft clamping bolt	22	3.0
Central tube flange-to-clutch bellhousing.................	30	4.2
Transmission mount-to-body	30	4.2
Transmission mount-to-transmission.......................	18	2.5
Clutch lever bolt	11	1.5

	ft-lb	m-kg
Support-to-transmission	30	4.2
Clamp assembly-to-central tube	14	2.0

5-speed transmission (016 Z, 016 Z Turbo):

Main shaft collar nut, large	159 to 174	22 to 24
Main shaft collar nut, small	116 to 130	16 to 18
Pinion collar nut	145 to 159	20 to 24
Joint flange-to-differential	34 to 36	4.7 to 5.0
Shift detent-to-final drive housing and transmission case ...	11 to 13	1.5 to 1.8*
Transmission case cover	16 to 18	2.2 to 2.5
Ring gear bolts	109 to 116	15 to 16
Lock plate bolt	5.8 to 7	0.8 to 1.0
Back-up light switch	18 to 23	2.5 to 3.2
Oil filler plug	14 to 18	2.0 to 2.5
Oil drain plug	14 to 18	2.0 to 2.5
Clamping plate, final drive housing	16 to 18	2.2 to 2.5
Starter gear ring bolt	16 to 18	2.2 to 2.5
Transmission mount-to-transmission.....................	30	4.2
Transmission mount-to-rear axle cross tube	30	4.2
Central tube-to-transmission case	61	8.5
Shift rod-to-inner shift rod	13	1.8
Guide-to-shift center section	6.5	0.9
Ball socket-to-guide rod	17	2.3

Automatic transmission:

Oil filler plug, differential	14	2.0
Axle shaft flange center bolt	18	2.5
Selector lever guide-to-selector lever support............	6.5	0.9
Detent plate bolt	6 + 1	0.8 + 0.2
Selector lever support bolt	6 + 1	0.8 + 0.2
Bracket-to-transmission	15	2.1
Cable-to-console coupling	6 ± 1	0.8 ± 0.1
Cable-to-bracket	6 ± 1	0.8 ± 0.1
Cable-to-transmission lever	4 ± 1	0.5 ± 0.1
Roler-to-holder	6.5	0.9
Roller bracket bolts....................................	6.5	0.9
Throttle pressure cable-to-holder	4	0.5
Throttle pressure cable-to-transmission bracket...........	22	3.0
Hose clamps, throttle pressure cable-to-drive shaft tube	1	0.14
Rubber stop nut on throttle lever	6.5	0.9
Rubber stop-to-lever	6.5	0.9
Brace-to-roller holder	6.5	0.9
Brace-to-crankcase	15	2.1
Accelerator pedal-to-floor	4	0.5

1 Transmission and transaxle – overview

1 Since its inception in 1976, the Porsche 924 has been equipped with five different transmissions. Together with the final drive differential, which is housed in the same casting as the transmissions, these make up the transaxle system. As the final drive is the same for all transaxles, this chapter will concentrate primarily on the transmissions, which are the main point of difference.

2 The transaxle is mounted at the rear of the 924's body, connected to the engine via a drive shaft tube. Together, the engine, drive shaft tube, and transaxle form a rigid center section, around which the 924's body is hung.

3 The US market was offered the 4-speed transmission as standard from 1976 through 1978. 1977 saw the introduction of the RL-series automatic transmission as optional equipment, and it has remained an option to date.

4 European-market 924's have carried the 4-speed transmission as standard equipment since 1976, and still do. In 1978, the 016 Z-series 5-speed transmission was offered as an option in the European market, and subsequently became standard equipment in the 1979 US range, although it remained an option in Europe. This transmission differed from the earlier 4-speed in that its gearbox cluster lay ahead of the differential instead of behind, as in the earlier transmission.

5 The three transmission types remained unchanged through the 1979 model year. In 1980, the transmission offerings were changed once again for all markets.

6 The European-market standard model retained its 4-speed transmission, but the optional 5-speed (standard in the US) was changed to the 016/9 series. Basically similar in appearance to the 4-speed, the 016/9 transmission carries its gearbox cluster behind the differential and uses a modified shift pattern from the 4-speed. Turbo models were equipped with a modified version of the 016 Z series transmission and have different gear ratios than the one installed in the earlier standard models. The automatic transmission offering remained unchanged.

7 This chapter is divided into five separate parts: Part A, 4-speed transmissions; Part B, 5-speed transmissions (016 Z series); Part C, 5-speed transmissions (016/9 series); Part D, automatic transmissions; and Part E, drive shaft and transmission linkage.

8 Those tasks which are the same for all transmissions will be covered only once in Part A. There are appropriate references for these points in the text.

Part A: 4-speed transmission

1 4-speed transmission – general description

1 The 4-speed transmission is housed within two castings, the differential casting and the end plate, which houses the gearbox.

2 The gearbox consists of two shafts, the main shaft and pinion shaft. The main shaft rides in needle and ball bearings and is directly linked to the drive shaft by a clamp. The pinion shaft runs on taper roller bearings and transmits the power from the gears to the differential.

3 Because the pinion shaft is part of the transmission and the final drive, adjustments and changes of transmission parts necessitate adjustment of the ring and pinion gear relationship. If you do not have the tools or are not prepared to take on this critical task, we suggest that you seek the help of your Porsche dealer or a qualified transmission specialist.

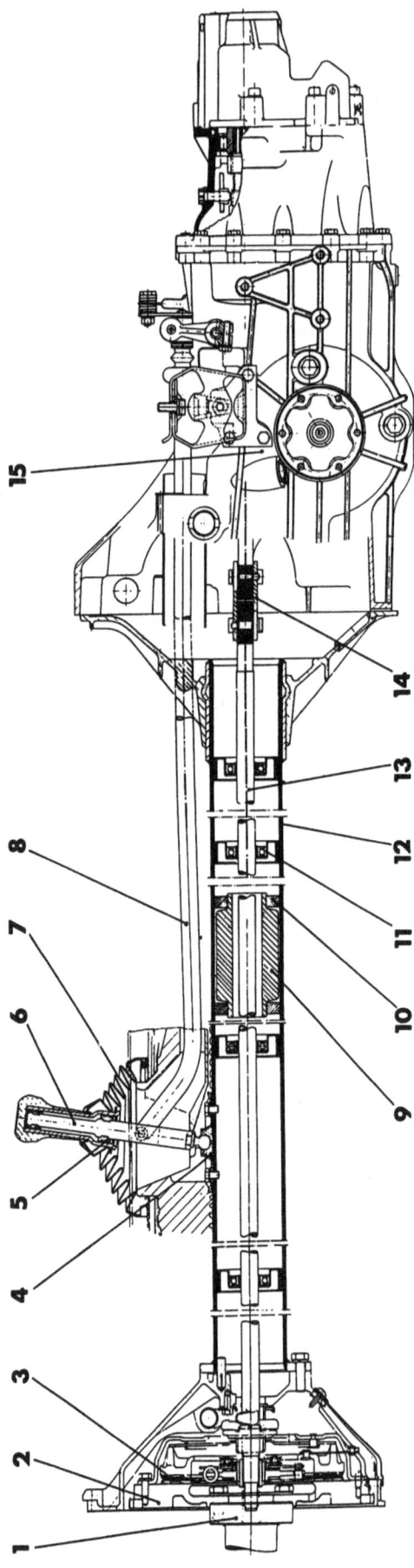

Fig. 7.1a Components of the power transmission assembly (4-speed, 5-speed [type 016/9], automatic)

1	Crankshaft	4	Shift lever base	8	Shift rod
2	Flywheel	5	Noise and vibration damper	9	Drive shaft vibration
3	Clutch (manual	6	Shift lever		damper (1978 – on)
	transmission)	7	Shift boot		

10 Flexible mount   13 Drive shaft
11 Guide bearing   14 Connecting sleeve
12 Central tube   15 Transmission

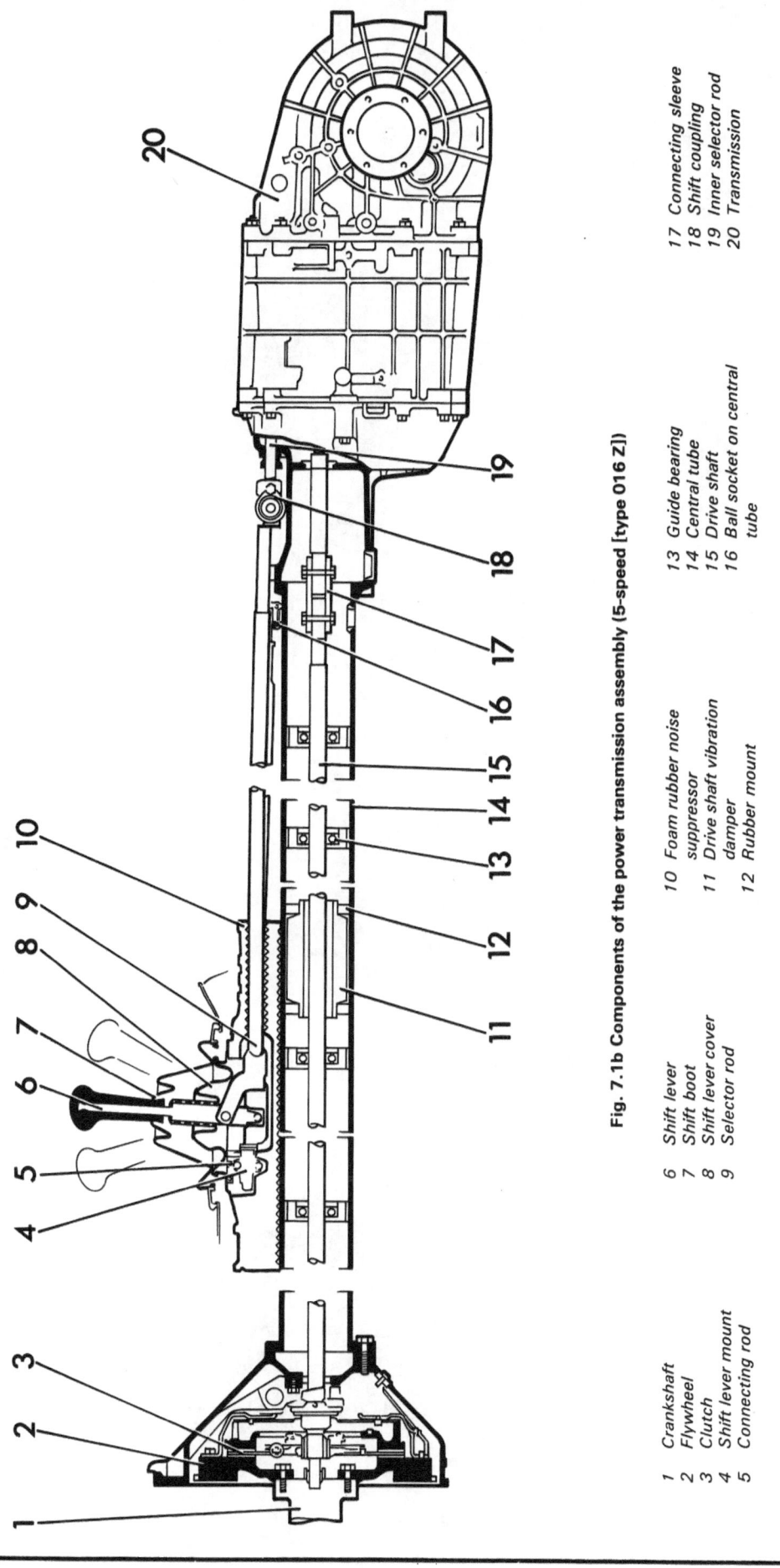

Fig. 7.1b Components of the power transmission assembly (5-speed [type 016 Z])

1 Crankshaft
2 Flywheel
3 Clutch
4 Shift lever mount
5 Connecting rod

6 Shift lever
7 Shift boot
8 Shift lever cover
9 Selector rod

10 Foam rubber noise
   suppressor
11 Drive shaft vibration
   damper
12 Rubber mount

13 Guide bearing
14 Central tube
15 Drive shaft
16 Ball socket on central
   tube

17 Connecting sleeve
18 Shift coupling
19 Inner selector rod
20 Transmission

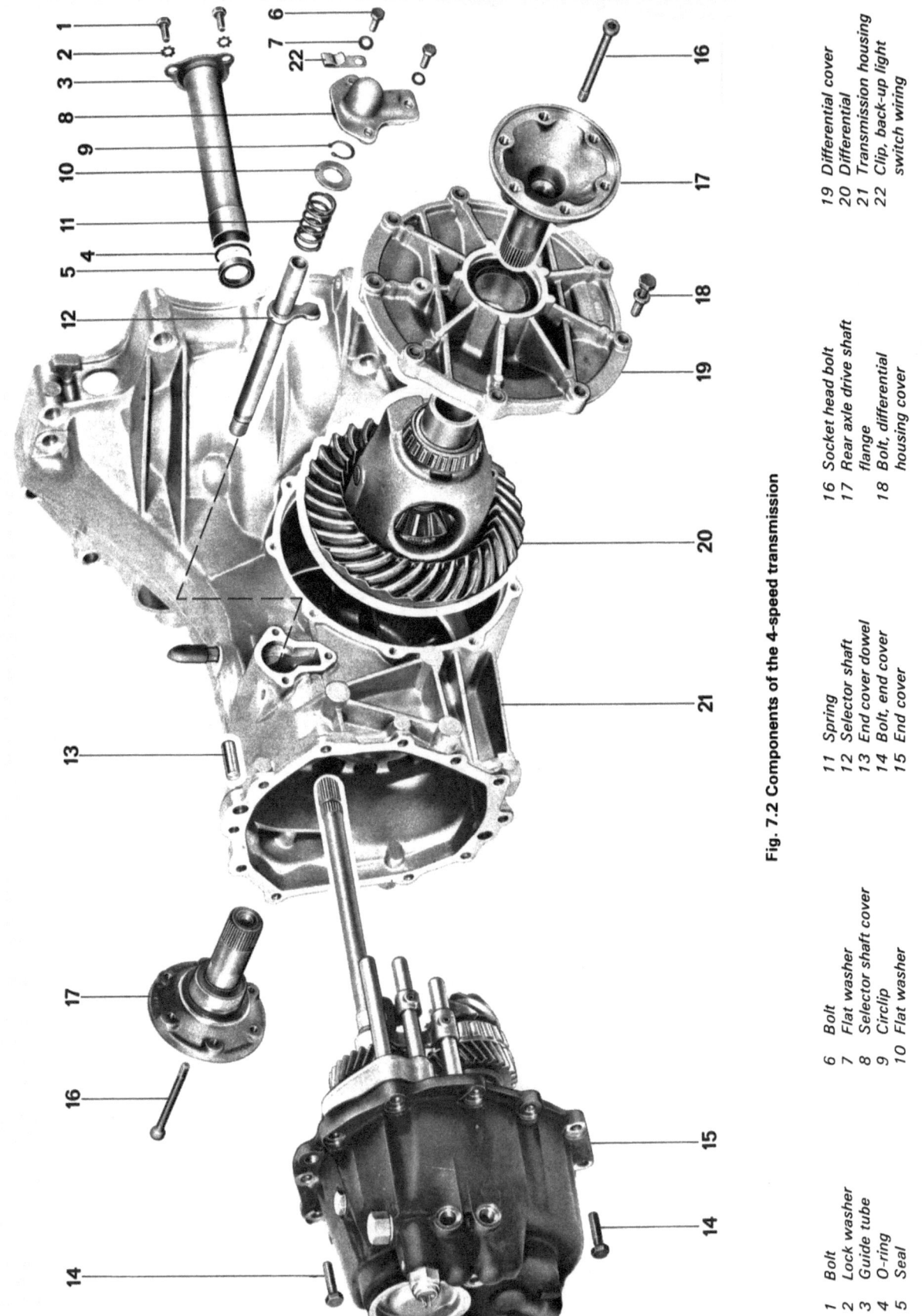

Fig. 7.2 Components of the 4-speed transmission

1 Bolt
2 Lock washer
3 Guide tube
4 O-ring
5 Seal

6 Bolt
7 Flat washer
8 Selector shaft cover
9 Circlip
10 Flat washer

11 Spring
12 Selector shaft
13 End cover dowel
14 Bolt, end cover
15 End cover

16 Socket head bolt
17 Rear axle drive shaft
   flange
18 Bolt, differential
   housing cover

19 Differential cover
20 Differential
21 Transmission housing
22 Clip, back-up light
   switch wiring

2 4-speed transmission – removal and installation

1 Disconnect the negative lead from the battery.
2 Raise the vehicle and place it on jack stands.
3 Cut the lockwire off the selector rod clamping screw and loosen the screw (photo).
4 Unsnap the shift lever boot from the center console and remove the boot and shift lever cover. It may be difficult to pull the shift lever cover directly off the shift lever as it is centered by a rubber locating block. If this is the case, wiggle the shift lever cover back and forth while pulling up to release the grip of the block.
5 Remove the circlip at the selector rod pivot on the shift lever. Remove the selector rod and the wave washer from the pivot (photo).
6 Pop the shift lever ball end from the socket by levering it with a screwdriver.
7 Press down on the foam rubber seal material between the drive shaft tube and the drive shaft tunnel and slide the selector rod forward about 300 mm (11.8 in).
8 Remove the exhaust system from the flange at the front exhaust pipe back (Chapter 3).
9 Unplug the back-up light switch and unclip the wires from the transmission (photo).
10 Remove the back-up light switch to prevent damage in the following steps (photo).
11 Unbolt the rear axle shafts at the transmission and suspend the shafts with wire or string in a horizontal position to prevent damage to the bearings (Chapter 10).
12 Open the inspection hole in the transmission bellhousing and remove the clamping bolt from the clamping sleeve (photo).
13 Mount Special Tool US 618/1 on a floor jack and raise the transmission slightly. If this tool is not available, you may use a floor jack with a thick piece of plywood, but you will need at least one strong assistant to help lower the transmission safely.
14 Remove the transmission bellhousing bolts (photo).
15 Unbolt the transmission mounts at the body and then at the transmission (photo).

16 The selector rod is guided through the transmission bellhousing by a plastic tube which is a press fit into the inside of the transmission and transmission bellhousing. Back the transmission and jack slightly to the rear. Support the guide tube and back and lower the transmission carefully, so the tube is not broken. When the transmission can be backed enough to allow a hand to be inserted between the two sections, pull the guide tube out and remove it.
17 Be careful not to foul any brake lines or stray electrical wiring. Replace any brake line which is crushed.
18 Installation is the reverse of the removal procedure.
19 Raise the transmission into place, locating the guide tube and the splined clamp on the driveshaft. Push the transmission forward until it matches with the bellhousing.
20 Install the bellhousing bolts and tighten them until snug. Install the transmission mounts, first to the transmission and then to the body. Tighten the bolts snug.
21 Remove the floor jack.
22 Torque the transmission mount-to-body bolts to 30 ft-lb (4.2 m-kg) and the transmission mount-to-transmission bolts to 18 ft-lb (2.5 m-kg). Torque the large transmission bellhousing bolts to 61 ft-lb (8.5 m-kg) and the smaller bolts to 30 ft-lb (4.2 m-kg).
23 Install the back-up light switch and torque it to 22 ft-lb (3 m-kg).
24 Install the socket head screw in the drive shaft clamp and torque it to 22 ft-lb (3 m-kg).
25 Adjust the shift linkage (Section 15).

3 4-speed transmission – gearbox removal and installation

1 Bolt the transmission to a transmission stand. If a transmission stand is not available, all steps but the one which follows may be done on a workbench, as long as the transmission is held steady by several blocks of wood.
2 Drain the transmission oil from the transmission. The drain plug is hex head socket screw which is removed with a large Allen-type wrench.
3 Remove the axle shaft flange mounting bolts. To keep the flange from turning, insert a punch through one of the holes on the flange

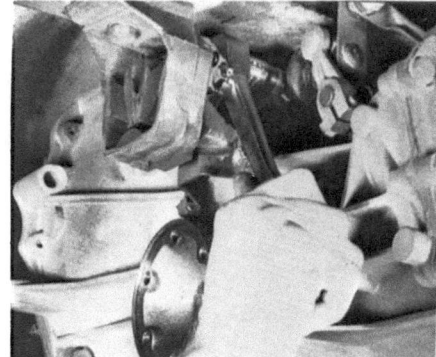
2.3 Loosening the selector rod screw

2.5 Removing the circlip at the selector rod pivot

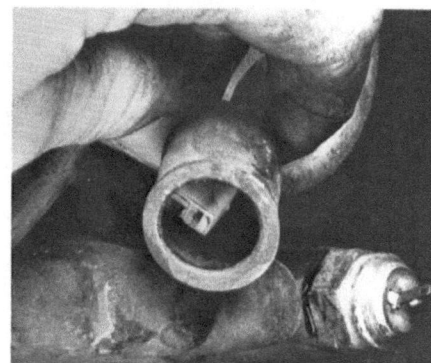
2.9 Unplugging the back-up light switch

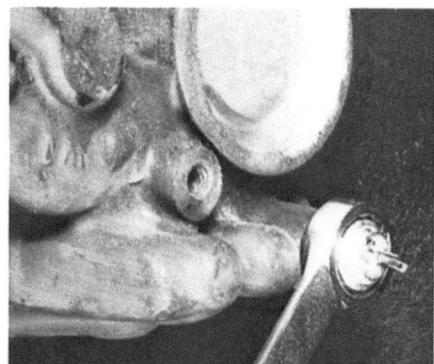
2.10 Removing the back-up light switch

2.12 Removing the clamping bolt from the clamping sleeve

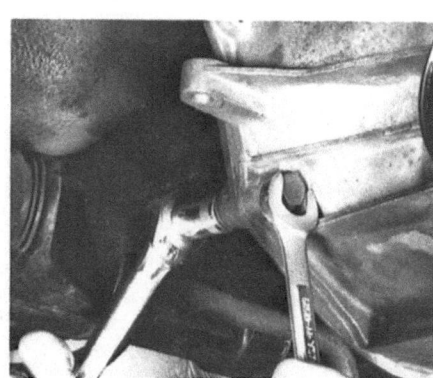
2.14 Removing the transmission bellhousing bolts

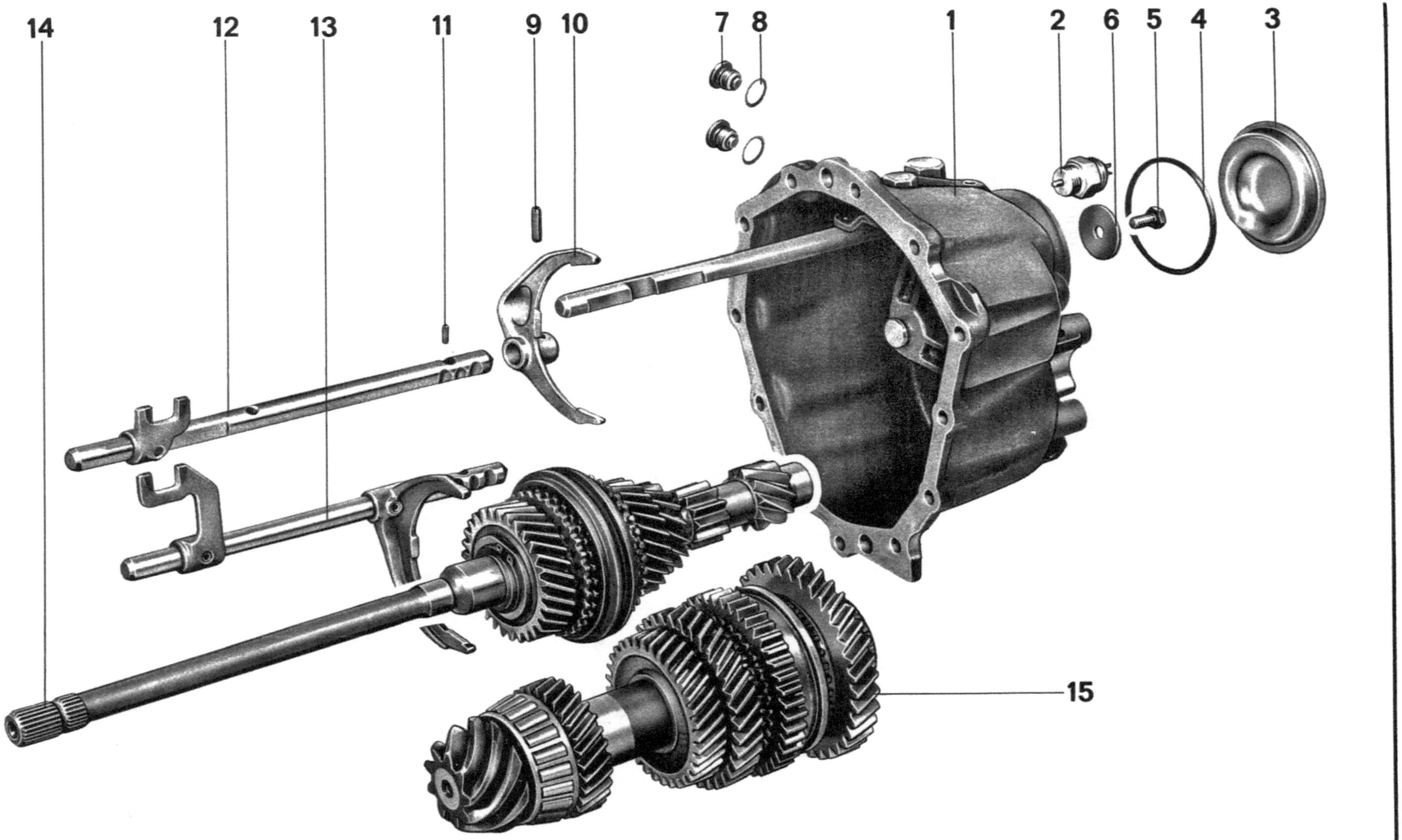

Fig. 7.3 End cover assembly and gear shafts

1	End cover	5	Bolt
2	Back-up light switch	6	Flat washer
3	End plate	7	Stop screw
4	O-ring	8	Seal

9	Selector fork key	11	Gear lock pin
10	Selector fork, 3rd and 4th gears	12	Selector rod, 3rd and 4th gears
13	Selector rod, 1st and 2nd gears		
14	Main shaft		
15	Pinion shaft		

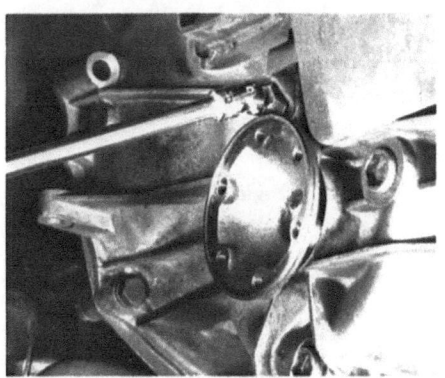

2.15 Unbolting the transmission mounts at the transmission

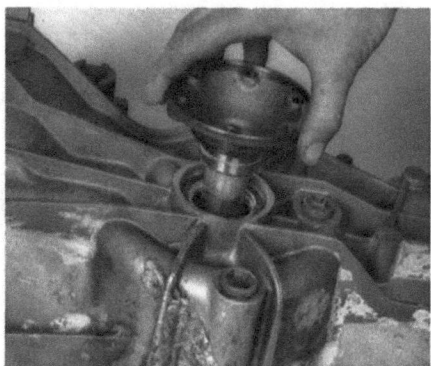

3.3 Removing the rear axle flange

3.4a Unbolting the guide tube

3.4b Withdrawing the guide tube

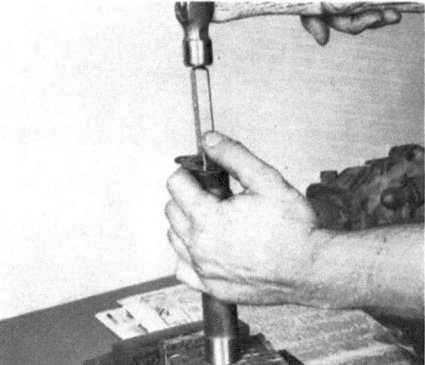

3.5 Driving the seal and O-ring from the guide tube

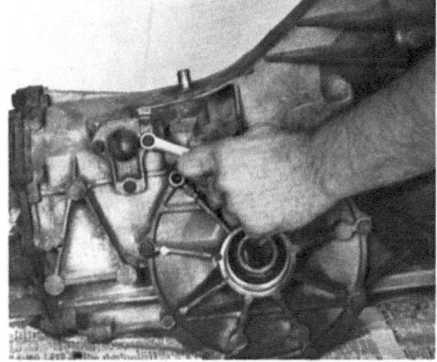

3.6a Removing the selector shaft cover

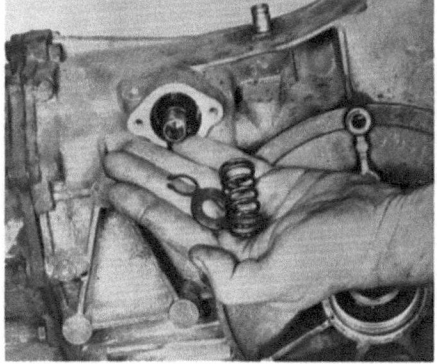

3.6b Removing the spring and components from the selector shaft

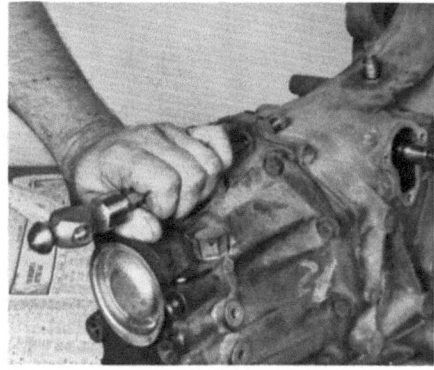

3.7 Driving out the end cover dowels

and hold it against one of the cast-in strengthening ribs. Remove the axle shaft flanges (photo).

4 Remove the three bolts on the main shaft guide tube inside the bellhousing and lever the guide tube forward with an angled screwdriver. Be careful not to bend the flange on the guide tube and to draw the tube straight out of the transmission housing (photos).

5 Insert a large screwdriver into the guide tube from the flange (forward) end. Locate the end of the screwdriver over the seal at the rear of the guide tube and drive the seal and O-ring out of the tube by striking the screwdriver with a mallet (photo).

6 Remove the cover and spring for the selector shaft on the upper right side of the transmission housing, just above the differential cover. Do not lose the clip which holds the back-up light wiring in place. The spring is held on the shaft with a circlip and washer. Relieve spring tension gradually when loosening the circlip. Press the selector shaft into the transmission housing as far as it will go (photos).

7 Drive the two dowels which locate the cover on the transmission

casting toward the front of the transmission housing. Do not drive the pins all the way out. Allow them to remain with the transmission housing, but they must be completely out of the end cover (photo).

8 Remove the end cover mounting bolts.

9 Remove the end cover, complete with the gear set installed.

10 Installation is the reverse of the removal procedure.

11 Slide the selector shaft in as far as possible.

12 Coat the sealing surfaces between the transmission and end cover with an oil-based gasket sealer. Apply a thin coat and follow the manufacturer's directions on drying.

13 Insert the end cover in the transmission. Make sure that the main shaft and pinion shaft are properly located.

14 Align the sealing surfaces between the transmission and the end cover and drive the dowels into place. This will properly locate the cover.

15 Install the end cover mounting bolts, and torque to 17 ft-lb (2.4 m-kg). To ensure proper seating of the end cover torque the bolts in a cross pattern.

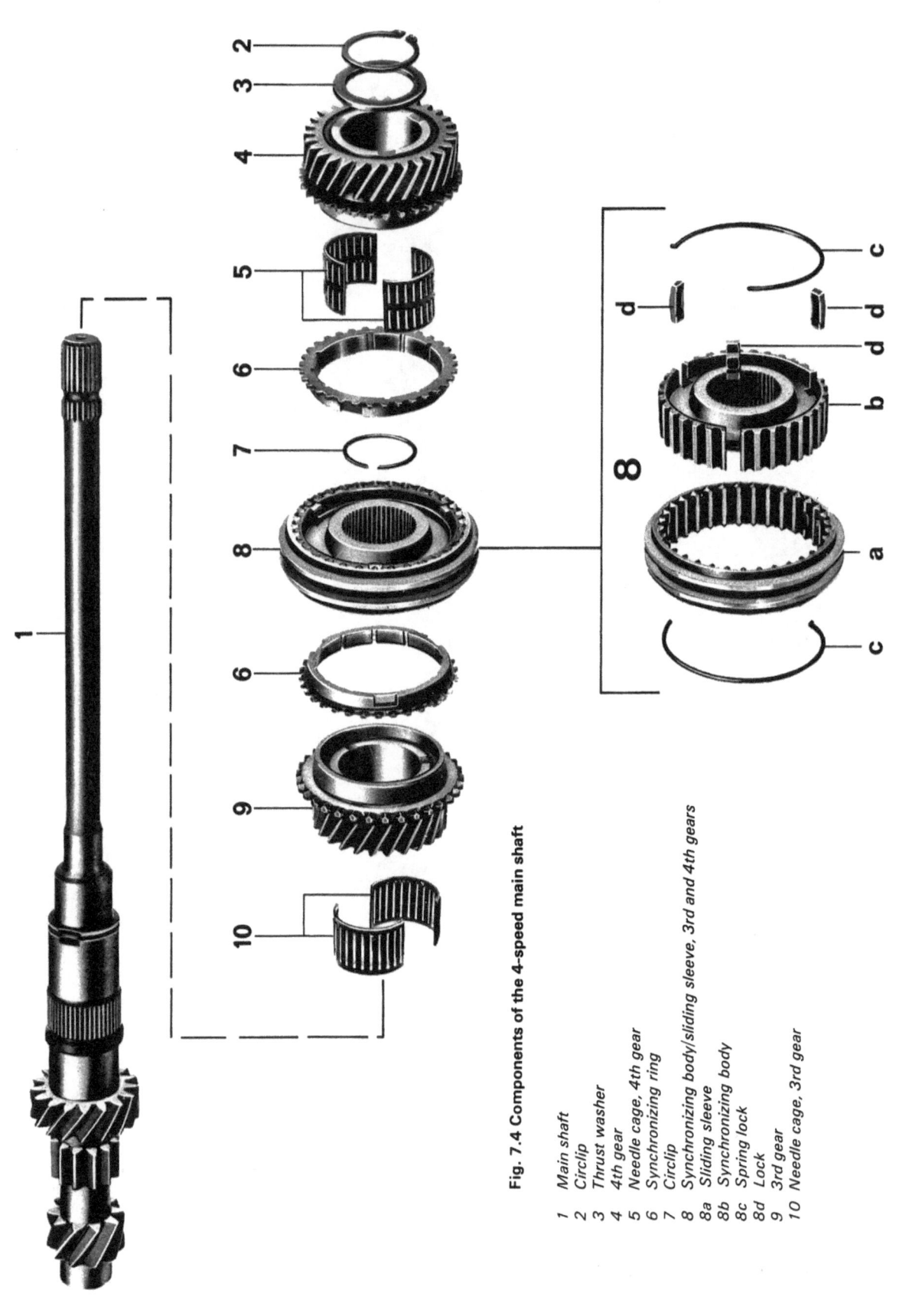

Fig. 7.4 Components of the 4-speed main shaft

1 Main shaft
2 Circlip
3 Thrust washer
4 4th gear
5 Needle cage, 4th gear
6 Synchronizing ring
7 Circlip
8 Synchronizing body/sliding sleeve, 3rd and 4th gears
8a Sliding sleeve
8b Synchronizing body
8c Spring lock
8d Lock
9 3rd gear
10 Needle cage, 3rd gear

16 Drive the new seal into the guide tube with Special Tool 9119 or another appropriate seal installation tool. There is a seal and O-ring which must be installed, and their order must not be mixed up (Fig. 7.2).

17 Special Tool 9113 is a sleeve which fits over the splined end of the main shaft and allows the guide tube to be installed without damaging the seals. If you do not have this tool, wrap several layers of masking tape over the splines, making sure that there is enough over the end of the shaft to round off the edge and prevent tearing of the seal. Slide the guide tube into place carefully. Install the three bolts on the flange and torque them to 9 ft-lb (1.2 m-kg). Remove the tool or the masking tape from the main shaft.

4 Gearbox - shaft removal and installation

1 Remove the gearbox from the transmission housing (Section 3).

2 Using a screwdriver and mallet, drive the end plate off the end cover (photo).

3 Clamp the splined end of the main shaft in the protected jaws of a vise.

4 Remove the main shaft bolt (photo).

5 Reposition the end cover in the vise, holding the flange in the jaws (photo).

6 Drive out the key for the 3rd/4th gear selector fork with a drift and hammer. Have an assistant hold another hammer on the side opposite the direction of the driving blows to prevent damage to the rod and bearings (photo).

7 Remove the selector rod stop screws from the outside of the end cover (photo).

8 Pull the 3rd/4th gear selector rod. Make sure that the reverse gear and the 1st/2nd gear gearshift sleeve are in the neutral position. Although the rod is removed, the 3rd/4th gear selector fork remains in the sliding sleeve.

9 Press the main shaft out of the grooved ball bearing with an extractor.

10 Pull out the main shaft with its selector fork, simultaneously with the pinion shaft and its selector fork. It will be necessary to swing the pinion shaft slightly to clear the shift gear for reverse.

11 Installation is the reverse of the removal procedure.

12 Inspect the end cover to be sure that the detent pins and locks are properly positioned in the end cover (Section 8).

13 Insert the pinion shaft with its 1st/2nd gear selector fork, and the main shaft with the 3rd/4th gear selector fork together as a unit. The pinion shaft must be swung over slightly during installation to clear the reverse shift gear. There is an opening in the 3rd/4th gear selector fork into which the reverse gear selector rod is inserted at the time of installation (photo).

14 Make sure the reverse gear selector rod is in neutral and insert the 1st/2nd gear selector rod into the bore of the end cover. Slide the entire assembly into the end cover as far as possible.

15 Clamp the main shaft in the protected jaws of a vise so the end cover may move.

16 Installing the main shaft in the end cover bearing requires the following: a bolt, which must be of the same thread pattern as the one normally installed, but about 13 mm (½ in) longer; a nut which fits that bolt; and a new washer to fit at the rear of the shaft and which holds it to the bearing.

17 Install the old washer, which was previously removed, and the bolt with its nut threaded high up on the threads. Thread the bolt into the end of the main shaft as far as possible. While holding the bolt head with one wrench, unscrew the nut with a second wrench. This will press against the washer and pull the main shaft into the bearing. Loosen the nut, threading the bolt deeper into the shaft for a firmer grip, if necessary. When the main shaft is pulled into the bearing as far as possible, remove the bolt, nut and washer.

18 Install the new washer and the proper bolt at the end of the main shaft. Torque the bolt to 17 ft-lb (2.4 m-kg).

19 Install a new O-ring on the end plate and install it so that the notch in the end plate is aligned with the oil feed bore in the end cover. This oil bore lubricates the tapered roller bearing in the end cover and must be kept open.

20 Slide the 3rd/4th gear selector fork into place and install the

4.2 Removing the end cover end plate

4.4 Clamping the main shaft in a vise and removing the end bolt

4.5 Repositioning the end cover for continued stripdown

4.6 Driving out the selector fork keys. Note the positioning of the second hammer

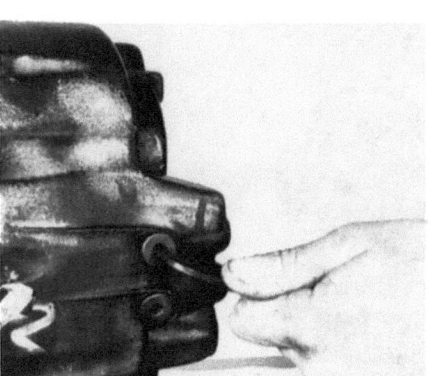
4.7 Removing the selector rod stop screws

4.13 Setting the gear shafts into the end cover

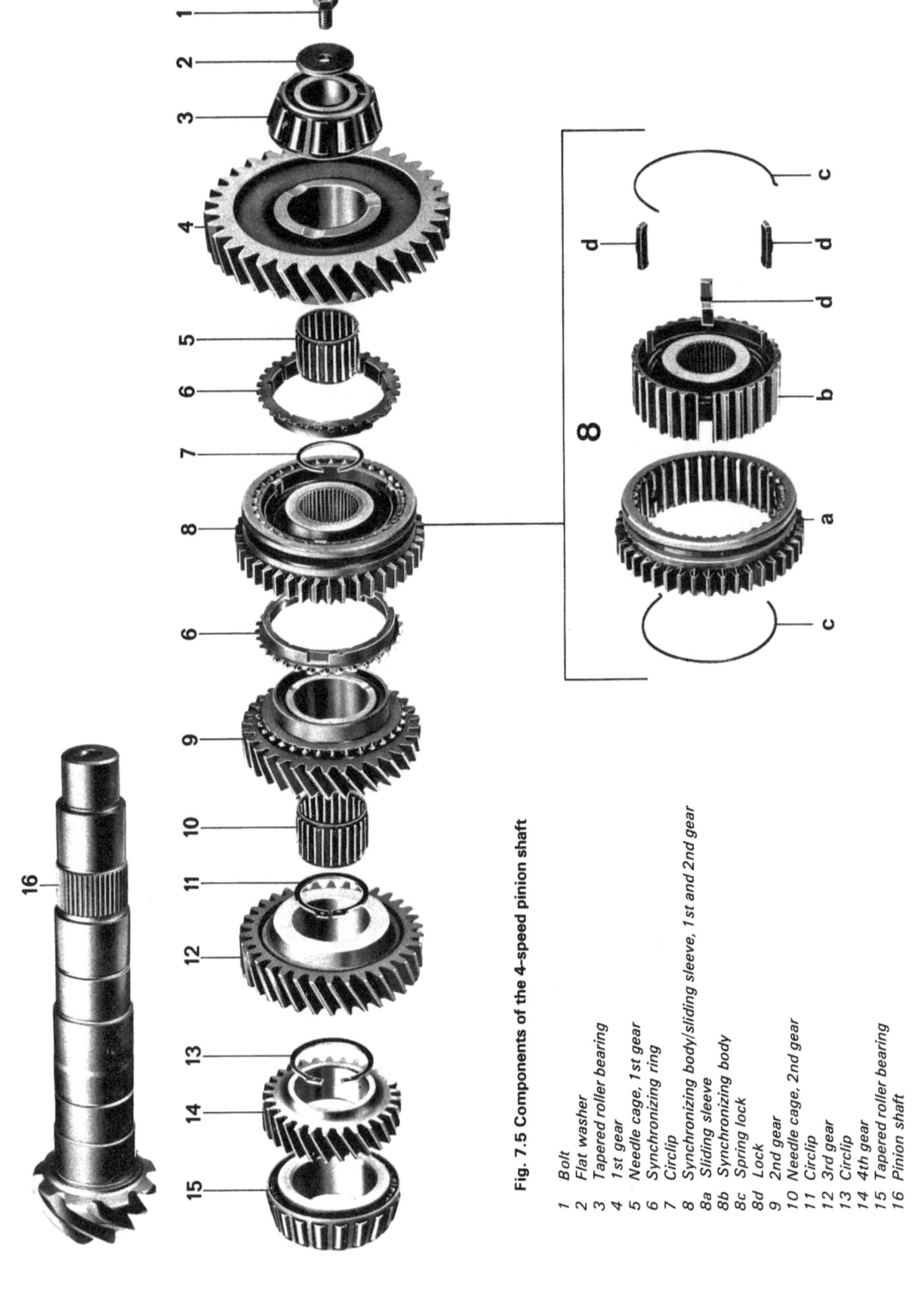

Fig. 7.5 Components of the 4-speed pinion shaft

1   Bolt
2   Flat washer
3   Tapered roller bearing
4   1st gear
5   Needle cage, 1st gear
6   Synchronizing ring
7   Circlip
8   Synchronizing body/sliding sleeve, 1st and 2nd gear
8a Sliding sleeve
8b Synchronizing body
8c Spring lock
8d Lock
9   2nd gear
10 Needle cage, 2nd gear
11 Circlip
12 3rd gear
13 Circlip
14 4th gear
15 Tapered roller bearing
16 Pinion shaft

dowel pin. Have an assistant hold another hammer on the side opposite the direction of the driving blows to prevent damage to the rod and bearings.

21 Install new seals on the selector rod stop screws and install the screws in the end plate. Torque the screws to 22 ft-lb (3 m-kg).

---

5 Main shaft and pinion shaft - inspection

1 Before stripping the gear shafts, make a careful visual inspection of the gears and synchronizers.

2 Check each gear for pitting on the faces of the teeth and wear patterns which indicate misalignment. Look for sections of the teeth narrower than others; grooves, breaks, and chips. Make sure none of the gears are blued or otherwise discolored. If you are in doubt as to the cause of the discoloration or wear, ask your Porsche dealer for assistance.

3 Bluing is an indication of heat buildup in the gearbox and usually means that the gearbox was run low on oil at some time in the past. Other colors have a variety of meanings which an expert mechanic will be able to judge best.

4 Do not remove any more parts from either gear shaft than is necessary to complete the replacement of a part. Check all clearances in the assembly directions, but make no changes unless indicated to be necessary.

5 Stripping of the gear shafts will require the use of an hydraulic press and an oven. If you do not have access to these, we recommend that you seek the services of a qualified transmission specialist or your Porsche dealer.

---

6 Main shaft - stripdown and assembly

1 Begin parts removal from the splined end of the main shaft. This is the 4th gear end.

2 Remove the circlip (photo).

3 Slide the thrust washer, 4th speed gear with its synchronizing ring, and the needle cage from the main shaft (photo).

4 Using a flat blade screwdriver, release the circlip tension and remove it.

5 Install the main shaft in an hydraulic press and press off the sliding sleeve/synchronizing body along with the 3rd gear. Be careful not to damage the needle cage inside the 3rd gear.

6 Scribe a mark across the sliding sleeve and synchronizing body so that they may be properly matched when reassembled. It is essential that these components be matched exactly for proper transmission operation.

7 Disassemble the sliding sleeve/synchronizer unit for inspection. Remove the circlip and press the sliding sleeve from the body.

8 Inspect all parts for wear after they have been thoroughly cleaned.

9 Reassemble the synchronizing body by placing the three lock pieces in the gaps on the body and placing the body in the sliding sleeve. Install the circlips so that the open ends are offset 120 degrees.

10 Inspect the needle cages. There are two types of cage which are used interchangeably. One type is the two-piece cage with has

matched halves; all slots in the cage should have rollers installed. The other type is a nylon cage split along one side for ease of installation. This type of cage has several spots at which no rollers are installed. The open slots serve as oil reservoirs and should not be altered.

11 Needle cage wear should be light. If grooving is noted or if the rollers are thinning in the middle, replace the cages.

12 Install the 3rd gear roller cage and the 3rd gear.

13 Install the 3rd gear synchronizing ring.

14 Press on the sliding sleeve/synchronizing body assembly and turn the synchronizing ring so that the three slots in the ring align with the locks on the sliding sleeve/synchronizing body. The sliding sleeve/synchronizing body is properly installed when the groove in the synchronizing body faces the 4th gear.

15 Install the 4th gear synchronizing ring.

16 Measure the gap between the teeth of the sliding sleeve and the synchronizing ring. New, the gap should be 1.0 to 1.7 mm, and used, the gap may fall to a minimum of 0.5 mm. If the gap (measured from the tip of the sliding sleeve to the flat at the ring) is at or less than the minimum wear limit, the ring must be replaced. Synchronizing rings may be replaced separately.

17 Remove the 4th gear synchronizing ring and adjust the end play on the synchronizing body. Measure the width of the circlip slot on the main shaft and the thickness of the proper circlip. All measurements are in millimeters; inch measurements are not appropriate for this task (photo). Subtract the circlip measurement from the gap measurement. The difference must be between 0.0 and 0.5 mm. If this is the case, install the circlip. If the difference is greater than 0.5 mm, a new circlip must be installed. Porsche offers three different circlips:

Part number	thickness
088 311 317	1.50 mm
088 311 317 B	1.56 mm
088 311 317 C	1.62 mm

Choose the circlip whose thickness will allow a gap of less than 0.5 mm end play in the circlip groove. If none of the circlips will allow proper adjustment of the end play, the main shaft will be replaced.

18 Measure the amount of play between 2nd and 3rd gear. The measured value must be between 0.1 and 0.35 mm. If the gap is larger, check the installation and adjustment of the synchronizing body. If the gap betwen 2nd and 3rd gear and the end play of the synchronizing body cannot be adjusted, the main shaft must be replaced (photo).

19 Install the 4th gear needle cage, the 4th gear, the thrust washer, and the circlip.

20 Check the end play of the 4th gear. Insert a feeler gauge between the circlip and the thrust washer. The gap must be between 0.20 and 0.35 mm, with the lower figure being the most desirable. If the value is different than this, the end play may be adjusted with available circlips. They are as follows:

Part number	thickness
088 311 287	1.65 mm
088 311 287 A	1.70 mm
088 311 287 B	1.75 mm

6.2 Removing the 4th gear circlip from the main shaft

6.3 Removing the 4th gear and ancillary parts from the main shaft

6.17 Measuring the end gap for synchronizer adjustment; main shaft

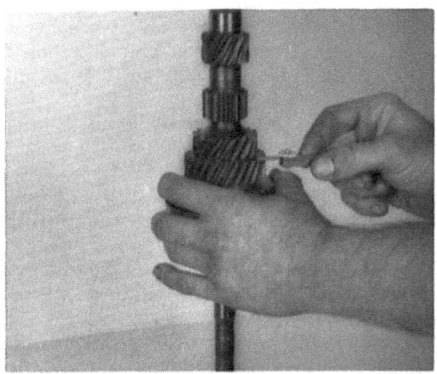

6.18 Measuring the free play between 2nd and 3rd gears; main shaft

6.20 Measuring 4th gear end play; main shaft

7.17 Measuring 4th gear end play; pinion shaft

Choose the circlip which will provide the proper clearance. If the gap remains too large with the available circlips, the main shaft must be replaced. If the gap is too small, recheck all previous adjustments and measurements (photo).
21 The main shaft is now rebuilt and ready for installation.

---

7 Pinion shaft – stripdown and assembly

---

1 Clamp the pinion shaft in the protected jaws of a vise, clamping on the open section between the 4th gear and the 3rd gear with the bolt end facing up.
2 Remove the bolt and washer.
3 Press the taper roller bearing and 1st gear with an hydraulic press.
4 Remove the 1st gear needle cage and synchronizing ring.
5 Press off the 2nd gear with the synchronizing ring attached.
6 Remove the circlip from the 3rd gear and press off the gear.
7 Remove the circlip from 4th gear and press off the gear.
8 Press off the taper roller bearing.
9 Clean the gears and shaft with a greaseless solvent, such as laquer thinner, until all parts are free of oil. Do not wash the bearings or synchronizers in this way. Thoroughly dry all parts before reassembly is begun.
10 Inspect the synchronizer body/sliding sleeve according to the directions in Section 6.
11 Assembly is the reverse of the stripdown procedure.
12 Heat the 4th gear and the taper roller bearing for the pinion end of the shaft to a temperature between 120° and 140°C (250° and 280°F).
13 Press on the taper roller bearing with the narrow end facing the pinion.
14 Make sure that there are no fingerprints on the shaft surface or on the thrust surface of the 4th gear. Oil from the skin on these surfaces will prevent a tight, firm fit of the gear on the shaft and may impair the gear's ability to transmit torque from the engine to the wheels.
15 Press the 4th gear into place. It must be installed with the large collar facing away from the pinion. Hold the gear under pressure for two minutes to allow the temperature to balance itself.
16 Allow the gear to cool before continuing.
17 Adjust the axial play of the 4th gear. Install the circlip and measure the end play between the collar and the circlip (photo). The end play must be between 0.0 and 0.02 mm, with the lower figure being the most desirable. If this is not the case, remove the circlip and measure its thickness. Choose the thickest possible circlip from the chart in Fig. 7.6 which will give you the necessary end play. If this cannot be done with any of the circlips listed, the pinion shaft must be replaced.
18 Heat the 3rd gear to 120° to 140°C (250° to 280°F).
19 Make sure the shaft and gear are free of fingerprints and grease before installing the gear. Press the 3rd gear into place with the collar facing away from the pinion. Allow the temperature to equalize for two minutes before removing the force of the press.
20 Adjust the 3rd gear end play with the circlip in the manner described above. The end play must be between 0.0 and 0.4 mm, and can be adjusted with the following circlips:

Part No.	Thickness (mm)
088 311 363	1,59
088 311 363 A	1,61
088 311 363 B	1,63
088 311 363 C	1,65
088 311 363 D	1,67
088 311 363 E	1,69
088 311 363 F	1,71
088 311 363 G	1,73
088 311 363 H	1,75

from 1977 model, modified circlip

088 311 363 AA	2,34
088 311 363 AC	2,36
088 311 363 AE	2,38
088 311 363 AG	2,40
088 311 363 AJ	2,42
088 311 363 AL	2,44
088 311 363 AN	2,46
088 311 363 AQ	2,48
088 311 363 AS	2,50

Fig. 7.6 Circlip range for 4th gear end play adjustment

Part number	thickness
088 311 287	1.65 mm
088 311 287 A	1.70 mm
088 311 287 B	1.75 mm

If the proper clearance cannot be obtained with these circlips, the pinion shaft must be replaced.
21 Assemble the sliding sleeve/synchronizing body as described in Section 6.
22 Install the synchronizing ring on the 2nd gear side of the sliding sleeve/synchronizer body, turning the ring so that the grooves align with the locks in the body.
23 Install the 2nd gear needle cage and press on the 2nd gear.
24 Install the sliding sleeve/synchronizer body with the 2nd gear synchronizing ring installed. Press the unit into place against the 2nd gear.
25 Install the 1st gear synchronizing ring and check the gaps between the rings and the sliding sleeve as described in Section 6 (photo).
26 Adjust the end play of the synchronizing body in the manner described above. Allowable end play may be between 0.0 and 0.4 mm and may be adjusted by using the following circlips:

Part number	thickness
088 311 327	1.50 mm
088 311 327 A	1.55 mm
088 311 327 B	1.60 mm

If the end play cannot be adjusted using these circlips, the pinion shaft must be replaced if the gap is too large, and the installation of the 2nd gear must be checked if the gap is too small for the smallest circlip.

27 Install the 1st gear needle cage and the 1st gear.

28 Press the taper roller bearing inner race into place with the taper facing away from the pinion.

29 Check the end play between the 1st gear and the taper roller bearing (photo). The free play must be between 0.10 and 0.40 mm. If the free play is more, check that all parts are pressed on fully up to their stops. If the free play is less, check the adjustment of the synchronizer body.

30 Install a new washer at the end of the pinion shaft, along with a new bolt. Torque the bolt to 17 ft-lb (2.4 m-kg).

8 End cover – stripdown and assembly

1 The following task requires the use of an oven to heat the end cover to uniform temperature. This is necessary for proper bearing race installation. If you do no have access to an oven which may be used for this purpose, take the transmission end cover to your Porsche dealer or a qualified transmission specialist.

2 Remove the threaded cap from the reverse gear stop. Use a magnet to remove the stop and spring. Remove the stops and springs from the two selector rod stop screw holes and set them aside (photo).

3 Remove the reverse gear operating fork bolt (photo).

4 Remove the bolt which holds the shaft on which the reverse gear rides and pull out the shaft (photo). The gear should fall free, so catch it in your hand to prevent damage to the gear teeth.

5 Remove the reverse gear operating fork (photo).

6 Remove the reverse gear selector rod (photo).

7 Remove the outer tapered roller bearing race with an internal extractor and a gear puller.

8 Drive out the main shaft's grooved ball bearing with an appropriate extractor.

9 Assembly is the reverse of the stripdown procedure.

10 Heat the end cover casting to 150°C (302°F).

11 Install the same shims removed from the tapered roller bearing race and then drive in the taper roller bearing outer race.

12 Drive in the grooved ball bearing with the appropriate driving tool and a hammer.

13 Allow the casting to cool to room temperature.

14 Coat the three selector shaft stops with a coating of multipurpose grease and install them, with their springs in their appropriate holes.

15 Insert the reverse gear selector rod.

16 Hold the reverse gear in its proper location and slide its shaft into place. Installation may be made easier by lightly coating the shaft with mulipurpose grease before inserting it in the end cover.

17 Install the bolt which holds the reverse gear shaft and torque it to 15 ft-lb (2.1 m-kg).

18 Attach the reverse gear operating fork to the reverse gear selector shaft and install it over the reverse gear so that the gear rides between the forks.

19 Install the bolt and lock washer to secure the operating fork. Apply pressure to the operating fork so that it is being pulled squarely into the end case interior. Tighten the operating fork pivot bolt until it jams on the operating fork. Press the operating fork toward the ouside of the end cover and loosen the bolt not more than one turn. Torque the bolt to 25 ft-lb (3.5 m-kg) (photo).

20 Operate the selector rod several times to ensure smooth operation of the reverse gear and its operating fork. If the fork binds, remove the operating fork pivot bolt and reinstall again to the above directions.

9 End cover – shim selection for end cover replacement

1 If the end cover is broken or will not accept replacement bearings or races, it must be replaced with a new unit. Do not attempt to replace the end cover with one removed from a scrapped transmission or crashed car.

7.29 Measuring 1st gear end play; pinion shaft

8.2 Removing the threaded cap from the reverse gear stop

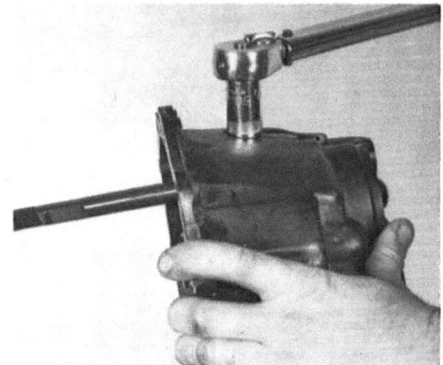
8.3 Removing the reverse gear operating fork bolt

8.4 Removing the reverse gear and shaft

8.5 Removing the reverse gear operating fork

8.6 Removing the reverse gear selector rod

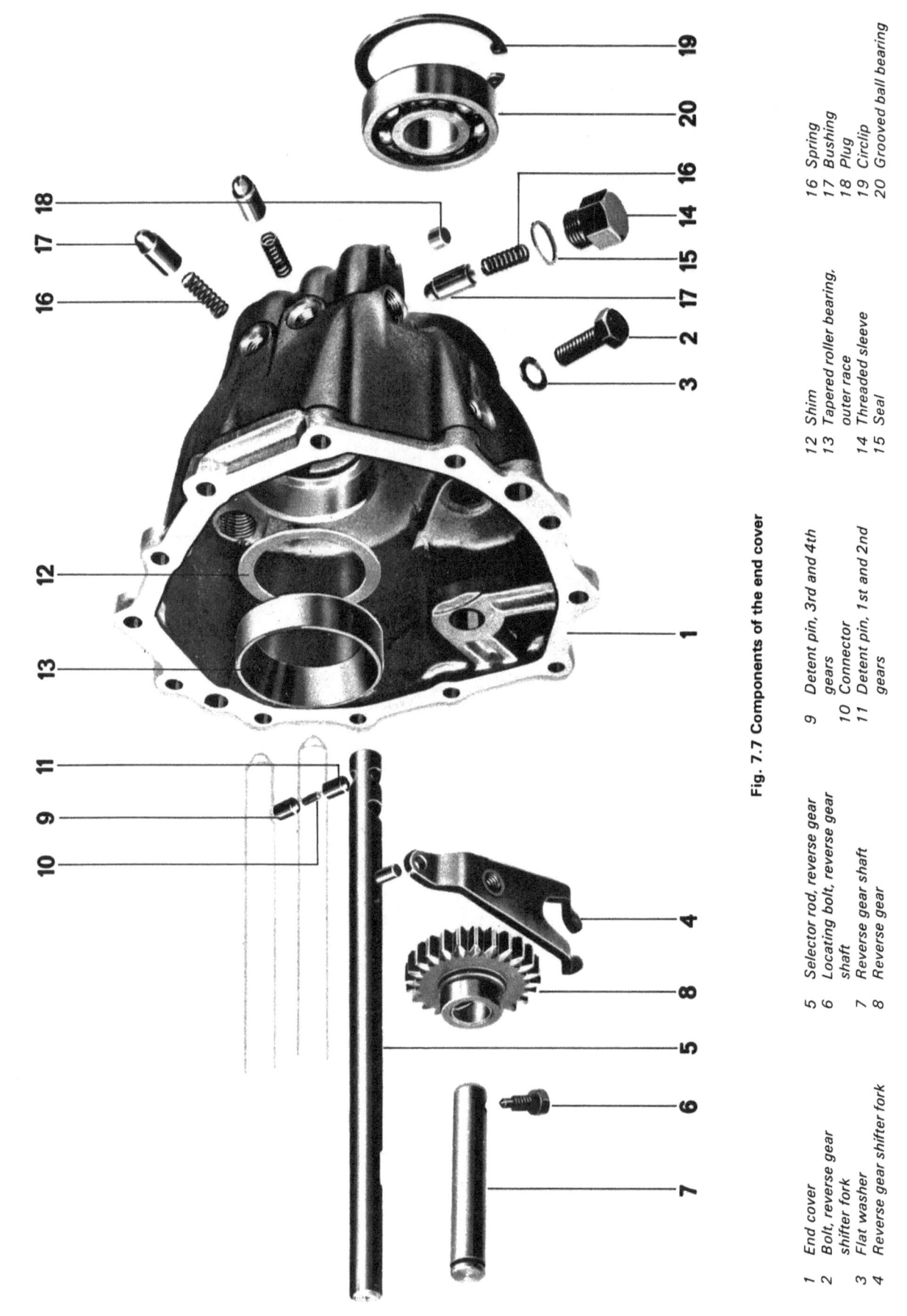

Fig. 7.7 Components of the end cover

1 End cover
2 Bolt, reverse gear shifter fork
3 Flat washer
4 Reverse gear shifter fork
5 Selector rod, reverse gear
6 Locating bolt, reverse gear shaft
7 Reverse gear shaft
8 Reverse gear
9 Detent pin, 3rd and 4th gears
10 Connector
11 Detent pin, 1st and 2nd gears
12 Shim
13 Tapered roller bearing, outer race
14 Threaded sleeve
15 Seal
16 Spring
17 Bushing
18 Plug
19 Circlip
20 Grooved ball bearing

8.19 Adjusting the operation of the reverse gear selectors

2   It is necessary to preload the taper roller bearing for the pinion shaft. The proper thickness of shims must be determined by comparing the new end cover with the old, assuming no other changes are being made.

3   Place a straight edge across the mounting flange of the end plate and measure the depth of the case from the lower edge of the straight edge to the machine surface in the outer bearing race boss. Record this measurement for both end covers.

4   All calculations must be figured to 0.05 mm accuracy (inch equivalents must not be used). A mistake in calculation will result in excessive wear of the final drive gearing, so take your time and work for accuracy.

5   If the new end cover is deeper than the old, add the difference between the two depth figures to the measured thickness of the shims you removed from the old end cover. If the old case is deeper, subtract the difference from the measured thickness of the shims. The basic calculations should look like the two examples which follow:

a. new case is deeper

old end cover case depth	119.10 mm
−new end cover case depth	119.35 mm
difference	0.25 mm
old shim thickness	0.95 mm
+difference for deeper case	+0.25mm
new shim thickness	1.20 mm

b. old case is deeper (same figures as above)

old shim thickness	0.95 mm
−difference for shallower case	−0.25 mm
new shim thickness	0.70 mm

Part No.	Thickness (mm)
088 311 393	0.24
088 311 393 A	0.27
088 311 393 B	0.30
088 311 393 C	0.33
088 311 393 D	0.36
088 311 393 E	0.39
088 311 393 F	0.42
088 311 393 G	0.45
088 311 393 H	0.69
088 311 393 J	0.93
088 311 393 K	1.17
088 311 393 L	1.41

Fig. 7.8 Available shims for end cover replacement

6   The total shim thickness could require more than one shim to give the correct spacing. Fig. 7.8 gives an accounting of the various shims available. Combine the various shim thicknesses to reach the proper shim thickness for the new end cover.

10   Differential – removal and installation

1   Remove the gearbox (Section 2).

2   Remove the bolts from the differential cover and remove the cover (photo).

3   Remove the O-ring from the differential cover and dispose of it (photo).

4   The entire differential assembly may be lifted straight out of the transmission housing (photo).

5   Installation is the reverse of the removal procedure.

6   Set the differential unit into the transmission housing so that the tapered roller bearing seats on its outer race.

7   Install a new sealing O-ring on the differential cover.

8   Position the cover so that the magnet in the cover is located at the bottom of the cover when the transmission is installed.

9   Install the differential cover bolts and torque them in a cross pattern to 20 ft-lb (2.7 m-kg).

11   Transmission housing – stripdown and assembly note

1   The performance of the task which follows requires two special tools to complete; an hydraulic press and an oven.

2   If these are not available to you, we suggest that you take the transmission housing, with the gearbox and differential removed (Sections 2 and 10) to your Porsche dealer or a qualified transmission specialist and have the bearing races removed and installed for you. Read through the instructions carefully and note that there are still three seals which you will have to install after the bearing races are installed.

10.2 Removing the differential cover

10.3 Removing the differential cover O-ring

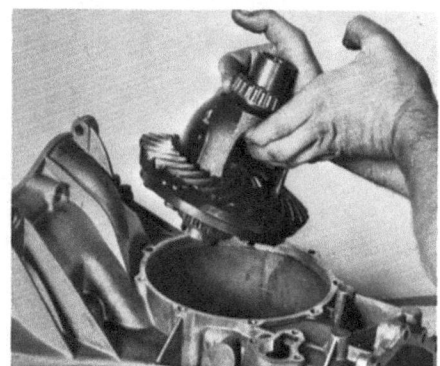

10.4 Removing the differential

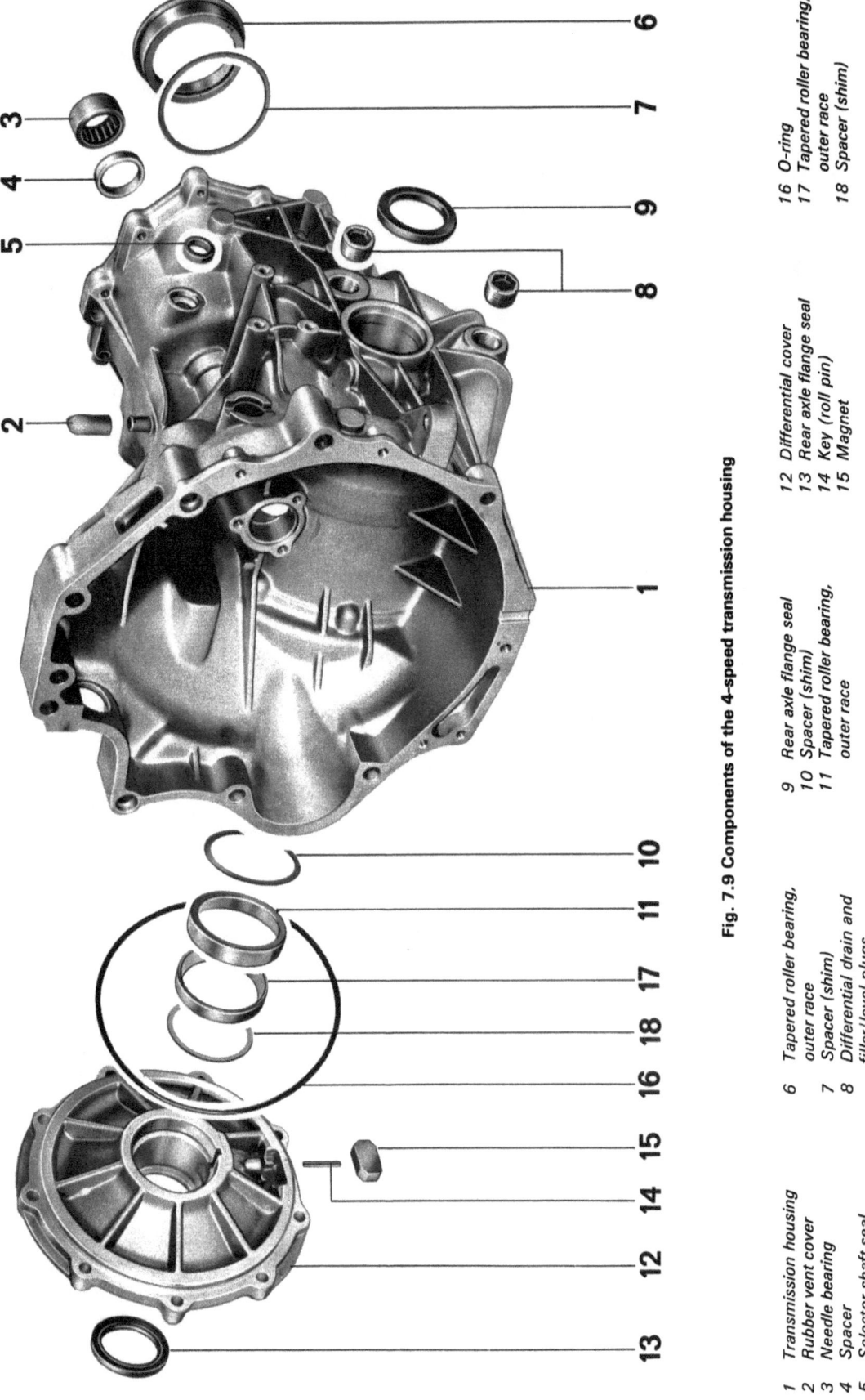

Fig. 7.9 Components of the 4-speed transmission housing

1 Transmission housing
2 Rubber vent cover
3 Needle bearing
4 Spacer
5 Selector shaft seal

6 Tapered roller bearing, outer race
7 Spacer (shim)
8 Differential drain and filler/level plugs

9 Rear axle flange seal
10 Spacer (shim)
11 Tapered roller bearing, outer race

12 Differential cover
13 Rear axle flange seal
14 Key (roll pin)
15 Magnet

16 O-ring
17 Tapered roller bearing, outer race
18 Spacer (shim)

12 Transmission housing – stripdown and assembly

1 The following steps include stripdown and assembly of the differential cover.
2 Remove the gearbox (Section 2).
3 Remove the differential (Section 10), but retain the cover close by for further work.
4 Remove the seals for the rear axle flanges by levering them out. Be careful not to damage any of the sealing surfaces.
5 Lever the selector shaft seal out of the transmission housing. Observe the same precautions above.
6 Pull the main shaft needle bearing from the transmission housing with an extractor and slide hammer.
7 Pull the pinion shaft taper roller bearing outer race with an extractor and slide hammer. The race is a tight fit in the case and it may be best to heat the surrounding case before pulling the race. If you do this, be sure to heat the transmission housing and not the bearing race.
8 Remove the small taper roller bearing outer race with an extractor and a slide hammer.
9 Remove the larger taper roller bearing outer races for the differential/axle shaft flange. One race must be pulled from the transmission housing and the other from the differential cover. In each case, the bearing race is pulled into the differential. Use an extractor and a threaded bearing puller for this task.
10 Assembly is the reverse of the stripdown procedure.
11 Because the bearing races are such a tight fit in the transmission housing, the casting should be heated to at least 150°C (302°F) and not more than 180°C (356°F). The heat must be even and the entire casting must be thoroughly heat soaked, therefore the transmission housing must be placed in an oven and 'baked' for approximately half an hour. Work on a surface which is heat resistant and do not allow bare skin to contact the casting.
12 Insert the pinion taper roller bearing outer race in the transmission with an hydraulic press to prevent the race tipping and damaging the bore. Hold the pressed load for about two minutes to allow heat transfer to take place.
13 Drive the main shaft needle bearing into place with a driving tool. The lettering on the bearing race must face to the rear of the installed transmission (into the end cover).
14 Press the bearing races for the differential/axle shaft flange bearing in the transmission housing and the differential cover.
15 When the differential cover and the transmission housing have cooled to room temperature, install the selector shaft seal in to its stop. Install the rear axle flange seals after the differential has been installed.

13 Differential – adjusting the ring and pinion

1 If you change one of the following items, your differntial must be adjusted. We recommend that you have your Porsche dealer perform the necessary work, as the alignment is quite complicated and requires several special tools which are not normally available to the home mechanic.
2 The conditions under which you should see you Porsche dealer

for work are:

> Replacement of any of the transmission/transaxle cases.
> Replacement of any of the differential gears.
> Replacement of the pinion shaft.

For the most part, replacement of bearings and bearing races not on the pinion shaft or differential housing should not affect the relationship between the ring and pinion gears, nor should the simple removal and installation of the differential. If you are in doubt, ask your Porsche dealer for advice.

14 Differential – replacing rear axle flange seal

1 Disconnect the negative lead from the battery.
2 Raise the vehicle and place it on jack stands.
3 Remove the axle shafts at both mounting flanges and remove them.
4 Unscrew the socket head bolt in the center of the flange at the transmission. To prevent the flange from turning, insert a punch into one of the holes on the flange and hold it against one of the cast-in strengthening ribs of the transmission case. Pull out the flange (photo).
5 Remove the seal by levering with the hooked end of a pry bar. Pull the seal out evenly and do not score the walls of the casting (photo).
6 Install the new seal with Special Tool VW 195 or another appropriate seal driving tool (photo).
7 Pack the cavity between the sealing and dust lips with MoS_2-base multi-purpose grease.
8 Install the flange, being careful not to tear the new seal.
9 Insert the punch back into one of the flange holes and hold it against one of the cast-in ribs of the transmission case. Install the bolt and torque it to 18 ft-lb (2.1 m-kg).

15 4-speed transmission – adjusting shift linkage

1 This task must be performed whenever the shift linkage is disconnected and whenever the shift pattern seems indistinct.
2 Make sure that the transmission is in neutral. Have an assistant operate the clutch and adjust the selector pivot arm on the transmission. Although the gear shift lever may indicate neutral, the only way to assure proper placement is as above.
3 Install the selector pivot arm on the selector shaft so that the pivot arm leans toward the rear of the vehicle about 5 degrees (Fig. 7.10). Tighten the pinch bolt on the pivot lever.
4 Move the pivot arm to the middle of the neutral travel.
5 Loosen the bolt which holds the support rod to the link plate. Move the bolt until the link plate is vertical over the transmission housing. Tighten the nut.
6 Loosen the mounting plate for the shift plate and install the shift lever and install the shift rod on the lever.
7 Adjust the mounting plate so that the shift lever forms an 82 degree angle with the drive shaft tube (Fig. 7.11).
8 Complete assembly of the console and shift components as the reverse of the removal procedure detailed in Section 2.

14.4 Removing the rear axle flange bolt, counterholding with a punch

14.5 Levering the seal from the transmission housing

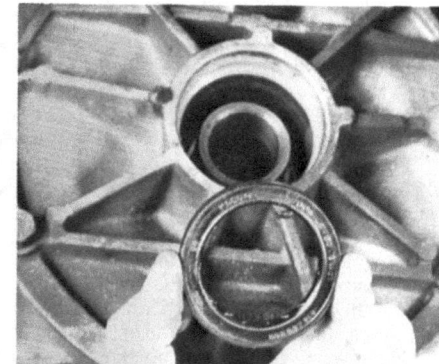
14.6 Installing the new seal

Fig. 7.10 Correct positioning of the pivot lever

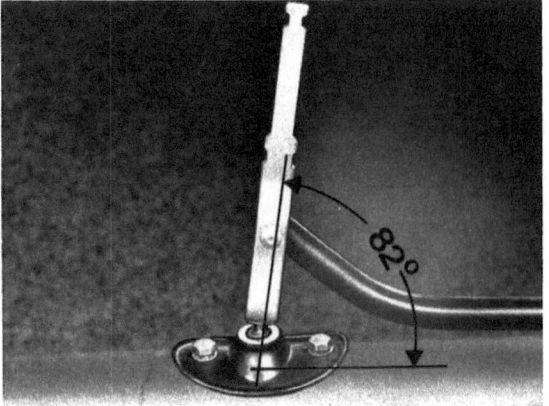

Fig. 7.11 Correct positioning of the shift lever

Part B: 5-speed transmission, type 016 Z

16 5-speed transmission – general description (type 016 Z)

1   This transmission differs from all other transmission versions in that the differential lies at the rear of the gearbox section, rather than ahead.

2   The transmission consists of three cast housings made of silumin alloy. The main shaft runs on ball and roller bearings. The pinion shaft is supported by two separate bearings in the differential housing. A cylindrical roller bearing takes up radial forces from the pinion teeth and a four-point ball bearing is employed to take up axial forces.

3   Shift linkage has been changed to a two-rod design which does not transmit road shocks to the transmission teeth. This has been achieved by mounting the shift rod supports to the body instead of the drive shaft housing.

4   Because the pinion shaft is part of the transmission and the final drive, adjustments and changes of transmission parts necessitate adjustment of the ring and pinion gear relationship. If you do not have the tools or are not prepared to take on this critical task, we suggest that you seek the help of your Porsche dealer or a qualified transmission specialist.

17 5-speed transmission – removal and installation (type 016 Z)

1   Disconnect the negative lead from the battery.
2   Raise the vehicle and place it on jack stands.
3   Remove the exhaust system behind the catalytic converter.
4   Unplug the wires on the back-up light switch.
5   Remove the reinforcement strut at the rear suspension tube to facilitate work procedures.
6   Engage 5th gear. Remove the rubber cap from the front transmission cover, immediately ahead of the torsion bar tube. Position the clamping bolt on the drive shaft clamp by turning one of the rear wheels while the other one is held in place. The bolt is of the socket head type and requires a very long socket wrench extension to loosen. Remove the bolt. Keep the transmission engaged in 5th gear.
7   Detach the axle shafts and suspend them with wire or string in a horizontal position to avoid damage to the bearings (Chapter 10).
8   Remove the self-locking nuts from the transmission mounts and dispose of them. Replace them with new ones when installing the transmission.
9   Position an universal transmission jack or a floor jack with a thick piece of plywood beneath the transmission and secure the transmission with a rubber strap to prevent its falling. It is advisable to keep an assistant by the transmission at all times during the next steps, to prevent the transmission falling.
10 Unscrew the bolts from the sides of the rubber/metal mounts. Raise the transmission slightly and remove the mounts. The left, rear brake line is immediately above the selector rod. Do not raise the transmission too far or the brake line will be crushed. If the

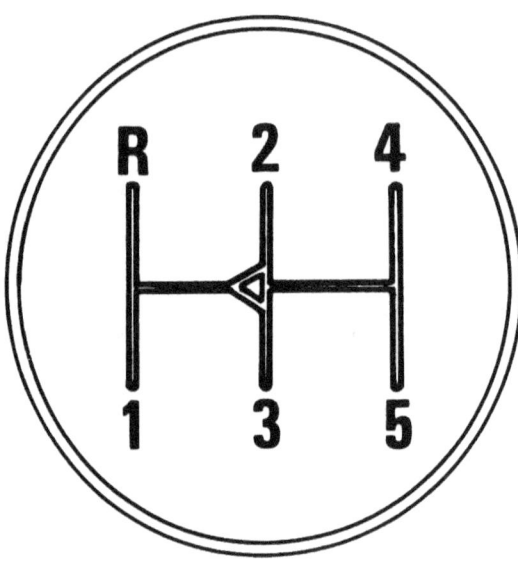

Fig. 7.12 The shift pattern of the type 016 Z transmission readily separates it from the other 5-speed models

brake line is deformed in any way, replace it (Chapter 9).
11 Remove the lower transmission mounting bolts from the flange at the drive shaft tube.
12 Lower the transmission until the front transmission cover rests on the torsion bar tube.
13 Push the transmission to the right of the vehicle and remove the conical bolt at the selector shaft. Separate the selector rod and the selector shaft in the transmission.
14 Remove the two upper transmission mounting bolts from the flange at the drive shaft tube.
15 Lift the transmission slightly, pull it to the rear, lower and remove.
16 Installation is the reverse of the removal procedure.
17 Raise the transmission into place and roll the transmission jack forward so that the drive shaft is engaged in the clamp.
18 Install the four transmission mounting bolts into the flange at the drive shaft tube and torque them in a cross pattern to 61 ft-lb (8.5 m-kg). If this is not done at this point, you will not be able to install or tighten the top left bolt.
19 Slide the transmission to the right and slip the selector rod into the selector shaft. Install the conical bolt and torque it to 15 ft-lb (2.1 m-kg).
20 Install the rubber/metal mounts and torque the side bolts to 30 ft-lb (4.2 m-kg). Install new lock nuts on the lower studs and torque them to 30 ft-lb (4.2 m-kg).
21 Remove the transmission jack.

22 Adjust the transmission linkage (Section 24) when all other components are installed.

18 5-speed transmission – stripdown and assembly (type 016 Z)

1 The transmission may be bolted into a transmission stand by manufacturing a plate from 10 mm (approx. 3/8 in) sheet steel drilled to accept the mounting points of the standard mount and drilled to accept the mounting points of the transmission at the rear of the differential housing.
2 Drain the oil from the unit. The plug is located beneath the differential gearing in the rear of the case.
3 Remove the bolts from the front cover and pull it off.
4 Engage 1st and 5th gears with the shift forks and remove the collar nut from the pinion shaft with a deep well socket.
5 Remove the inner shift rod at the top of the cluster by twisting the shaft clockwise to disengage the upper fork from the lower fork, then withdrawing the shaft.
6 With 1st and 5th gears still engaged, remove the collar nut from the main shaft.
7 Drive the pins from 2nd/3rd gear shift fork with a mallet and drift. Pull the fork from the selector rod.
8 Remove the free-running gear for the 1st gear set from the guide sleeve on the pinion shaft.
9 Remove the guide sleeve from the pinion shaft.
10 Remove the first gear from the pinion shaft with its roller cage. If the gear does not lift right off, use a gear puller to speed removal.
11 Remove the 2nd/3rd gear selector fork by first removing the bolt from the selector rod stop and removing the spring and stop. A magnet may help removal of the stop. Pull the fork and its shaft free.
12 Remove the thrust washer from the main shaft.
13 Pull the double reverse gear from the reverse shaft with a gear puller. Remove the roller cages and spacer for the gear from the shaft.
14 Remove the thrust bearing and thrust washer.
15 Remove the bolts from the transmission case and pull the case from the final drive case.
16 Inspect all of the gears and synchronizers for wear (Section 5).
17 If no work needs to be performed on the transmission gears and the shaft bearings in the final drive case are tight, remove no more parts. Go to paragraph 68 in this section and continue.
18 If work on the gears, shafts, or bearings in the final drive housing needs to be performed, continue the steps below.
19 Install a large gear puller on the main shaft and pull the 1st gear, roller bearing, and 2nd gear from the shaft.
20 Drive the locating pins from the 2nd/3rd gear shift forks and remove the shift fork.
21 Install the puller on the pinion shaft and remove the 2nd gear, needle cage, and roller bearing. Parts may fall from the synchronizer. Watch for parts and catch them before they fall to avoid deforming them or getting them dirty.
22 Pull 3rd gear, 4th gear, and the guide sleeve from the pinion shaft, then do the same for the main shaft.
23 Drive the locating pins from the 4th/5th gear shift fork and remove the shift fork.
24 The 5th gear components are keyed to a splined shaft and should just pull off.
25 If you do not need to inspect or change the bearings in the final drive case, and if the shafts are not in need of replacement (and removal) stop at this point and continue with assembly at paragraph 51.
26 If the bearings in the final drive case need replacement or if the shafts must be removed, continue with the steps below.
27 Unscrew the nuts on the clamping plate and remove the main shaft and pinion shaft together with the plate.
28 Remove the shims from the pinion shaft bearing race. Measure the shim thickness and record that figure. Set the shims aside together. To keep all of the shims in the same place, wrap a piece of masking tape around them so they are held together.
29 Remove the gear shafts from the clamping plate.
30 Continue the stripdown, first with the main shaft.
31 Place the splined end of the main shaft into Special Tool P 37 which is installed in a vise. If this tool is not available, place two thick softwood blocks between the vise jaws and clamp the splined end in place.

32 Unscrew the collar nut.
33 In order to press off the 5th gear inner race and the ball and roller bearings, obtain a spare guide sleeve for the synchronizer. Slide the guide sleeve on to the splined end of the shaft and install the main shaft, drive spline end down, in an hydraulic press jig. Press the shaft out of the race and bearings.
34 To remove the bearings from the pinion shaft, place the shaft, pinion end down, in a jig which consists of a tube slightly larger on the inside diameter than the outside diameter of the pinion and press the shaft out of the bearings with an hydraulic press.
35 Removal and installation of the bearing races in the final drive housing is covered in Section 21. If this work is performed, the transmission's ring and pinion gears must be checked by a competent transmission specialist for alignment when the transmission shafts are installed (but with no gears installed) and the differential gears are installed.
36 Clean all parts which are to be pressed together with a solvent which degreases and has no oil base, such as lacquer thinner. Dry all parts thoroughly before beginning assembly. Do not touch the shafts or the inner surfaces of any parts to be pressed on as the oil from you skin will lubricate the surface and prevent optimum torque transfer through the gears and shafts.
37 Heat the roller bearing for the pinion shaft to 120°C (248°F) and drive it on the pinion shaft. The bearing is installed with the collar of the metal cage facing the pinion.
38 Heat the ball bearing inner race to 120°C (248°F) and drive it on to the pinion shaft so that the beveled side of the race faces away from the pinion. Install the ball bearing, followed by the second inner race, heated to the same temperature and installed with the beveled edge facing the pinion.
39 Heat the needle bearing inner race for the main shaft to 120°C (248°F) along with the two ball bearing inner races and the roller bearing.
40 Install the needle bearing inner race and drive it tightly against the machined shoulder of the main shaft.
41 Install the thrust washer with the ground side facing the needle bearing.
42 Drive on the inner race for the ball bearing with the beveled edge of the race facing the threaded end of the shaft. Slide the ball bearing into place, followed by the other heated inner race. Drive the inner race into place with the beveled edge facing the splined end of the main shaft.
43 Install the roller bearing and drive it into place. The inner race of the roller bearing must come flush with the end of the threaded portion of the shaft.
44 Allow all bearings and shafts to cool. Make sure that all alignments are correct when the bearings have cooled and drive them in further, if necessary.
45 Install the main shaft in the Special Tool P 37 or clamp it between two soft wood blocks as in the removal procedure.
46 Install a new collar nut on the final drive end of the main shaft and torque to 159 to 174 ft-lb (22 to 24 m-kg). When this torque has been reached, lock the nut by punching the collar into the recess on the main shaft end with a prick punch and hammer.
47 Install the same thickness of shims on the final drive housing as the ones you removed.
48 Install the main shaft and pinion shaft in the clamping plate and install the entire assembly in the final drive housing. Double check the shimming before you continue. Install the nuts on the clamping plate and torque the nuts in a cross pattern to 16 to 18 ft-lb (2.2 to 2.5 m-kg).
49 If you have replaced any of the bearings which are now installed in the final drive case, or if you have changed the pinion shaft and ring, take the final drive housing with the gear shafts and differential installed to you Porsche dealer and have the alignment of the ring and pinion checked.
50 Once the alignment of the ring and pinion has been checked and corrected, the assembly of the shafts may commence.
51 Install the 5th gear main shaft needle cage on the inner race and slide the 5th gear into place over it. If the fit is too tight for slipping on, heat the gear to 120°C (248°F) and drive it into place.
52 Install the synchronizer guide sleeve onto the splines of the main shaft and slip the operating sleeve over it, locating the three wide splines of the guide sleeve in the slots of the operating sleeve.
53 Install the 4th/5th gear shift fork and drive in the locating pins.
54 Install the needle bearing inner race on the splines of the main

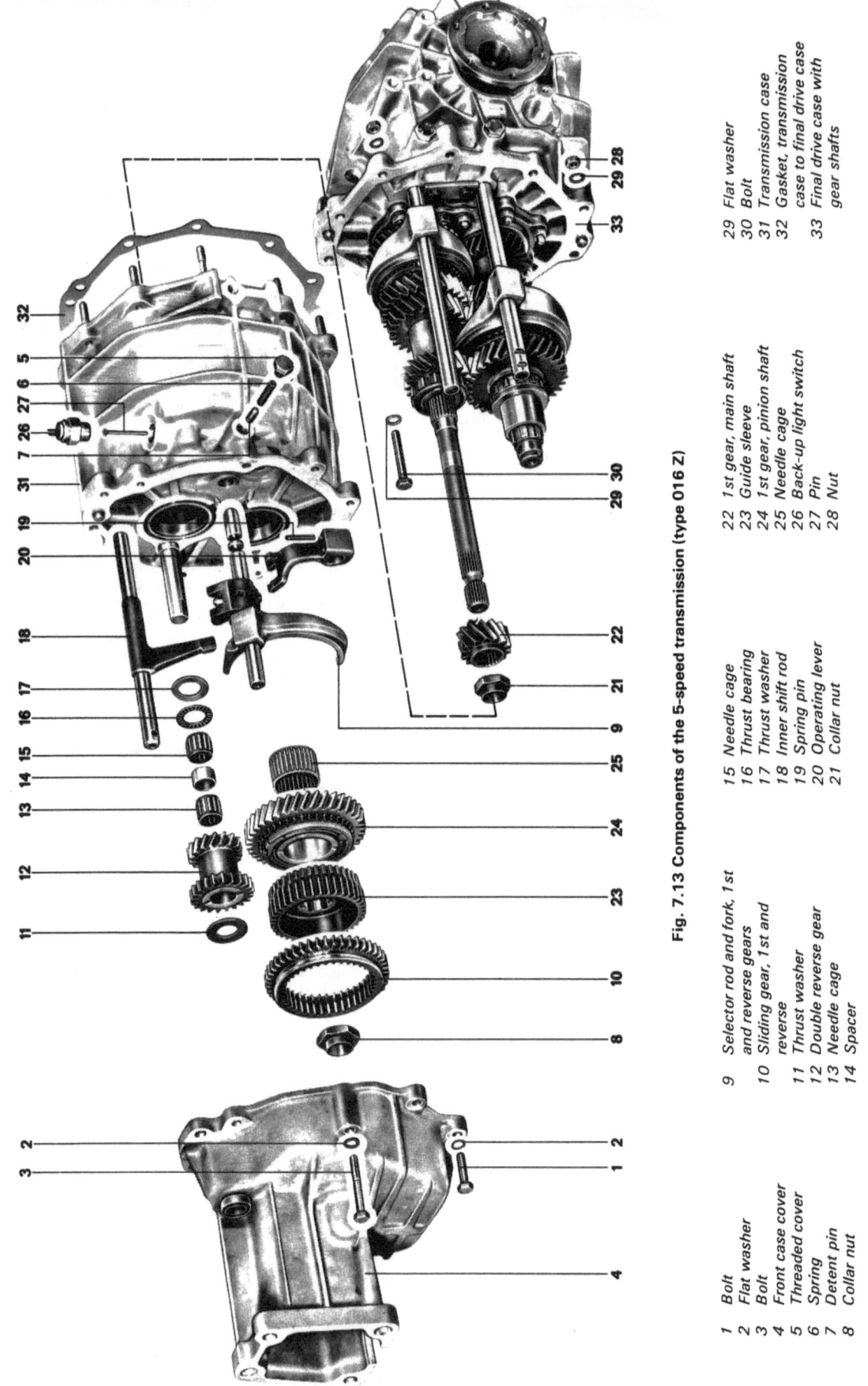

Fig. 7.13 Components of the 5-speed transmission (type 016 Z)

1 Bolt
2 Flat washer
3 Bolt
4 Front case cover
5 Threaded cover
6 Spring
7 Detent pin
8 Collar nut

9 Selector rod and fork, 1st and reverse gears
10 Sliding gear, 1st and reverse
11 Thrust washer
12 Double reverse gear
13 Needle cage
14 Spacer

15 Needle cage
16 Thrust bearing
17 Thrust washer
18 Inner shift rod
19 Spring pin
20 Operating lever
21 Collar nut

22 1st gear, main shaft
23 Guide sleeve
24 1st gear, pinion shaft
25 Needle cage
26 Back-up light switch
27 Pin
28 Nut

29 Flat washer
30 Bolt
31 Transmission case
32 Gasket, transmission case to final drive case
33 Final drive case with gear shafts

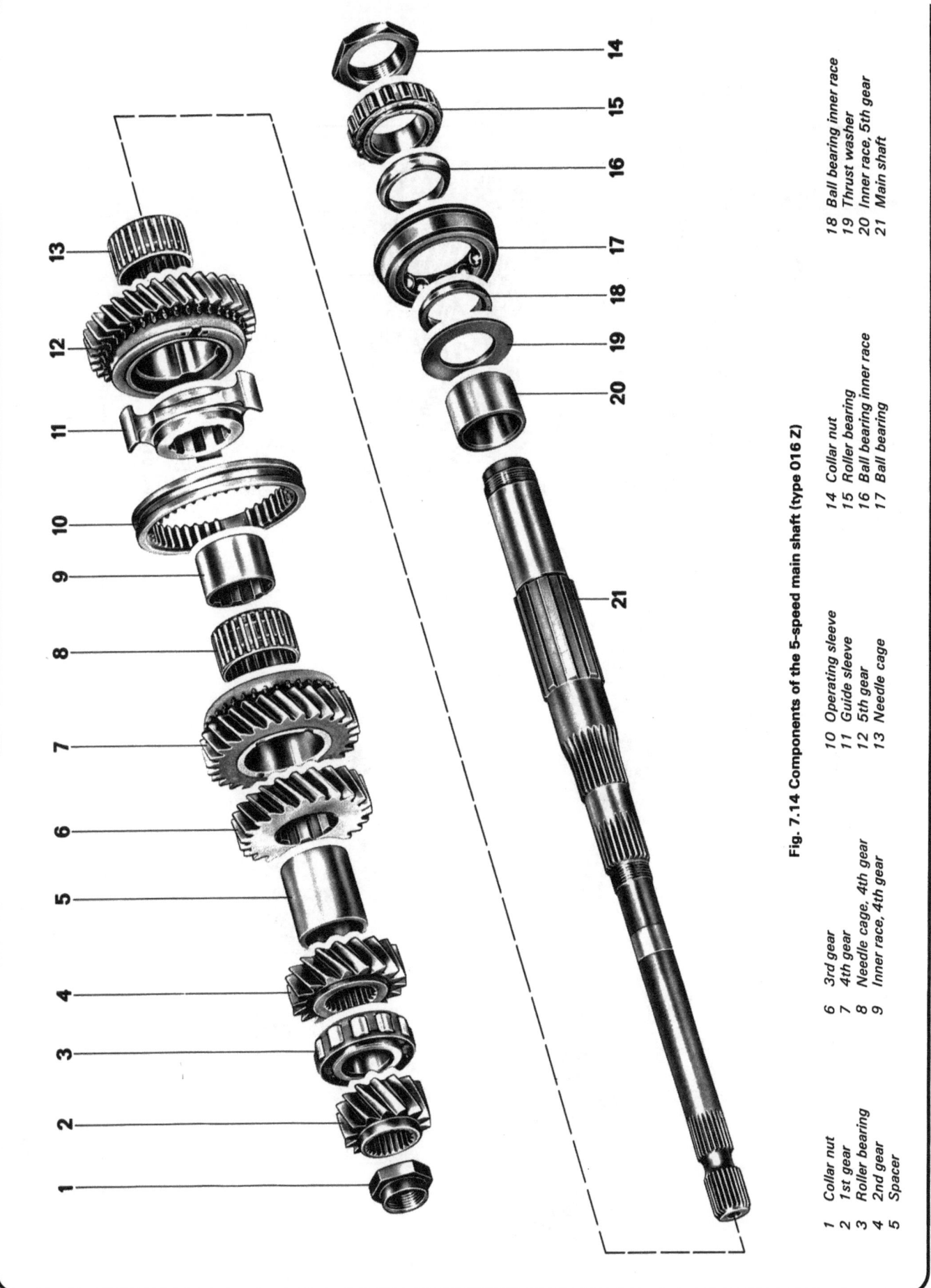

Fig. 7.14 Components of the 5-speed main shaft (type 016 Z)

1 Collar nut
2 1st gear
3 Roller bearing
4 2nd gear
5 Spacer

6 3rd gear
7 4th gear
8 Needle cage, 4th gear
9 Inner race, 4th gear

10 Operating sleeve
11 Guide sleeve
12 5th gear
13 Needle cage

14 Collar nut
15 Roller bearing
16 Ball bearing inner race
17 Ball bearing

18 Ball bearing inner race
19 Thrust washer
20 Inner race, 5th gear
21 Main shaft

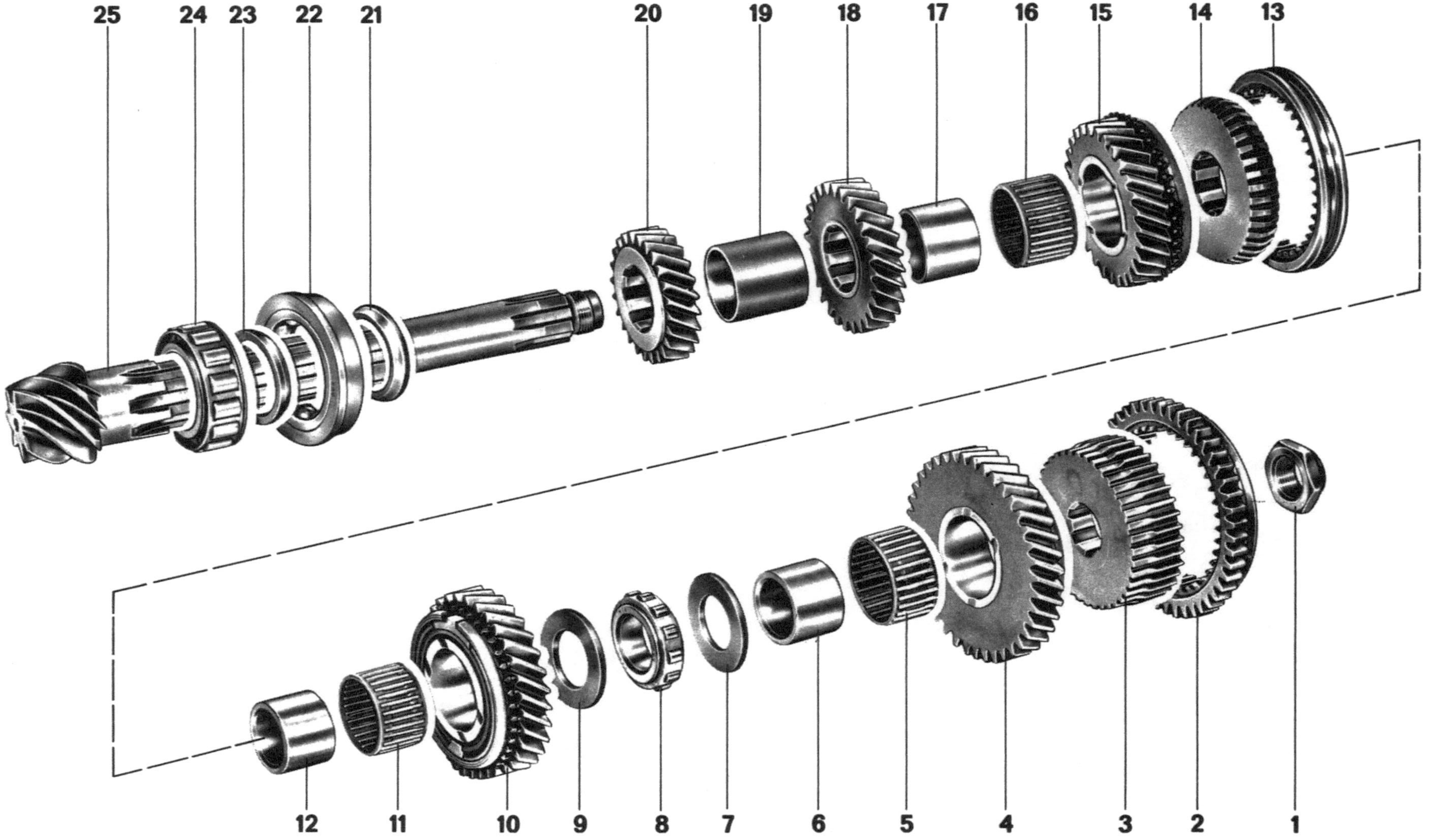

172

Fig. 7.15 Components of the 5-speed pinion shaft (type 016 Z)

1 Collar nut
2 1st synchro sleeve with
   reverse gear
3 Guide sleeve
4 1st gear
5 Needle cage, 1st gear

6 Inner race, 1st gear
7 Thrust washer
8 Roller bearing
9 Thrust washer
10 2nd gear
11 Needle cage, 2nd gear

12 Inner race, 2nd gear
13 Operating sleeve
14 Guide sleeve, 2nd and
    3rd gears
15 3rd gear

16 Needle cage, 3rd gear
17 Inner race, 3rd gear
18 4th gear
19 Spacer
20 5th gear

21 Ball bearing inner race
22 Ball bearing
23 Ball bearing inner race
24 Roller bearing
25 Pinion shaft

shaft. Install the needle cage on the inner race and then install the 4th gear over the needle bearing. If the gear requires press fitting, heat it to 120°C (248°F) and drive it into place.

55 Install the 5th gear on the pinion shaft. The large machined shoulder faces the ball bearing. If the fit is tight, heat the gear to 120°C (248°F) and drive it on.

56 Install the spacer between 5th gear and 4th gear. Install the 4th gear on the pinion shaft, heating as above and driving it on if necessary. The ground shoulder of the 4th gear faces away from the 5th gear.

57 Install the needle cage inner race on the pinion shaft, followed by the needle cage and 3rd gear. The small teeth of the synchronizer ring face away from 4th gear. If the fit is tight, heat the gear as above and drive it on.

58 Install the 3rd gear on the main shaft. If it is a tight fit, heat to the temperature above and drive it on.

59 Install the spacer between 2nd and 3rd gear on the main shaft and then install the 2nd gear. If necessary, heat the gear to the temperature above and drive it on.

60 Install the roller bearing on the main shaft. It may require heating to the above temperature before driving on.

61 Install the 1st gear on the main shaft. It may require heating to the above temperature before driving on.

62 Install the synchronizer guide sleeve on the pinion shaft. Locate the operating sleeve over the guide sleeve.

63 Install the 2nd/3rd gear shift fork and drive in the locating pins.

64 Install the needle bering inner race on the pinion shaft, heating to the above temperature if necessary for driving on. Install the needle bearing cage and 2nd gear, heating the gear to the above temperature, if necessary, before driving it into place.

65 Install the thrust washer on the pinion shaft. Install the roller bearing on the pinion shaft. Heating the bearing to 120°C (248°F), if

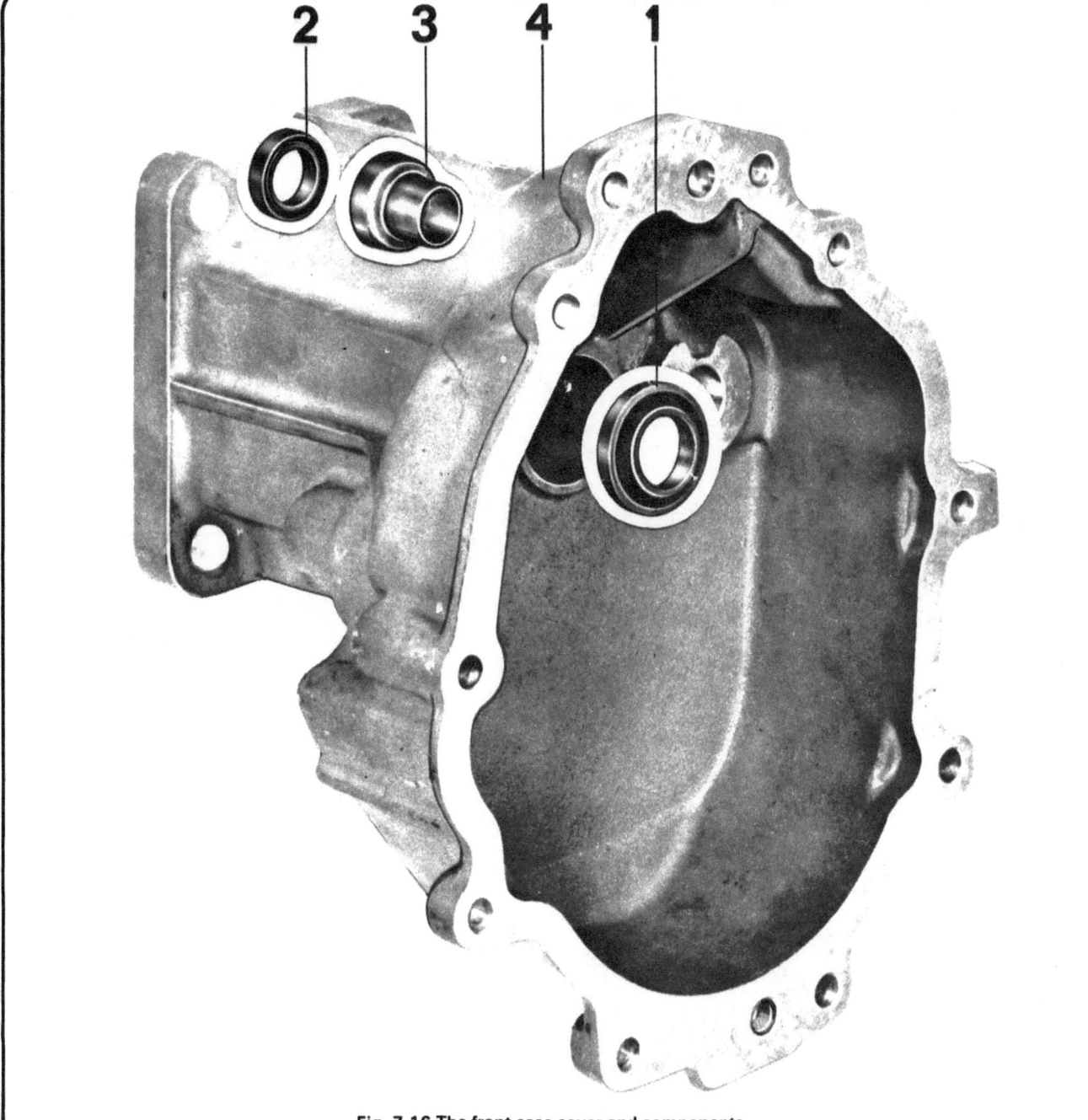

Fig. 7.16 The front case cover and components

| 1 Seal | 2 Seal | 3 Guide bushing | 4 Front case cover |

necessary, before driving it into place.

66 Adjust the gear selectors so that the gears are locked in 3rd gear. Install the collar nut on the main shaft and torque to 116 to 130 ft-lb (16 to 18 m-kg). Make sure that the collar faces the splined end of the main shaft. Lock the nut in place by punching the collar into the recess on the main shaft end with a prick punch and hammer.

67 Coat the gasket for the transmission-to-final drive case flange with a lght coat of silicone gasket sealer (non-hardening) and place the gasket on the flange of the final drive case.

68 Install the transmission case and align the bolt holes between the cases at the flange. Install the transmission case bolts and torque to 16 to 18 ft-lb (2.2 to 2.5 m-kg).

69 Install the inner bearing race for the 1st gear needle bearing on the pinion shaft. Heat it to the temperature above and drive it on if necessary.

70 Install the needle cage on the inner face and then install the 1st gear. It may be necessary to heat the gear to 120°C (248°F) before driving it on.

71 Slide the guide gear onto the pinion shaft with the cutaway teeth facing the 2nd gear, and install the 1st/reverse sleeve over the gear. The collar on the sleeve should face the threaded end of the shaft.

72 Install the operating lever on the lower shift guide rod and drive

in the locating pins.

73 Install the 1st/reverse selector rod and fork. Install the stop and spring in the transmission case and then install the bolt at the stop and torque to 11 to 13 ft-lb (1.5 to 1.8 m-kg).

74 Install the components for the reverse gear on the reverse gear shaft in the following order: thrust washer; thrust bearing; needle cage; spacer; needle cage; followed by the installation of the double reverse gear over the needle cages and the spacer. Install the thrust washer at the end of the shaft, at the double reverse gear.

75 Install the inner shift rod and locate the lever end in the notch at the top of the 1st/reverse shift fork.

76 Lock the gears in 1st and 5th gears at the same time and install the pinion shaft collar nut with the collar facing away from the pinion. Torque the nut to 145 to 159 ft-lb (20 to 22 m-kg) and lock the nut by punching the collar into the recess on the shaft with a flat ended punch.

77 Before installing the front case cover, Special Tool 9113 must be installed over the splines on the main shaft to prevent damage to the seal in the cover. If this tool is not available, wrap the splines with several layers of masking tape, rounding the front portion to allow clean passage of the shaft through the seal.

78 Coat the sealing flanges of the transmission case and the front case cover with silicone gasket sealer (non-hardening), as there is

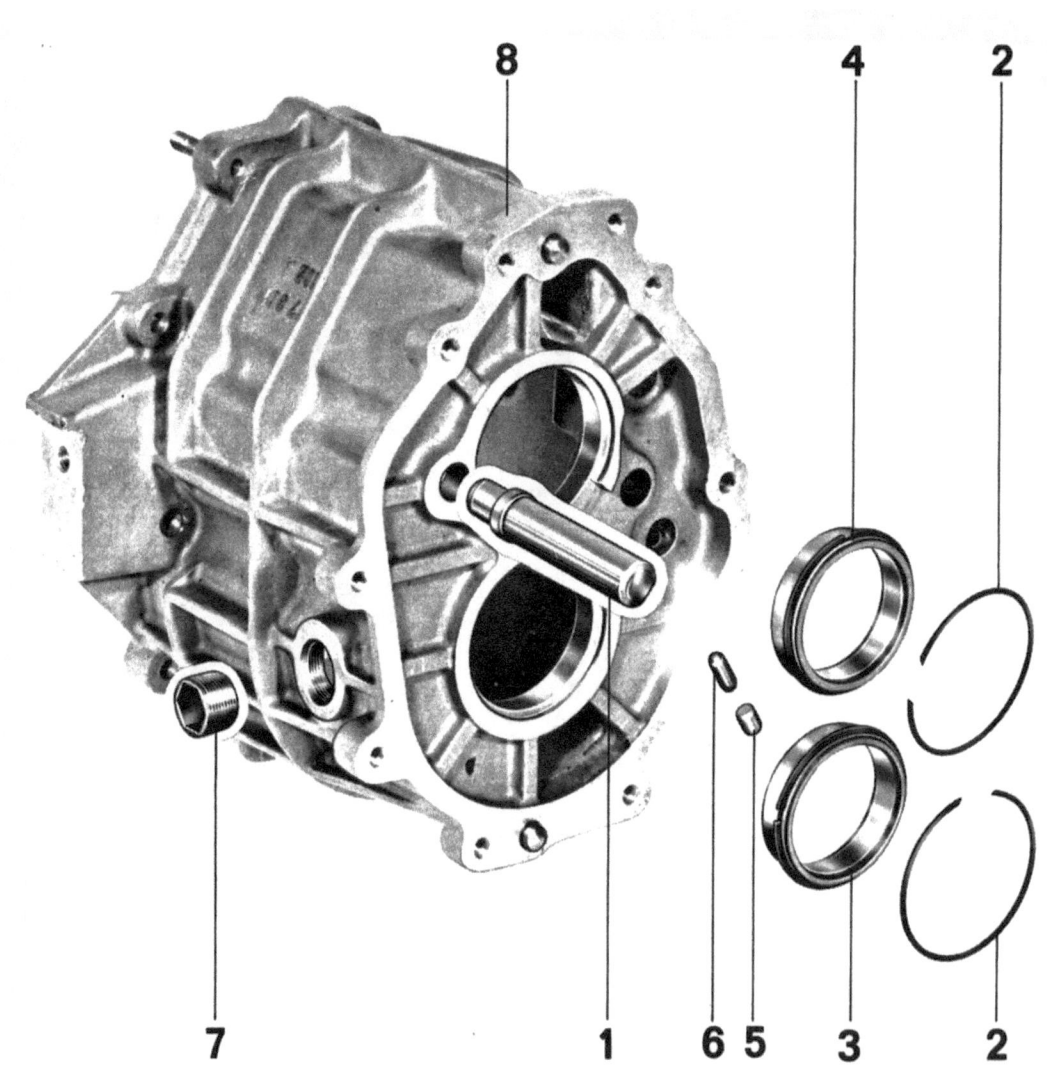

Fig. 7.17 The transmission case and components

1	Shaft	3	Bearing outer race with snap ring	4	Bearing outer race with snap ring
2	Snap ring			5	Plug

1 Shaft
2 Snap ring
3 Bearing outer race with snap ring
4 Bearing outer race with snap ring
5 Plug
6 Lock pin
7 Filler/level plug
8 Transmission case

no gasket for this join.

79 Install the front cover and the bolts which hold it to the transmission case. Torque the bolts to 16 to 18 ft-lb (2.2 to 2.5 m-kg).

80 Before installing the transmission fill it with oil, and make sure that the stop light switch and the drain plugs are properly installed and torqued to the correct value.

19 Front case cover - stripdown and assembly

1 Remove the front case cover (Section 18).

2 Drive the main shaft seal from the cover with a screwdriver and mallet. The seal is driven out toward the back of the cover.

3 Pry the guide seal out of the bushing with a screwdriver.

4 Remove the guide bushing from the case cover in a manner which will not damage the cover. We recommend grasping the outer collar of the bush with a pair of channel lock pliers and twisting the bush out of the case. Be careful not to damage the boss for the bush.

5 Assembly is the reverse of the stripdown procedure.

6 Place a new guide bushing into place and drive it into the case cover by placing the cover flange and the bush in the protected jaws

of a vise and then closing the vise to drive the bush into place, flush against the cover.

7 Install a new guide seal with an appropriate seal driver and pack the space between the dust and sealing lips with multipurpose grease.

8 Install a new main shaft seal. Press it in until the seal contacts the shoulder in the case.

20 Transmission case - stripdown and assembly

1 Remove the transmission case (Section 18).

2 Drive out the reverse gear shaft with a mandrel and hammer.

3 Remove the snap rings for the two bearing outer races with a screwdriver. Drive the outer races from the case from the inside out.

4 Assembly is the reverse of the stripdown procedure.

5 Install the snap rings on the bearing outer races and heat the transmission case to 120°C (248°F). Install the bearing races with an appropriate driver to the snap rings. Note that the bearing races have different inside diameters, the race with the larger diameter being for the main shaft (upper location).

6 Drive in the shaft for the reverse gear. It must be installed with

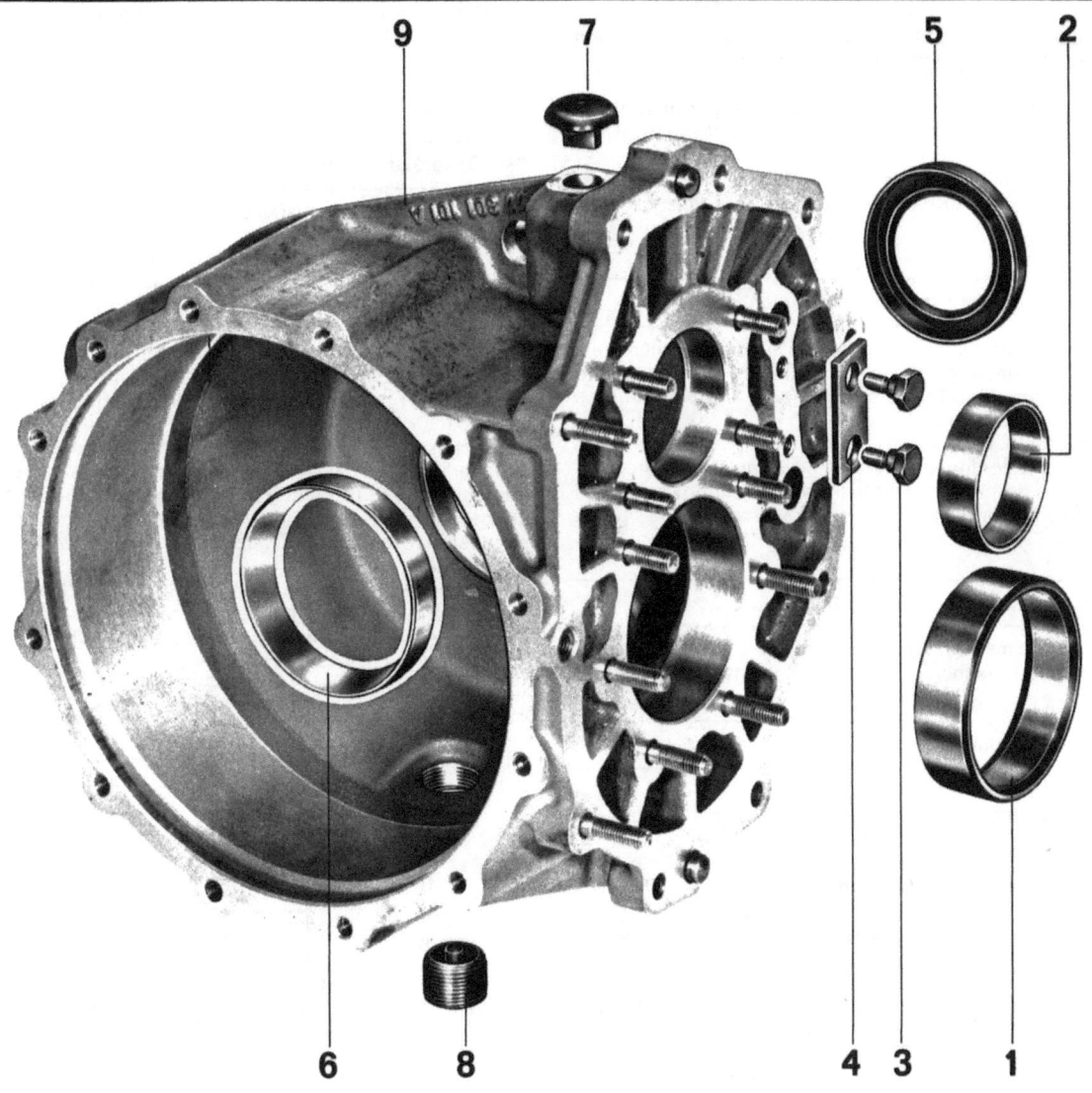

Fig. 7.18 The final drive case and components

1	Roller bearing, outer race	4	Lock plate	6	Tapered roller bearing,	7	Vent cover
2	Roller bearing, outer race	5	Seal		outer race	8	Drain plug
3	Bolt					9	Final drive case

the milled surface faces 30 degrees to the right of vertical when the transmission case is installed.

21 Final drive case - stripdown and assembly

1   Remove the cover plate from the differential and lift the differential from the final drive case.
2   Remove the O-ring from the differential cover and throw it away. A new O-ring must be used on assembly.
3   Pull the bearing race from the differential cover with an internal extractor and a gear puller. Remove the axle flange seal.
4   Remove the axle flange seal from the final drive case. Drive out the axle flange bearing race with a mandrel and hammer.
5   Pull the two gear shaft outer races from the case with internal extractors and gear pullers. The races are pulled toward the front of an installed transmission (into the transmission case).
6   Assembly is the reverse of the stripdown procedure.
7   Heat the final drive case and differential cover to 120°C (248°F).
8   Drive the bearing outer race into the differential cover.
9   Drive in the bearing outer race for the pinion shaft with an appropriate tool.
10 Drive in the bearing outer race for the main shaft with an appropriate tool.
11 Drive in the bearing outer race for the axle flange from the inside of the differential housing with an appropriate tool.
12 Install the differential.
13 Place a new O-ring on the differential cover and install the cover. Install the cover bolts and torque in a cross pattern to 20 ft-lb (2.7 m-kg).
14 Install the rear axle flange seals after the differential and the ring and pinion have been adjusted for proper clearance by your Porsche dealer.

22 Differential - adjusting the ring and pinion

1   The ring and pinion gears have a specific alignment which must be preserved at all times. Your Porsche dealer is the best place to have this work done, due to the special tools and calculations necessary for this procedure.
2   As a rule of thumb, the alignment of the ring and pinion must be checked any time a component behind the clamping plate on the final drive housing is changed. This includes all bearings and races in the final drive housing.

23 Differential - replacing rear axle flange seal

1   The removal and installation of the rear axle flange seal is common to all Porsche transmissions. This task is covered in Section 14.

24 Adjusting shift linkage

1   Remove the drive shaft tube (Section 40).
2   Remove the insulation base from the drive shaft tube. Clean off any residual tape and adhesive from the tube.
3   Pry the guide rod from the ball stud on the drive shaft tube. Turn the guide rod so that it extends beyond the tube and lever it off the ball stud.
4   Adjustment of the assembly is begun with length adjustment on the guide rod.
5   The guide rod must be adjusted to a length of 782 ± 1.5 mm between the center of the guide rod pivot pin and the center of the ball socket. Mark these center points on the socket and place the center mark for the pin on the top surface of the guide tool.
6   Place the guide rod in the protected jaws of a vise with the pivot pin facing you and approximately horizontal. The shaft and guide rod must also be horizontal. Measure the rod between the two previously mentioned points. If the length must be altered, loosen the locknut and turn the ball socket until the points are within the length limits above and the ball socket opening faces down.
7   Remove the guide rod from the vise and set it on a workbench with the ball socket to your right and the pivot pin facing toward

you. Clamp the ball socket to the bench top with the open end of the socket facing down and the pivot pin still pointing toward you.
8   Double check the measured length of the guide rod before continuing its adjustment.
9   Set an inclinometer (protractor with spirit levels built in) to 15 degrees. Place the inclinometer base on the top edge of the pivot pin and turn the pin until the bubble in the spirit level is centered and the pin is that many degrees down from horizontal. Tighten the lock nut and torque to 17 ft-lb (2.3 m-kg). Make a final check of the length of the rod and the angle of the pin.
10 Lubricate all bearing surfaces with a light coating of MoS$_2$ base multipurpose grease.
11 Install the guide rod on the ball stud of the drive shaft housing. Center the ball socket over the ball stud and strike it with a hammer to set in place.
12 Push the locknut spring and guide plate on the end of the guide rod. There should be a distance of 29 ± 0.3 mm from the face of the guide plate and the flat face of the guide rod end. This will provide automatic positioning of the insulation base.
13 Place the shift rod in the insulation base and align the guide plate. Secure the insulation base to the drive shaft tube with heavy tape, wrapping each side several times.
14 Install the drive shaft tube (Section 40).
15 Attach the locknut spring to the guide plate.
16 Install the shift lever.

Part C: 5-speed transmission (type 016/9)

25 General description

1   This transmission shares a strong external appearance with the 4-speed transmission.
2   The transmission case consists of a differential housing of cast aluminum similar to the 4-speed, a cast iron gear carrier, and an aluminum cover casting bolted to the end of the gear carrier.
3   The main shaft runs on three bearings, a needle bearing located in the differential housing, a cylindrical roller bearing in the gear carrier, and a four-point grooved ball bearing in the end cover. The pinion shaft runs on two tapered roller bearings which absorb the axial loads of the pinion.
4   Because the pinion shaft is part of the transmission and the final drive, adjustments and changes of the transmission parts necessitate adjustment of the ring and pinion gear relationship. If you do not have the tools or are not prepared to take on this critical task, we suggest that you seek the help of your Porsche dealer or a qualified transmission specialist.
5   Since the 016/9 version of the transmission is so similar to the 4-speed, all the relevant text is to be found in Part A of this chapter. Differences in work for the 5-speed are negligible.

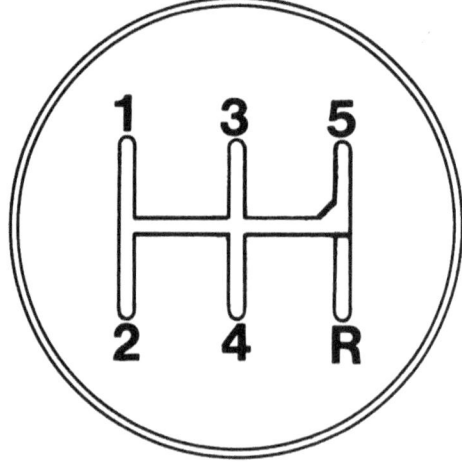

Fig. 7.19 The shift pattern of the type 016/9 transmission readily separates it from other 5-speed models

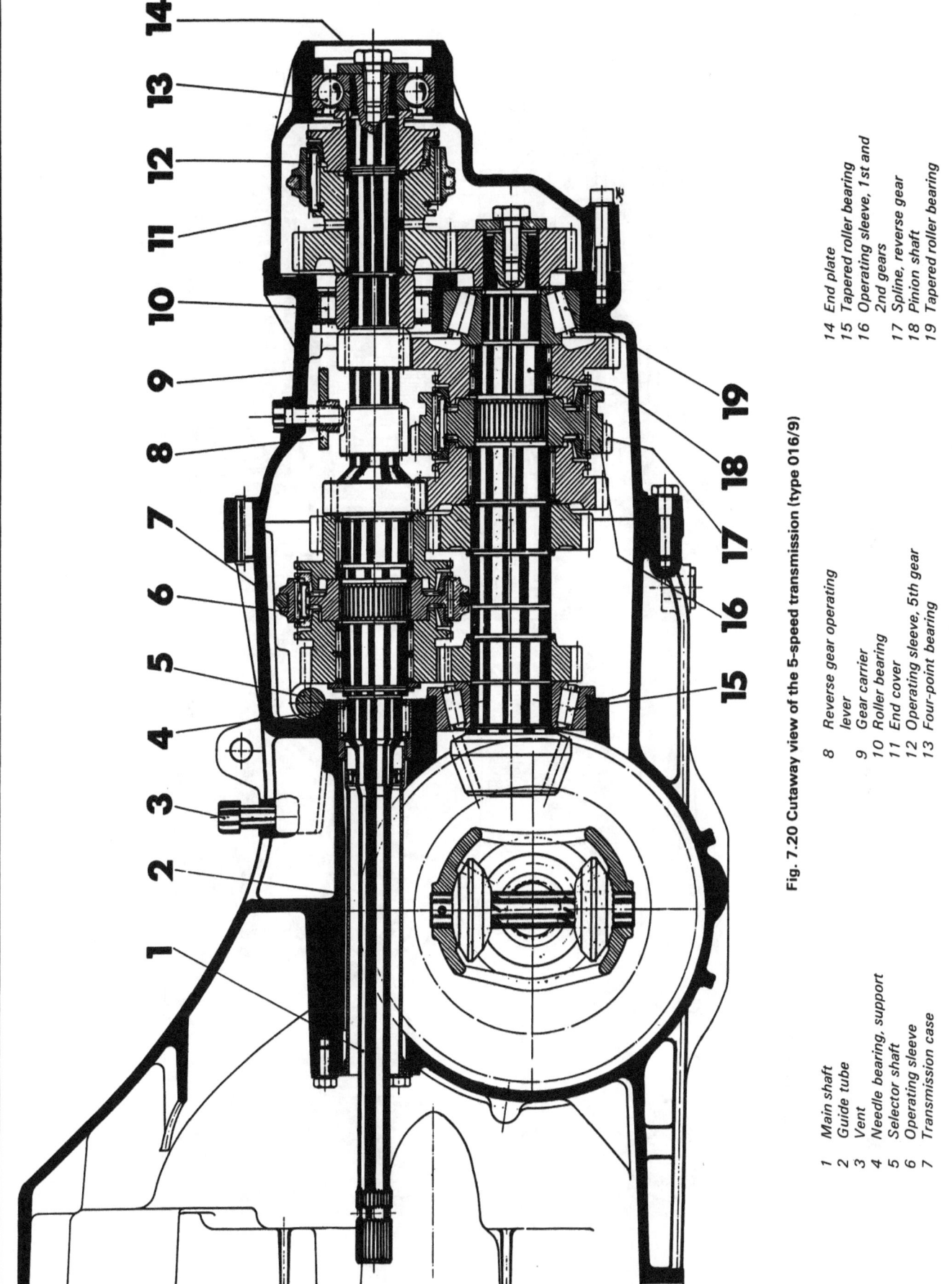

Fig. 7.20 Cutaway view of the 5-speed transmission (type 016/9)

1 Main shaft
2 Guide tube
3 Vent
4 Needle bearing. support
5 Selector shaft
6 Operating sleeve
7 Transmission case
8 Reverse gear operating
lever
9 Gear carrier
10 Roller bearing
11 End cover
12 Operating sleeve, 5th gear
13 Four-point bearing
14 End plate
15 Tapered roller bearing
16 Operating sleeve, 1st and
2nd gears
17 Spline, reverse gear
18 Pinion shaft
19 Tapered roller bearing

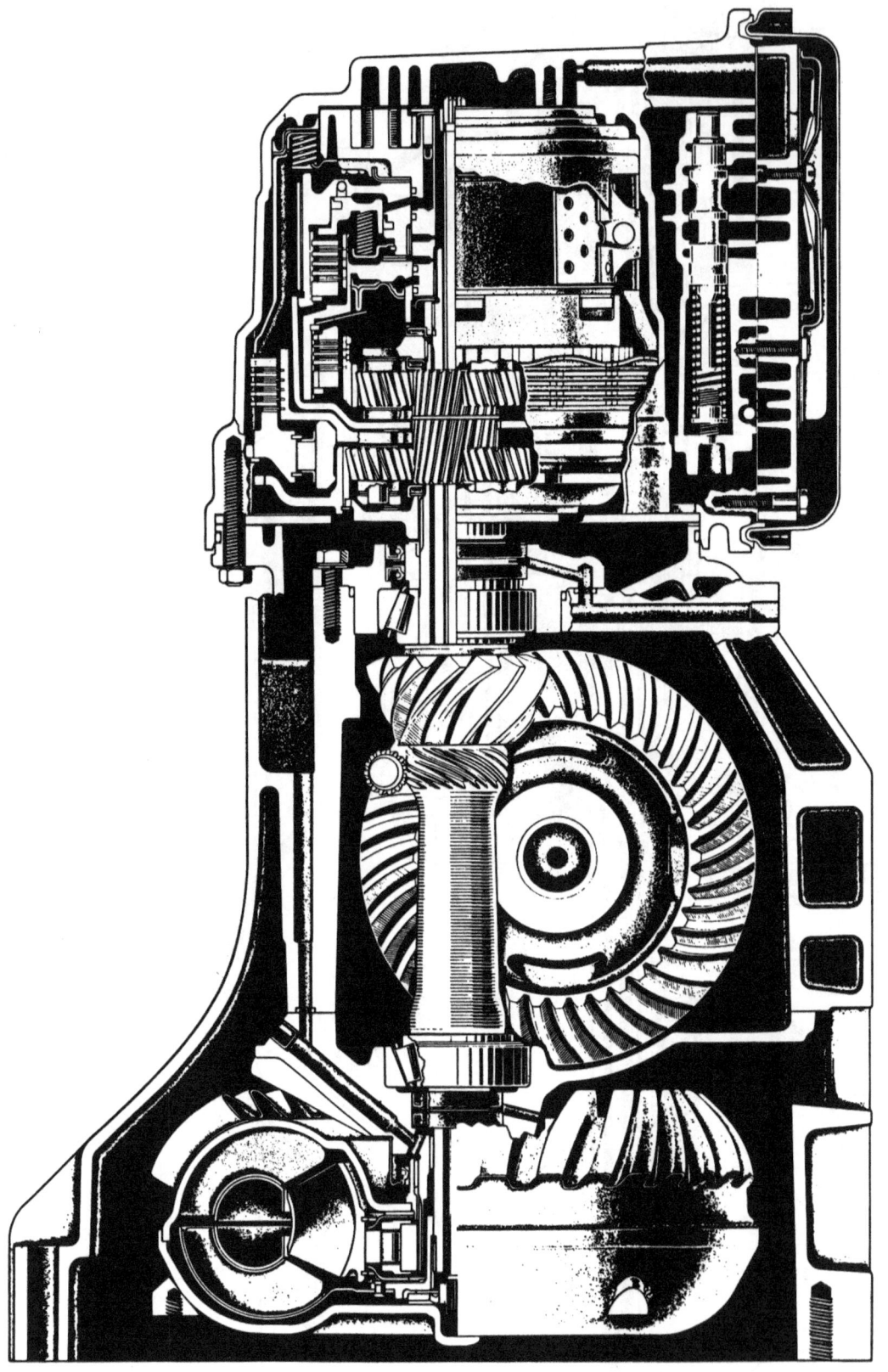

Fig. 7.21 Cutaway view of the automatic transmission

Part D: Automatic transmission

26 General description

1   The automatic transmission of the Porsche 924 is a precision instrument which relies on the hydraulic operation of check valves and the rotating mass of a torque converter to change engine power into forward motion. To safely rebuild the unit requires totally clean conditions and many special tools as well as a thorough understanding of the theory of automatic transmission design. Because of this we recommend that you seek the services of a trained automatic transmission specialist, either through your Porsche dealer or an independent shop. The costs involved in acquiring the proper tools, the time in stripdown and rebuilding by the home mechanic, and the problems in proper operation of the unit should any dirt or other foreign object be introduced into the unit, make a visit to the specialist the most economical choice.
2   This chapter part covers the basic adjustment of external cables and filling of the transmission fluid. The troubleshooting section of the Introduction chapter will give you basic troubleshooting procedures, based on the information available in this manual. If the suggested solutions do not correct the defect you have noticed, seek aid from your Porsche dealer or a specialist.

27 Gearbox – removal and installation

1   Disconnect the negative lead from the battery.
2   Raise the vehicle and place it on jack stands.
3   Remove the heat shield and rear muffler bracket (Chapter 3).
4   Detach the axle shafts at the transmission and suspend them in a horizontal position to prevent damage to the universal joints (Chapter 10).
5   Remove the protective shield from the transmission oil filler. This is held in place by two nuts.
6   Detach the selector lever and transmission lever cables. The transmission lever cable has a locking ball at its head to prevent the cable from springing off.
7   Open the inspection hole in the rear bellhousing and remove the torque converter mounting bolts. There are three torque converter mounting bolts.
8   If you do not have a transmission jack for supporting the transmission during the next steps, a floor jack and several flat boards may be employed to take the weight of the transmission from its mounts. Place the floor jack, protected with the wood, or the transmission jack beneath the central section of the transmission, between the axle shaft flanges, and raise the transmission slightly.
9   Remove all bolts from the transmission bellhousing and the transmission mounts. If you are using a floor jack, it may be best to have an assistant balance the transmission during this operation. When these bolts have been removed, the transmission will be supported only by the floor jack. Do not let it fall.
10 Move the floor jack and transmission slightly back and push the torque converter into the transmission, to separate it from the drive shaft. The torque converter should be secured in the transmission to prevent it from dropping. This may be accomplished by making three steadies from 4 in long pieces of heavy iron strap, drilled at one end and held in place by the three transmission bellhousing bolts. Another short-term solution is to enlist the aid of an assistant to hold the torque converter in place while the transmission is lowered.
11 Move the transmission to the rear of the vehicle while lowering so that all parts of the transmission clear the components on the underside of the vehicle. Be especially careful not to crush the brake lines which cross just above the transmission.
12 When the transmission has been lowered, slide the torque converter from its splined mounting and set it aside.
13 Installation is the reverse of the removal procedure.
14 Install the torque converter by sliding it into the splined shaft.
15 Raise the transmission into place. Do not crush the brake lines, and take care not to foul any of the other underside components.
16 Remove the torque converter steadies and arrange one tab on the torque converter and one of the holes of the mounting plate to align in the inspection hole of the transmission bellhousing.

Fig. 7.22 The transmission oil filler with level lines shown

17 Install the transmission-to-body mounting bolts and the mount-to-transmission mounting bolts and tighten them until snug.
18 Install the transmission bellhousing bolts and tighten them until snug.
19 Torque all transmission mounting bolts to 30 ft-lb (4.2 m-kg). Torque the large transmission bellhousing bolts to 61 ft-lb (8.5 m-kg) and the small bolts to 30 ft-lb (4.2 m-kg).
20 Install the first of the three bolts in the torque converter and tighten until snug, and then turn the converter to install the other two. Turn the converter and tighten each bolt until tight.
21 Install the selector lever and transmission lever cables.
22 Install the transmission oil filler protective shield and torque the nuts to 14 ft-lb (2 m-kg).
23 Install the axle shafts (Chapter 10).

28 ATF level – checking and filling

1   Park the vehicle on a level surface.
2   Move the selector lever to N and set the parking brake.
3   Start the engine and let it run at idle speed.
4   Remove the protective shield from the transmission oil filler at the rear of the transmission. Wipe the filler with a rag to remove all dirt accumulations.
5   Allow the engine to run and wait until the transmission body feels warm to the touch (about 40° to 60°C or 104° to 140°F). Thermal expansion will cause testing at any other temperature range to result in incorrect levels of ATF being indicated.
6   ATF levels indicated must be between the upper and lower marks on the transmission oil filler. The amount indicated between the two lines is 0.4 liter (1 US pint). Fill to the top line, but not beyond, whenever this amount is indicated. Do not overfill the transmission, as this will also cause problems in the transmission operation.
7   Replace the filler cap and tighten.
8   Install the protective shield and torque the nuts to 14 ft-lb (2 m-kg).
9   Move the selector lever through all gear ranges, and shut off the engine.

29 Differential oil – checking and changing

1   The level of the differential oil is checked by removing the large socket head cap from the oil filler hole. This is located on the left side of the differential, just behind the axle flange.
2   The oil level must just touch the bottom of the lowest thread. If there is too little, top up with the recommended lubricant (Specifications). If the oil level is too high and you have kept careful track of

differential oil levels, an exchange of oil between the automatic transmission and the final drive is indicated.

3   Oil may be changed by draining the differential through the drain plug in the casting beneath the differential location, replacing the plug and filling with fresh oil of the proper type (Specifications).

4   The drain plug and filler plug are torqued to 14 ft-lb (2 m-kg) when installed.

30   Selector lever cable – removal and installation

1   Disconnect the negative lead from the battery.

2   Remove all portions of the exhaust system from the catalytic converter back, including the converter (Chapter 3).

3   Loosen the cable at the clamping sleeve and holder. Remove all mounting parts.

4   Bend back the metal clip holding the cable housing to the drive shaft housing with a screwdriver or tire iron.

5   Remove the selector lever knob, pull the cover out of the center console, and pull off the selector lever sleeve. Set these aside.

6   Unplug the bulb holder and remove it.

7   Mark the location of the selector support on all attaching points on the drive selector shaft cover. Unbolt the selector support and remove the guide plates.

8   Lift the front of the selector support and pull the entire assembly

forward. Disconnect the selector cables at the base and at the bottom of the selector lever.

9   Hook a long piece of wire or strong string to the forward end of the selector cable and draw the cable out of the vehicle from the back. Allow the string or wire to remain. This will enable you to pull the new cable through the insulation blanket without damaging the blanket or the cable.

10   Installation is the reverse of the removal procedure.

11   Place a rubber grommet on the cable sleeve and coat the front dust cover with rubber lubricant (See position of part 24a in Fig. 7.23).

12   Fasten the clamping sleeve on the cable.

13   Have an assistant help you with the following step. Hook the string or wire used in the removal process to the forward end of the cable and have one person draw the cable into the passenger compartment while the other works from the rear of the vehicle to feed cable through the insulation sheet. Pull the cable forward, far enough to allow room to install the cable on the selector support.

14   Install the cable end at the bottom of the selector lever and hook the other end of the bellows in the mount on the selector support. Before installing the cable end, place a rubber washer between the cable end and the selector level. This will allow quiet operation of the selector level.

15   Bolt the selector support and guides into place and torque the bolts to 6 ± 1 ft-lb (0.8 ± 0.2 m-kg).

16   Push the rear cable end through the opening of the bracket.

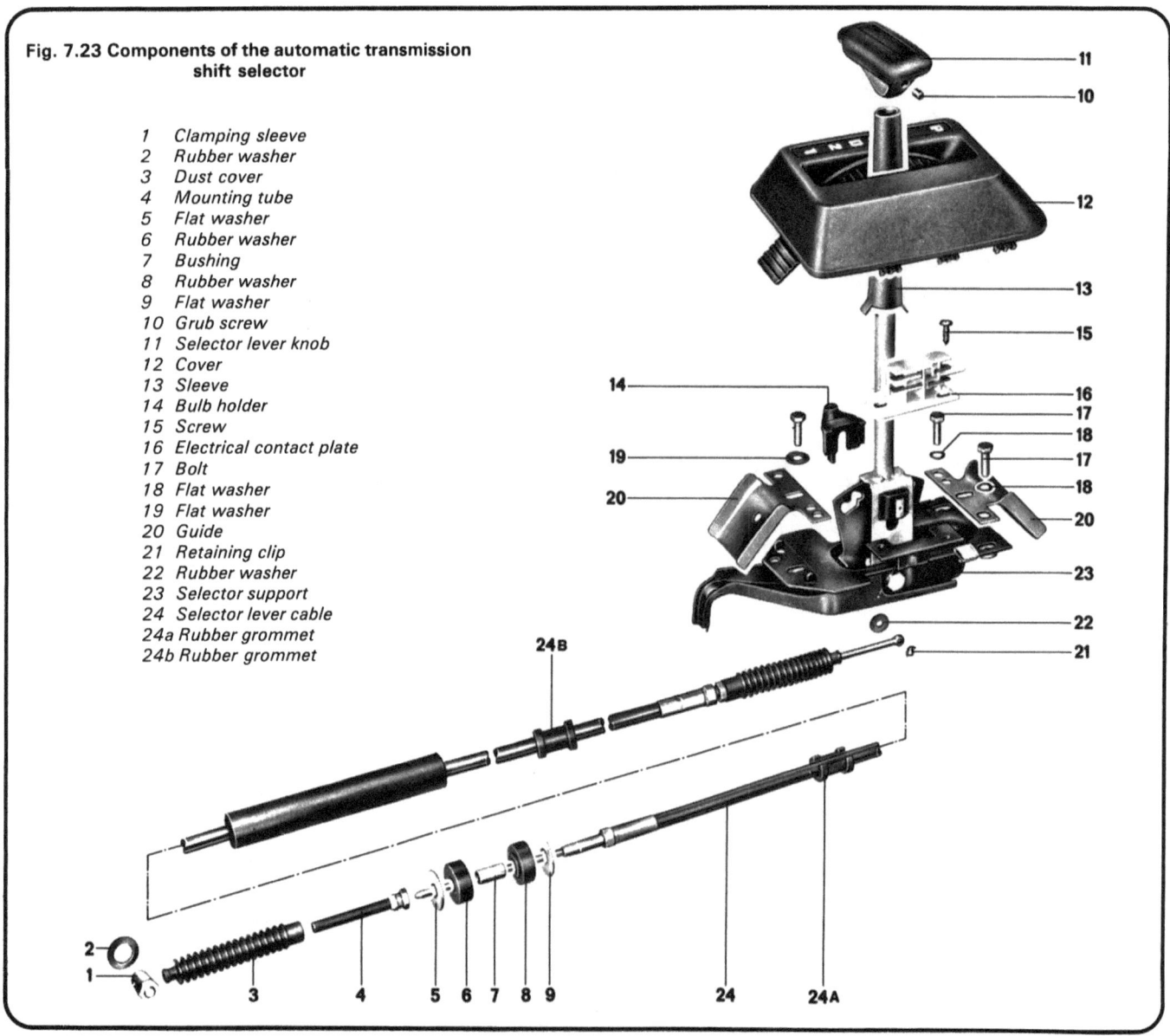

Fig. 7.23 Components of the automatic transmission shift selector

1   Clamping sleeve
2   Rubber washer
3   Dust cover
4   Mounting tube
5   Flat washer
6   Rubber washer
7   Bushing
8   Rubber washer
9   Flat washer
10   Grub screw
11   Selector lever knob
12   Cover
13   Sleeve
14   Bulb holder
15   Screw
16   Electrical contact plate
17   Bolt
18   Flat washer
19   Flat washer
20   Guide
21   Retaining clip
22   Rubber washer
23   Selector support
24   Selector lever cable
24a Rubber grommet
24b Rubber grommet

Install a rubber washer on the clamping sleeve and hook it onto the transmission lever.

17 Install a rubber grommet in the opening of the bracket to eliminate noise.

18 Adjust the rubber grommets on the cable covers so that the cable cannot touch the driveshaft housing. Close the clamp.

19 When all components are reinstalled, adjust the selector lever cable (Section 31).

31 Selector lever cable – adjusting

1 The following task requires two people.

2 Move the selector lever to the P position.

3 Loosen the nut on the clamping sleeve.

4 While one person holds the selector lever in P, adjust the operating lever on the transmissin by pressing it back against its stop into its corresponding P position.

5 Tighten the nut on the clamping sleeve and torque it to 4 ± 1 ft-lb (0.5 ± 0.1 m-kg)

6 Have the person beneath the vehicle get out, then start the engine. Hold one foot on the brake and move the selector lever in and out of all positions. An engagement jolt should be felt in positions R, D, 2, and 1 about 5 seconds after engaging that gear.

32 Throttle cable and throttle pressure cable – removal and installation (1976-78)

1 Movement of the accelerator pedal is transferred by two cables; one to the throttle valve and one to the throttle pressure lever.

2 Fig. 7.24 shows the complete layout of these cables and the pertinent parts of this system.

3 Basic directions for removal and installation of these components will be found in Section 34. The only major difference between the two methods of throttle valve and throttle pressure lever coordination is the use of two separate cables in the earlier system.

4 Never attempt to drive your car with either of the cables disconnected, as damage to the transmission will result.

33 Throttle cable and throttle pressure cable – adjustment (1976-78)

Initial adjustments

1 The accelerator pedal should be at the idle stop position with the rubber stop touching its stop plate.

2 The throttle valve must be fully closed.

3 The throttle pressure lever at the transmission must be at its rest position against its stop.

4 The safety yoke must lie flat on the bracket on the upper accelerator lever.

Final adjustments

5 Adjust both cables so that they are attached to the safety yoke without tension or slack. The throttle cable is adjusted at the mounting on the intake manifold (as in standard transmission vehicles – Chapter 3). The throttle pressure cable is adjusted at the mounting bracket on the transmission.

6 The safety yoke has been specially designed to eliminate the possibility of the vehicle being operated while only one cable is hooked up. If a cable disconnects or breaks, the other will detach, avoiding damage to the transmission.

7 There are two operational checks which must be made before concluding this task.

8 The full throttle check is performed by depressing the accelerator pedal down until the first pressure point is noticed. The throttle valve should be fully open.

9 The kickdown position check is performed by depressing the accelerator pedal to full stop. The throttle pressure lever at the transmission should have approximately 2 mm (0.079 in) of free play left before the end of its travel. If necessary, readjust the throttle pressure cable at the transmission bracket.

10 If the results above are not found in your operational checks,

make sure that the carpets, floor mats, or other obstructions are not blocking the travel of the pedal.

34 Accelerator pedal and throttle pressure cable – removal and installation (1979-on)

1 From 1979-on, the throttle and throttle pressure cables are actually a single cable with the action running through a bellcrank to coordinate the opening of the throttle valves with the opening of the valves in the transmission (Fig. 7.25).

2 Detach the throttle cable end from the accelerator pedal.

3 Detach the throttle valve pushrod from the bellcrank and turn it so that it is out of the way.

4 Remove the locking clip from the shorter cable and loosen the lock nut on the longer cable at the holder.

5 Press the rubber sealing grommet out of the firewall with a screwdriver. Be careful not to puncture the grommet. Press from the passenger compartment so that the cable end may be pulled into the engine compartment.

6 Remove the exhaust system from the front exhaust pipe mounting flange back (Chapter 3).

7 Press out the ball socket at the transmission lever and loosen the lock nut at the cable holder.

8 The cable is held to the drive shaft tube by hose clamps and a cable sleeve. Mark their position before removing them for ease in reassembly. This will also reduce the amount of time necessary for adjusting the cable when it is installed.

9 Pull the cable away from the bellcrank roller and remove the cable from the holder.

10 Remove the cable by pulling it downward along its entire length between the central tube and the insulation sheet. Do not bend the cable. Try to lower it along its length, easing back the insulation sheet with a putty knife or similar dull edged tool to prevent damage to the insulation sheet.

11 Installation is the reverse of the removal procedure.

12 Screw in the ball socket and the sleeve adjuster on the transmission end of the cable.

13 Hold the cable in its proper location along the drive shaft tube and push it between the tube and the insulation sheet. Use a putty knife again to keep the insulation from being ripped during installation.

14 Push the cable ends through to the transmission lever at the rear and the roller at the front.

15 Align the cable sleeve according to the marks made during disassembly and install the holder and its hose clamps. When you are sure that the central portion of the cable is properly located, torque the clamps to 1 ft-lb (0.14 m-kg).

16 Attach the cable and ball socket on the transmission.

17 Thread the front section of the cable through the holder and back the adjusting nut back all the way. Wrap the uncovered cable segment through the roller and set the other end into the clip. Push the cable through the firewall and press the grommet into place. If the grommet sticks or balks, lubricate it with rubber lubricant and press it into place.

18 Attach the cable to the accelerator pedal.

19 When all components have been replaced, adjust the throttle cable (Section 35).

35 Accelerator pedal and throttle pressure cable – adjustment (1979-on)

1 The following tools will be needed in addition to normal wrenches and screwdrivers: a protractor with a built-in level (inclinometer), a flat, clear plastic protractor.

2 Screw the cable sleeve mounting nut and the nut on the ball end of the transmission lever into their housings. Torque the cable sleeve nut to 22 ft-lb (3 m-kg) and the nut on the ball end to 4 ft-lb (0.5 m-kg).

3 Loosen the three bolts which hold the roller bracket to the engine and push the bracket fully forward. Torque the bolts to 15 ft-lb (2.1 m-kg).

4 Completely loosen the short cable at the firewall and the long cable at the bracket. Slip the cable out of the roller.

5 Remove the protective cap from the top of the roller and turn the

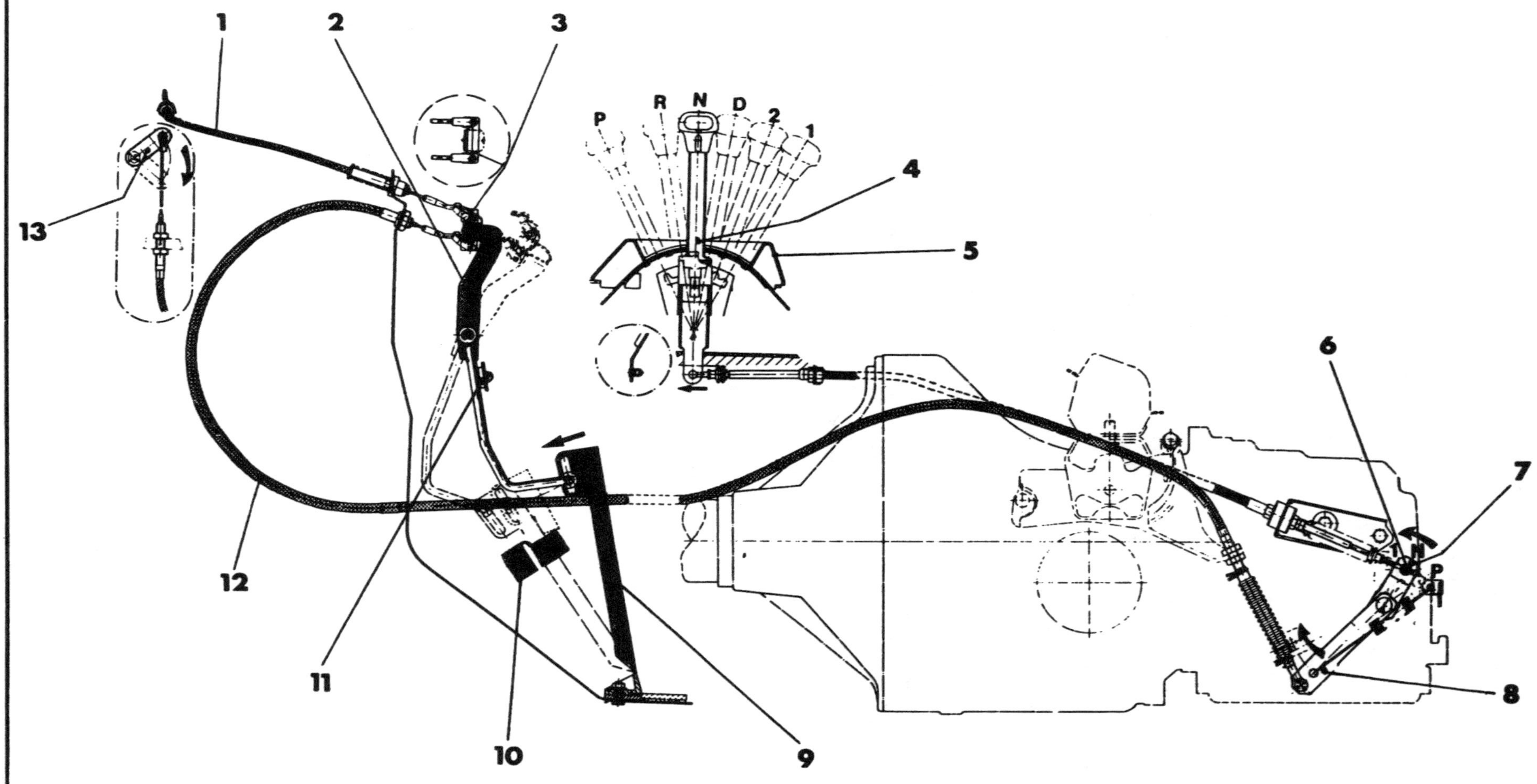

Fig. 7.24 The throttle cable and throttle pressure cable assemblies (1976-78)

1 Throttle cable
2 Upper accelerator lever
3 Safety yoke
4 Selector lever

5 Selector gate
6 Clamping bolt
7 Transmission lever

8 Throttle pressure lever
9 Accelerator pedal
10 Pedal kickdown stop

11 Pedal idle stop
12 Throttle pressure cable
13 Throttle valve

Fig. 7.25 From 1979, the safety yoke is eliminated and roller is installed

Fig. 7.26 Adjusting the roller. Angle A = 29°

roller so that an imaginary line, perpendicular to the engine, and another imaginary line running through the center of the nut of the roller and ball on the lever, form a 29° angle. It may help your measurement of this angle if you mask half of the nut and ball with masking tape, forming one of the two lines. The plastic protractor will help your determination of the proper angle. Note that proper turning of the roller will bring the slot for the cable into line with the reinforcement rib of the holder (Fig. 7.26).

6   Install the throttle pushrod while the roller is held in the position described above. The pushrod must just fit over the control ball without tension in this position. If the throttle pushrod needs adjustment to achieve this, loosen the lock nut on the ball cup end of the pushrod and adjust the pushrod length. Tighten the lock nut and torque it to 6.5 ft-lb (0.9 m-kg).

7   Locate the metal drum fitting in the slot of the roller and slip the cable into the roller.

8   Adjust the long cable sleeve until the metal drum fitting just rests in the slot without tension. There should be no slop in the cable, either.

9   Adjust the tension on the cable at the accelerator pedal by operating the adjuster at the firewall. The cable should be adjusted so that it rests without tension or slop.

10 When the cable has been adjusted properly, the accelerator pedal should rest in the neutral position of 11°30'. This may be checked with an inclinometer. The throttle valve will be closed and the lever on the transmission will be at bottom stop position.

11 There are two operational checks which must be made before concluding this task.

12 The full throttle check is performed by depressing the accelerator pedal until the first noticeable pressure point is felt. The throttle should be fully open.

13 The kickdown position check is performed by depressing the pedal down to its full stop position and checking the operation of the operating lever on the roller. The roller stop should have lifed off the operating lever approximately 6 mm (0.24 in). The lever on the transmission should be at full stop, or within 1° of the stop.

36 Differential – replacing rear axle flange seal

1   The removal and installation of the rear axle flange seal is common to all Porsche transmissions. This task is covered in Section 14.

Part E: Drive shaft tube and drive shaft

37 Drive shaft tube – general description

1   The drive shaft tube forms a rigid connection between the engine and the transaxle, completing the backbone around which the body is hung.

2   The drive shaft tube also provides enclosure for the drive shaft, which rides in ball bearings inside the tube.

38 Drive shaft tube – removal and installation (4-speed transmission and 5-speed transmission, type 016/9, and automatic)

1   Disconnect the negative lead from the battery.

2   Raise the vehicle and place it on jack stands.

3   Install an engine hoist and raise the engine by its lifting straps so that the weight of the engine rests on the lift and not on the engine mounts.

4   Place your homemade wood block spacing tool (Chapter 6) between the drive shaft tube and the reinforcing brace.

5   Remove the transmission (Section 2).

6   Detach the drive shaft tube from the clutch bellhousing.

7   Pull back the drive shaft tube about 100 mm (approximately 4 in).

8   Remove the rear cross brace in the transmission tunnel.

9   Remove the mounting bolts from the torsion bar tube and carefully lower the tube (Chapter 10).

10 Pull the selector rod out toward the rear of the vehicle.

11 Pull out the drive shaft tube to the rear of the vehicle.

12 Installation is the reverse of the removal procedure.

13 Slide the drive shaft tube into position so that it is about 100 mm (approx. 4 in) from the clutch bellhousing.

14 Slide the selector rod into place on top of the drive shaft tube.

15 Install the torsion bar tube mounting bolts and torque them to the required specification (Chapter 10).

16 Install the rear cross brace to the body and tighten the bolts evenly.

17 Slide the drive shaft into the clutch bellhousing and make sure that it engages the clutch disc. Torque the mounting bolts to 30 ft-lb (4.2 m-kg).

39 Drive shaft – checking (4-speed transmission)

1   Place a straight edge across the flange of the transmission bellhousing. The drive shaft must extend 13 ± 0.5 mm from the flange surface. This distance may be corrected by tapping the drive shaft from either end with a soft-faced mallet.

2   Check the condition of the drive shaft bearings by turning the drive shaft. Hard spots and gritty feel indicate bearings which have gone bad. If the bearings or the shaft are damaged, the drive shaft tube, drive shaft and bearings must be replaced as a single assembly.

3   1978 and later models have a vibration damper mounted between the second and third bearings on the drive shaft. Earlier units without the damper may be replaced with the later style, when replacement is necessary.

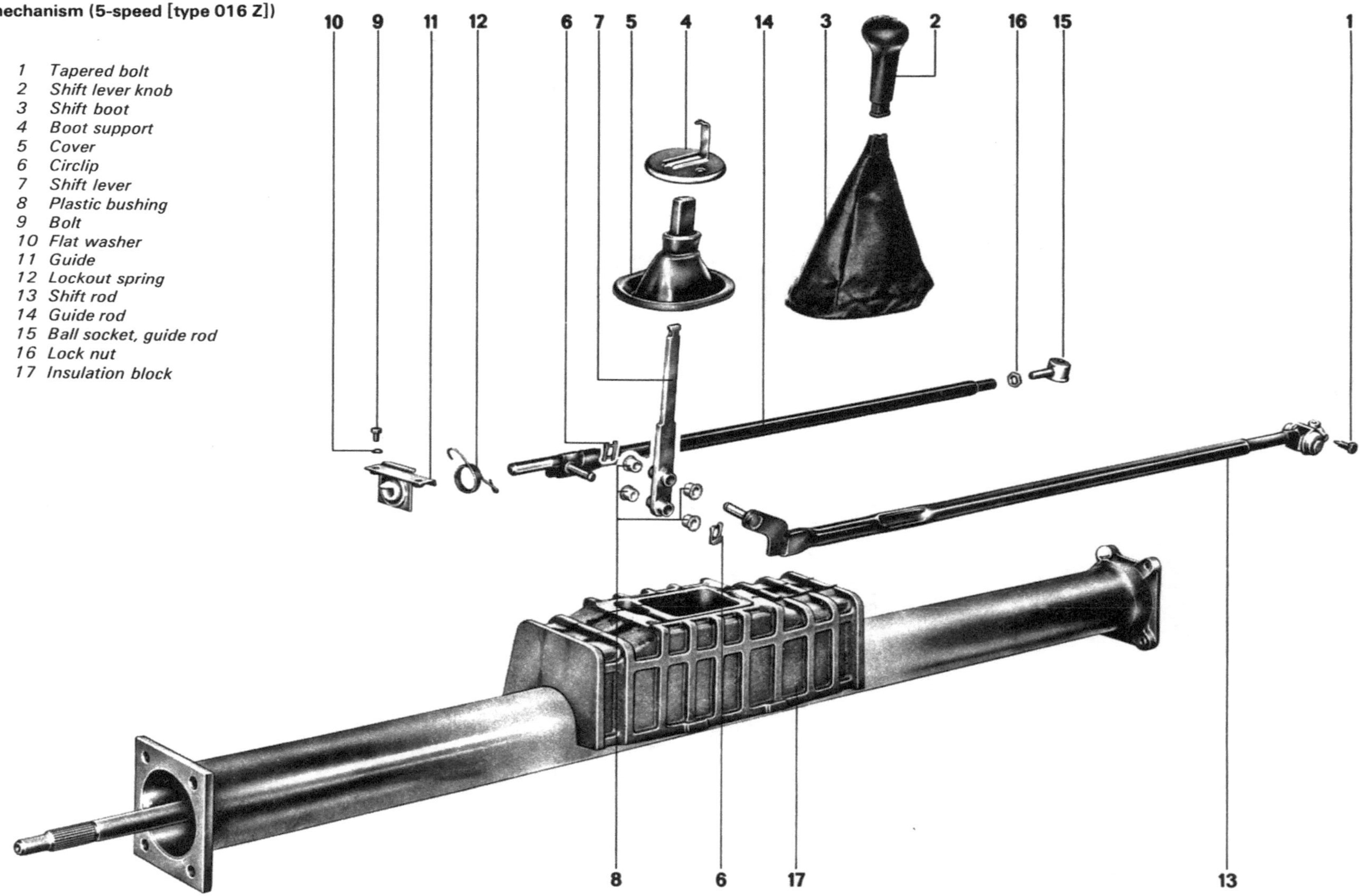

Fig. 7.27 The drive shaft tube and two-rod shift mechanism (5-speed [type 016 Z])

1   Tapered bolt
2   Shift lever knob
3   Shift boot
4   Boot support
5   Cover
6   Circlip
7   Shift lever
8   Plastic bushing
9   Bolt
10 Flat washer
11 Guide
12 Lockout spring
13 Shift rod
14 Guide rod
15 Ball socket, guide rod
16 Lock nut
17 Insulation block

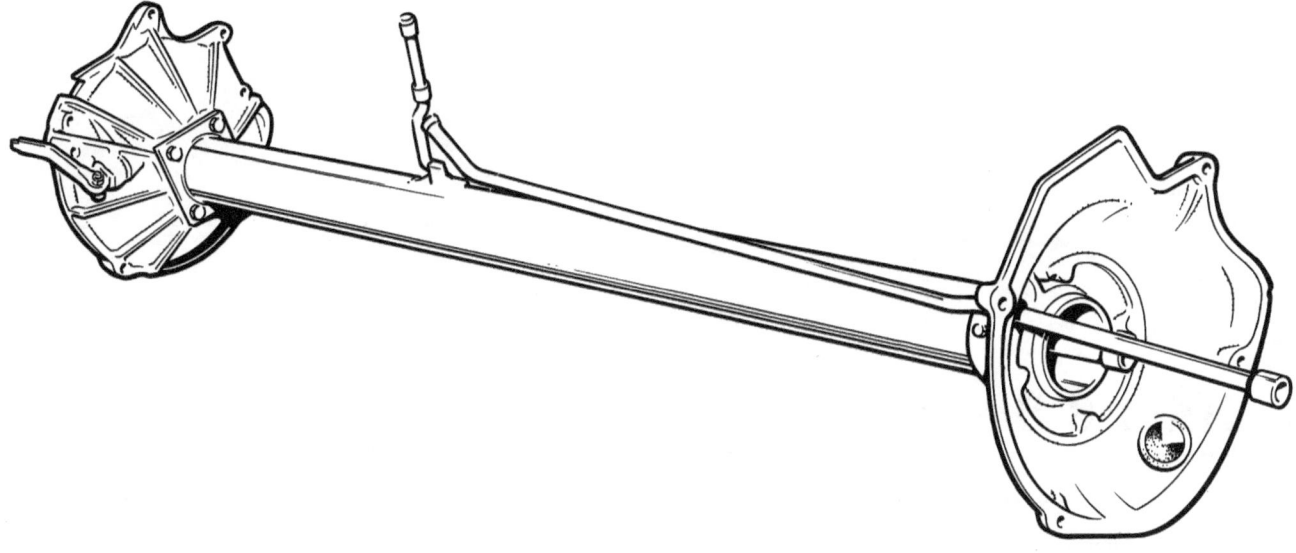

Fig. 7.28 The drive shaft tube with bellhousing and shift linkage installed (4-speed and 5-speed (type 016/9))

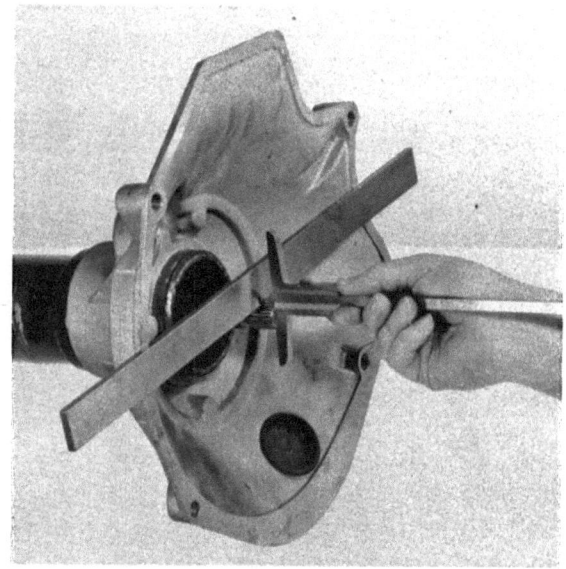

Fig. 7.29 Checking the driveshaft measurements (all transmissions)

40   Drive shaft tube – removal and installation (5-speed transmission type 016 Z)

1   Remove the transmission (Section 17).
2   Unbolt the drive shaft tube from the clutch bellhousing.
3   Remove the drive shaft tube cross brace at the rear of the transmission tunnel.
4   Remove the drive shaft tube by pulling it down and forward.
5   Installation is the reverse of the removal procedure.
6   Tighten the cross brace bolts in a cross pattern.

41   Drive shaft – checking (5-speed transmission, type 016 Z)

1   Place a straight edge across the flange at the rear of the drive shaft tube. The flat end of the drive shaft must be inside the drive shaft tube 19.5 ± 0.5 mm from the outer edge of the flange. Make small corrections with a soft-faced mallet or brass drift.
2   Check the condition of the bearings by twisting the drive shaft in its bearings. If any hard spots or binding are felt, the bearings are bad. The drive shaft tube, drive shaft and bearings must be replaced as an assembly.
3   Adjust the shift linkage before installing the drive shaft tube.

Chapter 8 Steering

Contents

Specifications

Type .... Rack and pinion

Steering wheel diameter
    Standard .... 383 mm
    Turbo .... 380 mm
    Turbo and M-471 option................................. 360 mm

Steering wheel ratio
    Standard and Turbo..................................... 19.15 : 1
    M-471 option .... 22.39 : 1

Turning circle
    Standard and Turbo..................................... 10.08 meters
    M-471 option .... 10.30 meters

Track circle diameter
    Standard and Turbo..................................... 9.21 meters
    M-471 option .... 9.50 meters

Steering wheel turns, lock to lock
    All models... 4.02

Raw settings for alignment
    6 mm machined surface on cup of cup and ball connector .... 68 ± 0.5 mm
    13 mm machined surface on cup of cup and ball connector ... 65 ± 0.5 mm
    Spacer sleeve clearance................................ 41 mm from top face of spacer to top face of the steering column

Torque specifications

	ft–lb	m–kg
Tie rod to steering knuckle	22 to 36	3 to 5
Steering column to steering gear assembly	18 to 25	2.5 to 3.5
Steering gear assembly to cross member	14 to 17	2.0 to 2.4
Adjuster screw plate	4 to 6	0.6 to 0.8
Cup and ball joint to tie rod	22 to 29	3 to 4
Ball pivot to tie rod	22 to 29	3 to 4
Steering wheel to steering column	25 to 40	3.5 to 5.5
Pinch bolt, ignition switch casing	8 to 14	1.1 to 2.0
Bearing cover and support to body	4	0.5
Steering column, clamping bolt	25	3.5

1 Steering – general description

1   The steering of the Porsche 924 is of the rack and pinion type.
2   When the steering wheel is turned, the steering column operates a gear within the steering gear assembly. This gear meshes with a toothed rail, called the rack, which moves beneath the stationary gear and, through the offset mounting of the steering knuckle, turns the wheels.

2 Steering knuckle – general notes

1   The steering knuckle, although it turns with the steering gear and therefore allows the wheels to turn, is basically a part of the braking and suspension systems.
2   Refer to Chapters 9 and 10 for full details on inspection, removal, and installation.

3 Ball joints – general notes

1   Although the operation of the ball joint can have a direct effect on the precision and accuracy of steering, it is a component of a major suspension piece. Its inspection, removal and replacement are covered in Chapter 10.

4 Ball pivot – checking wear

1   The ball pivot consists of a metal ball in a spring loaded shell.
2   To check the ball pivot for wear, raise the front end of the vehicle and place jack stands under the appropriate frame locations (see Introduction Sections).
3   Block the rear wheels and set the parking brake.
4   Remove the bolts from the lower engine guard and remove the guard.
5   Slide beneath the vehicle.
6   Grasp the tie rod firmly with both hands and push and pull the tie rod toward the steering gear assembly and then toward the outboard end of the ball pivot. Direct force only along the line created by the long side of the tie rod (longitudinal pressure). If any movement from side to side is noticed in the ball pivot, it must be replaced. It will be very easy to twist the tie rod, and this is normal action. It is the side to side (or inboard to outboard) play which indicates need for replacement.

5 Ball pivot – removal, inspection, replacement, and installation

1   Disconnect the negative lead from the battery.
2   Raise the vehicle and place it on jack stands.
3   Remove the bolts from the lower engine guard and remove the guard.
4   Remove the front wheels from the vehicle (see Chapter 9).
5   Remove the cotter pin from the threaded shaft of the ball joint.
6   Remove the castellated nut.
7   Use a gear puller (if you have one of the appropriate size) or a 'pickle fork' (small-bone wedge) extractor to separate the ball pivot from the steering knuckle (photo).
8   Even if your wear testing has proven the ball pivot to appear to be sound, check the condition of the rubber dust boot and if it is dry, cracked, or torn the ball pivot must be replaced.
9   If you have found the ball pivot to need replacement, carefully measure the distance between the inboard edge of the ball pivot lock nut to the inboard edge of the chamfer which is at the end of the threaded end of the tie rod. Make a written note of this figure.
10   Loosen the lock nut (photo).
11   Unscrew the ball pivot assembly with a wrench on the cast-in flats of the ball pivot.
12   Install the new ball pivot in the reverse of the removal directions.
13   Thread the new ball pivot into place with a wrench on the flats of the casting.
14   Screw the new ball pivot in until it is in the same approximate location as the old one and the threaded stud faces up.
15   Tighten the lock nut snug with a wrench and measure the distance between the inboard side of the lock nut and the inboard edge

of the chamfer at the end of the threaded end of the tie rod. Adjust the ball pivot until the same figure is found as the old measurement. Torque the lock nut to 22 to 29 ft-lb (3 to 4 m-kg) (photo).
16   Install the threaded stud of the ball pivot into the steering knuckle. If the cotter pin hole is not parallel to the dust guard at the rear of the brake discs, adjust the stud until it is.
17   When installing the castellated nut, it must be torqued so that one of the spaces between the castellations aligns with the cotter pin hole in the stud. To achieve this, first torque the castellated nut to 22 ft-lb (3 m-kg). If there is no alignment of the slot and the hole, raise the applied torque in 2 ft-lb (approx. 0.3 m-kg) increments until alignment occurs. If you reach the maximum torque figure of 36 ft-lb (5 m-kg) before the hole and slot line up, loosen the nut and torque it to 22 ft-lb (3 m-kg) and begin the process again. When alignment is made and the applied torque does not exceed the maximum limit, install the cotter pin and fold back its ends.
18   Your front wheels are now only in approximate alignment. Take your car to a certified alignment shop or your Porsche dealer as soon as possible. Alignment is a task which cannot be done accurately enough by the home mechanic in the case of the 924 model. A special tool and jig are necessary for the task and these cannot be procured or made with any real savings resulting.

6 Tie rod – removal and installation

1   Disconnect the negative lead from the battery.
2   Raise the vehicle and place it on jack stands.
3   Remove the bolts from the lower engine guard and remove the guard as well.
4   Remove the front wheels (see Chapter 9).
5   Remove the cotter pin from the threaded end of the ball joint.
6   Remove the castellated nut.
7   Remove the ball pivot from the steering knuckle with a gear puller (if you have one which fits) or a 'pickle fork' (small-bone wedge) extractor.
8   Loosen the clip on the rubber bellows and slide the bellows back to expose the cup and ball connector.
9   Loosen the jam nut on the inboard side of the cup (photo).
10   Remove the cup and ball connector by unscrewing the cup with a wrench which fits across the machined-in flats of the cup.
11   Do not allow the tie rod to fall off. Make the final turns on the cup with your hand while holding the tie rod (photo).
12   Inspect the ball pivot and replace if necessary (see Section 5).
13   Check the rubber bellows for cracking and other signs that the rubber has dried out. If there are deep cracks or breaks in the bellows, replace them. There are several brands of rubber protectant on the market which help prevent the bellows from drying out and cracking. A coating of one of these liquids on an occasional basis will

5.7 Removing the ball pivot from the steering knuckle

5.10 Loosening the ball pivot lock nut

5.15 Applying the specified torque to the ball pivot lock nut

6.9 Tie rod; loosening the jam nut on the cup

6.11 Removing the cup by hand

6.18 Removing the steering gear plug

6.19a Measuring the tie rod clearances, right side

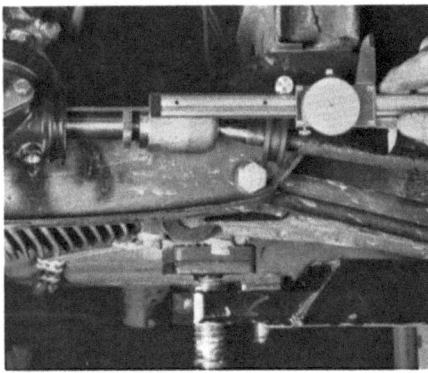
6.19b Measuring the tie rod clearances, left side

6.19c Measuring the width of the machined shoulder

6.19d The new-style stop ring

prolong the life of the protective bellows and prevent dirt from getting in the rack and pinion gears and wearing them out.

14 If the tie rod is bent or otherwise in need of replacement note the following when ordering a new tie rod from your parts supplier. There are two types of tie rod. The later type, which is the only one available for replacement, is identified by the width of the shoulder machined on the inboard side of the cup. On the older versions, this shoulder was 6 mm. The replacement tie rods have a 13 mm machined surface and will require a new rubber stop ring, too, if the tie rod you are replacing meets the older specification.

15 Replacement tie rods come with a new ball joint and cup and ball connector installed.

16 Installation is the reverse of the removal procedure.

17 Before starting the installation procedure the steering must be centered.

18 Remove the plug from the threaded boss at the bottom of the rack and pinion assembly and insert centering bolt 9116 (photo). An example of this tool can be made by taking a plain bolt of the same

diameter and thread, and grinding the threaded end to a 45° conical angle, so that there is a point at the center. Screw this bolt into place and turn the steering wheel back and forth slowly until the groove in the rack aligns with the point on the bolt. Screw the bolt home so that the rack is held in this location.

19 Screw on the tie rod evenly. With the centering tool installed and the rubber stop rings in place (photo), adjust cups so that there is 65 ± 0.5 mm distance between the inboard ridge on the stop ring and the outboard edge of the steering housing (right side), and the same distance between the inboard edge of the stop ring and the shoulder inside the casting on the left side (photos). If the cups on your particular model have 6 mm machined surfaces instead of the 13 mm surfaces of the later style cups, the measurements between the same points should be 68 ± 0.5 mm (photo).

20 Torque the jam nuts to 22 to 29 ft-lb (3 to 4 m-kg).

21 Recheck all of the measurements above once the jam nuts have been tightened to make sure nothing has moved. The stop surface on the rubber stop ring may move up to 1 mm under compression, so

adjustment may be necessary to bring these measurements back into the specified limits.

22 Adjust the steering by loosening the lock nut and screwing in the adjusting screw until it just touches the thrust washer in the rack and pinion assembly. If you are in doubt, loosen the adjusting screw and tighten it again until you can feel contact. Hold the adjusting screw tightly and tighten the locknut (photo).

23 Remove the centering tool and replace the plug.

24 Before installing the ball joint on the steering knuckle, line up the cotter pin hole so that it will be parallel to the dust guard on the disc brake. This will make it easier to install the cotter pin.

25 Press the ball pivot studs into place on the steering knuckle.

26 Install the castellated nut and torque to 22 ft-lb (3 m-kg). Sight through the castellations to locate the cotter pin hole. Raise the torque in 2 ft-lb (approx. 0.3 m-kg) increments until the cotter pin hole is seen squarely in between two castellations. The maximum torque which can be reached is 36 ft-lb (5 m-kg). If you reach this figure before the cotter pin hole is aligned, back off the nut, bring the torque back up to 22 ft-lb (3 m-kg) and begin the process again. Install the cotter pin when possible and fold back the ends. Do not exceed the maximum torque figures.

27 Place the rubber bellows back in their proper locations and tighten the clamp on the inboard side of the right bellows.

28 Your front end is not in alignment. Proper alignment of the Porsche 924 requires a special adjusting tool which must be used in conjunction with a light-type alignment bench. Have the front end alignment checked by a competent shop as soon as possible. Driving your car with the wheels out of line will cause excessive wear to your tires.

7 Steering gear – removal, stripdown, and installation

1 The rack and pinion gears in the steering assembly are manufactured and sold in matched sets. If you are removing the steering gear assembly for purposes of replacement, you must purchase the entire steering gear assembly as a unit.

2 Disconnect the negative lead from the battery.

3 Raise the vehicle and place it on jack stands.

4 Remove the front wheels (see Chapter 9).

5 Remove the bolts attaching the lower engine guard and remove the engine guard.

6 Remove the tie rods (see Section 6).

7 Remove the clamping bolt which holds the lower end of the steering column to the serrated shaft on the steering gear assembly. Pull the steering column free (photo).

8 The steering gear assembly is held to the cross member by four bolts. Remove the bottom two bolts and then have an assistant support the steering gear assembly while you remove the top two bolts (photo).

9 If you are replacing the steering gear assembly, a few parts must be stripped from the old unit for use in the new one. Remove the two bolts from the adjuster plate. This plate is under spring load, so loosen each bolt one turn at a time, alternating between the two bolts until pressure is evenly removed. Remove the adjuster plate, with the adjuster screw and lock nut installed; the spring; thrust washer; and

the pressure disc. Inspect the pressure disc for wear in the form of metal erosion (one spot deeper than the others), grooves and cracks. Replace if any of these conditions are noted.

10 Before installing these parts in the new steering gear assembly, lubricate the steering gears with multipurpose grease.

11 Lightly grease the rubbing surface of the pressure disc with the same multipurpose grease as used in the task above. Install the pressure disc with the longer side of the curved surface at the top and facing the steering gears.

12 Install the thrust washer and spring in the cup of the pressure disc.

13 Loosen the lock nut on the adjusting screw and back the adjusting screw out of the adjuster plate until one or two threads show on the innner side of the plate.

14 Install the adjuster plate and tighten its bolts evenly. Torque the bolts to 4 to 6 ft-lb (0.6 to 0.8 m-kg).

15 Tighten the adjusting screw only until contact can be felt when tightening with the fingers. Set the lock nut finger tight as well.

16 Installation of the steering gear assembly is the reverse of the removal procedure.

17 Have an assistant hold the steering gear assembly in place while you loosely install the mounting bolts. Tighten the bolts in a cross pattern and torque them, also in a cross pattern, to 14 to 17 ft-lb (2.0 to 2.4 m-kg).

18 Slide the serrated shaft of the pinion gear into the clamp on the steering column. Torque the nut to 18 to 25 ft-lb (2.5 to 3.5 m-kg).

19 Install the tie rods, set the basic steering alignment, and adjust the steering according to the instructions in Section 6.

8 Steering wheel – removal and replacement

1 Disconnect the negative lead from the battery.

2 Remove the impact pad from the steering wheel and disconnect the horn wire. Remove the springs (photo).

3 If the front wheels of the car are not pointing straight ahead, center the steering before you continue.

4 With an indelible marker, draw a line from the center of the steering column to one outside edge of the hole in the center of the steering wheel. This will help you align parts when installing the steering wheel.

5 Remove the nut from the steering column (photo).

6 Remove the washer and then pull the steering wheel free (photo).

7 Installation is the reverse of the removal procedure.

8 Line up the marks you made before removing the wheel. The bars of the steering wheel should be horizontal when the front road wheels are pointing straight ahead. Make any necessary adjustments.

9 Install the spring washer and nut. Torque the nut to 25 to 40 ft-lb (3.5 to 5.5 m-kg). In the case of the Turbo model these figures should be 33 ± 7 ft-lb (4.5 ± 1.0 m-kg) (photo).

10 Plug the horn wire into its proper spot, install the spring and press the pad into place.

11 Connect the battery leads and check the operation of the horn and turn signals. If there are any malfunctions, refer to Chapter 11.

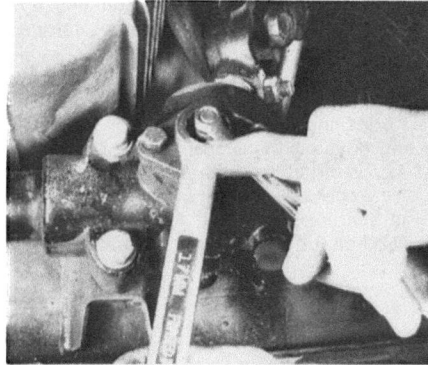
6.22 Adjusting the tension on the steering gear

7.7 Removing the clamping bolt from the steering gear

7.8 Removing the steering gear

8.2 Removing the impact pad and disconnecting the horn wire

8.5 Removing the steering column nut

8.6 Removing the steering wheel

8.9 Applying the specified torque to the steering wheel nut

9 Steering column – removal and installation

1   Disconnect the negative lead from the battery.
2   Raise the vehicle and place it on jack stands.
3   Remove the bolts from the engine guard and remove the lower engine guard.
4   Remove the pinch bolt on the upper universal joint and pull the universal joint free of the steering column.
5   Remove the steering wheel (see Section 8).
6   Remove the steering column switchgear and steering lock (see Section 10).
7   All models with the Oxygen Sensor System of emission control (Turbo and all 1980 standard models) must have the oxygen sensor control box removed before work can be continued (see Chapter 3).
8   Drill out the two shear bolts and remove the steering column and casing tube as a unit.
9   Check the needle bearing installed in the firewall for wear and damage. Replace it if necessary, or lubricate it with multipurpose grease.
10 Inspect the metal cylinder section of the steering column for signs of compression. Replace if necessary.
11 Installation is the reverse of the removal procedure.

12 Coat the rubber bearing at the forward end of the steering column with a light coat of silicone grease or talcum powder and slide it and the bearing support on to the casing tube.
13 Slide the casing tube and bearing support on to the steering column.
14 Slide the steering column and casing tube into place beneath the dashboard. Make sure that the forward end of the steering column fits squarely in the needle bearing on the firewall.
15 Install the shear bolts in the casing tube's mounting plate. Align the bolts with the holes in the mounting bracket beneath the dashboard and tighten the shear bolts finger-tight.
16 Install the switchgear and drive on the spacer sleeve. Make sure that there is a distance of 42.5 mm between the face of the steering column and the rear face of the spacer sleeve (photos).
17 Torque the bolts on the bearing support to 4 ft-lb (0.5 m-kg).
18 Torque the socket head bolt on the switchgear to 8 to 14 ft-lb (1.1 to 2.0 m-kg).
19 Install the oxygen sensor control unit on appropriate models (see Chapter 3).
20 Install the steering wheel and torque the center nut to 25 to 40 ft-lb (3.5 to 5.5 m-kg).
21 Check that the steering wheel hub to column switch clearance is between 2.0 and 4.0 mm, then tighten the shear bolts until their heads break off.

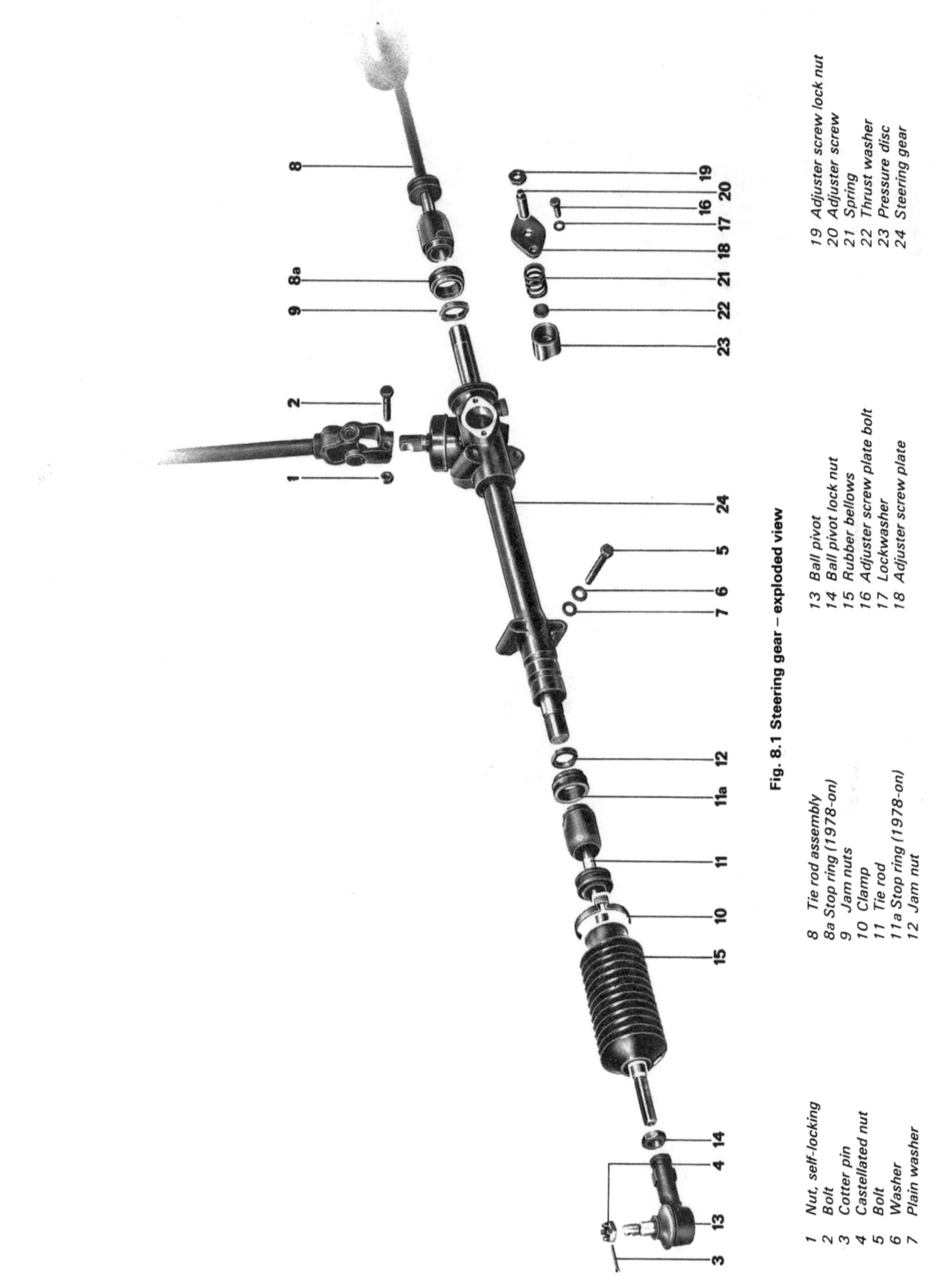

Fig. 8.1 Steering gear – exploded view

1	Nut, self-locking	8	Tie rod assembly	13	Ball pivot	19	Adjuster screw lock nut
2	Bolt	8a	Stop ring (1978-on)	14	Ball pivot lock nut	20	Adjuster screw
3	Cotter pin	9	Jam nuts	15	Rubber bellows	21	Spring
4	Castellated nut	10	Clamp	16	Adjuster screw plate bolt	22	Thrust washer
5	Bolt	11	Tie rod	17	Lockwasher	23	Pressure disc
6	Washer	11a	Stop ring (1978-on)	18	Adjuster screw plate	24	Steering gear
7	Plain washer	12	Jam nut				

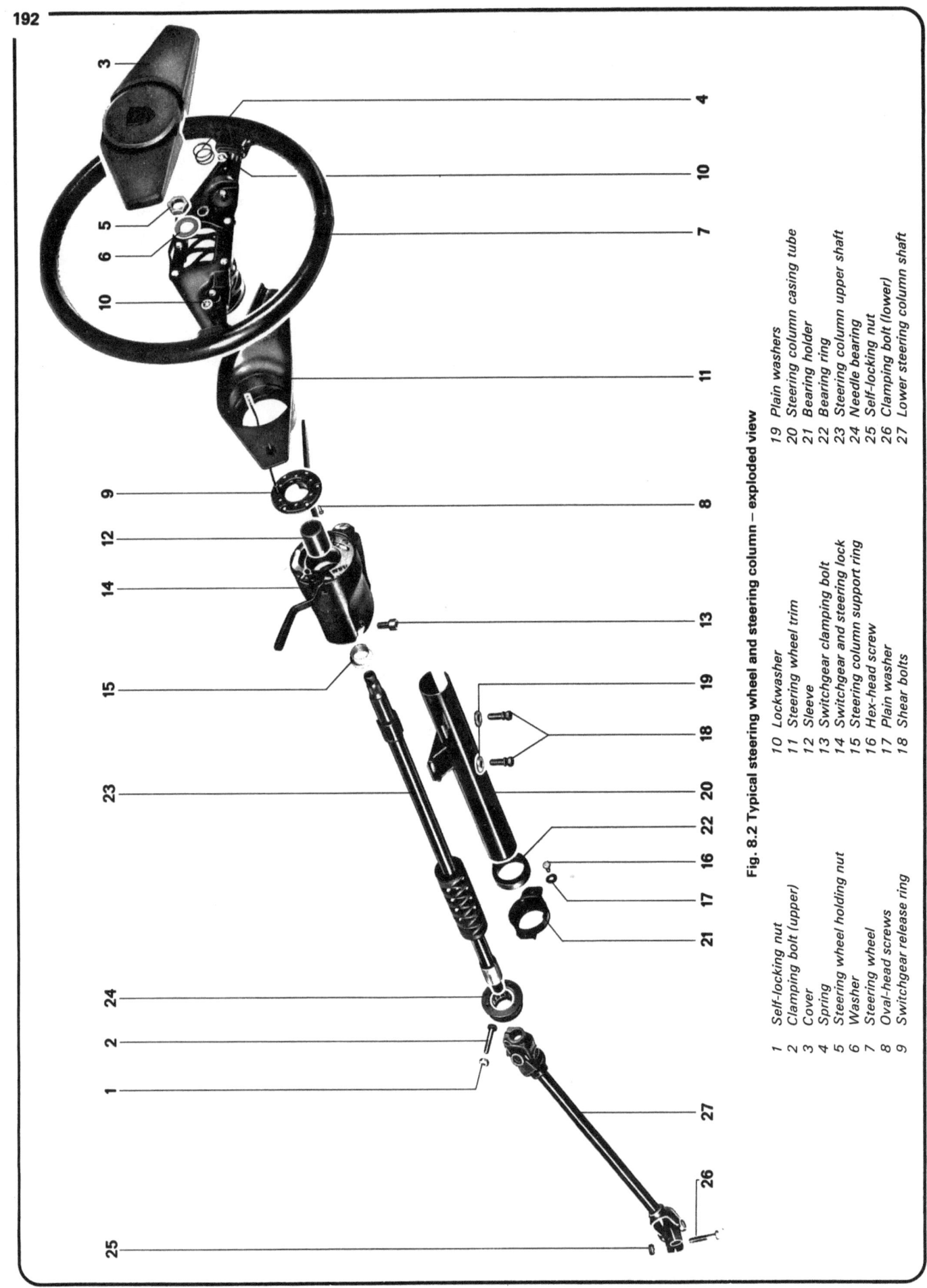

Fig. 8.2 Typical steering wheel and steering column — exploded view

1 Self-locking nut
2 Clamping bolt (upper)
3 Cover
4 Spring
5 Steering wheel holding nut
6 Washer
7 Steering wheel
8 Oval-head screws
9 Switchgear release ring
10 Lockwasher
11 Steering wheel trim
12 Sleeve
13 Switchgear clamping bolt
14 Switchgear and steering lock
15 Steering column support ring
16 Hex-head screw
17 Plain washer
18 Shear bolts
19 Plain washers
20 Steering column casing tube
21 Bearing holder
22 Bearing ring
23 Steering column upper shaft
24 Needle bearing
25 Self-locking nut
26 Clamping bolt (lower)
27 Lower steering column shaft

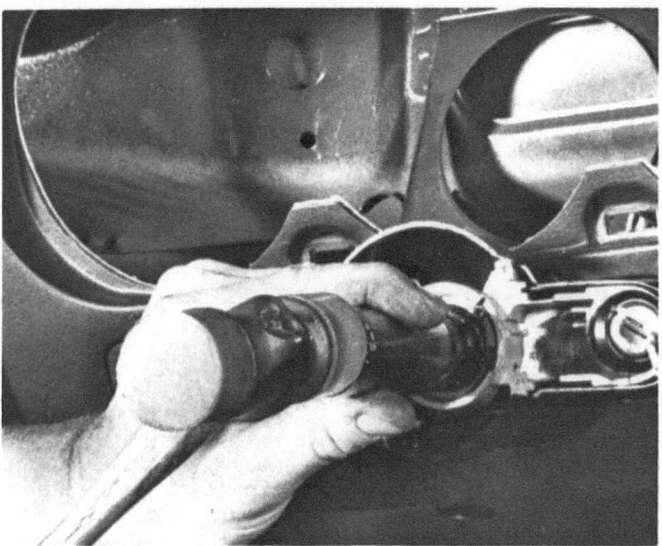

9.16a Driving the spacer on to the steering column

9.16b Measuring spacer clearance

10 Switchgear and steering lock – removal and installation

1 Disconnect the negative lead from the battery.
2 Remove the steering wheel (see Section 8).
3 Place the stalks of the switches in their 'off' positions.
4 Remove the plastic spacer piece from the steering column.
If it does not slide free, split it along one side with a sharp knife or razor blade and remove it.
5 Remove the four bolts holding the switch assemblies to the steering lock cylinder.
6 Reach behind the dashboard and carefully unplug the switch pin connectors (photo).
7 Gently pull the switch assemblies off the steering column (photos).
8 Unsnap the cover from the ignition switch and lock cylinder.
9 Loosen the clamp on the steering lock and ignition switch casting with a socket head wrench. Access to the socket head bolt is through the hole beneath the plastic housing.
10 Reach behind the dashboard once again and disconnect the plug connector from the ignition switch.
11 Remove the switch, casting and housing together. Grasp the housing firmly and slide the entire assembly off the steering column.
12 Check the bearing in the casting for smooth operation and the absence of radial play. If the bearing is in need of replacement, remove the circlip and drive out the bearing. Install the new bearing with the proper installation tool until it seats firmly on the stepped surface inside the casting, then install the circlip.
13 Installation is the reverse of the removal procedure.
14 Torque the socket head bolt on the switchgear clamp to 8 to 14 ft-lb (1.1 to 2.0 m-kg).
15 There is no specified torque for the four bolts attaching the switches to the casting. Before tightening the bolts, make sure that the stalks on the switches are in their 'off' positions, so that you will not damage the operating cams when tightening the screws. Tighten the screws in a cross pattern until they hold the switches firmly against the casting. Make sure that the screws are tight enough to prevent the switches from rocking or moving when the stalks are operated.

10.6 Unplugging the switch pin connectors

10.7a Pulling the switch assemblies from the steering column

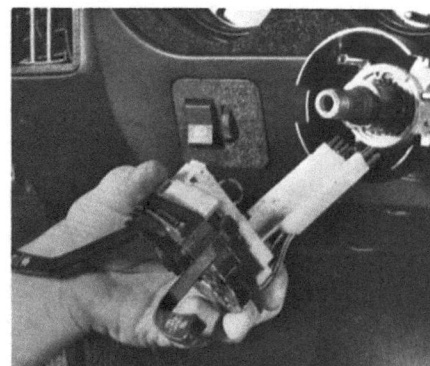

10.7b The switch assemblies removed from the steering column

Chapter 9 Braking system

For modifications, and information applicable to later models, see Supplement at end of manual

Contents

Specification

Brakes, 1976 to 1979 models

General
System type .... Hydraulic, disc front and drum rear with cable operated parking brake utilizing the trailing shoe within the brake drum

Front brakes
Rotor type... Solid
Rotor diameter .... 10.12 in (257 mm)
Rotor thickness.. New 0.512 in (13 mm)
Minimum, 0.472 in (12 mm)
Wear limit, 0.453 in (11.5 mm)
Pad lining thickness .... New, 0.551 in (14 mm)
Wear limit, 0.079 in (2 mm)
Caliper piston diameter .... 1.890 in (48 mm)

Rear brakes
Brake drum diameter .... New, 9.055 in (230 mm)
Maximum, 9.094 in (231 mm) using oversize linings
Wear limit, 9.114 in (231.5 mm)
Lining thickness .... New std. 0.150 to 0.157 in (3.8 to 4.0 mm)
New o/size, 0.169 to 0.177 in (4.3 to 4.5 mm)
Wear limit, 0.098 in (2.5 mm)
Wheel cylinder diameter .... 0.75 in (19.05 mm)

Hydraulic components
Brake booster .... Diameter, 7 in (177.8 mm)
Boost factor, 2.5:1
Master cylinder .... Diameter, 0.813 in (20.64 mm)
Stroke, 0.630 to 0.551 in (16 to 14 mm)
Recommended brake fluid .... SAE J 1703 or DOT 3

Brakes, 1980 models standard system
As above except for:

Hydraulic components
Brake booster .... Diameter, 9 in (228.6 mm)
Boost factor, 2.5:1
Master cylinder .... Diameter, 0.937 in (23.81 mm)
Stroke, 0.669 to .590 in (17 to 15 mm)

Brakes, M-471 option and standard on Carrera GT
As 1980 standard system except for:

General
System type .... Hydraulic, disc front and rear, with cable operated parking brake utilizing an internally expanding shoe drum brake on both rear wheels

Front brakes
Rotor type.. Ventilated
Caliper piston diameter .... 2.126 in (54 mm)

Rear brakes
Rotor type.. Ventilated
Caliper piston diameter .... 1.417 in (36 mm)

Parking brake
Drum diameter.. 7.087 in (180 mm)

Wheels and tires, 1976 to 1979 models

Standard, stamped steel wheel
Wheel size .... 5½ J x 14
Tire size... 165 HR 14
Cold tire pressure, front and rear .... 2.0 bar (29 psi)

Optional, spoked cast alloy wheel (Standard US, 1979)
Wheel size .... 6 J x 14
Tire size... 185/70 HR 14
Cold tire pressure, front and rear .... 1.8 bar (26 psi)

Winter tire recommendations
Standard wheel... 165 SR 14 M + S
Optional wheel .... 185/70 SR 14 M + S
(Tire pressures as above, M+S = mud and snow)

Spare tire
All standard spare tires are the same as the wheels above, ie, standard wheeled cars have standard wheel mounted spares. The exception is the 924 models with collapsible spare. This is mounted on a steel rim regardless of wheel type. Cars equipped with cast wheels and collapsible spare have a spare set of mounting bolts appropriate to the steel wheel.

Wheels and tires, 1980 models

Standard, spoked cast alloy wheel (except Turbo)
Wheel size .... 6 J x 14
Tire size... 185/70 HR 14
Cold tire pressure, front and rear .... 2.0 bar (29 psi)

Optional, 4-bolt cast alloy, wire wheel pattern (except Turbo)
Wheel size .... 6 J x 15
Tire size... 205/60 HR 15
Cold tire pressure, front and rear .... 2.0 bar (29 psi)

Standard, 4-bolt cast alloy, wire wheel pattern (Turbo)
Wheel size .... 6 J x 15
Tire size... 185/70 VR 15
Cold tire pressure, front .... 2.0 bar (29 psi)
                          rear .... 2.5 bar (36 psi)

Optional, M-471 option, 5 bolt mounting (all models)
Wheel size .... 6 J x 16
Tire size... 205/55 VR 16
Cold tire pressure, front .... 2.0 bar (29 psi)
                          rear .... 2.5 bar (36 psi)
Collapsible spare tire pressure (front or rear) .... 2.2 bar (32 psi)

Winter tire recommendations

All 924 except Turbo .... 165 SR 14 M+S on rims 5½ J x 14
                                                        185/70 SR 14 M+S on rims 5½ J x 14 or 6 J x 14
                                                        185/65 SR 15 M+S on rims 6 J x 15
All Turbo.. 165 SR 14 M+S on rims 5½ J x 15
                                                        185/70 SR 15 M+S on rims 5½ J x 15 or 6 J x 15
All 924 with M-471 option .... 205/55 SR 16 M+S on rims 6 J x 16
(Tire pressures as above, M+S = mud and snow)

Torque specifications

Parking Brake	ft-lb	m-kg
Parking brake lever to body	15	2.1
Brake cable to yoke	6	0.85
Parking brake cable to lock	6	0.85
Parking brake cable holder to drum brake backing plate	15	2.1

Brake Caliper (Front)		
Bleeder screw to caliper	3	0.4
Guard to steering knuckle	7	1.0
Clamping nut with socket head bolt	9 to 11	1.3 to 1.6
Caliper to steering knuckle	60	8.5
Hydraulic hose to caliper	9	1.2
Wheel rim to brake disc (cast alloy)	94	13
Wheel rim to brake disc (steel)	80	11

Brake Drum (Rear)		
Bearing cover and backing plate to diagonal arm	42	5.8
Brake cylinder to brake backing plate	15	2.1
Bleeder screw to wheel brake cylinder	3	0.4
Brake pressure line to brake cylinder	10	1.2
Parking brake cable holder to drum brake backing plate	15	2.1
Brake drum to wheel shaft (castellated nut)	217 to 289	30 to 40
Wheel rim to brake drum (cast alloy)	94	13
Wheel rim to brake drum (steel)	80	11

Hydraulic Components		
Brake pressure booster to console	15	2.1
Stop light switch to dual master cylinder	14 to 22	2 to 3
Dual master cylinder to brake pressure booster	9	1.3
Brake pressure line to dual master cylinder, brake hose, and distributor	10	1.4

1 Brakes - general description

1 The Porsche 924 models utilize an hydraulic system with vacuum boost for greater braking efficiency. A mechanical handbrake is included.

2 From the beginning of production in 1976 through 1979 inclusive, all models are equipped with floating caliper, single piston, disc brakes on the front and simplex (single leading shoe) drum brakes on the rear. For the 1980 model year, the M-471 package was included as an option and utilizes ventilated rotor disc brakes from the 911 SC, as well as floating caliper, single piston disc brakes with ventilated rotors on the rear. Vehicles with this option installed will have five-bolt, 16 inch wheels.

3 In all models with simplex drum rear brakes, pulling up on the handbrake lever activates another lever within the brake drum housing. This second lever presses the trailing edge (top edge) of the rearmost brake shoe against the surface of the brake drum. A cable connects the handbrake lever to the parking brake actuating levers in each drum. The M-471 equipped models have small (180 mm) drum brakes included in the rear brake assemblies which act as the parking brake. As in the previous type, they are activated via cable connection to the handbrake lever.

4 Braking system circuitry is of the dual-diagonal type. Two complete braking circuits, consisting of separate chambers in the brake fluid reservoir, brake master cylinder, one front brake and the rear brake on the side opposite, act together under normal operating conditions. In the event of a failure in one of the braking circuits, depressing the brake pedal will cause a warning light to illuminate in the combination instrument on the dashboard, alerting the driver; the front brake and the rear brake diagonally opposite in the undamaged circuit will slow the vehicle in a straight line. This, in combination with the negative roll characteristic of the suspension (see Chapter 10) will ensure straight line stopping of the vehicle while it is being driven to the nearest repair station. Under no circumstances should a vehicle with one damaged braking circuit be driven, except to a place of repair. The impaired braking performance means that the vehicle will require greater distances for stopping.

5 Under normal operation, depressing the brake pedal causes the dual master cylinder to pressurize by way of a connecting rod which passes from the end of the brake pedal lever, through the vacuum boost unit and connects to the plunger on the master cylinder. Hydraulic pressure is applied to the brakes in each circuit.

6 When ordering parts for your 924, be sure to provide the engine number, chassis number, year of manufacture, and model to your spare parts supplier. If you intend your Porsche 924 for hard driving or competition use, your Porsche dealer will be best equipped to advise you on modifications to improve braking performance.

7 Throughout the production life of the 924, several types of wheel have been offered. These may be broken into two specific types—cast alloy and steel. Both types require a specific type of mounting bolt (see Fig. 9.1). A chart is provided, outlining the various available wheels.

2 Brake master cylinder - removal and installation

1 Raise the hood and disconnect the negative lead from the battery. If removal and installation of the master cylinder is to be done without any work on the brakes, it is not necessary to raise the car or place it on stands. It is advisable, then, to set the parking brake and/or place the transmission in gear (standard transmission models).

2 Remove the two electrical plugs from the stop light swtches on the underside of the master cylinder body. Place them out of the way so they will not have brake fluid dripped on them. Some models have the wires bundled together and held with a nylon zip tie—if this is the case, it is necessary to cut the tie to get the plugs far enough away from the master cylinder so they won't be dripped on.

3 Using a flare nut wrench, loosen the three brake line nuts on the master cylinder body.

4 Place a drip pan beneath the car at the appropriate spot. Brake fluid will discolor and damage paint as well as being poisonous to pets and people. Clean up any drips immediately.

5 Remove the two nuts which hold the master cylinder to the booster unit.

6 Double check the location of the electrical connectors.

7 Remove the nuts and flare connectors of the brake lines from the master cylinder body.

8 Remove the master cylinder body from the car (photo).

9 Pump the master cylinder piston rod several times while holding

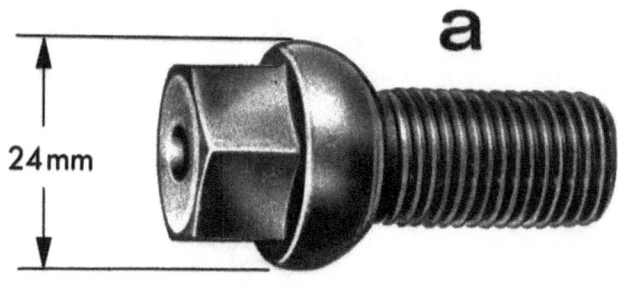

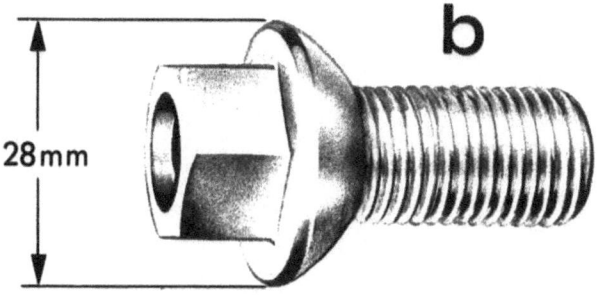

Fig. 9.1 Wheel bolt types

a   Steel wheels   b   Cast alloy wheels

the master cylinder over a drip pan to purge excess brake fluid from the assembly.

10 Before moving on to other tasks, make sure that no brake fluid has dripped onto any painted surfaces.

11 Installation is the reverse of the removal process with the following points to be observed:

12 Torque the two nuts which hold the master cylinder to the booster unit to 15 ft-lb (2.1 m-kg).

13 After refilling the master cylinder it will be necessary to bleed the brake system (Section 18).

14 If the brake master cylinder has been removed only to gain access to the brake booster, make sure that the O-ring which seals the master cylinder to brake booster join is not dried out and is free from cuts, tears, and breaks. This will be replaced in the normal course of a master cylinder rebuild but must be checked any time the master cylinder is removed.

3 Brake master cylinder - overhaul

1 When the master cylinder has been drained of excess fluid, place jaw protectors over the clamping jaws of a bench vise (or use wood blocks) and clamp one of the flanges in the jaws with the stop light sender switches facing up.

2 Remove the two stop light sender switches with a wrench (photo).

3 Remove the master cylinder body and place it in the vise with the pump rod facing up. Do not clamp the cylinder body in the vise jaws too tightly or deformation of the body will occur.

4 Remove the snap ring from the cylinder body at the pump rod end (photo).

5 Pump the pump rod up and down several times to free the washer and seal from the body, then remove the washer and seal. Note the direction the lip of the rubber seal faces when installed in the body.

6 Remove the retainer bolt from the cylinder body. It is located between the brake fluid reservoir and the cylinder body (photo).

7 Withdraw the pump rod and valve assemblies from the cylinder body. To aid in reassembly, lay out the various parts of the valve assembly on a clean sheet of absorbent paper in the order in which they were removed.

8 Inspect the inner surfaces of the cylinder body for evidence of scratching, "chattering", gouges, and longitudinal scoring. If evident, renew the master cylinder complete.

9 Make sure the new cylinder body is one of the same manufacture as the brake booster.

10 Place the cylinder body in the jaws of the vice. Do not over-tighten the jaws and make sure they are covered with jaw protectors.

11 Open the master cylinder rebuild kit you have purchased and lay out the parts of the new kit alongside those you have removed. Note that there are two thicknesses of seal cups which are not interchangeable. There are also two springs which upon close inspection will prove to be different. Separate these to avoid improper installation. There are also two different dust seal configurations available in rebuild kits. Each may be replaced by a new dust seal of any other configuration, but only with all other rebuild parts from the same kit. If any rebuild parts appear to be missing, obtain another kit from your parts supplier. Do not substitute old brake parts (photos).

12 Install the seal spacer in the smaller end of the tapered spring. Set it aside (photo).

13 Place one of the thin valve discs (washer) over the six holes of the valve body with the long, tapered, end adjacent the valve holes (photo).

14 Inspect the four seal cups. Note that one has a wider sealing surface (edge) than the others. Install this seal cup on the tapered end of the valve body with the open end facing the taper and the closed end against the valve disc.

15 Lightly lubricate the installed seal cup and the three unmounted seal cups with clean, new, brake fluid.

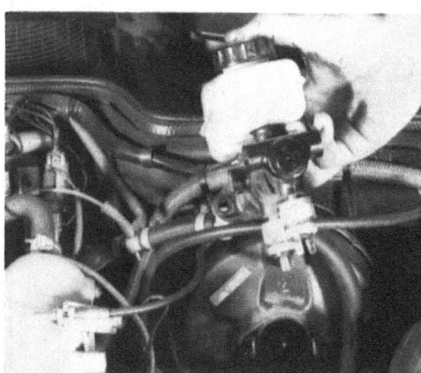

2.8 Removing the brake master cylinder

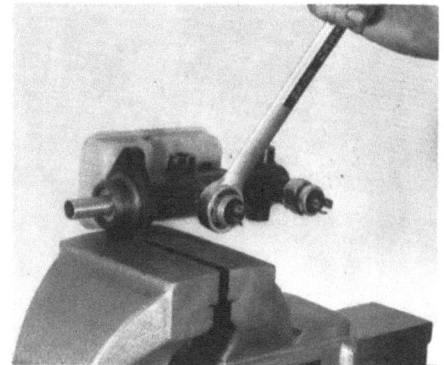

3.2 Removing the brake light pressure switches from the master cylinder body

3.4 Removing snap ring from cylinder body at pump rod end

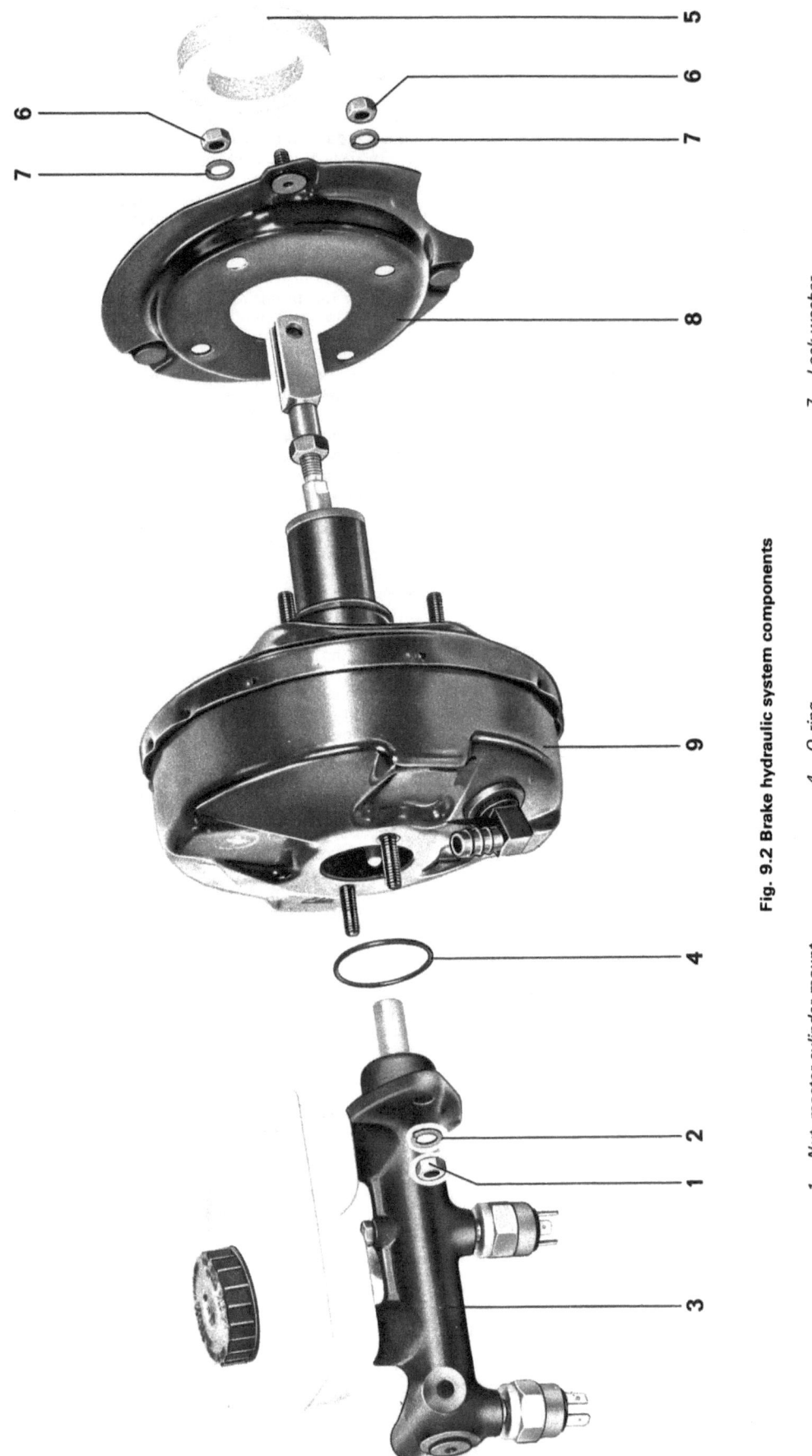

Fig. 9.2 Brake hydraulic system components

1 Nut, master cylinder mount
2 Lock washer
3 Brake hydraulic master
   cylinder

4 O-ring
5 Foam gasket
6 Nut, brake booster-to-
   console

7 Lock washer
8 Console
9 Brake booster

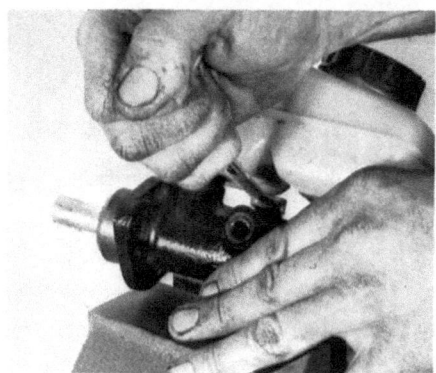

3.6 Removing retainer bolt

3.11a Laying out the new replacement parts in the same order as those removed saves time and confusion

3.11b Note that there are two thicknesses of seal cups, and separate them

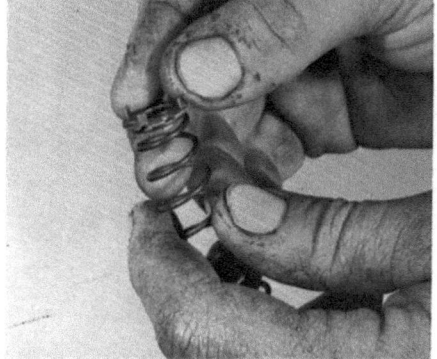

3.12 Installing the seal spacer

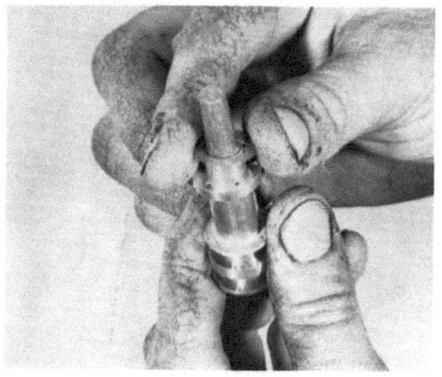

3.13 Installing the valve disc on the tapered end of the valve body

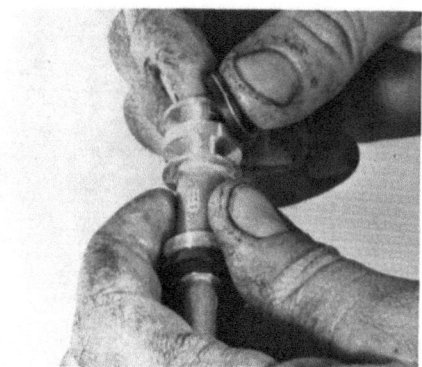

3.16 Installing the first of the double seals on the valve body

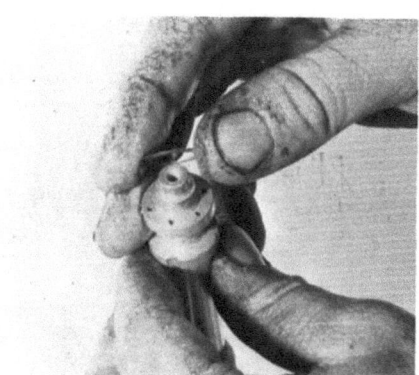

3.17 Installing the valve disc on the stepped end of the valve body

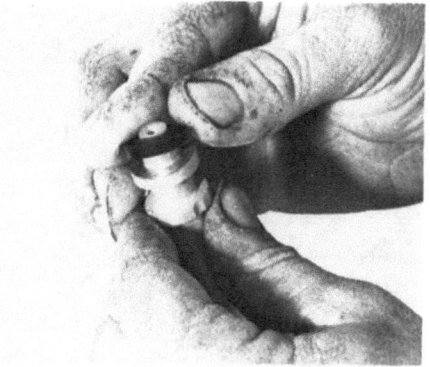

3.18 Installing the seal cup on the stepped end of the valve body

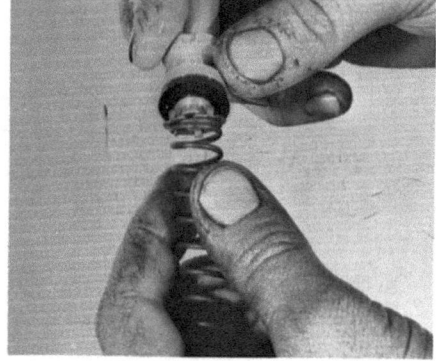

3.19 Installing the constant wound spring on the valve body

16 Select the two unmounted seal cups which have sealing surfaces (edges) of the same width and install them in the two grooves at the end of the valve body opposite the installed cup. The open ends of these cups should face the ends of the valve body with the closed ends facing each other (photo). Set the completed forward valve assembly aside.

17 Place the remaining valve disc (washer) over the six valve holes at the stepped end of the rear valve body (photo).

18 Install the remaining seal cup against the valve disc with the open end facing the end of the valve body and the closed end against the valve disc (photo).

19 Install the remaining seal spacer at one end of the constant-wound spring and place this assembly, seal spacer end first, into the seal cup of the rear valve assembly (photo).

20 Install the shouldered bolt into the flange end of the travel limiting sleeve and then install it in the open end of the constant wound spring (photos). Compress the spring and engage the threads of the

bolt in the rear valve assembly. Tighten the bolt until the shoulder firmly contacts the valve assembly. The lubricated assembly many be difficult to hold during tightening of the bolt. It may be held in a vise with protected jaws for ease in tightening.

21 Lubricate the seal surfaces, piston rubbing surfaces, and inner cylinder surfaces with clean, new, brake fluid or brake assembly lubricant.

22 Insert the tapered spring, wide end first, into the cylinder body.

23 Insert the tapered end of the forward valve assembly into the center hole of the seal spacer (tapered end of the spring) and gently press the assembly into the cylinder body (photo).

24 Install the rear valve assembly, spring end first, into the cylinder body. Press it in until only the hollow end of the pushrod shows over the edge of the cylinder body (photo).

25 Lubricate the pushrod shaft with brake fluid. Install a metal washer, the rubber dust seal, and a second metal washer on the shaft (photo). Compress the entire assembly until the locating

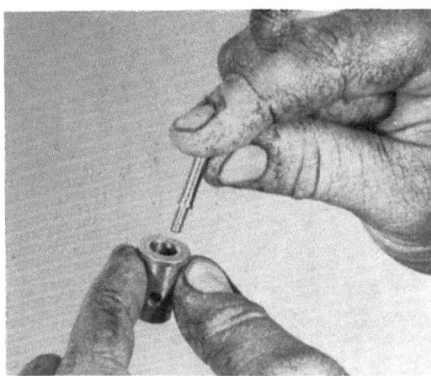

3.20a Placing the shouldered bolt into the limiting sleeve

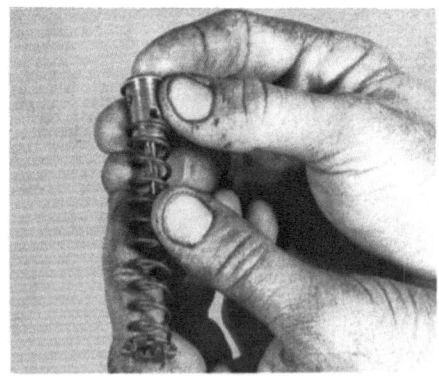

3.20b Installing the limiting sleeve and bolt into the constant wound spring

3.23 Installing the tapered spring and forward valve assembly into the cylinder body

3.24 Installing the rear valve assembly

3.25a Installing the rubber dust seal and metal washers

3.25b Fitting the circlip in its groove in the cylinder bore

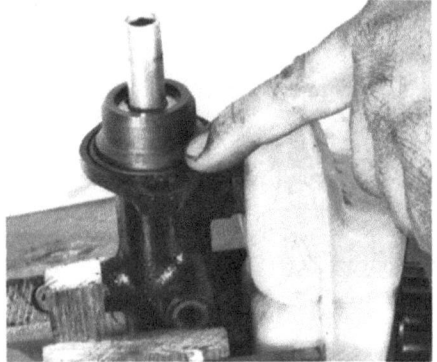

3.26 Do not forget to replace the O-ring

4.5 Removing the brake booster vacuum hose with the check valve installed

4.9 Removing the brake booster and its console

groove for the circlip appears. Install the circlip (photo). Heavily lubricating the dust seal will make compression of the valve assemblies much easier.

26 Remove the O-ring which seals the master cylinder to the brake booster. This is found in a shallow groove close to the master cylinder mounting flange (photo). Install the new O-ring from the rebuild kit in the groove. A light coat of brake fluid will ease installation and prevent damage to the seal when the master cylinder is reinstalled on the brake booster.

27 Before installing the rebuilt master cylinder in the car, bench bleed the cylinder. Place one of the mounting flanges of the master cylinder in the protected jaws of the vise so that the brake fluid reservoir is in a full upright position. Partially fill the brake fluid reservoir with clean, new, brake fluid. Pump the pushrod shaft in and out until all hydraulic connecting holes are pumping out brake fluid at the same rate. Note that brake fluid is poisonous and will damage paint. Allow the brake fluid to run out but do not pump so hard and fast that fluid is sprayed throughout the workshop.

28 Following installation of the rebuilt master cylinder, bleed the brake system (Section 18).

4 Brake booster - removal and installation

1   Disconnect the negative lead from the battery.
2   Remove the brake master cylinder.
3   Remove the left seat from the passenger compartment. This is held in place by four bolts (Chapter 12).
4   Loosen the clamp on the vaccum hose at the elbow fitting on the brake booster housing.
5   Loosen the clamp which holds the above vacuum hose to the tee fitting. Remove the hose, leaving the check valve assembly in the hose. The check valve assembly is a plastic housing mounted in-line in this hose (photo).
6   Cut the soundproofing blanket in the passenger compartment from the top edge of the blanket down about six inches, or enough

so that the blanket may be pulled clear of the accelerator cable. The two alternatives to this are removal of all foot-operated controls or removal of the dashboard.

7 Locate three nuts in the upper, front section of the firewall which are in approximately the ten, five, and two o'clock positions (when viewed full on by a sitting person) and remove the nuts and washers.

8 Remove the pivot pin which connects the brake pedal lever to the brake booster rod. This is snapped on to the brake booster rod. Unclip and pull the pivot pin free.

9 Lift the booster body and its mounting console from the firewall (photo).

10 Remove the four nuts which mount the booster body to the firewall mounting console.

11 Holding the actuating shaft across the machined-in flats, loosen the jam nut which prevents the clevis on the actuating shaft from turning. Remove the clevis and jam nut.

12 Installation of the brake booster is the reverse of the removal procedure. The following points should be observed:

13 The console which attaches the brake booster to the firewall can line up with the three mounting holes in the firewall in only one way. Before mounting the brake booster to the console make sure they are in the proper relationship to one another, ie. so that the elbow fitting is in the lower left corner of the booster unit when the console is bolted up to the firewall.

14 Torque the brake booster-to-console bolts to 15 ft-lb (2.1 m-kg).

15 Install the jam nut and clevis, but do not tighten them until final adjustment of the brake pedal can be carried out.

16 Carefully reinstall the booster/console assembly on to the firewall. The brake booster rod also acts as the piston. Scratching, scoring, or bending the rod will mean replacement of the booster.

17 Torque the console to firewall nuts to 15 ft-lb (2.1 m-kg).

18 Adjustment of the brake pedal is accomplished by threading the clevis on the brake booster shaft in our out until ¼ to $\frac{5}{16}$ in (6 to 8 mm) free movement of the brake pedal, measured at the pedal, is achieved. Once this adjustment has been made, tighten the jam nut and clip the pivot pin to the brake booster rod.

19 Test the check valve before re-installing the vacuum hose.

20 Re-install the master cylinder (Section 2). The brake system will require bleeding when brake work is completed.

5 Brake booster vacuum check valve - testing

1 The check valve is located in the vacuum hose which runs from the tee fitting on the brake booster.

2 Efficiency of the check valve is tested by blowing air through the hose in the direction of the arrow molded on the check valve case. This should cause the leaf valve to lift off its seat and air to pass through. Blowing air through the hose in the opposite direction should cause the valve to close completely.

3 If the check valve doesn't work in the manner above, replacement is necessary.

6 Brake booster - checking

1 With the engine shut off, pump the brakes several times. This uses up the vacuum in the booster.

2 Hold the brake pedal in the braking position (depressed) and start the engine. If the brake booster is working properly, there will be a slight drop of the pedal. Medium pressure on the pedal will produce the best results for this test.

3 The brake booster is not rebuildable by the home mechanic. In the event that replacement is necessary, purchase a new or rebuilt unit which is of the same original manufacture as the master cylinder. This must be done to achieve proper clearances between the booster rod and the master cylinder pushrod.

4 If the clearances are too small, the brakes will lock and may remain locked. Clearances which are too great will result in a sharp decrease in braking efficiency.

7 Front disc brakes - checking brake pad thickness

1 The brake pads cannot be checked for lining thickness without

removing the wheels. This task can most easily be done by placing the entire front end on jack stands and removing both front wheels. Do not forget to apply the parking brake to the rear wheels.

2 Turning the steering wheel full lock to the right will provide access to the brake pads on the left caliper, and vice-versa.

3 New brake pads have a layer of friction material 14 mm thick. Pads must be replaced when the friction material is worn to 2 mm thickness. This thickness can be checked by measuring the distance from the brake pad backing plate and the inner edge of the material layer.

8 Front disc brakes - pad replacement

1 Raise the front of the vehicle and support in on jack stands. If no work is to be performed on the rear brakes, only the front needs to be raised. The parking brake should be engaged and the transmission placed in first gear (standard transmission) or in park (automatic). If work is to be performed on the rear brakes, place the rear of the vehicle on jack stands as well.

2 Remove the front wheels and set them aside.

3 For 1980 models, remove the pull out retainer clips which hold the brake pad retaining pins in position. They will be found on the inboard side of the caliper and may be removed with pliers.

4 With a hammer and soft metal drift, drive out the brake pad retaining pins from the outboard side of the caliper. Removal of the brake pad retaining pins will free the cross clip, which may fall free or be removed with simple finger pressure (photo).

5 If brake pads are being removed in conjunction with other brake work and you intend to re-install the same pads, set aside an area where the removed brake pads may be laid out and marked for replacement in the caliper. Mixing of the brake pads will give poor braking and could lead to loss of vehicle control in certain conditions. This step will be unnecessary to those replacing the brake pads.

6 With a brake pad hook tool, remove the inboard brake pad. If this tool is not available, the pad may be removed with a Phillips head screwdriver. Taking great care not to score the face of the caliper, raise each side of the brake pad in turn until the pad has been "walked" out far enough to be pulled out with the fingers (photos).

7 The outboard brake pad is held in place by a tang on the caliper frame. To remove the outboard brake pad, pry gently between the brake pad and caliper back with a large, flat bladed screwdriver. This should be sufficient to allow the pad to free itself from the tang. Remove the brake pad with a brake pad tool or a Phillips head screwdriver (photos).

8 It is necessary to retract the brake caliper pistons only far enough to allow easy brake pad removal and installation. Retracting of the brake pads will cause an overflow of the brake master cylinder reservoir. Brake fluid may be removed with a siphon used only for brake fluid. Never suck brake fluid into a hose as this substance is poisonous. Any dripping of fluid should be cleaned up immediately as it will remove paint from any painted surface if left unattended.

9 Cleaning of the piston and surrounding surfaces should be done with acetone or spirits. No cleaner containing mineral oils should ever be used in or around any braking system component.

10 Inspect the brake pads for oil spattering, brake fluid coating, loosening of the brake pad material, or deep cracking of the pad material. If any of the above conditions are found, replace all four brake pads with new units.

11 Installation of the brake pads is the reverse of removal, with special attention to be paid to the following points:

12 Replacement brake pads usually come with uninstalled paper gaskets with adhesive backing. These should be placed on the backs of the brake pads with the central hole in alignment with the depression in the brake pad back (photo).

13 Install the outboard brake pads first and press on the caliper frame after installation to set the tang on the frame in the depression in the brake pad back (photo).

14 Porsche recommends the replacement of the cross clips and retaining pins. This is most necessary when installing new brake pads, but in every case, the retaining pins should be examined for wear and bending.

15 Depress the brake pedal several times to return the pads to their operating position.

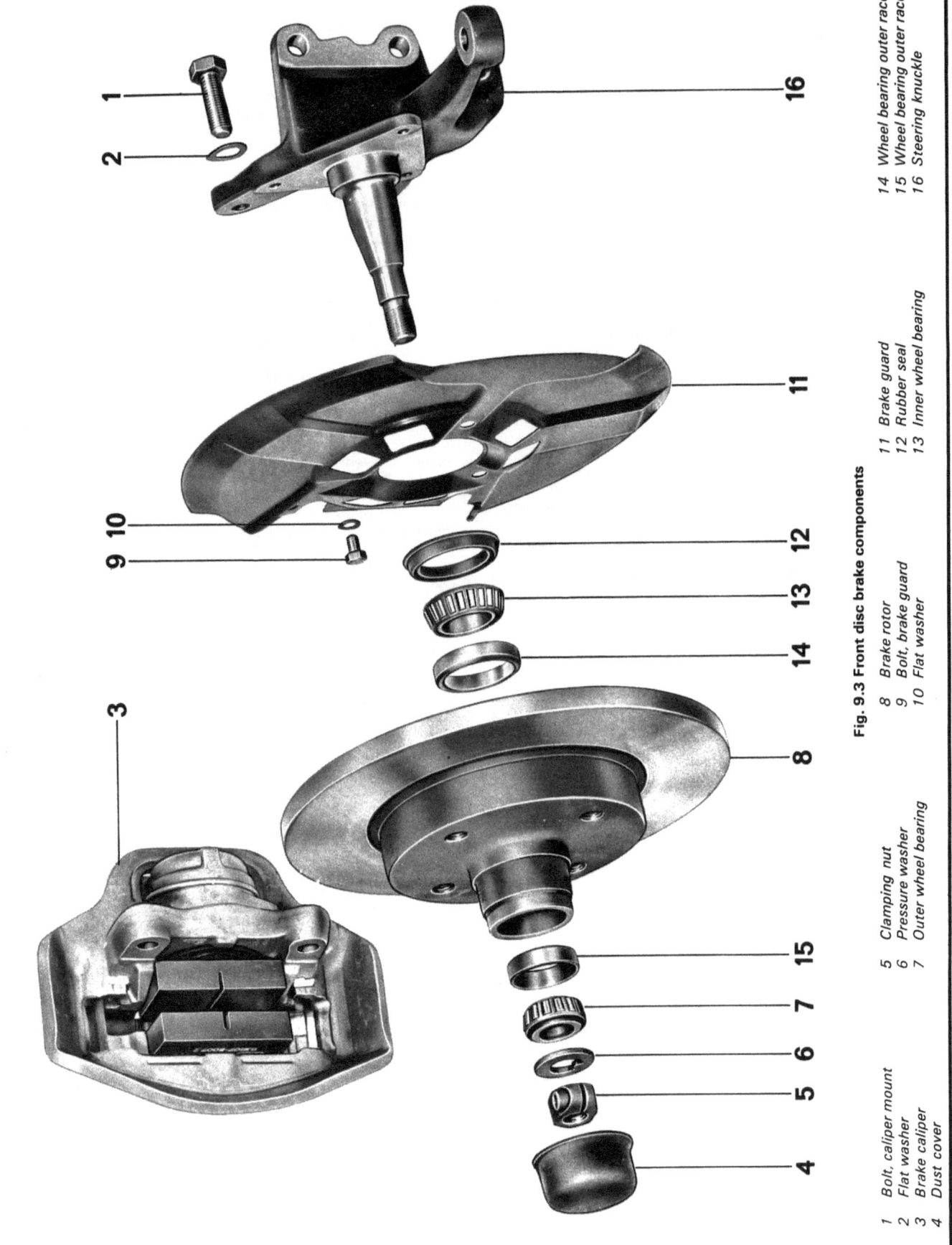

Fig. 9.3 Front disc brake components

1 Bolt, caliper mount	8 Brake rotor
2 Flat washer	9 Bolt, brake guard
3 Brake caliper	10 Flat washer
4 Dust cover	11 Brake guard
5 Clamping nut	12 Rubber seal
6 Pressure washer	13 Inner wheel bearing
7 Outer wheel bearing	14 Wheel bearing outer race
	15 Wheel bearing outer race
	16 Steering knuckle

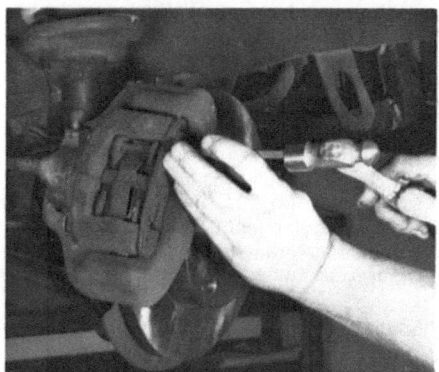

8.4 Driving out the brake pad retaining pins with a metal drift

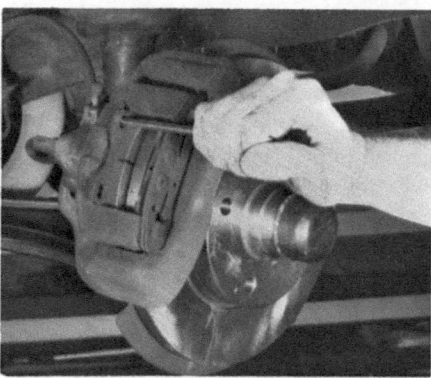

8.6a Using a Phillips head screwdriver to lever out the brake pads

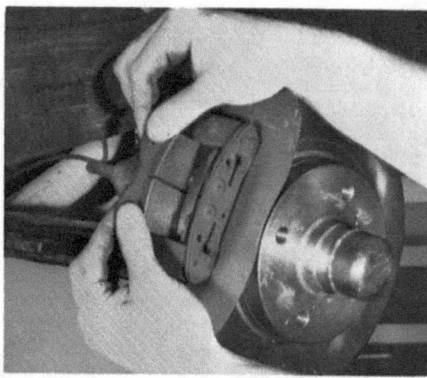

8.6b Final removal of the brake pads should require only fingers

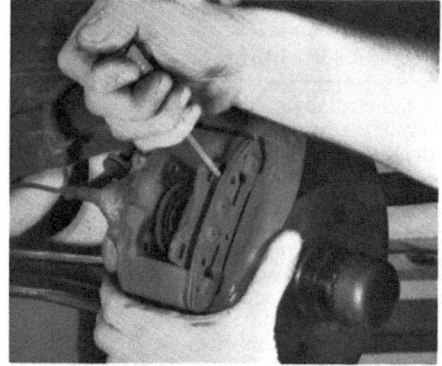

8.7a Using a flat bladed screwdriver to separate the outboard brake pad from the tang on the frame

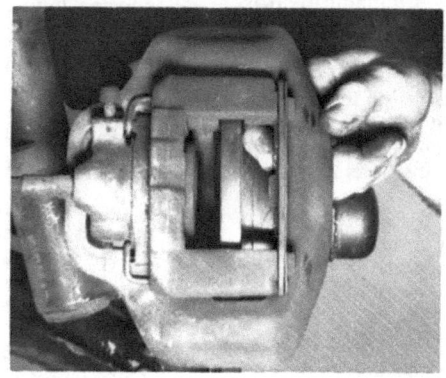

8.7b Location of the brake pad mounting tang

8.12 Installing the brake pad paper gaskets

8.13 Pressing the caliper frame to set the mounting tang into the brake pad back

9.4 The caliper may be hung out of the way of other work on a bent coathanger

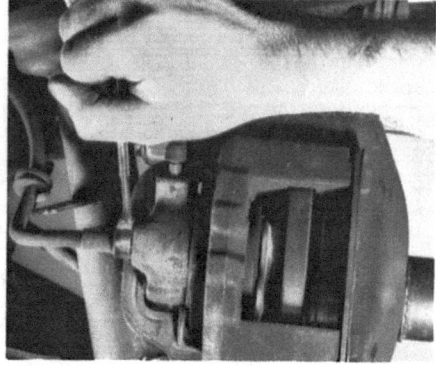

9.7 Loosening the hydraulic connection on the caliper wth a flare nut wrench

16 New brake pads are not at full efficiency for a period of about 120 traveling miles (200 km). During this period the brakes should be fully applied only in emergency situations. Average pedal pressure and long periods of time between pedal applications will give best break-in results.

9 Front disc brakes - caliper removal and installation

1 Raise the front of the vehicle and support it on jack stands.
2 Remove the front wheels and set them aside.
3 Remove the brake pads and set them aside (Section 8).
4 If the caliper is being removed only to gain access to other parts of the braking system or suspension and no caliper rebuild work is anticipated, it will not be necessary to disconnect the caliper from the hydraulic lines. In this instance, disconnect the rubber hose retainer from the fitting on the front suspension strut and remove the two bolts which attach the caliper to the steering knuckle. To

hang the caliper out of the way, bend a wire coathanger into a double hook (one hook at each end) and hang the caliper from the front suspension strut spring or another out-of-the-way location (photo).
5 If the caliper is being removed for renewal of the piston seals or replacement of other caliper parts, it will be necessary to disconnect the caliper from the hydraulic lines.
6 Plug the hole in the top of the master cylinder reservoir cap with a small amount of silicone seal or other flexible plasticine material. This will prevent drainage of the brake hydraulic system. Do not attempt to seal the cap by placing a sheet of plastic wrap over the master cylinder fluid reservoir filler hole and then replacing the cap. Although this will serve the same purpose, volatile elements of the brake fluid will leach various chemical compounds from the plastic wrap, which will cause gumming up of hydraulic lines and other unwanted sediments forming throughout the braking hydraulic system.
7 With a flare nut wrench, loosen—but do not remove—the

hydraulic line nut at the caliper body (photo).

8   Remove the two bolts which attach the caliper to the steering knuckle (photo).

9   Disconnect the rubber hose retainer from the fitting on the front suspension strut (photo).

10 Remove the caliper from the brake hydraulic line by twisting the caliper (unscrewing) and holding the hydraulic line in the same position. This will prevent kinking of the brake hydraulic line and also eliminate the possibility of internal breakup of the brake hose, which could lead to eventual hydraulic line failure. If in doubt as to the condition of brake lines, replace them.

11 Plug the end of the hydraulic line with a soft rubber plug. These plugs are available from most automotive parts dealers. This will prevent the draining of the hydraulic system and also keep dirt from entering the system.

12 Hang the brake line in an out-of-the-way location with the open (nut) end pointing upward.

13 Installation is the reversal of the removal procedure with the following items to be noted:

14 If the brake hydraulic lines have been removed, reinstall them by screwing the caliper onto the brake hydraulic line. Do not twist the brake hydraulic line excessively.

15 If the brake hydraulic lines have not been removed, take care not to twist the hydraulic line when placing the caliper on the steering knuckle.

16 Install the caliper-to-steering knuckle attaching bolts in the caliper and tighten to finger tightness. Torque the bolts to 60 ft-lb (8.5 m-kg), torquing the top bolt first.

17 Once the caliper has been properly installed, torque the brake hydraulic line nut to 9 ft-lb (1.2 m-kg). Do not do this until the caliper-to-steering knuckle bolts are torqued down.

10   Front disc brakes - rotor removal and installation

1   Raise the front of the vehicle and support it on jack stands.

2   Remove the front wheels and set them aside.

3   Remove the brake pads and set them aside (Section 8).

4   Remove the caliper (Section 9).

5   Remove the dust cover by gently levering it out toward you. The right side dust cover is plain, but the left side dust cover has a speedometer drive piece installed in the hub. This will protrude slightly from the end of the dust cap. Remove it once the dust cap is taken off and scrape the sealing compound from the dust cap before setting aside (photos).

6   With a socket head wrench (Allen type) loosen the threaded clamping nut and remove the nut, thrust washer, and the inner bearing race and caged roller assembly of the outboard wheel bearing (photo). If the bearing pieces do not fall out, pull the brake rotor toward you (outboard) and then push it back, doing this several times to "walk" the inner race out.

7   Remove the brake rotor from the steering knuckle. This is done by pulling the rotor outboard evenly to prevent "chattering" damage to the spindle and bearing surfaces (photo).

8   Remove the rotor guard by removing the three bolts which hold it to the steering knuckle (photo).

9   Clean the rotor and its guard with acetone or other cleaners which are approved for this purpose. Never clean brake parts with any solvents which contain mineral oils.

10 Installation of the brake rotor is the opposite of removal, with the following points to be observed:

11 Torque the three bolts holding the guard to the steering knuckle to 7 ft-lb (1.0 m-kg).

12 Lightly grease the spindle with a suitable bearing grease before installing the rotor (photo). This will help the inboard seal remain flexible. Grease the plain bearing surface inside the rotor with the same type of wheel bearing grease.

13 Slide the rotor onto the spindle shaft. A slight resistance will be felt as the seal stretches slightly to go over the plain bearing surface.

14 Lightly grease the outer bearing race on the outboard wheel bearing with wheel bearing grease. Place a small amount of this grease in the palm of one hand and pack the inner bearing race and rollers by pressing the edge of the roller cage into the grease, forcing grease out between the rollers and the cage (photo).

15 Install the inner race of the wheel bearing into the tapered outer race.

16 Install the thrust washer, taking care to align the tang on the thrust washer with the slot on the wheel spindle.

17 Screw on the clamping nut and spin the brake rotor. Continue tightening the nut and spinning the rotor between tightenings to seat the bearings squarely in their races. When resistance is felt twice in a row (ie. when the nut does not loosen between turns of the rotor and the nut is snug, not tight), back the nut one half turn and tighten until the thrust washer can just be moved by pressing with the blade of a flat screwdriver. No twisting or levering of the screwdriver should take place, as this will lead to overtightening (photo).

18 Torque the socket head bolt (Allen type) 9 to 11 ft-lb (1.3 to 1.6 m-kg).

19 Install the dust cover. On the left side dust cover remember to install the speedometer drive piece first. The dust cover may be seated by tapping gently around the top edge with a soft faced mallet. Seal the speedometer drive piece outside the dust cover with silicone seal (photos).

11   Front disc brakes - inspection of the rotor

1   Once the rotor has been removed and thoroughly cleaned, insert a spindle of the proper diameter and place both spindle ends in vee blocks or one end of the spindle in a vise if vee blocks are not available.

2   Inspect the braking surfaces of the rotor for evidence of grooving, gouging, chatter marks, and cracks. With a straight edge, check at least three points of the rotor braking surface (on a line from the outer edge through the center of the disc) for evidence of cupping. Check—also at these points—both surfaces to see if they are parallel to each other.

3   If any of the above conditions exist, check to see if they may be eliminated by removing material from the braking surfaces (turning the rotor) without exceeding the minimum rotor thickness of 12 mm. Both rotors must be turned down to the same thickness to assure proper braking. If material is removed from both sides of one rotor, the same amount must be removed from the other rotor of the same axle.

4   In the event of only one brake rotor needing replacement, it is still necessary to replace both brake rotors on the same axle to prevent the car from pulling to one side when braking.

5   Before taking the brake rotors to an authorized brake repair shop for turning down, check the rotor for lateral runout (warpage). With a dial indicator placed against the outer third of the rotor braking surface, slowly turn the brake rotor on the installed spindle and watch the dial for indications of warpage (high spots and low spots). Minimal warpage may be corrected by turning the rotor down, but ensure that correction of this warpage will not exceed the minimum rotor thickness of 12 mm.

6   As in the situations above, both rotors must be replaced if one is found to be outside the tolerances.

7   Brake rotor turning must be done on a lathe with special tools. It is best to seek the services of a qualified brake repair shop for this task.

12   Front disc brakes - caliper rebuild

1   Place the caliper frame in a vice with jaw protectors or wood blocks installed and press out the mounting frame with finger pressure only (photos).

2   Set the mounting frame aside and reposition the caliper frame in the vise so that the cylinder's piston faces downward. Slip a block of wood between the vise jaws and the cylinder to prevent damage to the piston face during the following step.

3   With a soft metal drift drive the cylinder off the caliper frame by striking the drift at both sides of the cylinder. Make sure that the cylinder comes off squarely. Remove the cylinder frame from the vise and set it aside (photo).

4   Detach the guide spring from the cylinder body (photo).

5   Remove the rubber dust cap from the cylinder bleed fitting, then unscrew the bleed fitting (photo).

6   Place the cylinder in a vise with protected jaws, with the piston facing up.

9.8 Removing the caliper mounting bolts from the steering knuckle

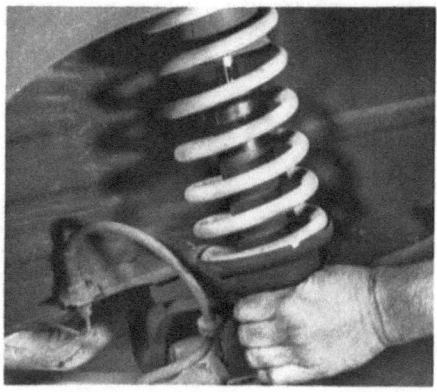

9.9 Disconnecting the rubber hose retainer

10.5a Removing the front wheel bearing dust cover

10.5b The right side dust cover showing the speedometer drive piece

10.6 Removing the clamping nut

10.7 Removing the brake rotor

10.8 Removing the rotor guard

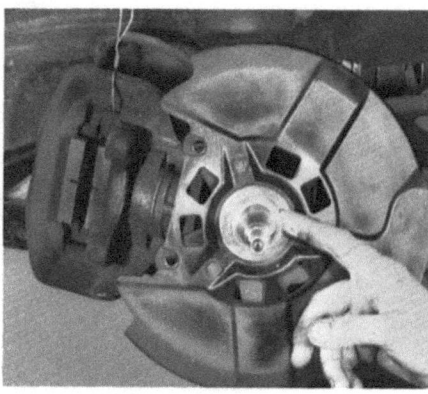

10.12 Lubricating the spindle surface

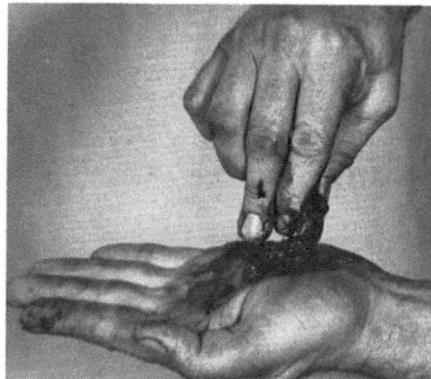

10.14 The proper way to pack wheel bearings

10.17 Checking the clamping nut tightness with a screwdriver

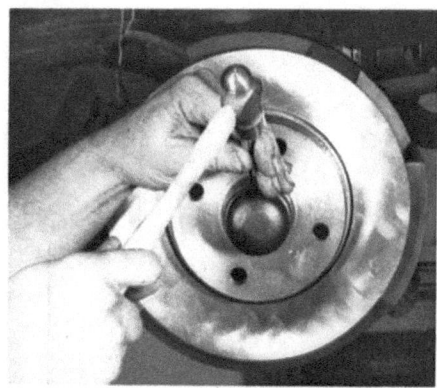

10.19a Installing the front wheel bearing dust cover

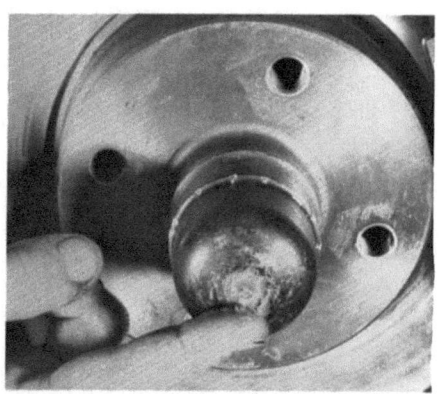

10.19b Sealing the speedometer drive piece with silicone seal

12.1a Installing the brake caliper assembly in a vise

12.1b Removing the mounting frame

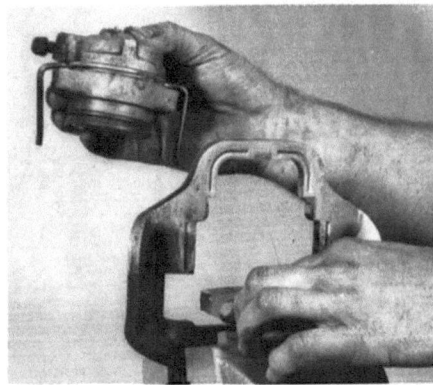

12.3 Driving the caliper cylinder from the caliper frame with a soft metal drift

12.4 Detaching the guide spring

12.5 Removing the bleed fitting

12.7a Prying the clip from the dust seal

12.7b Removing the dust seal

12.8 Removing the piston from the cylinder

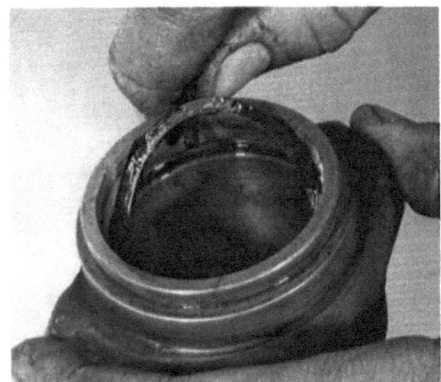

12.10 Removing the cylinder inner bore seal

12.12 The proper way to lubricate the cylinder bore

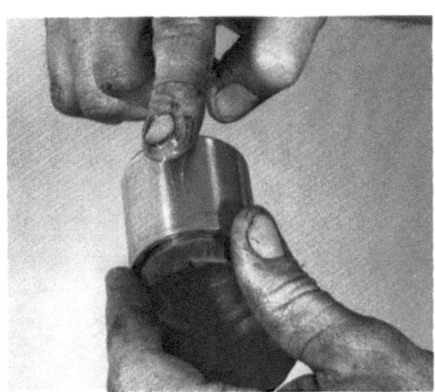

12.14a Lubricate the piston sides thoroughly

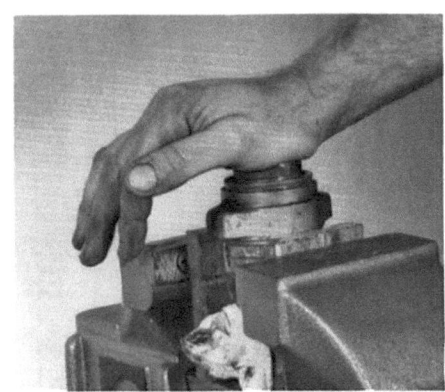

12.14b Pushing the piston to at least the inner seal

7 Pry the clip which retains the dust seal (bellows) from the cylinder and remove the dust seal (photos).

8 Remove the cylinder from the vise and place it piston side down on a block of wood. Hold the cylinder firmly with one hand, covering the bleed screw hole with one finger. Fill the cylinder with compressed air, forcing the air through the hydraulic brake hose fitting. Hold the cylinder firmly and allow the piston to slide out slowly. It may be necessary to temporarily replace the bleed screw in order to provide sufficient pressure in the cylinder. Do not allow the piston to shoot out quickly as it may damage its operating surfaces. A hand- or foot-operated tyre pump will usually be satisfactory (photo).

9 Inspect the piston and cylinder surfaces for gouges, chatter marks, nicks, and deep scratches. If any are found, do not attempt to re-use the damaged part.

10 Remove the seal from the inner bore of the cylinder. Auto parts stores carry plastic rods for this purpose. If this rod is not readily available, the seal may be removed with a sewing needle. Poke the needle in the seal, making sure not to contact the metal surfaces of the cylinder with the sharp point of the needle, as this may scratch the cylinder surface (photo).

11 Open the cylinder repair kit and lay out the new parts.

12 Carefully coat the inner cylinder surfaces and the new inner seal with brake assembly lubricant or brake fluid. Remember that brake fluid is poisonous and will remove paint. It is important to keep the work area free of dirt and grit during assembly of the cylinders, and to clean up the area of brake fluid drips immediately after completing this task (photo).

13 Install the new inner seal with the fingers and work it squarely into its groove.

14 Coat the outer surfaces of the piston with brake assembly lubricant or brake fluid. Set the piston squarely in the bore of the cylinder and push it in with your fingers until it contacts the inner seal (photos).

15 Open the jaws of your vise wide enough to accept the entire cylinder and piston assembly between the jaws with protectors installed. Place the piston squarely against one jaw and the back of the cylinder against the other jaw. Slowly close the vise, making sure that the piston is entering the cylinder squarely and is not galling the inner bore. Close the vise until the seal groove on the piston appears just above the top edge of the cylinder (photo).

16 Lubricate the inner edge of the new dust seal and install it in the

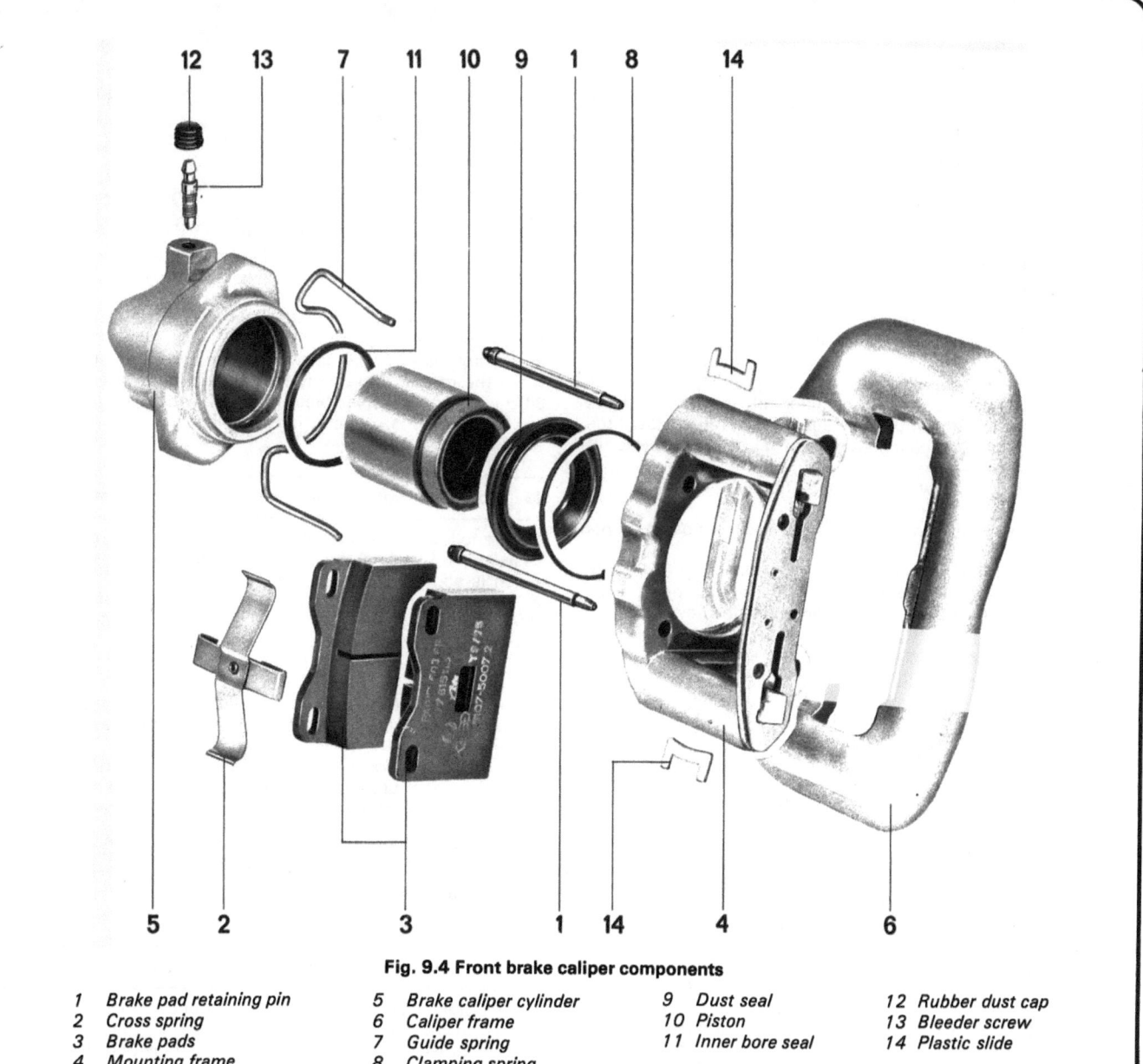

Fig. 9.4 Front brake caliper components

1 Brake pad retaining pin	5 Brake caliper cylinder	9 Dust seal	12 Rubber dust cap
2 Cross spring	6 Caliper frame	10 Piston	13 Bleeder screw
3 Brake pads	7 Guide spring	11 Inner bore seal	14 Plastic slide
4 Mounting frame	8 Clamping spring		

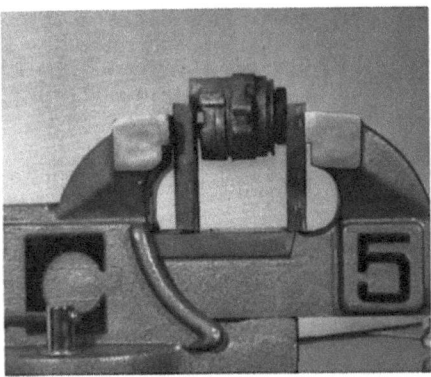

12.15 Using a vise to press the piston down to the seal groove

12.16 Installing the dust seal

12.21 Removing the old plastic slides from the caliper frame

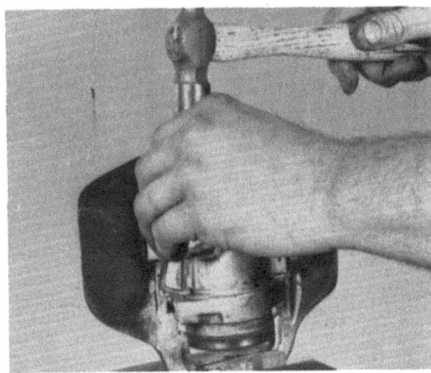

12.27 Driving the cylinder onto the caliper frame

13.4 Using a soft metal drift to remove old bearing races

13.6 Driving in new bearing races. A seal and bearing driver would make this job easier

groove on the piston. With your fingers locate the outer edge of the dust seal over the cast-in lip of the cylinder and install the clip (photo).

17 Place the cylinder assembly back into the protected jaws of the vise and retract the piston into the cylinder until it is flush with the edge of the cylinder housing. Once again, be careful to seat the piston squarely in the cylinder body and not gall the inner surface of the cylinder.

18 Install the bleed screw and its rubber cover.

19 Install the guide spring.

20 Lightly grease all rubbing surfaces on the cylinder body, caliper frame, and mounting frame.

21 The mounting frame has two plastic slides installed on its rubbing surfaces. Caliper rebuild kits normally include new plastic slides, so remove the old slides, lightly lubricate the new slides and install them in the mounting frame (photo).

22 Place the cylinder assembly in front of you on the workbench with the bleed screw end of the casting to your left and the bleed screw boss in the upper-rear position. Note also that the groove which locates the cylinder to the caliper frame should be parallel to the work surface.

23 Pick up the caliper with one hand and slip the guide spring into the locating groove on the cylinder body. The loop should be beneath the cylinder (open end up) and the two legs of the spring parallel to the cylinder body.

24 Set the cylinder back down in the position described above, with the spring installed.

25 Take the caliper frame and set it alongside the cylinder assembly with the "cupped" side facing down and the cylinder mounting bracket to your left. This is how the cylinder and caliper frame will be related to each other when they are mounted together.

26 Slip the grooved end of the cylinder housing onto the caliper frame. The bleed screw should be in the corner away from you and above the curved surfaces of the caliper frame. The guide spring 'arms' should be resting on the side of the caliper frame facing you.

27 When you are sure of the mounting arrangement, use a soft drift and hammer to drive the cylinder assembly squarely into the caliper frame (photo).

28 Install the mounting frame on the caliper frame, being careful not to damage the plastic slides.

29 Do not install brake pads now. This will be much easier to do when the caliper is properly located on the steering knuckle.

30 It will be necessary to bleed the brake hydraulic system once the braking system is properly reassembled.

13 Front disc brakes – rotor stripdown and assembly

1 The following instructions must be followed for replacement of bearings and seals or for removing re-useable parts from a rotor which is about to be scrapped.

2 Place jaw protectors or blocks of wood on top of the vise jaws. Open the jaws of the vise slightly wider than the diameter of the rotor's spindle hole.

3 Place the rotor on the vise jaws with the hole centered over the open jaws and the inboard (flat) side down.

4 With a soft drift, drive out the inboard bearing and seal. Alternate blows from one side to the other to prevent the bearing race from jamming against the sides of the bore (photo).

5 Turn the rotor over and drive out the outer bearing race of the outboard wheel bearing. Use the soft drift and hammer, placing the drift in the machined-in slots and alternating blows from side to side.

6 Intallation is simply the reverse of removal. Care should be taken, however, to set the seal with a proper size seal driver, rather than with a hammer and drift (photo).

14 Rear drum brakes – brake shoe inspection

1 The brake lining may be checked through two inspection holes located in the brake backing plate.

2 New brakes (standard linings) carry linings of 0.15 in to 0.16 in (3.8 to 4.00 mm). All brake linings may be allowed to wear to a thickness of 0.10 in (2.5 mm).

15 Rear drum brakes - brake lining replacement

1   Raise the rear of the vehicle. It is suggested, for the sake of safety, that the front be raised and placed on jack stands while the rear brakes are set (handbrake) and then the rear wheels raised. There are no parking brakes installed on the Porsche 924's front wheels, therefore some blocking arrangement would be required to prevent the vehicle from rolling forward. The four jack stand arrangement provides the most stable way of working on the rear brakes.

2   Remove the rear wheels and set aside.

3   Remove the cotter pin (split pin) from the castellated nut (photo).

4   The castellated nut is difficult to remove as it has been torqued to a high force. Automotive parts and accessory stores which cater to the Volkswagen trade may sell a tool which has the proper size hexagonal hole in the center (for the castellated nut), a 1/2 in. square hole for the addition of a long breaker bar, and flats for striking with a hammer to jar the nut loose. An example of this tool in use is found in the illustrations (photo). Remove the nut.

5   Release the emergency brake (handbrake) and back down the brake adjusters (paragraph 21), then remove the brake drum.

6   If the brake linings are in need of repair, the drum braking surface should also be inspected for grooving, and a possible out-of-round condition. Brake drums may be turned down on a lathe to restore roundness and smoothness to the braking surfaces. This may be done as long as the resulting inside diameter of the drum is 231 mm or less and the remaining surface is smooth. At this diameter oversize brake linings must be installed.

7   If the brake drums cannot be turned down to give a smooth surface within the tolerances above, drum replacement is necessary. As with disc brakes, the drums must be turned down to the same diameter on each side, or both must be replaced. Failure to do this will lead to uneven braking and a possiblity of skidding in certain weather conditions.

8   Linings also require complete replacement in the event of one being worn beyond the wear limit. If all four brake linings are not renewed at the same time, the problem is again one of skidding or loss of braking ability.

9   With a special spring removal tool compress the spring and spring retainer found about the center of the brake shoe. Twist the retaining pin approximately 90 degrees and remove the pin, spring, and spring retainer (photo).

10 Remove first the lower, then the upper brake return springs, clip, and pressure rod assembly from the upper spring location (photo).

11 Detach the forward brake shoe first, and lift off the spring, clip, and pressure rod assembly from the upper spring location.

12 Unhook the emergency brake cable from the emergency brake actuating lever and remove the rear brake shoe.

13 Remove the clip which holds the emergency brake actuating lever pivot pin and press out the pivot pin and actuating lever. Both brake shoes may now be removed (photo).

14 It is possible to exchange old, worn brake shoes for renewed brake shoes with bonded linings. This method eliminates the problems inherent with riveted linings.

15 In the event bonded exchange shoes are not available, riveted linings must be installed. Care must be taken to ensure that the liings are held tightly to the brake shoe by the rivets and that the rivets themselves are tightly driven home.

16 Before reassembling the rear brakes, screw the brake shoe adjusters to their fully withdrawn position.

17 Assembly is now the opposite of teardown. The only special note to be observed here is the torque on the castellated nut. Required torque is 220 to 290 ft-lb (30 to 40 m-kg). Tightening must be done in the following manner:

18 Torque the castellated nut to the lowest torque value given (220 ft-lb or 30 m-kg). Note the position of the castellations relative to the cotter pin hole. Raise the torque force on your torque wrench in 5 ft-lb (0.75 m-kg) increments until the slot between two castellations and the cotter pin hole align and the maximum torque of 290 ft lb (40 m-kg) has not been reached. If the upper limit is reached before the hole and slot align, back the castellated nut off and begin from the 220 ft-lb (30 m-kg) figure again. If you pass the point

15.3 Removing the brake drum cotter pin

15.4 Loosening the castellated nut with the special brake drum nut tool described in the text

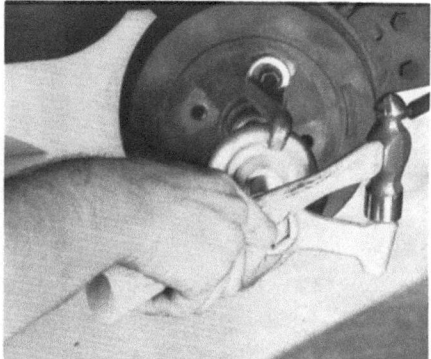

15.5a Loosening the brake drum with a standard puller

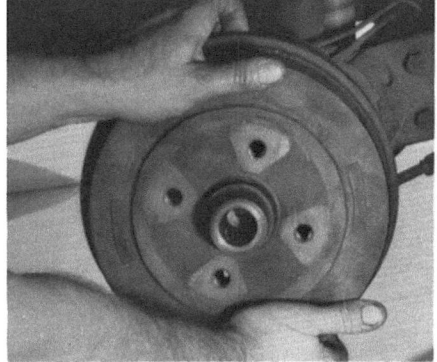

15.5b Use your hands for final removal of the brake drum

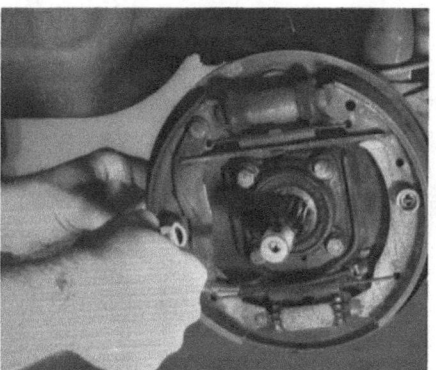

15.9 Removing a retaining pin and clip.

15.10 Using pliers to remove the brake return springs

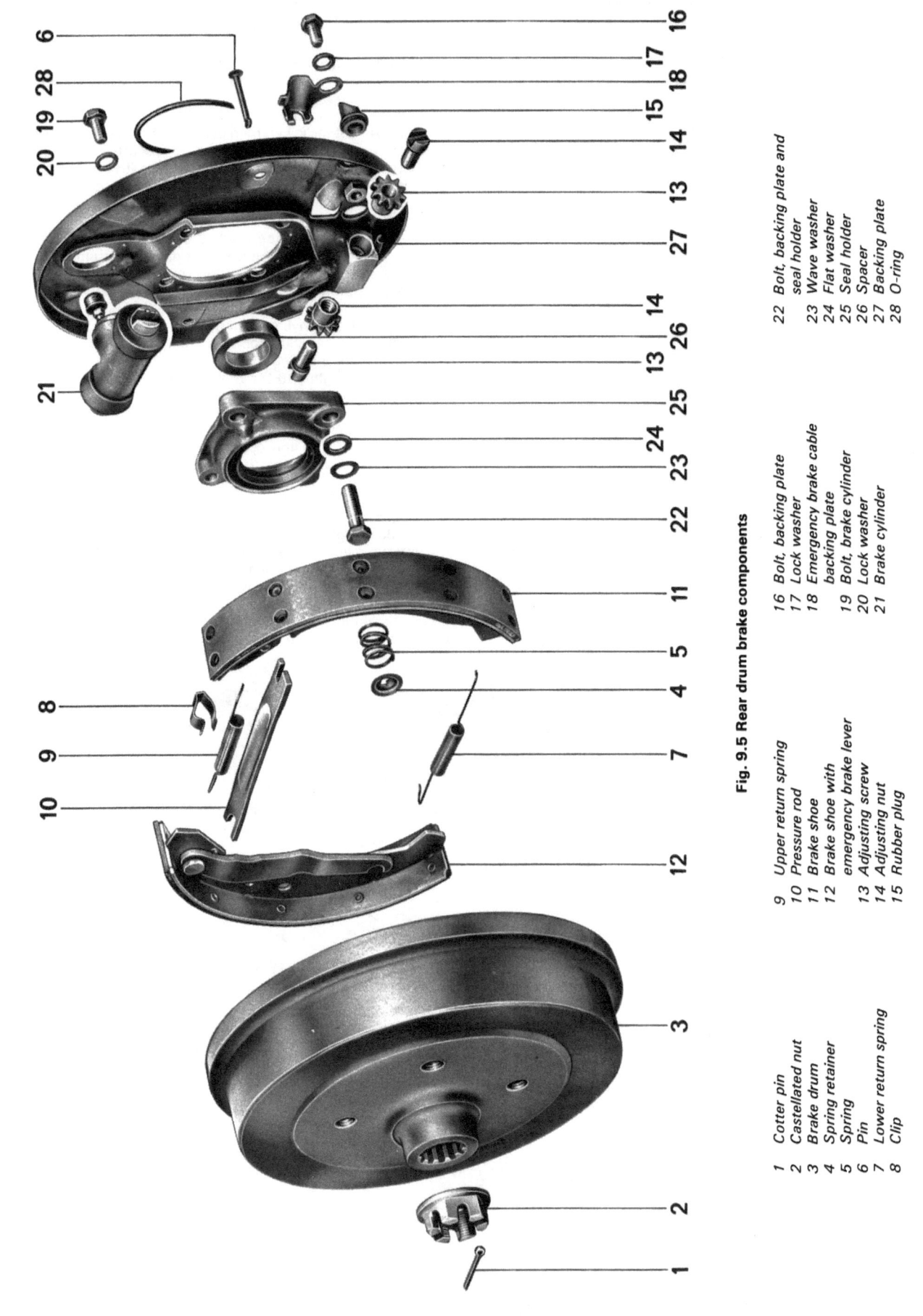

Fig. 9.5 Rear drum brake components

1 Cotter pin
2 Castellated nut
3 Brake drum
4 Spring retainer
5 Spring
6 Pin
7 Lower return spring
8 Clip

9 Upper return spring
10 Pressure rod
11 Brake shoe
12 Brake shoe with emergency brake lever
13 Adjusting screw
14 Adjusting nut
15 Rubber plug

16 Bolt, backing plate
17 Lock washer
18 Emergency brake cable backing plate
19 Bolt, brake cylinder
20 Lock washer
21 Brake cylinder

22 Bolt, backing plate and seal holder
23 Wave washer
24 Flat washer
25 Seal holder
26 Spacer
27 Backing plate
28 O-ring

15.13 Removing the brake shoes

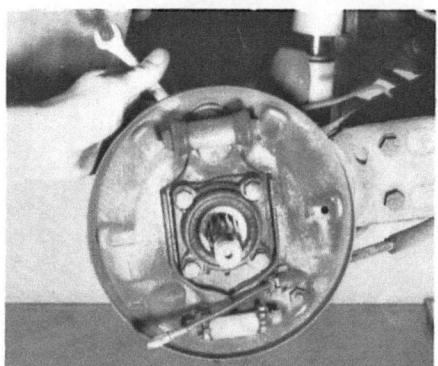

16.5 Loosening the hydraulic connection on the brake cylinder

16.10 Removing the emergency brake cable and backing plate

of alignment, back the castellated nut down and work you way back up to the torque force reading obtained before passing the alignment point, then proceed to raise the torque force adjustment of the torque wrench in 1 ft-lb (about 0:13 m-kg) increments.
19 Install the cotter pin and fold back the pieces of the pin.
20 Install the rear wheels. Do not take the vehicle off its jack stands yet.
21 Using a flat bladed screwdriver as a lever, reach through the adjustment holes in the backing plate and adjust the brake shoes out until the linings firmly contact the brake drum. Back the front and rear adjusters down by equal amounts until the wheel can be turned freely by hand.
22 Remove the vehicle from its jack stands.

16 Rear drum brakes – backing plate stripdown and build up

1   NOTE: Backing plate removal is necessary only when rear suspension work is required. Removal of the components of the drum brake will be necessary any time brake cylinder work is contemplated.
2   Raise the vehicle and place on jack stands.
3   Remove the brake drum and brake shoes (Section 15).
4   Use a small amount of silicone seal or other similar plasticine material to plug the hole in the top of the brake fluid reservoir filler cap. Do not attempt to seal off the filler hole with a sheet of plastic wrap screwed between the reservoir body and cap. Although it will serve the same purpose, volatile elements in the brake fluid will leach chemical compounds from the plastic wrap and these will lead to sludge deposits throughout the braking system.
5   With a flare nut wrench, loosen, but do not remove the hydraulic fitting connecting the brake line to the wheel cylinder (photo).
6   Remove the single bolt holding the wheel cylinder to the backing plate.
7   Carefully pull the wheel cylinder out and rotate it around the hydraulic fitting to unscrew the wheel cylinder. This will prevent kinking of the hydraulic hoses and eliminate the possibility of internal breakup of the hydraulic line.
8   Plug the hose and hang it on a suspension arm with the pressed end up.
9   If the apparent condition of any hydraulic line is in doubt, replace the hose.
10 Unbolt and remove the emergency brake cable backing plate and remove the cable and plate (photo).
11 Remove the four bolts attaching the brake backing plate and the seal holder to the rear suspension arm. When removing the bolts, remove also the two washers from each bolt hole. There is a machined spacer sleeve between the seal holder and the rear suspension arm which may be removed once the seal holder and backing plate are pulled free.
12 Clean the brake parts with acetone or a cleaner which is approved for brake cleaning. Never use solvents containing mineral oils to clean any brake part.
13 The brake adjusters, which were left installed on the backing plate, require no attention unless thread stripping or excessive

'chewing up' of the adjuster nut is noted. Replace these items as necessary.
14 Building up of the brake backing plate is the reverse of the stripdown. The following points should be noted:
15 The seal in the seal holder may be reused if not torn or cracked. Be careful in the placement of the seal lip when installing.
16 Torque the four bolts which mount the seal holder and backing plate to the suspension member in a crossing (diagonal) pattern. The torque is 42 ft-lb (5.8 m-kg).
17 Torque the bolt holding the emergency brake cable backing plate to 15 ft-lb (2.1 m-kg) after threading the emergency brake cable through and installing the plate.
18 Thread the brake line back on to the wheel cylinder before installing the wheel cylinder mounting bolt and torquing it to 15 ft-lb (2.1 m-kg).
19 Torque the nut on the hydraulic fitting to 9 ft-lb (1.2 m-kg).
20 Continue brake drum reassembly as detailed above (Section 15).

17 Rear drum brakes – wheel cylinder rebuild

1   Clean the outer surfaces of the wheel cylinder body with brake fluid and wipe dry. Check the outer surfaces for evidence of cracking or galling.
2   Remove the dust cap and piston from one end. There is a lip on the dust cap which fits into a groove on the cylinder body. The piston may be pulled out (photo).
3   Remove the piston and dust cap from the other end. With a finger, push out the guides, spring and cups (photo).
4   Remove the bleed screw cap and the bleed screw.
5   Blow dry all orifices with compressed air if available, then wipe all edges with a lint free cloth. Remember that the vapour blown off the cylinder is brake fluid and is poisonous when inhaled.
6   Inspect the inner surfaces of the wheel cylinder for evidence of scoring, galling, or chattering. If any is found, it will be necessary to replace the unit.
7   Check the bleed screw for obstructions and clean it thoroughly. Replace the bleed screw and its rubber cap.
8   Open the wheel cylinder rebuild kit and lay out the new parts.
9   Lubricate the cylinder walls with brake fluid (photo).
10 Lubricate the new guides with brake fluid and place them on either end of the spring.
11 Lubricate the rubber cups and place them over the guide pieces. The cupped portions should face each other.
12 Press this entire assembly into one end of the cylinder taking care to properly seat the last cup in and ensuring that the sealing edge is not torn or cut during installation. Center these pieces in the cylinder (photo).
13 Install one piston and cover with the dust cover. The lip of the dust cover will slide into its groove easily if it is lubricated with brake fluid. Install the other piston and dust cover (photo).
14 Never rebuild a single wheel cylinder; both should be done at the same time for maximum braking efficiency.
15 When the brake drums are reassembled, the brake hydraulic system must be bled before using the vehicle.

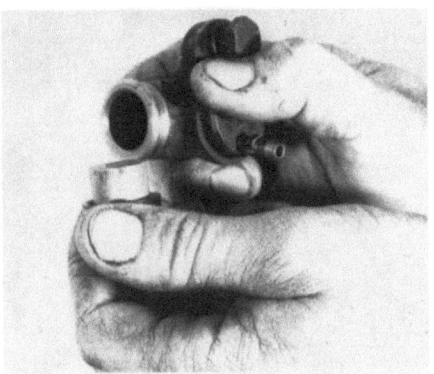

17.2 Removing the piston from the brake cylinder

17.3 The parts which must be removed from the cylinder

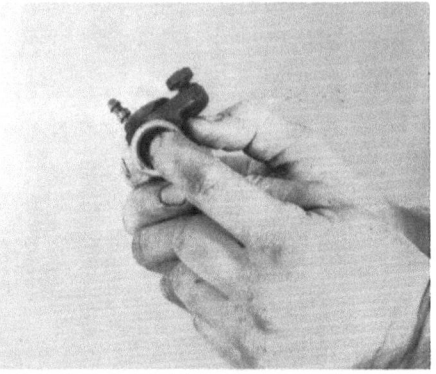

17.9 Lubricating the cylinder walls for re-assembly

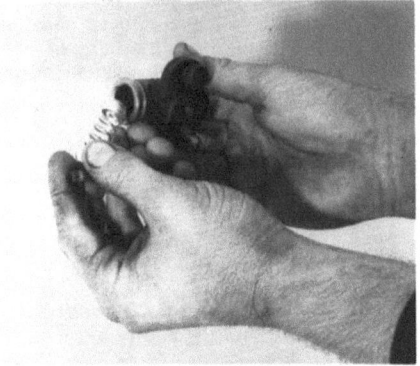

17.12 Installing all parts at the same end into the cylinder

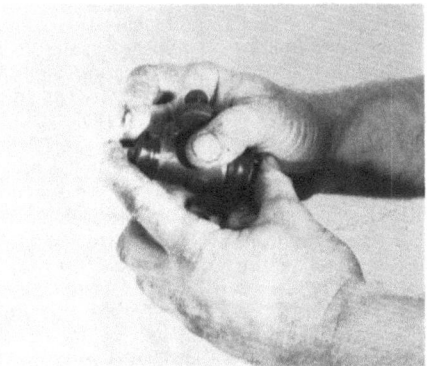

17.13 Installing the dust cover to complete the rebuild

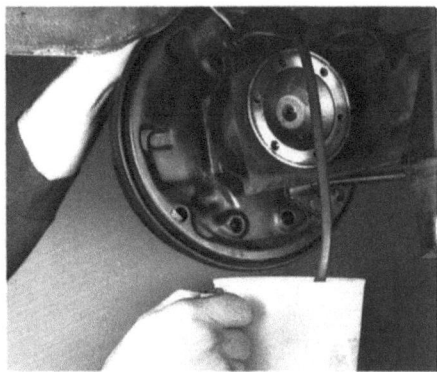

18.9 Bleeding the brake hydraulic system

18 Bleeding the brake hydraulic system

1   This is not a routine operation, and will only be required if the brake pedal feels spongy, or when the hydraulic fluid is being renewed by bleeding at the specified intervals. The spongy feel is usually caused by the presence of air in the hydraulic fluid. Air bubbles are highly elastic and compressible while the hydraulic fluid is not.

2   When work is performed to the hydraulic components at the ends of the system (calipers and wheel cylinders) it will be necessary to bleed only those particular items provided the directions on plugging the hydraulic lines and the proper precautions against system drainage have been followed.

3   Cleanliness is the key to this task. Brake hydraulic fluid is poisonous and removes paint. In addition the bleed screw nipples should thoroughly be wiped clean with a rag or paper towel before beginning the bleeding operation. This will prevent the introduction of dirt into the brake hydraulic system.

4   The following equipment will be required for the bleeding operation: a medium-size glass jar with a screw on cap; about 12 in (300 mm) of rubber or plastic tubing (clear plastic tubing works best) which will fit snugly over the bleeder screw nipple; a wrench of the proper size to fit the bleeder screw; enough new brake fluid of SAE J 1703 or DOT 3 specification to complete the bleeding procedure; and one additional person to assist in the bleeding.

5   The brake hydraulic fluid used in this task should come from a new container with a previously unbroken seal.

6   The brake bleeding procedure starts with the locating of the bleed screws, removing the rubber protection caps, and cleaning all dirt and grit from the nipples. The bleed screws are located on the rear, inboard side of the brake calipers and the top, inboard side of the wheel cylinders. Note again that it will only be necessary to bleed those sections of the brake hydraulic system which have just been

worked on.

7   Remove the silicone seal or plasticine plug from the cap on the brake fluid reservoir and top up the brake fluid reservoir. There are two sections of the reservoir, divided by a partial wall. Make sure that both sides of the reservoir are topped up.

8   The order for bleeding of the system is: Left-hand drive: right rear; left rear; right front; left front. Right-hand drive: left rear; right rear; left front; right front.

9   Pour about one inch (25 mm) of brake fluid into the jar. Submerge one end of the hose in the brake fluid and fit the other end to the appropriate nipple. Ensure that the hose is firmly held in place and that the nipple is fully covered by the hose (photo).

10 Have your assistant pump the brake pedal several times to build pressure in the system.

11 Open the bleed screw about one half turn, then have your assistant depress the pedal with a firm, sharp stroke. When the pedal is at full down travel, close the bleed screw and have your assistant raise the pedal.

12 Continue this procedure, pumping the brake pedal until firm, then opening the bleed screw until the stroke is completed. When two or three successive downward strokes of the brake pedal produce no more air bubbles in the brake fluid, the bleeding procedure is complete for that one hydraulic unit.

13 Do not allow the level of the fluid in the reservoir to fall below the 'Minimum' line as you will stand the risk of introducing air into the master cylinder and this will require bleeding all brake calipers and wheel cylinders again. When topping up the master cylinder reservoir, use new brake fluid. Never use the fluid which has been drained from the system into the glass jar.

14 Every two years or 30,000 miles, completely drain the brake hydraulic system and fill it with fresh fluid. In the event that bleeding the brakes does not cure spongy pedal symptoms, or if the

sponginess returns in a matter of weeks, carefully check all components of the brake hydraulic system for leaks, cracks, or breakages. Replace any hoses which are defective and rebuild any cylinders or calipers which show signs of bad seals (weeping or 'mist' covered).

15 A recent innovation in brake fluid is the DOT 5 specification. This silicone-based fluid is non-hygroscopic and does not damage paint. Porsche does not recommend this specification for the 924 braking system; however, if you make a personal decision to switch over, the entire brake hydraulic system must be thoroughly flushed with isopropyl alcohol or methylated spirits before introducing any brake fluid of a different type into the system.

16 Dispose of used brake fluid in a sealed container. It is illegal to dump out or bury containers holding brake fluid. Check with your local gas station or mechanic for proper disposal advice.

19 Emergency brake – adjustment

1   Make sure that the rear brake drums are properly adjusted (Section 15). This will require the raising of the vehicle and placing it on jack stands.
2 Pull the emegency brake lever up by two teeth in the ratchet assembly.
3   You should be able to turn the wheels, but only with a great

amount of force being required. If this isn't the case the emergency brake is either too tight (wheels cannot be turned at all) or too loose (wheels turn too easily).
4   Remove the driver's side seat (Chapter 12). This is not absolutely necessary, but the seat is held by only four nuts and the seat removal will cut your work time by over half.
5   Pull back the carpeting at the end of the emergency brake. Locate the locknut, adjusting nut, and the yoke which are attached to the end of the cable.
6   Loosen the locknut and adjust the cable tension until the rear wheels can be just turned with a great deal of force being applied to the rear wheels with the ratchet set at two clicks.
7   Torque the locknut to 6 ft-lb (0.85 m-kg).
8   Replace the carpeting.
9   Replace the seat.
10 Lower the vehicle from the jack stands.

20 Emergency brake – lever removal and installation

1   The emergency brake (handbrake) lever need only be removed when the ratchet mechanism is worn. It is not necessary to remove this item at any other time.
2   Remove the driver's seat. This is not necessary, but it will significantly reduce working time on this task.

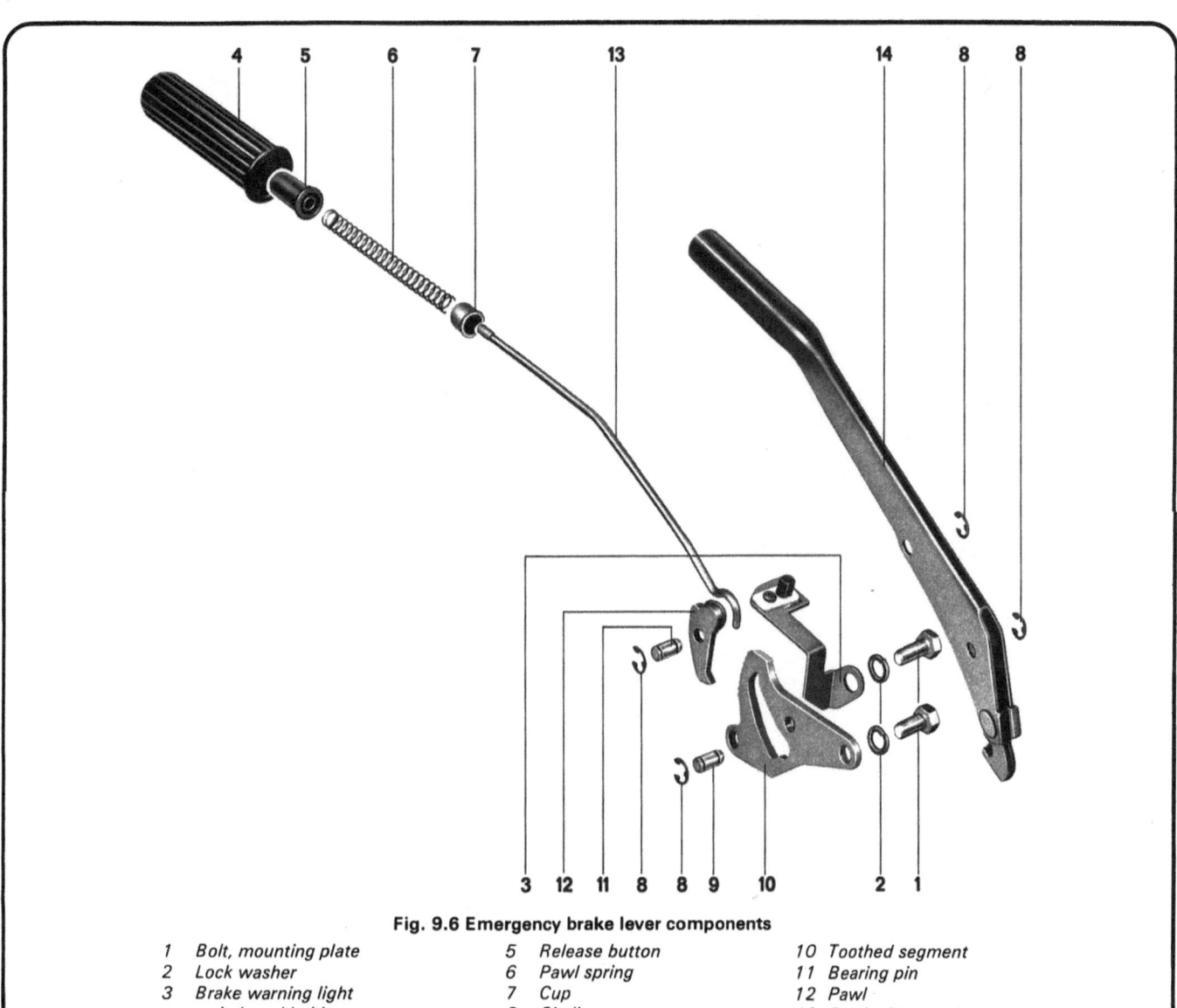

Fig. 9.6 Emergency brake lever components

1 Bolt, mounting plate	5 Release button	10 Toothed segment
2 Lock washer	6 Pawl spring	11 Bearing pin
3 Brake warning light switch and holder	7 Cup	12 Pawl
4 Hand grip	8 Circlip	13 Pawl release rod
	9 Bearing pin	14 Emergency brake lever

3 Pull back the carpeting around the lever assembly base.
4 Disconnect the spade connector for the emergency brake light switch.
5 Remove the two bolts which hold the toothed segment to the vehicle body.
6 Remove the lower bolt which holds the shoulder strap to the body.
7 Lift the lever assembly away from the body and unhook the lever end from the cable yoke.
8 Installation is the reverse of removal.
9 Torque the two bolts which attach the toothed segment to the body to 15 ft-lb (2.1 m-kg).

21 Emergency brake – lever stripdown and rebuild

1 Remove the inboard spring clips from each of the bearing pins. Push the pins out and remove the toothed section.
2 Remove the second bearing pin and the ratchet pawl.
3 Remove the grip from the lever. This is a press-on fit.
4 Remove the ratchet release push button and actuating rod from the lever. Unscrew the push button and separate the button, spring and retaining collar from the actuating rod.
5 Assembly is the reverse of stripdown. Make sure to lubricate all sliding and rubbing parts before assembly.

22 Emergency brake – cable replacement

1 The cables which connect the emergency brake lever to the brake actuating levers on the rear brake drums consist of woven wire cables which run inside armoured outer housings. Pulling up on the brake lever pulls on the cable, which in turn pulls on an equalizing yoke. The action of this yoke allows both rear brake shoes (one on each side of the vehicle) to be pulled against their respective brake drums with equal pressure.
2 This assembly must be replaced as a unit. Causes for replacement include inner cable breakage, seizing of the inner cable due to grit or dirt, or stretching of the inner cable to the point that adjustment at the yoke on the brake lever has no effect on emergency brake performance.
3 To remove the emergency brake cables, raise the vehicle and place it on jack stands. Remove the rear wheels and rear brake drums (Section 15). Disconnect the cable ends from the brake shoe actuating levers, remove the brake cable backing plate and pull the cables through the brake drum backing plate.
4 Remove the driver's seat, pull back the carpeting, and unbolt the locknut and adjusting nut from the cable end. Remove the cable and unhook the yoke.
5 Crawling beneath the vehicle, locate the point at which the cable assembly exits the body. This should look like a metal plug with the other cable housing coming out of the center. Pull sharply to loosen the plug and pull the cable assembly from the body.
6 The two branches of the cable assembly are held in place on the body by two clips. These clips are located beneath the body and are mounted on the vertical wall behind the passenger jump seats. Carefully pry these clips open and remove the remainder of the cable assembly.
7 Installation of the new cable assembly is the reverse of the removal procedure.

Chapter 10 Suspension

For modifications, and information applicable to later models, see Supplement at end of manual

Contents

Specifications

Front suspension

Type...	MacPherson strut, single control arm (wishbone) and spring strut per side.
Strut type...	Boge or Koni (Koni standard 1980 – on)

Stabilizer bar

1976 – 1977	20 mm (optional)
1978	22 mm (optional)
1979	23 mm (optional)
1980	21 mm (standard) 23 mm (optional)
1981	20 mm (standard) 21.5 mm (optional)

Alignment and adjusting values

Total toe (vehicle weight on wheels, suspension not compressed) ...	+'10 ± 5'
Camber	
1976 – 1977	–20' ± 10'
1978 – on	–20' ± 15'
Maximum camber difference between left and right.............	10'
Camber difference angle at 20° lock	–1° ± 20'
Castor..	2°45' ± 30'
Maximum difference between left and right caster	30'

Rear suspension

Type...	Independent with rear wheels suspended on diagonal control arms (trailing arms). Suspension controlled by torsion bars mounted in a transverse tube. Shock absorbers are of the double acting hydraulic type.
Shock absorber type	Fichtel & Sachs or Boge
optional type	Koni

Torsion bar

standard, 1976 – 1979	22 mm
optional, 1978 – 1979	23.5 mm
standard, 1980 – on	23.5 mm

Stabilizer bar

1976 – 1977	18 mm (optional)
1978 – on	14 mm (standard on 23.5 mm torsion bars)
	14 mm (optional on 22 mm torsion bars)

Alignment and adjusting values

Total toe	0° ± 10'
Maximum difference between left and right...................	10'
Camber	–0° 30' ± 0° 10'
Maximum difference between left and right..................	30'

Spring plate settings
    22 mm torsion bar without stabilizer bar
        1976 – 1977 .... 23°
        1978 – on .... 23° 40'
        23.5 mm torsion bars with stabilizer all years.............. 19°
    Maximum difference between left and right..................... 0.5°
    Height adjustment
        1976 – 1977 .... 1° change in spring setting = 20' change in rear wheel camber
        1978 – on
        Center of torsion bar below wheel center line .... 8.00 to 10 mm
        Maximum difference between left and right................ 10 mm

NOTE: a change in spring plate inclination 1° means a change of approximately:
      6 mm change in car height for 22 mm torsion bars
      5 mm change in car height for 23.5 mm torsion bars

Torque specifications

Front suspension	ft–lb	m–kg
Control arm forward, inboard pivot bolt-to-cross member ...	40 to 54	5.5 to 7.5
Control arm rear, inboard pivot clamp bolts	30	4.2
Control arm-to-steering knuckle............................	36 to 43	5.0 to 6.0
Ball joint mounting bolts..................................	18	2.5
MacPherson strut, upper mount..............................	15 to 21	2.1 to 2.9
MacPherson strut-to-steering knuckle	51 to 72	7.0 to 10.0
MacPerson strut, top nut	56 to 58	7.7 to 8.0
Stabilizer clamp-to-body	9	1.3
Stabilizer-to-control arm	11 to 18	1.5 to 2.5
Rear suspension (early style)		
Torsion bar tube-to-body	54	7.5
Torsion tube end plate bolts	25	3.5
Control arm pivot bolt	44	6.1
Control arm-to-spring plate	76 to 90	10.5 to 12.5
Shock absorber lower mount	44	6.1
Shock absorber upper mount	44	6.1
Axle shaft splined bolts..................................	30	4.2
Rear suspension (late style)		
Mounting flange bolts	33	4.6
Mounting flange-to-body...................................	51	7.0
Mounting flange-to-torque strut	33	4.6
Upper torque strut-to-body	33	4.6
Lower torque strut mount-to-body	33	4.6
Lower torque strut-to-strut mount	17	2.3
Camber eccentric on spring plate	65	9.0
Control arm-to-spring plate	75	10.3
Control arm-to-torsion bar hub	177	24.5
Stabilizer bar shackle-to-spring plate and stabilizer bar end.	33	4.6
Stabilizer bar mounting clamp	17	2.3

1 Front suspension – general description

1   The front suspension of the Porsche 924 is of the MacPherson strut type and is considered to be fully independent.
2   Road shocks are transmitted through the wheels to the steering knuckle. The up and down movement of the wheel is controlled by the arc of the control arm and the movement is damped by the hydraulic MacPherson strut.
3   The front suspension has few rebuildable parts and most work in this area will be replacement tasks.

2 Negative roll radius

1   A special design feature of the 924's suspension is the negative roll characteristic, which, in combination with the dual diagonal braking system (Chapter 9) ensures straight line braking under adverse conditions.
2   An explanation of the negative roll radius characteristic is best shown in figures. Examine Figs. 10.2 through 10.3.
3   Fig. 10.2a shows that the front wheel pivots around axis 'a'. If the angle of the suspension is vertical, the pivot point would be immediately below 'a', and the distance 'r' (a + b) is the roll radius.
4   When the pivot axis is vertical (Fig. 10.2b), the line through the suspension and the pivot point falls inside the centerline of the tire and the roll radius 'r' is positive.
5   In the case of the 924, the suspension is at a sharper angle to the outside and the pivot point strikes the ground at a point outside the centerline of the tire. This is negative roll radius. (Fig. 10.2c)
6   Negative roll radius works in the following way: in an instance where one front brake works better than the other (as in the case of the failure in one of the braking circuits), the working brake will pivot the car to the side of that brake. In Fig. 10.3a, the right front brake is working better than the left. The vehicle will try to pull to the right. The vehicle in this figure has positive roll radius, which in combination with the better braking on the right throws the whole vehicle into a right-hand turn.
7   In Fig. 10.3b, the vehicle has the same better-working right front brake, but negative roll radius. The right brake will cause the wheel to turn right, but leverage on the negative roll radius will cause the wheel to turn left. These two forces cancel out one another and the vehicle stops in a straight line.

3 Suspension alignment and adjustment

1   The alignment and adjustment of the Porsche 924's suspension requires special tools and equipment beyond the financial capabilities of many small garages as well as the home mechanic.

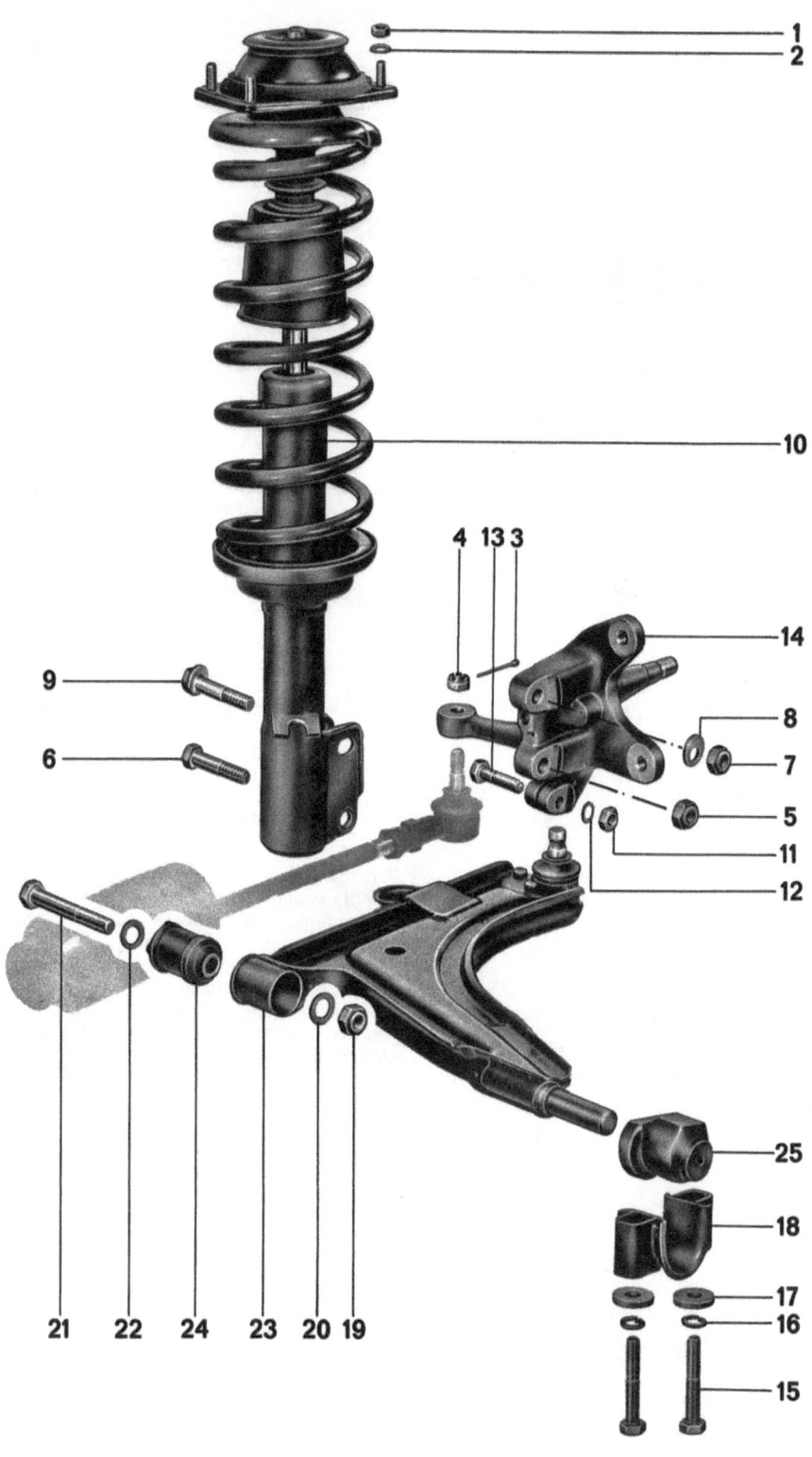

Fig. 10.1 Components of the front suspension

1	Nut	8	Eccentric disc	14	Steering knuckle	20	Flat washer
2	Flat washer	9	Eccentric bolt	15	Bolt	21	Bolt
3	Cotter pin	10	MacPherson strut	16	Lock washer	22	Flat washer
4	Castellated nut	11	Nut	17	Flat washer	23	Control arm
5	Self-locking nut	12	Lock washer	18	Clamp	24	Rubber/metal mount, front
6	Bolt	13	Bolt	19	Self-locking nut	25	Rubber/metal mount, rear
7	Self-locking nut						

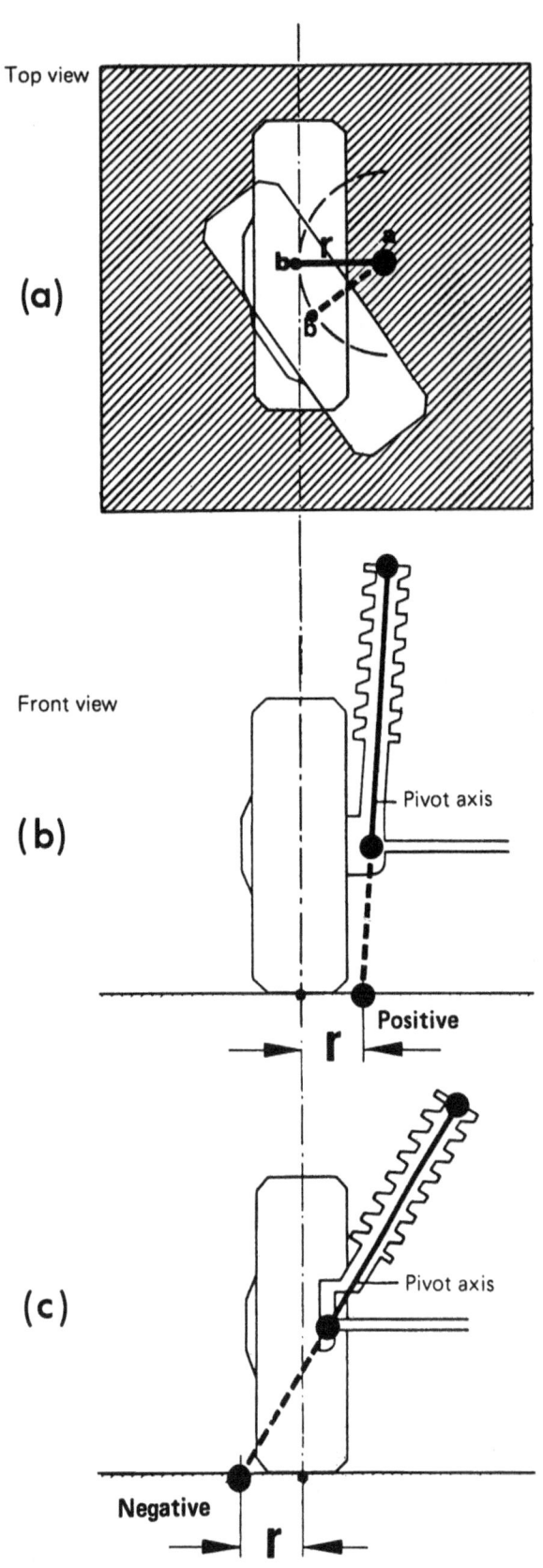

Top view

(a)

Front view

(b)

Pivot axis

r   **Positive**

(c)

Pivot axis

Negative   r

Fig. 10.2 Diagrammatic views of steering geometry

    a   The axis of front wheel pivoting
    b   Positive roll radius
    c   Negative roll radius

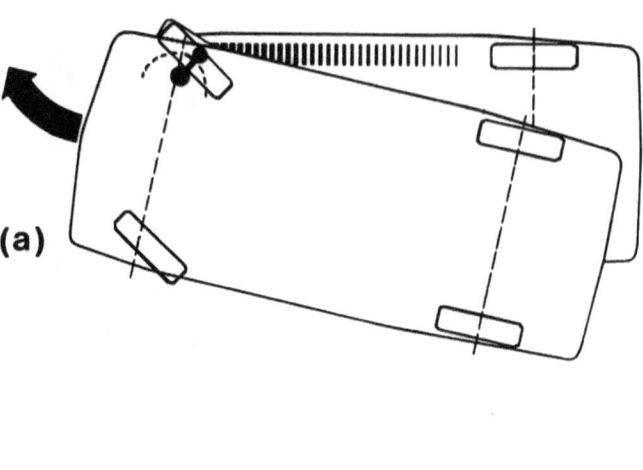

(a)

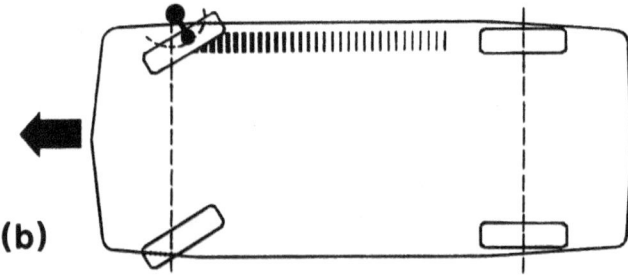

(b)

**Fig. 10.3 Diagrammatic views of vehicle control using negative
and positive roll radius**

    a   Positive roll radius   *b   Negative roll radius*

2   This chapter gives you the basic information necessary to work on the suspension of your vehicle and to make the basic adjustments which will allow you safely to drive your car to a reputable alignment shop. Unless stated in the text, the tasks below will not require a visit to a specialist.
3   Do not operate your vehicle for any extended period of time after performing these tasks without having the alignment of your wheels checked (unless otherwise noted, of course). Failure to do so may lead to unusual wear patterns in your tires, shortened tire life, and the possibility of steering and control problems.

4   Control arms – checking

1   The following task is performed with the control arms installed.
2   If you cannot lie comfortably beneath the vehicle when it is sitting on its wheels, raise the vehicle and place it on jack stands.
3   Inspect the area around the round hole in the 90 degree corner of the control arm for bends and creases. If any are found, front end damage has occurred to your car and the front suspension parts should be thoroughly checked.
4   Check the top, bottom, and leading edges of the control arm with a straight edge. These edges should be straight. If you are in doubt as to the straightness of these edges, compare your control arm (removed) with a new unit, or have a check performed by a qualified Porsche mechanic (photo).

5   Ball joints – checking

1   Raise the vehicle and place it on jack stands.
2   Make sure that the front wheels are pointing straight ahead. Make any necessary corrections.
3   You will need a socket from a socket wrench set and a large screwdriver (about 18 in in length) for this test. The socket and screwdriver should just slide into the space between the wheel rim and the ball joint without putting any pressure on the ball joint.
4   Insert a sliding caliper between the upper edge of the control arm and the lower edge of the steering knuckle mounting bolt.

4.4 Checking the control arm edges for straightness

5.5 Checking the play in the ball joints

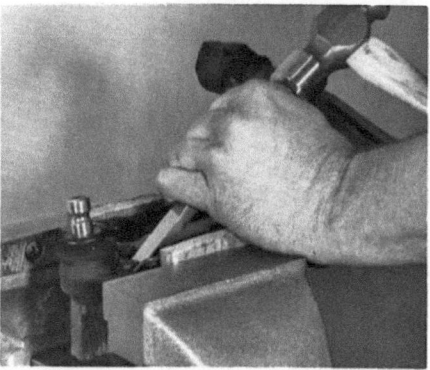

6.4 Removing ball joint rivets with a chisel

7.6 Removing the rear pivot clamp

7.7 Removing the self-locking nut from the forward, inboard, pivot

7.8a Removing the clamping bolt and nut from the steering knuckle

Record the measured distance.
5   Replace the caliper in the same location and lever out the ball joint free play by pressing down on the end of the screwdriver (photo).
6   New ball joints should have no free play. If the difference between the first distance measured and the second distance measured with the free play levered out is greater than 2.5 mm (0.10 in) the ball joint must be replaced.

6   Ball joints - replacement

1   Remove the control arm (Section 7).
2   Place the control arm in the protected jaws of a vise with the pivot end of the ball joint facing up.
3   Drill through the rivets with a 6 mm (¼ in) drill. Do not drill through the control arm. If you elongate any of the ball joint mounting holes in the control arm, you must replace the control arm as well.
4   Chisel off the rivet heads. Do not groove or scratch the control arm. These scratches and grooves will become the site of fatigue cracks and breaks. Replace a deeply grooved control arm (photo).
5   Drive out the remaining rivet pieces with a soft metal drift and remove the old ball joint.
6   Install the new ball joint with the pivot end of the ball joint facing up.
7   Install the mounting bolts for the new ball joint through the top of the control arm and install the nuts on the bottom.
8   Torque the nuts to 18 ft-lb (2.5 m-kg). One flat of the bolt heads must face the ball joint squarely. Adjust the bolts before applying torque.
9   If the ball joint is the only item to be replaced, the control arm may simply be reinstalled without any adjustment to the caster and camber.

7   Front control arms - removal, stripdown, rebuild, installation

1   Disconnect the negative lead from the battery.
2   Raise the vehicle and place it on jack stands.
3   Remove the wheel (Chapter 9).
4   Remove the disc brake caliper and hang it out of the way (Chapter 9).
5   Remove the disc brake rotor and dust guard (Chapter 9).
6   Remove the mounting bolts and clamp on the rear, inboard pivot (photo).
7   Remove the bolt and self locking nut from the forward, inboard pivot. Dispose of the self locking nut and replace it with a new one when installing the control arm (photo).
8   Remove the clamping bolt and nut from the steering knuckle and remove the control arm. If the nut on the clamping bolt is of the self locking type, replace the nut. Some versions have a standard nut and lock washer instead (photos).
9   The bonded bushings must be pressed from the control arm with an hydraulic press. If there is no evidence of bonding separation between the rubber and metal portions of the bush and the metal portions are not elongated, do not remove them.
10 Installation is the reverse of the removal procedure.
11 If the new rubber/metal bonded bushes are being installed, press the forward bush into the control arm so that the rubber beading on the bush faces forward when installed. The rear bush is pressed on with the round portion against the control arm and the square section facing upward when installed in the vehicle.
12 Torque the bolts on the rear, inboard pivot clamp to 30 ft-lb (4.2 m-kg).
13 Torque the pivot bolt's self locking nut at the forward bushing to 40 to 50 ft-lb (5.5 to 7.5 m-kg). Remember to use a new self locking nut.
14 Torque the clamping nut on the steering knuckle to 36 to 43 ft-lb (5 to 6 m-kg). Remember to use a new self locking nut.

7.8b Removing the control arm

8.11 Checking the tie rod boss on the steering knuckle for roundness

9.3a Removing the clamps from the stabilizer bar

9.3b Removing the stabilizer bar end pieces

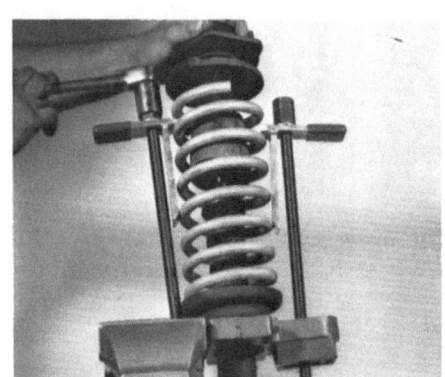

11.2 The strut compressor assembled and placed in a vise

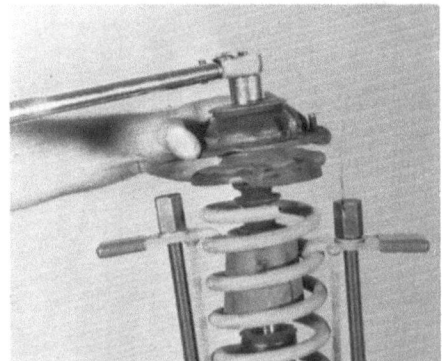

11.4 Removing the self-locking nut

15 Consult Chapter 9 for the remainder of the brake and wheel installation directions.

8 Steering knuckle – removal, inspection, installation

1 Disconnect the negative lead from the battery.
2 Raise the vehicle and place it on jack stands.
3 Remove the front wheels (Chapter 9).
4 Remove the disc brake caliper and hang it in an out of the way location (Chapter 9).
5 Remove the disc brake rotor and dust shield (Chapter 9).
6 Disconnect the tie rod end (Chapter 8).
7 The upper mounting bolt on the MacPherson strut is an eccentric cam. Paint or scribe a line across the cam and the strut mounting plate on both the bolt head and nut sides of the plate. Remove the nuts from the two MacPherson strut mounting bolts, but do not remove the bolts. These two nuts are self locking. Dispose of them and replace both of them with new nuts upon installation.
8 Remove the clamping bolt and nut from the control arm (ball joint) mount. Dispose of the self locking nut and install a new nut on assembly.
9 Hold the steering knuckle with one hand while extracting the bolts from the MacPherson strut mounting plate with the other. Remove the steering knuckle.
10 Inspect the steering knuckle for cracking and gouges. Replace the steering knuckle as necessary.
11 To test the roundness of the tie rod mounting boss, place a steel rule against the machined edge of the steering knuckle, immediately beneath the spindle. Place a caliper on the steering knuckle with one edge against the inside edge of the steel rule and the other against the farther side of the tie rod boss. The caliper should be parallel to the steering knuckle and should pass through the hole in the tie rod boss at its diameter. The steering knuckle is still useable if the distance measured in the above manner is as follows:

    1976 - 1979: 30.20 to 30.70 mm (1.19 to 1.21 in).
    1979 - on: 28.40 to 28.90 mm (1.12 to 1.14 in).

Double check your work and replace the steering knuckle as necessary (photo).
12 Installation of the steering knuckle is the reverse of the removal procedure.
13 Install the steering knuckle and all bolts. Remember to use new self locking nuts on the appropriate bolts.
14 Set the eccentric cams back in their marked locations and torque the nuts on the MacPherson strut mounting plate to 51 to 72 ft-lb (7 to 10 m-kg).
14 Torque the nut on the ball joint clamping bolt to 36 to 43 ft-lb (5 to 6 m-kg).
15 Install the tie rod end and torque the castellated nut according to the instructions in Chapter 8.
16 Install the front disc brake components and the wheels according to the instructions in Chapter 9.
17 Aligning the eccentric cam adjusters with their previous marks will give you basic camber and toe settings so that the car may be safely driven to a qualified alignment specialist for final adjustment. Do not operate your car on these settings for long, as unusual wear patterns in the tires and problems with the steering and control of your vehicle may be the result.

9 Steering stabilizer – removal and installation

1 The steering stabilizer was a piece of optional equipment for all models through the 1979 production year. 1980 and later models, including the Turbo, have them as standard equipment.
2 The steering stabilizer is held in place by two clamps which hold it to the body inside a rubber piece and two end pieces which attach it to the control arms.
3 Removal of the stabilizer bar is accomplished by removing first the four clamp bolts from the body and then the two pieces at the control arm (photos).
4 The four clamp bolts are torqued to 9 ft-lb (1.3 m-kg) and the control arm ends to 11 to 18 ft-lb (1.5 to 2.5 m-kg).

10 MacPherson strut - removal and installation

1 Disconnect the negative lead from the battery.

2 Loosen each of the strut mounting bolts in the engine compartment about two turns. Do not loosen them excessively and do not remove them.

3 Raise the vehicle and place it on jack stands.

4 Remove the front wheels.

5 Pull the rubber brake hose holder from the clip on the strut.

6 The upper bolt on the strut mounting plate is an eccentric cam, as is the washer on the nut side. Scribe or paint a thin line on the cam and mounting plate for reassembly purposes. This will give you a general alignment setting.

7 Remove the self locking nuts and bolts from the MacPherson strut mounting plate. Dispose of the self locking nuts and replace them with new ones when installing the strut. Pull the strut free from the mounting plate.

8 Loosen the upper nuts on the wheel wells in a cross pattern about two turns at a time to lower the strut squarely out of the body and prevent damage to the threads of the studs. It is best to have an assistant holding and controlling the strut, but a single person can remove the strut by holding it in one hand and removing nuts with the other.

9 Remove the strut.

10 Installation is the reverse of the removal procedure.

11 Locate the four mounting studs in the holes on the wheel well and install the nuts. It will be easier to have an assistant hold the strut in place, but one person can do this task alone. Tighten the nuts about two turns each in a cross pattern until the nuts are snug and the upper mount is firmly in place. At this time do not tighten the nuts to the specified torque; leave them loose enough to allow for a bit of 'give' in the plate.

12 Slide the mounting plate onto the steering knuckle and install the new self locking nuts finger tight. Align the marks on the eccentric cams with the marks on the mounting plate and torque the nut to 51 to 72 ft-lb (7 to 10 m-kg). Inspect the alignment of the two marks and make any necessary corrections before applying the same torque to the self locking nut on the lower bolt.

13 Now torque the upper mount nuts to 15 to 21 lb-ft (2.1 to 2.9 m-kg). Tighten and torque them in a cross pattern.

14 Push the rubber brake hose grommet into the clip on the strut body.

15 Replace the wheel according to the instructions in Chapter 9.

16 The basic adjustment of the eccentric cams and aligning them with their old marks will give you basic camber and toe settings so that the car may be safely driven to a qualified alignment specialist for final adjustment. Do not operate your car for long on these settings as unusual wear patterns in the tires and problems with the steering and control of your vehicle may be the result.

11 MacPherson strut - stripdown and rebuild

1 Disassembly of MacPherson struts requires a special type of spring compressor. If you do not have this tool, do not attempt to jury-rig other tools for this purpose. Most experiments of that type have harmful or fatal results. Take the struts to a local garage which has the proper tool and have them disassemble the struts for you. The cost will be minimal and the risk nil.

2 If you do not have the proper tool, check to see whether it is the type which requires that the tool or the strut be placed in the protected jaws of a vise. Place whichever is appropriate in the vise and install your compressor according to the manufacturer's instructions (photo).

3 Compress the spring until the spring retainer can be moved approximately ¼ in up and down.

4 Loosen the self locking nut. Dispose of this nut and replace it with a new one when reassembling the unit (photo).

5 Remove the stop, rubber seal, and bearing flange.

6 Remove the spring compressor. Ease the pressure from the spring evenly.

7 Remove the bearing, spring retainer, and the spring. This will give access to the rubber boot and protective sleeve which may also be removed.

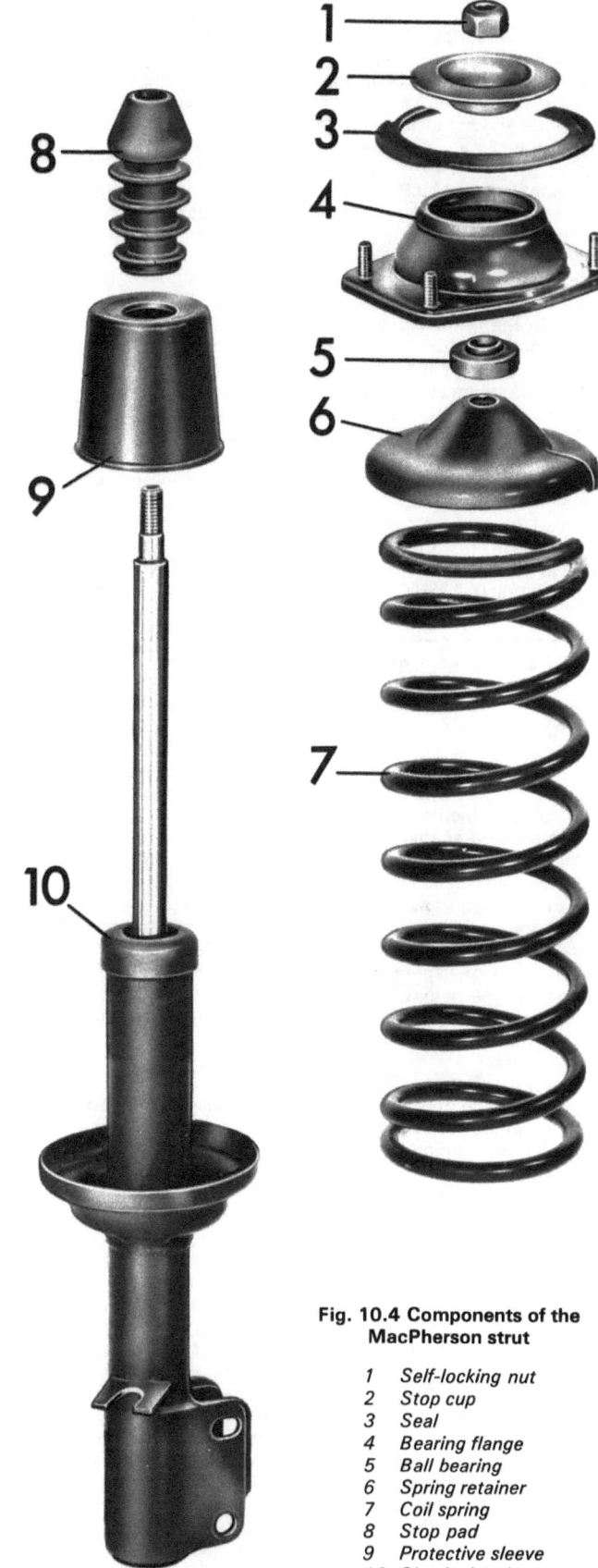

Fig. 10.4 Components of the MacPherson strut

1 Self-locking nut
2 Stop cup
3 Seal
4 Bearing flange
5 Ball bearing
6 Spring retainer
7 Coil spring
8 Stop pad
9 Protective sleeve
10 Shock absorber

8   Check the damping action of the strut shock absorber by pulling and pushing on the piston rod. The shock absorber must be right side up (piston rod at the top) and the pressure up and down should be kept as constant as possible. The piston rod should move firmly and evenly throughout its entire stroke without sticking, speeding up, or binding. If you are in doubt as to the performance of your shock absorbers, compare with a new strut. Remember that new units must be pumped several times before they are working properly and the action must be the same all the way to the end of the stroke of the piston. Worn strut shock absorbers make a rumbling sound in use.
9   Assembly of the MacPherson strut is the opposite of stripdown.
10 Make sure that the springs you have are matched according to rate. They will have red or green stripes in several combinations, depending on the rate and weight value. The stripe combinations should match. Replace as necessary.
11 The coil springs are installed with the straight-cut wire end installed in the lower spring retainer.
12 Slide the protective sleeve and the rubber boot on to the strut's piston rod and slide them down as far as they will go.
13 Install the spring compressor and compress the spring to a point approximately equal to the point it was when you disassembled the strut.
14 Install the spring retainer and place the rounded end of the spring wire in the depression in the retainer. Install the bearing, bearing flange, seal, and stop.
15 Thread the new self locking nut on to the end of the piston rod and tighten down with a wrench. Loosen the spring compressor slightly to provide resistance to the nut. Torque the self locking nut to 56 to 58 ft-lb (7.7 to 8.0 m-kg).

12   Rear suspension – general description

NOTE: Review this section before beginning work on your vehicle's rear suspension.
1   There are two types of rear suspension used in the 924 models. They are quite similar in design and performance. Basically, the rear suspension consists of control arms (sometimes called trailing arms), which are connected to the wheel hubs at one end and torsion bars at the other. The spring of the torsion bars is controlled by hydraulic shock absorbers. With the same assembly on each rear wheel, suspension action is independent.
2   There are two variations on the above design. Both can be removed and installed using a little common sense, and by following the exploded figures and the directions. The major difference between the two suspension types is that the later style must be adjusted for ride height out of the chassis before installation. A separate section is provided for that information. A description of the two variations follows immediately below.

Early style, 1976 - 1978 (Fig. 10.5)
3   The early style of 924 rear suspension is solidly mounted to the body. The spring plates are of a single-piece design and the spring plate cover bolts directly to the end of the torsion bar carrier tube.
4   This style of rear suspension has its beginnings in the Volkswagen Beetle and is a proven design.

Late style, 1978-on (Fig. 10.6)
5   The late style rear suspension is actually a modification of the previous design. It utilizes a two-piece spring plate with cam type adjusters, and an enlarged spring plate cover which bolts to the end of the torsion bar carrier tube and also has a long arm which bolts to a plate on the carrier tube. This prevents twisting of the carrier tube under load.
6   The new rear suspension also is rubber mounted to the chassis. Rubber mounts are located on the torsion bar carrier tube mounting points as well as the four anti-torque arms (two at the ends of the carrier tube and two farther inboard). This design modification allows additional dampening of suspension vibrations transmitted to the body without the problem of additional flexing of the suspension components under load.
7   The rear suspension has specific settings for caster and camber. Whenever you remove a major component from the rear suspension or adjust the ride height, have your alignment checked by a qualified specialist. The rule of thumb to use in determining whether or

not to see an alignment specialist after working on your vehicle's suspension is: see a specialist after the removal or replacement of any item between the brake backing plates, except the shock absorbers.

13   Shock absorbers – inspection

1   The most common test of the shock absorber's damping is simply to bounce the rear corners of the vehicle several times and observe whether or not the car stops bouncing once the action is stopped by you. A slight rebound and settling indicates good damping, but if the vehicle continues to bounce several times, the shock absorbers must be replaced.
2   If your shock absorbers stand up to the bounce test, crawl beneath your car and visually inspect the shock body for signs of fluid leakage, punctures or deep dents in the metal of the body, and that the shock absorber is straight from several angles. If the piston rod is bent, you will not be able to see that it is. A bend in the shock body or signs of the upper portion of the shock body rubbing on the lower section will let you know. Replace any shock absorber which is leaking or damaged, in spite of proper damping indicated in the bounce test.
3   When you have removed a shock absorber, pull the piston rod out and push it back in several times to check for smooth operation throughout the travel of the piston rod. Replace the shock absorber if it gives any signs of hard or soft spots in the piston travel.
4   When you install a new shock absorber, pump the piston rod fully in and out several times to lubricate the seals and fill the hydraulic sections of the unit.

14   Shock absorbers – removal and installation

1   Disconnect the negative lead from the battery.
2   Raise the vehicle and place it on jack stands.
3   Place a jack beneath the control arm at the point where the spring plate is bolted. Do not raise the jack as yet.
4   Remove the nut from the upper mounting bolt of the shock absorber. Raise the control arm until the upper mounting bolt can be pulled out of its hole (photo).
5   Compress the shock absorber to its shortest length.
6   Remove the nut and bolt from the lower shock absorber mount. Remove the shock absorber by lifting it out from between the mounts (photos).
7   Installation is the reverse of the removal procedure.
8   Make sure that the mounting bolt nuts have lockwashers installed. Torque the nuts to 44 ft-lb (6.1 m-kg).
9   Always replace your shock absorbers in pairs.

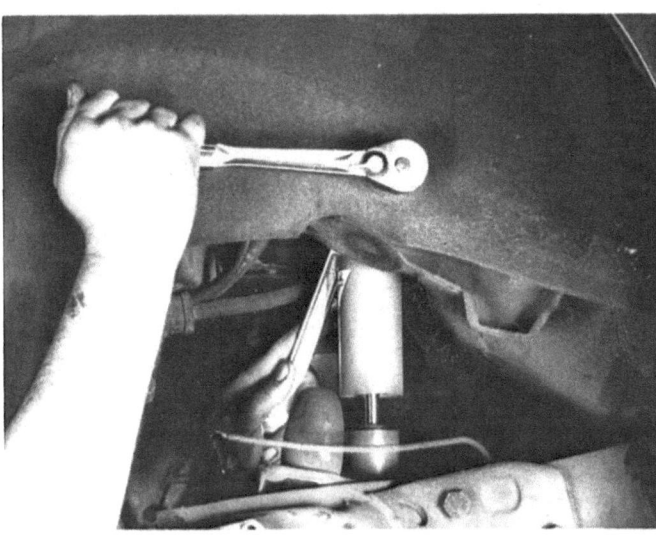

14.4 Removing the upper shock absorber mounting bolt

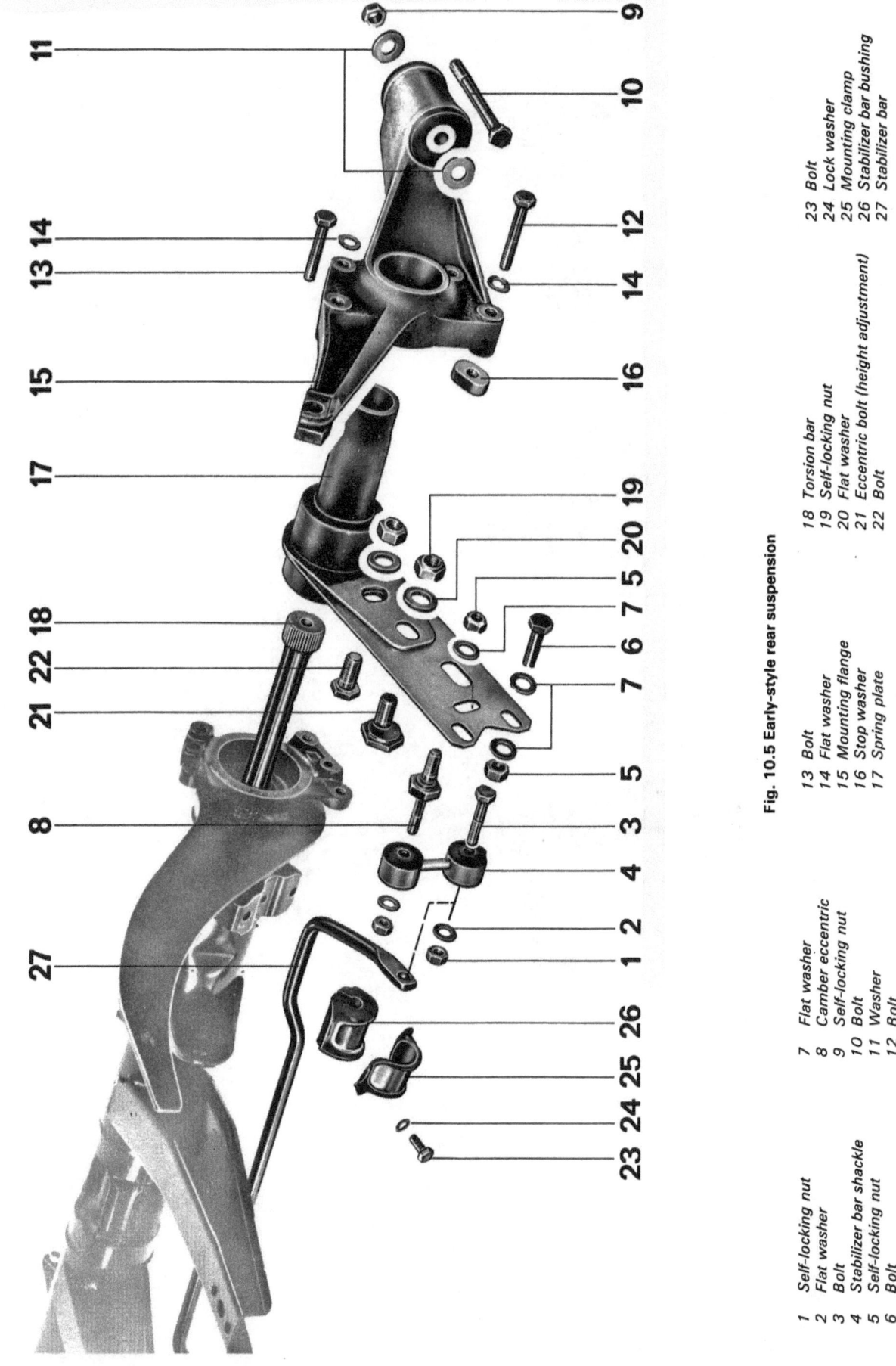

Fig. 10.5 Early-style rear suspension

1 Self-locking nut
2 Flat washer
3 Bolt
4 Stabilizer bar shackle
5 Self-locking nut
6 Bolt

7 Flat washer
8 Camber eccentric
9 Self-locking nut
10 Bolt
11 Washer
12 Bolt

13 Bolt
14 Flat washer
15 Mounting flange
16 Stop washer
17 Spring plate

18 Torsion bar
19 Self-locking nut
20 Flat washer
21 Eccentric bolt (height adjustment)
22 Bolt

23 Bolt
24 Lock washer
25 Mounting clamp
26 Stabilizer bar bushing
27 Stabilizer bar

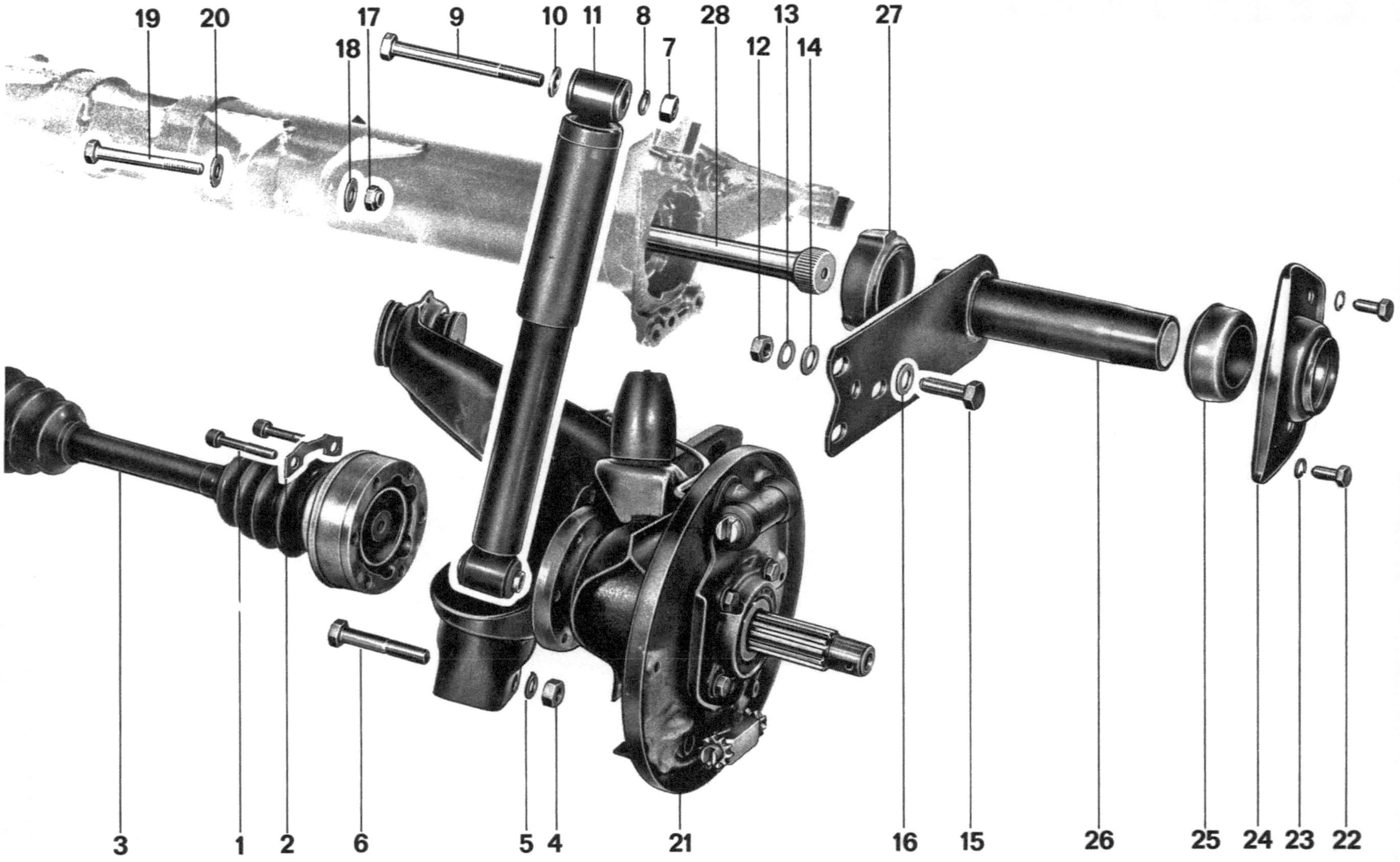

Fig. 10.6 Late-style rear suspension

1 Phillips head screw
2 Plate
3 Rear axle shaft
4 Nut
5 Lock washer
6 Bolt

7 Nut
8 Lock washer
9 Bolt
10 Flat washer
11 Shock absorber
12 Nut

13 Lock washer
14 Flat washer
15 Hex head screw
16 Flat washer
17 Self-locking nut
18 Flat washer

19 Bolt
20 Flat washer
21 Trailing arm
22 Bolt
23 Lock washer

24 Cover
25 Rubber mount, outer
26 Spring strut
27 Rubber mount, inner
28 Torsion bar

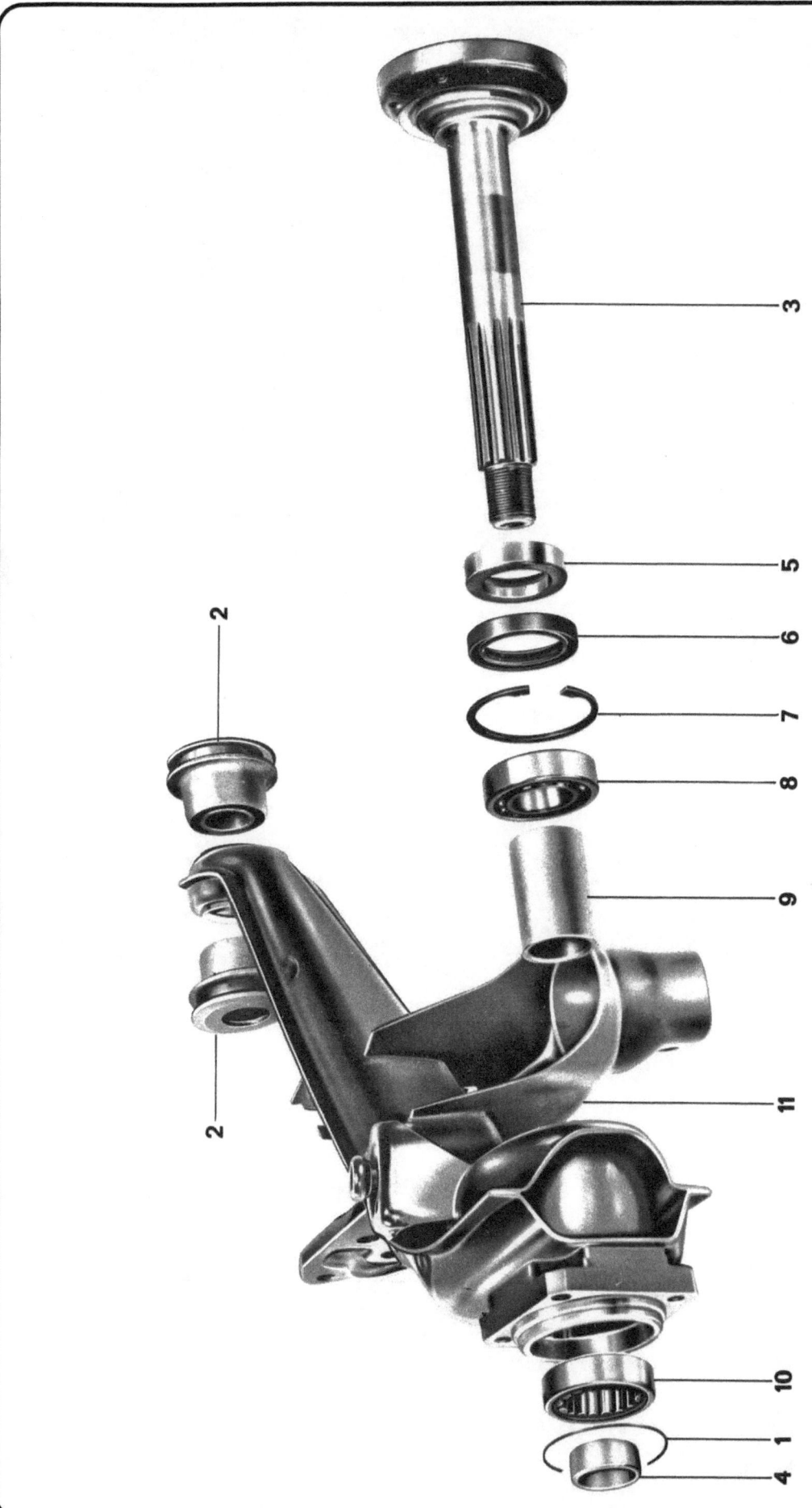

Fig. 10.7 Components of the rear control arm

1	O-ring	5	Spacer, inner	10 Roller bearing
2	Rubber bushings	6	Seal	11 Trailing arm
		7	Circlip	
3	Rear wheel shaft	8	Grooved ball bearing	
4	Bearing inner race	9	Spacer	

14.6a Removing the lower shock absorber mounting bolt

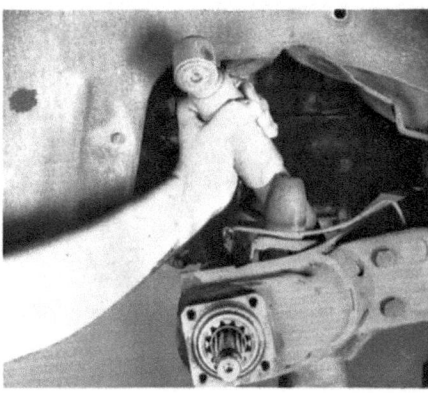

14.6b Removing the compressed shock absorber

15.5 Disconnecting the outboard end of the driveshaft

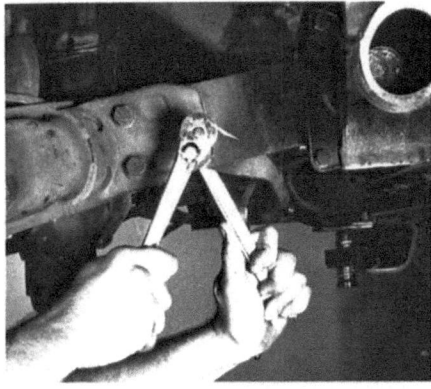

15.7 Loosening the nuts on the spring plate

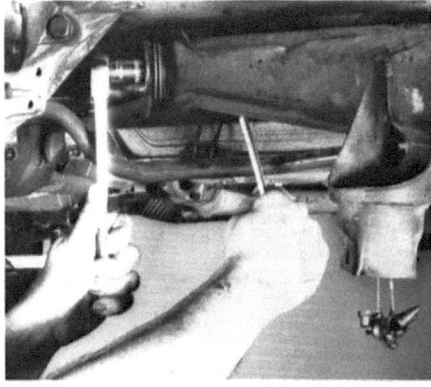

15.9 Removing the self-locking nut from the inboard pivot

15.10 Supporting the control arm for removal

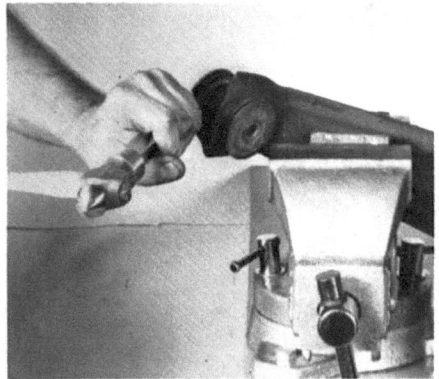

16.1 Driving out the 'Silentbloc' bushings from the control arm

16.8a Driving the inboard bearing into place

16.8b Installing the circlip on the inboard bearing

16.10 Installing the spacer in the control arm

16.11 Installing the outboard bearing

16.16 Ensuring the 'Silentbloc' bearings are squarely installed

15 Rear control arm – removal and installation

1 Disconnect the negative lead from the battery.
2 Raise the vehicle and place it on jack stands.
3 Remove the wheels.
4 Remove the brake drum and brake backing plate (Chapter 9).
5 Remove the outboard end of the drive shaft and suspend the shaft from the body to prevent the bearings from being damaged (photo).
6 Scribe a line around the mounting plate on the control arm to mark its location on the spring plate. This will ease reassembly problems.
7 Remove the two bolts which form a vertical line on the control arm to spring plate mounting flange. Remove the nut from the third bolt, but do not remove the bolt (photo).
8 Remove the bolt from the lower shock absorber mount and compress the shock absorber (photo 14.6a).
9 Remove the self locking nut from the inboard pivot bolt. Dispose of the locknut and replace it with a new one on installation of the control arm (photo).
10 Support the control arm with one hand while removing the bolts from the spring plate and the inboard pivot with the other. Do not drop the control arm (photo).
11 Installation is the reverse of the removal procedure.
12 Align the control arm mounting plate with the line on the spring arm. Do this after you have installed the inboard pivot bolt, the lower shock absorber mounting bolt, and pressed the three spring plate bolts into their holes. Do not install any nuts on the bolts.
13 When the single forward bolt on the spring plate is installed and the mounting plate aligns with the scribed mark, thread a nut onto the single bolt and tighten it snug to hold the pieces in their proper relationship to each other.
14 Install the nuts on the other two spring plate bolts and the nut on the lower shock absorber mounting bolt.
15 Install the new lock nut on the inboard pivot bolt and tighten it snug. This will be the last nut torqued down.
16 Torque the nuts on the three spring plate to mounting plate bolts to 76 to 90 ft-lb (10.5 to 12.5 m-kg).
17 Torque the lower shock absorber mounting bolt to 44 ft-lb (6.1 m-kg).
18 Install the driveshaft bolts and torque them to 30 ft-lb (4.2 m-kg).
19 Install the brake hub and wheel (Chapter 9).
20 Lower the vehicle and let it stand on its wheels.
21 Once the weight of the car is on all four of its wheels the inboard pivot bolt's lock nut may be torqued to 44 ft-lb (6.1 m-kg). b)

16 Rear control arm – stripdown and assembly

1 The two 'Silentbloc' bushings in the forward end of the control arm are removed by levering them out with a chisel or a large, flat bladed screwdriver. Lever on alternate sides so that the bushings come out squarely (photo).
2 The axle stub is removed with a two or three legged bearing puller. If one of these is not available, the stub may be driven out of the control arm with a mallet and a block of wood. Be sure to drive the stub out squarely.
3 Remove the inner spacer.
4 Lever the inner seal out of the control arm with a tire iron or a large, flat bladed screwdriver.
5 Remove the circlip. The bearings may be driven out from the inside outward by the careful use of a drift and hammer. Strike the bearing races on opposite sides to 'walk' the races out.
6 Clean the cavity of the control arm thoroughly. If you use any degreasing solvents, flush the cavity thoroughly and allow it to dry before reassembly.
7 Assembly is the reverse of the stripdown procedure.
8 Drive the inboard bearing into place. It must come flush against its inner stop and the chamfered edge of the bearing outer race must face out. Install the circlip (photos).
9 Turn the control arm so that the outboard side of the stub axle bearing housing is facing up. Pack the cavity in the control arm with about 80 gm of multipurpose grease.
10 Install the spacer in the cavity and locate it about the center of the inner bearing (photo).

11 Install the outboard bearing. It may be driven squarely into place with the chamfered edge facing out (photo).
12 If you do not have an hydraulic press to press the inner and outer bearings together, open the jaws of a bench vise wide enough to accept the control arm width at the bearing faces with the jaws protected. Close the protected jaws tightly to drive the bearings in toward one another.
13 Install the inboard seal with a seal driver or other appropriate tool. Install the inner spacer.
14 Install the inner race in the outboard bearing.
15 The stub axle should be installed in the control arm with an hydraulic press. If a press is not available, drive the axle into the control arm bearings with a mallet and a block of wood. Drive squarely and firmly. Do not allow the stub axle to twist to one side or another.
16 Install new 'Silentbloc' bushings in the forward pivot by driving them in squarely with a block of wood and a mallet. Make sure that the flanges of the bushing are tight against the control arm (photo).

17 Rear suspension – removal, adjusting, installation (early style)

1 Disconnect the negative lead from the battery.
2 Raise the vehicle and place it on jack stands.
3 Remove the brake drum and brake backing plate.
4 Remove the shock absorbers (Section 14).
5 Remove the control arms (Section 15).
6 Remove the round plate from the body panel ahead of the wheel opening. The plates are held on by one of two types of clip; one is bolted in place and the other is a snap clip (photo).
7 Remove the four bolts from the carrier tube end plate and carefully lever the end plate from its rubber mount (photo).
8 Lever the spring strut out with a long flat blade screwdriver or a tire iron. The strut is under tension and when released will snap in a downward direction. Take care not to get in its way.
9 Remove the spring strut from the body by passing the end of the strut through the hole in the body panel and turning the strut through 90 degrees (photo).
10 The torsion bars can be removed by pulling them straight out and passing them through the holes in the body panel. The torsion bars are marked with an 'R' or 'L' for the side of the vehicle they are installed on. Do not mix up the bars (photo).
11 Assembly and adjustment of the rear suspension is basically the reverse of the removal procedure.
12 Grease the splines of the torsion bars and install them on their proper sides. The bars are installed with their identification letters facing the outboard sides and are placed in the right and left sides as seen from the rear of the vehicle facing toward the front. Install the torsion bars far enough into the splines of the torsion bar carrier tube so that they are fully engaged. Do not force the torsion bars beyond this point or you will go beyond the splined area inside the tube.
13 Install the inner rubber mount. Lubricate it with a rubber lubricant to allow it to slide easily into place.
14 Coat the outboard end of the torsion bar with a thick coating of multipurpose grease in all of the splines and slide the spring plate into place over the splines. Do not hook the spring plate up onto its stop as yet.
15 Adjusting the rear suspension involves setting a pre-load angle on the spring plate, then compressing the spring plate so that it passes over the top of the torsion bar carrier tube.
16 To perform the adjusting task, you will need two long bolts of the same thread pitch as the torsion bar carrier tube's end plate and a protractor tool with a built-in spirit level. A spring compressor of the type illustrated (photo) is also necessary to pull the spring over its preload stop.
17 Place the protractor tool on the door sill of the vehicle, about four inches from the leading edge of the seat. Adjust the angle tester until the bubble in the level glass is in the center of the glass. Record the indicated angle.
18 Add to the body angle the required spring plate angle for your vehicle's rear suspension type (Specifications). Turn the protractor face in its carrier until the angle found in the above computations is indicated by the line on the carrier body. This is the angle at which the spring plate must be set in order for the inner level to indicate a level condition.

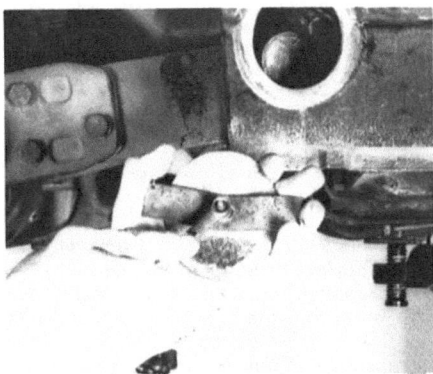
17.6 Removing the round body plates

17.7 Removing the end plate mounting bolts

17.9 Removing the end plate

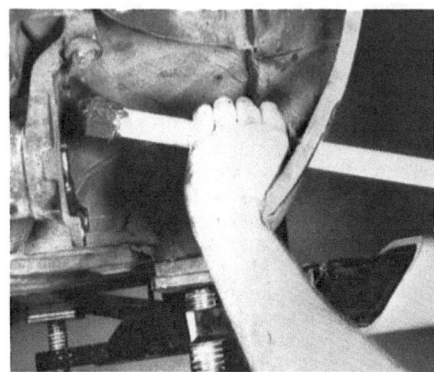
17.10 Removing the torsion bar

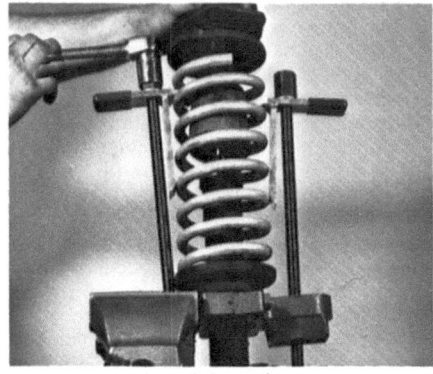
17.16 Installation of the spring strut compressor

19 If the placement of the spring plate is not correct when the protractor tool is in place on its upper edge, the following steps must be performed to adjust the spring plate angle:

20 There are two different numbers of teeth on the torsion bar's splined ends. The internal spline has 40 teeth and the external spline has 44 teeth. Turning the internal splines one tooth gives a change in spring plate height of 9°, and turning the external splines one tooth gives a change of 8° 10'. The smallest adjustment which can be made, then, is 50' (9° forward and 8° 10' back = 50').

21 Once you have determined the amount that the angle of the spring plate deviates from the desired angle, figure out on a piece of paper the moves you will have to make on the torsion bar splines to raise or lower the spring plate as required.

22 Make your calculated adjustments and install the two long bolts in diagonal corners from one another on the end plate and tighten the end plate onto the springplate until the bolts are snug. Re-check your angles and make any necessary corrections.

23 Using the proper type of spring compressor (photo 17.16), raise the spring plate up until the plate may be pressed over the stop on the torsion bar carrier. Tighten the long bolts to hold the spring plate over the stop, then install two of the standard end plate bolts in the other two holes and tighten them until they are snug.

24 Remove the two long bolts and install the remaining two standard bolts in their proper holes. Torque the bolts in a cross pattern to 25 ft-lb (3.5 m-kg).

25 Perform the same procedure on the other side of the vehicle.

26 Install the control arms. The angle created by the join of the spring plate and the control arm mounting plate must be less than 180 degrees.

27 Install the round plates in the body panels.

28 Install the shock absorbers.

29 Install the brake drum and backing plate.

---

18 Rear suspension - removal and installation (late style)

1 Disconnect the negative lead from the battery.

2 Raise the vehicle and place it on jack stands.

3 Remove the brake drum and brake backing plate.

4 Remove the shock absorbers (Section 14).

5 Remove the control arms (Section 15).

6 Remove the bolts at the ends of the carrier tube end plate which hold the end plates to the vehicle body.

7 Have an assistant hold the torsion bar carrier tube while you remove the bolts from the four rubber mounts for the torsion bar carrier tube.

8 Lift the torsion bar carrier tube from the vehicle and place it in the protected jaws of a vise with the straight edges of the torsion arms nearly parallel to the floor.

9 Most of the remaining bolts on the spring plate and stabilizer bar are eccentric bolts. Mark each of the bolts on the spring plate and stabilizer bar with paint or a scribed line so that these bolts may be replaced in the same spots, giving basic suspension adjustments.

10 Remove the lock nut from the steering stabilizer eccentric bolt and the standard bolt immediately beneath it on the spring plate. Dispose of the lock nuts and replace them with new ones upon reassembly.

11 Remove the two locknuts from the bolts which hold the two sections of the spring plate together. Dispose of the locknuts and replace them with new ones when reassembling the suspension.

12 Remove the mounting flange bolt from the torque arm. Remove the four bolts from the end plate and remove the endplate.

13 Remove the spring struts.

14 Remove the torsion bars.

15 Assembly of the rear suspension is the reverse of the dismantling procedure.

16 Assemble the two piece spring struts and torque the new lock nuts to 177 ft-lb (24.5 m-kg).

17 Adjust the suspension as outlined in Section 19.

18 Have an assistant hold the rear suspension carrier tube in place while you install the bolts and nuts in the mounts.

19 Torque the upper mount-to-body bolts to 33 ft-lb (4.6 m-kg).

20 Torque the torque strut mount bolts to 33 ft-lb (4.6 m-kg).

21 Torque the new lock nut on the mounting flange-to-body

mounting bolt to 51 ft-lb (7.0 m-kg).
22 Install the control arm.
23 Install the brake drum and backing plate.
24 Install the rear wheels.

19 Adjusting ride height – late style

1 This task requires a protractor with a bubble level. Do not attempt this task without the above tool.
2 Place the torsion bar carrier tube in the protected jaws of a vise. The torque struts should face up with the flat edge nearly horizontal with the floor.
3 Place a steel rule on the flat edge of the torque strut and place the protractor tool on top of the rule. Adjust the protractor until the bubble in the glass level is centered between the lines. Record the angle indicated by the protractor.
4 Rotate the level from this position by the specified adjusting level of the spring plate (Specifications). For example: if your vehicle has 22 mm torsion bars and no stabilizer, the adjusting level is 23° 40'. Adding the value you read at the torque strut, your problem should look like the one below

    Measured value at strut: 1° 30'
    + Specified level, spring plate:23° 40'
    = Value to be set on protractor:25° 10'

5 Install the torsion bars in the torsion bar carrier tube. The bars are stamped with a letter "R" or "L" at the end and that end must face outboard and be installed on the right or left side as seen with the carrier tube installed in the vehicle and the viewer facing toward the front of the car from the rear.
6 Assemble the spring plates, aligning the eccentric bolts with the marks you made at disassembly. Remember to use new self-locking nuts. Torque the nuts to 177 ft-lb (24.5 m-kg).
7 Engage the spring plate on the teeth of the torsion bar. Place the protractor on the upper straight edge of the spring plate. Check that the value set in the step above is still the one read.
8 Adjust the spring plate until the bubble in the level of the protractor is centered between the two marks on the glass.
9 There are two different numbers of teeth on the torsion bar's splined ends. The internal spline has 40 teeth and the external spline has 44 teeth. Turning the internal splines one tooth gives a change in spring plate height of 9°, and turning the external splines one tooth gives a change of 8° 10'. The smallest adjustment which can be made, then is 50' (9° forward and 8° 10' back = 50'). Once you have determined the amount that the angle of the spring plate deviates from the desired angle, figure out on a piece of paper the moves you will have to make on the torsion bar splines to raise or lower the spring plate as required.

10 Lubricate the rubber bushes on the spring-plate with a silicone preservative or lubricant and install the mounting flange over the outboard side of the bush.
11 Install the three short bolts on the mounting flange and tighten them until the long bolt on the stop washer can be inserted.
12 Install the bolt which holds the mounting flange to the torsion arm and tighten it slightly. This will prevent damage to the mounting flange in the following steps.
13 Compress the spring plate slightly with a spring compressor such as the one shown in photo 17.16. Slide the long bolt on the mounting flange far enough out so that the stop washer may be installed. Push the bolt back into place and tighten the bolt until snug.
14 Remove the spring compressor. This will set the stop washer in its proper position.
15 Torque the four bolts on the mounting flange to 33 ft-lb (4.6 m-kg). Tighten them uniformly and apply final torque in a cross pattern.
16 Tighten the bolt on the torque arm to 33 ft-lb (4.6 m-kg).
17 The torsion bar carrier tube assembly is ready for installation in the chassis.

20 Rear axle shafts – general description

1 The wheel shafts are mounted on the rear suspension trailing arms. The drive shafts are equipped with a constant velocity universal joint at each end and are coupled by flanges onto the axle shafts and transmission. Apart from the improved road holding this design means that the axle shafts, wheel bearings and transmission may be removed for servicing separately with comparative ease.

21 Rear axle shafts – removal

1 The drive shaft cap screws are best removed with a splined key to fit the socket. It is however, possible to use a hexagonal section key provided it is a dead fit and made of best quality hard steel (photo). If the screw sockets are damaged the greatest difficulty will be experienced in getting them out with any sort of key.
2 Before removing all the screws make sure that there are no accumulations of dirt around which could get into the joints. If any dirt gets in it will have to be cleaned out and the joints repacked with special molybdenum grease.
3 With all the screws removed the shafts may be removed (photo).

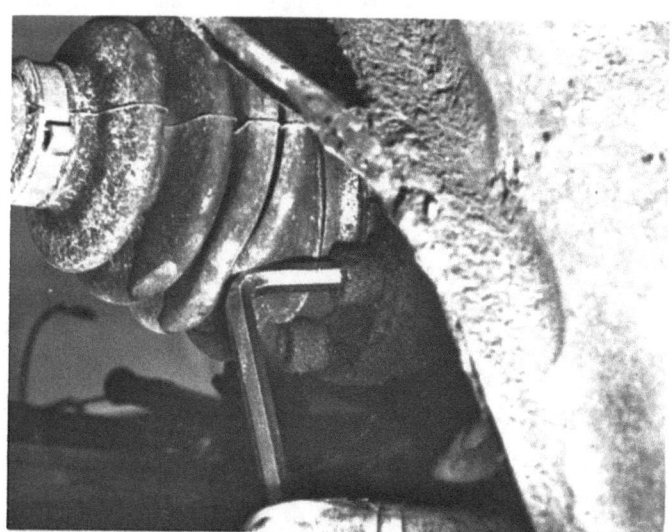
21.1 Removing the splined bolts with an hex-head key (see photo 15.5 for removal with the proper splined key)

21.3 Removing the axle shaft

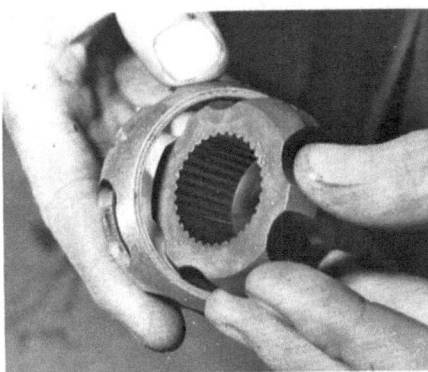

22.6 Fitting the splined hub to the ball cage

22.7 Snapping the balls into the ball cage

22.8 Installing the ball cage assembly in the outer cage

22.9 Installing the concave washer on the hub spline

22.10 Installing the universal joint on the splined shaft

22.11 Installing the circlip on the splined axle end

22 Rear axle shafts – rebuilding

1 If the constant velocity joints have a noticeable amount of back-lash they must be replaced completely. If the protective boot has split it is possible to dismantle and flush them, repack with grease and fit new boots.

2 First remove the drive shaft as described in the previous section.

3 It is not necessary to remove the rubber boot. Drive the metal cover from the joint which is a press fit. Before going any further clean off the face of the joint and note any forge marks on each of the components or any other features which will enable you to ensure they all face the same way again on reassembly. If none is apparent scratch some marks of your own.

4 Remove the circlip from the end of the shaft. If the joint is now supported by vise jaws the shaft can be tapped out. Recover the concave washer from behind the joint on the shaft.

5 Flush the joint out thoroughly, let it dry and then repack it with approximately 60 grams of molybdenum grease, working it well in from both sides.

6 If the inner cage of the joint is dismantled or falls apart it must be

correctly reassembled. First fit the splined hub inside the ball cage — it will only go in if two grooves are lined up (photo).

7 Then press the balls into the cage. They should be a snap fit unless the cage is worn badly (photo).

8 Place the ball and hub assembly into the outer cage so that the chamfered edge of the hub splines will be in a position against the shaft shoulder when the joint is eventually replaced on the shaft (photo). This means that it has to be the right way round in the outer cage because the outer cage goes on so that the protective boot assembly can be tapped back in position on the non-shouldered side.

9 Put the concave washer back on the shaft, concave side towards the joint (photo).

10 Put the joint back on the shaft (photo).

11 Refit the circlip (photo). In order to force the joint against the concave washer sufficiently to get the circlip in the groove, support the shaft in a vise and drive the circlip down with a suitably sized socket.

12 Having repacked the joint with grease tap the boot retainer plate back on to the joint. Use a screw to line up the holes in the joint and plate.

Chapter 11 Electrics

For modifications, and information applicable to later models, see Supplement at end of manual

Contents

Specifications

Battery	12 V, 63 Ah
Alternator	
Polarity	Negative ground
Output	1050 W, 75 A
Bulbs	
Sealed beam headlamp	50 W/40 W
Turn signal/marker light, front	21 W/5 W
Turn signal, rear	21 W
Brake light/running light, rear	21 W/5 W
Back-up light	21 W
Engine compartment light	10 W
Interior light	10 W
Luggage compartment light	10 W
Glove compartment light	3 W
Battery charge light	3 W
All other lights, including instrument lights, indicator lamp, etc	1.2 W

1 General description

1 The various models have a common system of electric wiring and accessories although the number and exact type of accessories depends on the option package and year of the vehicle. In most cases wiring and fixing provision is already built into models not fitted with extras such as fog lamps, and fitting of these extras is a simple task. All such extras must be grounded to the chassis with a separate connector.

2 A very marked step in technique is evident. The fuse and relay console under the dashboard contains 15 fuses and a number of relays. The purpose of these relays is two-fold. Firstly, the heavy current required for headlamps, fog lamps, air-conditioner, horn, rear window heater and flashers, may be routed only from the generating circuit, via the relay, to the accessory. The operation of the relay switching on the current is by a much smaller current from the switch on the dashboard (fascia) which enables the second step. Indeed it would not be very difficult to install all the accessories if the main current had to be lead to switches on the fascia.

3 Measuring instruments on the fascia have a controlling voltage stabilizer built into the instrument.

4 All vehicles have a built in tachometer (rev counter), oil pressure gauge and voltmeter fitted as standard.

5 All models have single round headlamps on each side.

6 The speedometer is included in this Chapter because it is part of the fascia.

7 Guide lines are given concerning the fitting of fog lamps, radios and provisions for lighting to trailers. If items other than VW/Porsche/Audi accessories are fitted the owner may be confronted with problems we cannot forsee so comment is confined mainly to what not to do in such cases.

8 Current flow type wiring diagrams with a short explanation of how to use them, are included.

2 Battery - removal and installation

1   On LHD cars the battery is located within the engine compartment (photo). On RHD cars, the battery is located in a well within the luggage compartment. Remove the ground strap (negative) and the positive cable terminal. The battery is held in position by a clamp which fits over a rim at the base.

2   Lift the battery out and clean the battery platform. Any sign of corrosion should be neutralized with an alkali solution. Ordinary baking powder will do the job. If the corrosion has reached the metal, scrape the paint away to give a bright surface and repaint right away.

3   Installation is the reverse. Smear the terminals with a little petroleum jelly (vaseline). Do not use grease.

3 Battery - maintenance and inspection

1   Normal weekly battery maintenance consists of checking the electrolyte level of each cell to ensure that the separators are covered by ¼ inch of electrolyte. If the level has fallen, top up the battery using distilled water only. Do not overfill. If a battery is overfilled or any electrolyte spilled, immediately wipe away the excess as electrolyte attacks and corrodes any metal it comes into contact with very rapidly.

2   As well as keeping the terminals clean and covered with petroleum jelly, the top of the battery, and especially the top of the cells, should be kept clean and dry. This helps prevent corrosion and ensures that the battery does not become partially discharged by leakage through dampness and dirt. If topping up the battery becomes excessive and the case has been inspected for cracks that could cause leakage, but none are found, the battery is being overcharged and the voltage regulator should be checked.

3   When removing the battery be careful not to strain the terminal posts. If these are twisted too much they may cause the plates inside to move with consequent battery failure.

4   With the battery on the bench at the three monthly interval check, measure its specific gravity with a hydrometer to determine the state of charge and condition of electrolyte. There should be very little variation between the different cells and if a variation in excess of 0.025 is present it will be due to either:

   a) *Loss of electrolyte from the battery at some time caused by spillage or a leak, resulting in a drop in the specific gravity of electrolyte when the deficiency was replaced with distilled water instead of fresh electrolyte.*

   b) *An internal short circuit caused by buckling of the plates or a similar malady pointing to the likelihood of total battery failure in the near future.*

5   The correct readings for the electrolyte specific gravity at various states of charge and conditions are:

	Temperate	Tropical
Fully charged	1.285	1.23
Half charged	1.20	1.14
Discharged	1.12	1.08

6   The hydrometer is a glass tube tapered at one end and fitted with a rubber bulb at the other end. Inside it there is a float. The tapered end of the tube is inserted into the filler hole of the cell to be tested and the bulb squeezed. When it is released acid is drawn into the tube. Enough must be drawn to allow the float to float freely. The float has a scale on it and where the surface of the acid meets the float is the point to be read on the scale.

7   It is rare indeed for a battery to freeze but it can happen. If the battery is discharged and the specific gravity is low it may happen more easily. It will not happen while the engine is running so the first intimation will be a refusal to start, for a frozen battery will not supply current. Remembering that there is a solid lump of acid, take care how it is handled. It must be thawed slowly. If it can be removed from the car so much the better, but if it is frozen in, any attempt to remove it by force will break the case. Indeed, the case may have split due to the expansion of the electrolyte so watch carefully as it does thaw or there may be an acid leak of considerable proportions which will do a lot of damage. If this happens take

2.1 Location of the battery (LHD)

the battery out of the car as quickly as possible, but wear rubber gloves, to avoid being burned.

8   If the battery thaws out and no leaks appear then it will be of use again. However, check the specific gravity and charge if necessary.

9   For interest value, acid at specific gravity 1.120 (ie. the battery is discharged) will freeze at –11°C (12°F), at 1.200 S.G. at –27°C (–17°F) and a fully charged battery at 1.285 is safe until –90°C (–68°F), so keep the battery well charged in cold weather, and if you do have to leave the car in a snowdrift get the battery out before it freezes.

10 If the battery loses its charge repeatedly then it is probably sulphated or damaged internally. First check the specific gravity of each cell. If some are high (1.285) and the odd one is lower, then that is where the trouble lies. The S.G. throughout the six cells should not vary by more than 0.025.

4 Battery - charging

1   In winter, when heavy demand is placed upon the battery such as when starting from cold and much electrical equipment is continually in use, it is a good idea occasionally to have the battery fully charged from an external source at the rate of 3.5 to 4 amps. Always disconnect it from the car electrical circuit when charging.

2   Continue to charge the battery at this rate until no further rise in specific gravity is noted over a four hour period.

3   Alternatively, a trickle charger, charging at the rate of 1.5 amps, can safely be used overnight. Disconnect the battery from the car electrical circuit before charging or you will damage the alternator.

4   Specially rapid 'boost' charges which are claimed to restore the power of the battery in 1 to 2 hours can cause damage to the battery plates through over-heating.

5   While charging the battery note that the temperature of the electrolyte should never exceed 37.8°C (100°F).

6   Make sure that your charging set and battery are set to the same voltage.

5 Battery - electrolyte replenishment

1   If the battery has been fully charged but one cell has a specific gravity of 0.025 or more, less than the others it is most likely that electrolyte has been lost from the cell at some time and the acid over diluted with distilled water when topping-up.

2   In this case remove some of the electrolyte with a pipette and top up with fresh electrolyte. It is best to get this done at the Service

Station, for making your own electrolyte is messy, dangerous, and expensive for the small amount you need. If you must do it yourself add 1 part of sulphuric acid (concentrated) to 2.5 parts of water. Add the acid to the water, not the other way round, or the mixture will spit back and you will be badly burned. Add the acid a drop at a time to the water.

3 Having added fresh electrolyte recharge and recheck the readings. In all probability this will cure the problem. If it does not then there is a short circuit somewhere.

4 Electrolyte must always be stored away from other fluids and should be locked up, not left about. If you have children this is even more important.

6 Alternator - safety precautions

1 The alternator has a negative ground circuit. Be careful not to connect the battery the wrong way or the alternator will be damaged.

2 Do not run the alternator with the output wire disconnected.

3 When welding is being done on the car the battery and the alternator output cable should be disconnected and the battery removed.

4 If the battery is to be charged in-situ both the leads of the battery should be disconnected, before the charging leads are connected to the battery.

5 Do not use temporary test connections which may short circuit accidentally. The fuses will not blow, the diodes will burn out.

6 When replacing a burnt out alternator clear the fault which caused the burn out first or a new alternator will be needed a second time.

7 Alternator - drivebelt adjustment

1 The alternator is driven by a belt from the crankshaft pulley. The belt also drives the water pump.

2 The alternator has two lugs on its casing. A bolt threaded through these is mounted in a bracket bolted to the cylinder block. This bolt forms the hinge on which the alternator is mounted. The head of the bolt is a hexagon which is accessible just beneath the timing belt cover (beneath the fuel lines-Turbo). This bolt must be slackened before the alternator belt tension may be adjusted.

3 On the top of the alternator is yet another lug, through which a bolt is fitted to a slotted strap. The strap is hinged on the cylinder block.

4 Thus the alternator may be rotated about the hinge bolt to tighten the drivebelt. The tension in the drivebelt is correct when the belt may be depressed with a thumb a distance of ⅜ in (9.5 mm) halfway between the crankshaft and alternator pulleys. The bolts should be tightened to hold the alternator in this position.

8 Alternator – testing

See also Chapter 5, Section 5.

1 Without the proper equipment, testing of the alternator is a difficult task, and in most cases is beyond the scope of the home mechanic.

2 If a fault is suspected in the alternator, your first check should be the drivebelt which turns the alternator pulley. Open the hood and visually inspect the condition of the belt. If it is broken, frayed or has a glazed appearance, the belt should be replaced with a new one.

3 The tension of the belt is also an important consideration. Check the tension as outlined in Section 7 and adjust as necessary.

4 Hand-held testing equipment is available for further diagnosis, however the operation of this equipment varies greatly between manufacturers. If this avenue is chosen, consult the instructions supplied with the tester for proper operation.

5 Possibly the best choice for the home mechanic is to remove the alternator from the engine and take it to a Porsche dealer or reputable repair shop equipped with bench testing equipment.

9 Headlamps - general

1 The fixing and beam adjustment for all 924 models is generally the same. The main differences are in the type of bulb and method of renewal.

10 Headlamps - removal and installation

1 Raise the headlights.

2 Disconnect the negative lead from the battery.

3 Remove the Phillips head screws from the headlight trim and lift the trim away (photo). Do not operate either of the adjusting screws.

4 Remove the Phillips head screws from the sealed beam carrier frame. Pull the headlight toward you and disconnect the plug (photo).

5 Remove the locating clip, screws, and spring. Separate the frame pieces and remove the sealed beam lamp.

6 Installation is the reverse of the removal procedure.

7 Adjust the headlight beams after lamp replacement (Section 18).

11 Headlamp raising assembly - maintenance and repair

Lubricate all moving parts of the headlamp raising system regularly, and particularly after the car has been through a car wash.

1 Disconnect the negative lead from the battery.

2 Raise the headlights by turning the knob on top of the motor. If a rubber shroud is installed, it will have to be removed to raise the headlights.

3 Check the operation of all bellcranks, bearings, and attachment points. If binding is noted in the bellcrank assembly when the raising knob is operated, check the condition of the bearings and the adjustment of the cranks (photo). If the bellcrank assembly is binding, have your Porsche dealer correct the alignment of the components. This requires a special jig.

4 If the headlights do not raise when the switch is turned on, there are two checks which should be performed before contemplating replacement of the motor.

5 First, check the plug for good contact and clean contact points within the plug itself. Clean any rusted or corroded contact points with sandpaper or an emery board for fingernails.

6 If the plug contacts are clean and the contact is firm, check the condition of the relay mounted on the side of the motor. If the relay proves to be in working order, the motor must be replaced.

7 Disconnect the plug from the motor and remove the relay (photo).

8 Remove the nut at the end of the operating shaft, then remove the three bolts which hold the motor to the raising assembly (photos).

9 Before installing the new motor, disconnect the negative lead from the battery (if not done before), plug in the power plug and the relay, turn the headlight switch to the off position, and touch the negative lead to the negative post of the battery. This will move the motor to its off/lowered position.

10 Install the motor and secure all bolts and nuts removed.

11 Connect the negative lead of the battery and raise the headlamps. If they do not raise fully, adjust the operating lever by pressing it to different splines on the motor shaft.

12 Check the headlamp adjustment. When the headlamps are raised, the rubber bumper should rest on the metal sheet, so that the headlamps are firmly held in place. If the headlight beams are in the approximate height position, adjust the rubber bumpers by screwing them in or out as required.

13 Check the aiming of the headlight beams.

12 Fog lamps - installation guidelines

1 Fog lamps are installed on some cars when new and as optional equipment for most 924s in the USA.

2 If fog lamps are to be added at a later date, it should be noted that a blank space for the switch exists on the console. Push out this blank space and the switch can be installed.

10.3 Removing the headlight trim

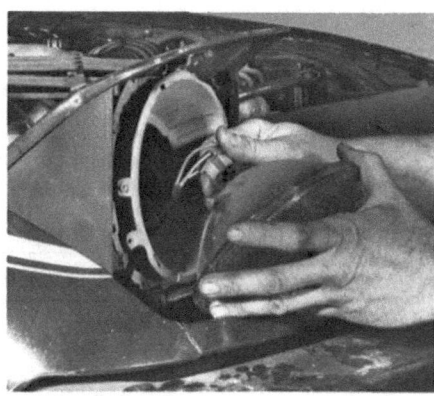

10.4 Removing the sealed beam carrier and unplugging the lamp

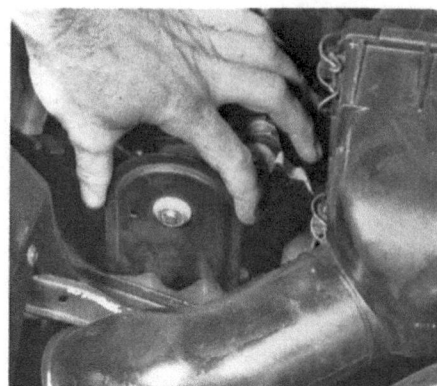

11.3 Checking the bearings in the headlight raising bellcrank for binding and operation

11.7 Unplugging the headlamp raising motor

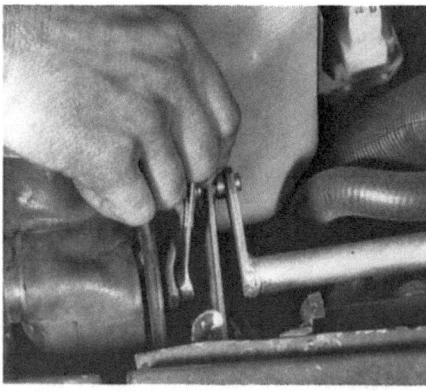

11.8a Removing the nut from the operating shaft

11.8b Removing the headlight raising motor mounting bolts

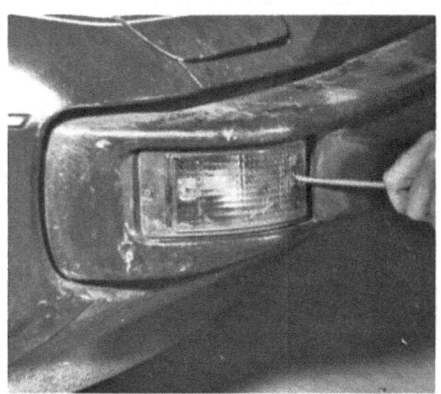

13.1 Removing the turn signal lens for bulb replacement

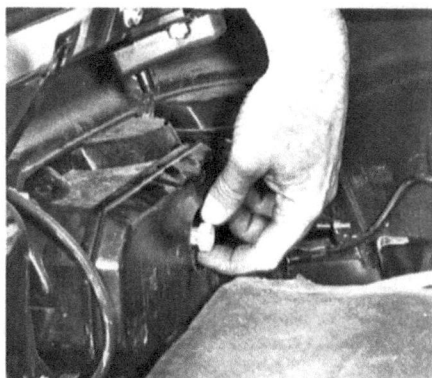

14.1a Loosening the knurled knob to gain access to the rear light cluster

14.1b The light cluster bulbs may be changed individually

17.1a Removing the side marker light mounting screws

17.1b Pressing the marker light from the body gives access to the bulbs

3 Depending on the model production date, some vehicles will also have complete wiring for the fog lamps in place ready for the hook-up. A close examination of the wiring diagrams will reveal the locations and color-coding for the optional fog lamps. This will greatly ease the installation procedure.

13 Turn signal lamps (front) – bulb replacement

1 Remove the two screws holding the lens to the bumper bar (photo). The bulb may then be pressed into the holder, turned to the left and extracted. A new bulb may then be fitted. When replacing the lens see that the gasket is in good condition. Do not tighten the screws too much or you will crack the lens.

14 Light cluster (rear) – bulb replacement

1 Remove the tire cover in the luggage compartment. The bulb holder may be removed by unscrewing the knurled nut and lifting the plate from the light unit (photo). The bulbs may be individually removed from the plate (photo).
2 Do not remove the plastic lens from the outside unless it is broken. When fitting a new one tighten the screws very carefully and make sure the joint between the lens and the vehicle body is water tight.

15 Interior light – bulb replacement

1 These are held into the linings by screws. The fitting may be levered out of the lining using a small screwdriver. Be careful not to damage the lining. The festoon bulb may then be extracted and replaced. Install the housing at the switch end first and engage the lug. Now press the other end until the spring clip engages.

16 Licence plate light – bulb replacement

1 Undo the screws holding the lens in place and remove the lens. The bulb may then be replaced. For some reason this light seems to collect more mud than the others and should be wiped clean frequently.

17 Side markers (USA) – bulb replacement

1 On the USA version, there are four lights; two yellow (front) and two red (rear); one of each on each side. Each one is fastened to the body by two screws. Remove these and gently pull the lens away from the body (photos). The bulb may then be removed and a new one fitted. Be careful when refitting the lens that the joint is made water tight, these lamps get more than their share of spray in wet weather from passing traffic.

18 Headlamp – beam adjustment

1 Refer to Figs. 11.1a and 11.1b. The screws arrowed are the adjusting screws which tilt the reflector horizontally and vertically.
2 Because of the many different local regulations and the increasing argument about what is, and what is not, a correctly aimed headlamp beam we are not offering any advice as to where the beam should point, only how to make it point in that direction. The actual focus point should be obtained from your local dealer or police authority.
3 Having ascertained how the beam is to be aimed on dip, whether it must swing to the right or left when dipped, and the measurements of the displacement, set the car on level ground about 20 feet (6 meters) from a vertical wall or door. The vehicle tire pressures should be correct and there should be the equivalent of the driver's weight in the driving seat.
4 Mark with relation to the center-line of the car and the height of the lamps from the ground, the equivalent positions of the lamps on the wall. Using this information mark the area to which the lights should be directed on dipped beam. Cover one light and switch on.

European models

North American models

Fig. 11.1 Location of the headlight adjusting screws

A = up-and-down adjustment
B = side-to-side adjustment

Using the adjusting screws direct the beam to the area required. Cover that light and repeat with the other one.
5 When the beams are correctly focused on dip the high beams will automatically be correct.

19 Direction indicators and emergency flashers – general

1 The direction indicators are controlled by the left-hand column switch.
2 A switch on the dashboard operates all four flashers simultaneously and although the direction indicators will not work when the ignition is switched off the emergency switch over-rides this and the flasher signals continue to operate.
3 All the circuits are routed through the relay on the console and its fuse.
4 If the indicators do not function correctly, a series of tests may be done to find which part of the circuit is at fault.
5 The most common fault is in the flasher lamps, defective bulbs, and dirty or corroded contacts. Check these first, then test the emergency switch. Remove it from the circuit and check its operation. If the switch is in good order replace it and again turn on the emergency lights. If nothing happens then the relay is not functioning properly and it should be renewed. If the lights function on emergency but not on operation of the column switch then the wiring and column switch are suspect.

20 Switches (lighting) – testing, removal and installation

1 You cannot repair the switches; either they work or they don't. If you suspect the switch then the only way to test it is to take out the

instrument panel. Disconnect the battery ground strap before you start. Squeeze the dovetail clips of the switch and extract it from the panel (photo), make a diagram of the wiring to the switch and pull off the connectors. Use a meter to test the operation of the switch. If it does not work satisfactorily, fit a new one.

21 Dashboard instruments – removal and installation

1 All three instruments in the dashboard are removed and installed in the same way. The three instruments consist of a speedometer, tachometer, and an information light panel.
2 Reach behind the dashboard and locate the instrument you wish to remove.
3 Press the instrument rearward, into the passenger compartment. Be careful not to let it drop.
4 Disconnect the wiring and drive cables. Be sure to label each of the connections with a piece of tape and an indelible pen for ease in reassembly.
5 Installation is the reverse of the removal procedure.
6 When pressing the instruments into the dashboard, do not press on the clear cover glass as this will break the cover. Apply pressure to the rim only.

20.1 Removing procedure for instrument panel switches

22 Console instrument panel – removal and installation

1 Disconnect the negative lead from the battery.
2 Remove the two Phillips head screws from the corners above the instruments and pull the top of the fascia toward you.
3 Lift the bottom of the plate slightly and pull the entire panel toward you (photo).
4 Instruments are removed and installed by loosening or installing the knurled nuts on the holding brackets seen at the rear of the panel (photo). When removing instruments, be sure to label all connections for ease of reassembly.
5 Installation is the reverse of the removal procedure.

23 Fuse and relay panel – removal and installation

1 Disconnect the battery ground strap. If you forget to do this something is bound to burn out this time.
2 Undo the screws holding the panel in place and lower it away from the bulkhead.
3 The underside of the board is shown in Fig. 11.3. Unplug the main multipin plugs 'A' to 'F'. Tag them as you pull them off.
4 The usual faults are loose connections in the multipin plug connector to the socket in the plate. Bent pins may be straightened but if the pins have spread then the plate may need replacement.
5 On vehicles without the intermittent wash wipe relay contacts '19' and '21' are connected with a bridge.

24 Heater (passenger compartment) – removal and installation

1 Disconnect the negative lead from the battery.
2 Remove the heat exchanger (Chapter 2).
3 Remove the console and the glovebox from the dashboard (Chapter 12).
4 Remove the radio from the dashboard, if one is fitted. Since there are many brands of radio installed, you must rely on the specific information provided by the shop which installed your particular radio.
5 Remove the radio speaker grille and the radio speaker from the dashboard.
6 The clamping bar on the heater flap box should now be visible through the radio speaker hole. Insert a flat blade screwdriver behind the dashboard and pry the clamping bar away from the heater flap box. It should now be possible to remove the flap box by lowering it into the passenger side of the vehicle. It may be necessary to pull hoses and ducts from the heater flap box in order to pull it free.
7 Installation is the reverse of the removal procedure.

22.3 Removing the console instrument panel

22.4 Individual instruments are removed by loosening the knurled nuts

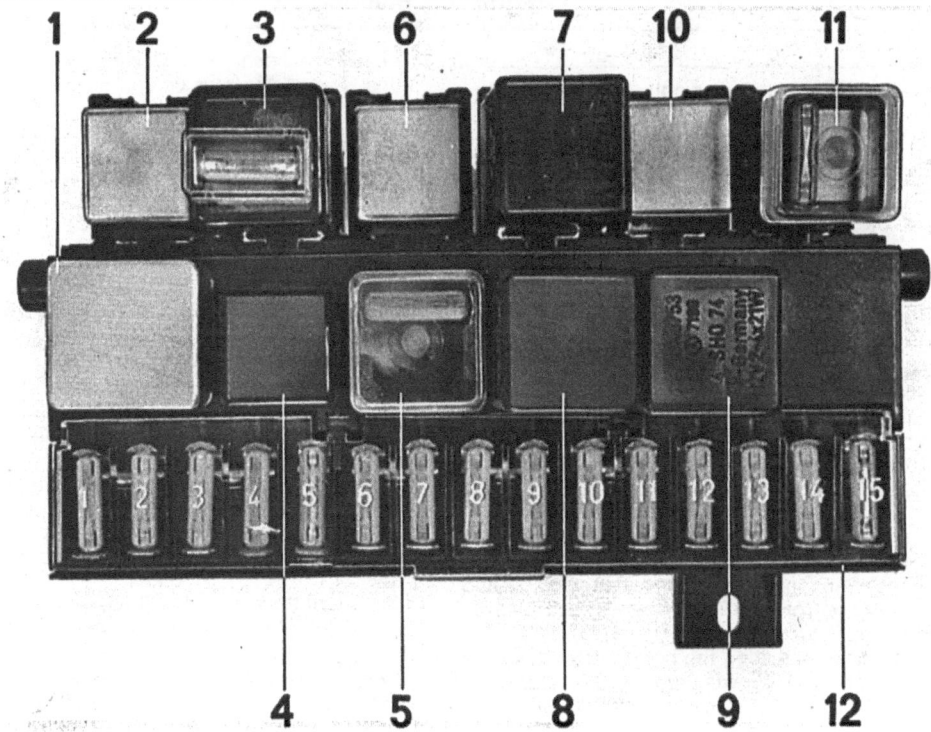

Fig. 11.2 Fuse and relay panel, top view

1　Headlight flasher and low beam relay
2　Horn relay
3　Fuel pump relay
4　Extra headlight relay
5　Blower relay
6　Fog lamp relay (option)
7　Headlight washer relay
8　Intermittent wiper relay
9　Flasher relay
10　Headlight flasher changeover relay
　　(Europe)
　　Warning and timer relay, seat belts

(U.S.A.)
Control unit for catalytic converter
control (Japan)
11　Rear window defogger relay
12　Fuses S1 through S15

Fuses (from left)

1　Headlight – dipped (Left)
2　Headlight – dipped (Right)
3　Headlight – high beam (Left)
4　Headlight – high beam (Right)

5　Additional headlights
6　Interior light, retractable headlights
7　Emergency flashers
8　Back-up lights, horn
9　Direction indicators, brake warning light
10　Fresh air blower
11　Windshield wipers
12　Luggage compartment light, licence
　　plate lights
13　Side marker light (Right)
14　Side marker light (Left)
15　Fan

**Fig. 11.3 Fuse and
relay panel, bottom
view**

A　Ivory plug,
　　engine
　　compartment
　　harness
B　Red plug,
　　engine
　　compartment
　　harness
C　White plug,
　　engine
　　compartment
　　harness
D　Blue plug,
　　instrument panel
　　harness
E　Black plug,
　　instrument panel
　　harness
F　Yellow plug,
　　rear light
　　harness
G　Male plugs
　　(see current
　　flow diagram)

Note: The current flow diagrams identify the female plugs
shown with the nomenclature 'TA', 'TB', and so on.

25 Heater flap box - stripdown and assembly

1 The heater flap box is held together by clips. Lever these clips from the box and it may be split into halves.
2 Remove the shut off flap from its pivots at the top of the box.
3 Lift the fan motor and fan from the box, disconnecting the wiring loom and marking the connections.
4 Assembly is the reverse of stripdown.

26 Horn – fault diagnosis

1 The Porsche 924 has twin horns. To remove the horns, disconnect the battery ground cable, pull off the electrical connectors at each horn, and then remove the horns from their respective brackets. When installing, make sure the horn body does not touch any body sheet metal or frame components as this will cause vibration noises when the horns are sounded.
2 If the horn blows continuously, or intermittently when the steering wheel is turned, disconnect the negative battery cable and remove the appropriate fuse from the fuse panel. Do not reinstall the fuse until the fault has been corrected.
3 The easiest method of fault-testing the horn system is with a standard electrical test light. The following process will isolate the fault as occuring in the horn itself or in the wiring system leading to the horn.
4 Your first check when troubleshooting the horn system is the fuse. If the fuse for that circuit is in good condition, proceed to the next step.
5 Disconnect the electrical wiring connectors at the horn. Now place the probe of your test light against the end of the wire and have an assistant depress the horn button. If the test light glows, current is reaching the horn in which case the horn itself is defective. If the test light proves that no current is evident at this point, the fault lies in the wiring system before the horn. Use the wiring diagram to follow the horn circuit through to find the fault.

27 Radio - fitting guidelines

1 The fitting of a radio to the Porsche 924 presents no problems. It may be fitted in the dashboard in the space provided.
2 Manufacturers provide a choice of radios to suit the taste and pocket. Pushbutton or manual control are available, and another option with a built in cassette tape player, speakers, a lockable antenna and suppression kits is available.
3 There does not seem to be any point in going elsewhere as fitting a set which is not tailored to suit will mean cutting the dashboard about and building separate supports which will get in the way of things in an already crowded space.
4 It is important to get advice from the local experts as to the best set for your requirements. If you do a lot of long distance work a set which functions well at home may be unsuitable in other areas.
5 If 'electrical noise' appears then it is probably due to some unit of the electrical system which is badly worn. Sparking at the alternator slip rings, a defective voltage regulator, a faulty ignition lead, fan motor or blower motor. The only way to find out is to isolate each item until the noise disappears and then overhaul that item.
6 It is recommended that a small two amp fuse be inserted in the supply cable.

28 Heated rear window - general

1 This item is a standard fitting throughout the range.
2 A switch on the dashboard activates a relay 'J9' on the fuse/relay plate. There is a heavy fuse in the heater power circuit and a smaller one in the switch/warning light circuit. The circuit is easily followed in the circuit diagram.

3 It will be seen that the window element is connected to two plugs 'T1d' in the rear compartment.
4 Testing is mainly following the circuit through. However, before starting to work on the system disconnect the battery and only reconnect it to do specified tests.
5 The current consumption is large (about 8 amps) so turn the heater off as soon as the window is clear.

29 Windshield wiper and washer - general description

1 The early basic vehicle was fitted with a two speed wiper and an electric pump for the washer system.
2 Subsequent models have an electric washer pump and an intermittent wiper control as well as two speed continuous wiping.
3 The early models may be converted by the installation of a different switch in the column switch set up. It is also necessary to fit a relay. The wiring circuit is shown in the various current flow diagrams. Details of the modification should be obtained from the dealer.
4 Some of the models are fitted with headlamp washers. A general description of this circuit is given in Section 34 and a current flow diagram in Fig. 11.19 for those who already have the system fitted.
5 A rear window wiper and washer is also available as an optional extra. The circuit diagram is shown in the current flow diagram.
6 The wiper/washer is controlled from the right-hand steering column switch. The speed control is fixed by the horizontal movement of the lever and the washer works when the lever is lifted towards the steering wheel.

30 Windshield wiper mechanism - removal, inspection and replacement

1 The nut holding the wiper arm is covered by a plastic cap. Prise this out and remove the nut. The arm may now be removed (photo). Under the wiper boss is a splined shaft and a rubber boot.
2 Remove the boot and the gland nut is accessible (photo). If you intend to dismantle any more remove the battery earth strap. Undo the nut and repeat the operation for the other spindle.
3 Unplug the connector from the motor terminals .
4 The wiper motor and frame are all held in position by a nut on a bracket (photo). Remove this nut and lift the motor and frame away from the car (photo). The mechanism may now be examined.
5 The motor may be removed from the frame by undoing two nuts. Alternatively, the motor may be removed from the frame while the frame is still in position but we do not see the point in this as having got so far one might as well have a look at the frame joints as well.
6 Check that all the levers and pins are secure, not worn and are well lubricated.
7 Do not remove the crank from the motor unless the motor is to be replaced with a new one. If this is to be done, connect the multipin plug to the motor before installing the motor, switch on and let the motor run for four minutes. Switch off and the motor will stop in the parking position. Install the crank.
8 Repair is by replacement. Whatever is wrong with the electrical components may only be cured by fitting new ones. The replacement of the column switch is discussed in Chapters 8 and 12. The brush gear is not a service part so the motor must be replaced if faulty.
9 Inspect the linkage for wear or corrosion. The parts of the linkage are replaceable, if required. However, the links are different on left-hand and right-hand drive vehicles.
10 If electrical 'noise' has caused problems with the radio the motor may be replaced by a fully suppressed one.
11 Replace is the reverse of removal. When assembling the arms they should be fitted to the splines in such a way that they come to rest the following distance from the bottom of the windshield glass:
    25 + 5 mm (driver's side)
    36 + 5 mm (passenger's side)
Tighten the wiper arms to 5 lb-ft (0.7 m-kg).

30.1 Prying the plastic cover from the windshield wiper base

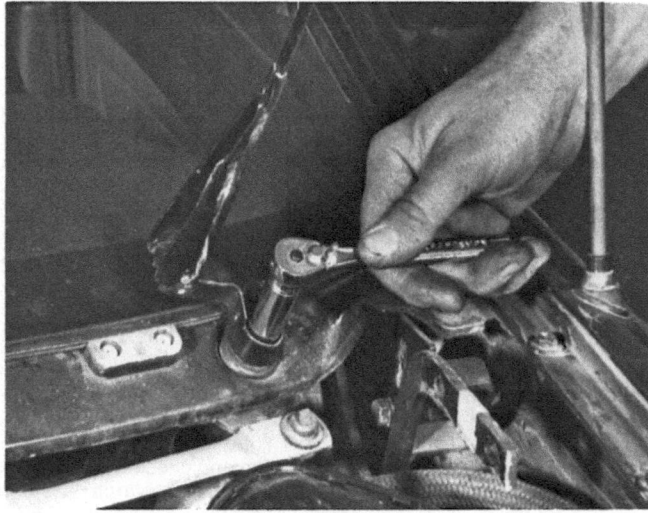

30.2 Removing the wiper gland nut

30.4a Removing the nuts from the wiper motor clamp

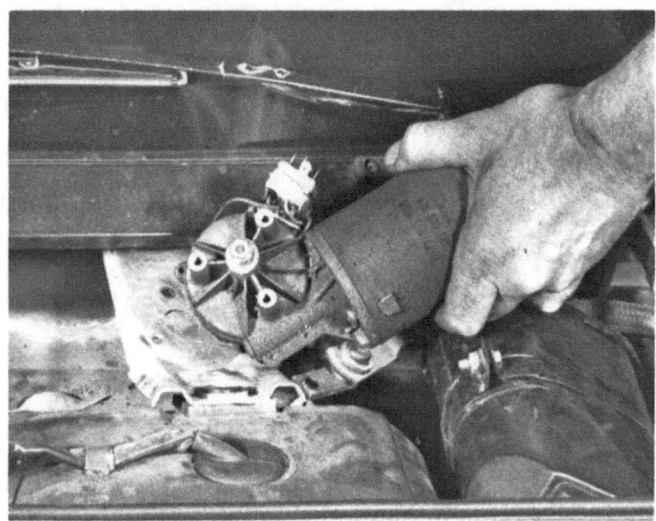

30.4b Removing the wiper motor

31 Windshield wiper (two stage without intermittent wiping) - fault diagnosis

1 Check that the bridge between contacts '53a' and '53m' is installed on the relay plate. The fresh air blower motor should be working to show that the fuse system is in order and the ignition should be switched on for each test.

2 *The motor is not working at all.* Check the voltage at terminal '53' on the wiper motor. Pull the multipin plug off the motor, set the switch lever to stage 1 and check the voltage at connection '53' (green/black). If there is voltage then the motor is defective. Connect a wire from terminal '53' of the motor to the battery ' + ve' and from the terminal '31' to ground. If the motor does not work now a new motor is needed. If it does work then the ground wire requires renewal.

3 If there was no voltage at terminal '53' when the connector was checked then the fault is probably in the wiper switch. Pull the multipin plug off the wiper column switch. Two wires, black/grey and black/green are connected to terminals '53' and '53a' of the plug. Slot these two out by connecting them with a piece of wire. If the motor now works a new column switch is needed. If it still does not work then there is a fault in wire '53' or wire '53a' which go to the relay plate. Disconnect the battery ground strap, pull connector 'E'

off the relay plate and bridge contacts 'E 15' and 'E 16'. It will be necessary to remove the relay plate to do this (Section 23). Reconnect the battery and try again. If the motor works this time then wires '53' or '53a' are defective. Replace them. If the motor still does not work then there is a fault in the relay plate. It must be removed and checked. Circuits 'E 16' to 'C 9' and 'E 15' to 'C 13' are the ones to test. If there is an open-circuit on these lines then a new relay plate is needed. If the circuits are in order then the wiring from the relay plate to the motor is at fault.

4 *The motor works on stage I, but not on stage II.* Set the lever to stage II. Connect terminal '31' on the motor to ground and terminal '53b' to the battery positive (+). If the motor works now then the fault is in the wiper switch. If the motor does not work then a new motor is needed. To test the switch: Fit the connector plug back on the motor and pull off the plug from the wiper switch. Bridge terminals '53a' and '53b' (wires black/grey and green/yellow). If the motor now works a new wiper switch is needed. If it does not then the problem is in the relay plate, between 'C16' and 'E21' (wire '53b'). The only way to find this out is to take the relay plate out, disconnect multiplugs 'C' and 'E' and check contacts 'C16' and 'E21' for continuity. If there is a break in the circuit a new relay plate is needed. If the relay plate circuit is in order then check wire '53b' from the plate to the switch. If the break is in the wire then fit a new wire. If the wire is in order then the wiring from the relay to the

motor must be renewed.

5 *The motor works on stage I and II, but not on intermittent wipe.*
If both stages I and II are in order then the relay is suspect. Fit a new
one. If the motor works now then the relay was faulty. If it does not
put the old relay back and pull the connector off the wiper switch.
Check switch contact 'S1'. It should be connected to ground with
the lever at intermittent wipe. If it is connected to ground (zero
resistance) then a new wiper switch is needed. If the 'S1' connection
is not grounded properly then the 'S1' wire to the relay plate is
shorted to ground. This time detach connector 'E' from the relay
plate and check wire 'S1' for a short to ground. If it is defective
replace the wire. If there is an open circuit, then the relay plate
requires renewal.

32 Windshield washers - general

1 The standard models have the electric pump fitted and a two-
speed wiper. The pump is situated on a bracket at the side of the
container. Keep the hoses and joints in good condition. If the motor
does not work pull off the connector plug and check whether there
is voltage at the ' + ' terminal when the lever switch is set to
'wash' and the ignition is switched on. Check also that the ground
side is in order.

2 If there is voltage then the motor is defective and the complete
pump/motor unit must be replaced. To be quite certain rig a 12v
supply and a ground wire to the motor terminals as a separate test.
If there is no voltage the circuit must be traced back to the switch.
There is no relay, the relay space on the board is bridged. The
washer motor is in current track '92'. The probable circuit trouble is
that the bridge on the relay/fuse panel has become dislodged.
Check for voltage here, and finally at the wiper switch plug. If the
fuse was blown and you cannot find the fault check the fuse frequently. If it blows again then consult your Porsche dealer.

3 If the vehicle has an intermittent wash/wipe then the bridge is
replaced by relay 'J31' and the turn signal switch has had a lug
removed at a pre-determined breaking point to expose the location
for intermittent wash/wipe to the wiper switch. There is also a variation in the wiring. Fault finding works the same way with the additional complication of the relay.

33 Rear window wipe/wash - fitting guidelines

1 A very desirable addition is a rear window wipe/wash. This may
be supplied by Porsche as an optional extra, or a kit may be purchased from Hella. The kit comprises switch motor, wiper arm,
pump and washer unit with wire and hose. Full fitting instructions
are supplied. It is not cheap, and requires holes to be drilled in the
bodywork. It is not a job for the beginner, but it can be done with
care and patience by the average mechanic. Do not fit a wiper
without a washer, you will scratch the rear window this way.

2 For those who do have a service installed rear wiper a word of
warning. If for some reason the motor must be disconnected, the
reconnection is very important or the diode will be destroyed and a
new motor required. If the wires to terminal '53' and '53a' are interchanged then this disaster will happen when the motor is switched
off.

34 Headlamp washer system - general

1 This system is fitted to the higher range of vehicles only. See
Fig. 12.1 for an illustration of the hose and nozzle installation.

2 The system washes only, and does not wipe. An extra pump is
installed which is operated by a relay allowing a jet for 0.3 seconds.
The emission is further controlled by a pressure valve set at 35 psi
(2.6 bar).

3 When the system is filled the lines must be bled (as with brakes).
This is done by pulling off the hose at the junction leading to the
headlamp jets until liquid emerges. Then reconnect the hose,
switch on the ignition and the headlights and operate the column
switch until water emerges from the jets. Be careful that all connections are correctly installed and use only the Porsche special water
hose.

4 Training the jet is a difficult job unless the correct tool (VW 819)
is available. This is a cylindrical mandrel which fits in the jet hole

and reaches up to the lens. The top of the tool is moved about until
it contacts the lens with certain limits.

35 Wiring diagrams - explanation of the circuit structure

1 The vehicles of several years ago were mostly supplied with
current by D.C. generators. This effectively kept the charging rate
down and in particular gave small charge at low engine rpm. The
maximum speed of the generator was governed by commutator
integrity problems. With the advent of the A.C. generator much
better charging characteristics became possible, and greater load-
ing of the electrical circuits without incurring cold starting problems due to uncharged batteries. At the same time miniaturization
of relays made it possible to use smaller and multi-contact
switches. The possible number of appliances which could be used
became much greater, and the number of circuits involved multip-
lied accordingly. Thus a vehicle of the Porsche 924 type which
formerly would have rubbed along with four fuses now appears with
fifteen fuses and a number of relays as well.

2 To date we have produced old fashioned circuit diagrams for all
the Porsche family but they are rapidly becoming so involved that
there is more black ink than white paper!

3 A circuit diagram bears little or no resemblance to the actual
wiring of the car, for on the car all the wires are bunched in harness
and the diagram may only be used to trace the terminal ends of the
wiring, that is if your eyesight is good and you have a liking for
finding your way in a maze. Some time ago Porsche took a firm line
on this and produced a new idea called the Current Flow Diagram,
which we reproduce in this book.

4 To understand the Current Flow Diagram it is necessary first to
appreciate the change in wiring layout that has taken place.

5 The ends of the wires terminate in plugs of various types ranging
from multipin connectors to simple single pin or in the case of earth
connections, eyelets. If you know how, the installation of a new
harness is simply a matter of dismantling these plugs and refitting a
new harness, but it is not a job for the amateur.

6 There are a number of single wire connections, mostly heavy
duty cable, some of which are ground connections. These are very
important as it is vital that there be minimal volts drop on the
ground connections carrying large current loads.

7 A sample wiring harness is shown in Fig. 11.5. This one is an
engine harness.

8 Under the dashboard on the left-hand side of the vehicle is the
fuse and relay plate (Fig. 11.2). This has six terminal plates 'A' to 'F'
into which the wiring harnesses plug in, a section 'H1' to 'H4' all of
which are connected to terminal '30', the main supply point in the
starter circuit, and 'G1' to 'G10' which is provided for single wire
contacts such as the oil pressure switch, ignition/starter switch
terminal '15', all of which for some reason are better served with
single wires. The board is so organized as to include the fuses in the
correct circuits.

9 Relays, as required are plugged in to the face of the plate, the
multipin connectors of the relays making the correct contacts
automatically.

10 A table showing the connections is given in Figure 11.4

36 Wiring diagrams - explanation of usage

1 Before looking at the diagram study Fig. 11.4. This gives the
explanation of the symbols used in the diagram. The majority of
them are straightforward. The wire junction, fixed, means what it
says - wires soldered or otherwise permanently fixed together. The
wire junction separable is a pull off tag or an eyelet held under a
screw and washer. The wire connector is a plug and socket have
one, two, or a multipin, connector which may be pulled apart easily,
and assembled easily. These are referred to in the wiring key under
letter 'T' and the type and location given.

37 Wiring diagrams - general advice

1 One of the truest things ever said is that a little knowledge is a
dangerous thing. If you have read and understood the previous two
Sections then you have a rough idea of how the connections are

arranged. If you are an electrical engineer or an automotive electrician then we have supplied all you need. If you do not have this expertise you can still check connections and find out whether voltage is getting to the right point, but there you will stop if you are wise. Refer to the various Sections of this book to see what can and cannot be done to components but do not take the wiring out of the car. You can convert a simple fault which the electrician will quickly locate and correct, into a nightmare for which there is no logical reason, in a matter of seconds. We do not wish to be blamed for this. You will rightly feel foolish if the radiator fan does not work because the connector has pulled apart and only needs pushing together, but if you go to the expert and say that you have checked the circuit as far as possible, that 'T2b' is connected properly but that 'J26' does not seem to work or 'F18' (the thermo-switch) is doubtful then he will regard you with much more respect. But if you replace 'J26' without finding out what is really wrong (eg; a short circuit in the motor), and reintroduce current to where it should not go, then the electrician may not say anything, but he will think it, and we wouldn't like that. Although they are up-to-date at the time of publication it would be wise to consult your Porsche dealer about possible modifications.

242

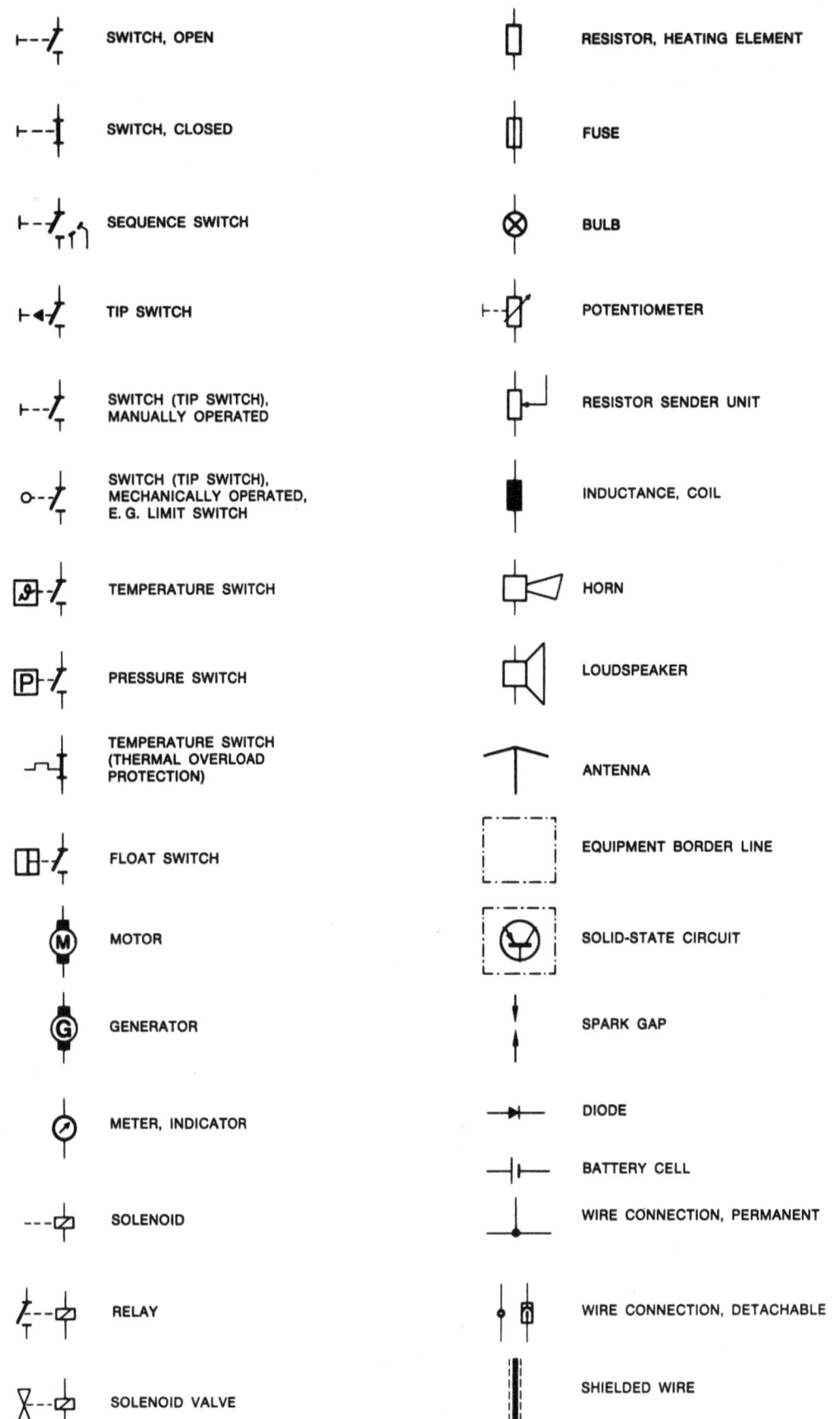

Fig. 11.4 Explanation of the symbols used in the current flow diagrams

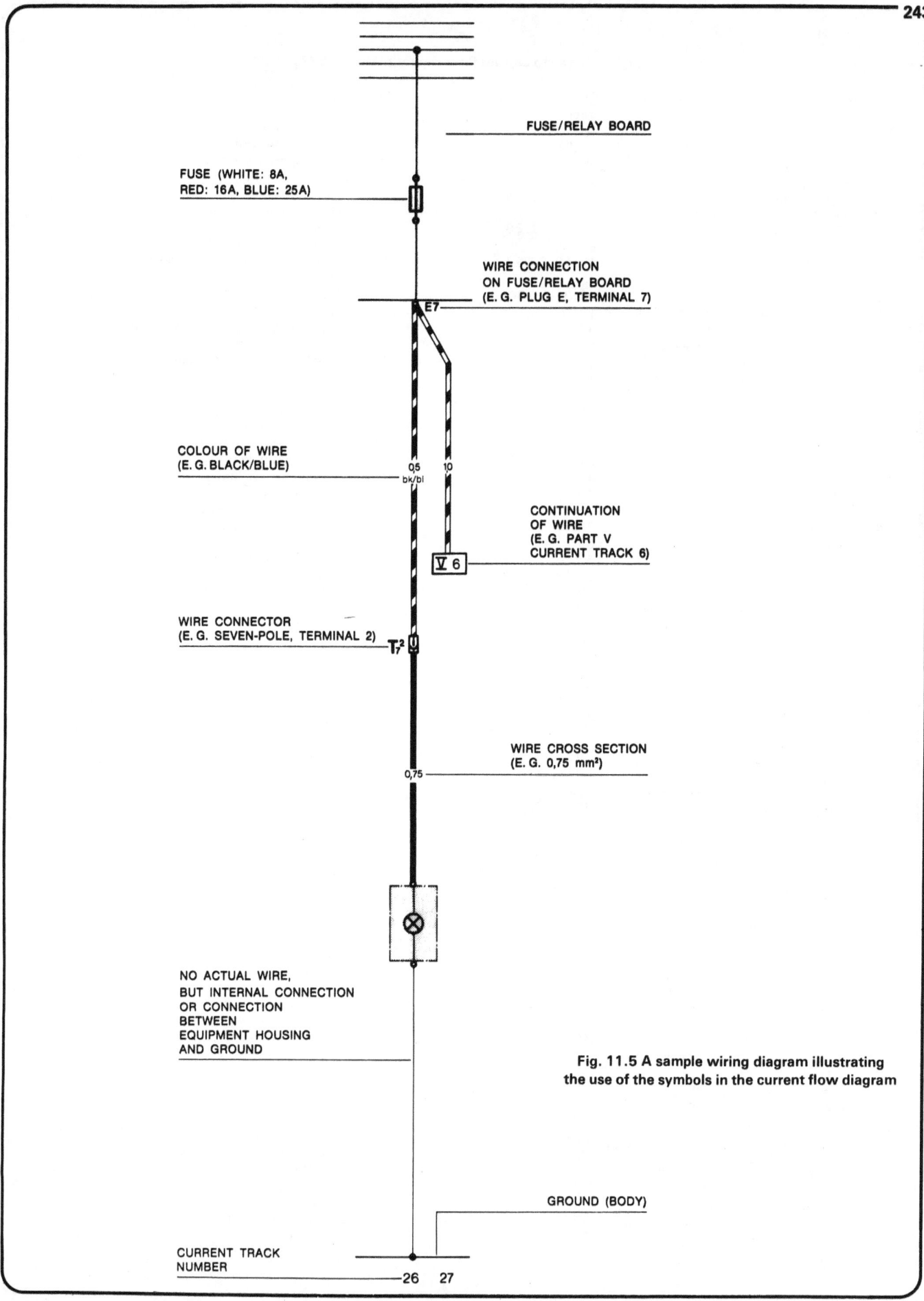

FUSE/RELAY BOARD

FUSE (WHITE: 8A, RED: 16A, BLUE: 25A)

WIRE CONNECTION ON FUSE/RELAY BOARD (E. G. PLUG E, TERMINAL 7)

E7

COLOUR OF WIRE (E. G. BLACK/BLUE)

0,5
bk/bl

1,0

CONTINUATION OF WIRE (E. G. PART V CURRENT TRACK 6)

V 6

WIRE CONNECTOR (E. G. SEVEN-POLE, TERMINAL 2)

T7²

WIRE CROSS SECTION (E. G. 0,75 mm²)

0,75

NO ACTUAL WIRE, BUT INTERNAL CONNECTION OR CONNECTION BETWEEN EQUIPMENT HOUSING AND GROUND

Fig. 11.5 A sample wiring diagram illustrating the use of the symbols in the current flow diagram

GROUND (BODY)

CURRENT TRACK NUMBER

26   27

Fig. 11.6 Key to current flow diagram, 1976–1977½

Description		Current track
A	– Battery	98
B	– Starter	96, 97
C	– Generator	99
C1	– Voltage	99
D	– Ignition/starter switch	71, 72, 73, 74
E	– Windshield wiper switch	85, 86, 87, 88, 89
E1	– Headlight switch	17, 18, 20, 21
E2	– Turn signal switch	33
E3	– Emergency flasher switch	29, 31, 32, 34
E4	– Dimmer/headlight flasher switch	1
E9	– Fresh air blower switch	93
E15	– Rear window defogger switch	82
E19	– Parking light switch	19
E20	– Instrument panel illumination potentiometer	22
E24	– Seat belt switch	74
F	– Stop light switch	46, 47
F2	– Left door switch	52
F3	– Right door switch	51
F4	– Back-up light switch	43
F9	– Parking brake switch	49
F18	– Thermo-switch for radiator fan	95
F26	– Thermo-switch for cold start valve	75, 75
F27	– Mileage counter switch (EGR)	65
F34	– Brake fluid level contact	50
G	– Fuel sender unit	66, 67
G1	– Fuel gauge	68
G2	– Coolant temperature sender unit	63
G3	– Coolant temperature indicator	62
G5	– Tachometer	60
G6	– Fuel pump	79
G8	– Oil temperature sender unit	60
G9	– Oil temperature indicator	60
G10	– Oil pressure sender unit	58, 59
G11	– Oil pressure indicator	59
G19	– Air meter contact	78
H	– Horn switch	39
H1	– Horn	40, 41, 42
J	– Dimmer/headlight flasher relay	1, 2
J1	– Hazard/turn signal flasher	32, 32, 33
J4	– Horn relay	40, 41
J9	– Rear window defogger relay	82, 83
J17	– Relay for fuel pump	77, 78, 79
J26	– Relay for radiator fan	94
J31	– Relay for intermittent wiper operation	88, 89
J34	– Seat belt warning system relay	72, 73, 74
J37	– Retractable headlight relay	24
K1	– High beam indicator light	18
K2	– Generator charge indicator light	64
K3	– Oil pressure indicator light	57
K5	– Turn signal indicator light	61
K6	– Hazard flasher indicator light	34
K7	– Brake warning light	48
K10	– Rear window defogger indicator light	81
K16	– Low fuel warning light	66
K19	– Seat belt warning light	48
K22	– EGR warning light	69
L1	– Left headlight	2, 4
L2	– Right headlight	3, 5
L6	– Speedometer illumination light	21
L7	– Fuel gauge illumination light	21
L8	– Clock illumination light	31
L9	– Headlight switch illumination light	17
L15	– Ashtray illumination light	28

Description		Current track
L16	– Heater control assembly illumination light	32
L24	– Oil temperature indicator illumination light	32
L26	– Tachometer illumination light	21
L27	– Oil pressure indicator illumination light	32
L29	– Engine compartment light	6
L30	– Coolant temperature indicator illumination light	21
M2	– Right rear light	13
M4	– Left rear light	9
M5	– Left front turn signal parking light	7, 35
M6	– Left rear turn signal	36
M7	– Right front turn signal, parking light	11, 36
M8	– Right rear turn signal	38
M9	– Left stop light	45
M10	– Right stop light	46
M11	– Front side marker light	8, 12
M12	– Rear side marker light	10, 14
M16	– Left back-up light	43
M17	– Right back-up light	44
N	– Ignition coil	104
N6	– Register for ignition coil	104
N9	– Warm up for regulator	80
N17	– Cold start valve	75
N21	– Supplementary air valve	81
N39	– Resistor for radiator fan	95
N41	– Electronic ignition unit	100, 101, 102
O	– Distributor	101, 103-106
P	– Spark plug connector	103-106
Q	– Spark plug	103-106
S1 to S4	– Fuses	2, 3, 4, 5
S5	– Fuses	101
S6 to S9	– Fuses on the fuse	52, 30, 28, 41
S10	– and	93
S11	– relay	84
S12	– board	24
S13 to S15	– Fuses on the fuse	11, 7, 95
S18	to and relay	83, 79, 94
S19	– board	22
T1	– Cable connector, single	
	a–near fuse and relay board	10, 12, 40, 42
	b–near brake booster	10, 12
	c–near windshield wiper motor	6
	d–behind radio	27
T1	– Cable connector, single	
	a–near fuse and relay board	73, 79
	f–in centre panel	93
	g–near gas lift cylinder	83
T2	– Cable connector double	
	a–near left front turn signal	8
	b–near right front turn signal	12
	e–left side markers	10
	f–near right side markers	14
T2	– Cable connector, double	
	d–near radiator fan	95
	g–near left seat	73, 74

Fig. 11.6 Key to current flow diagram, 1976 – 1977½ (continued)

Description		Current track		Description		Current track
T3	Cable connector, triple			T7	– Cable connector, sevenfold	58, 59, 60, 63, 76
	a–near left front turn signal	7, 35			in engine compartment	78, 80
	b–near right front turn signal	11, 37		T7	– Cable connector, sevenfold	
T3	– Cable connector, triple				a–near left rear lights	9, 36
	e–in engine compartment	96, 97, 99			b–near right rear lights	13, 38
T4	– Cable connector, fourfold			T21	– Gas lift cylinder, left	83
	near fuse and relay board	44, 49		T22	– Gas lift cylinder, right	83
T4	– Cable connector, fourfold			U1	– Cigar lighter	29
	near fuse and relay board	66		V	– Windshield wiper motor	91, 92
T6	–Cable connector, sixfold			V2	– Fresh air blower	93
	a–behind instrument panel	60, 61, 100		V5	– Washer pump	90
	b–behind instrument panel	64, 70		V7	– Radiator fan	95
	c–behind instrument panel	57, 62, 66, 68, 69		V9	– Retractable headlight motor	23, 24, 44
	d–in centre panel	59, 60		W	– Interior light	52
	e–near fuse and relay board	59, 60, 100		W3	– Luggage compartment light	24
T6	– Cable connector, sixfold			W6	– Glove compartment light	26
	a–behind instrument panel	15, 22		X	– License plate light	25
	b–behind instrument panel	18, 22		Y	– Clock	30
	d–in centre panel	30, 31, 32		Z1	– Rear window defogger	83
	e–near fuse and relay board	47, 50				

Color Key

bk	black
bl	blue
br	brown
gn	green
gr	grey
re	red
vi	violet
wt	white
ye	yellow

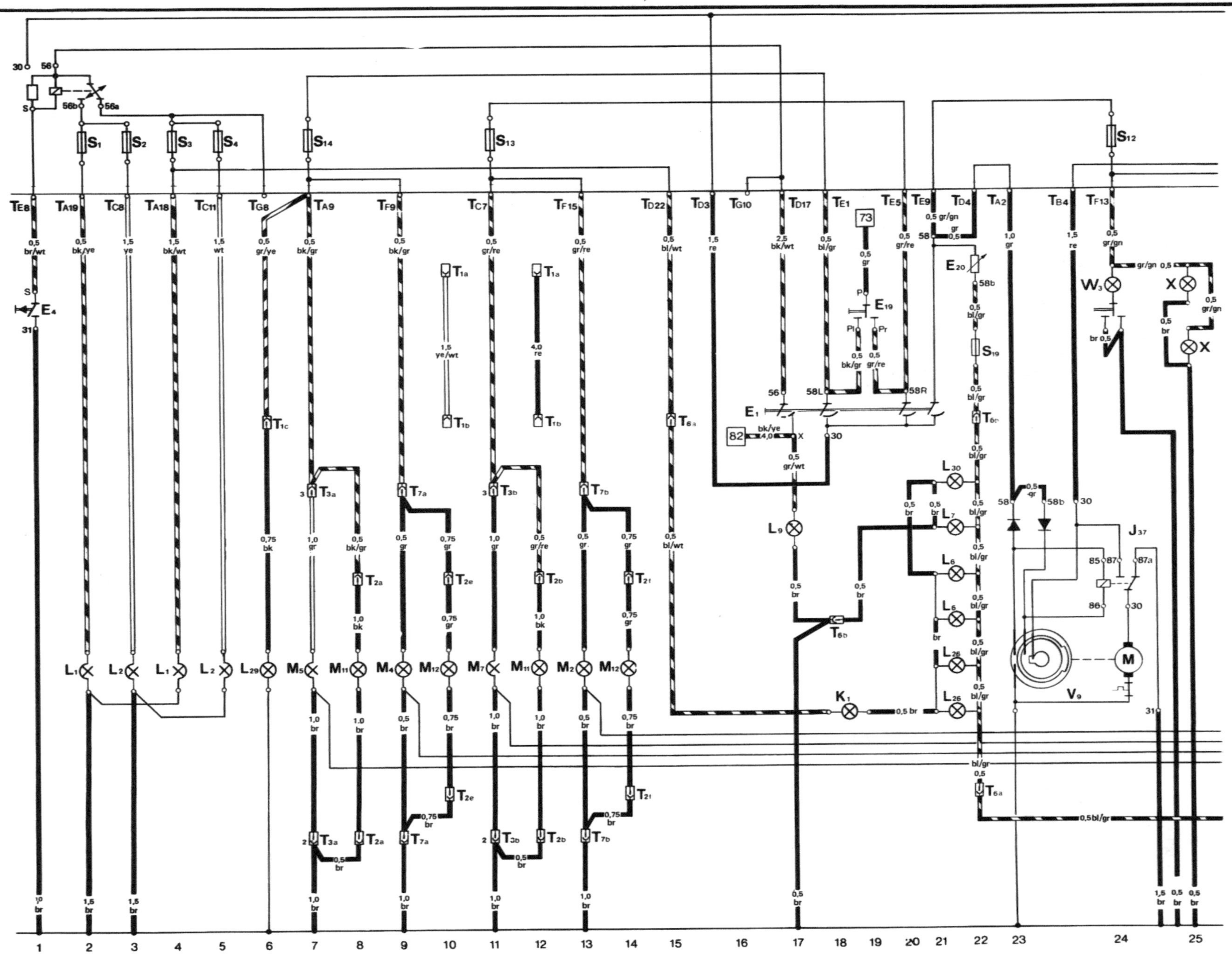

Fig. 11.7a Current flow diagram, 1976 – 1977½

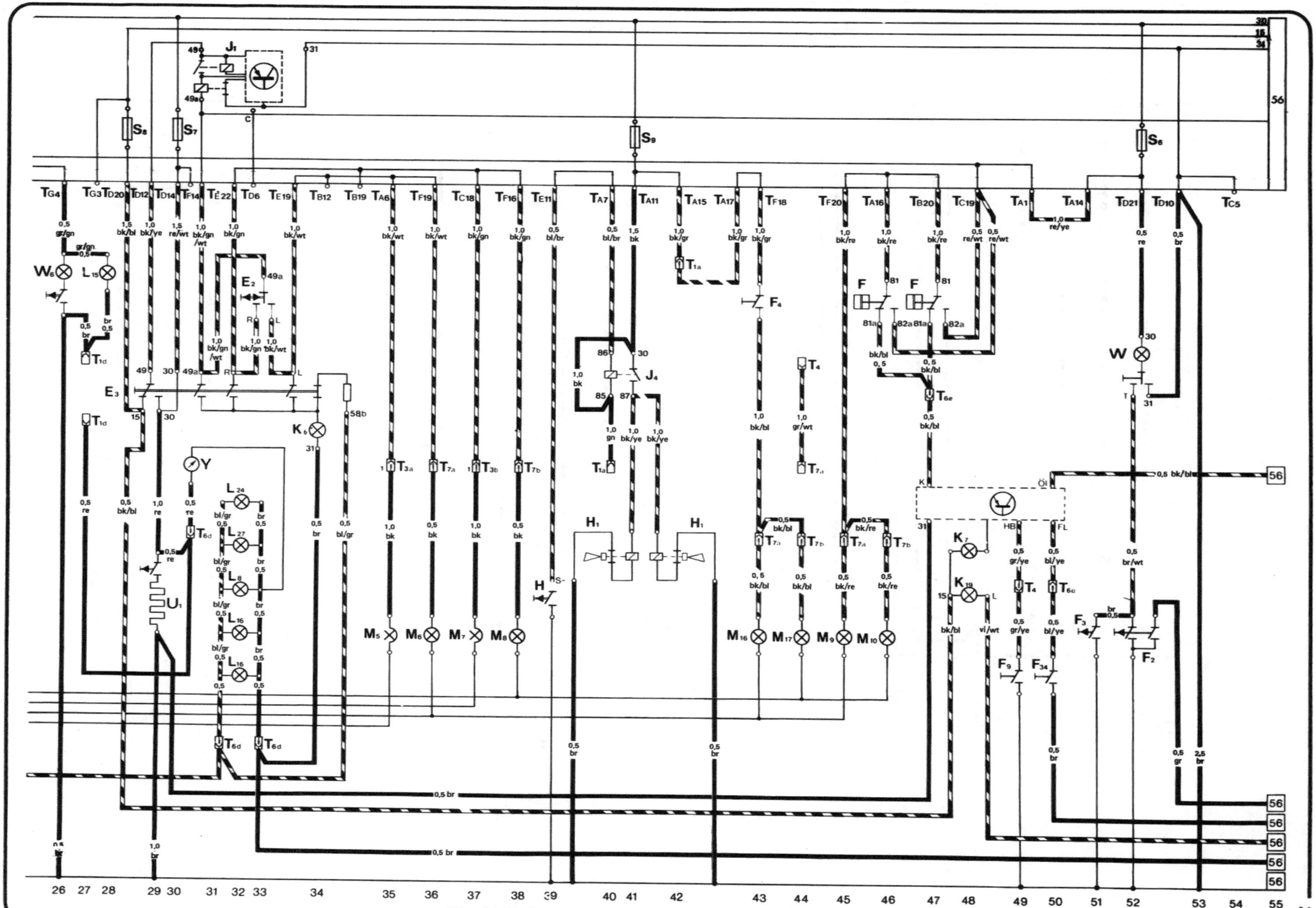

Fig. 11.7b Current flow diagram, 1976 – 1977½ (continued)

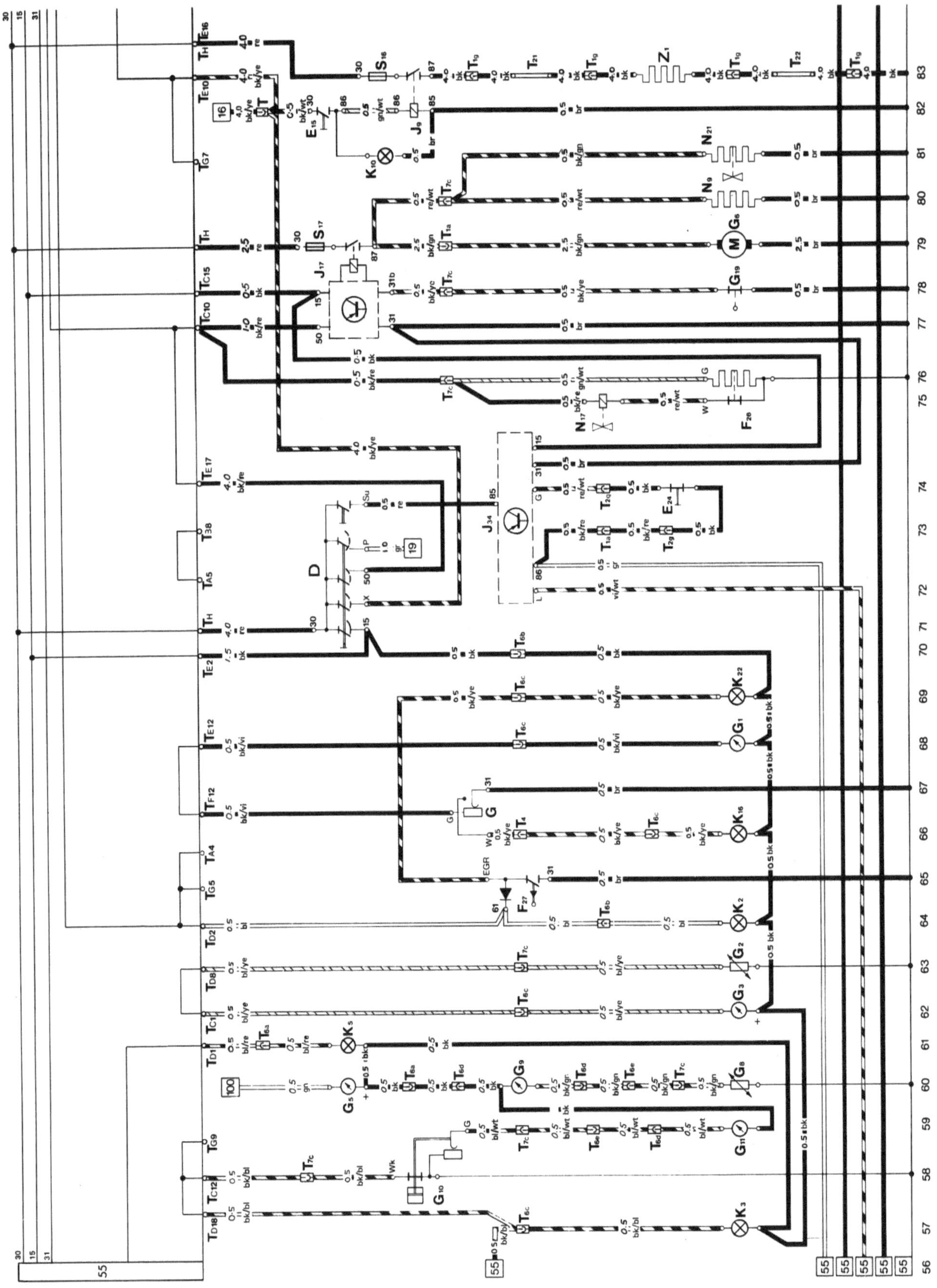

Fig. 11.7c Current flow diagram, 1976 – 1977½ (continued)

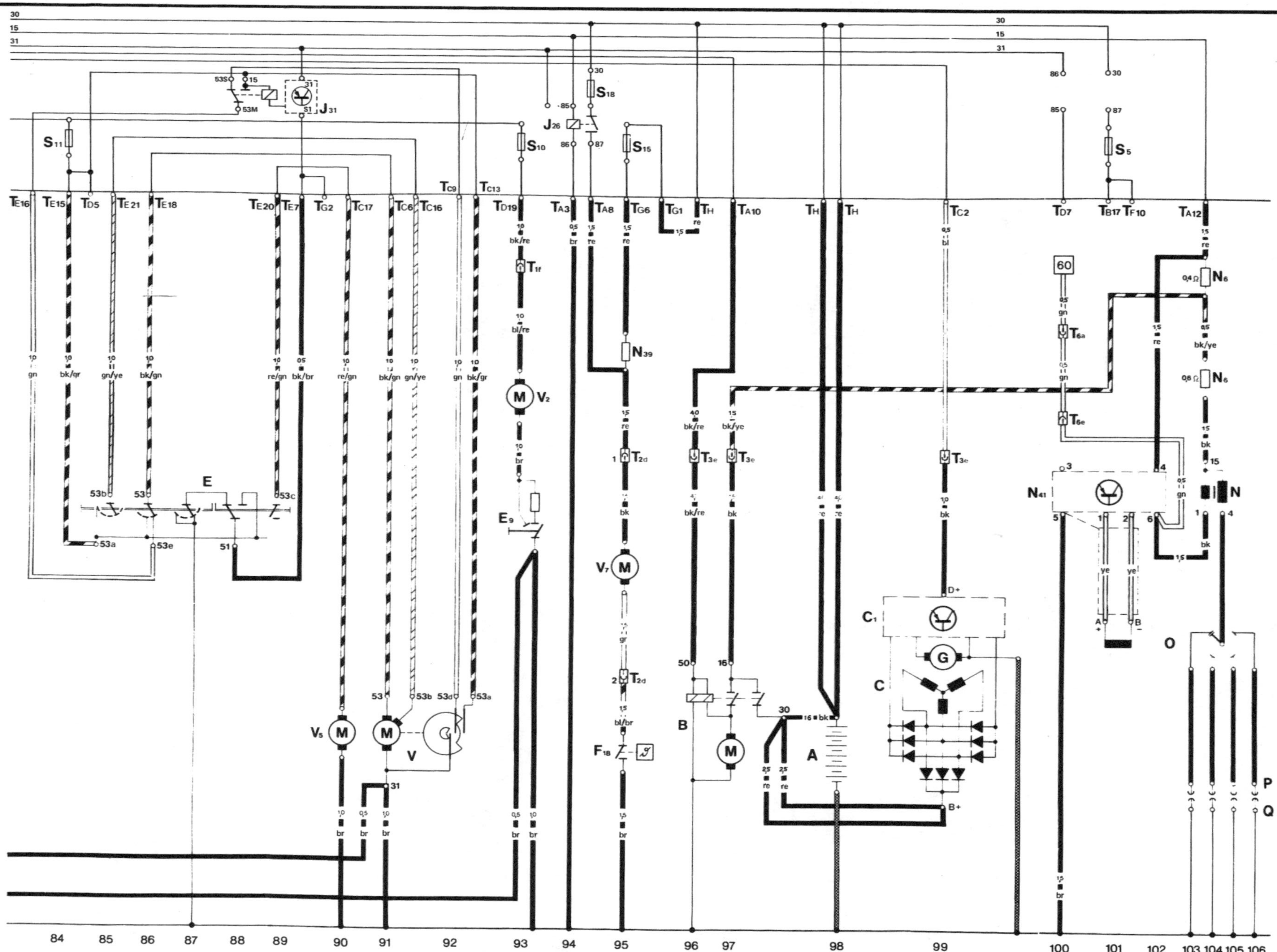

Fig. 11.7d Current flow diagram, 1976 – 1977½ (continued)

Fig. 11.8 Key to current flow diagram, 1977½ – 1978

Description		Current track		Description		Current track
A	– Battery	3		K19	– Seat belt warning light	24
B	– Starter	4, 5, 6		L1	– Left headlight	16, 17
C	– Generator	2		L2	– Right headlight	18, 19
C1	– Voltage regulator	2		L6	– Speedometer illumination	7
D	– Ignition/starter switch	14...17		L7	– Fuel gauge illumination	7
E	– Windshield wiper switch	2...6		L8	– Clock illumination	12
E1	– Headlight switch	2...7		L9	– Headlight switch illumination	3
E2	– Turn signal switch	11		L15	– Ashtray illumination	4
E3	– Emergency flasher switch	6...13		L16	– Heater control assembly illumination	12
E4	– Headlight dimmer switch	15		L22	– Fog light	12
E9	– Fresh air blower switch	11		L25	– Voltage illumination	12
E15	– Rear window defogger	19, 20		L26	– Tachometer illumination	7
E18	– Rear fog light switch	20		L27	– Oil pressure indicator illumination	12
E19	– Parking light switch	5		L29	– Engine compartment light	21
E20	– Instrument panel illumination potentiometer	8		L30	– Coolant temperature indicator illumination	7
E24	– Seat belt switch	17		M1	– Left parking light	23
E34	– Rear window wiper switch	26		M2	– Right rear light	28
F	– Stop light switch	21, 23		M3	– Right parking light	26
F2	– Left door switch	22, 23		M4	– Left rear light	30
F3	– Right door switch	24		M5	– Left front turn signal	24
F4	– Back-up light switch	17		M6	– Left rear turn signal	15
F9	– Hand brake warning switch	14		M7	– Right front turn signal	27
F18	– Temperature switch for cooling fan	21		M8	– Right rear turn signal	16
F26	– Thermo-time switch for cold start valve	11, 12		M9	– Left stop light	19
G	– Fuel sender unit	11, 12		M10	– Right stop light	20
G1	– Fuel gauge	13		M11	– Front side marker light	22, 25
G2	– Coolant temperature sender unit	9		M12	– Rear side marker light	29, 31
G3	– Coolant temperature indicator	8		M16	– Left back-up light	17
G5	– Tachometer	5		M17	– Right back-up light	18
G6	– Fuel pump	16		N	– Ignition coil	8
G10	– Oil pressure sender unit	2, 3		N6	– Ballast resistor	7
G11	– Oil pressure indicator	3		N9	– Warm-up regulator	17
G14	– Voltmeter	5		N17	– Cold start valve	11
G19	– Air flow sensor contact	15		N21	– Auxiliary air valve	18
H	– Horn switch	25		N39	– Series resistor for cooling fan	21
H1	– Horn	27, 28		N41	– Transistor ignition unit	9, 10
J	– Headlight dimmer relay	15, 16, 17		O	– Distributor	8, 9
J1	– Hazard/turn signal flasher	8, 9, 10		P	– Spark plug connector	8
J4	– Horn relay	26, 27		Q	– Spark plug	8
J5	– Fog light relay	12		R	– Radio	4
J9	– Rear window defogger relay	20, 21		S1	– Fuse	16, 17, 18
J17	– Fuel pump relay	14, 15, 16		S5	– Fuse	19, 20
J26	– Cooling fan relay	19, 20		S6	– Fuse	23
J31	– Interval wiping relay	4, 5		S7	– Fuse	5
J34	– Seat belt warning system relay	16, 17, 18		S8	– Fuse	6
J37	– Concealing headlights relay	12		S9	– Fuse	27
J39	– Headlight washer relay	14		S10	– Fuse	11
K1	– High beam indicator light	1		S11	– Fuse	1
K2	– Generator charge light indicator	10		S12	– Fuse	1
K3	– Oil pressure indicator light	1		S13	– Fuse	25
K5	– Turn signal indicator light	6		S14	– Fuse	22
K6	– Emergency flasher indicator light	13		S15	– Fuse	22
K7	– Brake system warning light	23		S16	– Fuse	21
K14	– Hand brake warning light	14		S17	– Fuse	16
K16	– Low fuel warning light	11		S18	– Fuse	20
				S18	– Fuse	8

Fig. 11.8 Key to current flow diagram, 1977½ – 1978 (continued)

Description	Current track
T1a – Wire connector, near fuse/relay board	12, 14
T1a – Wire connector, near fuse/relay board	16
T1a – Wire connector, near fuse/relay board	18
T1a – Wire connector, near fuse/relay board	18, 26
T1b – Wire connector, in engine compartment	21
T1c – Wire connector, near brake booster	12, 14
T1c – Wire connector, in instrument panel	20
T1d – Wire connector, in center console	4
T1d – Wire connector, in center console	11
T1e – Wire connector, on rear lid	21
T2a – Wire connector, two-pole near cooling fan	21
T2a – Wire connector, near left front turn signal	22
T2b – Wire connector, near right front turn signal	25
T2c – Wire connector, two-pole near left seat	17, 18
T2d – Wire connector, near right side markers	29
T2e – Wire connector, near left side markers	31
T3a – Wire connector, three-pole in engine compartment	1, 5, 6
T3b – Wire connector, near left headlight	16, 17
T3c – Wire connector, near right headlight	18, 19
T4 – Wire connector, four-pole near fuse/relay board	11, 14
T4 – Wire connector, four-pole near fuse/relay board	20
T6a – Wire connector, six-pole near fuse/relay board	3
T6a – Wire connector, six-pole near fuse/relay board	21
T6b – Wire connector, six-pole in instrument panel	1
T6b – Wire connector, six-pole in instrument panel	5, 6

Description	Current track
T6b – Wire connector, six-pole in instrument panel	10
T6c – Wire connector, six-pole in instrument panel	4, 8
T6c – Wire connector, six-pole in instrument panel	10, 14
T6d – Wire connector, six-pole in center console	3, 5
T6d – Wire connector, six-pole in center console	11, 13
T6e – Wire connector, six-pole in instrument panel	1, 8, 11, 13
T7a – Wire connector, seven-pole in engine compartment	3, 9
T7a – Wire connector, seven-pole in engine compartment	12, 15, 17
T7b – Wire connector, seven-pole near right rear lights	16, 18, 20
T7b – Wire connector, seven-pole near right rear lights	28
T7c – Wire connector, seven-pole near left rear lights	15, 17, 19
T7c – Wire connector, seven-pole near left rear lights	30
T21 – Left pneumatic spring	21
T22 – Right pneumatic spring	21
U1 – Cigarette lighter	7
V – Windshield wiper motor	7, 8
V5 – Washer pump	9
V7 – Cooling fan	21
V9 – Concealing headlight motor	10...14
W – Interior light	23
W3 – Luggage compartment light	1
W6 – Glove compartment light	3
X – License plate light	2
Y – Clock	12
Z1 – Rear window defogger	21

Color Key

bk	black
bl	blue
br	brown
gn	green
gr	grey
re	red
vi	violet
wt	white
ye	yellow

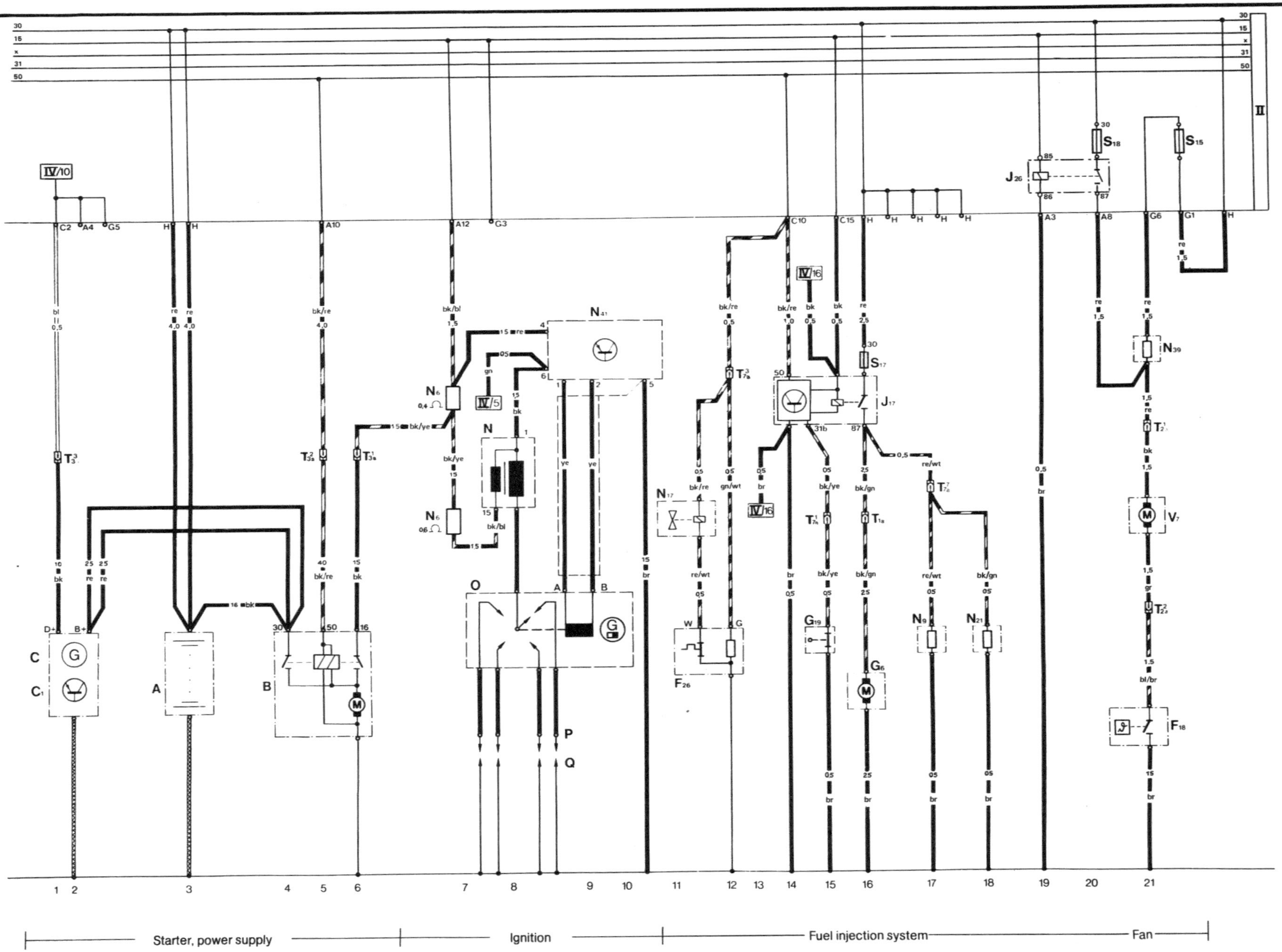

Fig. 11.9a Current flow diagram, $1977\frac{1}{2}$ – 1978

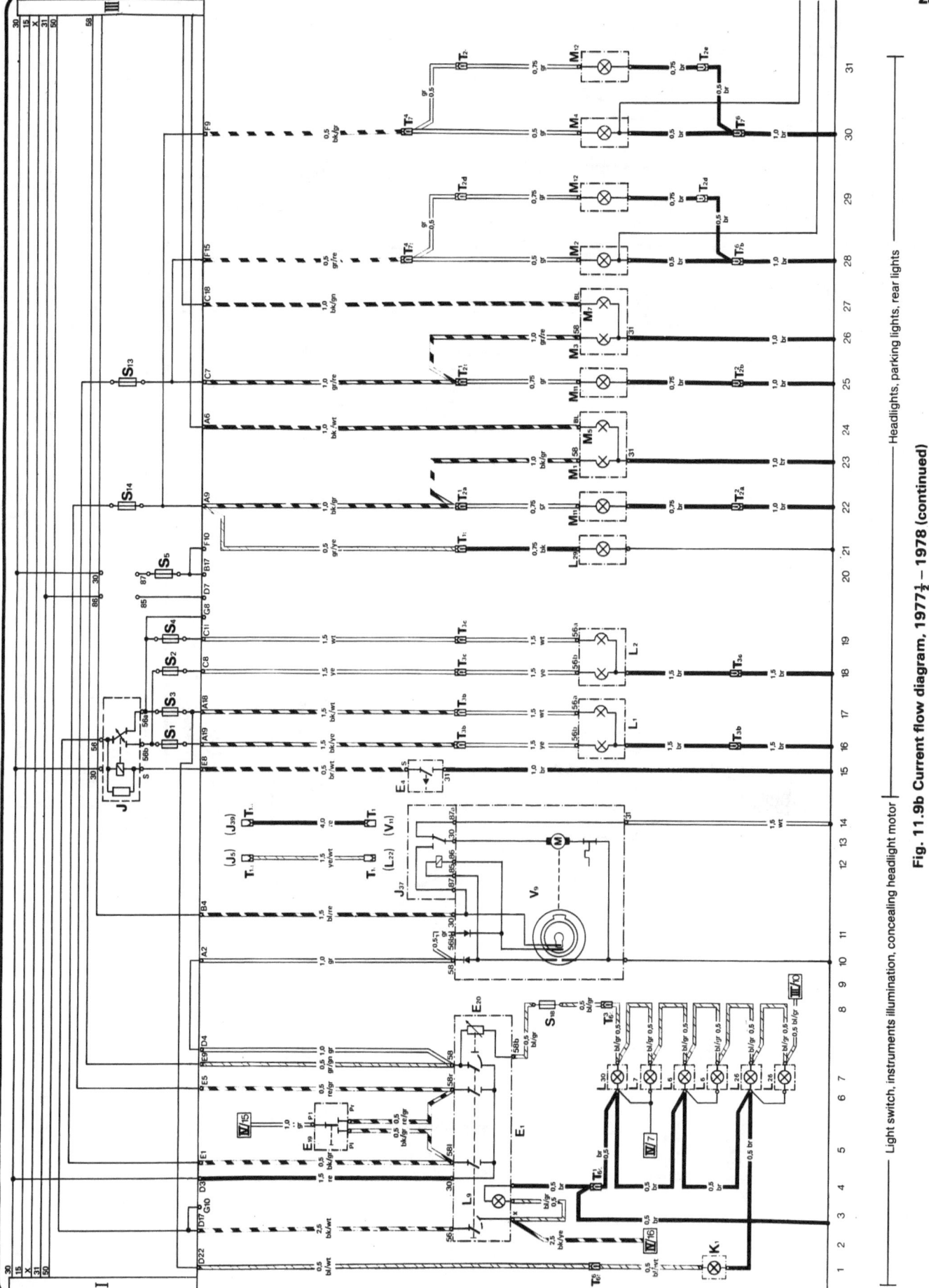

Fig. 11.9b Current flow diagram, 1977½ – 1978 (continued)

|— Light switch, instruments illumination, concealing headlight motor —|—— Headlights, parking lights, rear lights ——|

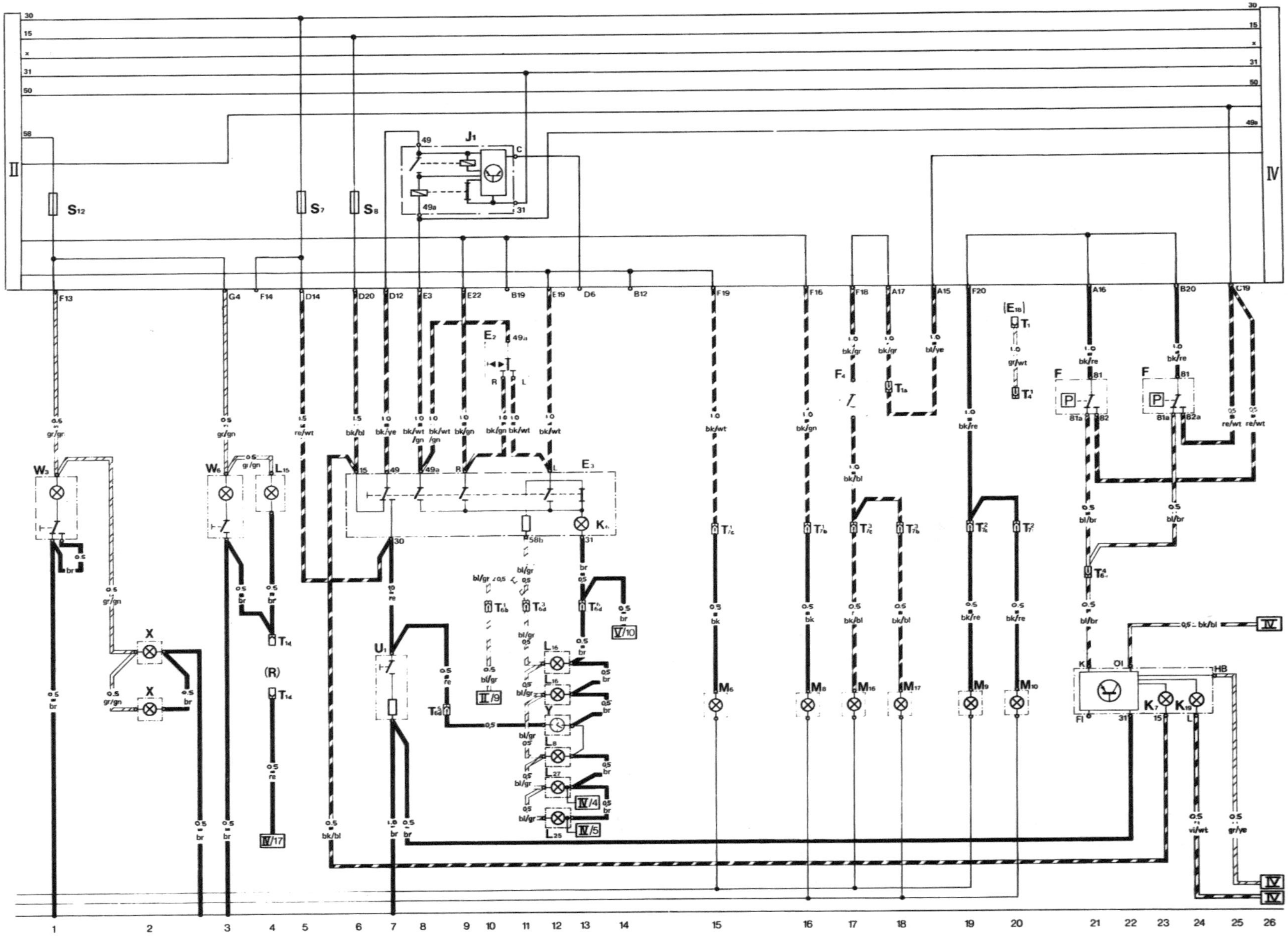

Fig. 11.9c Current flow diagram, 1977½ – 1978 (continued)

Interior lights, license plate light — Emergency flasher, instruments illumination center console — Turn signals, rear lights — Stop light switch

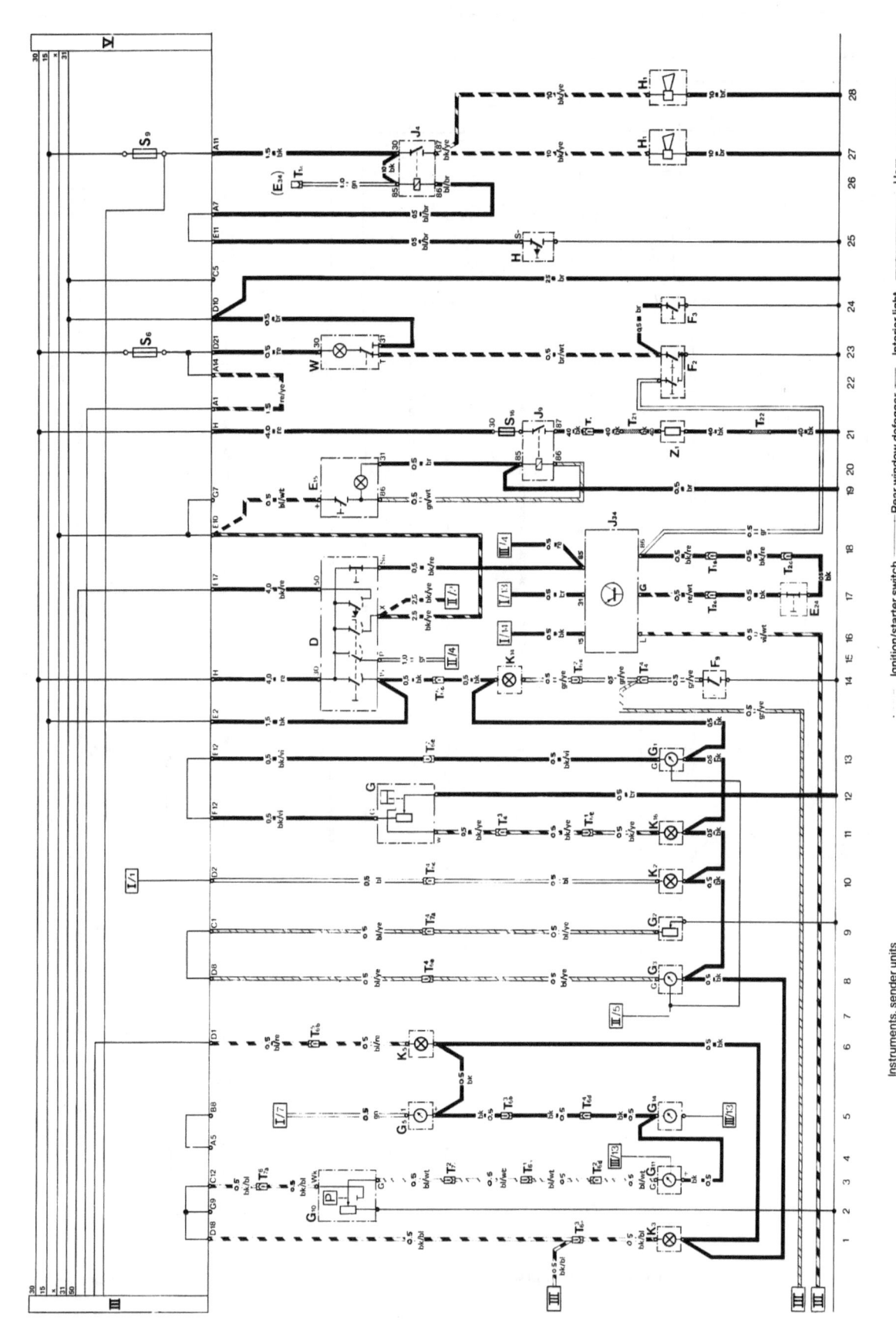

Fig. 11.9d Current flow diagram, 1977½ – 1978 (continued)

Instruments, sender units ———— Ignition/starter switch ———— Rear window defogger ———— Interior light ———— Horn

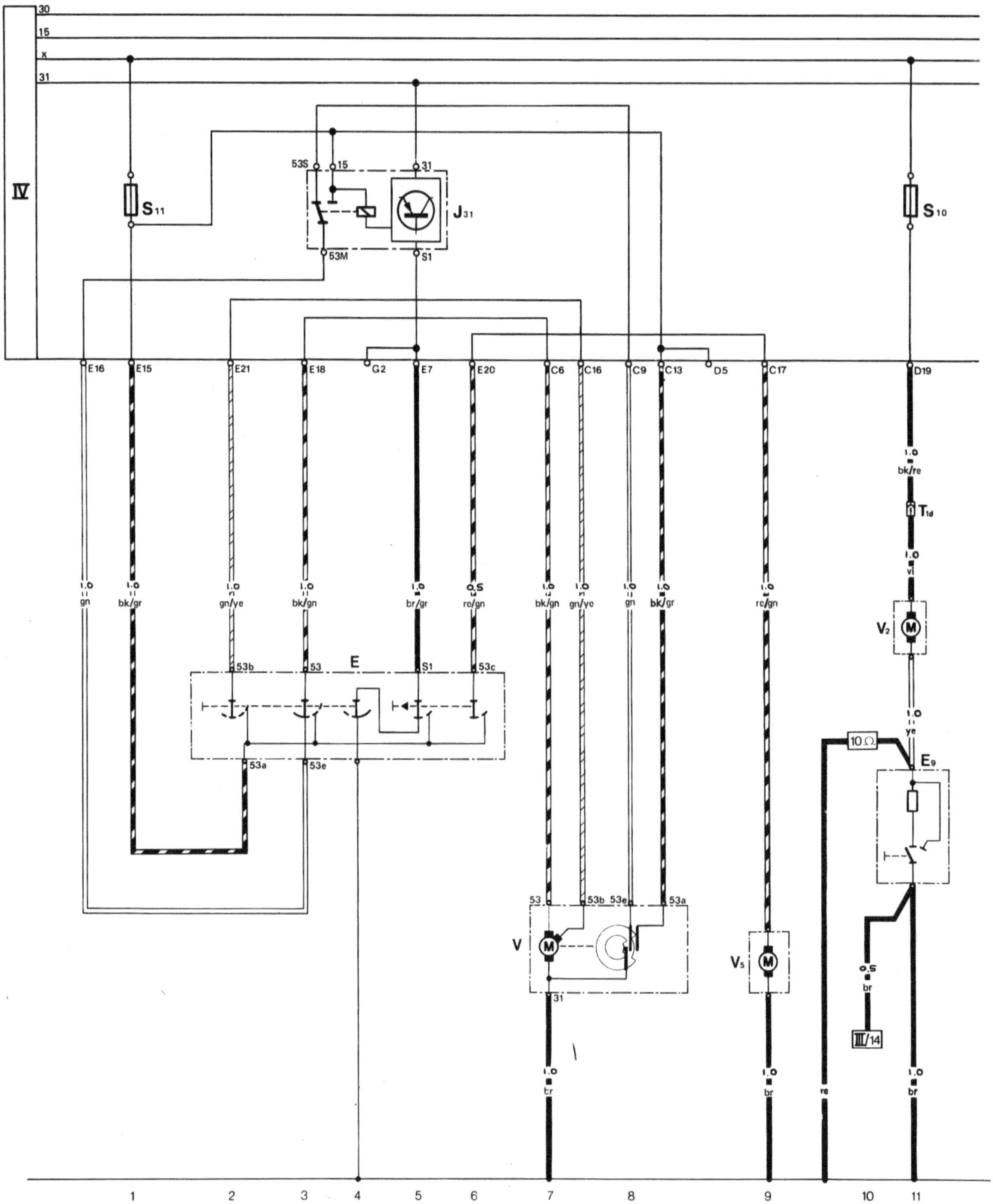

Windshield wipers, windshield washer pump

Fresh air blower

Fig. 11.9e Current flow diagram, 1977½ – 1978 (continued)

Part / Current-track

Part	Current-track	Component
IV	14	ASHTRAY LIGHT
III	21	BACK-UP LIGHT, LEFT
III	22	BACK-UP LIGHT, RIGHT
III	21	BACK-UP LIGHT, SWITCH
I	3	BATTERY
III	1	BRAKE LIGHT, LEFT
III	2	BRAKE LIGHT, RIGHT
III	6	BRAKE WARNING LIGHT
III	4	BRAKE LIGHT SWITCH
III	10	CIGARETTE LIGHTER
V	5	CLOCK
II	12	CONCEALING HEADLIGHT MOTOR
II	13	CONCEALING HEADLIGHT RELAY
IV	33	COOLANT TEMPERATURE SENDER UNIT
IV	27	COOLANT TEMPERATURE INDICATOR
II	15	DIMMER/HEAD LIGHT FLASHER SWITCH
I	13	DISTRIBUTOR
III	30	DOOR SWITCH, LEFT
III	31	DOOR SWITCH, RIGHT
III	13	EMERGENCY FLASHER SWITCH
II	22	ENGINE COMPARTMENT LIGHT
II	23	FAN MOTOR
I	23	FAN RELAY
V	32	FOG LIGHT
V	2	FRESH AIR BLOWER MOTOR
V	2	FRESH AIR BLOWER SWITCH
IV	31	FUEL GAUGE
I	18	FUEL PUMP
I	16	FUEL PUMP RELAY
IV	31	FUEL SENDER UNIT

FUSES

Part	Current-track	Fuse
II	17	1
II	20	2
III	18	3
V	21	4
III	22	5
IV	14	6
II	8	7
II	9	8
III	24	9
V	2	10
V	13	11
IV	1	12
II	27	13
II	24	14
II	32	15

FUSES — ADDITIONAL FUSE BOARD

Part	Current-track	Fuse
III	27	1
I	18	2
I	23	3
IV	5	4
	9	5
		6 (free)
		7 (free)
		8 (free)
		9 (free)

Part	Current-track	Component
I	2	GENERATOR
IV	23	GENERATOR CHARGE INDICATOR LIGHT
IV	13	GLOVE COMPARTMENT LIGHT
III	12	HAZARD/TURN SIGNAL FLASHER
III	18	HEADLIGHT, LEFT
I	18	HEADLIGHT RELAY
III	21	HEADLIGHT, RIGHT
IV	33	HEADLIGHT WASHER
V	3	HEATER CONTROL ASSEMBLY LIGHT
IV	26	HIGH BEAM INDICATOR LIGHT
III	28	HORN
III	26	HORN CONTACT
III	28	HORN RELAY

Part / Current-track

Part	Current-track	Component
I	12	IGNITION COIL
IV	9	IGNITION/STARTER SWITCH
IV	20	INSTRUMENT CLUSTER ILLUMINATION
IV	15	INSTRUMENT CLUSTER ILLUMINATION, POTENTIOMETER
IV	26	INSTRUMENT CLUSTER
III	30	INTERIOR LIGHT
V	17	INTERVAL WIPING, RELAY
IV	2	LICENCE PLATE LIGHT
IV	6	LIGHT SWITCH
IV	30	LOW FUEL WARNING LIGHT
IV	1	LUGGAGE COMPARTMENT LIGHT
V	10	OIL PRESSURE INDICATOR
IV	28	OIL PRESSURE INDICATOR LIGHT
V	9	OIL PRESSURE SENDER UNIT
III	25	OUTSIDE MIRROR
IV	22	PARKING BRAKE CONTACT
IV	22	PARKING BRAKE INDICATOR LIGHT
II	7	PARKING LIGHT CONTACT
II	24	PARKING LIGHT, LEFT
II	27	PARKING LIGHT, RIGHT
II	9	PNEUMATIC SPRING RIGHT
IV	9	PNEUMATIC SPRING LEFT
IV	14	RADIO
II	31	REAR LIGHT, LEFT
II	29	REAR LIGHT, RIGHT
IV	9	REAR WINDOW DEFOGGER
IV	8	REAR WINDOW DEFOGGER RELAY
IV	4	REAR WINDOW DEFOGGER SWITCH
III	25	REAR WINDOW WIPER
I	2	REGULATOR
I	20	RESISTOR
I	12	SPARK PLUG
IV	15	SPEEDOMETER
I	5	STARTER
I	8	START VALVE
I	21	SUPPLEMENTARY AIR VALVE
IV	5	SEAT BELT SWITCH
IV	5	SEAT BELT WARNING RELAY
II	23	SIDE MARKER, FRONT, LEFT
II	26	SIDE MARKER, FRONT, RIGHT
II	32	SIDE MARKER, REAR, LEFT
II	30	SIDE MARKER, REAR, RIGHT
I	10	SUPPLEMENTARY START VALVE
IV	19	TACHOMETER
I	10	TEMPERATURE SWITCH, SUPPLEMENTARY START VALVE
I	23	TEMPERATURE SWITCH, COOLING FAN
I	8	THERMO SWITCH FOR COLD START VALVE
II	13	TRANSISTOR IGNITION UNIT
II	25	TURN SIGNAL, FRONT, LEFT
II	28	TURN SIGNAL, FRONT, RIGHT
III	25	TURN SIGNAL INDICATOR LIGHT
III	18	TURN SIGNAL, REAR, LEFT
III	20	TURN SIGNAL, REAR, RIGHT
III	13	TURN SIGNAL SWITCH
V	12	VOLTMETER
I	20	WARM UP REGULATOR
V	21	WIND SHIELD WASHER PUMP
V	20	WIND SHIELD WIPER MOTOR
V	16	WIND SHIELD WIPER SWITCH

WIRE CONNECTORS

T1 - ONE-POLE
A - NEAR FUSE / RELAY BOARD
B - IN ENGINE COMPARTMENT
C - NEAR BRAKE BOOSTER
D - IN CENTER CONSOLE
E - ON REAR LID
F - BEHIND INSTRUMENT CLUSTER

T2 - TWO-POLE
A - NEAR LEFT PARKING LIGHT
B - NEAR RIGHT PARKING LIGHT
C - NEAR LEFT SEAT
D - NEAR RIGHT REAR LIGHT
E - NEAR LEFT REAR LIGHT
F - NEAR FAN

T3 - THREE-POLE
A - IN ENGINE COMPARTMENT
B - NEAR HEADLIGHT, LEFT
C - NEAR HEADLIGHT, RIGHT

T4 - FOUR-POLE
NEAR FUSE / RELAY BOARD

T6 - SIX-POLE
A - NEAR FUSE / RELAY BOARD
B - IN CENTER CONSOLE

T7 - SEVEN-POLE
A - IN ENGINE COMPARTMENT
B - NEAR RIGHT REAR LIGHTS
C - NEAR LEFT REAR LIGHTS

GROUND TERMINALS

(1) NEAR FUSE / RELAY BOARD
(2) IN LUGGAGE COMPARTMENT, NEAR LEFT REAR LIGHT
(3) NEAR DISTRIBUTOR
(4) NEAR LEFT HEADLIGHT
(5) NEAR RIGHT HEADLIGHT

WIRE COLORS

BK - BLACK	GN - GREEN	BR - BROWN
WT - WHITE	YE - YELLOW	BL - BLUE
RE - RED	GR - GREY	VI - VIOLET

Fig. 11.10 Key to current flow diagram, 1979

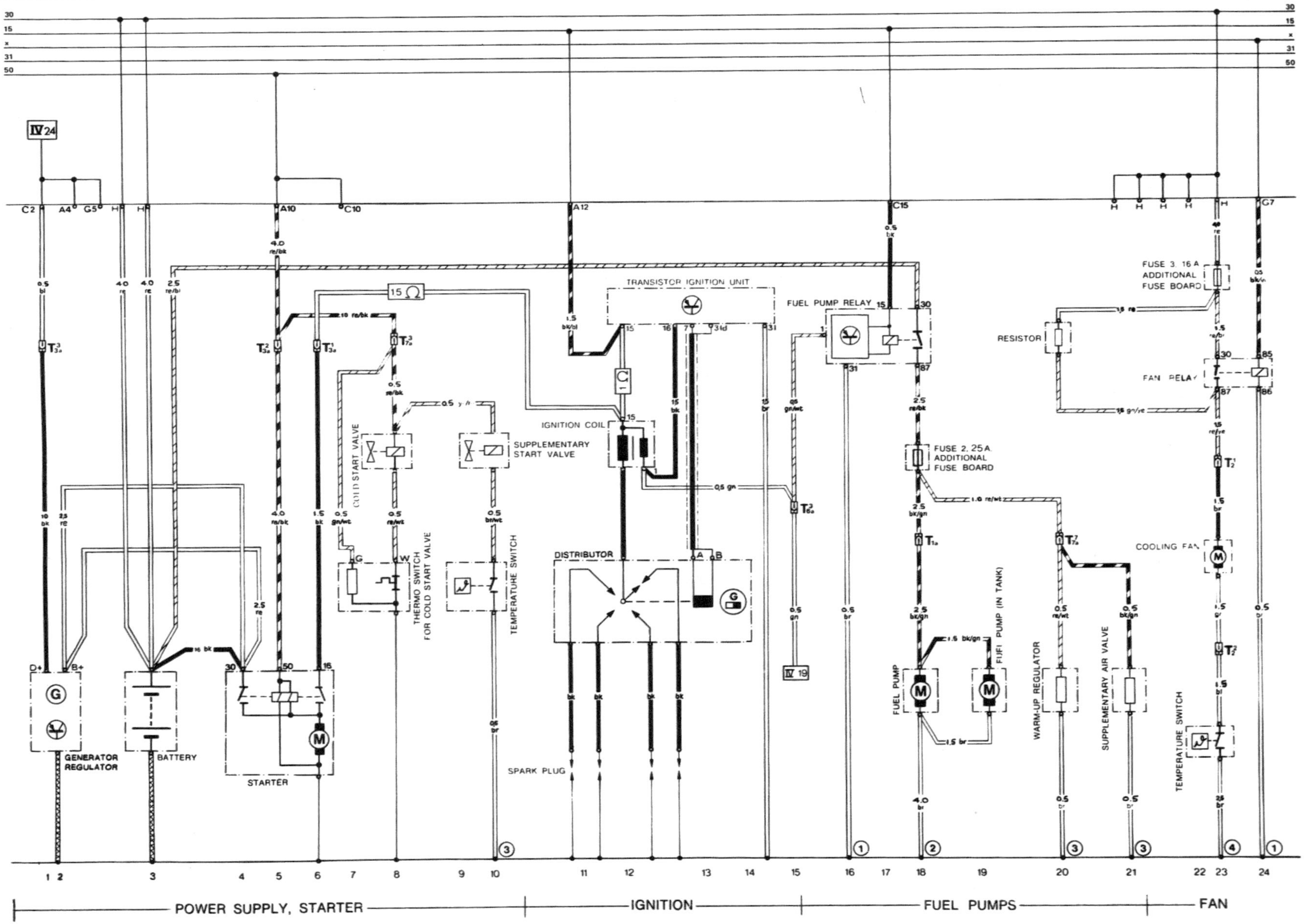

Fig. 11.11a Current flow diagram, 1979 (including all 1980 standard models, except Oxygen Sensor System)

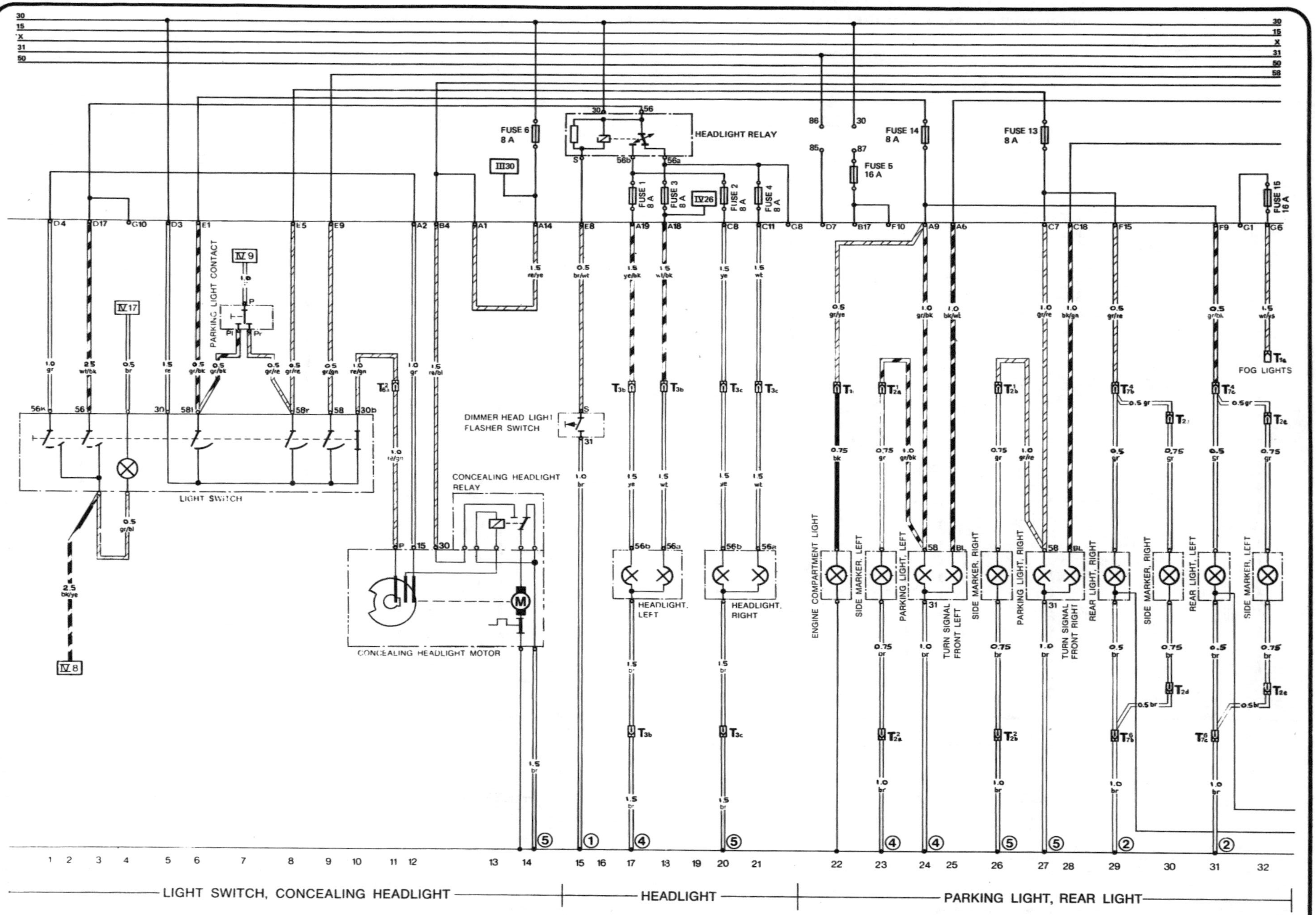

Fig. 11.11b Current flow diagram, 1979 (including all 1980 standard models, except Oxygen Sensor System) (continued)

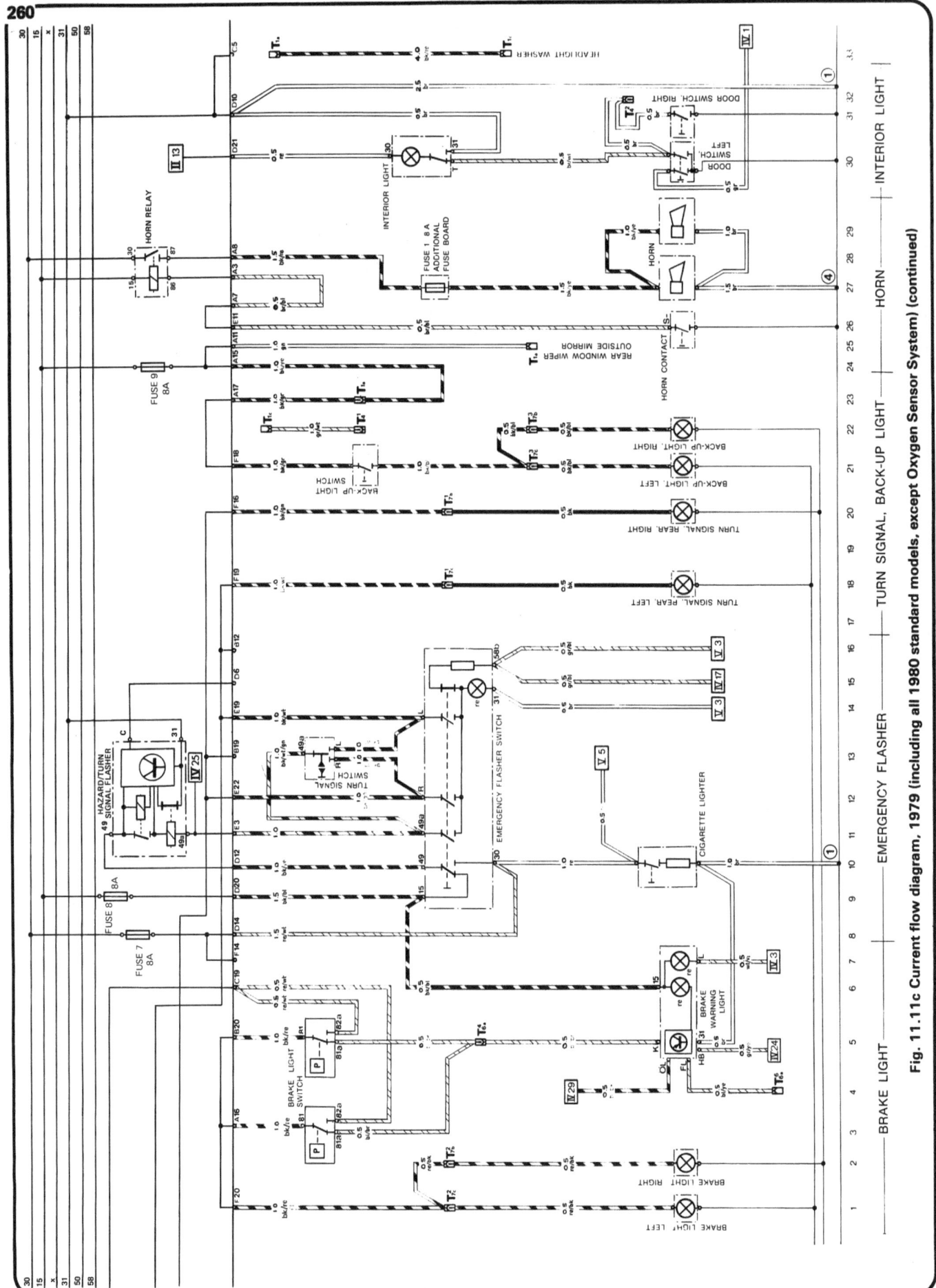

Fig. 11.11c Current flow diagram, 1979 (including all 1980 standard models, except Oxygen Sensor System) (continued)

BRAKE LIGHT — EMERGENCY FLASHER — TURN SIGNAL, BACK-UP LIGHT — HORN — INTERIOR LIGHT

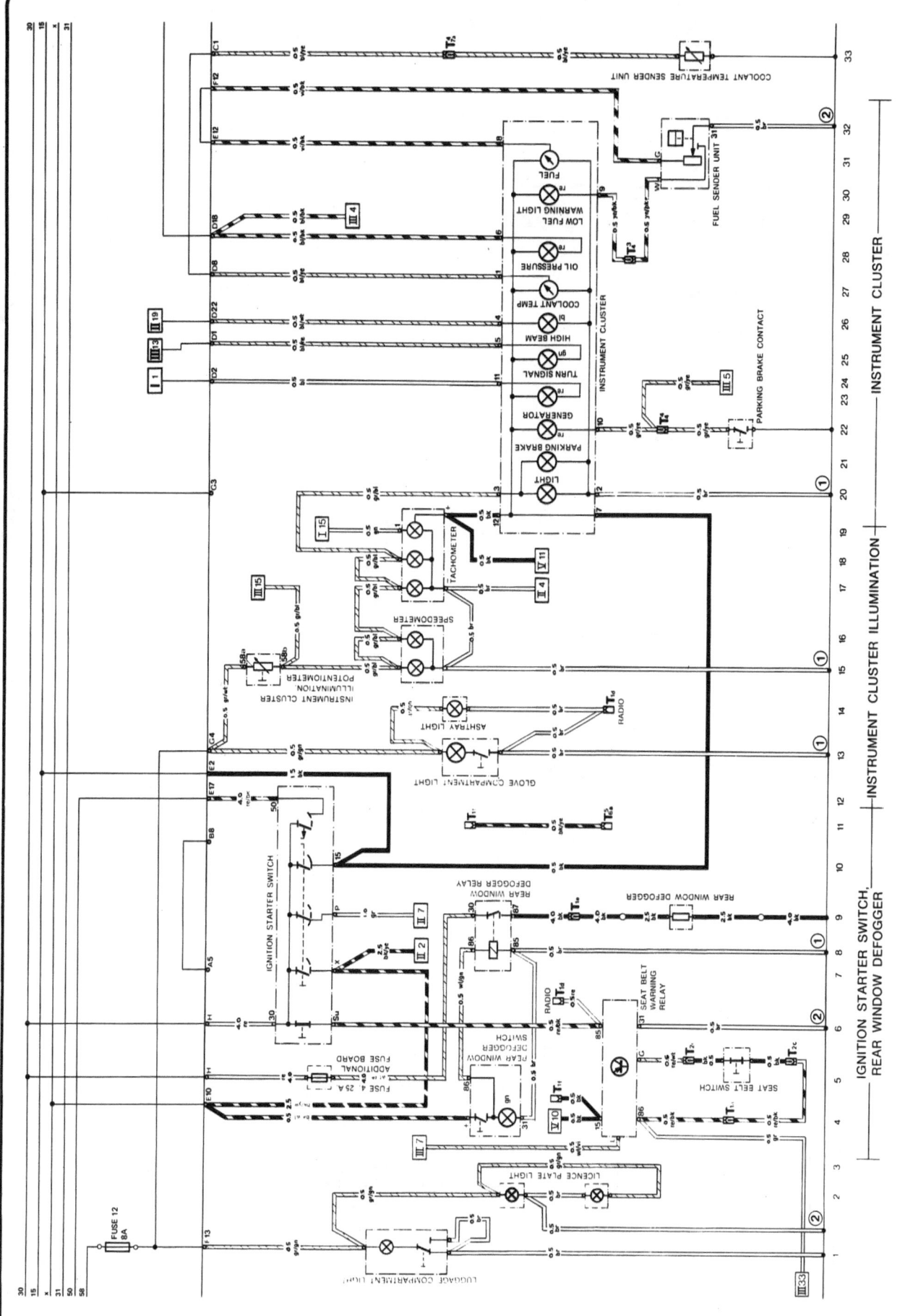

Fig. 11.11d Current flow diagram, 1979 (including all 1980 standard models, except Oxygen Sensor System) (continued)

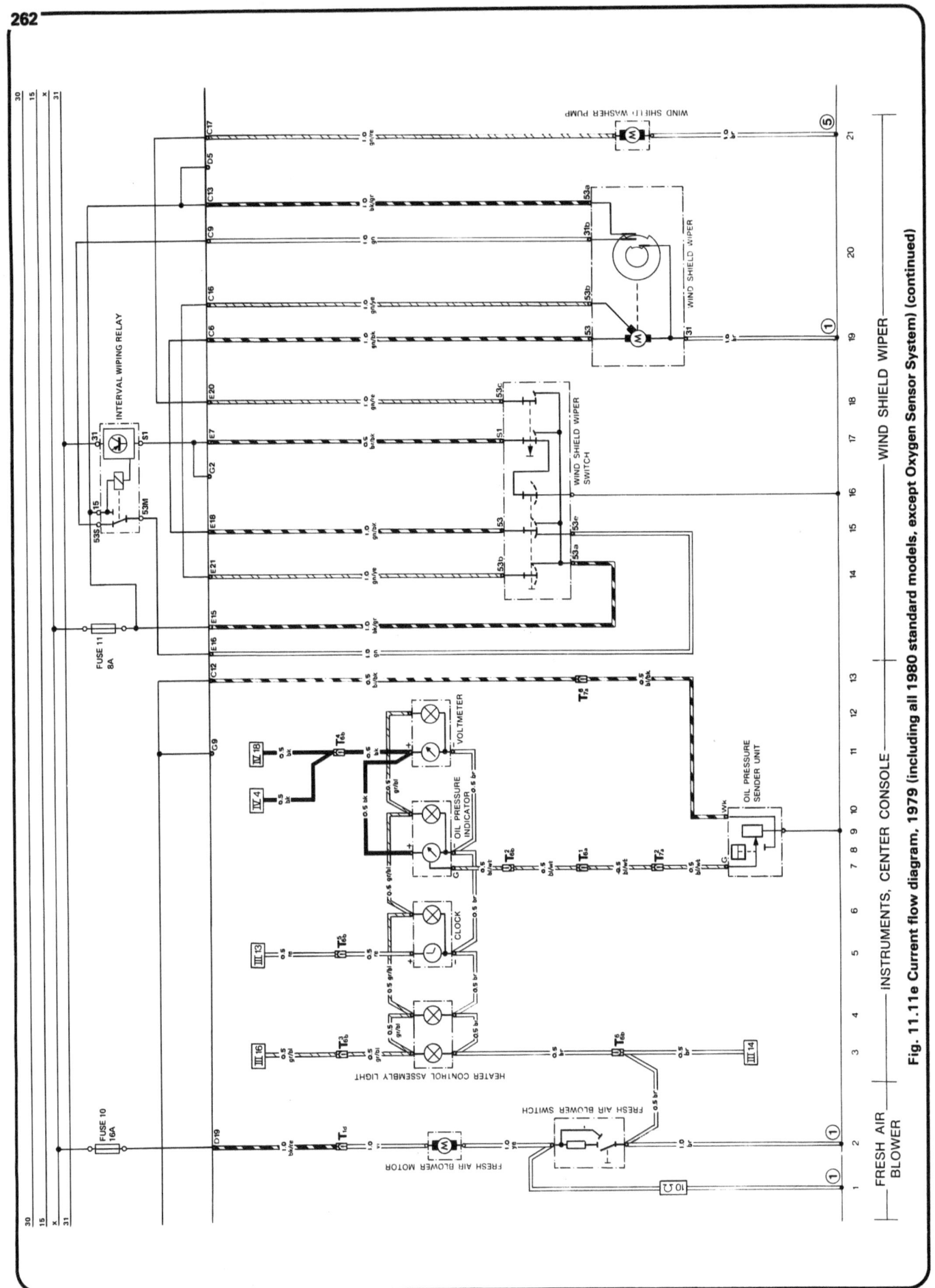

Fig. 11.11e Current flow diagram, 1979 (including all 1980 standard models, except Oxygen Sensor System) (continued)

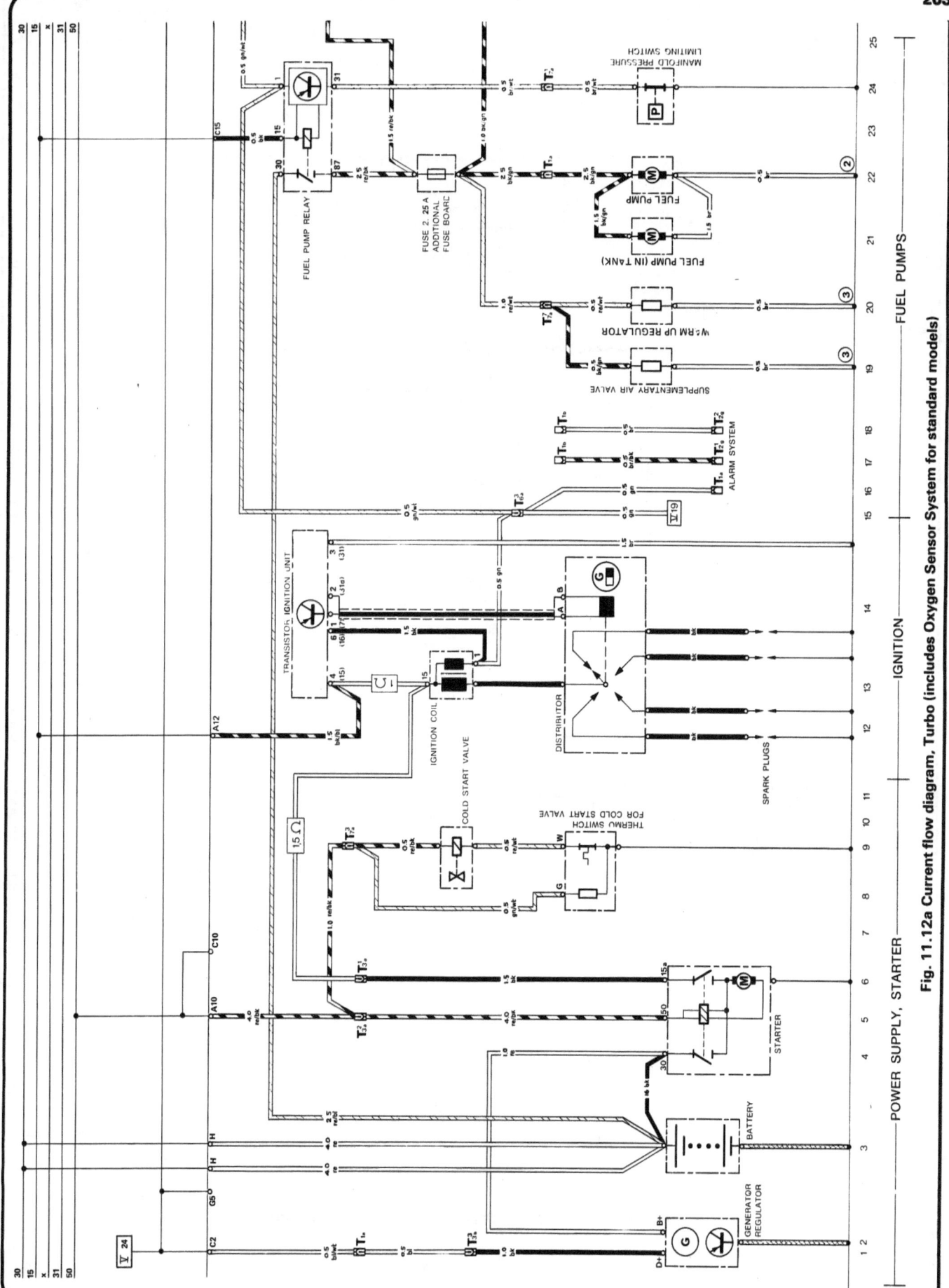

Fig. 11.12a Current flow diagram, Turbo (includes Oxygen Sensor System for standard models)

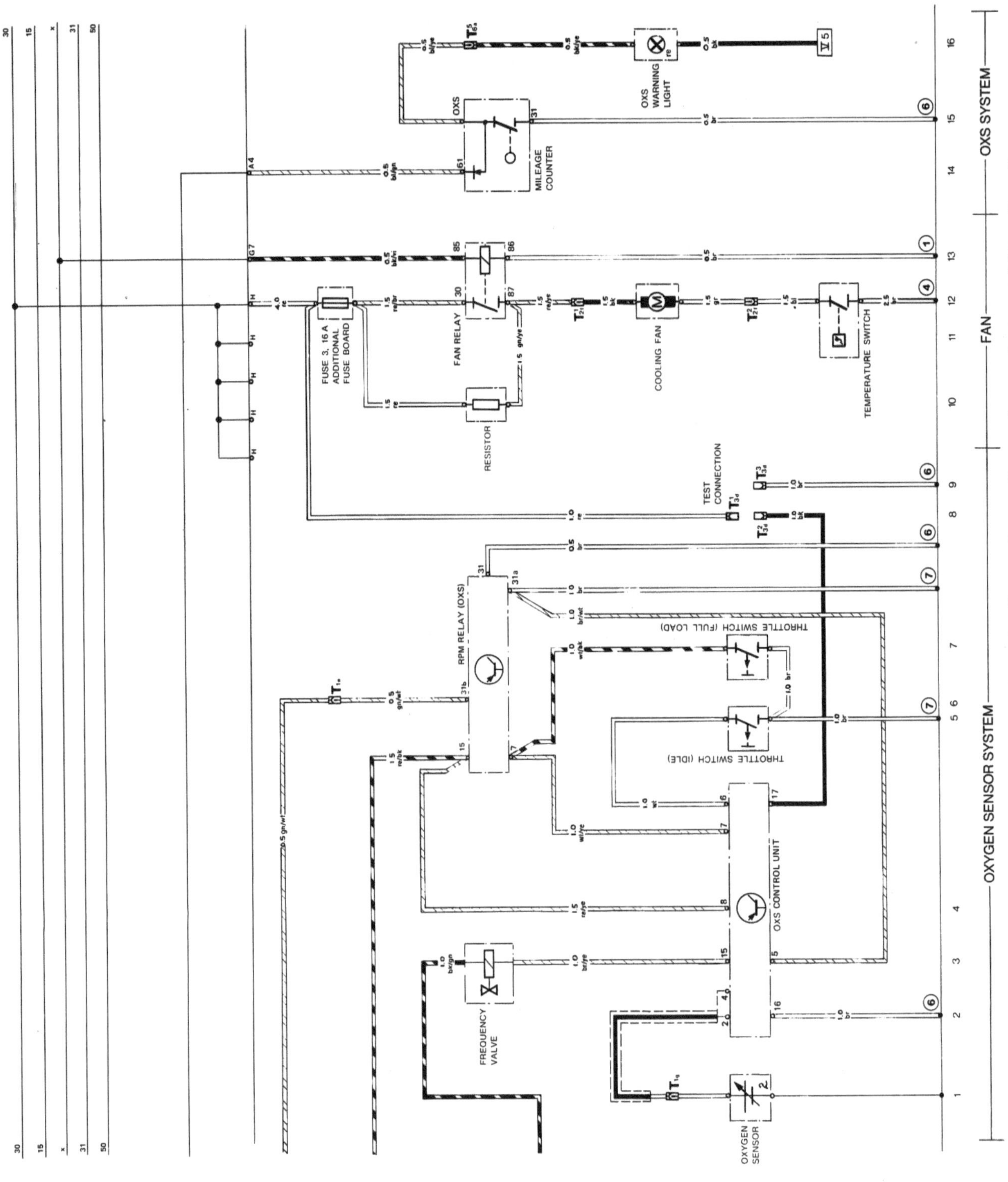

Fig. 11.12b Current flow diagram, Turbo (includes Oxygen Sensor System for standard models) (continued)

Continuation see current flow diagram type 924, 924 turbo, Model 80

Current track

A	1
D	4, 5
E[15]	2
E[43]	8, 9, 10, 11
J[4]	6, 7
K[10]	3
N[35]	13
S[9]	6
T[1]	7, 8
T[7]	8, 9, 12, 13, 14
	12, 13, 14
V[17]	14
Z[4]	12

Description

A — to battery
D — Ignition/starter switch
E[15] — Rear window defogger switch
E[43] — Mirror adjusting switch
J[4] — Horn relay
K[10] — Rear window defogger indicator light
N[35] — Magnetic clutch for mirror control
S[9] — Fuse
T[1] — Wire connector, near fuse/relay board
T[7] — Wire connector, seven-pole
  a – in door well, left
  b – in mirror housing
V[17] — Mirror control motor
Z[4] — Mirror defogger

Color Key

bk — black
bl — blue
br — brown
gn — green
gr — grey
re — red
vi — violet
wt — white
ye — yellow

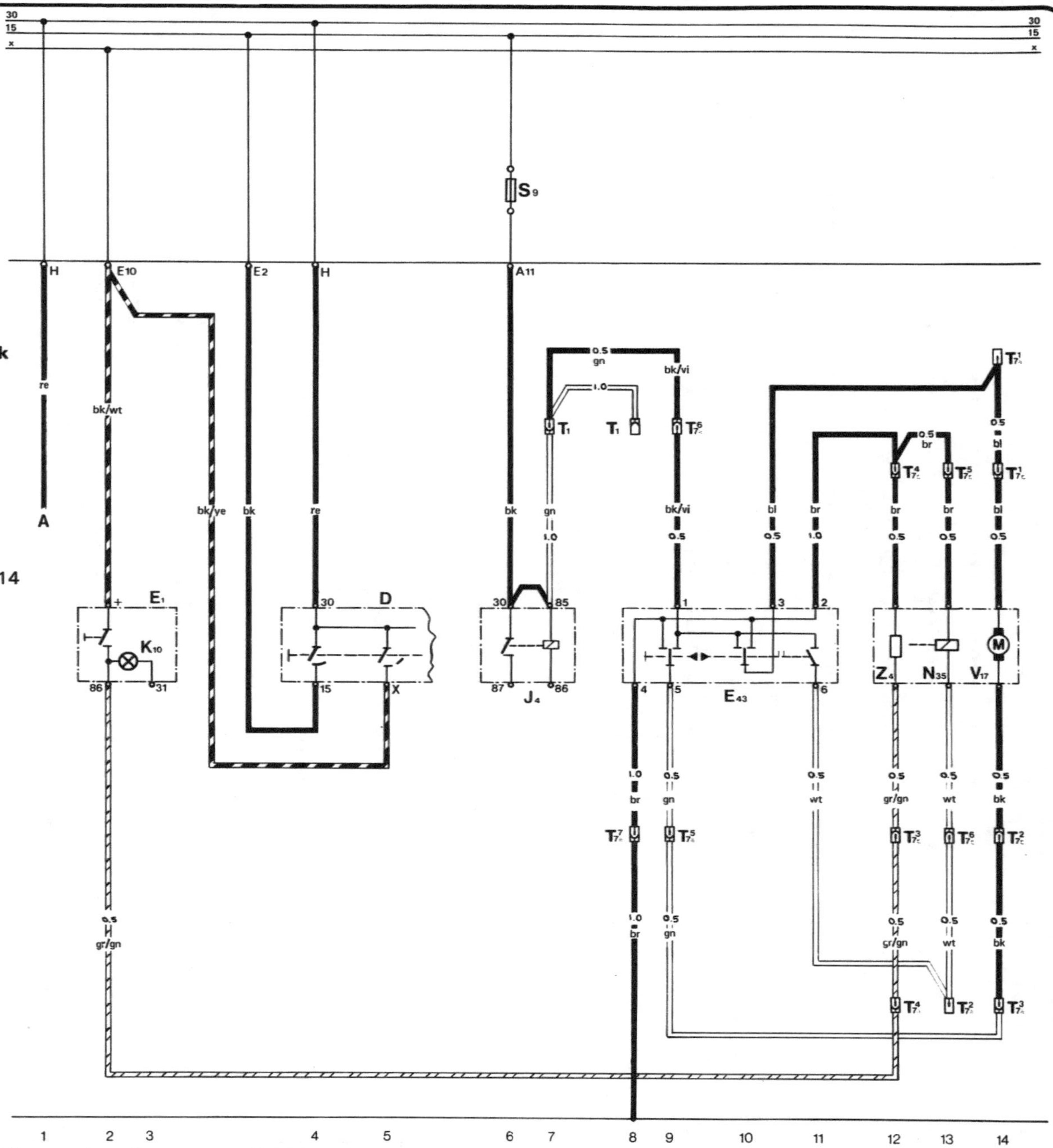

Fig. 11.13 Current flow diagram for adjustable outside mirror, driver's side

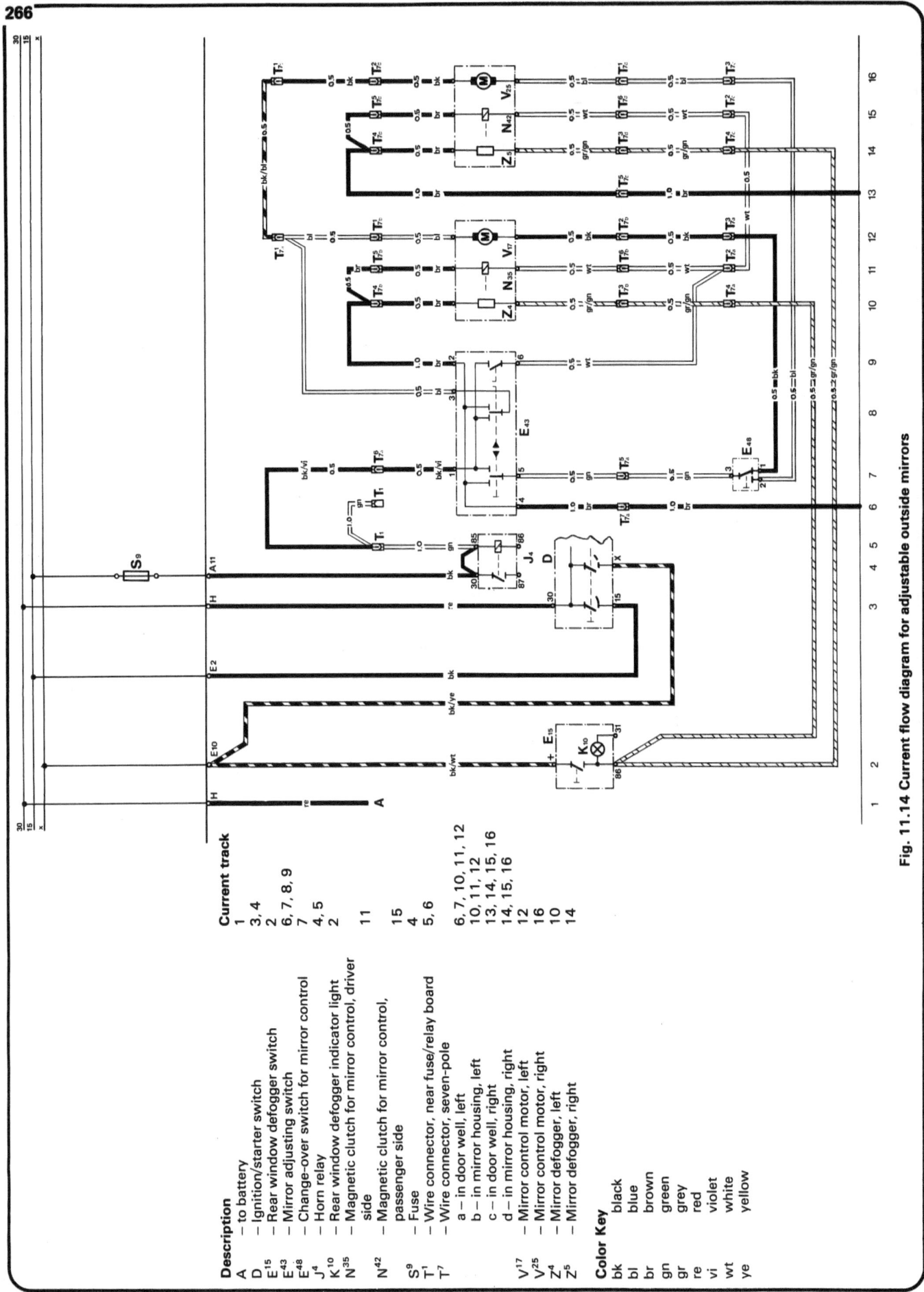

Fig. 11.14 Current flow diagram for adjustable outside mirrors

Current track

Description	Current track
A – to battery	1
D – Ignition/starter switch	3, 4
E^{15} – Rear window defogger switch	6, 7, 8, 9
E^{43} – Mirror adjusting switch	7
E^{48} – Change-over switch for mirror control	4, 5
J^4 – Horn relay	2
K^{10} – Rear window defogger indicator light	11
N^{35} – Magnetic clutch for mirror control, driver side	15
N^{42} – Magnetic clutch for mirror control, passenger side	4
S^9 – Fuse	5, 6
T^1 – Wire connector, near fuse/relay board	
T^7 – Wire connector, seven-pole	6, 7, 10, 11, 12
a – in door well, left	10, 11, 12
b – in mirror housing, left	13, 14, 15, 16
c – in door well, right	14, 15, 16
d – in mirror housing, right	12
V^{17} – Mirror control motor, left	16
V^{25} – Mirror control motor, right	10
Z^4 – Mirror defogger, left	14
Z^5 – Mirror defogger, right	

Color Key

bk	black
bl	blue
br	brown
gn	green
gr	grey
re	red
vi	violet
wt	white
ye	yellow

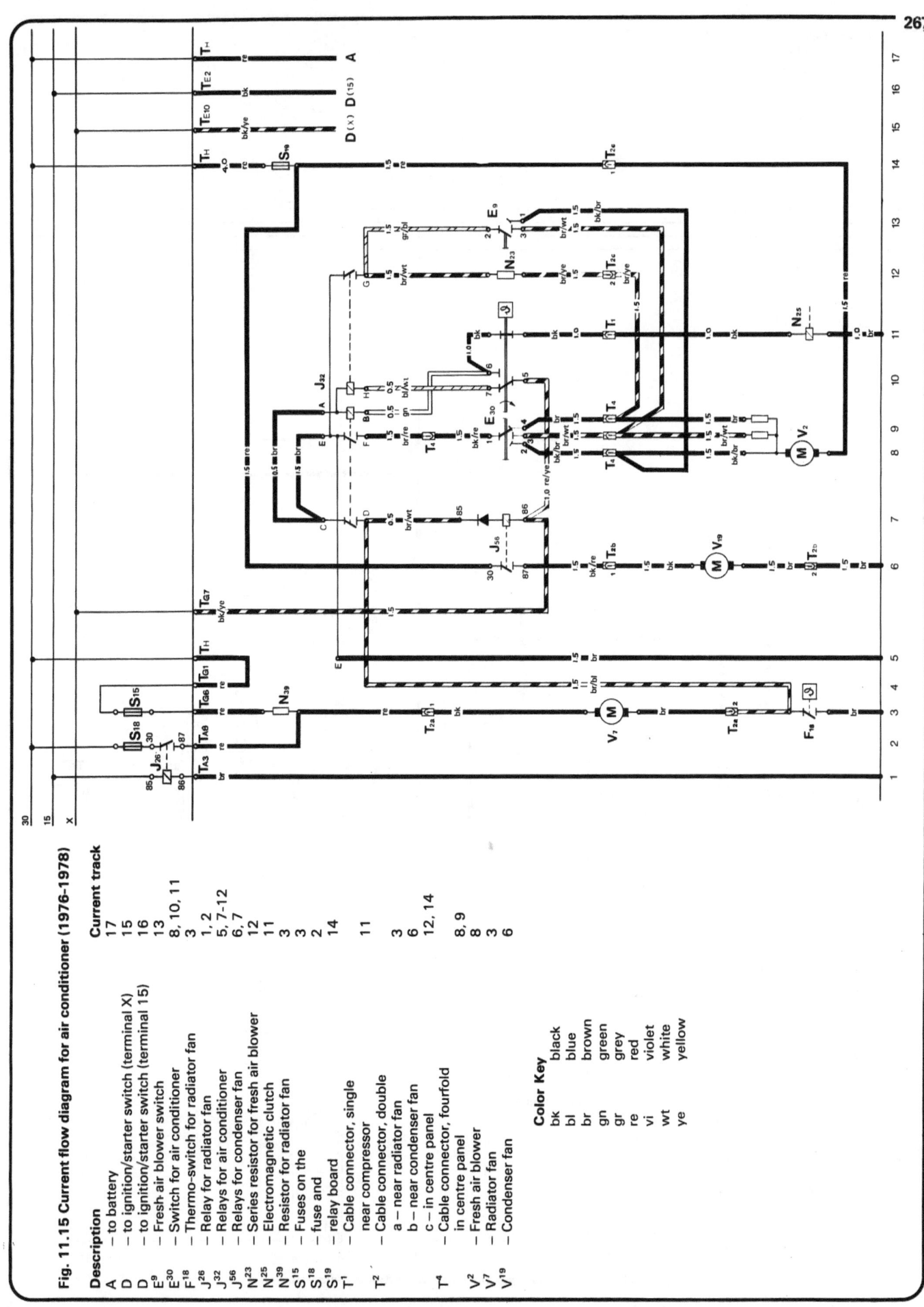

Fig. 11.15 Current flow diagram for air conditioner (1976-1978)

Description		Current track
A	– to battery	17
D	– to ignition/starter switch (terminal X)	15
D	– to ignition/starter switch (terminal 15)	16
E^9	– Fresh air blower switch	13
E^{30}	– Switch for air conditioner	8, 10, 11
F^{18}	– Thermo-switch for radiator fan	3
J^{26}	– Relay for radiator fan	1, 2
J^{32}	– Relays for air conditioner	5, 7–12
J^{56}	– Relays for condenser fan	6, 7
N^{23}	– Series resistor for fresh air blower	12
N^{25}	– Electromagnetic clutch	11
N^{39}	– Resistor for radiator fan	3
S^{15}	– Fuses on the	3
S^{18}	– fuse and	2
S^{19}	– relay board	14
T^1	– Cable connector, single	11
	near compressor	
T^2	– Cable connector, double	
	a – near radiator fan	3
	b – near condenser fan	6
	c – in centre panel	12, 14
T^4	– Cable connector, fourfold	
	in centre panel	8, 9
V^2	– Fresh air blower	8
V^7	– Radiator fan	3
V^{19}	– Condenser fan	6

Color Key

bk	black	
bl	blue	
br	brown	
gn	green	
gr	grey	
re	red	
vi	violet	
wt	white	
ye	yellow	

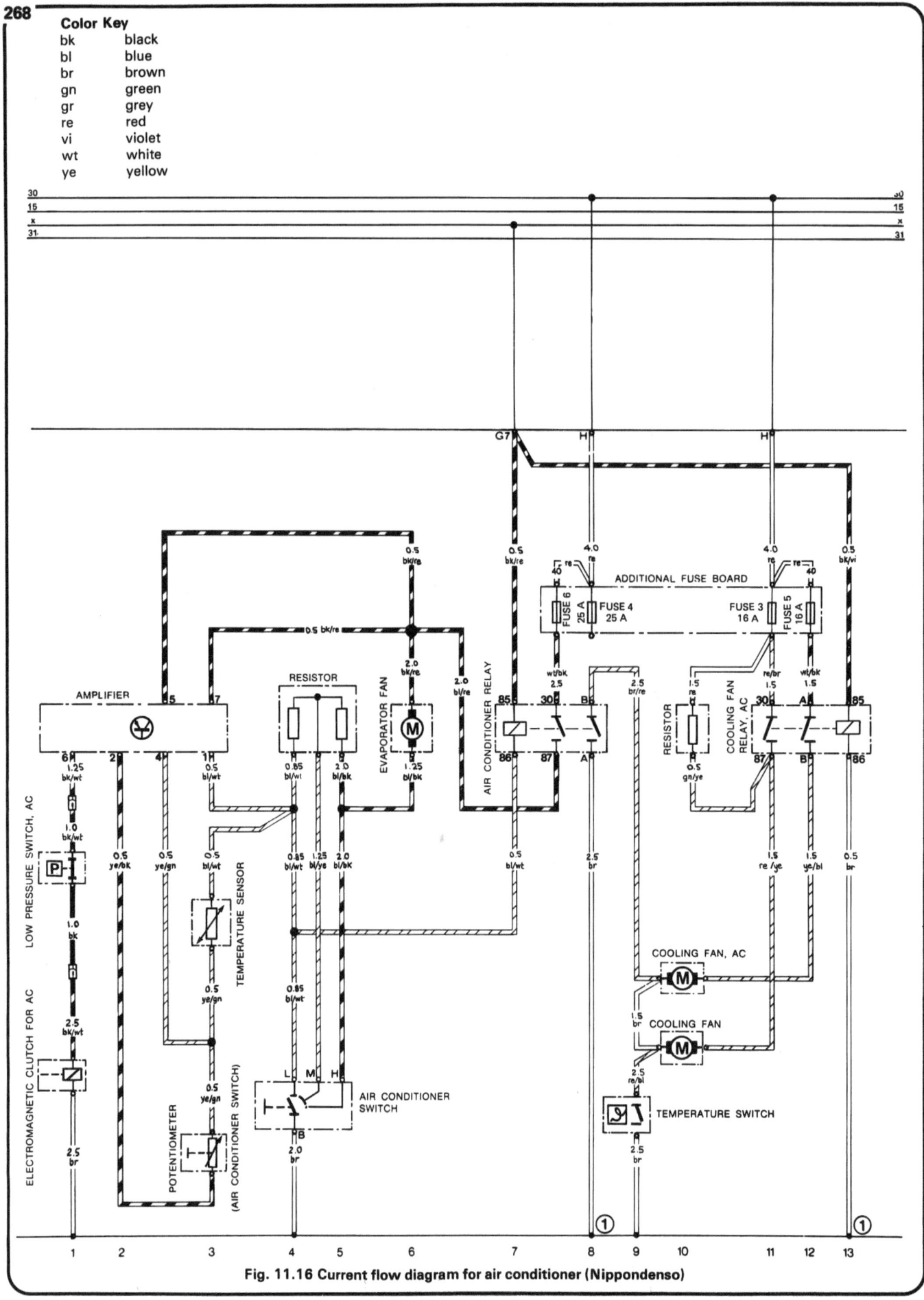

Color Key

bk	black
bl	blue
br	brown
gn	green
gr	grey
re	red
vi	violet
wt	white
ye	yellow

Fig. 11.16 Current flow diagram for air conditioner (Nippondenso)

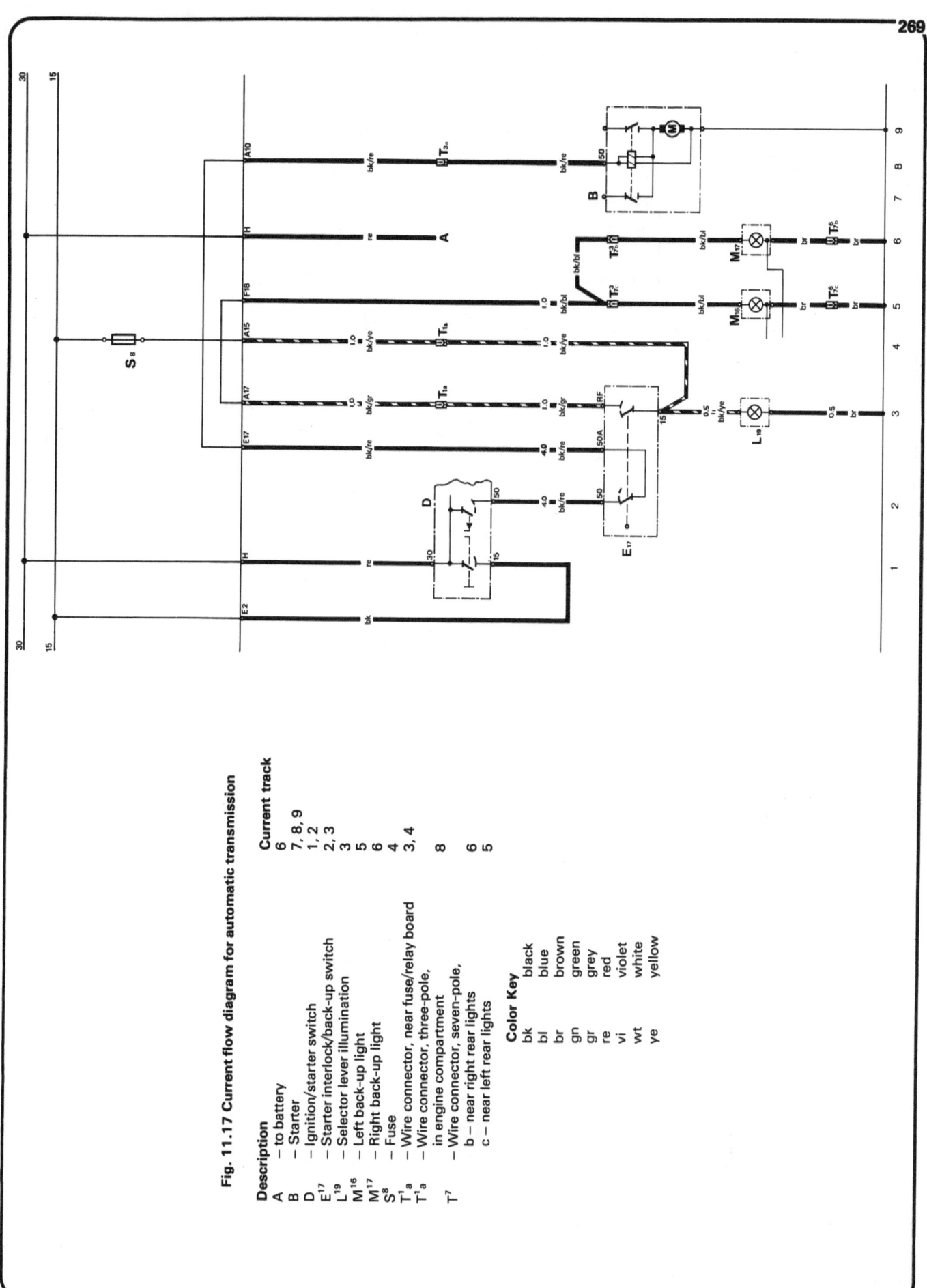

Fig. 11.17 Current flow diagram for automatic transmission

Description

		Current track
A	– to battery	6
B	– Starter	7, 8, 9
D	– Ignition/starter switch	1, 2
E[17]	– Starter interlock/back-up switch	2, 3
L[19]	– Selector lever illumination	3
M[16]	– Left back-up light	5
M[17]	– Right back-up light	6
S[8]	– Fuse	4
T[1]a	– Wire connector, near fuse/relay board	3, 4
T[1]a	– Wire connector, three-pole, in engine compartment	8
T[7]	– Wire connector, seven-pole,	
	b – near right rear lights	6
	c – near left rear lights	5

Color Key

bk	black
bl	blue
br	brown
gn	green
gr	grey
re	red
vi	violet
wt	white
ye	yellow

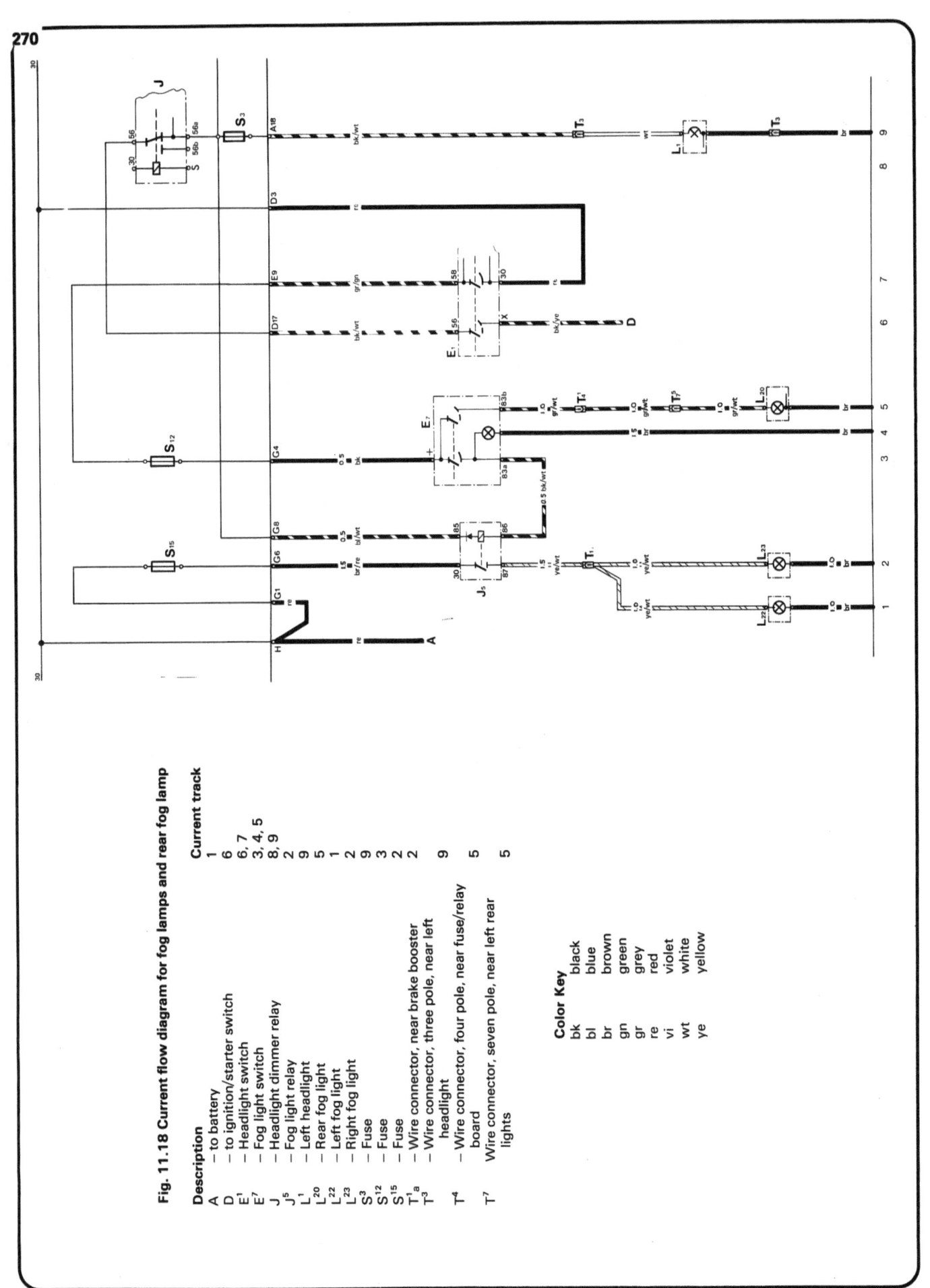

Fig. 11.18 Current flow diagram for fog lamps and rear fog lamp

Description		Current track
A	– to battery	1
D	– to ignition/starter switch	6, 7
E¹	– Headlight switch	6, 7
E⁷	– Fog light switch	3, 4, 5
J	– Headlight dimmer relay	8, 9
J⁵	– Fog light relay	2
L¹	– Left headlight	9
L²⁰	– Rear fog light	5
L²²	– Left fog light	1
L²³	– Right fog light	2
S³	– Fuse	9
S¹²	– Fuse	3
S¹⁵	– Fuse	2
T¹ₐ	– Wire connector, near brake booster	2
T³	– Wire connector, three pole, near left headlight	9
T⁴	– Wire connector, four pole, near fuse/relay board	5
T⁷	– Wire connector, seven pole, near left rear lights	5

Color Key

bk	black
bl	blue
br	brown
gn	green
gr	grey
re	red
vi	violet
wt	white
ye	yellow

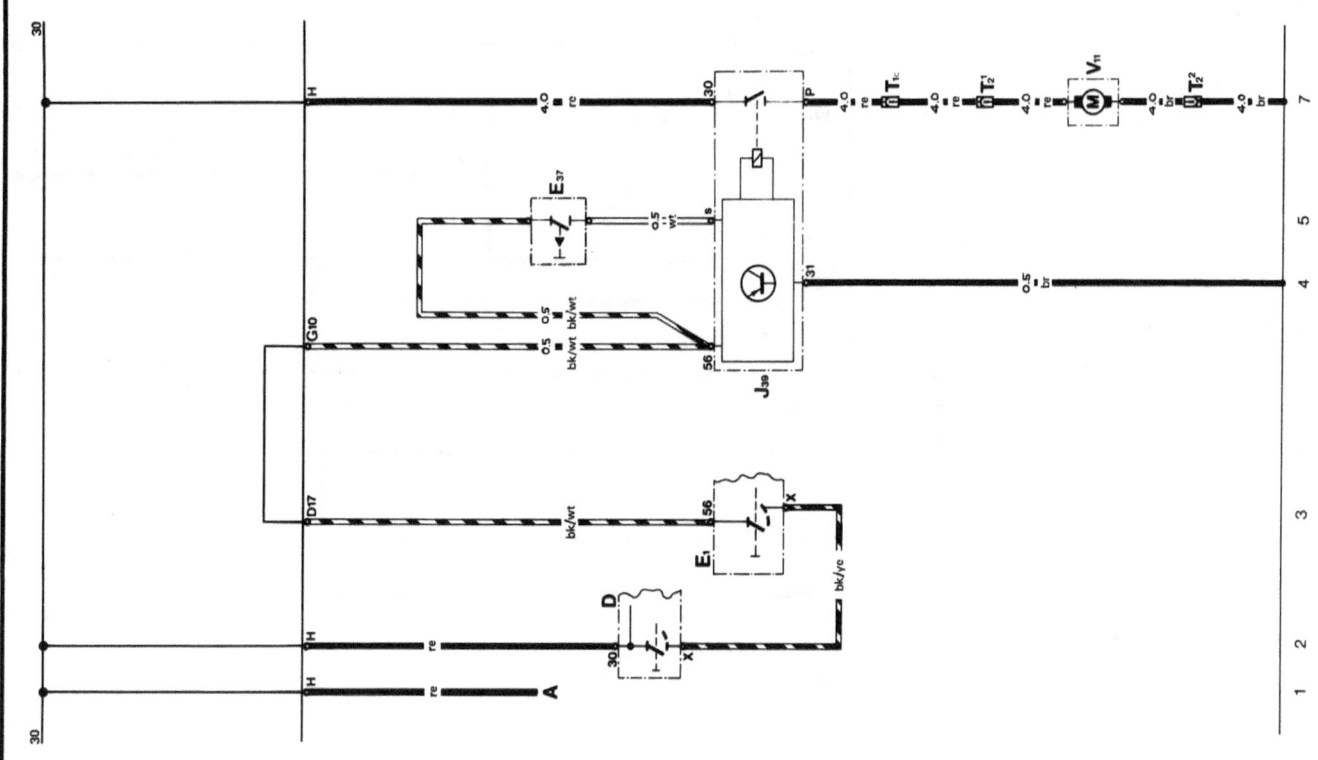

Fig. 11.19 Current flow diagram for headlight washer

Description		Current track
A	— to battery	1
D	— Ignition/starter switch	2
E[1]	— Headlight switch	3
E[37]	— Headlight washer switch	5
J[39]	— Headlight washer relay	4, 5, 7
T[1c]	— Wire connector, near brake booster	7
T[2]	— Wire connector, two-pole,	
	near headlight washer-pump	7
V[11]	— Headlight washer pump	7

Color Key

bk	black
bl	blue
br	brown
gn	green
gr	grey
re	red
vi	violet
wt	white
ye	yellow

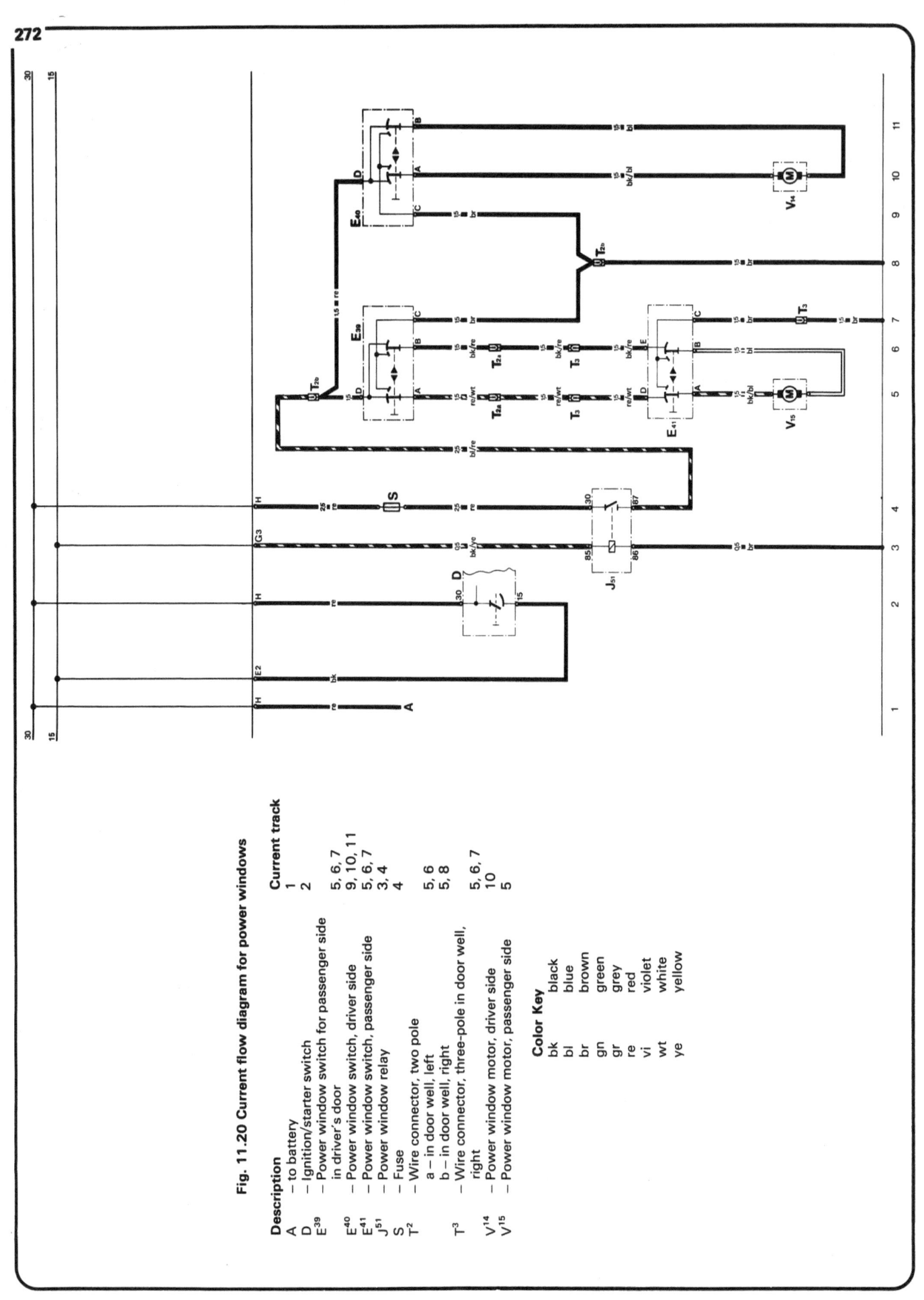

Fig. 11.20 Current flow diagram for power windows

Description		Current track
A	– to battery	1
D	– Ignition/starter switch	2
E^{39}	– Power window switch for passenger side in driver's door	5, 6, 7
E^{40}	– Power window switch, driver side	9, 10, 11
E^{41}	– Power window switch, passenger side	5, 6, 7
J^{51}	– Power window relay	3, 4
S	– Fuse	4
T^{2}	– Wire connector, two pole	
	a – in door well, left	5, 6
	b – in door well, right	5, 8
T^{3}	– Wire connector, three-pole in door well, right	5, 6, 7
V^{14}	– Power window motor, driver side	10
V^{15}	– Power window motor, passenger side	5

Color Key

bk	black
bl	blue
br	brown
gn	green
gr	grey
re	red
vi	violet
wt	white
ye	yellow

Fig. 11.21 Current flow diagram for rear window wiper

Description		Current track
A	– to battery	1
D	– Ignition/starter switch	7
E^{34}	– Rear window wiper switch	4
J^4	– Horn relay	2, 3
S^9	– Fuse	2
T^{1a}	– Wire connector, near fuse/relay board	4
T^2	– Wire connector, two pole, near rear window wiper	4, 5
V^{12}	– Rear window wiper motor	4, 5, 6

Color Key

bk	black
bl	blue
br	brown
gn	green
gr	grey
re	red
vi	violet
wt	white
ye	yellow

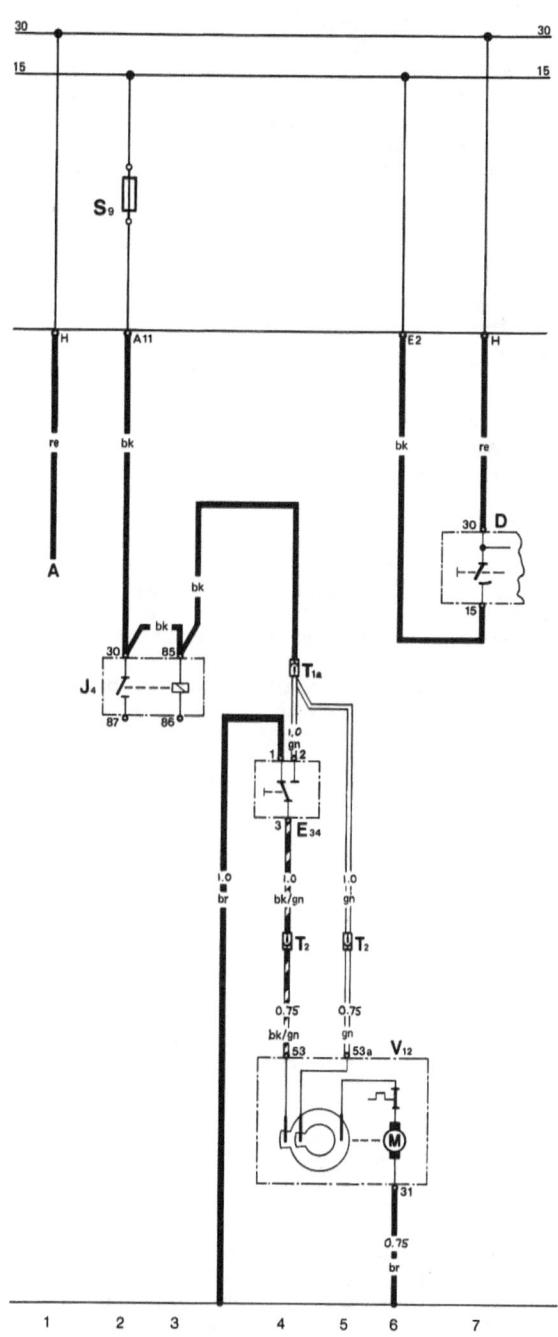

Chapter 12 Bodywork

For modifications, and information applicable to later models, see Supplement at end of manual

Contents

1 General description

1 The Porsche 924 range is a new body design. It is based on the lessons learned from the VW Experimental Safety Vehicle (ESV) and other safety vehicles which produced so much new technology for the safety of the people riding in the car. Fore and aft there are 'crumple zones' which take the brunt of any accident leaving the passenger compartment with minimum distortion. In the front this takes the form of two corrugated box sections in the scuttle and firewall.

2 The floor pan, suspension and steering are the same for all models.

3 All models have the large rear window hinged at the top. This is propped open by a gas filled telescopic strut. All models are two door sports hatchbacks.

4 The types of bumper fitted vary. In the USA and certain other countries shock absorbing bumpers are mandatory. Where this is not a legal requirement normal bolted-on types are fitted.

5 This chapter does not go into the detail differences of the various models but confines itself to those jobs which can be done by the owner.

2 Maintenance – bodywork and underframe

1 The general condition of vehicle's bodywork is the one thing that significantly affects its value. Maintenance is easy but needs to be regular and particular. Neglect, particularly after minor damage, can lead quickly to further deterioration and costly repair bills. It is important also to keep watch on those parts of the car not immediately visible, for instance, the underside and inside of all the wheel arches.

2 The basic maintenance routine for the bodywork is washing - preferably with a lot of water, from a hose. This will remove all the solids which may have stuck to the car. It is important to flush these off in such a way as to prevent grit from scratching the finish. The wheel arches and underbody need washing in the same way to remove any accumulated mud which will retain moisture and tend to encourage rust. Paradoxically enough, the best time to clean the underbody and wheel arches is in wet weather when the mud is thoroughly wet and soft. In very wet weather, the underbody is usually cleaned of large accumulations automatically and this is a good time for inspection.

3 Periodically it is a good idea to have the whole of the underside of the vehicle steam cleaned, so that a thorough inspection can be carried out to see what minor repairs and renovations are necessary. Steam cleaning is available at commercial vehicle garages but if not, there are one or two excellent grease solvents available which can be brush applied. The dirt can then be hosed off.

4 After washing paintwork, wipe it with a chamois leather to give an unspotted clear finish. A coat of clear protective wax polish will give added protection against chemical pollutants in the air. If the paintwork sheen has dulled or oxidised, this requires a little more effort, but is usually caused because regular washing has been neglected. Always check that drain holes are completely clear so that water can drain out. Chrome trim should be treated the same way as paintwork. Windshields and windows can be kept clear of the smeary film which often appears if a little ammonia is added to the water. If they are scratched, a good rub with a proprietary metal polish will often clear them. Do not use any form of wax or polish on glass.

3 Maintenance – upholstery and floor coverings

1 Mats and carpets should be brushed or vacuum cleaned regularly to keep them free of grit. If they are badly stained remove them for scrubbing or sponging and make quite sure they are dry before replacement. Seats and interior trim panels can be kept clean by a wipe over with a damp cloth. If they do become stained (which can be more apparent on light coloured upholstery) use a little liquid detergent and a soft nailbrush to scour the grime out of the grain of the material. Do not forget to keep the head lining clean in the same way as the upholstery. When using liquid cleaners inside the car do not over wet the surfaces being cleaned. Excessive damp could get into the seams and padded interior causing stains, offensive odours or even rot. If the inside of the car gets wet accidentally, it is worthwhile taking some trouble to dry it out properly, particularly when carpets are involved. Do not leave heaters inside for this purpose.

4 Minor body damage – repair

See also the photo sequence on pages 278 and 279.

Repair of minor scratches in the bodywork

1 If the scratch is very superficial and does not penetrate to the metal of the bodywork, repair is very simple. Lightly rub the area of

the scratch with a rubbing compound or a very fine cutting paste, to remove loose paint from the scratch and to clear the surrounding bodywork of wax polish. Rinse the area with clean water.

2   Apply touch-up paint to the scratch using a thin paint brush, continue to apply thin layers of paint until the surface of the paint in the scratch is level with the surrounding paintwork. Allow the new paint at least two weeks to harden, then blend it into the surrounding paintwork by rubbing the paintwork in the scratch area with a rubbing compound, or a very fine cutting paste. Finally apply wax polish.

3   If the car is painted with a two-coat metallic finish an entirely different technique is required. The materials may be obtained from an authorized Porsche dealer. Two types of repair are possible, the 80°C drying method and the Air-drying method. A 'wet-on-wet' procedure for the topcoat and clear laquer is used. The repair can be done satisfactorily only if the specified top coat and laquer are used with the specially developed synthetic thinner. After filling with Filler L145, if required sand down with 400-500 wet and dry paper. Apply the first top coat using synthetic resin metallic paint LKL or spraying viscosity 15-17 seconds (DIN cup 4 mm). Let the paint flash off for 25 minutes, then apply the second layer of Air-drying L100 clear varnish with hardener L101 mixed in proportion 8:1. This becomes unusable after six hours. The repair is dust dry after 30 minutes but requires up to 8 days for complete drying. As can be seen it is a complicated process and you are advised to go to your Porsche dealer for advice if you have not done the job before. If you have other than a metallic finish then proceed as follows.

4   Where a scratch has penetrated right through to the metal of the bodywork causing the metal to rust, a different repair technique is required. Remove any loose rust from the bottom of the scratch with a penknife, then apply rust inhibiting paint to prevent the formation of rust in the future. Using a rubber or nylon applicator fill the scratch with scratch filler paste. If required, this paste can be mixed with compatible paint thinners to provide a very thin paste which is ideal for filling narrow scratches. Before the paste in the scratch hardens, wrap a piece of smooth cotton rag around the tip of a finger. Dip the finger in a compatible paint thinners and then quickly sweep it across the surface of the paste in the scratch; this will ensure that the surface of the paste is slightly hollowed. The scratch can now be painted over as described earlier in this Section.

Repair of dents in the bodywork

5   When deep denting of the car's bodywork has taken place, the first task is to pull the dent out, until the affected bodywork almost attains its original shape. There is little point in trying to restore the original shape completely unless you are an experienced bodywork specialist, as the metal in the damaged area will have stretched on impact and cannot be reshaped fully to its original contour. It is better for the home mechanic to bring the level of the dent up to a point which is about 3 mm (1/8 inch) below the level of the surrounding bodywork. In cases where the dent is very shallow, it is not worth trying to pull it out at all.

6   If the underside of the dent is accessible, it can be hammered out gently from behind, using a mallet with a wooden or plastic head. While doing this, hold a suitable block of wood firmly against the impact from the hammer blows and thus prevent a large area of bodywork from being 'belled-out'.

7   Should the dent be in a section of the bodywork which has a double skin or some other factor making it inaccessible from behind, a different technique is called for. Drill several small holes through the metal inside the dent area - particularly in the deeper sections. Then screw long self-tapping screws into the holes just sufficiently for them to gain a purchase in the metal. Now the dent can be pulled out by pulling on the protruding heads of the screws with a pair of pliers.

8   The next stage of the repair is the removal of the paint from the damaged area, and from an inch or so from the surrounding 'sound' bodywork. This is accomplished most easily by using a wire brush or abrasive pad on a power drill, although it can be done just as effectively by hand using sheets of abrasive paper. To complete the preparations for filling score the surface of the bare metal with a screwdriver or the tang of a file, or alternatively drill small holes in the affected areas. This will provide a really good key for the filler paste.

9   To complete the repair see the Section on filling and respraying.

Repair of rust holes or gashes in the bodywork

10   Remove all paint from the affected area and from an inch or so of the surrounding 'sound' bodywork, using an abrasive pad or wire brush on a power drill. If these are not available a few sheets of abrasive paper will do the job just as effectively. With the paint removed you will be able to gauge the severity of the corrosion and therefore decide whether to replace the whole panel (if this is possible) or to repair the affected area. Replacement body panels are not as expensive as most people think and it is often quicker and more satisfactory to fit a new panel than to attempt to repair large areas of corrosion.

11   Remove all fittings from the affected areas except those which will act as a guide to the original shape of the damaged bodywork (eg; headlamp shells etc.,). Then using tin snips or a hacksaw blade, remove all loose metal and any other metal badly affected by corrosion. Hammer the edges of the hole inwards in order to create a slight depression for the filler paste.

12   Wire brush the affected area to remove the powdery rust from the surface of the remaining metal. Paint the affected area with rust inhibiting paint. If the back of the rusted area is accessible treat this also.

13   Before filling can take place it will be necessary to block the hole in some way. This can be achieved by the use of one of the following materials: Zinc gauze, Aluminum tape or Polyurethane foam.

14   Zinc gauze is probably the best material to use for the large hole. Cut a piece to the approximate size and shape of the hole to be filled, then position it in the hole so that its edges are below the level of the surrounding bodywork. It can be retained in position by several blobs of filler paste around its periphery.

15   Aluminum tape should be used for small or very narrow holes. Pull a piece off the roll and trim it to the appropriate size and shape required, then pull off the backing paper (if used) and stick the tape over the hole; it can be overlapped if the thickness of one piece is insufficient. Burnish down the edges of the tape with the handle of a screwdriver or similar to ensure that the tape is securely attached to the metal underneath.

16   Polyurethane foam is no longer generally used for automotive applications. In certain situations it can present a toxicity hazard.

Bodywork repairs - filling and painting

17   Before using this Section, see the Sections on dent, deep scratch, rust hole and gash repairs.

18   Many types of body filler are available, but generally speaking those proprietary kits which contain a tin of filler paste and a tube of resin hardener are best for this type of repair. A wide, flexible plastic or nylon applicator will be found invaluable for imparting a smooth and well contoured finish to the surface of the filler.

19   Mix up a little filler on a piece of card or board - use the hardener sparingly (follow the maker's instructions on the packet), otherwise the filler will set very rapidly. Check the packages for warnings before mixing these agents on paper. Some catalyzing agents produce enough heat to ignite paper when mixed.

20   Using the applicator, apply the filler paste to the prepared area; draw the applicator across the surface of the filler to achieve the correct contour and to level the filler surface. As soon as a contour that approximates the correct one is achieved, stop working the paste - if you carry on too long the paste will become sticky and begin to 'pick up' on the applicator. Continue to add thin layers of filler paste at twenty-minute intervals until the level of the filler is just above the surrounding bodywork.

21   Once the filler has hardened, excess can be removed using a "Surform" plane or "Dreadnought" file. From then on, progressively finer grades of abrasive paper should be used, starting with a 40 grade production paper and finishing with 400 grade 'wet-and-dry' paper. Always wrap the abrasive paper around a flat rubber, cork or wooden block - otherwise the surface of the filler will not be completely flat. During the smoothing of the filler surface the 'wet-and-dry' paper should be periodically rinsed in water. This will ensure that a very smooth finish is imparted to the filler at the final stage.

22   At this stage the dent should be surrounded by a ring of bare metal, which in turn should be encircled by the finely 'feathered' edge of the good paintwork. Rinse the repair area with clean water, until all of the dust produced by the rubbing-down operation is gone.

23 Spray the whole repair area with a light coat of gray primer - this will show up any imperfection in the surface of the filler. Repair these imperfections with fresh filler paste or scratch filler and once more smooth the surface with abrasive paper. If scratch filler is used, it can be mixed with compatible paint thinners to form a really thin paste which is ideal for filling small holes. Repeat this spray and repair procedure until you are satisfied that the surface of the filler, and the feathered edge of the paintwork are perfect. Clean the repair area with clean water and allow to dry fully.

24 The repair area is now ready for spraying. Paint spraying must be carried out in a warm, dry, windless and dust free atmosphere. This condition can be created artificially if you have access to a large indoor working area, but if you are forced to work in the open, you will have to pick your day very carefully. If you are working indoors, dousing the floor in the work area with water will 'lay' the dust which would otherwise be in the atmosphere. If the repair area is confined to one body panel, mask off the surrounding panels; this will help to minimise the effect of a slight mis-match in colours. Bodywork fittings (eg; chrome strips, door handles etc) will also need to be masked off. Use genuine masking tape and several thicknesses of newspaper for the masking operation.

25 Before commencing to spray, agitate the aerosol can thoroughly, then spray a test area (an old tin or similar) until the technique is mastered. Cover the repair area with a thick coat of primer; the thickness should be built up using several thin layers of paint rather than one thick one. Using 400 grade 'wet-and-dry' paper, rub down the surface of the primer until it is really smooth. While doing this, the work area should be thoroughly doused with water, and the 'wet-and-dry' paper periodically rinsed in water. Allow to dry before spraying on more paint.

26 Spray on the top coat, again building up the thickness by using several thin layers of paint. Start spraying in the centre of the repair area and then, using a circular motion, work outwards until the whole repair area and about 2 inches of the surrounding original paintwork is covered. Remove all masking material 10 to 15 minutes after spraying on the final coat of paint.

27 Allow the new paint at least 2 weeks to harden fully; then using a rubbing compound or a very fine cutting paste, blend the edges of the new paint into the existing paintwork. Finally apply wax polish.

5 Major body damage - repair

1 Where serious damage has occurred or large areas need renewal due to neglect it means, certainly, that completely new sections or panels will need welding in and this is best left to professionals. If the damage is due to impact it will also be necessary to check the alignment of the body structure. In such instances the services of an agent with specialist checking jigs are essential. If a body is left misaligned it is first of all dangerous as the car will not handle properly, and secondly, uneven stresses will be imposed on the steering, engine and transmission, causing abnormal wear or complete failure. Tire wear will also be excessive.

6 Front fenders - removal and installation

1 A badly damaged front fender may be removed complete and replaced by a new one. The fender is secured with bolts.
2 It will be necessary to remove the bumper before removing the fender. The screws fastening the fender are fitted very tightly and may not come out without considerable force. Do not use an impact screwdriver or you will distort the frame. It may be necessary to grind off the heads and drill out the shanks.
3 Once all the screws are out, the fender may be levered away pulling it out of the guides. If it does not come out easily it may be necessary to warm the line of the joint with a blow lamp to melt the adhesive underseal. Be careful how you do this, for apart from the fire risk to the car the adhesive is also inflammable.
4 When removing, lever the fender away from the wheel housing and the door pillar, work it to-and-fro, pulling it forwards to the front of the car a little.
5 Clean up the frame and paint with inhibitor if any rust is present. Use a good sealing tape along the line of the bolts before installing

the fender, and once the fender is securely in place treat the underside with underseal compound. Refer to Section 4 for painting techniques, (the last few paragraphs).

7 Radiator grille - removal and installation

1 The grille is held in position by screws. These are accessible from the front of the vehicle.

8 Rear hatch - strut removal and installation

1 Open the rear hatch.
2 Unplug the heater element wire from its connector.
3 Pop the snap caps open on the pivot ends and snap the ball sockets from the ball pivots. If you are removing both struts, be sure to set the window down slowly.
4 Installation is the reverse of the removal procedure.

9 Rear hatch - removal and installation

1 Remove the struts (Section 8).
2 Remove the soft plastic caps from the hinge plates along the rear edge of the vehicle roof (photo).
3 Remove the two inner bolts at the hinge (photo).
4 Have two assistants support the hatch window from the sides of the vehicle and remove the outside bolts from the hinges.
5 Lift the window from the body.
6 Installation is the reverse of the removal procedure.

10 Rear hatch - lock and latch removal and installation

1 Raise the rear hatch.
2 Remove the fascia from the rear of the luggage compartment and fold back the luggage compartment carpeting.
3 Unsnap the covers on the ball socket. Pop the ball sockets from the ball pivots on the rod.
4 Pull the latch operating rods toward the center and disconnect them from the lock cylinder.
5 The lock cylinder is held in place by two screws. If there is a problem with this item, remove it and take it to a Porsche dealer for service or replacement with a suitable new part (photo).
6 Remove the wedge-shaped gasket from the water traps at either side of the luggage compartment, and unbolt the reinforcement plate and the lid lock base (photo). Inspect the water trap and the water trap drain hose for plugging.
7 Installation is the reverse of the removal procedure.
8 If the latches allow the window to be loose or do not latch, adjust the catches on the window frame by loosening the lock nut and extending or retracting the arrowhead-shaped catch as required. Tighten the lock nut and secure the window.

11 Front bumper - removal and installation

1 Follow the wires from each of the park/running lights in the bumper and unplug the wires at the connector.
2 If headlight washers are fitted, pull the washer hose from the reservoir at the T-fitting.
3 The bumper is held in place by two bolts, one on either side of the license plates, just behind the bumperette pads. Insert the proper size socket wrench and ratchet drive into the access holes beneath the bumper and unbolt the bumper.
4 Remove the bolts, lock washers, and flat washers from each side.
5 Remove the bumper.
6 Installation is the reverse of the removal procedure.
7 There is no torque specification for the bumper bolts, but they must be tightened securely.
8 Be sure to align the plastic side covers with the body for a neat fit.

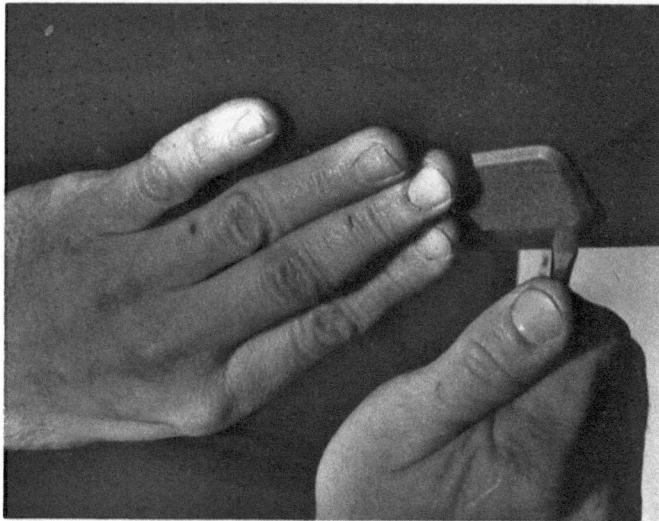

9.2 Prying the plastic caps from the hatch hinge bolts

9.3 Removing the hinge bolts

10.5 Removing the rear hatch lock cylinder

10.6 Disassembling the rear hatch water traps for inspection

12 Rear bumper - removal and installation

1   The rear bumper is mounted to its shock absorbers by two bolts.
2   Remove the two mounting bolts from the bumper and remove it. There is a square nut in a slot on the bumper mount on either side of the bumper which must be removed.
3   Installation is the reverse of the removal procedure.

13 Bumper shock absorbers - general note

1   The shock absorbers on the bumpers are specialized parts made for your vehicle. If they need adjustment or replacement see your Porsche dealer for this work.

14 Hood - removal and installation

1   The hood, or engine compartment cover, is hinged at the rear and held shut by a lock operated from inside the vehicle. It is held to the hinge by two bolts on each side. Mark around the hinges so the hood may be replaced in its original position, then remove the securing bolts. The hood may now be lifted off and taken away. Two people are needed to lift it, not because it is heavy but to avoid scratching the paint.
2   Installation is the reverse of the removal procedure.
3   The latch mechanism will require adjustment if the hood rattles or if the latch does not hold. A cone-shaped piece on a threaded shaft at the front of the hood is the adjustable piece in the latch assembly. To adjust the hood latch, loosen the lock nut on the threaded shaft and screw the cone out, if the latch is too tight; or in, if the latch is too loose. Make small adjustments, checking the latching often. When the hood latches and does not rattle, the latch mechanism is in proper adjustment. Remember to tighten the lock nut when the proper adjustment is achieved.

15 Door-mounted rear view mirrors - removal and installation

1   These instructions pertain only to the removal and installation of factory authorized and installed mirrors. If you are installing an aftermarket mirror, consult the directions enclosed with the part.
2   Carefully pry the plastic cover from the mirror base (photo).
3   Remove the bolts from the mirror base and remove the mirror (photo).
4   Installation is the reverse of the removal procedure.

This photographic sequence shows the steps taken to repair the dent and paintwork damage shown above. In general, the procedure for repairing a hole will be similar; where there are substantial differences, the procedure is clearly described and shown in a separate photograph.

First remove any trim around the dent, then hammer out the dent where access is possible. This will minimise filling. Here, after the large dent has been hammered out, the damaged area is being made slightly concave.

Next, remove all paint from the damaged area by rubbing with course abrasive paper or using a power drill fitted with a wire brush or abrasive pad. 'Feather' the edge of the boundary with good paintwork using a finer grade of abrasive paper.

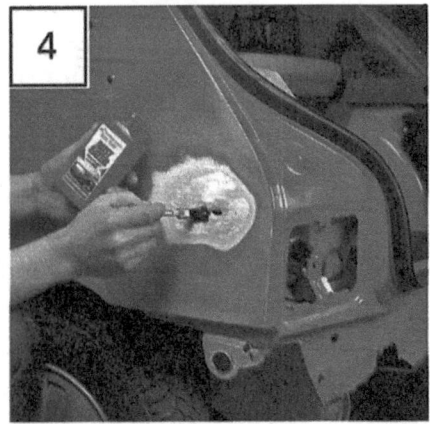

Where there are holes or other damage, the sheet metal should be cut away before proceeding further. The damaged area and any signs of rust should be treated with Turtle Wax Hi-Tech Rust Eater, which will also inhibit further rust formation.

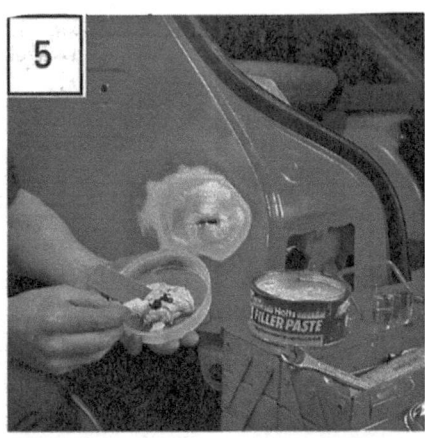

For a large dent or hole mix Holts Body Plus Resin and Hardener according to the manufacturer's instructions and apply around the edge of the repair. Press Glass Fibre Matting over the repair area and leave for 20-30 minutes to harden. Then ...

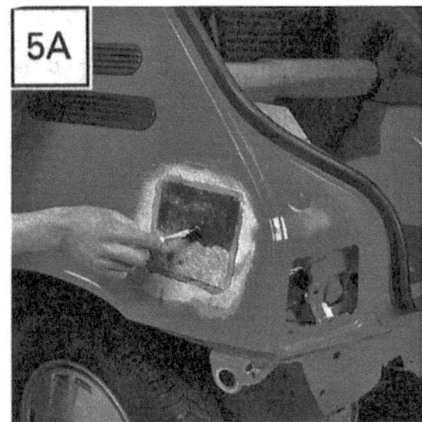

... brush more Holts Body Plus Resin and Hardener onto the matting and leave to harden. Repeat the sequence with two or three layers of matting, checking that the final layer is lower than the surrounding area. Apply Holts Body Plus Filler Paste as shown in Step 5B.

For a medium dent, mix Holts Body Plus Filler Paste and Hardener according to the manufacturer's instructions and apply it with a flexible applicator. Apply thin layers of filler at 20-minute intervals, until the filler surface is slightly proud of the surrounding bodywork.

For small dents and scratches use Holts No Mix Filler Paste straight from the tube. Apply it according to the instructions in thin layers, using the spatula provided. It will harden in minutes if applied outdoors and may then be used as its own knifing putting.

Use a plane or file for initial shaping. Then, using progressively finer grades of wet-and-dry paper, wrapped around a sanding block, and copious amounts of clean water, rub down the filler until glass smooth. 'Feather' the edges of adjoining paintwork.

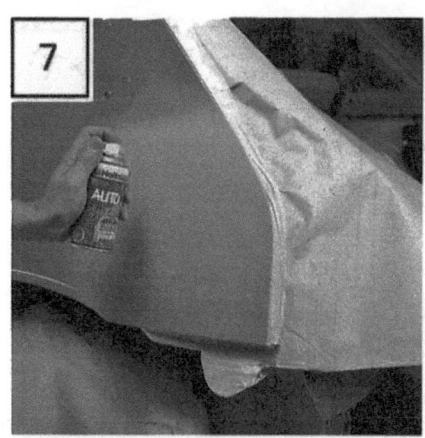

Protect adjoining areas before spraying the whole repair area and at least one inch of the surrounding sound paintwork with Holts Dupli-Color primer.

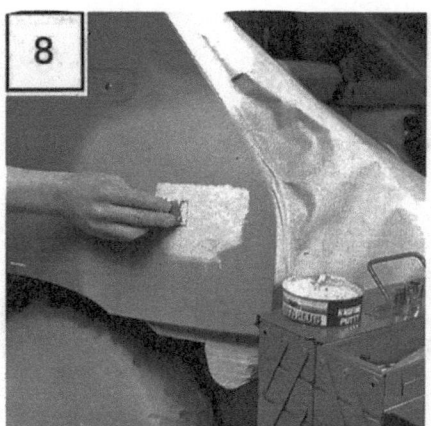

Fill any imperfections in the filler surface with a small amount of Holts Body Plus Knifing Putty. Using plenty of clean water, rub down the surface with a fine grade wet-and-dry paper - 400 grade is recommended - until it is really smooth.

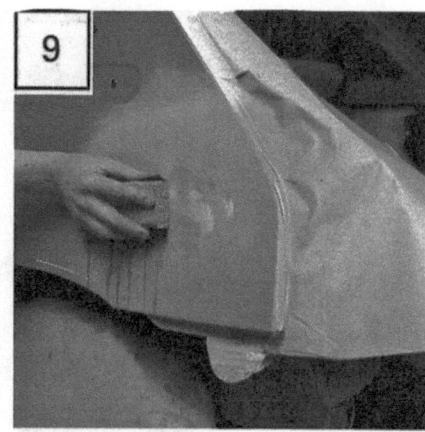

Carefully fill any remaining imperfections with knifing putty before applying the last coat of primer. Then rub down the surface with Holts Body Rubbing Compound to ensure a really smooth surface.

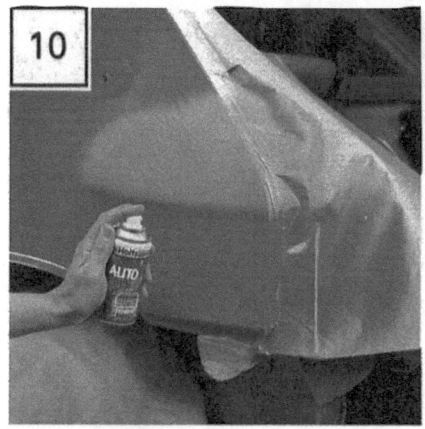

Protect surrounding areas from overspray before applying the topcoat in several thin layers. Agitate Holts Dupli-Color aerosol thoroughly. Start at the repair centre, spraying outwards with a side-to-side motion.

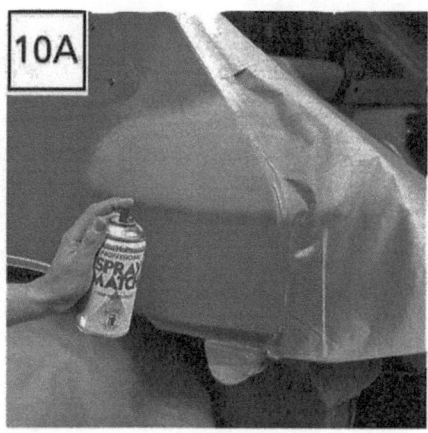

If the exact colour is not available off the shelf, local Holts Professional Spraymatch Centres will custom fill an aerosol to match perfectly.

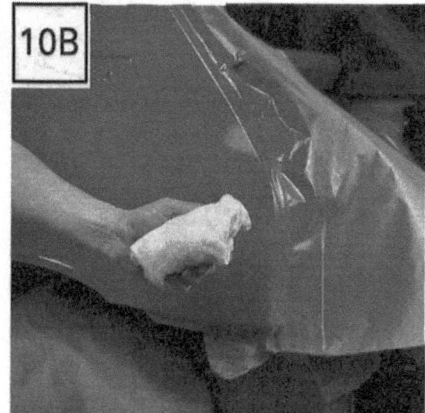

To identify whether a lacquer finish is required, rub a painted unrepaired part of the body with wax and a clean cloth.

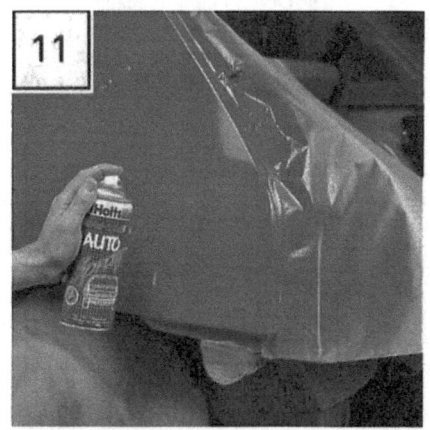

If *no* traces of paint appear on the cloth, spray Holts Dupli-Color clear lacquer over the repaired area to achieve the correct gloss level.

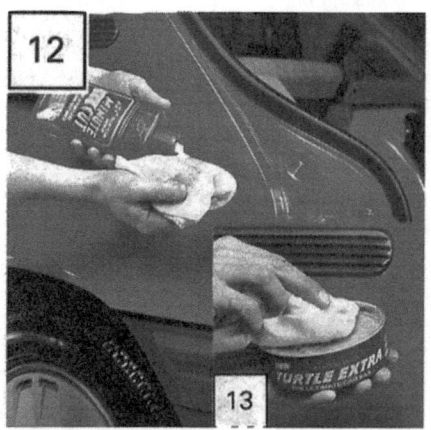

The paint will take about two weeks to harden fully. After this time it can be 'cut' with a mild cutting compound such as Turtle Wax Minute Cut prior to polishing with a final coating of Turtle Wax Extra.

When carrying out bodywork repairs, remember that the quality of the finished job is proportional to the time and effort expended.

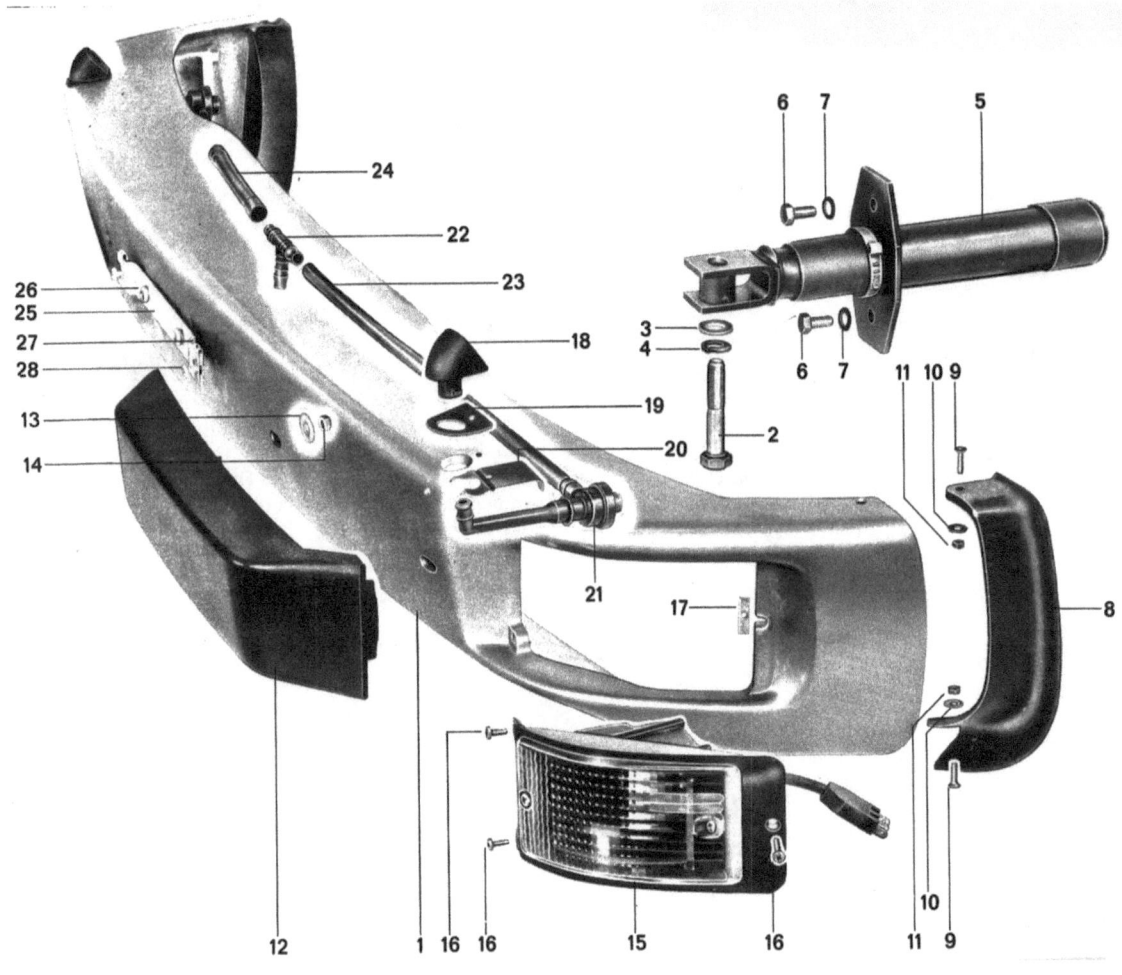

Fig. 12.1 Components of the front bumper

1 Bumper	10 Flat washer	washer)
2 Bolt	11 Nut	19 Adapter plate (optional
3 Flat washer	12 Override strip	washer)
4 Lock washer	13 Flat washer	20 Support bracket
5 Bumper shock absorber	14 Self-locking nut	(optional washer)
6 Bolt	15 Turn signal assembly	21 Adapter (optional
7 Lock washer	16 Phillips head screw	washer)
8 Flap	17 Threaded plate	22 T-adapter (optional
9 Bolt	18 Washer nozzle (optional	washer)

23 Hose, long (optional washer)	
24 Hose, short (optional washer)	
25 License plate bracket	
26 Phillips head screw	
27 Sheet metal nut	
28 Phillips head screw	

5   Adjust the tension of the spring so that the mirror may still be adjusted by hand.

16 Electric door mirrors – general note

1   If you experience problems with the operation of these mirrors, we suggest you seek the services of your Porsche dealer. Improper electrical hook-up and fault finding, in this case may affect the operation of the engine electrics.

17 Seats – removal and installation

1   The driver and passenger seats are held in place by four nuts. When these are removed, the seat and adjuster may be lifted and removed.
2   Installation is the reverse of the removal procedure.
3   Tighten the nuts evenly.

18 Doors – removal and installation

1   The hinges are secured to the pillar with shallow socket headed bolts which are very difficult to undo unless special tools are available. They are also in an awkward position. If the socket heads are damaged and the hexagon hole is converted into a round one then you are in serious trouble, as it will be necessary to drill the bolt and extract it with a special bolt extractor. For this reason we recommend that door hinges should be undone by professionals with the correct equipment. However, if you can undo these bolts the door is easily removed.
2   If power operated windows or electrically operated mirrors are fitted, the door trim panel must be removed and the wiring disconnected and fed through the flexible sleeve on the door edge.
3   Take the pin out of the check strap, slacken the hinge bolts, have someone hold the door while you remove the bolts, and lift the door away. Check the weather strip and fit a new one, if necessary.
4   When installing the door first remove the door striker bolt from the frame. You cannot adjust the hinge while this is in place. Fit the door to the pillar and tighten the hinge bolts enough to hold the

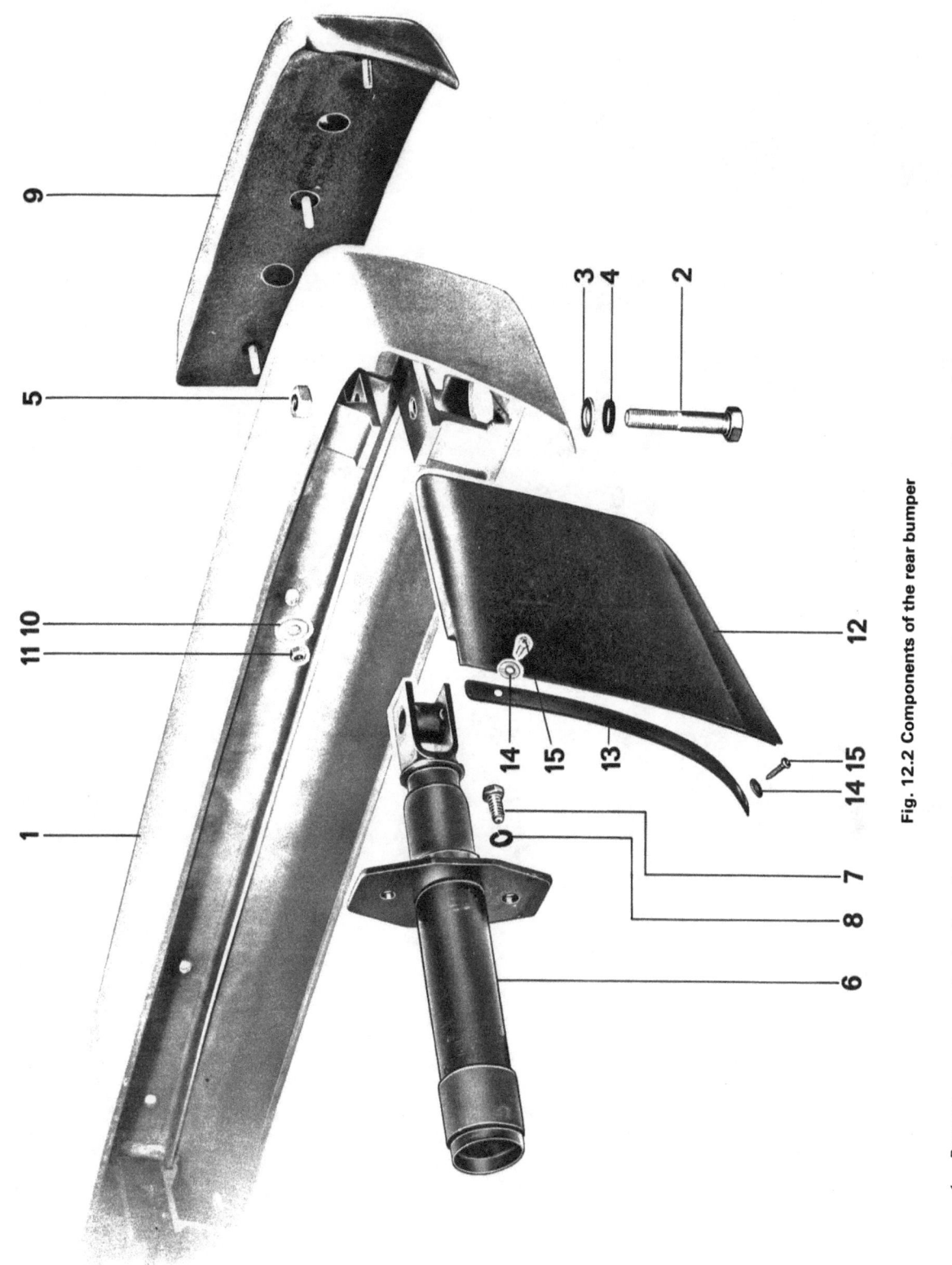

Fig. 12.2 Components of the rear bumper

1	Bumper	4	Lock washer	7	Bolt	10	Flat washer	13	Flap liner
2	Bolt	5	Square nut	8	Lock washer	11	Nut	14	Flat washer
3	Flat washer	6	Bumper shock absorber	9	Override strip	12	Flap	15	Phillips head screw

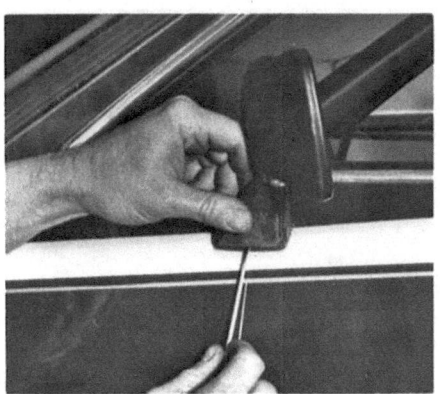

15.2 Prying the plastic cap from the mirror base

15.3 Unbolting the mirror

18.4 Adjusting the door lock and aligning the striker

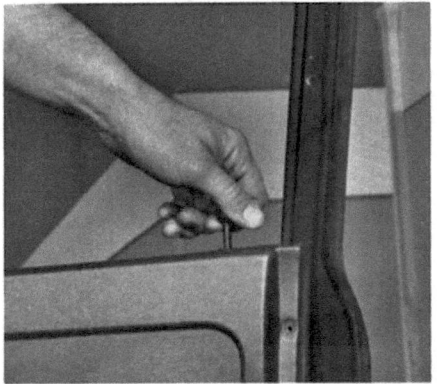

19.2 Unscrewing the lock knob

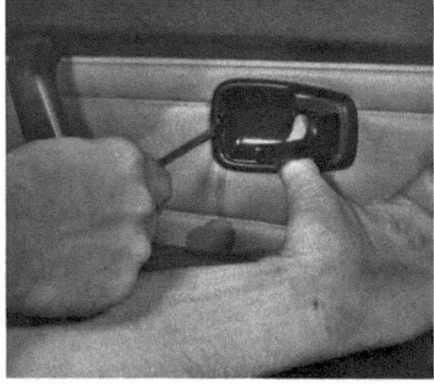

19.3a Prying the finger guard from the latch

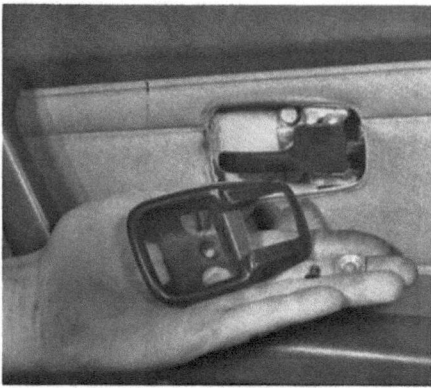

19.3b Removing the latch surround piece

19.4 Unbolting the window winder

19.5 Removing the map pocket

19.8 Prying the trim from the door

22.2 Unbolting the window glass at the support strap

24.3 Removing the heater control box fascia plate

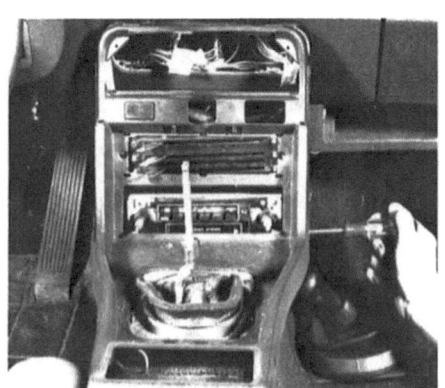

24.10a Removing the screws from the edge of the console

door in place. Close the door and check that the gap all round the edge is symmetrical. Adjust the hinge until it is correct then tighten the hinge bolts fully. Refit the striker bolt and adjust the lock if necessary (photo).

5   If the door is not flush with the body panels, it is permissible to fit shims between the hinges and carrier plates.

19   Door interior trim - removal and replacement

1   It is not necessary to remove the interior door trim to remove the exterior door handle.
2   Remove the knob from the lock by unscrewing (photo).
3   Remove the finger guard from the door latch by prying it carefully away and pulling out (photo). Remove the screw which holds the surround plate around the latch lever and lift the surround piece away (photo).
4   Note the position of the window winder and pull its rubber cover from the handle. Unbolt the handle and remove it (photo).
5   Remove the three screws which hold the map pocket in place and remove the pocket (photo).
6   Remove the three screws from the arm rest and allow the arm rest to hang by its upper mounting screw at the top of the door pull. This screw will not have to be removed.
7   Carefully pry the soft plastic caps from the trim pieces and remove the screws.
8   Beginning at the rear of the door, carefully pry the door clips from the door frame with a long, flat-bladed screwdriver (photo). When all clips have been removed, lift the trim from the door.
9   Installation is the reverse of the removal procedure. Make certain that the clips are aligned, then strike each one with the flat of the hand when installing to seat them squarely.

20   Door handle (exterior) - removal and installation

1   Lift the rubber moulding away from the door just above the door lock and remove the screw situated in the recess.
2   Push the door handle forward towards the hinge and extract the back of the handle first. The front end is held by a fork. The lock barrel may now be removed. If the lock is damaged take it to the Porsche dealer to have the correct lock installed to fit your door key.
3   When replacing the handle make sure the handle lever engages with the door lock.
4   When removing the barrel lock always leave the key in the lock or the tumblers and springs will fall out.

21   Door lock mechanism - servicing

1   Remove the interior trim (Section 19). Remove the plastic cover from the face of the door. Press the clip off the linkage inside the door.
2   Remove the two screws, holding the remote control lever in the centre of the door, disengage the long link and then disconnect it from the lock.
3   Undo the two screws holding the lock to the door and remove the lock through the door opening.
4   When assembling make sure the door handle operating lever engages with lock operating lever.
5   There is little that can be done to a faulty lock. The mechanism is mostly made of pressed parts which can neither be repaired nor renewed. The lock can be moved to the limits of the screws to engage the striker bolt more easily. The striker bolt may be rotated a little if worn.

22   Window winder mechanism - servicing

1   Remove the door trim and plastic sheet.
2   The window glass may be disconnected from the window by undoing the two bolts which secure the window support strip to the window bracket (photo).
3   The winder mechanism is tubular and is secured at the bottom

of the door by bolts. It proceeds from there vertically through the winder handle gear and then bends to the left inside the door along the top in clips and then descends vertically to the base of the door where it is secured again. In this leg the stirrup which is bolted to the base of the window glass operates.
4   By removing the screws which hold the winder handle mechanism and then feeling inside for the various clips and brackets which retain the winder cable it may be eventually be freed and withdrawn from the door. It is a fiddling job and because the cable is covered with grease you will get into a mess. The cable may be loose in the tube, which causes an annoying rattle and may be cured by closing the opening in the tube a little. When replacing the winder, or a new one, push and pull it roughly into position, connect the window loosely and then fit the winder handle to the door. Disconnect the window again and wind the bracket up and down, adjusting the position of the window in its clips until the bracket moves up and down freely. Now reconnect the window to the bracket and test it again. It is a question of patience rather than skill, and going softly for it is easy to damage a new winder when fitting it to the door.

23   Door window glass - removal and installation

1   Remove the door trim panel as described earlier.
2   Lower the glass far enough to be able to release the front lifting rail screw, accessible through the hole in the door inner panel. If power operated windows are fitted, disconnect the battery.
3   Detach the rear glass guide rail.
4   Disconnect the glass lifting arms from the glass channel.
5   Remove the weatherseals from the door waist glass slot.
6   Withdraw the glass upwards, turn it and remove it from the door cavity.
7   The window regulator can be unbolted and removed through the inner panel aperture.
8   Refitting is a reversal of removal, but apply grease to the regulator teeth and glass lower channel. Adjust the glass vertical guides.
9   Where power operated windows are fitted, the operations are similar, but electric lift motors are used instead of a mechanical regulator.

24   Console - removal and installation

1   Disconnect the negative lead from the battery.
2   Remove the instrument cluster. Mark all wires and connections with pieces of tape and an indelible ink pen before disconnecting the wires.
3   Remove the knobs from the heater controls and remove the fascia plate from the heater control box (photo).
4   Remove the radio, if one is installed. Removal procedure depends on the brand and type of radio installed in your vehicle.
5   Remove the screws from either side of the heater control box.
6   Remove the ashtray.
7   Reach behind the switches mounted in the console (if any), press out the switches and unplug the wires. Mark the wires for ease in reassembly.
8   Remove the shift lever cover and the shift lever boot. The lever cover is held in place by a rubber doughnut around the selector lever. It may be necessary to rock the cover back and forth while pulling upward to loosen it.
9   If your vehicle is equipped with a 5-speed transmission, remove the two bolts from the guide plate just ahead of the selector lever.
10 Remove the screws from the lower edge of the console and remove the console by lifting from the back edge of the unit and pulling back (photos).
11 Installation is the reverse of the removal procedure.

25   Dashboard - removal and installation

1   Remove the console (Section 24).
2   Open the glove compartment and unbolt the hinges and the limiting strap. Remove the glove compartment door.
3   Remove the four bolts for the glove compartment box and

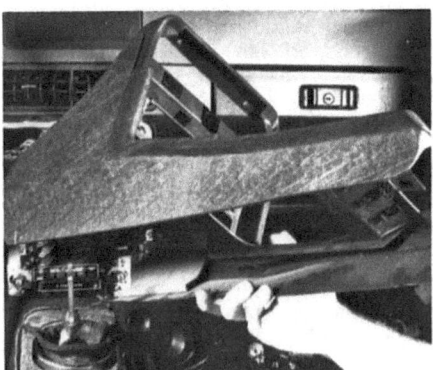

24.10b Removing the console

25.3 Removing the glove compartment box and unplugging the light

25.6 Pressing the entire instrument cluster from the dashboard

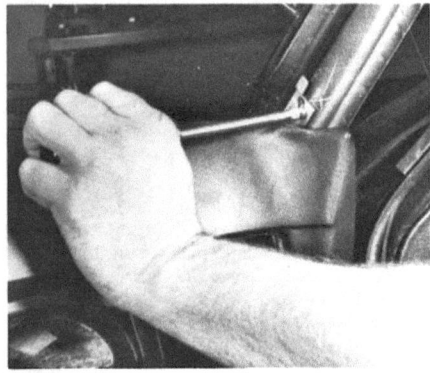

25.8 Removing the mounting screws on the windshield pillars

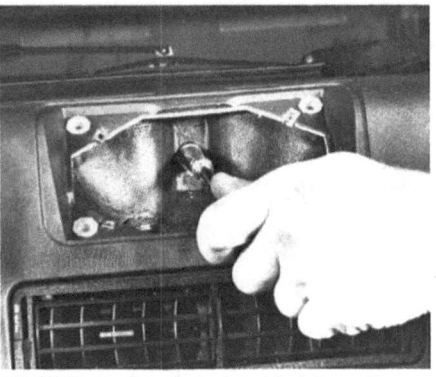

25.10 Removing the bolt behind the radio speaker

remove the box by pulling forward into the passenger compartment (photo).

4   Remove the sun visors and the padding strips from the windshield pillars. Access to the mounting screws is gained by prying back the soft plastic covers on the screws.

5   Remove the steering wheel and switchgear from the steering column (Chapter 8).

6   Press the instrument cluster out of the dashboard, mark and disconnect the wires before unplugging them, then remove the instrument cluster (Chapter 11) (photo).

7   Remove the radio speaker grille. Remove the radio speaker.

8   Remove the screws on the windshield pillars (photo).

9   Remove the side screw in the glove compartment.

10 Remove the bolt behind the radio speaker (photo).

11 Lift the dashboard away from the mounts and remove it.

12 Installation is the reverse of the removal procedure.

Chapter 13 Supplement:
Revisions and information on later models

Contents

1 Introduction

This Supplement contains information which is additional to, or a revision of, material in the first twelve Chapters. Although most of the material relates to later models, some items apply retrospectively to all models from the start of production.

The Sections in the Supplement follow the same order as the Chapters to which they relate. The Specifications are all grouped together for convenience, but they follow Chapter order.

It is recommended that, before any particular operation is undertaken, reference be made to the appropriate Section(s) of the Supplement. In this way any changes to procedure or components can be noted before referring to the main Chapters.

2 Specifications

The specifications below are revisions of, or supplementary to, those at the beginning of the preceding Chapters.

Engine
General (1981 on)

Compression ratio:
    924 .... 9.3:1
    Turbo 8.5:1
    Carrera GT 8.5:1
Maximum power:
    924 .... 92 kW (125 bhp) at 5800 rpm
    Turbo .... 130 kW (177 bhp) at 5500 rpm
    Carrera GT .... 154 kW (210 bhp) at 6000 rpm
Maximum torque:
    924 .... 165 Nm (122 lbf ft) at 3500 rpm
    Turbo .... 250 Nm (185 lbf ft) at 3500 rpm
    Carrera GT .... 280 Nm (207 lbf ft) at 3500 rpm

Lubrication system

Oil capacity, including filter (all models):
924 .... 5.0 litres (8.8 Imp pints) approx
Turbo and Carrera GT .... 5.5 litres (9.7 Imp pints) approx

Torque wrench settings (1980 on)

	Nm	lbf ft
Cylinder head bolts – splined type (engine cold):		
Stage 1	65	48
Stage 2	+ 180°	+ 180°

Fuel system (1981 on)
Idle adjustments

Idle speed:
924 .... 950 ± 50 rpm
Turbo and Carrera GT .... 900 rpm (electronically controlled)
CO level at idle .... 1.5 ± 0.5%

Injection system test values

Leak test (1984 on):
Minimum pressure after 10 minutes .... 2.0 bar (29 lbf/in²)
Minimum pressure after 20 minutes .... 1.7 bar (25 lbf/in²)
For other values, see Chapter 3 Specifications

Turbocharger
Boost pressure

Except Carrera GT .... 0.64 bar (9.28 lbf/in²)
Carrera GT .... 0.75 bar (10.88 lbf/in²)

Ignition system
Distributor – contact breaker type (1976)

Type .... Bosch
Contact breaker points gap .... 0.40 mm (0.016 in)
Dwell angle .... 44 to 50°
Timing (dynamic, at idle) .... 10° BTDC (vacuum hose disconnected)
Firing order 1–3–4–2

Spark plugs – all models

924 .... Champion N6YC or equivalent
Turbo and Carrera GT .... Champion N2G or equivalent
Electrode gap:
924 .... 0.7 mm (0.028 in)
Turbo and Carrera GT .... 0.6 mm (0.024 in)

Manual transmission (1981 on)
Ratios

	924	Turbo/Carrera GT
1st	3.600:1	3.166:1
2nd	2.125:1	1.777:1
3rd	1.458:1	1.217:1
4th	1.107:1	0.931:1
5th	0.857:1	0.706:1
Reverse	3.500:1	2.909:1
Final drive	3.889:1	4.125:1

Automatic transmission (all models)
Torque wrench settings

	Nm	lbf ft
Fluid pan screws	20	15
Fluid filter screws	4	2.5

Braking system
Carrera GT (1981 on)

Master cylinder diameter .... 19.1 to 23.8 mm (0.75 to 0.94 in)
Booster diameter .... 228.6 mm (9.0 in)

Suspension (1981 on)
Tyre sizes

Except Carrera GT:
Standard (steel wheel) .... 165 HR 14
Standard (alloy wheel) .... 185/70 HR 14
Option .... 205/60 HR 15
Carrera GT:
Standard .... 215/60 VR 15
Options .... 205/55 VR 16, 225/50 VR 16

Tyre pressures

924 (front and rear)	2.0 bar (29 lbf/in²)

Turbo and Carrera GT:

Front	2.0 bar (29 lbf/ft²)
Rear	2.5 bar (36 lbf/in²)
'Space saver' spare (when applicable)	2.2 bar (32 lbf/in²)

Front wheel alignment (vehicle at kerb weight)

Camber:

924	$-20' \pm 10'$
Turbo and Carrera GT	$-20' \pm 15'$
Maximum side-to-side difference	0°10'

Castor:

All models to 1983	$+2°45' \pm 30'$
1983 on	$+2°30' \; {+30' \atop -15'}$
Maximum side-to-side difference	0°30'

Rear wheel alignment

Toe	$0° \pm 10'$
Camber	$-0°25' \pm 30'$
Maximum side-to-side camber difference	0°30'

Height adjustment

Centre of torsion bar below wheel centre-line:

924 and Turbo (to 1983)	5 ± 10 mm (0.2 ± 0.4 in)
924 (1983 on)	3 mm (0.12 in)
Carrera GT	20 ± 20 mm (0.8 ± 0.8 in)

Rear spring strut angle

924 (1981 to 1983)	19°30'
924 (1983 on)	19°00'
Turbo (1981 on)	18°05'
Carrera GT (1981 on)	15°35'

General dimensions and weights
Dimensions

Overall length:

All models except Carrera GT	4213 mm (165.9 in)
Carrera GT	4320 mm (170.1 in)

Overall width:

All models except Carrera GT	1685 mm (66.3 in)
Carrera GT	1735 mm (68.3 in)

Overall height:

All models except Carrera GT	1270 mm (50.0 in)
Carrera GT	1275 mm (50.2 in)
Wheelbase	2400 mm (94.5 in)

Track (front):

924 and Turbo	1418 mm (55.8 in)
Carrera GT	1477 mm (58.1 in)

Track (rear):

924	1372 mm (54.0 in)
Turbo	1392 mm (54.8 in)
Carrera GT	1451 mm (57.1 in)

Weights

Kerb weight:

924	1130 kg (2492 lb)
Turbo and Carrera GT	1180 kg (2602 lb)

Maximum trailer load:

Brakes	800 kg (1764 lb)
Unbraked	500 kg (1102 lb)
Maximum roof rack load	35 kg (77 lb)

---

3 Routine maintenance

Maintenance intervals – all models

Maintenance intervals are based on a notional annual mileage of 15 000 miles. Vehicles covering a lower mileage should still have the 15 000-mile maintenance tasks performed every year, the 30 000-mile tasks every two years, and so on.

Older and high-mileage vehicles will benefit from more frequent maintenance, as will those operating under adverse conditions. 'Adverse conditions' include extremes of climate, full-time trailer towing or city driving, and driving on unmade roads.

Although not specified by the makers, it is recommended that the engine timing belt be renewed as a precautionary measure every 40 000 miles (64 000 km) or so. If the belt breaks or slips in service, extensive damage may result.

4   Engine

Cylinder head bolt tightening (1980 on)

1   The cylinder head bolts on later models are of splined socket type, and should be tightened by the angular method – see Specifications.
2   The bolt threads should be lightly oiled before installation. Renew the bolts each time they are removed. The bolts no longer require re-torquing after the initial running-in period.

Oil filter adapter – RHD vehicles

3   On RHD vehicles, if the position of the oil filter adapter is incorrect, the filter may foul adjacent components. If the adapter has been disturbed, adjust it *in situ* as follows.
4   With the filter adapter loose, fit a new filter and insert a wooden block 26 mm (1 in) thick, between the filter and the upper edge of the crossmember. Tighten the adapter bolt in this position, then remove the wooden block.

Valve clearance adjustment (all models)

5   A 3 mm Allen key may be substituted for one of the special adjusting tools shown in Fig. 1.12 (Chapter 1) (photos). Note that the adjusting screw must be moved in complete turns (360°); the screw will be felt to click home at the end of each turn.
6   The maker's special tools carry markings (shown by arrows in Fig. 1.12) which show when the screw has been turned to its limit. If the limit marking is passed, the tappet must be removed and a thicker or thinner adjusting screw fitted. There is no easy way of providing this limit indication with a home-made tool.

Piston rings (all models) – removal and refitting

7   The piston ring installation tool shown in Chapter 1 (photo 26.17) may be replaced by three old feeler blades as follows.
8   Carefully expand the top ring with the fingers and slide the feeler blades under the ring to stop it dropping back into the groove. The ring is brittle and will snap if expanded too far. Slide the ring off the piston, being careful not to scratch the piston with the ends of the ring.
9   Repeat the process on the second and third rings, moving the feeler blades down to stop the rings falling into the grooves above (photo).
10 Refit by reversing the removal operations. If the rings carry 'TOP' markings, these must face upwards.

Flywheel (924 Turbo, 1981 on) – modified fitting

11 The flywheel on these models is an interference fit on the end of the

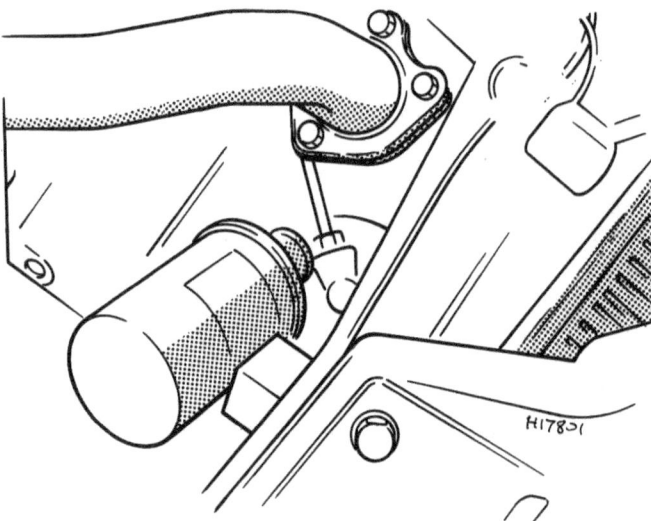

Fig. 13.1 A block of wood between the oil filter and the crossmember (Sec 4)

4.5A Adjusting valve clearance with an Allen key

4.5B Tappet removed and inverted to show engagement of Allen key

4.9 Piston ring removal using three feeler blades

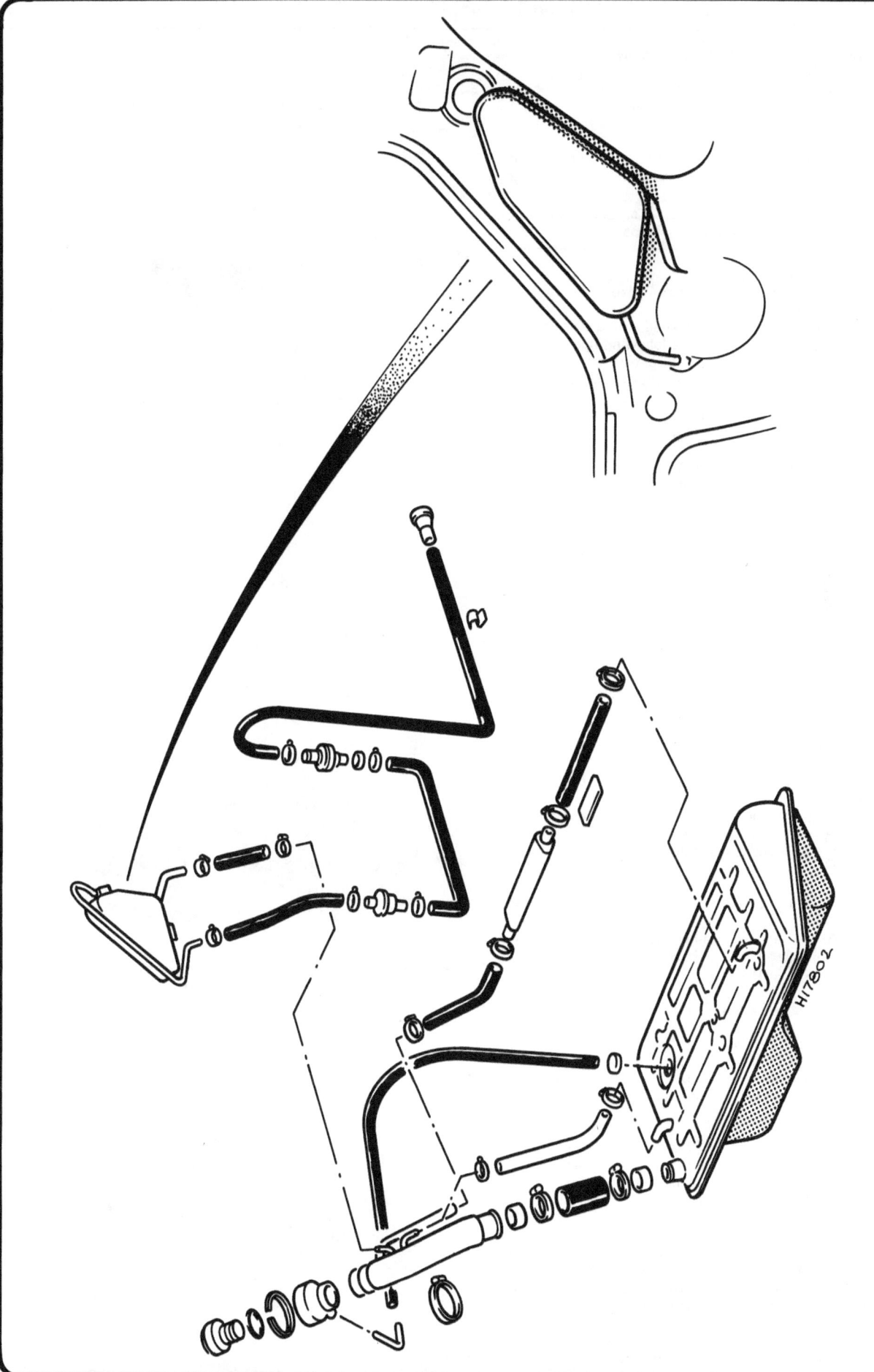

Fig. 13.2 Fuel expansion tank components and location (Sec 5)

crankshaft (as well as being bolted on). A new flywheel must be heated before installation.

12 Securing bolts for this type of flywheel are 2 mm (0.08 in) shorter than those used previously. The new bolts are identified by having a hole 4 mm (0.16 in) in diameter in their heads. Old and new bolts must not be interchanged.

13 The position of the flywheel on the crankshaft determines the ignition timing. Make sure that alignment marks are made before disturbing it.

5 Fuel, emission control and exhaust systems

Fuel system expansion tank

1 On 1982 and later models, the fuel system expansion tank is located in the right-hand body C-pillar.

2 Access to the expansion tank can be obtained after disconnecting the battery negative lead and carrying out the following operations.

3 Remove the trim panel from the right-hand rear pillar inside the car. The seat back holder must be unbolted to provide clearance for withdrawal of the panel.

4 Partially withdraw the sidewall carpet from around the fuel filler neck area.

5 Remove the fuel filler pipe neck cover.

6 Disconnect the hoses from the expansion tank, drain any fuel, and clean and blow out the tank. Reconnect hoses and removed components.

7 If, for any reason such as a leak, the expansion tank must be removed, then this will necessitate removal of the side window and cutting out the inner body panel in accordance with the diagram, Fig. 13.3.

8 Use metal shears or a saw, not a gas torch. When fitting the new tank, spot-weld it to the panel and then weld the panel back with a continuous seam. Take care to insulate generously to prevent damage to the exterior paintwork.

9 As an interim measure, a leaking expansion tank can simply be bypassed by following paragraph 2 to 5 above, then disconnecting the hoses from the tank and joining the filler neck stub directly to the pressure relief valve. Plug the open stubs on the expansion tank.

Throttle switch (turbo models) – checking and adjustment
Checking

10 Connect a test lamp between the battery and the white/blue wire on the multiple pin plug.

11 The lamp should light. Move the throttle slowly by hand and make sure the lamp goes out at about 1°. This can be checked with a 0.2 to 0.5 mm (0.008 to 0.020 in) feeler gauge at the stop screw as shown in the illustration.
Adjustment

12 Remove the throttle housing and loosen the mounting screw on the switch.

13 Insert a 0.3 mm (0.012 in) feeler gauge between the stop screw and throttle stop and connect a test lamp between terminals 2 and 18.

14 Turn the switch until it just opens and the test lamp goes out. Tighten the screw.

15 Repeat the test and install the throttle housing.

Fuel injection systems – UK models

16 All non-turbo UK models are covered by the CIS information in Chapter 3 (Part A and Specifications). Turbo model specifications are as given in Chapter 3 for Lambda injection. Most of Parts B and C of Chapter 3 do not apply to UK models.

Auxiliary air regulator – testing (all models)

17 When testing the auxiliary air regulator (Chapter 3, Section 17), tap it lightly from time to time to encourage movement of the valve. In normal use, engine vibrations have the same effect.

Idle adjustment – models with DITC

18 The Digital Idle Timing Control system fitted to later Turbo models regulates idle speed by varying the ignition timing. More details of the system are given in Section 7. Idle adjustment is made using an exhaust gas analyser (CO meter), a tachometer and a timing light (stroboscope). Proceed as follows.

19 Unscrew the air intake temperature sensor from the intake manifold. Reconnect the sensor and place it in the area just behind the engine bulkhead, so that it is·exposed to a temperature of 50°C (122°

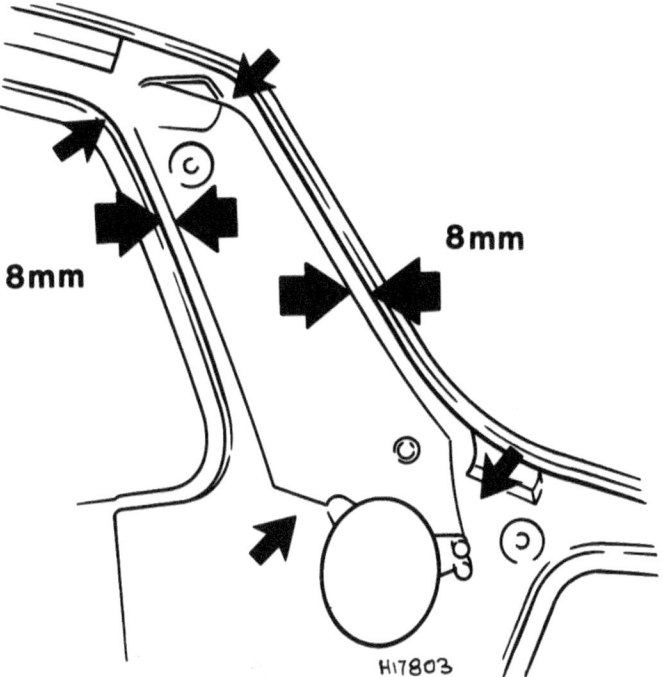

Fig. 13.3 Body panel cutting diagram (Sec 5)

Fig. 13.4 Checking throttle switch continuity with a test lamp (Sec 5)

Fig. 13.5 Checking throttle switch adjustment (Sec 5)

F) or less. Plug the hole in the manifold with a bolt, thread M14 x 1.5.

20 Run the engine to operating temperature and connect the test gears. Connect the timing light to No 1 cylinder spark plug lead. Switch off electrical loads (lights, heated rear window etc). Allow the engine to idle.

21 Adjust the bypass screw on the throttle housing, at the same time shining the timing light on the timing marks, until the flywheel timing mark is seen to be sometimes aligned with the reference mark and sometimes jumping away from it. This shows that the DITC is advancing the timing periodically to maintain the idle speed. At this point the idle speed should be 900 rpm or less.

22 Check the CO level and adjust if necessary.

23 Repeat the adjustments until both speed and CO level are correct, then stop the engine and disconnect the test gear.

Fuel system adjustments (all models) – caution

24 Some adjustment screws or orifices may be protected by 'tamperproof' plugs, caps or seals. The purpose of tamperproofing is to discourage, and to detect, adjustment by unqualified operators. In some EEC countries (though not yet in the UK) it is an offence to drive a vehicle without the necessary tamperproof devices fitted. Satisfy yourself that current legislation permits the removal of tamperproof devices before making adjustments, and fit new devices on completion when this is required. Note that removal of tamperproof devices may also invalidate any warranty, when applicable.

6 Turbocharger

Crankcase ventilation system

1 The layout of the crankcase ventilation system is shown in Fig. 13.6.

2 System hoses and traps should be cleaned periodically and checked for condition.

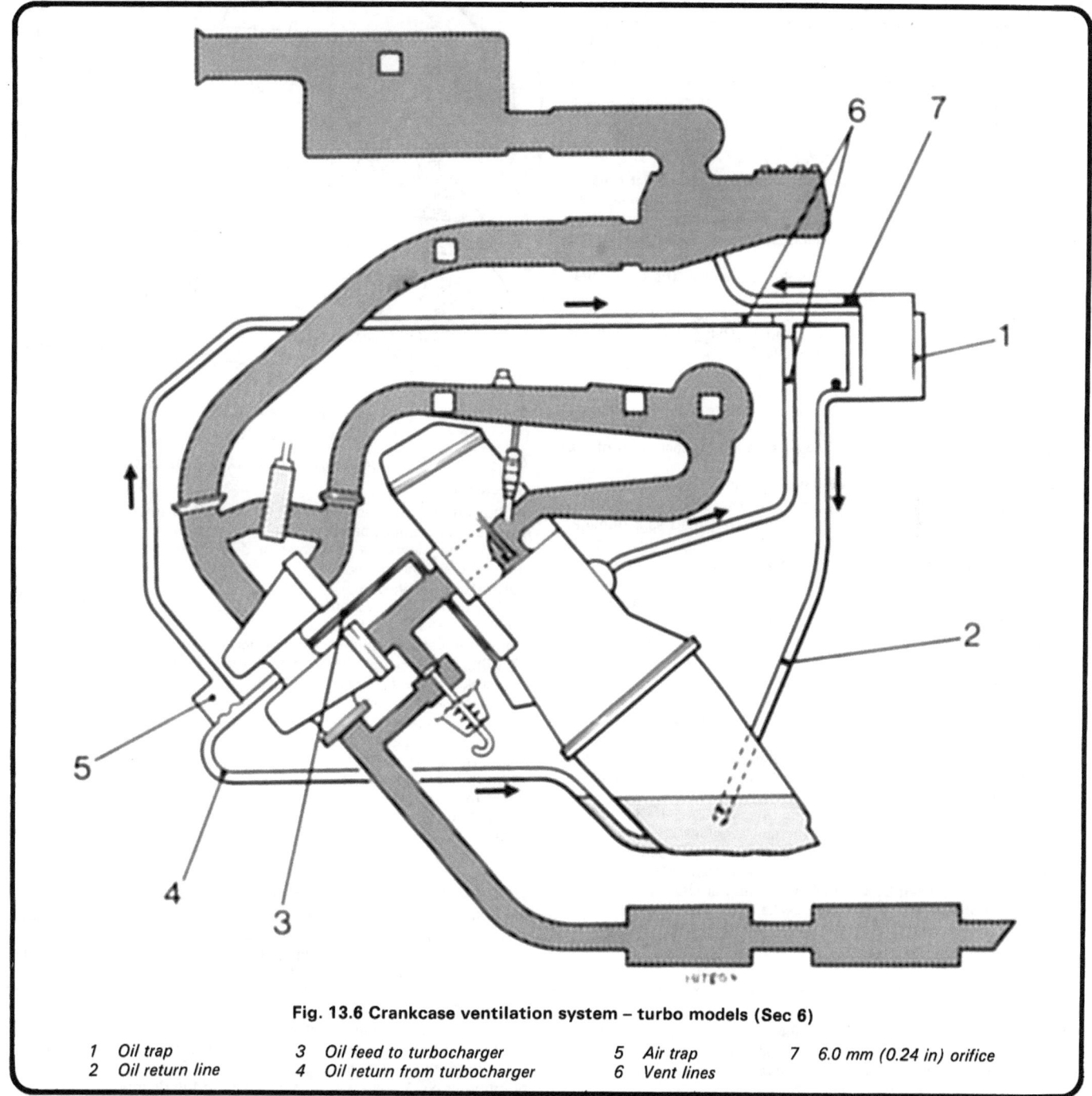

Fig. 13.6 Crankcase ventilation system – turbo models (Sec 6)

1	Oil trap	3	Oil feed to turbocharger	5	Air trap
2	Oil return line	4	Oil return from turbocharger	6	Vent lines
				7	6.0 mm (0.24 in) orifice

Turbocharger – 1981 on

3 On these models, a modified turbocharger is used, which has a lower boost pressure (see Specifications) and has new associated components including bypass valve, mixture control unit, coasting boost valve and throttle housing.

4 On Carrera GT models, an intercooler is fitted between the turbocharger and the intake manifold. This increases efficiency and power output by reducing the charge air temperature.

---

7   Ignition and starting systems

Distributor (contact breaker type) – description

1 The distributor fitted to the earliest 924 models is of conventional mechanical contact breaker type.

2 The distributor rotor is driven from a gear on the rear end of the overhead camshaft.

3 A vacuum diaphragm, connected to the inlet manifold, causes the ignition timing to be varied according to inlet manifold suction and therefore engine load, while a centrifugally operated cam varies the timing dependent upon engine speed. Some models have a vacuum connection to each side of the diaphragm so that the basic ignition timing can be either advanced, or retarded. This additional provision is to reduce exhaust pollution.

Contact breaker points – renewal

4 Every 15 000 miles (24 000 km), or annually, the contact breaker assembly should be renewed. It is not recommended that the contact points are refaced – the assembly should be renewed complete.

5 Release the two clips securing the distributor cap and remove the cap.

6 Pull the rotor arm off the cam spindle and remove the dust cover beneath the rotor arm.

7 Disconnect the contact breaker wire from the terminal inside the distributor. Remove the clamp screw and washer from the contact breaker assembly and remove the assembly.

8 Before fitting the new points, smear the distributor cam with grease and grease the pivot pin of the moving contact breaker contact.

9 Fit the contact breaker assembly and tighten the clamp screw so that the fixed contact is just clamped to the base plate. Rotate the crankshaft until the plastic cam follower is on the highest point of the cam.

10 With the cam follower on the highest point of the cam, lever the fixed contact plate until the contacts are at the specified gap and then tighten the clamp screw. This should only be regarded as a nominal setting. For optimum engine performance the setting of the contact breaker points should be checked with a dwell meter – see paragraph 12 onwards.

11 Ensure that the contact breaker lead is securely attached to the contact on the side of the distributor and then refit the distributor cover, rotor and cap. Check the ignition timing on completion.

Dwell angle – checking and adjustment

12 Connect a dwell meter in accordance with the manufacturers' instructions, which may require the engine to be idling, or to be cranked on the starter motor.

13 The dwell angle is the number of degrees through which the distributor cam turns during the period between the instants of closure and opening of the contact breaker points.

14 The correct dwell angle is as given in Specifications. If the angle is too large, increase the points gap, if too small, reduce the gap.

15 The dwell angle not only provides a more accurate setting of the contact breaker points gap but the method also evens out any variations in gap caused by wear in the distributor shaft or bushes or differences in the heights of the cam peaks.

16 Always check and adjust the dwell angle before checking or adjusting the ignition timing.

Ignition timing checking and adjustment – contact breaker type distributor

17 Have the engine at normal operating temperature, distributor vacuum hoses disconnected and a timing light (stroboscope) connected in accordance with the manufacturer's instructions.

18 Start the engine and let it idle.

19 Point the timing light at the aperture in the flywheel housing. The + mark on the edge of the flywheel should appear to be in alignment with the reference cut-out in the flywheel housing. This represents the specified 10° BTDC setting.

20 If the mark is not in alignment, release the distributor clamp nut and turn the distributor until it is. Tighten the nut, reconnect the vacuum hoses and switch off the engine.

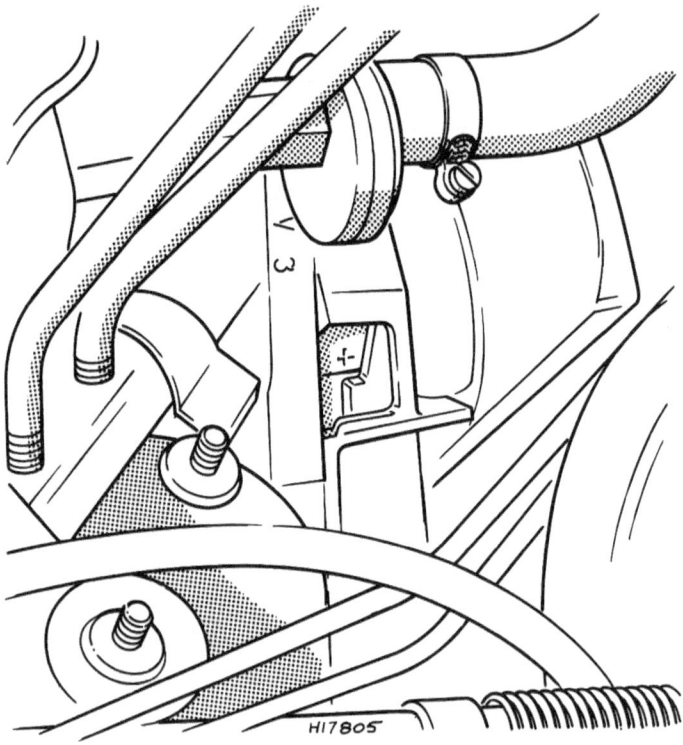

Fig. 13.7 Timing mark on flywheel – contact breaker distributor (Sec 7)

Automatic advance (contact breaker type distributor) – checking

21 It is difficult to check whether the amount of advance is within the manufacturer's specification unless special equipment is available, but the following tests are adequate for determining whether or not the automatic advance is working.

Centrifugal advance

22 Disconnect the vacuum hoses. When two vacuum hoses are connected, the retard hose, which is the one connected to the flatter side of the vacuum unit, must be sealed off with a plug.

23 With a timing light connected, proceed as for dynamic ignition timing described in the previous Section.

24 After checking that the timing is correct at idling speed, gradually increase the speed of the engine. At about 1000 to 1250 rpm the ignition should begin to advance and continue to advance as engine speed is increased to its maximum. The overall advance should be about 25° at maximum speed.

Vacuum advance

25 With the engine idling, apply vacuum to the advance (domed) side of the vacuum diaphragm. When vacuum is applied, the ignition should advance by about 10° and fall again when vacuum is released.

Distributor (contact breaker type) – removal and refitting

26 Pull the high tension connection from the centre of the ignition coil and remove the caps from the spark plugs.

27 Release the two spring clips securing the distributor cover, then remove the distributor cover with the ignition harness attached.

28 Remove the connection from the low tension lead to the contact breaker. Disconnect the vacuum hoses.

29 Turn the crankshaft until No 1 piston is at TDC. This can be established by noting the alignment of the camshaft sprocket timing mark, and the position of the distributor rotor, which should be pointing at No 1 spark plug lead contact in the distributor cap.

30 Mark the rim of the distributor body adjacent to the contact end of the rotor.
31 Mark the relationship of the distributor mounting plinth to the distributor drive housing.
32 Unscrew the distributor clamp plate fixing nut and withdraw the distributor.
33 To refit the distributor, first check that No 1 piston is still at TDC, and reset it if necessary.
34 Hold the distributor over its hole with the pedestal mark in alignment with the one on the drive housing.
35 Turn the rotor to align with the rim mark. When the distributor is installed, the rotor will turn a few degrees, due to the meshing of the drive gears, so anticipate this by turning the rotor so that it is a few degrees out of alignment with the rim mark before pushing the distributor into place.
36 Check that the distributor pedestal mark is in alignment with the one on the drive housing and fit the clamp plate and the nut.
37 Refit the distributor cap, reconnect the HT and LT leads and vacuum hoses.
38 Check the ignition timing as described earlier.

Distributor (contact breaker type) – overhaul
39 Remove the distributor as previously described.
40 Release the two spring clips retaining the cap and lift the cap off.
41 Pull the rotor arm off the cam spindle and then lift off the dust cover beneath it.
42 Disconnect the contact breaker lead from the terminal on the side of the distributor. Remove the clamp screw and washer from the contact breaker and lift the breaker assembly off the base plate.
43 Disconnect the condenser lead from the terminal on the side of the distributor. Remove the condenser fixing screw and take off the condenser.
44 Remove the small spring clip which secures the operating rod of

the vacuum unit to the pin on the contact breaker base plate. Remove the screw securing the vacuum unit to the distributor case and take off the vacuum unit. This is the limit of dismantling which should be attempted, because none of the parts beneath the contact breaker plate, nor the drivegear, can be renewed individually.
45 Inspect the inside of the distributor cap for signs of burning, or

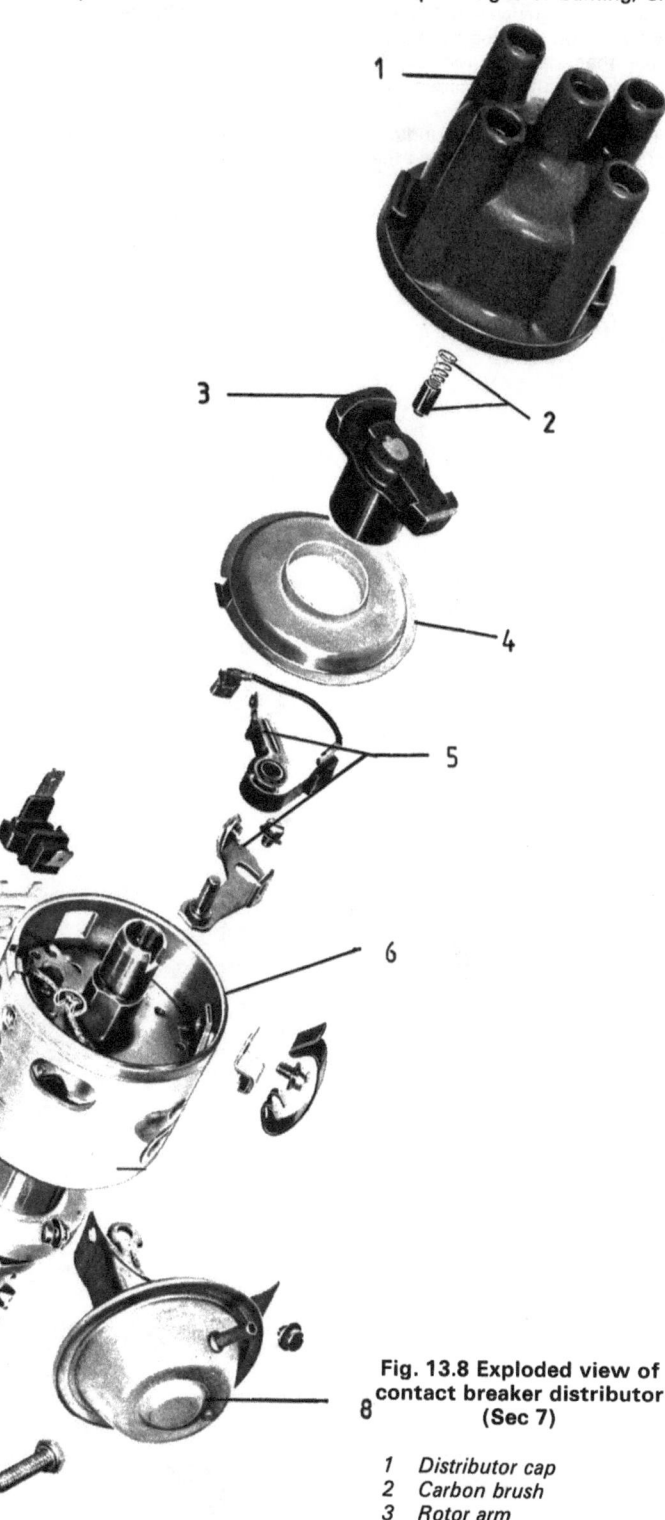

Fig. 13.8 Exploded view of contact breaker distributor (Sec 7)

1   Distributor cap
2   Carbon brush
3   Rotor arm
4   Dust cover
5   Contact breaker points
6   Distributor body
7   Condenser
8   Vacuum unit
9   Clamping plate
10 Distributor drive housing

tracking. Make sure that the small carbon brush in the centre of the distributor cap is in good condition and can move up and down freely under the influence of its spring.

46 Check that the rotor arm is not damaged. Use an ohm-meter to measure the resistance between the brass contact in the centre of the rotor arm and the brass contact at the edge of the arm. The measured value of resistance should be between 4000 and 6000 ohms.

47 Suck on the pipe connection to the vacuum diaphragm and check that the operating rod of the diaphragm unit moves. Retain the diaphragm under vacuum to check that the diaphragm is not perforated.

48 The contact breaker and condenser are relatively inexpensive items and it is recommended that the old ones are discarded and new ones fitted on reassembly.

49 Before reassembling, make sure that all the parts are clean and take great care not to get any oil, grease or dirt on the contacts. Smear the cam with grease and after fitting the vacuum unit, apply a single spot of oil to the junction of the operating rod and the pin on the contact breaker plate.

50 Fit and adjust the contact breaker as described earlier.

51 Refit the distributor as described earlier, check the dwell angle and the ignition timing.

Ignition systems (later models) – general

52 Later models are equipped with a different type of electronic ignition system from that described in Chapter 5. While the distributor

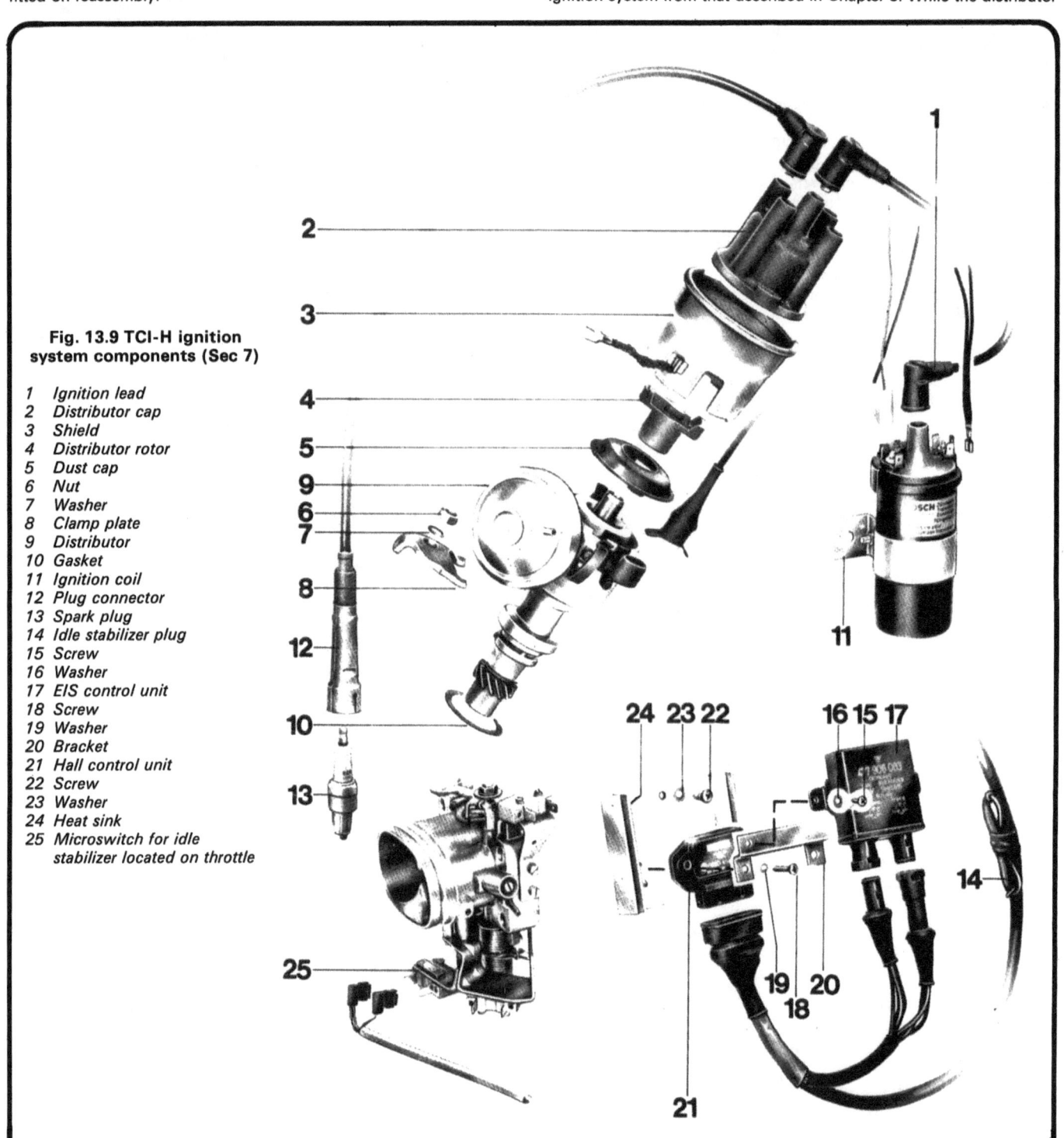

Fig. 13.9 TCI-H ignition system components (Sec 7)

1 Ignition lead
2 Distributor cap
3 Shield
4 Distributor rotor
5 Dust cap
6 Nut
7 Washer
8 Clamp plate
9 Distributor
10 Gasket
11 Ignition coil
12 Plug connector
13 Spark plug
14 Idle stabilizer plug
15 Screw
16 Washer
17 EIS control unit
18 Screw
19 Washer
20 Bracket
21 Hall control unit
22 Screw
23 Washer
24 Heat sink
25 Microswitch for idle stabilizer located on throttle

and some components differ from earlier models, many checking and adjustment procedures are unchanged.

53 Non-turbo engines are equipped with a TCI-H ignition system, while turbo engines are equipped with a Digital Ignition Timing Control System (DITC).

TCI-H ignition system

54 The TCI-H system uses a Hall transmitter and (on some models) an idle stabilizer in place of the induction transmitter on earlier models. To avoid damage to the system, the following precautions must be observed.

    (a) *The ignition should be off when testers or leads are connected or disconnected.*

    (b) *The distributor cap and dust cap spring retainers must not be allowed to hang down into the sensor system when the engine is being cranked.*

    (c) *A capacitor should never be connected to the coil.*

    (d) *The ignition coil must be replaced with a coil of the same specification.*

    (e) *Whenever the engine is cranked over without starting it, connect the coil wire to earth as shown in the illustration or unplug the Hall control unit.*

    (f) *Starting voltage should never exceed 16 volts.*

    (g) *Because the EIS control unit (when fitted) will affect idle speed, the unit must be disconnected during testing and adjustments. This is accomplished by detaching the plug located on the left wheel well housing in the engine compartment.*

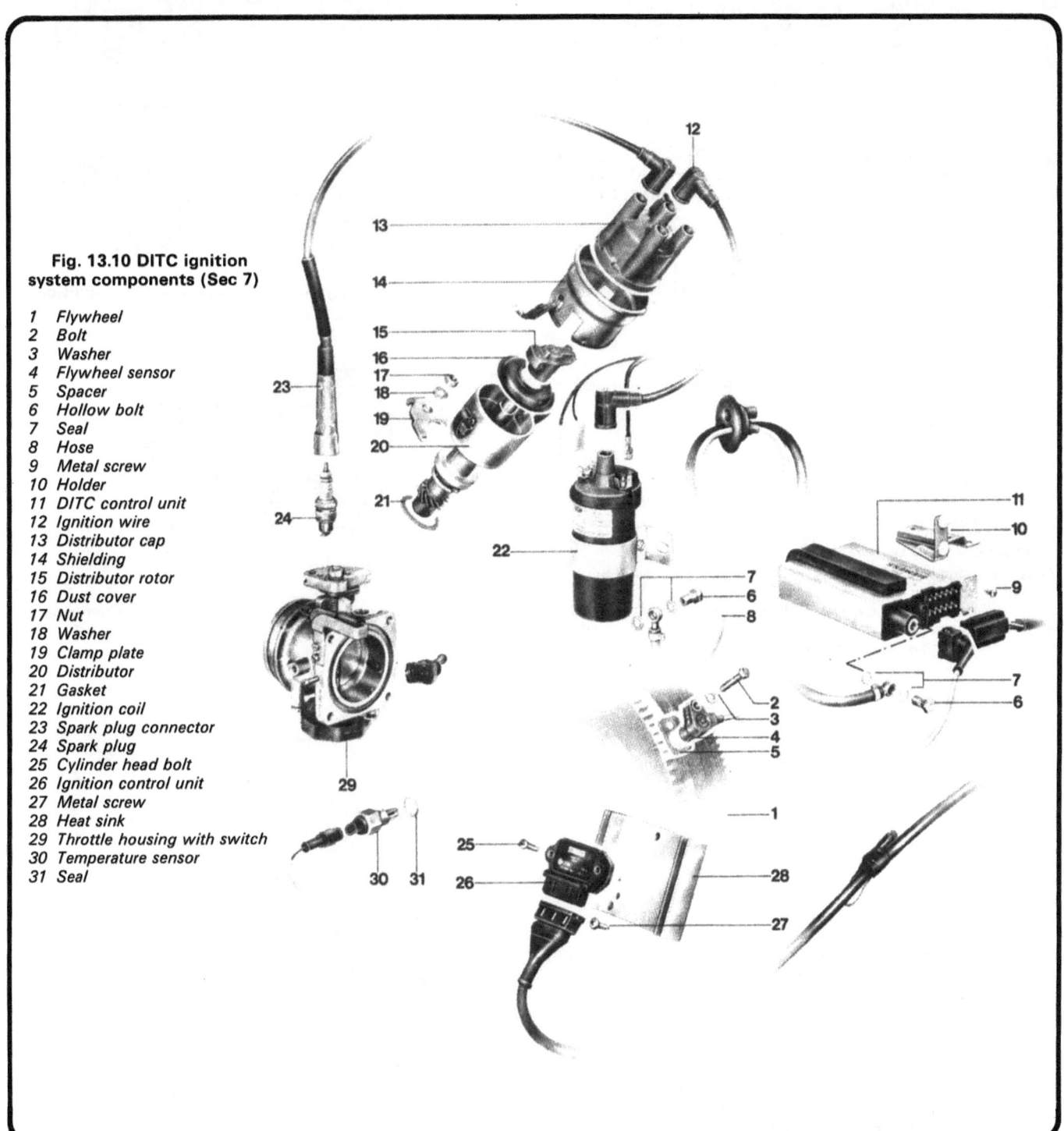

Fig. 13.10 DITC ignition system components (Sec 7)

1 Flywheel
2 Bolt
3 Washer
4 Flywheel sensor
5 Spacer
6 Hollow bolt
7 Seal
8 Hose
9 Metal screw
10 Holder
11 DITC control unit
12 Ignition wire
13 Distributor cap
14 Shielding
15 Distributor rotor
16 Dust cover
17 Nut
18 Washer
19 Clamp plate
20 Distributor
21 Gasket
22 Ignition coil
23 Spark plug connector
24 Spark plug
25 Cylinder head bolt
26 Ignition control unit
27 Metal screw
28 Heat sink
29 Throttle housing with switch
30 Temperature sensor
31 Seal

Ignition coil – checking

55 Disconnect the coil wires and remove the cap. Inspect the top of the coil to make sure the plug is secure and that no sealing compound is leaking. Replace the coil with a new one if the plug is damaged or missing.

56 Measure the resistance between terminal 1 and terminal 15. The resistance should be 0.52 to 0.76 ohms.

57 Measure the resistance between terminal 1 and terminal 4. The resistance should be 2.4 to 3.5 kilohms.

58 Replace the ignition coil with a new one if the resistance is not within the specifications.

Hall control unit – checking

59 Disconnect the idle stabilizer plug (when applicable).

60 Earth the ignition coil as described in the precautions in paragraph 54.

61 Unplug the Hall transmitter at the distributor.

62 Connect a voltmeter to ignition coil terminals 15 and 1 and turn the ignition on. The voltmeter should indicate between 5 and 6 volts, then after about 1 second, it should drop to zero.

63 With the voltmeter connected as described in paragraph 62, momentarily connect a wire between the green (centre) terminal of the Hall transmitter plug and a good earth. The voltage should rise and then drop to zero.

64 Measure the voltage between the outside terminals of the plug with the ignition on and make sure the reading is at least 10 volts.

65 Replace the control unit with a new one if it fails any of the tests.

Hall transmitter – checking

66 With the ignition coil earthed, connect a test lamp between terminals 1 and 15.

67 When the starter is operated, the test lamp should flicker. If it does not, the Hall transmitter is defective and must be replaced with a new one.

DITC system – description

68 The DITC system is unique in that LT pulses are not generated in the distributor, but by a flywheel sensor which responds to the passage of flywheel ring gear teeth. Basic ignition timing is therefore determined by the position of the flywheel.

69 Speed-related (centrifugal) and load-related (vacuum/pressure) advance values are determined electronically within the control unit, instead of mechanically within the distributor. Charge air temperature is also considered by the control unit.

70 The only function of the distributor in this system is the distribution of HT voltage to the spark plugs in the correct order.

71 As mentioned in Section 5, ignition timing will vary at idle in order to maintain a steady idle speed.

72 No adjustment of ignition timing is possible, other than the retard adjustment described in paragraph 91 onwards. This is intended for use if circumstances force the use of inferior fuel, with consequent pinking.

DITC system flywheel sensor – checking

73 Unplug the flywheel sensor plug at the control unit.

74 Use a test lamp to check for continuity between terminals 13 and 15, followed by terminals 14 and 15 of the sensor plug.

75 Replace the sensor with a new one if it fails either continuity test.

DITC system flywheel sensor – removal and refitting

Removal

76 Remove the ignition mark cover.

77 Remove the flywheel sensor mounting bolt and pull out the sensor and spacers (if equipped).

78 Remove the hollow bolts on the intake air distributor and timing control unit and disconnect the flywheel sensor plug.

79 Remove the sensor, grommet and hose. Remove the clamp to separate the hose from the grommet.

Refitting

80 Push the hose into the grommet and secure it with a new clamp.

81 Push the lines into the passenger compartment and install the grommet, making sure it fits tightly. It may be necessary to use body sealant.

82 Install the flywheel sensor and spacers (if equipped), tightening the bolt to 8 Nm (6 lbf ft).

83 Connect the hose to the air distributor and timing control unit, making sure the seals are not damaged. Route the hose in such a way that there are no sharp bends and tighten the hollow bolts to 9 Nm (7 lbf ft).

Distributor (electronic type) – removal and refitting

84 Position the number 1 piston at TDC with the mark on the flywheel aligned with the edge of the bellhousing and the marks on the camshaft sprocket and valve cover aligned as shown in the illustrations.

Fig. 13.11 Earthing the coil lead on the TCI-H ignition system (Sec 7)

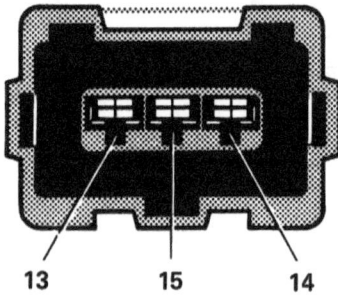

                    13   15   14

Fig. 13.12 DITC system flywheel sensor connector terminals (Sec 7)

Fig. 13.13 Flywheel timing mark on turbo models (Sec 7)

85 Remove the distributor cap and disconnect the earth wire at the shielding.
86 Remove the hold-down nut and withdraw the distributor from the engine.
87 Install the gasket on the distributor flange.
88 Insert the distributor carefully into the engine so that the cap locking groove is facing the flywheel and the mounting clips face the vehicle longitudinal axis and install the rotor as shown in the illustration.
89 Install the distributor cap.
90 Install the hold-down nut and tighten it securely.

Ignition retard – checking

91 Connect a timing light to the engine.
92 Start the engine, rev it up to approximately 1500 rpm and note the ignition timing. Shut the engine off.
93 Unplug the ignition retard connector shown in the accompanying illustration, Fig. 13.16.
94 Start the engine and check that the timing is now retarded by about 7°.
95 If the ignition timing is not retarded by the specified amount there is a fault in the wiring or timing control unit.

Timing control unit – removal and refitting

Removal
96 Unplug the multi-plug connector on the timing control unit and remove the hollow bolt from the hose.
97 Remove the bolts on the holder and withdraw the control unit toward the footwell.

Refitting
98 Push the timing control unit into place and tighten the bolts securely.
99 Carefully plug in the connector and install the hollow bolt. Tighten the bolt to 9 Nm (7 lbf ft).

Fault diagnosis – DITC system

100 The following points are unique to the DITC system and should be considered before making expensive replacements.
101 **Ignition excessively retarded** – this may be due to a disconnected or defective charge air temperature sensor, or to the retard connector (Fig. 13.16) being disconnected.
102 **Ignition excessively advanced** – this may be due to a leaking or disconnected vacuum/pressure hose between the intake manifold and the timing control unit. Do not drive hard in this instance, as destructive pre-ignition could occur.
103 If the throttle switch fails or is disconnected, idle stabilisation will not be available.
104 If the flywheel sensor fails, the engine will not fire or run, since no sparks will be generated.

8 Transmission and transaxle

Shift linkage – adjustment (type 016/9)

1   With the transmission in neutral, the intermediate selector lever can only be installed with one inclination as it is the only way it will fit on the shaft due to the changed design.

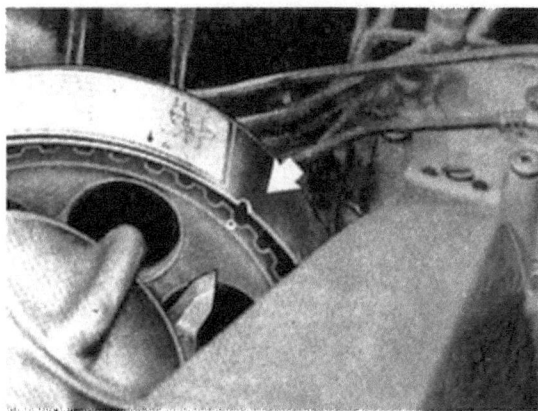

Fig. 13.14 Camshaft sprocket timing marks on turbo models (Sec 7)

Fig. 13.15 Distributor fitting diagram on turbo models – cap locking groove (arrowed) facing flywheel (Sec 7)

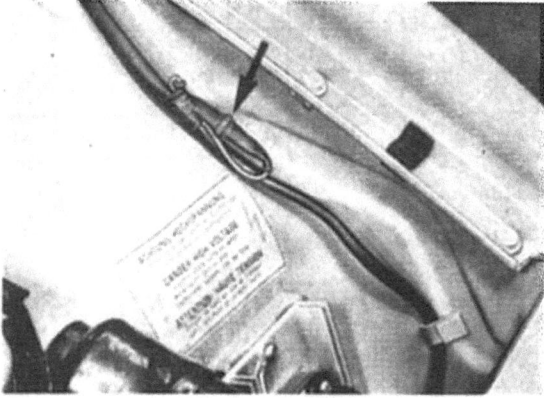

Fig. 13.16 Ignition retard connector – arrowed (Sec 7)

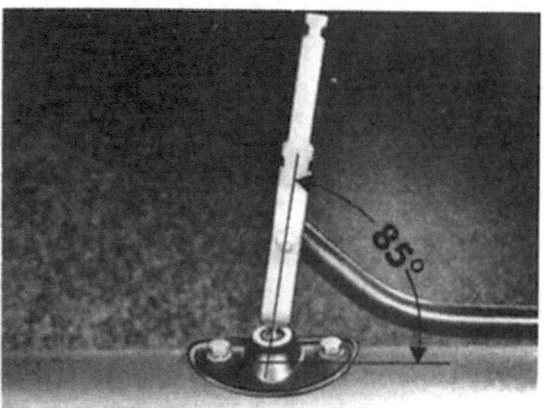

Fig. 13.17 Shift lever inclination (Sec 8)

Fig. 13.18 Transverse selector shaft (I) and intermediate selector lever – arrowed (Sec 8)

2   Move the base of the selector lever to adjust it to an angle of 85° as shown in the illustration.
3   With the selector lever in neutral, the transverse selector shaft I shown in the illustration will be held in the middle (3rd and 4th gear) by spring pressure. When correctly adjusted, the shift lever should not lean to the side. Adjustment is made at the intermediate selector lever.

Reverse gear lock – modification
4   As from 1981, the reverse gear lock has been relocated inside the transmission casing.
5   The design of the various components has been modified as shown in Fig. 13.19.

Manual transmission – topping-up and oil renewal
6   At the intervals specified in 'Routine Maintenance,' remove the socket-headed filler/level plug from the side of the transmission casing. The oil level should be just below the plug hole. Top up if necessary with the specified grade of lubricant.
7   At the specified intervals, drain the transmission oil – do this when the oil is hot.
8   Remove the filler/level and drain plugs and allow the oil to drain completely.
9   Refit the drain plug and fill with the correct grade and quantity of oil, then refit the filler/level plug.

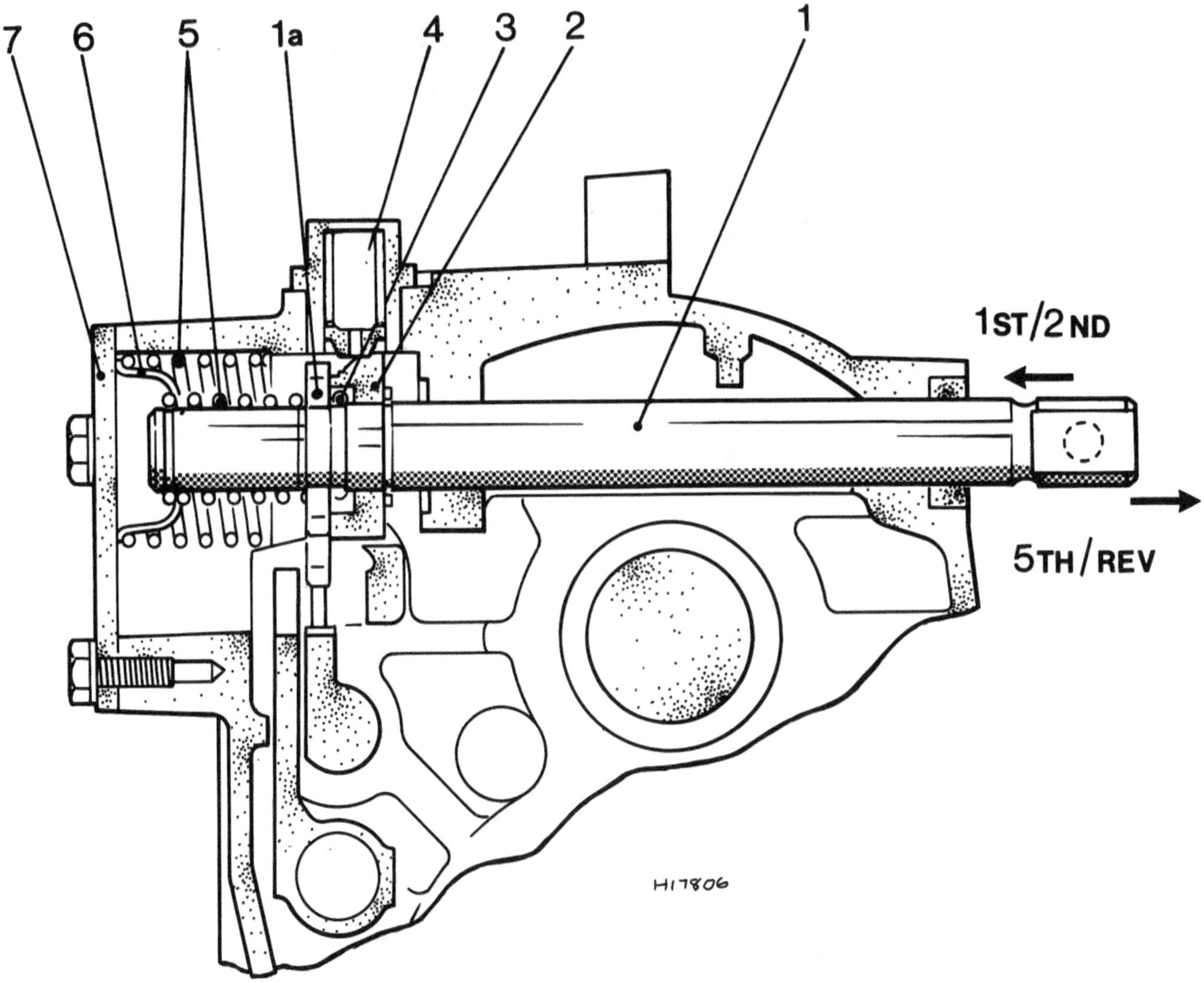

1ST/2ND

5TH/REV

H17806

Fig. 13.19 Sectional view of transmission casing showing integral reverse gear lock (Sec 8)

1 Selector shaft	2 Locking disc	4 Lockpin with housing	6 Spring retainer
1a Selector arm	3 Spring	5 Springs	7 Housing cover

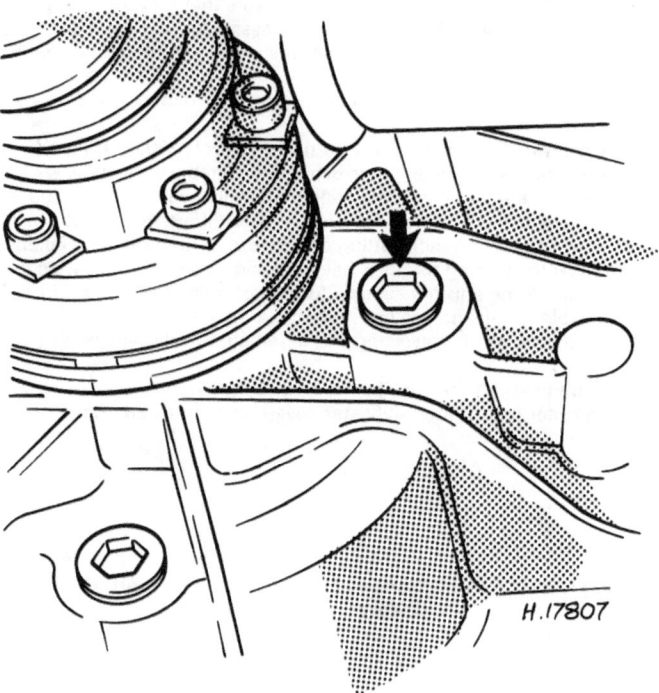

Fig. 13.20 Manual transmission filler/level plug – arrowed (Sec 8)

Automatic transmission – fluid renewal

10 At the specified intervals, the automatic transmission fluid should be drained hot.

11 To do this, unscrew the oil filler tube and the fluid pan screws, and then tilt the pan to drain the fluid into a suitable container. Take care not to scald yourself, as the fluid will be very hot.

12 Extract the filter fixing screws from the bottom of the valve block and withdraw the cover, filter screen and gasket.

13 Clean the screen in petrol and allow to dry. If it is badly contaminated, renew it.

14 Refit the removed components using a new filter gasket and pan gasket.

15 Tighten the screws to specified torque shown in the Specifications at the beginning of this Supplement, then refill the transmission using fresh ATF. (The final drive is lubricated separately with SAE 90 hypoid oil. See Chapter 7, Section 29.) Bring the transmission to operating temperature and check the fluid level as described in Chapter 7, Section 28.

Limited slip differential – overhaul

16 This is fitted as standard to some models, including automatic transmission versions, and is optionally available on others.

17 To dismantle the limited slip differential on manual transmission models, dismantle the transmission as described in Chapter 7 and then unbolt and remove the crownwheel.

18 Remove the bolts from the casing flange and withdraw the cover.

19 Remove all the individual components, keeping them in strict order as originally assembled.

20 Check every part for wear or distortion and renew those which are grooved or scored.

21 Smear each component with SAE 90 hypoid oil during reassembly and observe the following points.

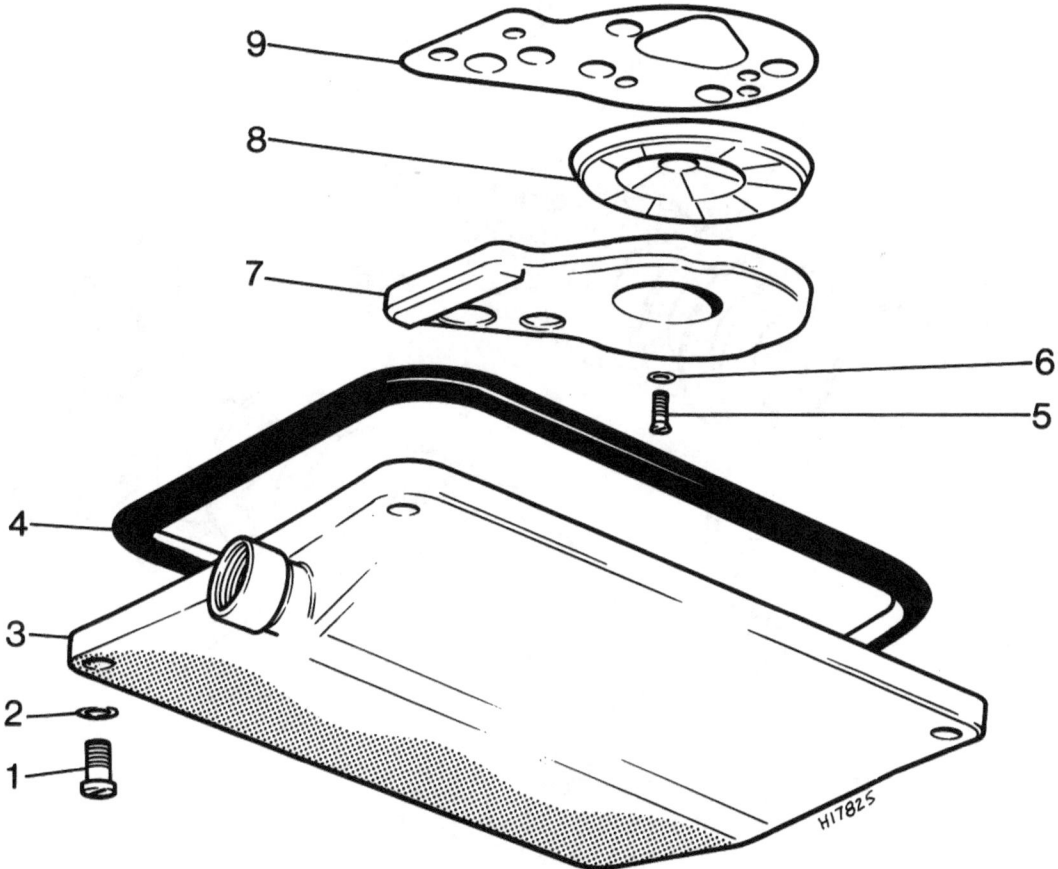

Fig. 13.21 Automatic transmission fluid filter (Sec 8)

1 Screw	4 Gasket	6 Washer	8 Filter screen
2 Washer	5 Screw	7 Filter casing	9 Gasket
3 Fluid pan			

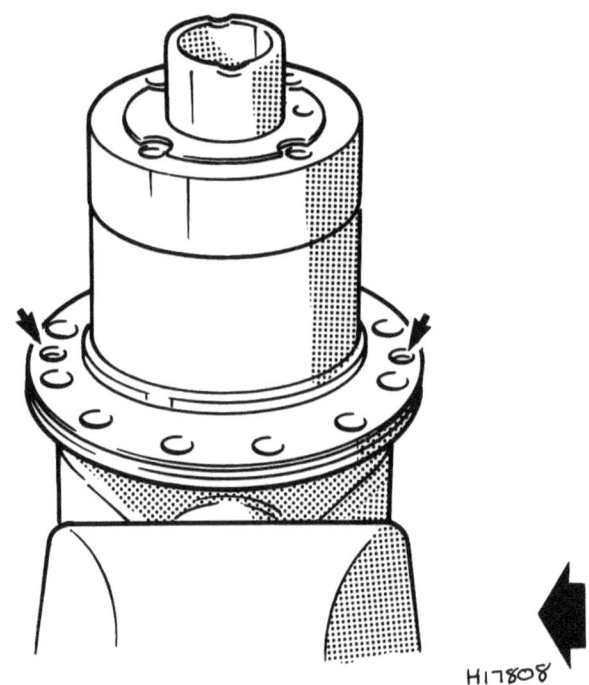

22 When fitting the thrust washers, make sure that they engage in the casing cover grooves. Apply grease if necessary to hold them in place.
23 Fit the diaphragm springs so that their convex side is towards the casing cover.
24 Once reassembly is complete, carry out the following slip torque test.
25 Secure the differential in a vice using two old flange bolts. With one differential gear held and one being free, turn the differential with a torque wrench. A suitable connecting plate will have to be made up to facilitate the use of the torque wrench. The differential should start turning at a torque wrench setting of between 35 and 60 Nm (26 and 44 lbf ft). If the turning torque is below the figure specified, change the outer plate on the appropriate side for one of greater thickness. Plates are available in thicknesses of 1.9, 2.0 and 2.1 mm.
26 Repeat the test by reversing the differential gears which are held and free.
27 Failure to reach the specified turning torque figures even with the thickest outer plates fitted indicates severe wear in all components.

H17808

Fig. 13.22 Casing flange bolts (arrowed) – limited slip differential (Sec 8)

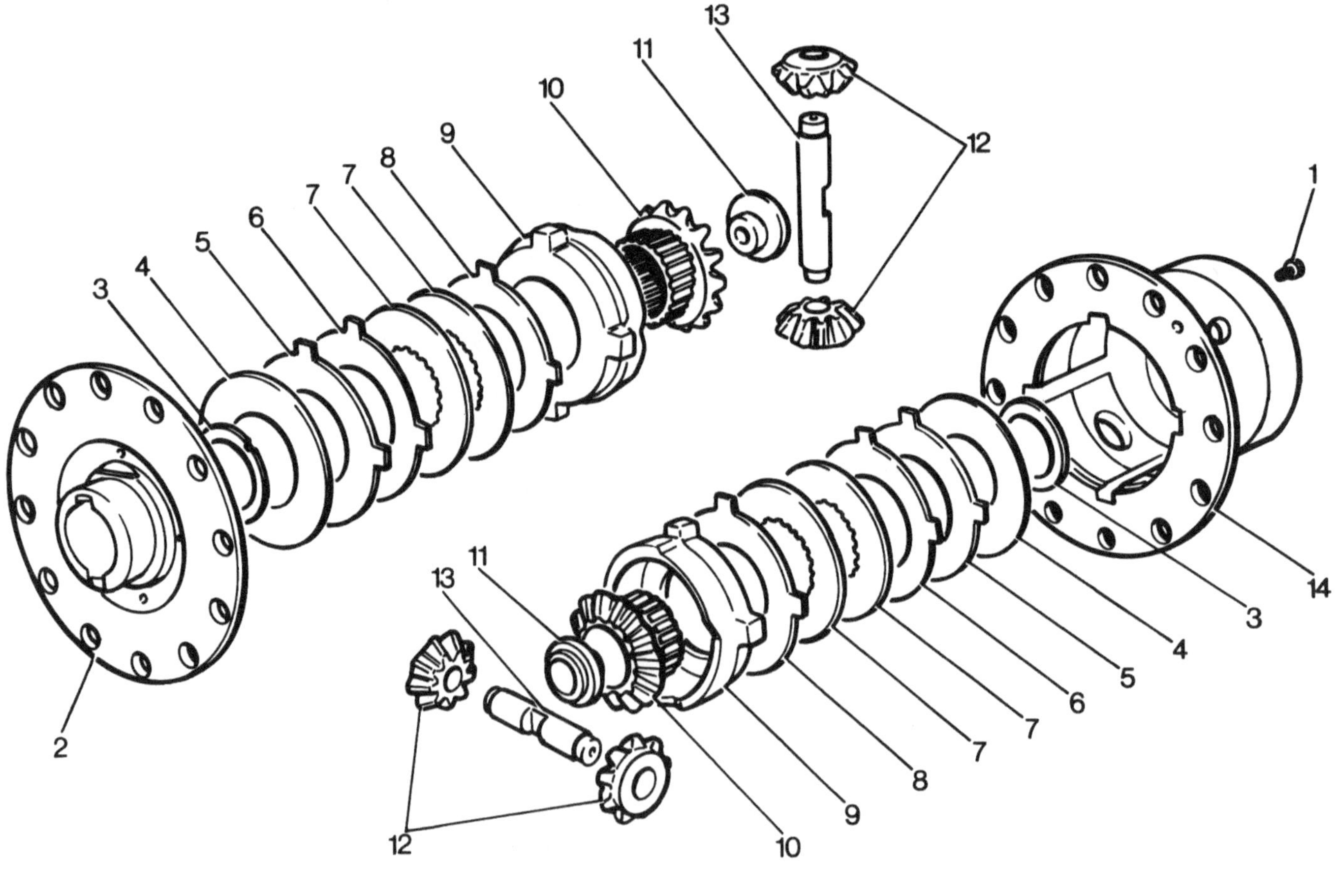

Fig. 13.23 Components of the limited slip differential (Sec 8)

1 Casing bolt	5 Blind plate
2 Cover	6 Outer plate
3 Thrust washer	7 Inner plate (molybdenum lined)
4 Diaphragm spring	

8 Outer plate	12 Differential pinion gear
9 Pressure ring	13 Pinion shaft
10 Differential gear	14 Case
11 Threaded plate	

9 Braking system

Stop-lamp switch – adjustment

1 On later models without master cylinder integral switches, the brake pedal stop-lamp switch should be adjusted, after releasing the switch locknuts, so that a 5.0 mm (0.2 in) gap exists between the switch body (plunger housing) and the brake pedal arm.

Hydraulic system – additional bleeding methods

2 In addition to the method described in Chapter 9, Section 18, one of the following bleeding procedures may also be used.

3 Before commencing operations, check that all system hoses and pipes are in good condition with all unions tight and free from leaks.

4 Take great care not to allow hydraulic fluid to come into contact with the vehicle paintwork as it is an effective paint stripper. Wash off any spilled fluid immediately with cold water.

5 As the system incorporates a vacuum servo, destroy the vacuum by giving several applications of the brake pedal in quick succession.

Bleeding – using one way valve kit

6 There is a number of one-man, one-way brake bleeding kits available from motor accessory shops. It is recommended that one of these kits is used wherever possible as it will greatly simplify the bleeding operation and also reduce the risk of air or fluid being drawn back into the system quite apart from being able to do the work without the help of an assistant.

7 To use the kit, connect the tube to the bleedscrew and open the screw one half a turn.

8 Depress the brake pedal fully and slowly release it. The one-way valve in the kit will prevent expelled air from returning at the end of each pedal downstroke. Repeat this operation several times to be sure of ejecting all air from the system. Some kits include a translucent container which can be positioned so that the air bubbles can actually be seen being ejected from the system.

9 Tighten the bleed screw, remove the tube and repeat the operations on the remaining brakes.

10 On completion, depress the brake pedal. If it still feels spongy repeat the bleeding operations as air must still be trapped in the system.

Bleeding – using a pressure bleeding kit

11 These kits too are available from motor accessory shops and are usually operated by air pressure from the spare tyre.

12 By connecting a pressurised container to the master cylinder fluid reservoir, bleeding is then carried out by simply opening each bleed screw in turn and allowing the fluid to run out, rather like turning on a tap, until no air is visible in the expelled fluid.

13 By using this method, the large reserve of hydraulic fluid provides a safeguard against air being drawn into the master cylinder during bleeding which often occurs if the fluid level in the reservoir is not maintained.

14 Pressure bleeding is particularly effective when bleeding 'difficult' systems or when bleeding the complete system at time of routine fluid renewal.

All methods

15 When bleeding is completed, check and top up the fluid level in the master cylinder reservoir.

16 Check the feel of the brake pedal. If it feels at all spongy, air must still be present in the system and further bleeding is indicated. Failure to bleed satisfactorily after a reasonable period of the bleeding operation may be due to worn master cylinder seals.

17 Discard brake fluid which has been expelled. It is almost certain to be contaminated with moisture, air and dirt making it unsuitable for further use. Clean fluid should always be stored in an airtight container as it absorbs moisture readily (hygroscopic) which lowers its boiling point and could affect braking performance under severe conditions.

Rear disc brakes – turbo models

18 Ventilated disc type rear brakes are fitted to these models. The discs incorporate drums for the parking brake shoes.

19 Although a shoe adjuster is fitted, it is rare for the shoes to require adjusting and even rarer for new shoes to be required.

20 Disc pad renewal is carried out in a similar way to that described in Chapter 9 for the front brakes.

21 To obtain access to the parking brake shoes, raise the car and remove the roadwheel and spacer.

22 Remove the caliper and tie it up out of the way.

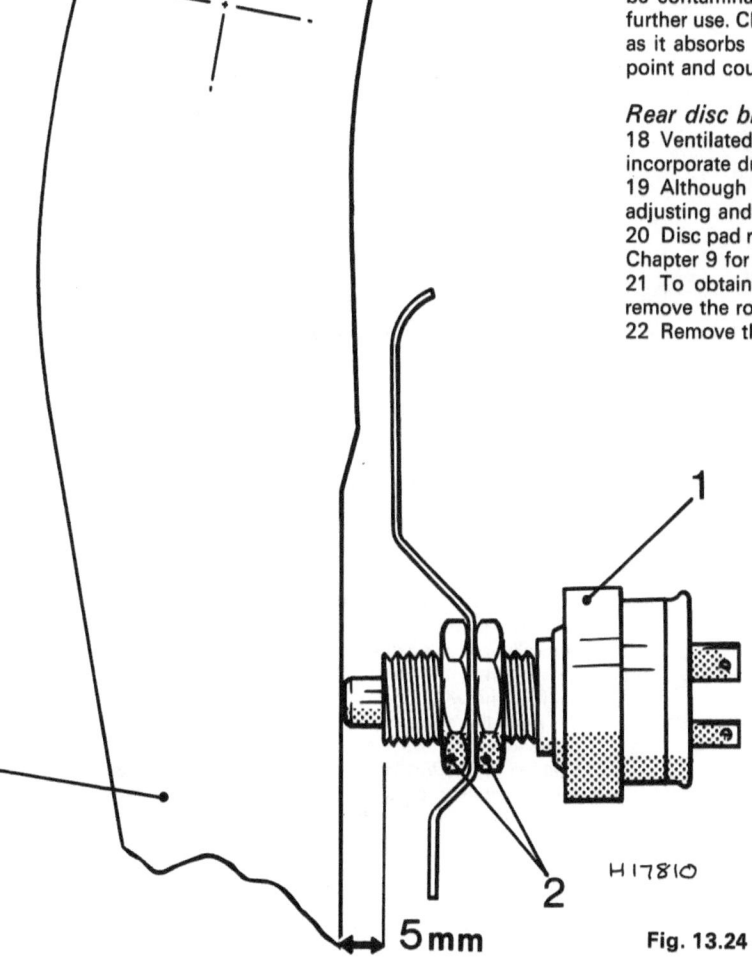

H17810

Fig. 13.24 Brake stop-lamp switch setting diagram (Sec 9)

1   Switch body   2   Locknuts   3   Pedal arm

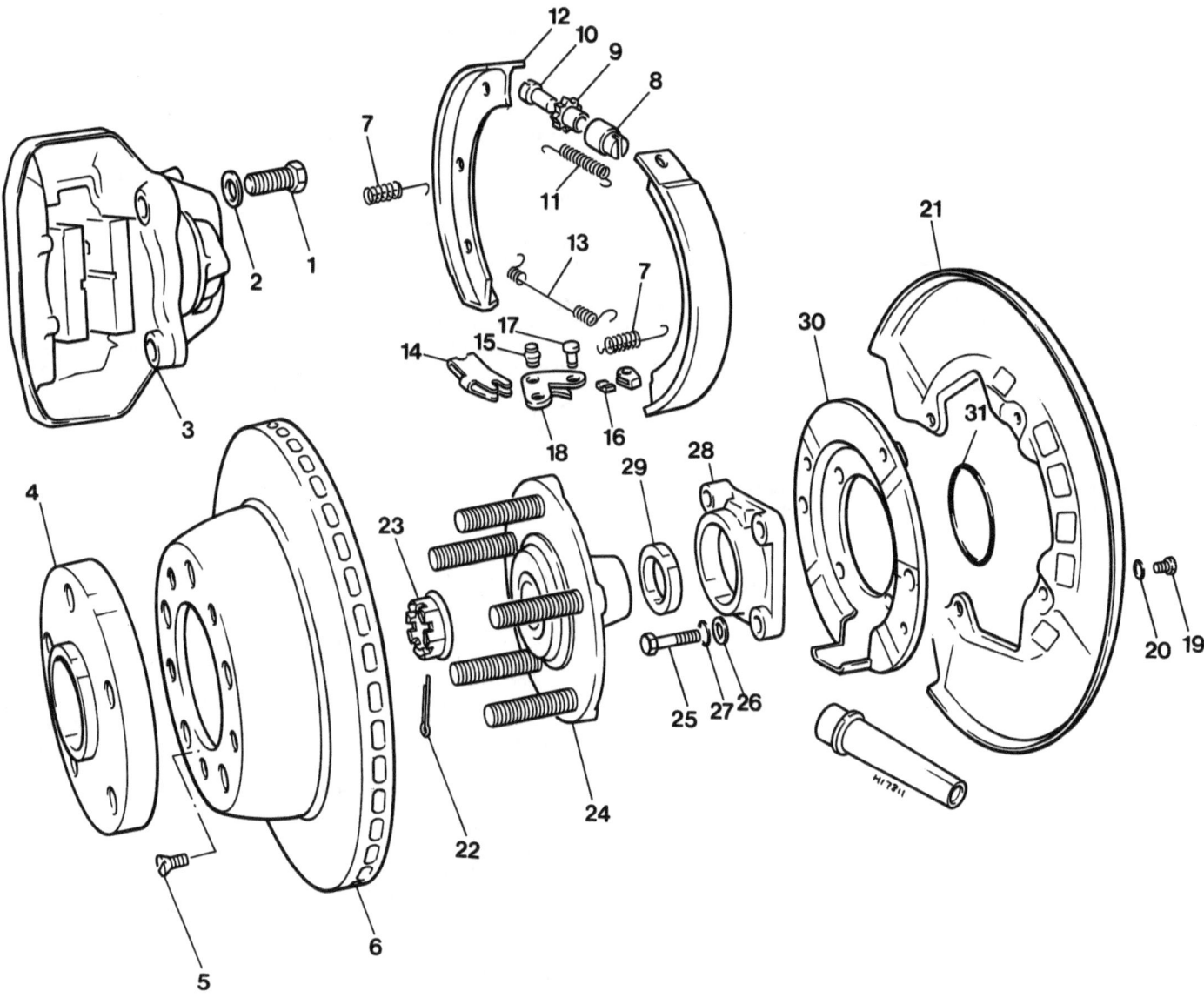

Fig. 13.25 Turbo model rear brake components (Sec 9)

1	Bolt	9	Starwheel adjuster	17	Clevis pin	25	Setscrew
2	Washer	10	Threaded sleeve	18	Handbrake lever	26	Plain washer
3	Caliper	11	Shoe return spring	19	Bolt	27	Spring washer
4	Spacer	12	Shoe	20	Washer	28	Cover
5	Screw	13	Shoe return spring	21	Backplate outer shield	29	Spacer
6	Disc/drum	14	Strut	22	Split pin	30	Backplate
7	Shoe hold-down spring	15	Pivot	23	Castellated nut	31	Seal
8	Tappet	16	Circlip	24	Hub		

23 Extract the two screws and withdraw the disc/drum asembly. If it is tight, insert a thin screwdriver in a hole in the disc and turn the starwheel adjuster.

24 Disconnect the shoe return springs and remove the shoes and adjuster.

25 Clean away dirt from the guard plate and smear the shoe rubbing high spots with high-melting-point grease.

26 Clean and lubricate the starwheel adjuster.

27 Reassemble the shoes, connect the lower return spring, locate the adjuster (fully retracted), then connect the upper return spring, in that order.

28 Refit the shoe hold-down springs.

29 Centre the shoes and fit the disc/drum.

30 Adjust the shoes so that the disc/drum will turn without binding.

31 Refit the caliper, then apply the brake pedal and parking brake lever two or three times.

32 Refit the roadwheel and lower the car.

Rear drum brakes – maintenance (all models)

33 Inspect the rear brake linings at every major service interval or annually, either as described in Chapter 9, Section 14, or (preferably) by removing the drum (Chapter 9, Section 15). The latter method enables the wheel cylinder to be inspected also.

34 Periodic adjustment of the drum brakes will be required to compensate for wear of the linings. This is carried out as described in Chapter 9, Section 15, paragraph 21. (Some models may be fitted with self-adjusting brakes, as described below; periodic adjustment is not required.) Need for adjustment is indicated by the brake pedal and handbrake lever travel becoming excessive.

Self-adjusting rear drum brakes – general

35 Some models may be fitted with self-adjusting rear drum brakes. The major components are shown in Fig. 13.27.

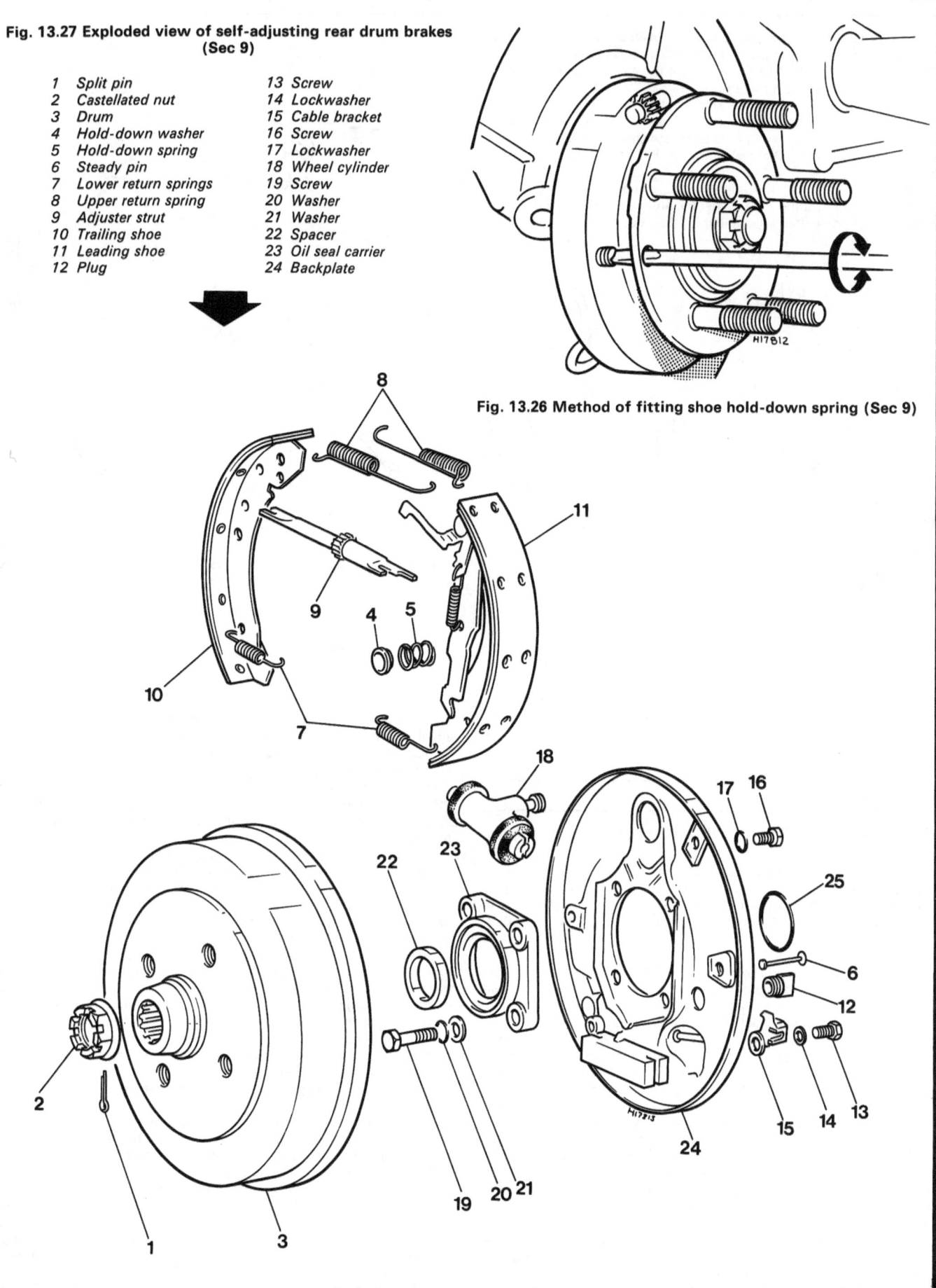

Fig. 13.27 Exploded view of self-adjusting rear drum brakes (Sec 9)

1 Split pin	13 Screw
2 Castellated nut	14 Lockwasher
3 Drum	15 Cable bracket
4 Hold-down washer	16 Screw
5 Hold-down spring	17 Lockwasher
6 Steady pin	18 Wheel cylinder
7 Lower return springs	19 Screw
8 Upper return spring	20 Washer
9 Adjuster strut	21 Washer
10 Trailing shoe	22 Spacer
11 Leading shoe	23 Oil seal carrier
12 Plug	24 Backplate

Fig. 13.26 Method of fitting shoe hold-down spring (Sec 9)

36 Except as noted here, inspection and overhaul procedures are as described for manually adjusted drum brakes in Chapter 9.

37 When removing a brake drum, release the adjuster by pressing the handbrake lever with a screwdriver inserted through the hole in the backplate (Fig. 13.28). Press the lever away from the brake shoe until a click is heard, showing that the lever is clear of the stop on the shoe.

38 Transfer the adjuster components to new shoes if applicable, using a new bearing pin. Do not mix up left-hand and right-hand components.

39 When refitting, turn the adjuster strut pinion in or out until the drum will just fit over the shoes. After the drum is fitted, apply the brake pedal several times until adjustment is taken up.

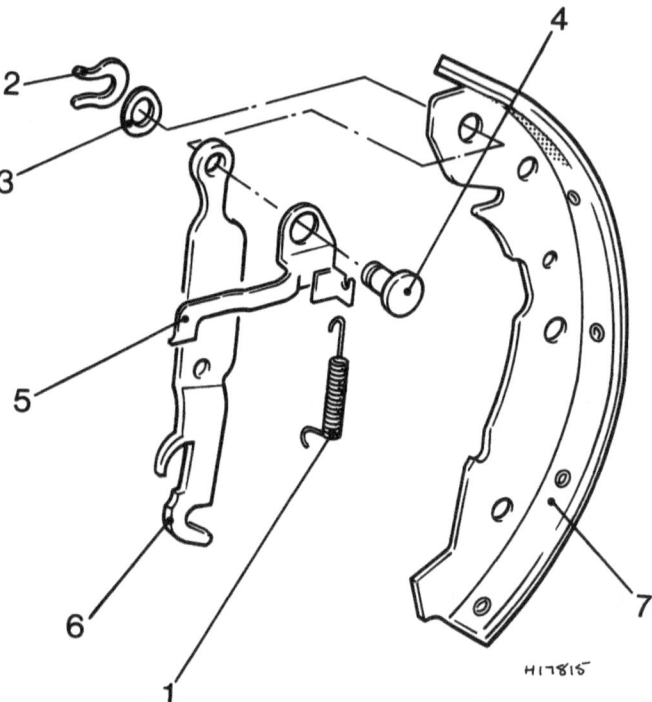

Fig. 13.29 Adjuster components must be transferred to new shoes (Sec 9)

1 Spring   5 Pinion lever
2 Retainer   6 Handbrake lever
3 Washer   7 Shoe
4 Bearing pin

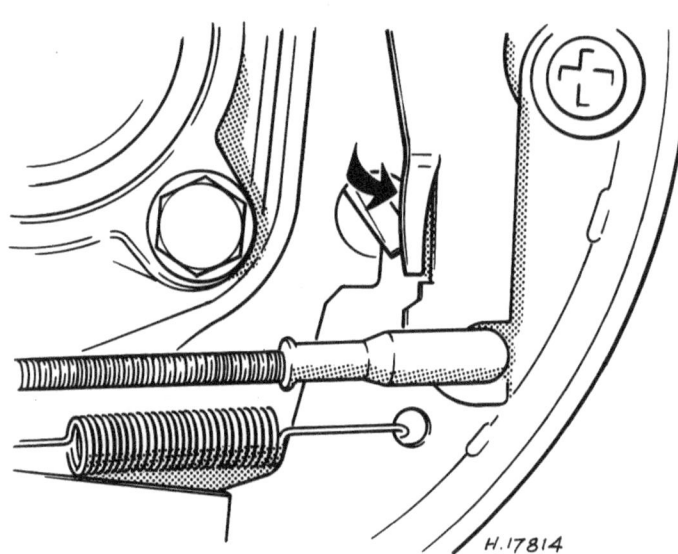

Fig. 13.28 Detail showing release of adjuster mechanism – drum removed for clarity (Sec 9)

10 Suspension

Rear control arm (Turbo, 1981 on) – bearing axial play adjustment

1 The inner bearing axial play may be adjusted if necessary by changing the circlip for one of different thickness. The bearing play should not exceed 0.05 mm (0.002 in). Circlips are available in thicknesses of 2.0, 2.05, 2.10, 2.15 and 2.20 mm (0.079, 0.081, 0.083, 0.085 and 0.087 in).

Wheels and tyres – general care and maintenance

2 Wheels and tyres should give no real problems in use provided that a close eye is kept on them with regard to excessive wear or damage. To this end, the following points should be noted.

3 Ensure that tyre pressures are checked regularly and maintained correctly. Checking should be carried out with the tyres cold and not immediately after the vehicle has been in use. If the pressures are checked with the tyres hot, an apparently high reading will be obtained owing to heat expansion. Under no circumstances should an attempt be made to reduce the pressures to the quoted cold reading in this instance, or effective underinflation will result.

4 Underinflation will cause overheating of the tyre owing to excessive flexing of the casing, and the tread will not sit correctly on the road surface. This will cause a consequent loss of adhesion and excessive wear, not to mention the danger of sudden tyre failure due to heat build-up.

5 Overinflation will cause rapid wear of the centre part of the tyre tread coupled with reduced adhesion, harsher ride, and the danger of shock damage occurring in the tyre casing.

6 Regularly check the tyres for damage in the form of cuts or bulges, especially in the sidewalls. Remove any nails or stones embedded in the tread before they penetrate the tyre to cause deflation. If removal of a nail *does* reveal that the tyre has been punctured, refit the nail so that its point of penetration is marked. Then immediately change the wheel and have the tyre repaired by a tyre dealer. Do *not* drive on a tyre in such a condition. In many cases a puncture can be simply repaired by the use of an inner tube of the correct size and type. If in any doubt as to the possible consequences of any damage found, consult your local tyre dealer for advice.

7 Periodically remove the wheels and clean any dirt or mud from the inside and outside surfaces. Examine the wheel rims for signs of rusting, corrosion or other damage. Light alloy wheels are easily damaged by 'kerbing' whilst parking, and similarly steel wheels may become dented or buckled. Renewal of the wheel is very often the only course of remedial action possible.

8 The balance of each wheel and tyre assembly should be maintained to avoid excessive wear, not only to the tyres but also to the steering and suspension components. Wheel imbalance is normally signified by vibration through the vehicle's bodyshell, although in many cases it is particularly noticeable through the steering wheel. Conversely, it should be noted that wear or damage in suspension or steering components may cause excessive tyre wear. Out-of-round or out-of-true tyres, damaged wheels and wheel bearing wear/maladjustment also fall into this category. Balancing will not usually cure vibration caused by such wear.

9 Wheel balancing may be carried out with the wheel either on or off the vehicle. If balanced on the vehicle, ensure that the wheel-to-hub relationship is marked in some way prior to subsequent wheel removal so that it may be refitted in its original position.

10 General tyre wear is influenced to a large degree by driving style – harsh braking and acceleration or fast cornering will all produce more rapid tyre wear. Interchanging of tyres may result in more even wear, but this should only be carried out where there is no mix of tyre types on the vehicle. However, it is worth bearing in mind that if this is completely effective, the added expense of replacing a complete set of tyres simultaneously is incurred, which may prove financially restrictive for many owners.

11 Front tyres may wear unevenly as a result of wheel misalignment. The front wheels should always be correctly aligned according to the settings specified by the vehicle manufacturer.

12 Legal restrictions apply to the mixing of tyre types on a vehicle. Basically this means that a vehicle must not have tyres of differing construction on the same axle. Although it is not recommended to mix tyre types between front axle and rear axle, the only legally permissible combination is crossply at the front and radial at the rear. When mixing radial ply tyres, textile braced radials must always go on the front axle, with steel braced radials at the rear. An obvious disadvantage of such mixing is the necessity to carry two spare tyres to avoid contravening the law in the event of a puncture.

13 In the UK, the Motor Vehicles Construction and Use Regulations apply to many aspects of tyre fitting and usage. It is suggested that a copy of these regulations is obtained from your local police if in doubt as to the current legal requirements with regard to tyre condition, minimum tread depth, etc.

'Space saver' spare type

14 Some models are equipped with a 'space saver' spare tyre, of smaller section than the four normal tyres. The spare may even be stored deflated, in which case a compressor is also supplied to inflate it when needed.

15 Handling may be adversely affected when this type of spare tyre is in use. Observe any speed restrictions which may be specified by the vehicle or tyre manufacturer, and also any applicable regulations imposed by national laws.

16 Refer to the Specifications for the recommended inflation pressure for the 'space saver' spare tyre.

11 Electrics

Electrically operated windows

1 The wiring circuit has been modified on later models to enable the windows to be power operated even with the ignition off and the doors open.

2 A modified regulator relay is located adjacent to the sliding roof control unit on the left of the fresh air duct on the centre console.

Battery (all models) – maintenance

3 Further to Chapter 11, Section 3, it should be noted that most modern batteries are of the low-maintenance or maintenance-free type. Topping-up of the electrolyte is rarely required on such batteries; maintenance-free types may have been filled for life and sealed so that further topping-up is impossible. Follow the battery maker's instructions.

Battery (all models) – charging

4 Battery charging from an external source should not be necessary except under exceptionally adverse conditions of use. Regular need for recharging suggests a fault in the battery, alternator or voltage regulator, or a short-circuit discharging the battery when not in use.

Headlight bulbs – renewal

5 According to model and market, headlight bulbs may be fitted instead of the sealed beam units shown in Chapter 11.

6 Renewal is as described in Chapter 11, Section 10, but additionally the bulb must be removed from the lens/reflector unit by releasing the spring clips.

7 Do not touch the glass of the new bulb with the fingers. Grease from the fingers can cause blackening and premature failure of the bulb. If the glass is accidentally touched, clean it with a tissue and some methylated spirit.

8 When fitting the new bulb, engage the lugs and cut-outs on the bulb rim with those in the reflector. Secure the bulb with the spring clips.

Windscreen washer nozzles – electrically heated type

9 Some 1985 models have electrically heated windscreen washer jets, which are actuated and temperature controlled as soon as the ignition is switched on.

10 No further information was available at the time of writing.

Wiring diagrams overleaf

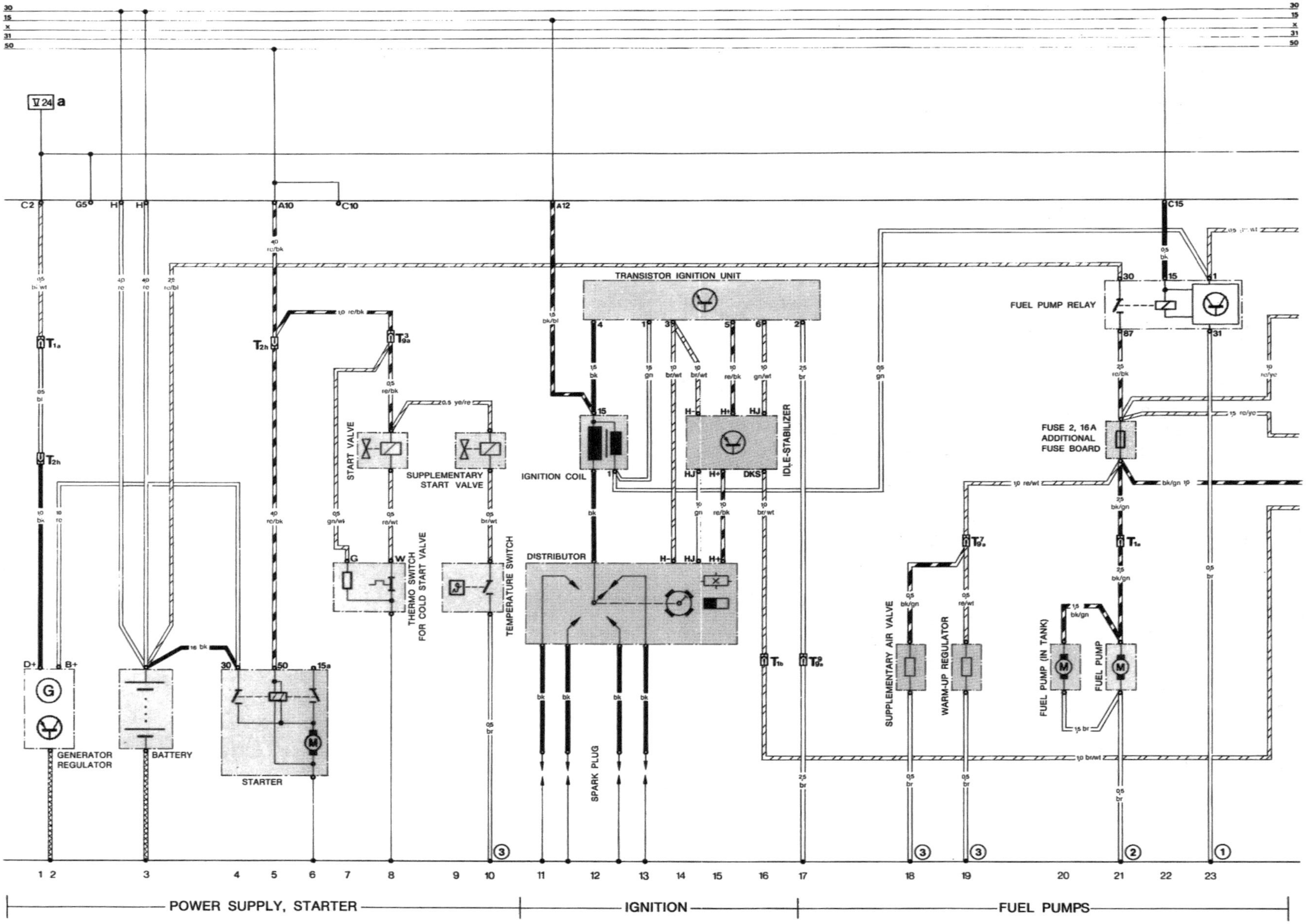

Fig. 13.30 Wiring diagram – starting, power supply, ignition and fuel pumps (1981 on)

For colour code, see p.245

POWER SUPPLY, STARTER — IGNITION — FUEL PUMPS

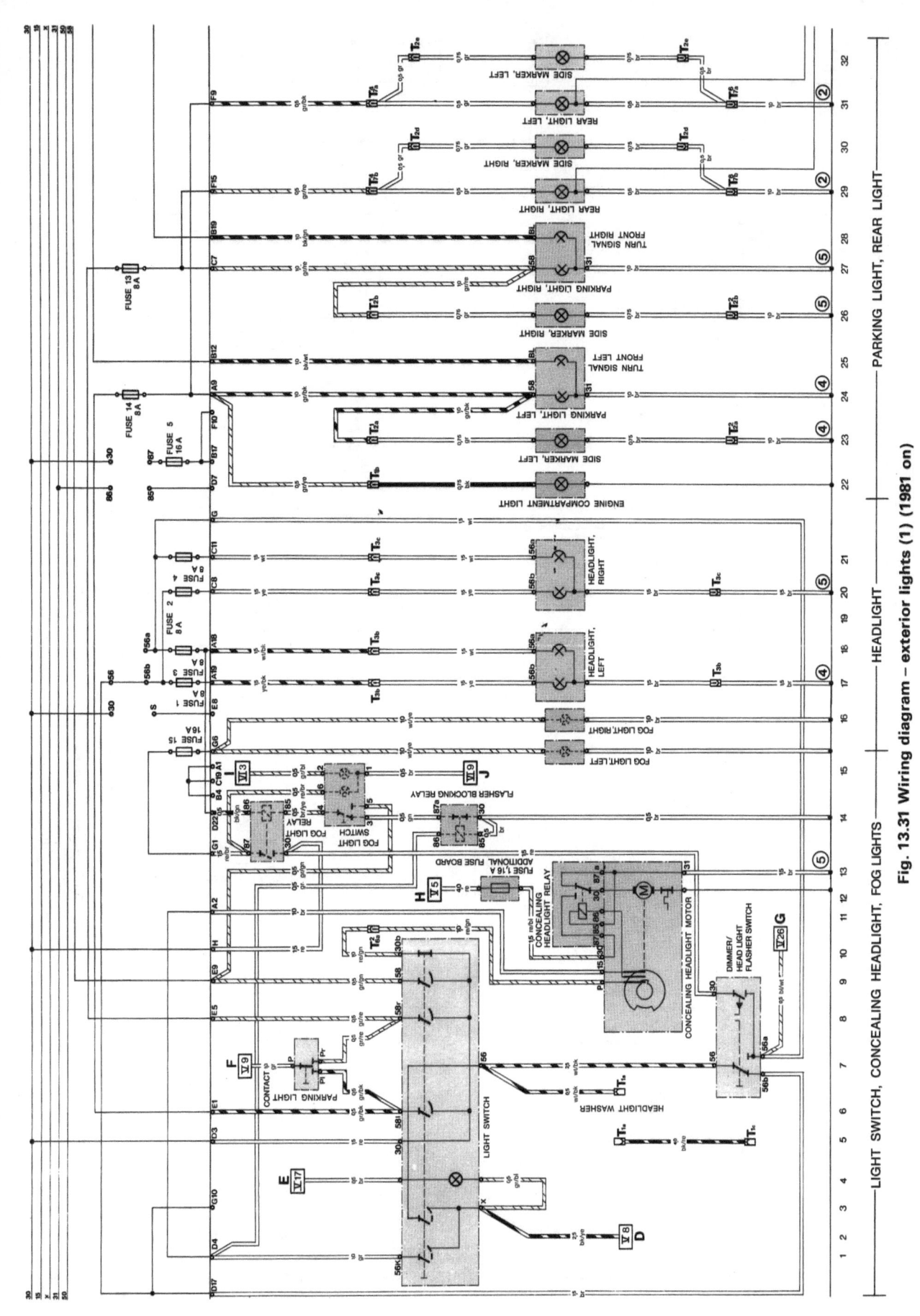

Fig. 13.31 Wiring diagram – exterior lights (1) (1981 on)

For colour code, see p. 245

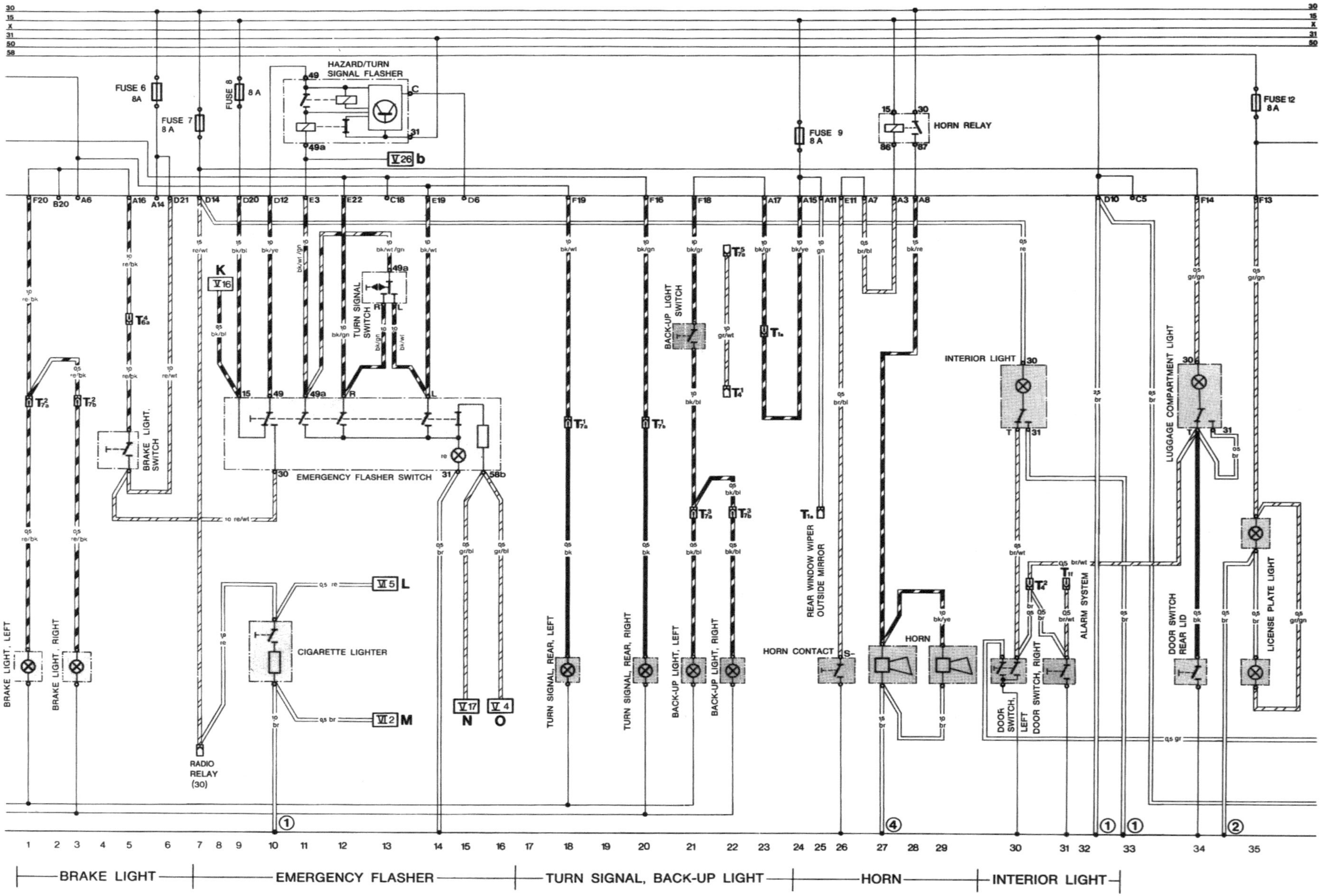

Fig. 13.32 Wiring diagram – exterior lights (2), horn and interior light (1981 on)

For colour code, see p. 245

FUSE 12 8A

LICENSE PLATE LIGHT

LUGGAGE COMPARTMENT LIGHT

DOOR SWITCH, REAR LID

ALARM SYSTEM

INTERIOR LIGHT

DOOR SWITCH, RIGHT

DOOR SWITCH, LEFT

HORN RELAY

FUSE 9 8A

HORN

HORN CONTACT

REAR WINDOW WIPER

OUTSIDE MIRROR

BACK-UP LIGHT SWITCH

BACK-UP LIGHT, RIGHT

BACK-UP LIGHT, LEFT

TURN SIGNAL, REAR, RIGHT

TURN SIGNAL, REAR, LEFT

HAZARD/TURN SIGNAL FLASHER

TURN SIGNAL SWITCH

EMERGENCY FLASHER SWITCH

CIGARETTE LIGHTER

RADIO RELAY (30)

FUSE 8 8A

FUSE 7

FUSE 6 8A

BRAKE LIGHT SWITCH

BRAKE LIGHT, RIGHT

BRAKE LIGHT, LEFT

BRAKE LIGHT — EMERGENCY FLASHER — TURN SIGNAL, BACK-UP LIGHT — HORN — INTERIOR LIGHT

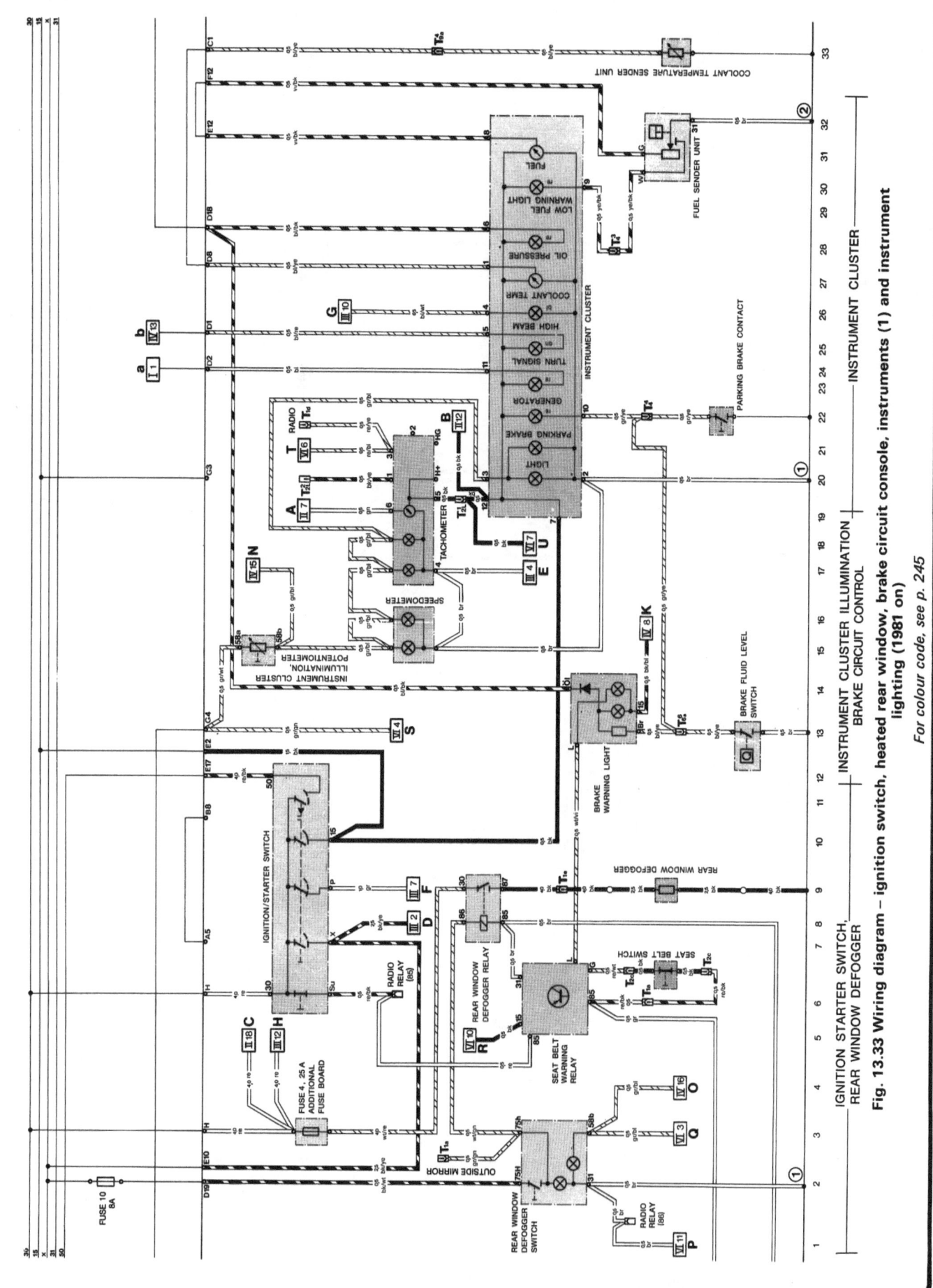

Fig. 13.33 Wiring diagram – ignition switch, heated rear window, brake circuit console, instruments (1) and instrument lighting (1981 on)

For colour code, see p. 245

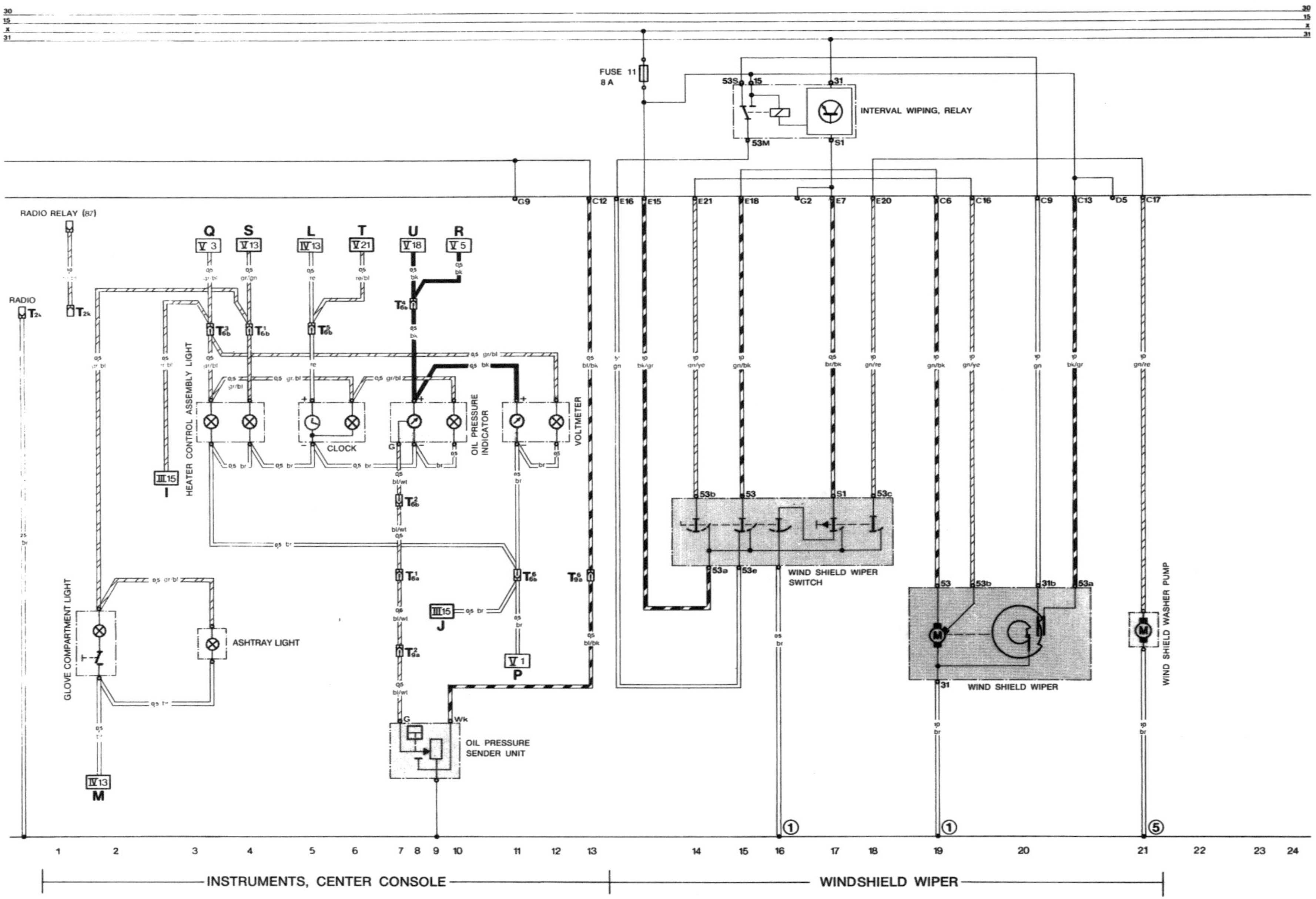

Fig. 13.34 Wiring diagram – instruments (2), centre console and windscreen wiper (1981 on)

For colour code, see p. 245

INSTRUMENTS, CENTER CONSOLE

WINDSHIELD WIPER

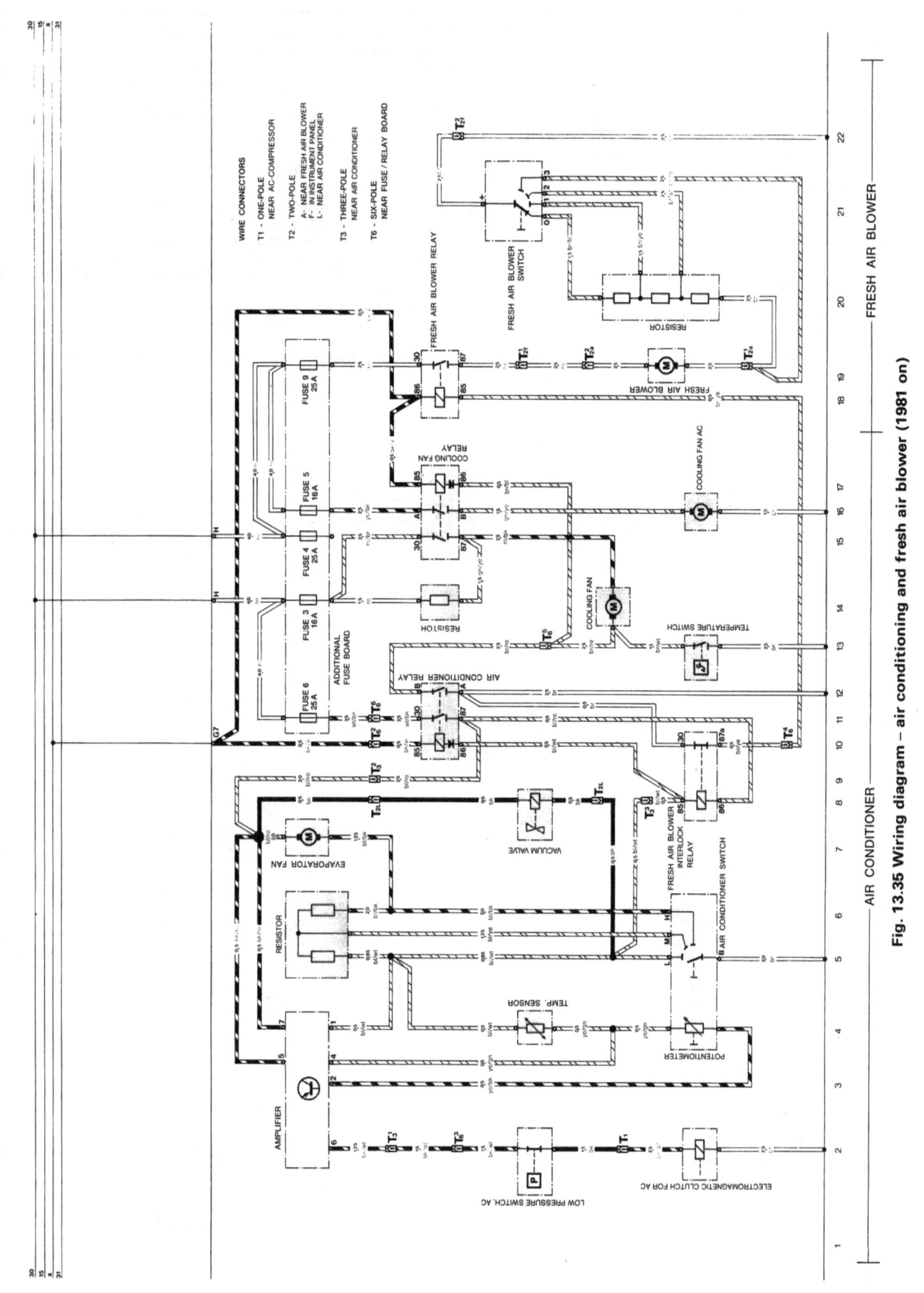

Fig. 13.35 Wiring diagram – air conditioning and fresh air blower (1981 on)

For colour code, see p. 245

12 Bodywork

Sunroof – electrically operated type
Sunroof panel – removal and refitting
1 Turn off the ignition and operate the sunroof control switch until the panel is unlocked.
2 Open the front fasteners, lift and remove the roof panel.
3 The panel can be refitted by sliding it at an angle from above the wind deflector and the front guides.
4 Lower the rear end of the panel.
5 Operate the control switch towards the right until the panel locks, then close the front fasteners.

Operating components
6 The main components of the system are located as follows.
7 The lifting motor, relays and cable drive are positioned behind the trim panel on the left-hand side.

8 The microswitches and their operating sliding gate are mounted on the back of the motor console.
9 A transfer box is located in the centre of the sliding roof rear frame. Short cables run from this box to the operating arc elements, which in turn move the bearing units which are fixed to the sliding panel.
10 A slip clutch is integral in the electric motor for safety reasons. The clutch friction torque is adjustable by means of the screw (a) (Fig. 13.37).
11 In the event of a failure in the electrical circuit, the sunroof panel can be closed in the following way.
12 Unscrew the clutch friction screw fully and remove it to expose the threaded spindle. Using a screwdriver, turn the threaded spindle anti-clockwise until the roof panel is closed.
13 Refit the friction screw and tighten it finger-tight only.
14 A supplementary microswitch is fitted on the left-hand front roof guide to indicate the open or closed position of the roof panel.
15 A control unit with integral radio relay is mounted on the fresh air duct on the left of the centre console.

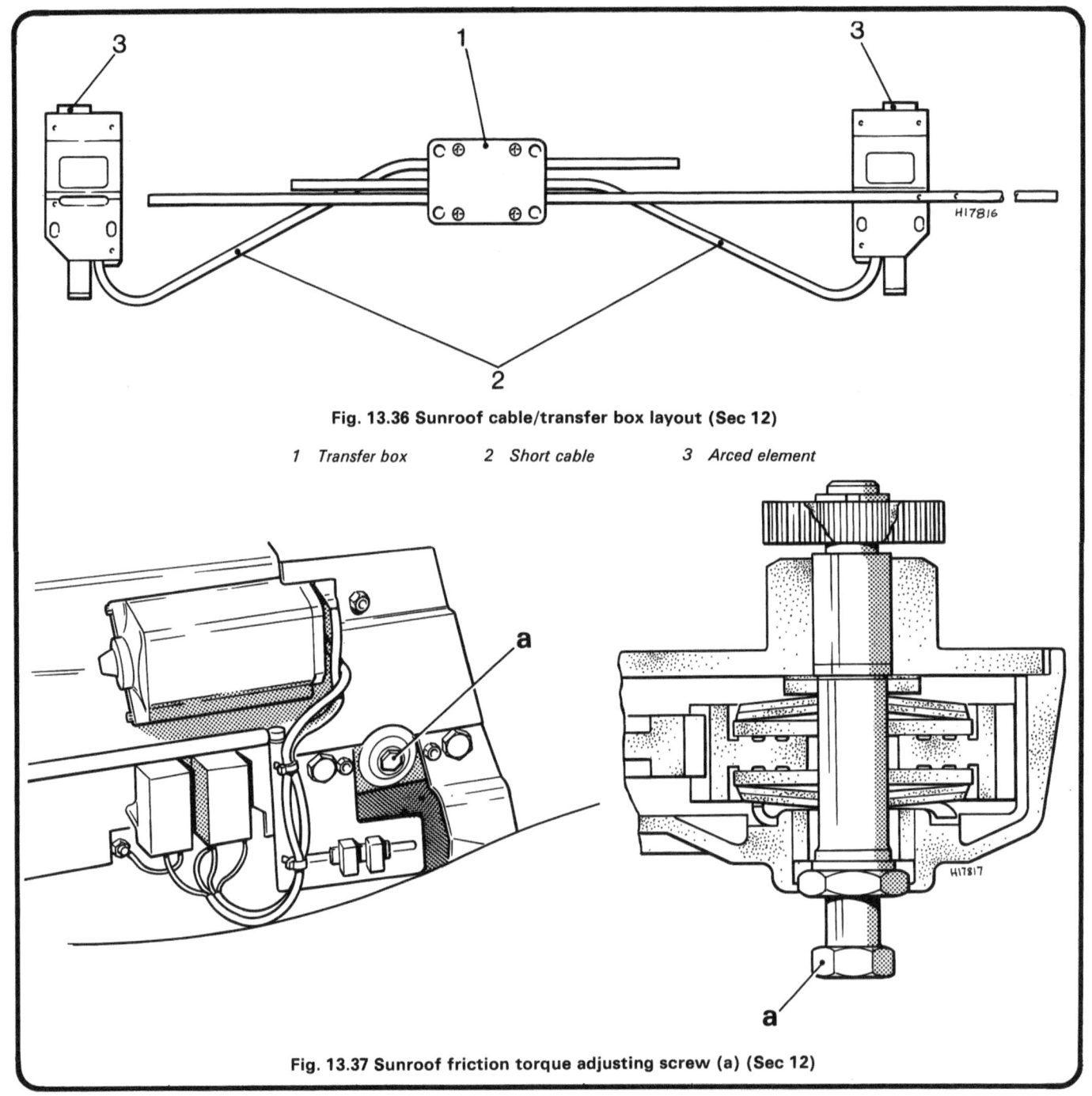

Fig. 13.36 Sunroof cable/transfer box layout (Sec 12)

1 Transfer box   2 Short cable   3 Arced element

Fig. 13.37 Sunroof friction torque adjusting screw (a) (Sec 12)

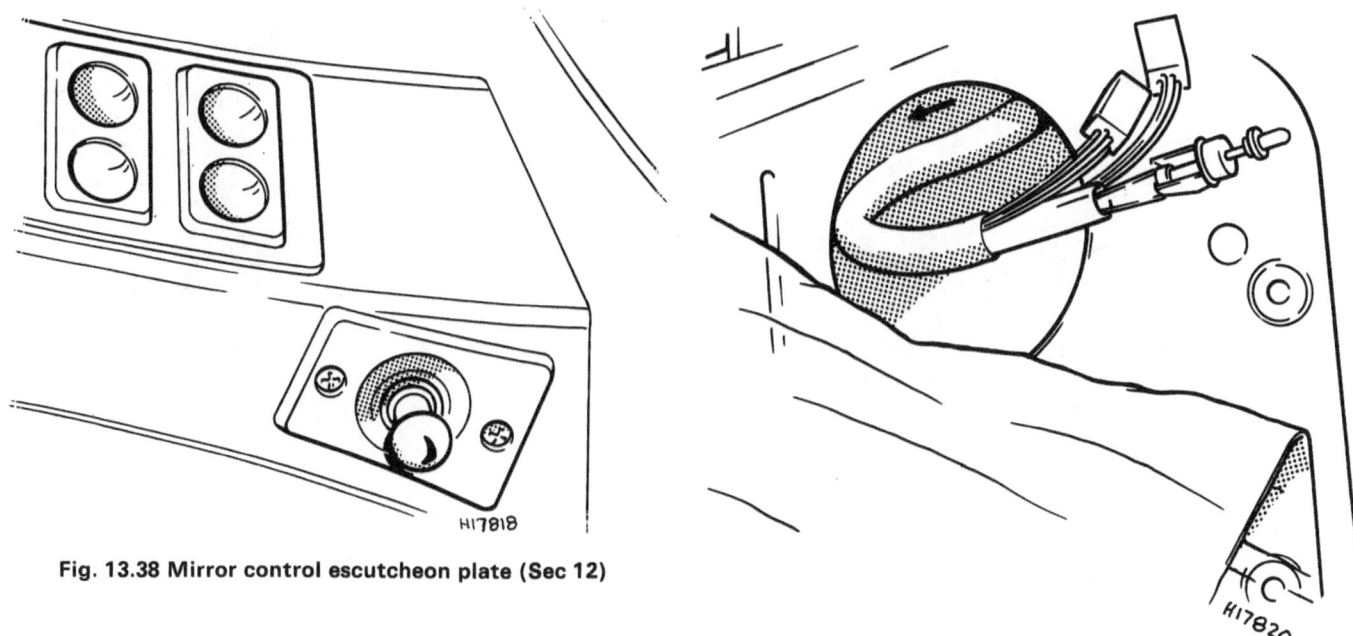

Fig. 13.38 Mirror control escutcheon plate (Sec 12)

Fig. 13.40 Exterior mirror remote control cable (Sec 12)

Tailgate lock – electrically operated type

16 As from 1984, the tailgate lock is electrically operated by a switch located adjacent to the bonnet release handle.

17 The tailgate lock can be opened in the normal way by using a key from outside.

Remote control rear view mirror – removal and refitting
Manually operated type

18 Extract the screws and release the control knob escutcheon plate.

19 Remove the knob, dust cover and clamping ring.

20 Using a pair of circlip pliers or similar tool, unscrew the threaded ring nut, then take off the escutcheon plate.

21 Remove the door interior trim panel and peel back the waterproof sheet from the mirror mounting area.

22 Guide the remote control cable around the door glass vertical guide into the door cavity.

Fig. 13.39 Exploded view of manually operated exterior mirror (Sec 12)

1	Mirror body	7	Screw
2	Liner	8	Threaded ring nut
3	Screw	9	Circlip
4	Cable	10	Dust cover
5	Control lever	11	Control knob
6	Escutcheon plate		

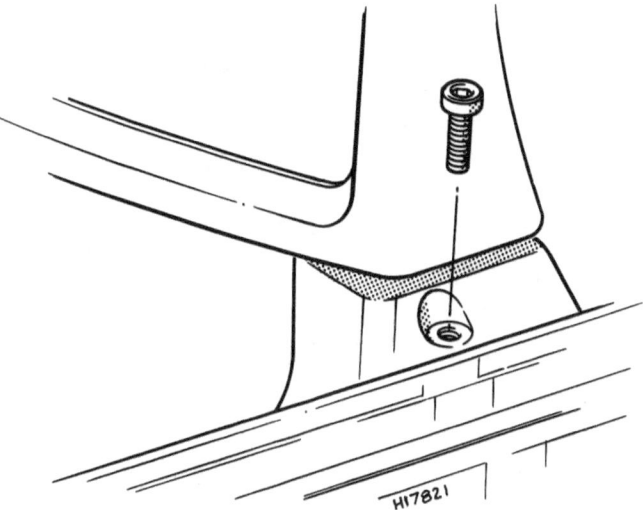

Fig. 13.41 Mirror mounting screw (Sec 12)

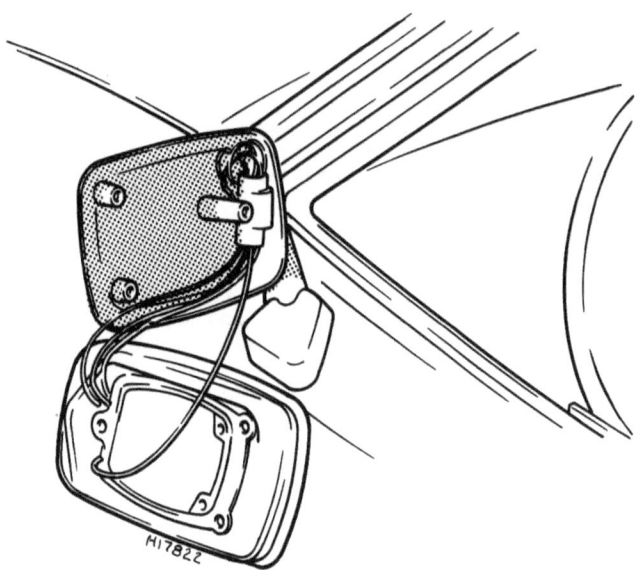

Fig. 13.42 Glass separated from mirror body – electrically operated type (Sec 12)

23 Extract the mirror mounting screw and withdraw the mirror and cable.
24 Refitting is a reversal of removal.

Electrically operated type
25 Using a thin blade, prise the glass from the mirror body. Pull evenly to avoid damaging the fixing pins.
26 Unscrew the carrier plate, note the cable colours and disconnect them.
27 Extract the mirror fixing screw and withdraw mirror with its wiring.
28 Remove the door switch from inside the door, then remove the door trim panel and peel back the waterproof sheet. Withdraw the wiring from the door cavity.
29 Refitting is a reversal of removal.

Seat belts – general
30 The inertia reel type seat belts should be inspected regularly for fraying, and renewed if fraying is evident.
31 If the belts have been subjected to strain as a result of a collision, renew them.

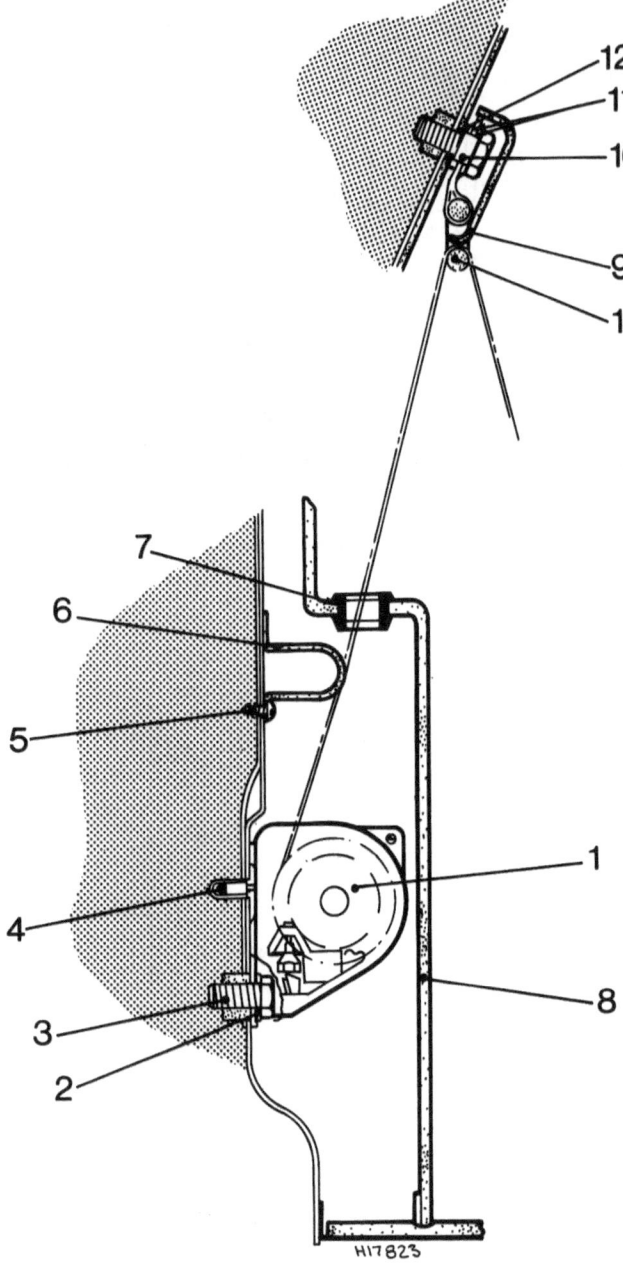

Fig. 13.43 Typical seat belt arrangement (Sec 12)

1	Reel/roller	7	Grommet
2	Lockwasher	8	Trim panel
3	Bolt	9	Cover
4	Lug	10	Anchor bolt
5	Screw	11	Plastic washer
6	Tab	12	Wave washer

32 To clean a belt use warm water and mild detergent only and prevent the belt retracting into its reel housing until it is dry.
33 The reels are located behind the rear quarter trim panels.
34 Whenever a belt or stalk anchorage is removed or refitted, make sure that the original fitted sequence of plate, spacer and wave washer is retained.

Rear interior quarter trim panel – removal and refitting

35 The fixed side window must first be removed by carefully pushing it out with its rubber surround.

36 Disconnect the seat belt upper anchorage.

37 Pull off the door aperture weatherseal.

38 Extract the screws (arrowed in Fig. 13.44).

39 Refitting is a reversal of removal. Lubricate the window surround with liquid soap to assist refitting.

Plastic components – repair

40 With the use of more and more plastic body components by the vehicle manufacturers (eg bumpers, spoilers, and in some cases major body panels), rectification of more serious damage to such items has become a matter of either entrusting repair work to a specialist in this field, or renewing complete components. Repair of such damage by the DIY owner is not really feasible owing to the cost of the equipment and materials required for effecting such repairs. The basic technique involves making a groove along the line of the crack in the plastic using a rotary burr in a power drill. The damaged part is then welded back together by using a hot air gun to heat up and fuse a plastic filler rod into the groove. Any excess plastic is then removed and the area rubbed down to a smooth finish. It is important that a filler rod of the correct plastic is used, as body components can be made of a variety of different types (eg polycarbonate, ABS, polypropylene).

41 Damage of a less serious nature (abrasions, minor cracks etc) can be repaired by the DIY owner using a two-part epoxy filler repair material. Once mixed in equal proportions, this is used in similar fashion to the bodywork filler used on metal panels. The filler is usually cured in twenty to thirty minutes, ready for sanding and painting.

42 If the owner is renewing a complete component himself, or if he has repaired it with epoxy filler, he will be left with the problem of finding a suitable paint for finishing which is compatible with the type of plastic used. At one time the use of a universal paint was not possible owing to the complex range of plastics encountered in body component applications. Standard paints, generally speaking, will not bond to plastic or rubber satisfactorily. However, it is now possible to obtain a plastic body parts finishing kit which consists of a pre-primer treatment, a primer and coloured top coat. Full instructions are normally supplied with a kit, but basically the method of use is to first apply the pre-primer to the component concerned and allow it to dry for up to 30 minutes. Then the primer is applied and left to dry for about an hour before finally applying the special coloured top coat. The result is a correctly coloured component where the paint will flex with the plastic or rubber, a property that standard paint does not normally possess.

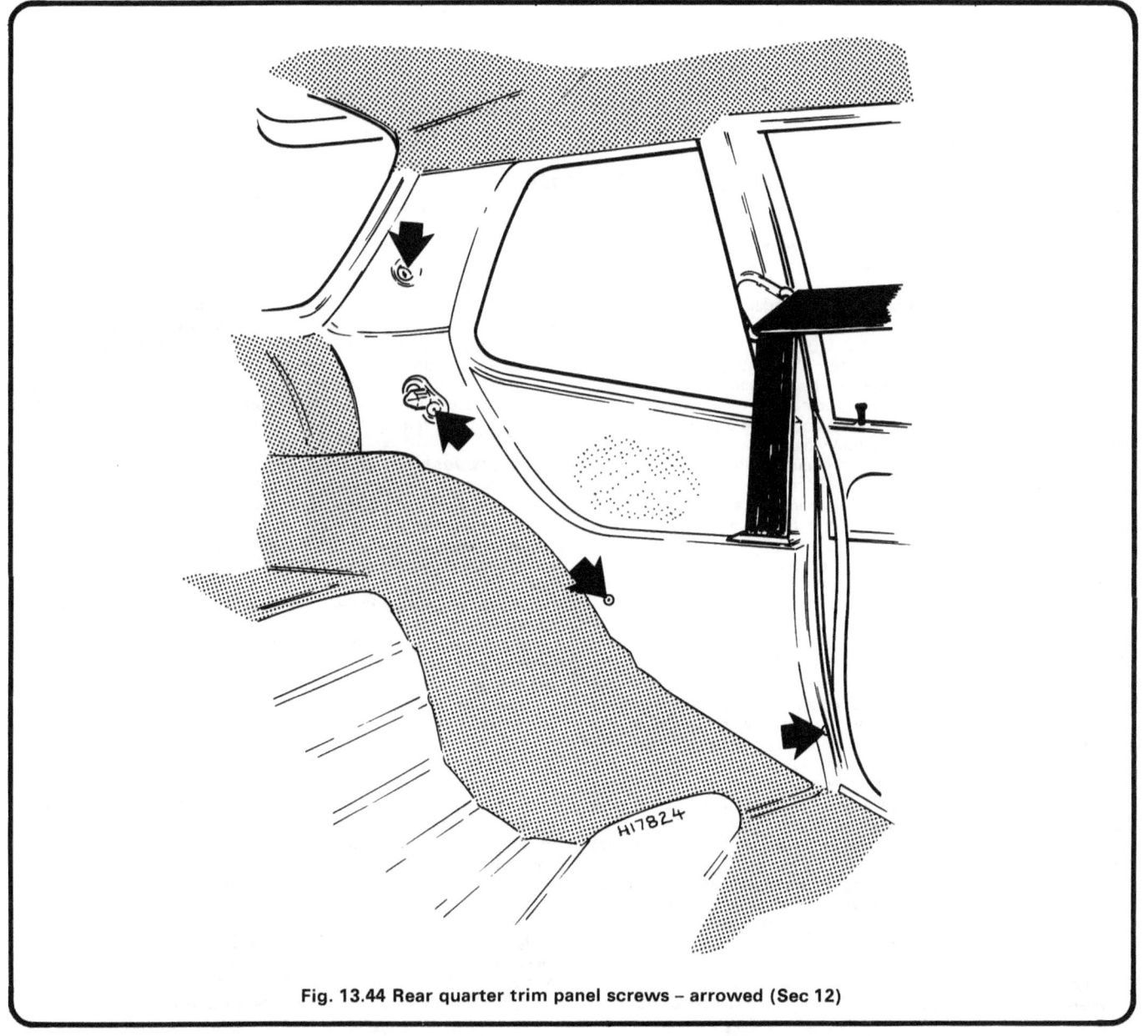

Fig. 13.44 Rear quarter trim panel screws – arrowed (Sec 12)

General repair procedures

Whenever servicing, repair or overhaul work is carried out on the car or its components, it is necessary to observe the following procedures and instructions. This will assist in carrying out the operation efficiently and to a professional standard of workmanship.

Joint mating faces and gaskets

Where a gasket is used between the mating faces of two components, ensure that it is renewed on reassembly, and fit it dry unless otherwise stated in the repair procedure. Make sure that the mating faces are clean and dry with all traces of old gasket removed. When cleaning a joint face, use a tool which is not likely to score or damage the face, and remove any burrs or nicks with an oilstone or fine file.

Make sure that tapped holes are cleaned with a pipe cleaner, and keep them free of jointing compound if this is being used unless specifically instructed otherwise.

Ensure that all orifices, channels or pipes are clear and blow through them, preferably using compressed air.

Oil seals

Whenever an oil seal is removed from its working location, either individually or as part of an assembly, it should be renewed.

The very fine sealing lip of the seal is easily damaged and will not seal if the surface it contacts is not completely clean and free from scratches, nicks or grooves. If the original sealing surface of the component cannot be restored, the component should be renewed.

Protect the lips of the seal from any surface which may damage them in the course of fitting. Use tape or a conical sleeve where possible. Lubricate the seal lips with oil before fitting and, on dual lipped seals, fill the space between the lips with grease.

Unless otherwise stated, oil seals must be fitted with their sealing lips toward the lubricant to be sealed.

Use a tubular drift or block of wood of the appropriate size to install the seal and, if the seal housing is shouldered, drive the seal down to the shoulder. If the seal housing is unshouldered, the seal should be fitted with its face flush with the housing top face.

Screw threads and fastenings

Always ensure that a blind tapped hole is completely free from oil, grease, water or other fluid before installing the bolt or stud. Failure to do this could cause the housing to crack due to the hydraulic action of the bolt or stud as it is screwed in.

When tightening a castellated nut to accept a split pin, tighten the nut to the specified torque, where applicable, and then tighten further to the next split pin hole. Never slacken the nut to align a split pin hole unless stated in the repair procedure.

When checking or retightening a nut or bolt to a specified torque setting, slacken the nut or bolt by a quarter of a turn, and then retighten to the specified setting.

Locknuts, locktabs and washers

Any fastening which will rotate against a component or housing in the course of tightening should always have a washer between it and the relevant component or housing.

Spring or split washers should always be renewed when they are used to lock a critical component such as a big-end bearing retaining nut or bolt.

Locktabs which are folded over to retain a nut or bolt should always be renewed.

Self-locking nuts can be reused in non-critical areas, providing resistance can be felt when the locking portion passes over the bolt or stud thread.

Split pins must always be replaced with new ones of the correct size for the hole.

Special tools

Some repair procedures in this manual entail the use of special tools such as a press, two or three-legged pullers, spring compressors etc. Wherever possible, suitable readily available alternatives to the manufacturer's special tools are described, and are shown in use. In some instances, where no alternative is possible, it has been necessary to resort to the use of a manufacturer's tool and this has been done for reasons of safety as well as the efficient completion of the repair operation. Unless you are highly skilled and have a thorough understanding of the procedure described, never attempt to bypass the use of any special tool when the procedure described specifies its use. Not only is there a very great risk of personal injury, but expensive damage could be caused to the components involved.

Conversion factors

Length (distance)

Inches (in)	X	25.4	= Millimetres (mm)	X	0.0394	= Inches (in)
Feet (ft)	X	0.305	= Metres (m)	X	3.281	= Feet (ft)
Miles	X	1.609	= Kilometres (km)	X	0.621	= Miles

Volume (capacity)

Cubic inches (cu in; in³)	X	16.387	= Cubic centimetres (cc; cm³)	X	0.061	= Cubic inches (cu in; in³)
Imperial pints (Imp pt)	X	0.568	= Litres (l)	X	1.76	= Imperial pints (Imp pt)
Imperial quarts (Imp qt)	X	1.137	= Litres (l)	X	0.88	= Imperial quarts (Imp qt)
Imperial quarts (Imp qt)	X	1.201	= US quarts (US qt)	X	0.833	= Imperial quarts (Imp qt)
US quarts (US qt)	X	0.946	= Litres (l)	X	1.057	= US quarts (US qt)
Imperial gallons (Imp gal)	X	4.546	= Litres (l)	X	0.22	= Imperial gallons (Imp gal)
Imperial gallons (Imp gal)	X	1.201	= US gallons (US gal)	X	0.833	= Imperial gallons (Imp gal)
US gallons (US gal)	X	3.785	= Litres (l)	X	0.264	= US gallons (US gal)

Mass (weight)

Ounces (oz)	X	28.35	= Grams (g)	X	0.035	= Ounces (oz)
Pounds (lb)	X	0.454	= Kilograms (kg)	X	2.205	= Pounds (lb)

Force

Ounces-force (ozf; oz)	X	0.278	= Newtons (N)	X	3.6	= Ounces-force (ozf; oz)
Pounds-force (lbf; lb)	X	4.448	= Newtons (N)	X	0.225	= Pounds-force (lbf; lb)
Newtons (N)	X	0.1	= Kilograms-force (kgf; kg)	X	9.81	= Newtons (N)

Pressure

Pounds-force per square inch (psi; lbf/in²; lb/in²)	X	0.070	= Kilograms-force per square centimetre (kgf/cm²; kg/cm²)	X	14.223	= Pounds-force per square inch (psi; lbf/in²; lb/in²)
Pounds-force per square inch (psi; lbf/in²; lb/in²)	X	0.068	= Atmospheres (atm)	X	14.696	= Pounds-force per square inch (psi; lbf/in²; lb/in²)
Pounds-force per square inch (psi; lbf/in²; lb/in²)	X	0.069	= Bars	X	14.5	= Pounds-force per square inch (psi; lbf/in²; lb/in²)
Pounds-force per square inch (psi; lbf/in²; lb/in²)	X	6.895	= Kilopascals (kPa)	X	0.145	= Pounds-force per square inch (psi; lbf/in²; lb/in²)
Kilopascals (kPa)	X	0.01	= Kilograms-force per square centimetre (kgf/cm²; kg/cm²)	X	98.1	= Kilopascals (kPa)
Millibar (mbar)	X	100	= Pascals (Pa)	X	0.01	= Millibar (mbar)
Millibar (mbar)	X	0.0145	= Pounds-force per square inch (psi; lbf/in²; lb/in²)	X	68.947	= Millibar (mbar)
Millibar (mbar)	X	0.75	= Millimetres of mercury (mmHg)	X	1.333	= Millibar (mbar)
Millibar (mbar)	X	0.401	= Inches of water (inH₂O)	X	2.491	= Millibar (mbar)
Millimetres of mercury (mmHg)	X	0.535	= Inches of water (inH₂O)	X	1.868	= Millimetres of mercury (mmHg)
Inches of water (inH₂O)	X	0.036	= Pounds-force per square inch (psi; lbf/in²; lb/in²)	X	27.68	= Inches of water (inH₂O)

Torque (moment of force)

Pounds-force inches (lbf in; lb in)	X	1.152	= Kilograms-force centimetre (kgf cm; kg cm)	X	0.868	= Pounds-force inches (lbf in; lb in)
Pounds-force inches (lbf in; lb in)	X	0.113	= Newton metres (Nm)	X	8.85	= Pounds-force inches (lbf in; lb in)
Pounds-force inches (lbf in; lb in)	X	0.083	= Pounds-force feet (lbf ft; lb ft)	X	12	= Pounds-force inches (lbf in; lb in)
Pounds-force feet (lbf ft; lb ft)	X	0.138	= Kilograms-force metres (kgf m; kg m)	X	7.233	= Pounds-force feet (lbf ft; lb ft)
Pounds-force feet (lbf ft; lb ft)	X	1.356	= Newton metres (Nm)	X	0.738	= Pounds-force feet (lbf ft; lb ft)
Newton metres (Nm)	X	0.102	= Kilograms-force metres (kgf m; kg m)	X	9.804	= Newton metres (Nm)

Power

Horsepower (hp)	X	745.7	= Watts (W)	X	0.0013	= Horsepower (hp)

Velocity (speed)

Miles per hour (miles/hr; mph)	X	1.609	= Kilometres per hour (km/hr; kph)	X	0.621	= Miles per hour (miles/hr; mph)

Fuel consumption*

Miles per gallon, Imperial (mpg)	X	0.354	= Kilometres per litre (km/l)	X	2.825	= Miles per gallon, Imperial (mpg)
Miles per gallon, US (mpg)	X	0.425	= Kilometres per litre (km/l)	X	2.352	= Miles per gallon, US (mpg)

Temperature

Degrees Fahrenheit = (°C x 1.8) + 32

Degrees Celsius (Degrees Centigrade; °C) = (°F − 32) x 0.56

*It is common practice to convert from miles per gallon (mpg) to litres/100 kilometres (l/100km),
where mpg (Imperial) x l/100 km = 282 and mpg (US) x l/100 km = 235

Use of English

As this book has been written in England, it uses the appropriate English component names, phrases, and spelling. Some of these differ from those used in America. Normally, these cause no difficulty, but to make sure, a glossary is printed below. In ordering spare parts remember the parts list may use some of these words:

English	American	English	American
Accelerator	Gas pedal	Locks	Latches
Aerial	Antenna	Methylated spirit	Denatured alcohol
Anti-roll bar	Stabiliser or sway bar	Motorway	Freeway, turnpike etc
Big-end bearing	Rod bearing	Number plate	License plate
Bonnet (engine cover)	Hood	Paraffin	Kerosene
Boot (luggage compartment)	Trunk	Petrol	Gasoline (gas)
Bulkhead	Firewall	Petrol tank	Gas tank
Bush	Bushing	'Pinking'	'Pinging'
Cam follower or tappet	Valve lifter or tappet	Prise (force apart)	Pry
Carburettor	Carburetor	Propeller shaft	Driveshaft
Catch	Latch	Quarterlight	Quarter window
Choke/venturi	Barrel	Retread	Recap
Circlip	Snap-ring	Reverse	Back-up
Clearance	Lash	Rocker cover	Valve cover
Crownwheel	Ring gear (of differential)	Saloon	Sedan
Damper	Shock absorber, shock	Seized	Frozen
Disc (brake)	Rotor/disk	Sidelight	Parking light
Distance piece	Spacer	Silencer	Muffler
Drop arm	Pitman arm	Sill panel (beneath doors)	Rocker panel
Drop head coupe	Convertible	Small end, little end	Piston pin or wrist pin
Dynamo	Generator (DC)	Spanner	Wrench
Earth (electrical)	Ground	Split cotter (for valve spring cap)	Lock (for valve spring retainer)
Engineer's blue	Prussian blue	Split pin	Cotter pin
Estate car	Station wagon	Steering arm	Spindle arm
Exhaust manifold	Header	Sump	Oil pan
Fault finding/diagnosis	Troubleshooting	Swarf	Metal chips or debris
Float chamber	Float bowl	Tab washer	Tang or lock
Free-play	Lash	Tappet	Valve lifter
Freewheel	Coast	Thrust bearing	Throw-out bearing
Gearbox	Transmission	Top gear	High
Gearchange	Shift	Torch	Flashlight
Grub screw	Setscrew, Allen screw	Trackrod (of steering)	Tie-rod (or connecting rod)
Gudgeon pin	Piston pin or wrist pin	Trailing shoe (of brake)	Secondary shoe
Halfshaft	Axleshaft	Transmission	Whole drive line
Handbrake	Parking brake	Tyre	Tire
Hood	Soft top	Van	Panel wagon/van
Hot spot	Heat riser	Vice	Vise
Indicator	Turn signal	Wheel nut	Lug nut
Interior light	Dome lamp	Windscreen	Windshield
Layshaft (of gearbox)	Countershaft	Wing/mudguard	Fender
Leading shoe (of brake)	Primary shoe		

Index

W

Water pump
inspection – 64
removal and installation – 63
removal and installation (Turbo) – 64
Wheel specifications – 195
Windshield washer
description – 238, 315
general – 240

Windshield wiper
description – 238
fault diagnosis – 240
mechanism – 238
Wiring diagrams
current flow diagrams – 244 to 273, 316 to 321
explanation of circuit structure, usage and general advice – 240 to 241
explanation of symbols – 242
sample wiring diagram – 243
Working facilities – 9

FSC
www.fsc.org
MIX
Papier | Fördert
gute Waldnutzung
FSC® C083411

Zeitfracht Medien GmbH
Ferdinand-Jühlke-Straße 7
99095 Erfurt, Deutschland
produktsicherheit@kolibri360.de